Portrait of

America

PORTRAIT OF AMERICA

SEVENTH EDITION

VOLUME I

From Before Columbus
to the End of Reconstruction

STEPHEN B. OATES

University of Massachusetts, Amherst

HOUGHTON MIFFLIN COMPANY   BOSTON   NEW YORK

Again, for Greg and Stephanie with my love

Sponsoring editor   Jeffrey Greene
Senior project editor   Rosemary Winfield
Production/design coordinator   Jennifer Waddell
Senior manufacturing coordinator   Sally Culler
Marketing manager   Sandra McGuire

Cover design by Diana Coe; cover image: The Underground Railroad, mural, Dolgeville, New York Post Office, 1940, by James Michael Newell, National Museum of American Art, Washington, D.C./Art Resource.

Printed in the U.S.A.
Library of Congress Catalog Card Number: 98-72072
ISBN: 0-395-90077-8
6 7 8 9-DC-05 04 03 02 01

CONTENTS

shaped a Constitution that has stood for more than two hundred years.

It happened with shattering suddenness, an explosion of black rage
that struck an obscure Virginia county like a tornado roaring out of
the southern night. In August 1831, a mystical slave preacher
named Nat Turner led a column of ax-wielding blacks on a bloody
rampage through the Virginia forests, leaving behind ghastly scenes
of hacked-up bodies. The insurrection plunged southeastern
Virginia into convulsions of racial violence that rocked the entire
South to its foundations, exacerbated sectional tensions, and pointed
the way to the Civil War thirty years later.

Southern whites blamed Nat Turner's insurrection on the balding,
bespectacled Garrison, Boston editor of the *Liberator*, thereby giving
him a national reputation. In the early 1830's, Garrison was one of
the most visible spokesmen of the nascent abolitionist movement,
thundering against slavery and slaveowners in a stunning display of
moral outrage and seeking to win converts through moral pressure.
Korngold not only brings Garrison brilliantly alive in the context of
his time, but also introduces other important figures in the
abolitionist crusade.

A top Jacksonian scholar disputes recent interpretations of Andrew
Jackson as a fraud who masqueraded as the people's hero, and
restores Old Hickory to a prominent place in history. Remini
argues that Jackson launched a revolt against aristocratic rule and
moved America toward a more democratic system.

Jackson's arch foe is just a name in most American history
textbooks. This portrait resurrects Clay's fascinating personality and
recounts his remarkable career as one of the great political figures of
the first four decades of the nineteenth century. Speaker of the
House, senator, compromiser, Jackson hater, perennial presidential
contender, and an antislavery slaveowner, Clay championed
Jefferson's scheme of gradual emancipation and colonization and
stood as the foremost spokesman of the "American System," which
became a casualty of the sectional controversy.

slaveholder, and an overseer on a slaveowning plantation. The Old South was a cruel system that sought to strip black people of all human rights, reducing them to the status of cattle, swine, wagons, and other "property." Yet the slaves found ways to retain their humanity and created survival mechanisms—their families, religion, and songs—that helped them endure the unendurable.

PREFACE

Like its predecessors, the Seventh Edition of this anthology stresses the human side of history, suggesting how the interaction of people and events shaped the course of the American past. I chose selections for *Portrait of America* that make history live and that were written for students, not for professional historians. The essays, narratives, and biographical portraits gathered here humanize American history, portraying it as a story of real people who actually lived, who struggled, enjoyed triumphs, suffered failures and anxieties, just like people in our own time. I hope that the anthology is an example of humanistic history at its best, the kind that combines scrupulous and engaging scholarship with a compelling narrative style. Since college survey audiences are not professional ones, they might enjoy reading history if it is presented in an exciting and readable form.

There is another reason why students will find *Portrait of America* edifying: it showcases the writings of some of America's most eminent historians. The prizes their work has won testify to their important places in the galaxy of American letters. Bruce Catton's incomparable books on the Civil War won the Pulitzer Prize, a special Pulitzer citation, the National Book Award, and the Presidential Medal of Freedom. James M. McPherson's *Battle Cry of Freedom: The Civil War Era*—a section of which is excerpted here—received the Pulitzer Prize for history. John Demos received the Bancroft Prize and was a nominee for the American Book Award. Oliver La Farge won the Pulitzer Prize and the O. Henry Memorial Prize. Robert V. Remini's biography of Andrew Jackson received the American Book Award and the Carl Sandburg Award for nonfiction, and Eric Foner's extraordinary new book on Reconstruction garnered the Bancroft Prize and the Francis Parkman Prize of the Society of American Historians. David Herbert Donald twice won the Pulitzer Prize for biography, and his recent life of Lincoln received the Abraham Lincoln Award. Page Smith and Richard B. Morris won Bancroft Prizes, and Walter LaFeber received the Albert Beveridge Prize. Richard N. Current garnered the Bancroft Prize, the O. Max Gardner Prize, and the George Bante Award. Benjamin Quarles's scholarship earned him a fellowship from the John Simon Guggenheim Foundation and an appointment as honorary consultant to the Library of Congress. Many of the other contributors also received significant literary and scholarly awards. Thus *Portrait of America* offers readers a unique opportunity to learn from a lineup of nationally recognized historians and writers.

The Seventh Edition has been extensively revised. It contains ten new sections and a reorganization of the sections on the Jacksonian era and the black struggle for freedom. The new readings are

- Oliver La Farge's trenchant discussion of the Native American cultures that flourished before Columbus and what the European contact did to them;
- John Demos's mesmerizing account of the 1704 Deerfield massacre, which was symbolic of the great struggle between France and England for supremacy in North America;
- Alexander Winston's sparkling portrait of Sam Adams and the coming of the Revolution;
- Stephen Oates's story of Nat Turner's bloody slave insurrection;
- Elaine Kendall's gracefully written account of the struggle to educate women in the early Republic;
- John W. Blassingame's powerful description of the Old South's cruel slave regime;

- Benjamin Quarles's engaging portrait of Harriet Tubman, the most famous conductor on the fabled Underground Railroad;
- Bruce Catton's knowledgeable and entertaining essay on Civil War soldiers;
- Eric Foner's brilliant essay on the new view of Reconstruction; and
- Richard N. Current's trenchant reassessment of the carpetbaggers of the Reconstruction era.

The Seventh Edition retains the best and most popular selections of the previous editions. I hope that *Portrait of America* remains as balanced as ever, for it offers samplings of virtually every kind of history— men's and women's, black and white, social and cultural, political and military, urban and economic, national and local—so that students can appreciate the rich diversity of the American experience.

Portrait of America contains several important features that help students learn from its contents. Each selection is preceded by a glossary that identifies important individuals, events, and concepts that appear in the reading. Introductions set the selections in proper context and suggest ways to approach studying them. They also tie all the selections together so that they can be read more or less as connected episodes. Study questions following the selections raise significant issues and encourage students to make comparisons and contrasts between the selections. The questions also help students review the readings and suggest points for class discussion.

The anthology is intended for use largely in college survey courses. It could be utilized as a supplement to a textbook or to a list of paperback readings. Or it could serve as the basic text. The book is organized into fifteen parts according to periods or themes; each part contains two related selections. This organization allows readers to make comparisons and contrasts between different events or viewpoints.

The Seventh Edition could not have been assembled without the help of others. My talented assistant, Karl Anderson, not only helped me choose the new selections, but helped me write the glossaries and the study questions for the new pieces and the synopses of the selections for the Table of Contents. Since he is an undergraduate history major, he proved to be invaluable in assessing whether a potential selection was suitable for students in college survey courses. My former assistants, Anne-Marie Taylor and Dr. Karen Smith, and Professor Betty L. Mitchell of the University of Massachusetts, Dartmouth, wrote the study questions for the other selections. I want to thank the following professors for reviewing one or both volumes.

John Duke, Alvin Community College
Brian Lister, University of Maine at Farmington
Geoffrey Plank, University of Cincinnati

S. B. O.

Portrait of

America

THE EUROPEAN DISCOVERY

1

Myths That Hide the American Indian

OLIVER LA FARGE

For many people, American history began in 1492 when Columbus "discovered" the New World. Every Columbus Day we commemorate the myth of the bold, visionary hero who defied superstition, plunged across a storm-tossed Atlantic against all odds, landed in America, and made the United States possible. In reality, of course, Columbus did not "discover" America; prehistoric people from Asia, the ancestors of the Native Americans, or Indians, had done that about 14,000 years earlier when they began migrating from Siberia to Alaska across the land bridge of the Bering Strait. Over the centuries, the first Americans fanned out across North and South America and the islands of the Caribbean until by Columbus's time they numbered approximately 40 million. These "pre-European" inhabitants spoke hundreds of different languages and created remarkably diverse cultures — there were 2 million people and a thousand different tribes in North America alone, ranging from nomadic bands on the Plains to collectivist, corngrowing pueblos in New Mexico and highly developed agricultural towns in the Southeast.

Who knows what this thriving, complex population of indigenous Americans might have become had Columbus not stumbled onto America in his search for the fabled Orient. What we do know is that the European arrival in the "New World" had profound consequences for the Western Hemisphere, Europe, and Africa. On his second voyage, Columbus established the first outpost of European civilization in the New World and inaugurated "the Columbian Exchange" — described by authors Lewis Lord and Sarah Burke — "a global swap of animals, plants, people, ailments and ideas" that altered the course of human history. Among other things, this exchange sent American corn to Africa and American tobacco, potatoes, beans, squash, tomatoes, and peanuts to Europe, and brought horses, cows, chickens, pigs, honeybees, coffee, wheat, and rice to the Americas.⌉

For the first Americans, to whom Columbus gave the name Indios, the introduction of European animals and plants was salutary. The horse, for example, spread rapidly among the buffalo-hunting tribes of the Plains, increasing their speed and range of locomotion and becoming their chief symbol of wealth. But in almost every other respect, the European invasion of the Indian world was a catastrophe. Columbus himself set the example for subsequent Europeans, initiating a policy of enslavement and killing that was to contribute to the near extermination of the first Americans. Even Columbus's otherwise sympathetic biographer, Samuel Eliot Morison, acknowledged that the "cruel policy" begun by Columbus and pursued by his successors amounted to genocide. To make matters worse, the Indians were not immune to the communicable diseases the Europeans carried to the New World. Epidemics of measles, typhoid, smallpox, and tuberculosis, not to mention dysentery and alcoholism, were to sweep through the original Americans, killing them by the countless thousands. By 1890, after four centuries of white conquest, only about 250,000 Indians remained in all of North America.

In the following selection, Oliver La Farge, anthropologist, novelist, and one of the all-time great historians of the Native Americans, goes behind the convenient myths the Europeans invented about the Indians and shows us the rich and complex indigenous cultures that thrived in North America before and after the Europeans made first contact. La Farge will introduce you to the mound builders, whose corn-growing civilization flourished in the southeastern woodlands before A.D. 1500. In the words of W. Michael Gear and Kathleen Gear, "This civilization embraced not only the most complex religious ceremonialism, social organization, and economic sophistication ever seen in prehistoric North America, but also the most expansive political influence heretofore known," with trade routes that extended across the entire continent. The Mississippians, as they are called, built towns of earthen mounds that could reach heights of a hundred feet, and they had sufficient grasp of astronomy and math to "align each of their mounds according to the exact position of the sun when it rose and set on the equinox and solstice." As he does with the other Indian cultures he discusses, La Farge does not hesitate to point out negative aspects of the mound builders, who were exceedingly warlike and perfectly willing to torture captives. When the Europeans came, however, this once powerful civilization had disappeared, having been overrun by marauders from the north and plagued by drought and famine. Their temple mound towns were completely empty now, leaving European immigrants to contemplate their mysteries.

La Farge's essay will also introduce you to the "Five Civilized Tribes" of the Southeast — the powerful Iroquois of the Northeast; the Pueblos, Navahos, and Apaches of the Southwest; the totemic, potlatch culture of the Indians of the Northwest coast; and the great horse-riding buffalo hunters of the Great Plains, whose war bonnets, war *dances, and tepees — prominently featured in the white man's Wild West shows — made them in white eyes the stereotype of the Native American. That stereotype contained the incongruous European myths of the noble red man and the ruthless savage that hid the American Indian for three hundred years.*

GLOSSARY

APACHES   See Athabascans.

ATHABASCANS   Invaders from Canada who spoke languages of the Athabascan stock and filtered into the American Southwest. They became the Navahos and the Apaches, who raided the Pueblo Indians and stole, traded, and learned from them. In time the Navahos became excellent weavers but continued to raid their Pueblo neighbors. The Apaches and Navahos did not glorify warfare but fought for profit.

DAKOTA SIOUX   Driven by the musket-carrying Chippewas out of wooded Minnesota into the Plains, they encountered horses in 1782 as they spread north, first eating and then riding them. This began the great horseback buffalo-hunting Sioux culture of the Plains.

FIVE CIVILIZED TRIBES   The Cherokee, Chickasaw, Choctaw, Creek, and Seminole tribes of the Southeast and the Mississippi Valley, which were ancestral to the great mound-building culture of earlier times.

HIAWATHA   Founder of the League of the Five Nations.

IROQUOIS   A confederation of closely knit, highly organized tribes of the Northeast that lived in "long houses" covered in bark and allowed women considerable power.

LEAGUE OF THE FIVE NATIONS   Formed in the sixteenth century by five Iroquois tribes: the Senecas, Onondagas, Mohawks, Cayugas, and Oneidas (the Tuscaroras joined later). The league was so successful a union that it was studied by the framers of the United States Constitution.

MOUND BUILDERS   Highly developed agricultural civilization of the Southeast woodlands. The mound builders lived in towns with thatched-roof houses and produced "really impressive art, especially in carving and modeling."

NATCHEZ   Highly developed Indian nation of Mississippi ruled by a sun king and divided into two classes: the aristocracy and the common people, called Stinkers. The Natchez were warlike and perfectly willing to torture captives to death. Other captives they adopted so as to replenish the supply of Stinkers.

NAVAHO   See Athabascans.

NOBLE RED MAN OR CHILD OF NATURE   First myth the Europeans invented about the Native American; it credited the Indian with either a penchant for flowery but dull oratory or an inability to communicate beyond "Ugh" and grunts.

NORTHWEST COAST INDIANS   Highly developed fishing, hunting, and gathering tribes on the Pacific coast who, because of the abundance of trees, made wooden houses, wooden armor, wooden ships, and wooden totem poles. Divided into chiefs, commoners, and slaves, they excelled at carving and woodworking and gained respectability by giving through the famous potlatch.

POTLATCH   Practice of the Northwest coastal tribes in which a chief, to demonstrate his lavishness and respectability, would give away generous piles of possessions to a rival chief and other guests; the chief might also burn some possessions and even slay a few slaves with a club called the "slave-killer." If the rival chief did not respond with an even more lavish potlatch, he would cease to be a chief.

PUEBLOS   Highly developed farming people of the Southwest who raised corn, lived in defensible villages consisting of interconnected adobe houses, and stressed the solidarity of the community at the expense of individuality. Their government was a theocracy in which priests ruled by the consent of the governed.

RUTHLESS SAVAGE   Second myth the Europeans invented about the Native American; later, when the "savages" were conquered, the myth was changed to "drunken, lazy good-for-nothings."

SIOUX, BLACKFEET, CHEYENNES, KIOWAS, COMANCHES, PIEGANS, ARAPHOS, CROWS   Nomadic buffalo-hunting tribes of the Great Plains whose culture was made possible by the Spaniards' introduction of the horse. These great horseback tribes depended on the buffalo for their food supply, using the hides to fashion winter robes and the skins to make their tepees. These Indians wore war bonnets, did war dances, and raided rival tribes for horses, their prize possessions.

Ever since the white men first fell upon them the Indians of what is now the United States have been hidden from white men's view by a number of conflicting myths. The oldest of these is the myth of the Noble Red Man or the Child of Nature, who is credited either with the habit of flowery oratory of implacable dullness or else with an imbecilic inability to converse in anything more than grunts and monosyllables.

That first myth was inconvenient. White men soon found their purposes better served by the myth of ruthless, faithless savages, and later, when the "savages" had been broken, of drunken, lazy good-for-nothings. All three myths coexist today, sometimes curiously blended in a schizophrenic confusion such as one often sees in the moving pictures. Through the centuries the mythical figure has been variously equipped; today he wears a feather headdress, is clothed in beaded buckskin, dwells in a tepee, and all but lives on horseback.

It was in the earliest period of the Noble Red Man concept that the Indians probably exerted their most important influence upon Western civilization. The theory has been best formulated by the late Felix S. Cohen, who, as a profound student of law concerning Indians, delved into early white-Indian relations, Indian political economy, and the white men's view of it. According to this theory, with which the present writer agrees, the French and the English of the early seventeenth century encountered, along the East Coast of North America from Virginia southward, fairly advanced tribes whose semi-hereditary rulers depended upon the acquiescence of their people for the continuance of their rule. The explorers and first settlers interpreted these ruler as kings, their people as subjects. They found that even the commonest subjects were endowed with many rights and freedoms, that the nobility was

Oliver La Farge, "Myths That Hide the American Indian," *American Heritage,* vol. 7, no. 6 (October 1955), pp. 4–9, 103–107.

European view of the Indian as a child of nature, the oldest myth about the Native-Americans. (Library of Congress, USZ62-572)

fluid, and that commoners existed in a state of remarkable equality.

Constitutional monarchy was coming into being in England, but the divine right of kings remained firm doctrine. All European society was stratified in many classes. A somewhat romanticized observation in Indian society and government, coupled with the idea of the Child of Nature, led to the formulation, especially by French philosophers, of the theories of inherent rights in all men, and of the people as the source of the sovereign's authority. The latter was

stated in the phrase, "consent of the governed." Both were carried over by Jefferson into our Declaration of Independence in the statement that "all men are created equal, that they are endowed by their Creator with certain unalienable Rights" and that government derive "their just powers from the consent of the governed. . . ."

Thus, early observations of the rather simple, democratic, organization of the more advanced coastal tribes, filtered through and enlarged by the minds of European philosophers whose thinking was ripe for

Sixteenth-century European drawing of Native-Americans as blood thirsty savages. This was one of the enduring myths that hid them from white people. (The Newberry Library, Chicago)

just such material, at least influenced the formulation of a doctrine, or pair of doctrines, that furnished the intellectual base for two great revolutions and profoundly affected the history of mankind.

In the last paragraph I speak of "the more advanced" tribes. Part of the myth about the first Americans is that all of them, or most of them, had one culture and were at the same stage of advancement. The tribes and nations that occupied North America varied enormously, and their condition was anything but static. The advent of the white men put a sudden end to a phase of increasingly rapid cultural

evolution, much as if a race of people, vastly superior in numbers, in civilization, and above all in weapons, had overrun and conquered all of Europe in Minoan times. Had that happened, also, the conquerors would undoubtedly have concluded, as so many white men like to conclude about Indians, that that peculiar race of light-skinned people was obviously inferior to their own.

Human beings had been in the New World for at least 15,000 years. During much of that time, as was the case in the beginning everywhere, they advanced but little from a Palaeolithic hunting culture. Somewhere around 2,500 B.C. farming began with the domestication of corn either in Peru or in Meso-America★ in the vicinity of western Guatemala. Farming brought about the sedentary life and the increased food supply necessary for cultural progress. By the time of the birth of Christ, the influence of the high cultures, soon to become true civilizations, in Meso-America was beginning to reach into the present United States. Within the next 1,500 years the Indians of parts of North America progressed drámatically. When the white men first landed, there were three major centers of high culture: the Southeast-Mississippi Valley, the Southwest, and the Northwest Coast. None of the peoples of these regions, incidentally, knew about war bonnets or lived in tepees.

The Southeast-Mississippi Valley peoples (for brevity, I shall refer to the area hereafter simply as "Southeast") seem to have had the strongest influences from Meso-America, probably in part by land along the coast of Texas, in part by sea across the Gulf of Mexico, whether direct from Mexico or secondhand through the peoples of the West Indies. There is a striking resemblance between some of their great earthen mounds, shaped like flat-topped pyramids, with their wood-and-thatch temples on top, and the stone-and-mortar, temple-topped pyramids of Meso-America. Some of their carvings and engravings strongly suggest that the artists had actually seen Meso-American sculptures. The list of similarities is convincingly long.

There grew up along the Mississippi Valley, reaching far to the north, and reaching also eastwards in the far south, the high culture generally called "Mound Builder." It produced a really impressive art, especially in carving and modeling, by far the finest that ever existed in North America. The history of advancing civilization in the New World is

like that of the Old — a people develops a high culture, then barbarians come smashing in, set the clock partway back, absorb much of the older culture, and carry it on to new heights. A series of invasions of this sort seems to have struck the Mound Builders in late prehistoric times, when they were overrun by tribes mainly of Muskhogean and Iroquoian linguistic stock. Chief among these were the ancestors of the well-know Five Civilized Tribes — the Seminoles, Creeks, Choctaws, Chickasaws, and Cherokees. When white men first met them, their culture was somewhat lower than that of the earlier period in the land they occupied. Nonetheless, they maintained, in Florida, Alabama, Mississippi, Louisiana, and Georgia, the highest level east of the Rockies. A late movement of Iroquoian tribes, close relatives of the Cherokees, among them the Iroquois themselves, carried a simpler form of the same culture into Pennsylvania, New York, Ohio, and into the edge of Canada.

All of these people farmed heavily, their fields stretching for miles. They were few in a vast land — the whole population of the present United States was probably not over a million. Hunting and fishing, therefore, were excellent, and no reasonable people would drop an easy source of abundant meat. The development of their farming was held in check quantitatively by the supply of fish and game. They farmed the choice land, and if the fields began to be exhausted, they could move. They moved their habitations somewhat more freely then do we, but they were anything but nomadic. The southern tribesmen lived neither in wigwams nor tepees, but in houses with thatched roofs, which in the extreme south often had no walls. They had an elaborate social structure with class distinctions. Because of their size, the white men called their settlements "towns." The state of their high chiefs was kingly. . . .

The Natchez of Mississippi had a true king, and a curious, elaborate social system. The king had absolute power and was known as the Sun. No ordinary man could speak to him except from a distance,

---

★Meso-America denotes the area in which the highest civilizations north of Peru developed, extending from a little north of Mexico City into Honduras.

shouting and making obeisances. When he went out, he was carried on a litter, as the royal and sacred foot could not be allowed to touch the ground. The Natchez nation was divided into two groups, or moieties: the aristocracy and the common people. The higher group was subdivided into Suns (the royal family), Nobles, and Honored Ones. The common people were known simply as Stinkers. A Stinker could marry anyone he pleased, but all the aristocrats had to marry out of their moiety, that is, marry Stinkers. When a female aristocrat married a Stinker man, her children belonged to her class; thus, when a Sun woman married a Stinker, her children were Suns. The children of the men, however, were lowered one class, so that the children of a Sun man, even of the Sun himself, became Nobles, while the children of an Honored One became lowly Stinkers.

This system in time, if nothing intervened, would lead to an overwhelming preponderance of aristocrats. The Natchez, however, for all their . . . civilization, their temples, their fine crafts and arts, were chronically warlike. Those captives they did not torture to death they adopted, thus constantly replenishing the supply of Stinkers (a foreigner could become nothing else, but his grandchildren, if his son struck a royal fancy, might be Suns).

The Indians of the Southeast knew the Mexican-West Indian art of feather weaving, by means of which they made brilliant, soft cloaks. The Sun also wore a crown of an elaborate arrangement of feathers, quite unlike a war bonnet. In cloak and crown, carried shoulder-high on a litter, surrounded by his retainers, his majesty looked far more like something out of the Orient than anything we think of ordinarily when we hear the word "Indian."

The Natchez were warlike. All of the southeasterners were warlike. War was a man's proper occupation. Their fighting was deadly, ferocious, stealthy if possible, for the purpose of killing — men, women, or children, so long as one killed — and taking captives, especially strong males whom one could enjoy torturing to death. It is among these tribes and their simpler relatives, the Iroquois, that we find the bloodthirsty savage of fiction, but the trouble is that he is not a savage. . . .

With the Iroquois, they shared a curious pattern of cruelty. A warrior expected to be tortured if captured, although he could, instead, be adopted, before torture or at any time before he had been crippled. He entered into it as if it were a contest, which he would win if his captors failed to wring a sign of pain from him and if he kept taunting them so long as he was conscious. Some of the accounts of such torture among the Iroquois, when the victim was a member of a tribe speaking the same language and holding to the same customs, are filled with a quality of mutual affection. In at least one case, when a noted enemy proved to have been too badly wounded before his capture to be eligible for adoption, the chief, who had hoped that the man would replace his own son, killed in battle, wept as he assigned him to his fate. At intervals between torments so sickening that one can hardly make one's self read through the tale of them, prisoner and captors exchanged news of friends and expressions of mutual esteem. Naturally, when tribes who did not hold to these customs, including white men, were subjected to this treatment it was not well received.

This pattern may have come into North America from a yet more advanced, truly civilized source. The Mexicans — the Aztecs and their neighbors — expected to be sacrificed if they were captured, and on occasion might insist upon it if their captors were inclined to spare them. They were not tortured, properly speaking, as a general rule, but some of the methods of putting them to death were not quick. What we find in North America may have been a debasement of the Mexican practices developed into an almost psychopathic pleasure among people otherwise just as capable of love, of kindness, of nobility, and of lofty thought as any anywhere — or what the conquistadores found in Mexico may have been a civilized softening of earlier, yet more fearful ways. The Aztecs tore fantastic numbers of hearts from living victims, and like the people of the Southeast, when not at war said, "We are idle." They were artists, singers, dancers, poets, and great lovers of flowers and birds.

The Iroquois and Muskhogeans had a real mental sophistication. We observe it chiefly in their social order and what we know of their religions. The Iroquois did not have the royalty and marked divisions of classes that we find farther south, but their well-organized, firmly knit tribes were what enabled them, although few in numbers, to dominate the Algonkians who surrounded them. The Iroquois came nearer to having the matriarchy that popular fable looks for among . . . [Indians] than any other American tribe. Actual office was held by the men, but the women's power was great, and strongly influenced the selection of the officers.

Five of the Iroquois tribes achieved something unique in North America, rare anywhere, when in the sixteenth century they formed the League of the Five Nations — Senecas, Onondagas, Mohawks, Cayugas, and Oneidas — to which, later, the Tuscaroras were added. The league remained united and powerful until after the American Revolution, and exists in shadowy form to this day. It struck a neat balance between sovereignty retained by each tribe and sovereignty sacrificed to the league, and as so durable and effective a union was studied by the authors of our Constitution.

The league was founded by the great leader Hiawatha. Any resemblance between the fictional hero of Longfellow's poem and this real, dead person is purely coincidental. Longfellow got hold of the name and applied it to some Chippewa legends, which he rewrote thoroughly to produce some of the purest rot and the most heavy-footed verse every to be inflicted upon a school child.

The Iroquois lived in "long houses," which looked like extended Quonset huts sheathed in bark. Smaller versions of these, and similarly covered, domed or conical structures, are "wigwams," the typical housing of the Northeast. Many people use the word "wigwam" as synonymous with "tepee," which is incorrect. A tepee, the typical dwelling of the Plains Indians of a later period, is a functional tent, usually covered with hides or, in recent years, canvas, and one of its essential features is that it is the shelter of constantly mobile people. A tepee, incidentally, is about the most comfortable tent ever invented, winter or summer — provided you have two or three strong, competent women to attend to setting it up and striking it.

The great tribes we have been discussing showed their sophistication in a new way in their response to contact with Europeans. Their tribal organizations became tighter and firmer. From south to north they held the balance of power. The British success in establishing good relations with many of them was the key to driving the French out of the Mississippi area; to win the Revolution, the Americans had to defeat the Iroquois, whose favor up to then had determined who should dominate the Northeast. The southern tribes radically changed their costume, and quickly took over cattle, slaves, and many arts. By the time Andrew Jackson was ready to force their removal, the Cherokees had a stable government under a written constitution, with a bicameral parliament, an alphabet for writing their language, printing presses, a newspaper, schools, and churches.

Had it not been for the white men's insatiable greed and utter lawlessness, this remarkable nation would have ended with a unique demonstration of how, without being conquered, a "primitive" people could adapt itself to a new civilization on its own initiative. They would have become a very rare example of how aborigines could receive solid profit from the coming of the white men.

After the Five Civilized Tribes were driven to Oklahoma, they formed a union and once again set up their governments and their public schools. Of course we could not let them have what we had promised them; it turned out that we ourselves wanted that part of Oklahoma after all, so once again we tore up the treaties and destroyed their system.

Nonetheless, to this day they are a political power in the state, and when one of their principal chiefs speaks up, the congressmen do well to listen.

The tribes discussed until now and their predecessors in the same general area formed a means of transmission of higher culture to others, east and west. Their influence reached hardly at all to the northwards, as north of the Iroquois farming with native plants was difficult or impossible. On the Atlantic Coast of the United States the tribes were all more or less affected. Farming was of great importance. Even in New England, the status of chiefs was definite and fairly high. Confederacies and hegemonies, such as that of the Narragansetts over many of the Massachusetts tribes, occurred, of which more primitive people are incapable. Farther south, the state of such a chief as Powhatan was royal enough for Europeans to regard him as a king and his daughter as a true princess.

To the westward, the pattern of farming and sedentary villages extended roughly to the line that runs irregularly through Nebraska and Kansas, west of which the mean annual rainfall is below twenty inches. In wet cycles, there were prehistoric attempts to farm farther west, and in historic times the Apaches raised fair crops in the eastern foothills of the southern tip of the Rockies, but only the white men combined the mechanical equipment and the stupidity to break the turf and exhaust the soil of the dry, high plains.

An essay as short as this on so large a subject is inevitably filled with almost indefensible generalizations. I am stressing similarities, as in the case of the Iroquois-Southeast tribes, ignoring great unlikenesses. Generalizing again, we may say that the western farmers, whose cultures in fact differed enormously, also lived in fairly fixed villages. In the southern part, they built large houses covered with grass thatch. At the northwestern tip of the farming zone we find the Mandans, Hidatsa, and Crows, who lived in semi-subterranean lodges of heavy poles covered with earth, so big that later, when

horses came to them, they kept their choice mounts inside. These three related, Siouan-speaking tribes living on the edge of the Plains are the first we have come to whose native costume, when white men first observed them, included the war bonnet. That was in the early nineteenth century; what they wore in 1600, no one knows.

The western farmers had their permanent lodges; they also had tepees. Immediately at hand was the country of the bison, awkward game for men on foot to hunt with lance and bow, but too fine a source of meat to ignore. On their hunting expeditions they took the conical tents. The size of the tepees was limited, for the heavy covers and the long poles had to be dragged either by the women or by dogs. Tepee life at that time was desirable only for a short time, when one roughed it.

The second area of Meso-American influence was the Southwest as anthropologists define it — the present states of New Mexico and Arizona, a little of the adjacent part of Mexico, and various extensions at different times to the north, west, and east. We do not find here the striking resemblances to Meso-America in numbers of culture traits we find in the Southeast; the influence must have been much more indirect, ideas and objects passing in the course of trade from tribe to tribe over the thousand miles or so of desert northern Mexico.

In the last few thousand years the Southwest has been pretty dry, although not as dry as it is today. A dry climate and a sandy soil make an archaeologist's paradise. We can trace to some extent the actual transition from hunting and gathering to hunting plus farming, the appearance of the first permanent dwellings, the beginning of pottery-making, at least the latter part of the transition from twining and basketry to true weaving. Anthropologists argue over the very use of the term "Southwest" to denote a single area, because of the enormous variety of the cultures found within it. There is a certain unity, nonetheless, centering around beans, corn, squashes, tobacco, cotton, democracy, and a preference for peace. Admitting the diversity, the vast differences between, say, the Hopi and Pima farmers, we can still think of it as a single area, and for purposes of this essay concentrate on the best-studied of its cultures, the Pueblos.

The name "Pueblo" is the Spanish for "village," and was given to that people because they lived — and live — in compact, defensible settlements of houses with walls of stone laid up with adobe mortar or entirely of adobe. Since the Spanish taught them how to make rectangular bricks, pure adobe construction has become the commoner type. They already had worked out the same roofing as was usual in Asia Minor and around the Mediterranean in ancient times. A modern Pueblo house corresponds almost exactly to the construction of buildings dating back at least as far as 600 B.C. in Asia Minor.

The Pueblos, and their neighbors, the Navahos, have become well enough known in recent years to create some exception to the popular stereotype of Indians. It is generally recognized that they do not wear feathers and that they possess many arts, and that the Pueblos are sedentary farmers.

Farming has long been large in their pattern of living, and hunting perhaps less important than with any people outside the Southwest. Their society is genuinely classless, in contrast to that of the Southeast. Before the Spanish conquest, they were governed by a theocracy. Each tribe was tightly organized, every individual placed in his niche. The power of the theocracy was, and in some Pueblos still is, tyrannical in appearance. Physical punishment was used to suppress the rebellious; now more often a dissident member is subjected to a form of being sent to Coventry. If he be a member of the tribal council, anything he says at meetings is pointedly ignored. If he has some ceremonial function, he performs it, but otherwise he is left in isolation. I have seen a once self-assertive man, who for a time had been a strong leader in his tribe, subjected to this treatment for several years. By my estimation, he lost some thirty pounds, and he became a quiet conformist.

The power of the theocracy was great, but it rested on the consent of the governed. No man could overstep his authority, no one man had final authority. It went hard with the individual dissident, but the will of the people controlled all.

The Pueblos had many arts, most of which still continue. They wove cotton, made handsome pottery, did fine work in shell. Their ceremonies were spectacular and beautiful. They had no system of torture and no cult of warfare. A good warrior was respected, but what they wanted was peace.

The tight organization of the Pueblo tribes and the absolute authority over individuals continues now among only a few of them. The loosening is in part the result of contact with whites, in part for the reason that more and more they are building their houses outside of the old, solid blocks of the villages, simply because they are no longer under constant, urgent need for defense.

It is irony that the peace-loving southwestern farmers were surrounded by the worst raiders of all the . . . tribes of North America. Around A.D. 1100 or 1200 there began filtering in among them bands of primitives, possessors of a very simple culture, who spoke languages of the Athabascan stock. These people had drifted down from western Canada. In the course of time they became the Navahos and the Apaches. For all their poverty, they possessed a sinew-backed bow of Asiatic type that was superior to any missile weapon known to the Southwest. They traded with the Pueblos, learned from them, stole from them, raided them. As they grew stronger, they became pests. The Navahos and the northeastern branch of the Apaches, called Jicarilla Apaches, learned farming. The Navahos in time became artists, above all the finest of weavers, but they did not give up their raiding habits.

These Athabascans did not glorify war. They made a business of it. Killing enemies was incidental; in fact, a man who killed an enemy had to be purified afterwards. They fought for profit, and they were about the only North Americans whose attitude toward war resembled professional soldiers'. This did not make them any less troublesome.

The last high culture area occupied a narrow strip along the Pacific Coast, from northern California across British Columbia to southern Alaska, the Northwest Coast culture. There was no Meso-American influence here, nor was there any farming. The hunting and fishing were so rich, the supply of edible wild plants so adequate, that there was no need for farming — for which in any case the climate was unfavorable. The prerequisite for cultural progress is a food supply so lavish that either all men have spare time, or some men can specialize in non-food-producing activities while others feed them. This condition obtained on the Northwest Coast, where men caught the water creatures from whales to salmon, and hunted deer, mountain sheep, and other game animals.

The area was heavily forested with the most desirable kinds of lumber. Hence wood and bark entered largely into the culture. Bark was shredded and woven into clothing, twined into nets, used for padding. Houses, chests, dishes, spoons, canoes, and boats were made of wood. The people became carvers and woodworkers, then carried their carving over onto bone and horn. They painted their houses, boats, chests, and their elaborate wooden masks. They made wooden armor, including visored helmets, and deadly wooden clubs. In a wet climate, they made raincloaks of bark and wore basketry hats, on the top of which could be placed one or more cylinders, according to the wearer's rank. The chiefs placed carvings in front of their houses that related their lineage, tracing back ultimately to some sacred being such as Raven or Bear — the famous, so-called totem poles.

I have said that the finest prehistoric art of North America was that of the Mound Builders; in fact, no Indian work since has quite equaled it — but that is, of course, a matter of taste. The greatest historic Indian art was that of the Northwest Coast. Their carvings, like the Mound Builder sculptures, demand comparison with our own work. Their art was highly stylized, but vigorous and fresh. As for all Indians, the coming of the white men meant ruin in the end, but at first it meant metal tools, the possession of which resulted in a great artistic outburst.

Socially they were divided into chiefs, commoners, and slaves. Slaves were obtained by capture, and slave-raiding was one of the principal causes of war. Generosity was the pattern with most Indians, although in the dry Southwest we find some who made a virtue of thrift. In the main, a man was respected because he gave, not because he possessed. The Northwest Coast chiefs patterned generosity into an ugliness. A chief would invite a rival to a great feast, the famous potlatch. At the feast he would shower his rival and other guests with gifts, especially copper disks and blankets woven of mountain sheep wool, which were the highest units of value. He might further show his lavishness by burning some possessions, even partially destroy a copper disk, and, as like as not, kill a few slaves.

If within a reasonable time the other chief did not reply with an even larger feast, at which he gave away or destroyed double what his rival had got rid of, he was finished as a chief — but if he did respond in proper form, he might be beggared, and also finished. That was the purpose of the show. Potlatches were given for other purposes, such as to authenticate the accession of the heir to a former chief, or to buy a higher status, but ruinous rivalry was constant. They seem to have been a rather disagreeable, invidious, touchy people. The cruelty of the southeasterners is revolting, but there is something especially unpleasant about proving one's generosity and carelessness of possessions by killing a slave — with a club made for that special purpose and known as a "slave-killer."

The Meso-American culture could spread, changing beyond recognition as it did so, because it carried its food supply with it. The Northwest Coast culture could not, because its food supply was restricted to its place of origin.

North and east of the Northwest Coast area stretched the sub-Arctic and the plains of Canada, areas incapable of . . . farming. To the south and east were mountains and the region between the Rockies and the Coastal ranges called the Great Basin. Within it are large stretches of true desert; most of it is arid. Early on, Pueblo influences reached into the southern part, in Utah and Nevada, but as the climate grew drier, they died away. It was a land to be occupied by little bands of simple hunters and gatherers of seeds and roots, not strong enough to force their way into anywhere richer.

In only one other area was there a natural food supply to compare with the Northwest Coast's, and that was in the bison range of the Great Plains. But, as already noted, for men without horses or rifles, hunting bison was a tricky and hazardous business. Take the year 1600, when the Spanish were already established in New Mexico and the English and French almost ready to make settlements on the East Coast, and look for the famous Plains tribes. They are not there. Some are in the mountains, some in the woodlands to the northeast, some farming to the eastward, within the zone of ample rainfall. Instead we find scattered bands of Athabascans occupying an area no one else wanted.

Then the white men turned everything upside down. Three elements were most important in the early influence: the dislodgment of eastern tribes, the introduction of the horse, and the metal tools and firearms. Let us look first at the impact on the centers of high culture.

White men came late to the Northwest Coast, and at first only as traders. As already noted, early contact with them enriched the life of the Indians and brought about a cultural spurt. Then came settlers. The most advanced, best organized tribes stood up fairly well against them for a time, and they are by no means extinct, but of their old culture there are now only remnants, with the strongest survivals being in the arts. Today, those Indians who are in the "Indian business," making money from tourists,

dress in fringed buckskin and war bonnets, because otherwise the tourists will not accept them as genuine.

The tribes of the Atlantic Coast were quickly dislodged or wiped out. The more advanced groups farther inland held out all through colonial times and on into the 1830's, making fairly successful adjustments to the changed situation, retaining their sovereignty, and enriching their culture with wholesale taking over of European elements, including, in the South, the ownership of Negro slaves. Finally, as already noted, they were forcibly removed to Oklahoma, and in the end their sovereignty was destroyed. They remain numerous, and although some are extremely poor and backward, others, still holding to their tribal affiliations, have merged successfully into the general life of the state, holding positions as high as chief justice of the state supreme court. The Iroquois still hold out in New York and in Canada on remnants of their original reservations. Many of them have had remarkable success in adapting themselves to white American life while retaining considerable elements of their old culture. Adherents to the old religion are many, and the rituals continue vigorously.

The British invaders of the New World, and to a lesser degree the French, came to colonize. They came in thousands, to occupy the land. They were, therefore, in direct competition with the Indians and acted accordingly, despite their verbal adherence to fine principles of justice and fair dealing. The Spanish came quite frankly to conquer, to Christianize, and to exploit, all by force of arms. They did not shilly-shally about Indian title to the land or Indian sovereignty, they simply took over, then granted the Indians titles deriving from the Spanish crown. They came in small numbers — only around 3,000 settled in the Southwest — and the Indian labor force was essential to their aims. Therefore they did not dislodge or exterminate the Indians, and they had notable success in modifying Indian culture for survival within their regime and contribution to it.

DRAWN BY FREDERIC REMINGTON.

THE CHARGE ON THE SUN-POLE.

ENGRAVED BY J. W. EVANS.

Frederick Remington's painting of Plains warriors on horseback. The myth of the Plains culture remains "embedded in our folk- *lore." (North Wind Picture Archives)*

In the Southwest the few Spaniards, cut off from the main body in Mexico by many miles of difficult, wild country, could not have survived alone against the . . . tribes that shortly began to harry them. They needed the Pueblo Indians and the Pueblos needed them. The Christian Pueblos were made secure in their lands and in their local self-government. They approached social and political equality. During the period when New Mexico was under the Mexican Republic, for two years a Taos Indian, braids, blanket, and all, was governor of the territory. Eighteen pueblos survive to this day, with a population now approaching 19,000, in addition to nearly 4,000

Hopis, whose culture is Pueblo, in Arizona. They are conservative progressives, prosperous on the whole, with an excellent chance of surviving as a distinctive group for many generations to come. It was in the house of a Pueblo priest, a man deeply versed in the old religion as well as a devout Catholic, that I first saw color television.

The Spanish, then, did not set populations in motion. That was done chiefly from the east. The great Spanish contribution was loosing the horses. They did not intend to; in fact, they made every possible effort to prevent Indians from acquiring horses or learning to ride. But the animals multiplied and ran wild; they

15

spread north from California into Oregon; they spread into the wonderful grazing land of the high Plains, a country beautifully suited to horses.

From the east, the tribes were pressing against the tribes farther west. Everything was in unhappy motion, and the tribes nearest to the white men had firearms. So the Chippewas, carrying muskets, pushed westward into Minnesota, driving the reluctant Dakotas, the Sioux tribes, out of the wooded country into the Plains as the horses spread north. At first the Dakotas hunted and ate the strange animals, then they learned to ride them, and they were off.

The Sioux were mounted. So were the Blackfeet. The semi-civilized Cheyennes swung into the saddle and moved out of the farming country onto the bison range. The Kiowas moved from near the Yellowstone to the Panhandle; the Comanches came down out of the Rocky Mountains; the Arapahos, the Crows, abandoning their cornfields, and the Piegans, the great fighting names, all followed the bison. They built their life around the great animals. They ate meat lavishly all year round; their tepees, carried or dragged now by horses, became commodious. A new culture, a horse-and-bison culture, sprang up overnight. The participants in it had a wonderful time. They feasted they roved, they hunted, they played. Over a series issue, such as the invasion of one tribe's territory by another, they could fight deadly battles, but otherwise even war was a game in which shooting an enemy was an act earning but little esteem, but touching one with one's bare hand or with a stick was the height of military achievement.

This influx of powerful tribes drove the last of the Athabascans into the Southwest. There the Apaches and the Navahos were also mounted and on the go, developing their special, deadly pattern of war as a business. In the Panhandle country, the Kiowas and Comanches looked westward to the Spanish and Pueblo settlements, where totally alien peoples offered rich plunder. The Pueblos, as we have seen, desired to live at peace. The original Spanish came

to conquer; their descendants, becoming Spanish-Americans, were content to hold what they had, farm their fields, and graze their flocks. To the north of the two groups were Apaches and Utes; to the east, Kiowas and Comanches; to the south, what seemed like unlimited Apaches; and to the west the Navahos, of whom there were several thousands by the middle of the seventeenth century.

The tribes named above, other than the Kiowas and Comanches, did not share in the Plains efflorescence. The Navahos staged a different cultural spurt of their own, combining extensive farming with constant horseback plundering, which in turn enabled them to become herdsmen, and from the captured wool develop their remarkable weaving industry. The sheep, of course, which became important in their economy, also derived from the white men. Their prosperity and their arts were superimposed on a simple camp life. With this prosperity, they also developed elaborate rituals and an astoundingly rich, poetic mythology.

The Dakotas first saw horses in 1722, which makes a convenient peg date for the beginning of the great Plains culture. A little over a hundred years later, when Catlin visited the Mandans, it was going full blast. The memory of a time before horses had grown dim. By 1860 the Plains tribes were hard-pressed to stand the white men off; by 1880 the whole pattern was broken and the bison were gone. At its height, Plains Indian culture was brittle. Materially, it depended absolutely on a single source of food and skins; in other aspects, it required the absolute independence of the various tribes. When these two factors were eliminated, the content was destroyed. Some Indians may still live in tepees, wear at times their traditional clothing, maintain here and there their arts and some of their rituals, but these are little more than fringe survivals.

While the Plains culture died, the myth of it spread and grew to become embedded in our folklore. Not only the Northwest Coast Indians but many others as unlikely wear imitations of Plains Indian costume and put on "war dances," to satisfy the believers in the myth. As it exists today in the public mind, it still contains the mutually incongruous elements of the Noble Red Man and the Bloodthirsty Savage that first came into being three centuries and a half ago, before any white man had ever seen a war bonnet or a tepee, or any Indian had ridden a horse.

QUESTIONS TO CONSIDER

1   Oliver La Farge discusses the myths devised by Europeans to hide the Native Americans and their cultures from the Europeans' view. Discuss these myths and explain why the Europeans created them. How did such myths influence the colonial interaction with Native Americans?

2   What were the significant cultural traits of the Indian civilizations of the Southeast before the coming of the Europeans? What was unique about the Natchez of Mississippi? How would you compare the Natchez to European civilizations at the time?

3   How did the introduction of European goods, livestock, horses, and disease affect the Native Americans? What Indian tribes were most profoundly changed by the introduction of the horse?

4   Why did the framers of the U.S. Constitution study the political structure of the Iroquois League of Nations? Is this action at odds with the myths that early European settlers perpetuated about the Indians?

5   La Farge is particularly fond of the sophisticated mound builders of the Southeast. Does he discuss other similarly sophisticated Native American cultures? If so, which ones? What were the unique cultural traits of the Indians of the Northwest coast? Which ones does the author find most disdainful? Do you find his criticism unfair in light of European atrocities against the Native Americans?

2

From These Beginnings

PAGE SMITH

The European arrival in the Americas brought about a clash of imperial energies as Spain, Portugal, France, and eventually England vied with one another in staking claims to the "New World." For a time, it seemed that Spain would become the dominant imperial power in the New World. While Portugal received Brazil, thanks to an edict from the Pope in 1493, Spain claimed the rest of South and Central America and sent out explorers to look for gold and silver there. By the 1550s, powerful Spain had a sprawling colonial empire that comprised most of South America, Central America, Mexico, the Caribbean islands, Florida, and the American Southwest from Texas to California. As one historian pointed out, Spain established "the largest and most populous empire the western world had seen since the fall of Rome." The industrious Spaniards introduced to the New World the cattle ranch, horses, cattle, sheep, goats, burros, swine, and most of the lingo of the cowboy (rodeo, lariat, mustang, cinch, bronco, and chaps). The Spanish home government, thanks to the eloquent entreaties of Father Bartolomé de las Casas, also tried to stop the brutal enslavement and extermination of the Native Americans, which the Spaniards themselves had begun.

Meanwhile French explorers searched eastern Canada for the Northwest Passage, a legendary waterway that was supposed to connect the Atlantic and Pacific Oceans and that, under France's control, would give France access to the luxuries of Asia. Unable to find such a passage, France was content to establish a fur-trading empire in Canada, with French explorers, traders, and missionaries advancing west to the Great Lakes and then southward down the Mississippi to New Orleans.

England, however, was slow to join the race for colonies, although John Cabot's voyage to North America in 1497 had given England a claim to the New World. Finally, under Queen Elizabeth, the English challenged Spain's rule of the oceans and domination of the New World. Adventurous "sea dogs" under John Hawkins raided Spanish commerce on both the Atlantic and the Pacific, and in 1588, in a dramatic sea battle, the English navy defeated the Spanish armada, a victory that gave England virtually undisputed control of the seas. Thanks to the persuasive arguments of Sir Walter Raleigh, Sir Humphrey Gilbert, and Richard Hakluyt, all champions of colonization, England at last began to build a New World empire. After an abortive attempt to found a colony on Roanoke Island, North Carolina, Queen Elizabeth and her successor James I authorized private corporations called joint stock companies to establish the Virginia (first known as Jamestown) Plymouth, and Massachusetts Bay colonies.

From the outset, the Indians, from the Pequots of Massachusetts to the Powhatans of Virginia, posed the biggest obstacle to English conquest and settlement in North America. How to deal with them? The London-based leaders of Massachusetts and Virginia directed their settlers to treat the Indians "humanely," to christianize, feed, and clothe them, instruct them in "the manual arts and skills," and to incorporate them into "the English community" so that they could enjoy the amenities of "civilization."

These instructions, of course, were based on the European misconception of the Indian as a savage. Although the Indians possessed a culture as old, as rich, and as religious as any in Europe, whites typically thought of them as "bad people, having little of humanity but shape, ignorant of civility or arts, or religion; more brutish than the beasts they hunt, more wild and unmanly than that unmanned wild country, which they range rather than inhabit." Racial prejudice fed that hostile attitude. In European eyes, these dark-skinned people were "pernicious creatures" and barbarians. Only violence would keep them in line. As one European man said, "Unless we bang the Indians stoutly, and make them fear us, they will never love us, nor keep the peace long with us."

And bang the Indians they did, killing off whole tribes and driving others into the interior, where they had to force their way into areas inhabited by other tribes. Some Indians — the Powhatans and Pequots, among them — resisted the colonists and were wiped out. Others, like the Piscataway Indians of Maryland, managed to accommodate themselves to the invaders and thus to preserve "their cultural integrity." Those Indians who did convert to Christianity and adopt the white man's way remained second-class citizens.

Writes historian James Freeman Hawke, "The white man took from the Indian what he could use. The Indian paths through the woods eventually became the settlers' ways and roads. Like the natives, they girdled trees to open up the forest to sunlight. They planted, harvested, and cooked native crops as the Indians did. The Indian taught them how to use snowshoes, how to convert animal pelts into warm winter clothing, how to make a dugout canoe and a pair of moccasins. . . . These borrowings helped to speed the white man's adjustment to the strange new world but did not fundamentally alter his culture." As we saw in the first selection, most of what the Indians got from the Europeans, especially their deadly diseases, virtually destroyed the Indian way of life.

As the number of colonies increased in the seventeenth century, a great migration began to English North America. That migration is the subject of this selection by historian Page Smith, who writes from the standpoint of the European immigrants, thus giving you a different perspective from that in the opening selection. With a vivid pen and an eye for telling detail, Smith discusses the remarkable hodgepodge of humanity that streamed into the English colonies from more than a dozen European countries. Among them, of course, were hardy farmers, aspiring merchants, indentured servants, and visionary religious groups in search of better secular and spiritual lives. But the unfortunate and the disreputable came as well, ranging from English boys who were stolen and sold into bondage, to convicted felons and "rogues and vagabonds" shipped out to the colonies by the British government. As Smith explains, "rogues and vagabonds" included a variety of outlawed folk — beggars, prostitutes, drunkards, dancers, fiddlers, fencers, actors, jugglers, dice players, minstrels, fortunetellers, charlatans, tinkers, peddlers, and loiterers, all of whom played some part in the drama of colonization. From farmers to felons, this diverse assortment of individuals went on to seize the eastern coast of North America and to forge a new nation in the wilderness.

GLOSSARY

CALVINISTS   Those who subscribed to the religious teachings of John Calvin (1509–1664), a French theologian and a leader in the Protestant Reformation, who stressed God's sovereignty, the supremacy of the Scriptures, and predestination — the notion that one's fate was already determined by an all-powerful God and that human beings could do nothing to achieve their salvation or alter their fate.

DURAND   French Protestant who described the love-making of indentured servants during a passage to colonial America.

GREAT AWAKENING   Religious revival that swept the English from about 1725 to 1770. Treated in detail in selection 5.

HUGUENOTS   European Protestants who fled from persecution in Catholic countries such as France.

INDENTURED SERVANT   A man or woman bound over to a master for a period of servitude; in exchange, the master paid the servant's way to the colonies and provided food and shelter.

MITTELBERGER, GOTTLIEB   German immigrant from Enzweiningen who provided a dramatic account of his voyage to America.

PENN, WILLIAM (1644–1718)   English Quaker who founded the colony of Pennsylvania as a refuge for Quakers.

REDEMPTIONERS   Bound servants similar to indentured servants, "they were carried to America by a ship captain with the understanding that after they reached the colonies, they would undertake to sell themselves to the highest bidder and then pay the captain the cost of their passage."

The American Colonists came from a variety of backgrounds. . . . What united them was the wilderness to which they came, a vast land . . . [that] was, literally, incomprehensible; it reached beyond the mind's imagining, threatening and promising, larger than all of Europe: coastal shelf and then mountains and endless plains and more mountains and, finally, the Pacific. No one could measure its extent. The English settlers for their part clung to its eastern margins, to the seacoast strip that faced the ocean highway to the Old World. Even here there were terrains, climates, and topographies as dramatically different as one could imagine — from the rocky, frigid shores of New Hampshire to the sunny beaches of South Carolina.

There was a kind of mad presumption about the whole venture: a few thousand, and then a few hundred thousand, and finally a few million souls scattered along almost two thousand miles of coastline. And in truth it could be said that those who made this strange odyssey to the New World were as diverse as the land they inhabited. Those from England itself represented every class and condition of men. And then there were the Swedes, who settled on the Delaware long before William Penn and his followers arrived, and the stolid and intractable Dutch, reputed to have bought Manhattan from the [Indians] for a few strings of beads — the most famous real estate deal in history. And the French Huguenots, Protestants fleeing from persecution in a Catholic country; the Catholics of Maryland, fleeing persecution in a Protestant country; the Quakers, fleeing the harassments of the Anglican establishment, the Church of England; and Germans from innumerable principalities, fleeing military draft and the various exactions of petty princes.

Within the British Isles themselves — Ireland, Scotland, England and Wales — there was striking

diversity among the New World emigrants. The Separatists — the Pilgrims under William Bradford — wanted, in essence, to be separate; the Puritans wanted to found a Bible Commonwealth and redeem a fallen world. When Cromwell and the Puritans dominated England and beheaded Charles I, certain Royalists found refuge in Virginia and New York. When the restoration of the monarchy brought Charles II to the English throne and re-established the Stuart line, the regicides — those involved in the execution of Charles I — found refuge in Puritan New England. When the Scottish Covenanters, or Presbyterians, so akin in spirit to the Puritans of New England, rose against the high-handed and tyrannical actions of the re-established monarchy, they were crushingly defeated . . . and cruelly repressed. Many, in consequence, came to America. And they continued to come for a hundred years. . . .

And then there were the Irish. They were a special case. They fled famine and rent-wracking landlords. . . . A Catholic people, they fled their Protestant masters. But above all they fled poverty, the poverty of a ruthlessly exploited peasantry. Generation after generation, the Irish came to the American colonies, primarily to Maryland and Pennsylvania, where they gravitated to the frontier areas. In addition to the Catholic Irish, Scotch-Irish Presbyterians came in substantial numbers to the colonies throughout the eighteenth century. The Scotch-Irish were those Covenanters, or militant Presbyterians, who had been forced by the bitter divisions in Scotland itself to seek the protection of the English armies in Northern Ireland (hence Scotch-Irish). For many of them, Ireland was little more than a way station to the colonies, where they showed a marked preference for Pennsylvania and settled, typically, on the frontier. . . .

So the immigrants came in an ever-growing tide — the hungry, the oppressed, the contentious, the ambitious, those out of power and out of favor, the losers, whether in the realm of politics or of eco-

Extracts from *A People's History of the American Revolution*, Vol. II: *A New Age Begins*, pages 28–47, copyright McGraw-Hill Publishing Company. Used by permission of the author.

German Immigrants in Georgia. "The immigrants came in an ever-growing tide," Page Smith writes, "the hungry, the oppressed, the contentious, the ambitious, those out of power and out of favor, the losers, whether in the realm of politics or of economics." (New York Public Library, Rare Book Room, Astor, Lenox and Tilden Foundations)

nomics. And America could accommodate them all: Irish peasant and his land-poor master, Scottish Highlander and Lowlander, persecuted Protestant and persecuted Catholic, fortune-seeker and God-seeker, they found their places, their kinfolk, the familiar accents of their home shires or counties or countries.

But the essence of them all, of all that human congress, the bone and marrow, the unifying principle, the prevailing and pervasive spirit was English. Like the others who came, the English came ... for a number of reasons. Most of them shared some particular expectation, whether for spiritual or material betterment or, happily, both. Many of those who came later shared, of course, the hopes of the original settlers. Many more came because conditions were desperately hard in England and Ireland for poor people, even for those who had not yet sunk into the pit of abandoned hopelessness that was the lot of the most wretched.

It has been estimated that London in the eighteenth century had 6,000 adult and 9,300 child beggars. In the entire country of some 10,000,000 persons, there were estimated to be 50,000 beggars, 20,000 vagrants, 10,000 idlers, 100,000 prostitutes, 10,000 rogues and vagabonds, 80,000 criminals, 1,041,000 persons on parish relief. Indeed, over half the population was below what we would call today "the poverty line," and many, of course, were profoundly below it — below it to the point of starvation. An estimate of the different classes — and class lines were almost impassable — in 1688 suggests that nobility, gentry, merchants, professionals, freeholders (those who held land on their own), craftsmen, and public officials constituted 47 per cent of the population; while common sailors and soldiers (recruited, for the most part, from the lowest levels of British society and enduring desperately hard conditions of service), laborers, servants, paupers, and all those other remarkable subdivisions that we have listed above such as rogues and vagrants made up 53 per cent of the population. The colonies, for their part, had a virtually inexhaustible demand for labor. Anyone willing to work could be put to worthwhile labor, and might (and often did) in a few years establish himself as an independent farmer or artisan.

Yet it was one thing to be an undernourished London apprentice who hated his master and another to find a way to get to America. Some indication of the situation of the working class in the larger cities may be discerned from the condition of pauper children in London in the early eighteenth century. Orphaned, or more frequently illegitimate and abandoned at birth, they were sent to workhouses and to parish nurses. A Parliamentary study found that of all such infants born or received in London's workhouses in a three-year period, only seven in every hundred were alive at the end of that time. As part of the "surcharge of necessitous people," orphaned and impoverished children who were public charges were sporadically dispatched to the colonies as indentured servants. People worked, typically, from six in the morning until eight at night for a pittance that barely supported life. They had no holidays except at Christmas, Easter, and on hanging days, when everyone might be entertained and edified by watching wretches hanged for crimes that, in many instances, would be classed as misdemeanors today.

Despite the cruelty of punishments, London had a large criminal class and was infested with prostitutes. The working class drowned its miseries in bad gin and beer. There were some 7,000 ginshops in the suburbs of London and, by 1750, 16,000 in the city itself (only 1,050 of which were licensed); most of them were in the poorest sections of the city, whose horrors are vividly recorded in Hogarth's etchings of Gin Lane. The hard liquor consumed in one year (1733) in London alone amounted to 11,200,000 gallons, or some 56 gallons per adult male.

Next to public hangings, the principal entertainments available to the poor — and enjoyed by the rich as well — were cockfighting, bullbaiting, and badger baiting. In such circumstances there was ample incentive to emigrate almost anywhere. . . . But to the penniless, the question was: How? The growing need for labor in the colonies supplied the answer, and a system of indenture, based on the long-established apprenticeship, was devised. Agents paid for the ship's passage of improvident men and women who were willing to contract themselves in America to work off the cost of their transportation. By this means, tens of thousands of English and Irish workers of both sexes found their way across the ocean.

The system was easily and often abused. A class of men "of the lowest order," called spirits and crimps, arose, who spirited away unwilling lads and sold them into bondage. . . . One spirit boasted that he had been spiriting persons for twelve years at a rate of five hundred persons a year. He would give twenty-five shillings to anyone who would bring him a likely prospect, and he could sell such a one to a merchant at once for forty shillings. Often spiriting was a profitable sideline for a brewer, hostler, carpenter, or tavern keeper. The tavern keeper was in an especially advantageous position, since a drunken patron was an easy victim. So dreaded were these dismal agents that mothers frightened their children into obedience by warning them that a spirit would carry them off if they were bad. It was no idle threat. In 1653 Robert Broome secured a warrant for the arrest of a ship's captain charged with carrying off his son, aged eleven, who had been spirited aboard. A few years later, a commission going aboard the *Conquer* found that eleven out of nineteen servants had been "taken by the spirits." Their average age was nineteen. Not all spirits were depraved men, however, and even the worst of them often performed a useful service in arranging transportation for a servant who wished to emigrate to the colonies against the wishes of parents or a master. . . .

For a time it proved easier to get women servants than men servants. . . . Mathew Cradock, captain of the *Abraham*, sailing for Virginia, made elaborate preparations for carrying a shipload of servants, men and women alike, to Virginia on a four-year indenture. On his ship's arrival in various English ports, . . . he rounded up forty-one men and twenty women, the latter "from 17 to 35 yeares and very lustye and strong Boddied. . . ."

Clothing, "peppar and Gingar," and three-and a-half pounds of tobacco for the men were all purchased before the ship set sail, and a midwife was hired to make sure none of the women were pregnant. Soon after the ship sailed it was driven into the harbor of Cowes, and it was a month before it got favorable winds. By that time, three of the women were pregnant and were sent home; some who were put ashore to do the washing ran away and had to be tracked down at a cost of ten shillings; and another was found "not fette to be entertained haveinge the frentche dizeas [gonorrhea]" and was sent packing.

If a female indentured servant became pregnant during her service, her misdeed represented a loss to her master, so that an indentured servant guilty of bastardy was required to pay the usual charges levied against unwed mothers as well as to indemnify her master for the loss of her services during the later stages of her pregnancy and her lying-in. Not infrequently, the master was the culprit. In Maryland, Jacob Lumbrozo [of Portugal] . . . alias Dr. John, was charged with having made persistent overtures to his maid, Elisabeth Weales, and when rebuffed, "hee tooke her in his armes and threw her upon the bed she went to Cry out hee plucked out his handerchif of his pocket and stope her mouth and force her whether shee will or noe when hee know that she was with Child he gave her fickes to distroy it and for anything shee know hee would distroy her too. . . ." By the time the case came to court, Lumbrozo had married Elisabeth Weales, who became a prominent if contentious figure in the affairs of the county. In Virginia, a statute was passed to prevent a master who had impregnated his servant girl from claiming extra service from her beyond her indenture: "Late experiments shew that some dissolute masters have gotten their maides with child, and yet claime the benefitt of their service." However, the maid got off no better. After the end of her indenture she was to be sold by the church wardens for the use of the parish for two years. . . .

The terms of indenture required the master to provide food and clothing for his servants and, often in the case of German or Swiss servants, to take the responsibility for seeing that they learned English during the term of their indenture. At the end of their terms they were to be provided with a stated sum of money and a suit of presentable clothes so that they could make a proper start in life. South Carolina required that a female servant at the expiration of her service be given a waistcoat and petticoat, a new shift of white linen, shoes and stockings, a blue apron and two white linen caps. In some colonies, indentured servants received land at the end of their term of indenture. Thus in North Carolina during the proprietary period a servant's "freedom dues" were fifty acres of land and afterward three barrels of Indian corn and two new suits of a value of at least five pounds. . . ."

Whether wickedly abused or treasured and re-warded — and certainly they experienced both cruelty and kindness — indentured servants made up more than half the immigrants to the middle and southern colonies. During the twenty-five-year period between 1750 and 1775, some 25,000 servants and convicts entered Maryland, and a comparable number arrived in Virginia. Abbott Smith estimates that during the same period at least twice as many servants and redemptioners entered Pennsylvania, of whom perhaps a third were German and the rest, in large part, Irish. The Irish ... were Catholics. To Protestants, this fact made the Irish the least desirable of all immigrant groups. The more substantial class of immigrants, especially the Germans and the Swiss, came as redemptioners. Redemptioners were carried to America by a ship captain with the understanding that after they reached the colonies, they would undertake to sell themselves to the highest bidder and then pay the captain the cost of their passage. Most of the redemptioners were craftsmen whose skills were much in demand in the colonies and who could thus sell themselves on favorable terms to a master. If they could not sell themselves, it was the shipmaster's right to undertake to sell them, often at highly disadvantageous terms. Since a master could buy much cheaper from a ship captain, collusion between prospective buyers and the captain was not uncommon.

The story of indentured servants is one of the most dramatic in colonial America. While many of those who came under indenture were the "scum and offscourings of the earth" — convicts, paupers, runaway apprentices, prostitutes and the like — many, particularly among the non-English, were respectable and decent people who had fallen on hard times or simply wished to improve their fortunes. We also know that in the rude conditions of colonial life, many of the dissolute were redeemed.

In seventeenth- and eighteenth-century England, crime was endemic. The alarm of the more prosperous classes was expressed in cries for law and order.

The penalty of death was prescribed for all felonies. In seventeenth-century England, almost three hundred crimes were classed as felonies; a conviction for anything, indeed, from housebreaking and the theft of goods worth more than a shilling must result in the sentence of death by hanging, since the judge had no discretionary power in felony cases. The benefit of clergy and royal pardon were the only mitigations. A convicted felon could "call for the book," usually a Bible, and if he could read it, he was freed of the penalty of death, branded on the thumb, and released. The practice stemmed from medieval times, when generally speaking only those in holy orders were able to read, and they were subject to their own ecclesiastical courts. The benefit of clergy was undoubtedly a great incentive to the development of a literate criminal class, but in a time when a vast majority of the poor were illiterate, it had little else to recommend it. The simple fact was that if you were poor and illiterate you might be hanged for stealing a few shillings' worth of cloth, while a villainous cutpurse who could decipher a simple text would be branded and then would go free. . . .

The royal pardon was the only amelioration of a murderous system. Again in a typically English accommodation, judges who thought sentences too severe could send up a list of those convicted felons they considered worthy of mercy, and these would be pardoned by the king. For many years more than half of those sentenced to hang were pardoned, and increasingly it came to be the practice to issue such pardons on the condition that the culprit agreed to leave the country. From the middle of the seventeenth century until early in the eighteenth, thousands of convicts left England under this arrangement. Of these, a substantial majority found their way to the English colonies in the West Indies and in North America. In 1717, Parliament passed a law permitting the "transportation" out of the realm of certain classes of offenders "in clergy." From 1619 to 1640 all felons reprieved by royal pardon were transported to Virginia to help make up the toll of those settlers lost by disease, and between 1661 and 1700 more than 4,500 convicts were dispatched to the colonies. In the years from 1745 to 1775, 8,846 convicts, 9,035 servants, and 3,324 slaves landed at Annapolis, Maryland.

Convicts were certainly not ideal settlers. In one contingent, twenty-six had been convicted for stealing, one for violent robbery, and five for murder. . . . The character of such settlers is indicated by the career of Jenny Voss, who was eventually hanged at Tyburn after having been transported to the colonies, where "she could not forget her old Pranks, but used not only to steal herself, but incited all others that were her fellow Servants to Pillfer and Cheat," so that her master was glad to be rid of her, the more so since "she had wheadled in a Son of the Planters, who used to Lye with her and supply her with Moneys. . . ."

Virginia and Maryland, which had been the principal outlets for transported felons, had passed laws forbidding their importation by the end of the seventeenth century. . . . But despite such [laws], Parliament in 1717 passed a statute that overrode colonial efforts to stem the tide of undesirables. A total of thirty thousand convicted felons were shipped from England in the fifty-year period prior to the Revolution, of whom the greater number apparently went to Maryland and Virginia. Since convicts were bound into servitude for seven or fourteen years, which often proved to be a lifetime, the colonists usually bid actively for the most likely ones. The men sold for from eight to twenty pounds or, roughly, twenty-five to fifty dollars. Women brought slightly less, while the old and infirm were given away or, if no taker could be found, a subsidy was paid to anyone who would take them in.

It was not a humane or enlightened system, and the most that can be said for it is that the majority of the transported felons who were sold into white semislavery were slightly better off alive than dead. For those who escaped their masters, fled to other colonies, and established themselves as respectable citizens, it was a handsome bargain. Those willing to work and fortunate enough to have a kind master, had a far better life than the one they had left behind in England. It is safe to surmise that a substantially higher proportion of women than men were redeemed to a decent life — from which it would presumably follow that a substantial number of Americans who trace their line of descent back to colonial times have an ancestress or two who arrived here as a convicted felon, a sneak thief, or a prostitute.

Three or four times a year, the convicts to be transported were marched in irons through the streets of London from Newgate Prison to Blackfriars. This procession provided, like hangings, a popular form of entertainment for mobs who would hoot at the convicts and, when the convicts replied with obscene epithets, sometimes pelt them with mud and stones. The more prosperous convicts could buy special privileges. Thus in 1736, four felons rode to the point of embarkation in two hackney coaches, and another, "a Gentleman of Fortune, and a Barrister at Law," convicted of stealing books from the Trinity College library, had a private coach to carry him in style. These men paid their own passage and shared a private cabin.

Besides the large number of convicted felons, there were many other Englishmen who fell in the rather commodious category of "rogues and vagabonds." Although they came from a very different economic stratum, these were the hippies and dropouts of seventeenth- and eighteenth-century English society, the men and women so alienated from the dominant culture that they had devised their own. They lived on the margins of the law, devoted to preying in a thousand ingenious ways on the public. A statute of Parliament defined them as [beggars, drunkards, prostitutes, dancers, fiddlers, fencers, actors, jugglers, dice players, minstrels, fortunetellers, charlatans, tinkers, peddlers, and loiterers]. . . . Punishments were meant to be exemplary and painful. All beggars were to be stripped to the waist and whipped until they were bloody, then sent home or to the grim confines of a house of correction. Moreover, any rogue who appeared to be a hardened and dangerous character would be sent to such places beyond the seas as the Privy Council might designate.

By these provisions, incorrigible lawbreakers could be shipped out of the mother country even more readily than convicts throughout the colonial period. How "manie Drunkards, Tossepottes, whoremoisters, Dauncers, Fidlers and Minstrels, Diceplaiers, & Maskers" were dispatched to the colonies is not revealed by British court records. On the other hand, we know of enough charlatans, fortunetellers, minstrels, jugglers, tinkers, and actors in the colonies to assume that a good many of these roguish varieties made their way to America and provided lively if not always discreet entertainment for the less sophisticated colonists. What seems remarkable is that the colonies (like Virginia and Maryland) receiving the largest numbers of indentured servants and convicted felons were not utterly submerged and demoralized by these successive waves of human flotsam. Vicious and depraved as many of them must have been, the great majority made the adjustment to colonial life with reasonable success. Otherwise it is hard to see how these colonies could have survived, let alone prospered in their material and spiritual endeavors.

The transatlantic voyage from England to America was a terrible ordeal for most of those who made the crossing. Indentured servants signed up by crimps and spirits embarked on small, poorly equipped, and often dirty sailing vessels that took from one to as much as five months, depending on prevailing winds, to make the crossing. The Sea-Flower, with 106 passengers aboard, took sixteen weeks; forty-six of her passengers died of starvation, and of these, six were eaten by the desperate survivors. The long crossing meant bad food; the water stank and grew slimy, meat spoiled, and butter turned rancid. If the captain or owner was a profiteer, the food was often rotten to begin with. In small boats tossed by heavy seas, seasickness was commonplace. One passenger on such a crossing wrote a crude verse describing the

effects of a storm on his fellow voyagers: Soon after the storm began, "there was the odest scene betwixt decks that I ever heard or seed. There was some sleeping, some spewing ... some damning, some Blasting their legs and thighs, some their liver, lungs, lights and eyes. And for to make the scene the odder, some curs'd Father, Mother, Sister, and Brother."

A French Protestant named Durand sailed for Virginia after the revocation of the Edict of Nantes and the resumption of active persecution of the Huguenots. There were fifteen prostitutes on board ship, headed, hopefully, for a new life in the New World. During the passage, they spent their time singing and dancing and making love with the sailors and the indentured servants aboard. Durand, kept awake by their revels, wrote: "Certainly their insolence wrought a change in my nature, for my acquaintances would no doubt impute to me, as my greatest failing, an exaggerated love of the fair sex, & to tell the truth I must admit that in my youth there was no injustice in this accusation. Not that I was ever low enough or coarse enough to feel an affection for prostitutes, but I am obliged to confess I did not abhor their debauchery as I should have.... But when I saw those wenches behave so shockingly with the sailors and others, in addition to the distress caused by their songs and dances, it awakened within me so intense a hatred of such persons that I shall never overcome it." Durand's wife died at sea, the food ran out, and the captain proved to be a knave and a bully. Their voyage took nineteen miserable weeks, long enough for weakness and hunger to quiet the gaiety of the prostitutes.

In the German principalities, the counterparts of the English "spirits" were the Newlanders, agents who tried to persuade guileless countryfolk to set sail for America. Gottlieb Mittelberger, a German immigrant from Enzweiningen who arrived in Philadelphia in 1750, gave a vivid account of his crossing of the Atlantic. He was bitter about the "sad and miserable condition of those traveling from Germany to the New World, and the irresponsible and merciless proceedings of the Dutch traders in human beings and their man-stealing emissaries—I mean the so-called Newlanders. For these at one and the same time steal German people under all sorts of fine pretexts, and deliver them into the hands of the great Dutch traffickers in human souls." The trip meant "for most who undertake it the loss of all they possess, of freedom and peace, and for some the loss of their very lives and, I can even go so far as to say, of the salvation of their souls." Mittelberger's journey took six months, the people "packed into the big boats as closely as herring. . . ." The water distributed to thirsty passengers was often "very black, thick with dirt and full of worms." Mittelberger's description of conditions on the ship refers to "smells, fumes, horrors, vomiting . . . boils, scurvy, cancer, mouthrot . . . caused by the age and the highly-salted state of the food, especially of the meat. . . . Add to all that shortage of food, hunger, thirst, frost, heat, dampness, fear, misery, vexation, and lamentation . . . so many lice . . . that they have to be scraped off the bodies. All this misery reaches its climax when in addition to everything else one must suffer through two or three days and nights of storm . . . all the people on board pray and cry pitifully together." Under such circumstances, what little civility there might have been collapsed completely. People grew so bitter "that one person begins to curse the other, or himself and the day of his birth, and people sometimes come close to murdering one another. Misery and malice are readily associated, so that people begin to cheat and steal from one another." It is hardly surprising that America, when the immigrants reached it, seemed a land of deliverance; "When at last after the long and difficult voyage the ships finally approach land," Mittelberger wrote, "for the sight of which the people on board had longed so passionately, then everyone crawls from below to the deck, in order to look at the land. . . . And the people cry for joy, pray, and sing praises and thanks to God. The glimpse of land revives the passengers, especially those who are half-dead of illness. Their spirits, however weak they had become, leap up, triumph, and rejoice. . . ."

As difficult as were the conditions under which indentured servants and redemptioners crossed the Atlantic, the circumstances of the prisoners were, as might be imagined, substantially worse. They were chained below decks in crowded, noisome ranks. One observer who went on board a convict ship to visit a prisoner wrote: "All the states of horror I ever had an idea of are much short of what I saw this poor man in; chained to a board in a hole not above sixteen feet long, more than fifty with him; a collar and padlock about his neck, and chained to five of the most dreadful creatures I ever looked on." Living conditions were little better than those obtaining on slave ships, and before the voyage was over it was not uncommon to lose a quarter of the human cargo, most frequently to the ravages of smallpox. (Only half as many women as men died on these hell ships, a fact attributed by merchants in the convict trade to their stronger constitutions.) Convicts so often arrived in the colonies more dead than alive that Parliamentary statutes finally set minimum allowances of bread, cheese, meat, oatmeal, and molasses per passenger—with two gills of gin issued on Saturdays.

The feelings of the colonists concerning the apparently endless stream of transported felons and vagabonds are indicated by a passage in the *Virginia Gazette* of May 24, 1751: "When we see our Papers fill'd continually with Accounts of the most audacious Robberies, the most cruel Murders, and infinite other Villanies perpetrated by Convicts transported from Europe," the correspondent wrote, "what melancholy, what terrible Reflections must it occasion! What will become of our Posterity? These are some of thy Favours, Britain! Thou are called our Mother country; but what good Mother ever sent Thieves and Villains to accompany her children; to corrupt some with their infectious Vices and murder the rest? . . . In what can Britain show a more Sovereign contempt for us than by emptying their Jails into our Settlements. . . ." Whatever the colonists' feelings, the English were delighted with the practice of transporting their convicts to America. By such a procedure, the criminal was separated from evil companions and from the usually deplorable conditions that had induced him to take up a life of crime.

Not all convicts appreciated, by any means, the opportunity afforded them to start life over in the colonies. Not a few found their way back home (risking certain death, if caught) and declared that they would rather be hanged than return to America.

Servants and convicts who had served out their indentures often drifted to the frontier areas of the colonies, particularly to the southern frontier. Some took up cattle ranching in western Carolina, where the cattle were turned loose to graze, rounded up yearly into pens (hence Cowpens, South Carolina), and driven to the seacoast markets for meat and hides. Some, like the Hatfields and the McCoys, would in time feud with each other for decades; others lived lives of lawlessness and banditry, preying on staid planters in more settled areas and becoming, in some instances, the ancestors of the southern mountain folk, who for successive generations resisted the incursions of tax collectors.

A number, of course, gathered in the seaport towns of Baltimore, Philadelphia, New York, Charles Town, and Boston, where they drank excessively, did occasional labor, committed petty crimes, rioted, and formed the nucleus of revolutionary mobs. The truth was that with few exceptions, they belonged to that class of people whose feelings lie very close to the surface. Violent and passionate by nature, they were peculiarly susceptible to both religious conversion and revolutionary ardor. Restless and rootless, they were readily swept up by any emotional storm. Many of them were converted at the time of the Great Awakening [a series of Protestant revivals lasting from about 1725 to 1770] into pious Presbyterians, Methodists, and, somewhat later, Baptists. These denominations, with their emphasis on personal experience, were perfectly suited to the psychological needs of such individuals. Thus a substantial number of servants and ex-convicts accommodated themselves to the Protestant Ethic and became in time indistinguishable from their orthodox neighbors.

Less colorful, but equally important, were those settlers who came on their own initiative and at their own expense. By a process of natural selection, such individuals were usually aggressive, ambitious, and, as we would say today, highly motivated. Prominent among them were the Scotch-Irish. . . . [They were] independent yeoman farmers who were stout Presbyterians, often shared a common Scottish aversion to the British, and were now removed in turn to the congenial atmosphere of the colonies, particularly Pennsylvania. Hardy, enterprising Calvinists, they made their way in large numbers westward, where land was plentiful and cheap. There, serving as "the guardians of the frontier," they were constantly embroiled with eastern land speculators or various Indian tribes over ownership of land.

There was a special affinity between native Lowland Scots and the inhabitants of the middle and eastern colonies. This led to a substantial immigration of Scotch-Irish in the middle years of the eighteenth century preceding the Revolutionary crisis. Never large in numbers, the Scots nonetheless, like the Jews and Huguenots, played a disproportionately important role in colonial affairs and were prominent in the patriot cause.

The Rhineland country in present-day Germany was in the eighteenth century divided into a number of principalities, including the Rheinpfalz or Rhenish Palatinate, Württemberg, Baden, and Brunswick. These petty states were constantly embroiled in European conflicts, and many German peasants, most of them pious Lutherans, fled from the exactions of their princes: from conscription, heavy taxes, and a condition of chronic insecurity. The majority came to Pennsylvania, with some in New York, Virginia, and the Carolinas. In Penn's colony, they established tight-knit, self-contained farming communities, where they clung to their language and their folk traditions. Travelers noted that they were stolid, hard-working, and usually more tidy than their English or Scotch-Irish neighbors. From *Deutsch,* they became Pennsylvania Dutch, developing their own patois and, by clinging stubbornly to their folk traditions, making their villages into small fortresses of cultural separatism. The most conspicuous and long-lived of the German immigrant groups that came to America were the Moravians, a pietist sect.... This group settled primarily in Salem, North Carolina, and Bethlehem, Pennsylvania, and to this day they preserve a rich tradition of church music, especially that of Johann Sebastian Bach. The Dunkers, who excelled in choral singing and bookmaking, and their close cousins the Mennonites also came largely to Pennsylvania. Today, forbidden by their religion to wear clothes with buttons, to drive cars, to use electricity, radios, or television, the Mennonite men with their chin hair, plain black clothes, and broad-brimmed black hats, and the women with their long skirts and bonnets, still farm the rich and carefully tended soil of central Pennsylvania and [have been] frequently embroiled with the state over their determination not to send their children to public schools....

As Protestant England had persecuted its Catholics, so Catholic France persecuted its Protestants (known as Huguenots). In consequence many Huguenots looked to the New World. Since they were denied entry into New France, a number were strung out from Boston to Charles Town, favoring the toleration and commercial opportunities offered by these port towns. Peter Faneuil, the rich merchant who built Faneuil Hall, Boston's "Cradle of Liberty," and who was both a good patriot and a public benefactor, was of Huguenot ancestry, as were Paul Revere and — in South Carolina — the Rhetts, the Gadsdens, the Ravenels, the Laurenses, the Deveaux and the L'Enfants.

A handful of Jews came to the American colonies in the seventeenth and eighteenth centuries, with Pennsylvania and Rhode Island as the preferred locations. The first American synagogue was built in Providence, Rhode Island. Aaronsburg, Pennsylvania, was founded by Jewish settlers, and in Philadelphia the wealthy Gratz family contributed generously to the patriot cause. A Jewish scholar taught Hebrew at Harvard in the middle of the eighteenth century.

[Ultimately] ... this collection of astonishingly diverse individuals, from a dozen countries and twice as many religious sects and denominations, spread out over a vast territory and coalesced into a nation and eventually into a united people....

QUESTIONS TO CONSIDER

1 Sixteenth-century immigrants to the American colonies came from England, Scotland, Ireland, France, Germany, Holland, and Sweden. What characteristics does Page Smith suggest they had in common?

2 How did conditions in seventeenth- and eighteenth-century England fuel emigration to the colonies? Describe the system of indenture. How did convicted felons, rogues, and vagabonds end up coming to America?

3 Describe the ordeal of the ocean crossing for indentured servants and for convicts. If they arrived safely, how did these immigrants make their way in American society? In what ways did the system of indenture discriminate against women?

4 By the mid-eighteenth century, established colonists had begun to protest the dumping of England's human refuse on American shores. Why do you suppose the colonies were not simply overwhelmed by the flood of undesirables? Where did these and other colonial protests against English high-handedness eventually culminate?

5 Page Smith says that many of the felons, rogues, and vagabonds were converted to solid citizens in the religious revivals of the mid-eighteenth century. In what ways were these immigrants particularly susceptible to conversion?

II

The First Century

3

Black People in a White People's Country

GARY B. NASH

In 1619, a year before the Pilgrims landed at Plymouth Rock, a Dutch ship deposited "twenty Negars" on the wharf of Jamestown Colony, in what became Virginia. These were the first Africans to enter colonial America, but their exact status is unknown. Like Africans subsequently imported until 1660, they were probably indentured servants whose period of servitude was temporary. After 1660, however, most Africans who came to America were slaves, purchased through a heinous business operation, the international slave trade. By the eighteenth century, every English colony from Carolina to Massachusetts had enacted "slave codes," bodies of law that stripped black people of all rights and reduced them to pieces of property, or "chattel," with their children inheriting that status.

The troubling question is why the Africans were enslaved and white indentures were not. In the selection that follows, Gary B. Nash, one of the leading experts on colonial America, argues that the answer lies in a combination of racial prejudice and labor needs in early America, particularly in the southern colonies. When faced with the problem of cultivating labor-intensive crops, Nash writes, English settlers "turned to the international slave trade to fill their labor needs." That white colonists viewed Africans as uncivilized barbarians only made it easier "to fasten chains upon them." The Africans, of course, were no more barbaric than were the Native Americans. As Nash observes, the Africans had been stolen from richly complex and highly developed cultures. The English settlers, of course, knew nothing about such cultures beyond that they were neither white nor Christian and were therefore "uncivilized."

As more and more Africans were imported to the English colonies, racial fears intensified in direct proportion to the number of blacks in a given area. Such fears were worse in the southern colonies, where the extensive cultivation of labor-intensive crops necessitated the purchase of large numbers of slaves. In the northern colonies, as Nash points out, "slavery existed on a more occasional basis" because labor-intensive crops were not so widely grown there and far fewer Africans were imported. This is a crucial point. It helps explain why slavery later disappeared in the North, during and after the Revolution.

In the colonial period, meanwhile, every colony in North and South alike enacted laws that severely regulated black people and made them slaves for life. Thus from the very outset, slavery served a twofold purpose: it was both a labor system and a means of racial control in a white people's country. This "mass enslavement of Africans," Nash points out, only reinforced racial prejudice in a vicious cycle. "Once institutionalized, slavery cast Africans into such lowly roles that the initial bias against them could only be confirmed and vastly strengthened."

To provide a fuller understanding of slavery in North America, Nash discusses the origins of African slavery itself and offers a graphic and painful portrait of the Atlantic slave trade, which involved "the largest forced migration in history" and was thus "one of the most important phenomena in the history of the modern world." Greed and profit kept the trade booming for four hundred years, with European entrepreneurs reaping fortunes at the expense of millions of human beings. The captain and crew of a slave ship, whether British, Dutch, Portuguese, or colonial American, had to be monstrously depraved and utterly inured to human suffering in order to carry out this brutal business. One such slave trader, Englishman John Newton, later repented, became a minister and an abolitionist, and wrote a hymn about his salvation, "How Sweet the Name of Jesus Sounds," popularly known as "Amazing Grace." Grace was indeed amazing, he said, to have saved "a wretch" like him.

The horrors of the middle passage, warns one historian, were "so revolting that a writer of the present day hesitates to give such details to his readers." On one slaver, said an eyewitness, "400 wretched beings" were chained and "crammed into a hold 12 yards in length . . . and only 3½ feet in height." Because of the hold's "suffocating heat" and stench, the Africans panicked and in their torment tried in vain to escape. The next morning, the crew lifted "fifty-four crushed and mangled corpses up from the slave deck." To keep the survivors in line, the crew beat and murdered other Africans. Such atrocities were commonplace on slave ships, and the captains could not have cared less, because "insurance companies bore part of the loss, and profits were so high that heavy risks were cheerfully assumed."

Driven to madness in the rat-filled, claustrophobic bowels of the slave ships, many Africans maimed themselves or committed suicide. Others starved to death or died of some white man's disease. And the women, too many of them, were humiliated in unspeakable ways by their white captors. If the Africans somehow survived the Atlantic passage, they found themselves dumped into some fly-infested slave pen in a port of the New World. We can imagine such a group in chains on the wharves of colonial New York City or Baltimore. Sick, starving, and frightened, they had to find some way to endure the unendurable in a strange new land. That such Africans salvaged much of their heritage, transforming it into a distinctly African American heritage, was a tribute to their power "to keep on keeping on."

"Thus," writes historian Carl Degler, "began in the seventeenth century the Negro's life in America. With it commenced a moral problem for all Americans which still besets us at the close of the twentieth century." As Nash observes, the emergence of slavery in colonial America was "one of the great paradoxes in American history — the building of what some thought was to be a utopia in the wilderness upon the backs of black men and women wrenched from their African homeland and forced into a system of abject slavery." That paradox, as we shall see, would persist through the American Revolution, the early Republic, and well into the nineteenth century, causing sectional tensions between the North and the South that finally plunged America into the most destructive war in its history.

GLOSSARY

BLACK CODES   Colonial laws that legalized and enforced slavery, depriving Africans of all rights and reducing them to pieces of property.

BLACK GOLD   The European expression for slaves.

DUTCH WEST INDIA COMPANY   A leading "international supplier of slaves."

GONÇALVEZ, ANTAM   Portuguese sea captain who made the first European Landing on the west African coast south of the Sahara and brought back the first kidnapped Africans to Portugal in 1441.

MACKRONS   Africans considered too old or too infirm to make good slaves.

MIDDLE PASSAGE   The route across the Atlantic from the African coast to the New World.

ROYAL AFRICAN COMPANY   An English joint stock company chartered by the Crown to carry slaves to the English colonies.

SEQUEIRA, RUY DO   The Portuguese captain who began the European slave trade in 1472.

The African slave trade, which began in the late fifteenth century and continued for the next 400 years, is one of the most important phenomena in the history of the modern world. Involving the largest forced migration in history, the slave trade and slavery were crucially important in building the colonial empires of European nations and in generating the wealth that later produced the Industrial Revolution. But often overlooked in the attention given to the economic importance of the slave trade and slavery is the cultural diffusion that took place when ten million Africans were brought to the western hemisphere. Six out of every seven persons who crossed the Atlantic to take up life in the New World in the 300 years before the American Revolution were African slaves. As a result, in most parts of the colonized territories slavery "defined the context within which transferred European traditions would grow and change." As slaves, Africans were Europeanized; but at the same time they Africanized the culture of Europeans in the Americas. This was an inevitable part of the convergence of these two broad groups of people, who met each other an ocean away from their original homelands. In addition, the slave trade created the lines of communication for the movement of crops, agricultural techniques, diseases, and medical knowledge between Africa, Europe, and the Americas.

Just as they were late in colonizing the New World, the English lagged far behind their Spanish and Portuguese competitors in making contact with the west coast of Africa, in entering the Atlantic slave trade, and in establishing African slaves as the backbone of the labor force in their overseas plantations. And among the English colonists in the New World, those on the mainland of North America were a half century or more behind those in the Caribbean in converting their plantation economies

From Gary B. Nash, *Red, White, and Black: The Peoples of Early North America* (3rd ed.), copyright © 1992, pp. 144–161, 208–225. Reprinted by permission of Prentice-Hall, Englewood Cliffs, New Jersey.

to slave labor. By 1670, for example, some 200,000 slaves labored in Portuguese Brazil and about 30,000 cultivated sugar in English Barbados; but in Virginia only 2,000 worked in the tobacco fields. Cultural interaction of Europeans and Africans did not begin in North America on a large scale until more than a century after it had begun in the southerly parts of the hemisphere. Much that occurred as the two cultures met in the Iberian colonies was later repeated in the Anglo-African interaction; and yet the patterns of acculturation were markedly different in North and South America in the seventeenth and eighteenth centuries.

☆·

THE ATLANTIC SLAVE TRADE

A half century before Columbus crossed the Atlantic, a Portuguese sea captain, Antam Gonçalvez, made the first European landing on the west African coast south of the Sahara. What he might have seen, had he been able to travel the length and breadth of Africa, was a continent of extraordinary variation in geography and culture. Little he might have seen would have caused him to believe that African peoples were naturally inferior or that they had failed to develop over time as had the peoples of Europe. This notion of "backwardness" and cultural impoverishment was the myth perpetuated after the slave trade had transported millions of Africans to the Western Hemisphere. It was a myth which served to justify the cruelties of the slave trade and to assuage the guilt of Europeans involved in the largest forced dislocation of people in history.

The peoples of Africa may have numbered more than 50 million in the late fifteenth century when Europeans began making extensive contact with the continent. They lived in widely varied ecological zones — in vast deserts, in grasslands, and in great forests and woodlands. As in Europe, most people farmed the land and struggled to subdue the forces of nature in order to sustain life. That the African population had increased so rapidly in the 2,000 years before European arrival suggests the sophistication of the African agricultural methods. Part of this skill in farming derived from skill in iron production, which had begun in present-day Nigeria about 500 B.C. It was this ability to fashion iron implements that triggered the new farming techniques necessary to sustain larger populations. With large populations came greater specialization of tasks and thus additional technical improvements. Small groups of related families made contact with other kinship groups and over time evolved into larger and more complicated societies. The pattern was similar to what had occurred in other parts of the world — in the Americas, Europe, the Middle East, and elsewhere — when the "agricultural revolution" occurred.

Recent studies of "pre-contact" African history have showed that the "culture gap" between European and African societies when the two peoples met was not as large as previously imagined. By the time Europeans reached the coast of West Africa a number of extraordinary empires had been forged in the area. The first, apparently, was the Kingdom of Ghana, which embraced the immense territory between the Sahara Desert and the Gulf of Guinea and from the Niger River to the Atlantic Ocean between the fifth and tenth centuries. Extensive urban settlement, advanced architecture, elaborate art, and a highly complex political organization evolved during this time. From the eighth to the sixteenth centuries, it was the western Sudan that supplied most of the gold for the Western world. Invasion from the north by the Moors weakened the Kingdom of Ghana, which in time gave way to the Empire of Mali. At the center of the Mali Empire was the city of Timbuktu, noted for its extensive wealth and its Islamic university where a faculty as distinguished as any in Europe was gathered.

Lesser kingdoms such as the kingdoms of Kongo, Zimbabwe, and Benin had also been in the process of growth and cultural change for centuries before Europeans reached Africa. Their inhabitants were skilled in metal working, weaving, ceramics, architecture, and aesthetic expression. Many of their towns rivaled European cities in size. Many communities of West Africa had highly complex religious rites, well-organized regional trade, codes of law, and complex political organization.

Of course, cultural development in Africa, as elsewhere in the world, proceeded at varying rates. Ecological conditions had a large effect on this. Where good soil, adequate rainfall, and abundance of minerals were present, as in coastal West Africa, population growth and cultural elaboration were relatively rapid. Where inhospitable desert or nearly impenetrable forest held forth, social systems remained small and changed at a crawl. Contact with other cultures also brought rapid change, whereas isolation impeded cultural change. The Kingdom of Ghana bloomed in western Sudan partly because of the trading contacts with Arabs who had conquered the area in the ninth century. Cultural change began to accelerate in Swahili societies facing the Indian Ocean after trading contacts were initiated with the Eastern world in the ninth century. Thus, as a leading African historian has put it, "the cultural history of Africa is . . . one of greatly unequal development among peoples who, for definable reasons such as these, entered recognizably similar stages of institutional change at different times."

The slave trade seems to have begun officially in 1472 when a Portuguese captain, Ruy do Sequeira, reached the coast of Benin and was conducted to the king's court, where he received royal permission to trade for gold, ivory, and slaves. So far as the Africans were concerned, the trade represented no strikingly new economic activity since they had long been involved in regional and long-distance trade across their continent. This was simply the opening of contacts with a new and more distant commercial partner. This is important to note because often it has been maintained that European powers raided the African coasts for slaves, marching into the interior and kidnapping hundreds of thousands of help-less and hapless victims. In actuality, the early slave trade involved a reciprocal relationship between European purchasers and African sellers, with the Portuguese monopolizing trade along the coastlands of tropical Africa for the first century after contact was made. Trading itself was confined to coastal strongholds where slaves, most of them captured in the interior by other Africans, were sold on terms set by the African sellers. In return for gold, ivory, and slaves, African slave merchants received European guns, bars of iron and copper, brass pots and tankards, beads, rum and textiles. They occupied an economic role not unlike that of the Iroquois middlemen in the fur trade with Europeans.

Slavery was not a new social phenomenon for either Europeans or Africans. For centuries African societies had been involved in an overland slave trade that transported black slaves from West Africa across the Sahara Desert to Roman Europe and the Middle East. But this was an occasional rather than a systematic trade, and it was designed to provide the trading nations of the Mediterranean with soldiers, household servants, and artisans rather than mass agricultural labor. Within Africa itself, a variety of unfree statuses had also existed for centuries, but they involved personal service, often for a limited period ... rather than lifelong, degraded, agricultural labor. Slavery of a similar sort had long existed in Europe, mostly as the result of Christians enslaving Moslems and Moslems enslaving Christians during centuries of religious wars. One became a slave by being an "outsider" or an "infidel," by being captured in war, by voluntarily selling oneself into slavery to obtain money for one's family, or by committing certain heinous crimes. The rights of slaves were restricted and their opportunities for upward movement were severely circumscribed, but they were regarded nevertheless as members of society, enjoying protection under the law and entitled to certain rights, including education, marriage, and parenthood. Most important, the status of a slave was not irrevocable and was not automatically passed on to his or her children.

Thus we find that slavery flourished in ancient Greece and Rome, in the Aztec and Inca empires, in African societies, in early modern Russia and eastern Europe, in the Middle East, and in the Mediterranean world. It had gradually died out in Western Europe by the fourteenth century, although the status of serf was not too different in social reality from that of the slave. It is important to note that in all these regions slavery and serfdom had nothing to do with racial characteristics.

When the African slave trade began in the second half of the fifteenth century, it served to fill labor shortages in the economies of its European initiators and their commercial partners. Between 1450 and 1505 Portugal brought about 40,000 African slaves to Europe and the Atlantic islands — the Madeiras and Canaries. But the need for slave labor lessened in Europe as European populations themselves began to grow beginning late in the fifteenth century. It is possible, therefore, that were it not for the colonization of the New World the early slave trade might have ceased after a century or more and be remembered simply as a short-lived incident stemming from early European contacts with Africa.

With the discovery of the New World by Europeans the course of history changed momentously. Once Europeans found the gold and silver mines of Mexico and Peru, and later, when they discovered a new form of gold in the production of sugar, coffee, and tobacco, their demand for human labor grew astonishingly. At first Indians seemed to be the obvious source of labor, and in some areas Spaniards and Portuguese were able to coerce native populations into agricultural and mining labor. But European diseases ravaged native populations, and often it was found that Indians, far more at home in their environment than white colonizers, were difficult to subjugate. Indentured white labor from the mother country was another way of meeting the demand for labor, but this source, it soon became apparent, was

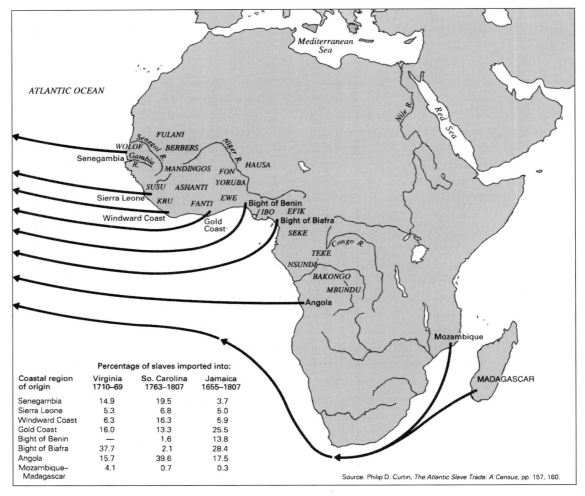

Coastal region of origin	Percentage of slaves imported into:		
	Virginia 1710–69	So. Carolina 1763–1807	Jamaica 1655–1807
Senegambia	14.9	19.5	3.7
Sierra Leone	5.3	6.8	5.0
Windward Coast	6.3	16.3	5.9
Gold Coast	16.0	13.3	25.5
Bight of Benin	—	1.6	13.8
Bight of Biafra	37.7	2.1	28.4
Angola	15.7	39.6	17.5
Mozambique–Madagascar	4.1	0.7	0.3

Source: Philip D. Curtin, *The Atlantic Slave Trade: A Census*, pp. 157, 160.

(Source: Philip D. Curtin, The Atlantic Slave Trade: A Census, *pp. 157, 160. Reprinted by permission of the University of Wisconsin Press.)*

far too limited. It was to Africa that colonizing Europeans ultimately resorted. Formerly a new source of trade, the continent now became transformed in the European view into the repository of vast supplies of human labor — "black gold."

From the late fifteenth to the mid-nineteenth centuries, almost four hundred years, Europeans transported Africans out of their ancestral homelands to fill the labor needs in their colonies of North and South America and the Caribbean. The most recent estimates place the numbers who reached the shores of the New World at about ten to eleven million people, although many million more lost their lives while being marched from the interior to the coastal trading forts or during the "middle passage" across the Atlantic. Even before the English arrived on the Chesapeake in 1607 several hundred thousand slaves had been transported to the Caribbean and South American colonies of Spain and Portugal. Before the slave trade was outlawed in the nineteenth century far more Africans than Europeans had crossed the Atlantic Ocean and taken up life in the New World. Black slaves, as one eighteenth-century Englishman put it became "the strength and the sinews of this western world."

Once established on a large scale, the Atlantic slave trade dramatically altered the pattern of slave recruitment in Africa. For about a century after Gonçalvez brought back the first kidnapped Africans to Portugal in 1441, the slave trade was relatively slight. The slaves whom other Africans sold to Europeans were drawn from a small minority of the population and for the most part were individuals captured in occasional war or whose criminal acts had cost them their rights of citizenship. For Europeans the African slave trade provided for modest labor needs, just as the Black Sea slave trade had done before it was shut off by the fall of Constantinople to the Turks in 1453. Even in the New World plantations, slaves were not in great demand for many decades after "discovery."

More than anything else it was sugar that transformed the African slave trade. Produced in the Mediterranean world since the eighth century, sugar was for centuries a costly item confined to sweetening the diet of the rich. By the mid-1400s its popularity was growing and the center of production had shifted to the Portuguese Madeira Islands, off the northwest coast of Africa. Here for the first time an expanding European nation established an overseas plantation society based on slave labor. From the Madeiras the cultivation of sugar spread to Portuguese Brazil in the late sixteenth century and then to the tiny specks of land dotting the Caribbean in the first half of the seventeenth century. By this time Europeans were developing an almost insatiable taste for sweetness. Sugar — regarded by nutritionists today as a "drug food" — became one of the first luxuries that was transformed into a necessary item in the diets of the masses of Europe. The wife of the poorest English laborer took sugar in her tea by 1750 it was said. "Together with other plantation products such as coffee, rum, and tobacco," writes Sidney Mintz, "sugar formed part of a complex of 'proletarian hunger-killers,' and played a crucial role in the linked contribution that Caribbean slaves, Indian peasants, and European urban proletarians were able to make to the growth of western civilization."

The regularization of the slave trade brought about by the vast new demand for a New World labor supply and by a reciprocally higher demand in Africa for European trade goods, especially bar iron and textiles, changed the problem of obtaining slaves. Criminals and "outsiders" in sufficient number to satisfy the growing European demand in the seventeenth century could not be found. Therefore African kings resorted to warfare against their neighbors as a way of obtaining "black gold" with which to trade. European guns abetted the process. Thus, the spread of kidnapping and organized violence in Africa became a part of maintaining commercial relations with European powers.

In the forcible recruitment of slaves, adult males were consistently preferred over women and children. Primarily this represented the preference of New World plantation owners for male field laborers. But it also reflected the decision of vanquished African villagers to yield up more men than women to raiding parties because women were the chief agriculturalists in their society and, in matrilineal and matrilocal kinship systems, were too valuable to be spared.

For the Europeans the slave trade itself became an immensely profitable enterprise. In the several centuries of intensive slave trading that followed the establishment of New World sugar plantations, European nations warred constantly for trading advantages on the West African coast. The coastal forts, the focal points of the trade, became key strategic targets in the wars of empire. The great Portuguese slaving fort at Elmina on the Gold Coast, begun in 1481, was captured a century and a half later by the Dutch. The primary fort on the Guinea coast, started by the Swedes, passed through the hands of the

Danes, the English, and the Dutch between 1652 and 1664. As the demand for slaves in the Americas rose sharply in the second half of the seventeenth century, European competition for trading rights on the West African coast grew intense. By the end of the century monopolies for supplying European plantations in the New World with their annual quotas of slaves became a major issue of European diplomacy. The Dutch were the primary victors in the battle for the West African slave coast. Hence, for most of the century a majority of slaves who were fed into the expanding New World markets found themselves crossing the Atlantic in Dutch ships.

Not until the last third of the seventeenth century were the English of any importance in the slave trade. Major English attempts to break into the profitable trade began only in 1663, when Charles II, recently restored to the English throne, granted a charter to the Royal Adventurers to Africa, a joint-stock company headed by the king's brother, the Duke of York. Superseded by the Royal African Company in 1672, these companies enjoyed the exclusive right to carry slaves to England's overseas plantations. For thirty-four years after 1663 each of the slaves they brought across the Atlantic bore the brand "*DY*" for the Duke of York, who himself became king in 1685. In 1698 the Royal African Company's monopoly was broken due to the pressure on Parliament by individual merchants who demanded their rights as Englishmen to participate in the lucrative trade. Thrown open to individual entrepreneurs, the English slave trade grew enormously. In the 1680s the Royal African Company had transported about 5,000 to 6,000 slaves annually (though interlopers brought in thousands more). In the first decade of free trade the annual average rose above 20,000. English involvement in the trade increased for the remainder of the eighteenth century until by the 1790s England had become the foremost slave-trading nation in Europe.

☆

CAPTURE AND TRANSPORT OF SLAVES

No accounts of the initial enslavement of Africans, no matter how vivid, can quite convey the pain and demoralization that must have accompanied the forced march to the west coast of Africa and the subsequent loading aboard ships of those who had fallen captive to the African suppliers of the European slave traders. As the demand for African slaves doubled and redoubled in the eighteenth century, the hinterlands of western and central Sudan were invaded again and again by the armies and agents of both coastal and interior kings. Perhaps 75 percent of the slaves transported to English North America came from the part of western Africa that lies between the Senegal and Niger rivers and the Gulf of Biafra, and most of the others were enslaved in Angola on the west coast of Central Africa. Slaving activities in these areas were responsible for considerable depopulation of the region in the eighteenth and nineteenth centuries.

Once captured, slaves were marched to the sea in "coffles," or trains. A Scotsman, Mungo Park, described the coffle he marched with for 550 miles through Gambia at the end of the eighteenth century. It consisted of 73 men, women, and children tied together by the neck with leather thongs. Several captives attempted to commit suicide by eating clay, another was abandoned after being badly stung by bees; still others died of exhaustion and hunger. After two months the coffle reached the coast, many of its members physically depleted by thirst, hunger, and exposure, where they were herded into fortified enclosures called barracoons.

The anger, bewilderment, and desolation that accompanied the forced march, the first leg of the 5,000-mile journey to the New World, was only increased by the actual transfer of slaves to European

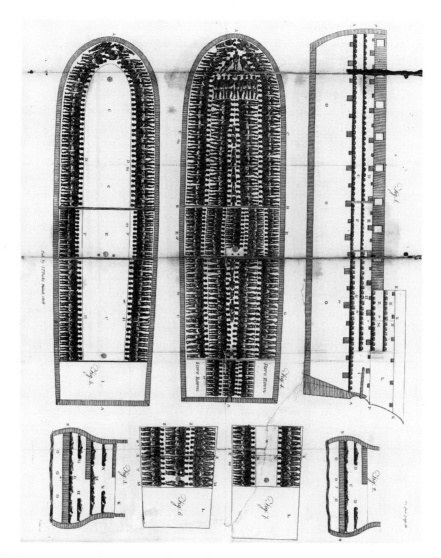

The international slave trade was such an unspeakably brutal business — especially the trip across the Atlantic — that even Southern slaveholders were anxious to outlaw it. Above is a diagram of a slave ship, showing arrangement and padlocks. In recounting a single night on such a ship, an eyewitness wrote of "400 wretched beings . . . crammed into a hold 12 yards in length . . . and only 3½ feet in height." He described how "the suffocating heat of the hold" drove the Negroes to panic in their attempts to escape to the upper air. The next day, he saw 54 "crushed and mangled corpses" lifted up from the slave deck. (Courtesy of The New York Public Library, The Arents Collection)

ship captains, who carried their human cargo in small wooden ships to the Americas. "As the slaves come down to Fida from the inland country," wrote one European trader in the late seventeenth century, "they are put into a booth or prison, built for that purpose, near the beach . . . and when the Europeans are to receive them, they are brought out into a large plain, where the [ships'] surgeons examine every part of every one of them, to the smallest member, men and women being all stark naked. Such as are allowed good and sound, are set on one side, and the others by themselves; which slaves so rejected are called Mackrons, being above 35 years of age, or defective in their lips, eyes, or teeth, or grown grey; or that have the venereal disease, or any other imperfection." Such dehumanizing treatment was part of the commercial process by which "merchandise" was selected and bargained for. But it was also part of the psychological process that attempted to strip away self-respect and self-identity from the Africans.

Cruelty followed cruelty. After purchase, each slave was branded with a hot iron signifying the company, whether Spanish, Portuguese, English, French, or Dutch, that had purchased him or her. Thus were members of "preliterate" societies first introduced to the alphabetic symbols of "advanced" cultures. "The branded slaves," one account related, "are returned to their former booths" where they were imprisoned until a full human cargo could be assembled. The next psychological wrench came with the ferrying of slaves, in large canoes, to the waiting ships at anchor in the harbor. An English captain described the desperation of slaves who were about to lose touch with their ancestral land and embark upon a vast ocean that many had never previously seen. "The Negroes are so wilful and loth to leave their own country, that they have often leap'd out of the canoes, boat and ship, into the sea, and kept under water till they were drowned, to avoid being taken up and saved by our boats, which pur-

sued them; they having a more dreadful apprehension of Barbadoes than we can have of hell." Part of this fear was the common belief that on the other side of the ocean Africans would be eaten by the white savages.

The kind of fear that inspired suicide while still on African soil was prevalent as well on the second leg of the voyage — the "middle passage" from the West African coast to the New World. Conditions aboard ship were miserable, although it was to the advantage of the ship captains to deliver as many slaves as possible on the other side of the Atlantic. The preservation rather than the destruction of life was the main object, but brutality was systematic, both in pitching overboard any slaves who fell sick on the voyage and in punishing offenders with almost sadistic intensity as a way of creating a climate of fear that would stifle insurrectionist tendencies. John Atkins, aboard an English slaver in 1721, described how the captain "whipped and scarified" several plotters of rebellion and sentenced others "to cruel deaths, making them first eat the Heart and Liver of one of them killed. The Woman he hoisted up by the thumbs, whipp'd and slashed her with Knives, before the other slaves, till she died." Though the naval architects of Europe competed to produce the most efficient ships for carrying human cargoes to the New World, the mortality on board, for both black slaves below decks and white sailors above, was extremely high, averaging between 10 and 20 percent on each voyage.

That Africans frequently attempted suicide and mutiny during the ocean crossing provides evidence that even the extraordinary force used in capturing, branding, selling, and transporting them from one continent to another was not enough to make the captives submit tamely to their fate. An eighteenth-century historian of slavery, attempting to justify the terroristic devices employed by slavers, argued that "the many acts of violence they [the slaves] have committed by murdering whole crews and destroying ships when they had it in their power to do so have made these rigors wholly chargeable on their own bloody and malicious disposition which calls for the same confinement as if they were wolves or wild boars." The modern reader can detect in this characterization of enslaved Africans clear proof that submissiveness was not a trait of those who were forcibly carried to the New World. So great was this resistance that special techniques of torture had to be devised to cope with the thousands of slaves who were determined to starve themselves to death on the middle passage rather than reach the New World in chains. Brutal whippings and hot coals applied to the lips were frequently used to open the mouths of recalcitrant slaves. When this did not suffice, a special instrument, the *speculum oris,* or mouth opener, was employed to wrench apart the jaws of a resistant slave.

Taking into consideration the mortality involved in the capture, the forced march to the coast, and the middle passage, probably not more than one in two captured Africans lived to see the New World. Many of those who did must have been psychologically numbed as well as physically depleted by the experience. But one further step remained in the process of enslavement — the auctioning to a New World master and transportation to his place of residence. All in all, the relocation of any African brought westward across the Atlantic may have averaged about six months from the time of capture to the time of arrival at the plantation of a European slave master. During this protracted personal crisis, the slave was completely cut off from most that was familiar — family, wider kinship relationships, community life, and other forms of social and psychological security. Still facing these victims of the European demand for cheap labor was adaptation to a new physical environment, a new language, new work routines, and, most important, a life in which bondage for themselves and their offspring was unending.

☆

THE DEVELOPMENT OF SLAVERY IN THE ENGLISH COLONIES

Even though they were long familiar with Spanish, Dutch, and Portuguese use of African slave labor, English colonists did not turn immediately to Africa to solve the problem of cultivating labor-intensive crops. When they did, it could have caused little surprise, for in enslaving Africans the English were merely copying their European rivals in attempting to fill the colonial labor gap. No doubt the stereotype of Africans as uncivilized made it easier for the English to fasten chains upon them. But the central fact remains that the English were in the New World, like the Spanish, Portuguese, Dutch, and French, to make a fortune as well as to build religious and political havens. Given the long hostility they had borne toward Indians and their experience in enslaving them, any scruples the English might have had about enslaving Africans quickly dissipated.

Making it all the more natural to employ Africans as a slave labor force in the mainland colonies was the precedent that English planters had set on their Caribbean sugar islands. In Barbados, Jamaica, and the Leeward Islands (Antigua, Monserrat, Nevis, and St. Christopher) Englishmen in the second and third quarters of the seventeenth century learned to copy their European rivals in employing Africans in the sugar fields and, through extraordinary repression, in molding them into a slave labor force. By 1680, when there were not more than 7,000 slaves in mainland North America and the institution of slavery was not yet unalterably fixed, upwards of 65,000 Africans toiled on sugar plantations in the English West Indies. Trade and communication were extensive between the Caribbean and mainland colonists, so settlers in North America had intimate knowledge concerning the potentiality of slave labor.

It is not surprising, then, that the North American colonists turned to the international slave trade to fill their labor needs. Africans were simply the most available people in the world for those seeking a bound labor force and possessed of the power to obtain it. What is surprising, in fact, is that the North American colonists did not turn to slavery more quickly than they did. For more than a half century in Virginia and Maryland it was primarily the white indentured servant and not the African slave who labored in the tobacco fields. Moreover, those blacks who were imported before about 1660 were held in various degrees of servitude, most for limited periods and a few for life.

The transformation of the labor force in the Southern colonies, from one in which many white and a relatively small number of black indentured servants labored together to one in which black slaves served for a lifetime and composed the bulk of unfree labor, came only in the last third of the seventeenth century in Virginia and Maryland and in the first third of the eighteenth century in North Carolina and South Carolina. The reasons for this shift to a slave-based agricultural economy in the South are twofold. First, English entry into the African slave trade gave the Southern planter an opportunity to purchase slaves more readily and more cheaply than before. Cheap labor was what every tobacco or rice planter sought, and when the price of slave labor dipped below that of indentured labor, the demand for black slaves increased. Also, the supply of white servants from England began to dry up in the late seventeenth century, and those who did cross the Atlantic were spread among a growing number of colonies. Thus, in the late seventeenth century the number of Africans imported into the Chesapeake colonies began to grow and the flow of white indentured servants diminished to a trickle. As late as 1671 slaves made up less than 5 percent of Virginia's population and were outnumbered at least three to one by white indentured servants. In Maryland the situation was much the same. But within a generation, by about 1700, they represented one-fifth of the population and probably a majority of the labor force. A Maryland census of 1707 tabulated 3,003 white bound laborers and 4,657 black slaves. Five years later the slave population had almost doubled. Within another generation white indentured servants were declining rapidly in number, and in all the Southern colonies African slaves made up the backbone of the agricultural work force. "These two words, *Negro* and *slave*," wrote one Virginian, had "by custom grown Homogenous and Convertible."

To the north, in Pennsylvania, New Jersey, and Delaware, where English colonists had settled only in the last third of the seventeenth century, slavery existed on a more occasional basis, since labor-intensive crops were not as extensively grown in these areas and the cold winters brought farming to a halt. New York was an exception and shows how a cultural preference could alter labor patterns that were usually determined by ecological factors. During the period before 1664 when the colony was Dutch, slaveholding had been practiced extensively, encouraged in part by the Dutch West India Company, one of the chief international suppliers of slaves. The population of New York remained largely Dutch for the remainder of the century, and the English who slowly filtered in saw no reason not to imitate Dutch slave owners. Thus New York became the largest importer of slaves north of Maryland. In the mid-eighteenth century, the areas of original settlement around New York and Albany remained slaveholding societies with about 20 percent of the population composed of slaves and 30 to 40 percent of the white householders owning human property.

As the number of slaves increased, legal codes for strictly controlling their activities were fashioned in each of the colonies. To a large extent these "black codes" were borrowed from the law books of the English West Indies. Bit by bit they deprived the African immigrant — and a small number of Indian slaves as well — of rights enjoyed by others in the society, including indentured servants. Gradually they reduced the slave, in the eyes of society and the law, from a human being to a piece of chattel property. In this process of dehumanization nothing was more important than the practice of hereditary lifetime service. Once servitude became perpetual, relieved only by death, then the stripping away of all other rights followed as a matter of course. When the condition of the slave parent was passed on to the child, then slavery had been extended to the womb. At that point the institution became totally fixed so far as the slave was concerned.

Thus, with the passage of time, Africans in North America had to adapt to a more and more circumscribed world. Earlier in the seventeenth century they had been treated much as indentured servants, bound to labor for a specified period of years but thereafter free to work for themselves, hire out their labor, buy land, move as they pleased, and, if they wished, hold slaves themselves. But, by the 1640s, Virginia was forbidding blacks the use of firearms. In the 1660s marriages between white women and black slaves were being described as "shameful Matches" and "the Disgrace of our Nation"; during the next few decades interracial fornication became subject to unusually severe punishment and interracial marriage was banned.

These discriminatory steps were slight, however, in comparison with the stripping away of rights that began toward the end of the century. In rapid succession slaves lost their right to testify before a court; to engage in any kind of commercial activity, either as buyer or seller; to hold property; to participate in the political process; to congregate in public places with more than two or three of their fellows; to travel without permission; and to engage in legal marriage or parenthood. In some colonies legislatures even prohibited the right to education and religion, for they thought these might encourage the germ of freedom in slaves. More and more steps were taken to contain them tightly in a legal system that made no allowance for their education, welfare, or future advancement. The restraints on the slave

owner's freedom to deal with slaves in any way he or she saw fit were gradually cast away. Early in the eighteenth century many colonies passed laws forbidding the manumission of slaves by individual owners. This was a step designed to squelch the strivings of slaves for freedom and to discourage those who had been freed from helping fellow Africans to gain their liberty.

The movement to annul all the slave's rights had both pragmatic and psychological dimensions. The greater the proportion of slaves in the population, the greater the danger to white society, for every colonist knew that when he purchased a man or woman in chains he had bought a potential insurrectionist. The larger the specter of black revolt, the greater the effort of white society to neutralize it by further restricting the rights and activities of slaves. Thus, following a black revolt in 1712 that took the lives of nine whites and wounded others, the New York legislature passed a slave code that rivaled those of the Southern colonies. Throughout the Southern colonies the obsessive fear of slave insurrection ushered in institutionalized violence as the means of ensuring social stability. Allied to this need for greater and greater control was the psychological compulsion to dehumanize slaves by taking from them the rights that connoted their humanity. It was far easier to rationalize the merciless exploitation of those who had been defined by law as something less than human. "The planters," wrote an Englishman in eighteenth-century Jamaica, "do not want to be told that their Negroes are human creatures. If they believe them to be of human kind, they cannot regard them . . . as no better than dogs or horses."

Thus occurred one of the great paradoxes in American history — the building of what some thought was to be a utopia in the wilderness upon the backs of black men and women wrenched from their African homeland and forced into a system of abject slavery. America was imagined as a liberating and regenerating force, it has been pointed out, but became the scene of a "grotesque inconsistency." In the land heralded for freedom and individual opportunity, the practice of slavery, unknown for centuries in the mother country, was reinstituted. Following other parts of the New World, North America became the scene of "a disturbing retrogression from the course of historical progress."

The mass enslavement of Africans profoundly affected white racial prejudice. Once institutionalized, slavery cast Africans into such lowly roles that the initial bias against them could only be confirmed and vastly strengthened. Initially unfavorable impressions of Africans had coincided with labor needs to bring about their mass enslavement. But it required slavery itself to harden the negative racial feelings into a deep and almost unshakable prejudice that continued to grow for centuries. The colonizers had devised a labor system that kept the African in the Americas at the bottom of the social and economic pyramid. Irrevocably caught in the web of perpetual servitude, the slave was allowed no further opportunity to prove the white stereotype wrong. Socially and legally defined as less than people, kept in a degraded and debased position, virtually without power in their relationships with white society, Afro-Americans became a truly servile, ignoble, degraded people in the eyes of the Europeans. This was used as further reason to keep them in slavery, for it was argued that they were worth nothing better and were incapable of occupying any higher role. In this long evolution of racial attitudes in America, nothing was of greater importance than the enslavement of Africans.

QUESTIONS TO CONSIDER

1   How did conditions in the New World transform the traditional character of the slave trade? why? What crop had a particular effect, and why did it become so important in international trade?

2   What effects did the sudden growth of the slave trade in the seventeenth century have on conditions in Europe? In Africa? What had African culture been like before the seventeenth century? How had it compared with European culture?

3   Describe the conditions of the Atlantic slave trade. What was the purpose of physical cruelty in the slave trade? What do you think it would have been like to be an African stolen from his or her native land and taken across the middle passage? What might be the physical and psychological effects of such an experience?

4   By what process did black slavery gradually become established in the British North American colonies? How were the colonies unusual in this? Why did it develop less in the North than in the southern colonies? Why was New York an exception?

5   How does Gary Nash believe that slavery and racial prejudice influenced each other? What are the implications of his conclusions for the subsequent history of America up to the present day?

4

The Deerfield Massacre

JOHN DEMOS

The massacre of a western Massachusetts town by the French and Indians one night in 1704 was symbolic of the great struggle between France and England for supremacy in North America. To understand that terrible night requires that the English colonists in New England and the French in Canada be explained and contrasted. In 1630, Separatist Puritans had founded Massachusetts Bay colony and sought, under the leadership of their first governor, even-tempered John Winthrop, to create a model Christian commonwealth — "a city on a hill" — that would stand as a beacon of inspiration for others to emulate. Each town had its own congregation and its own minister, whose sermons rang with Calvinist precepts (see the glossary in selection 2). The system of local congregations that selected their ministers and ran their own affairs became known as the Congregational church. In their wilderness Zion, ministers and government officials worked together to maintain holiness, purity, and order. Only church members — the elect — could vote and hold political office. The government, in turn, protected the church by levying taxes to support it on members and nonmembers alike and by making church attendance compulsory. The Puritans, as historian Edmund S. Morgan said, "not only endeavored themselves to live a 'smooth, honest, civil life,' but tried to force everyone within their power to do likewise."

On the surface, the Puritans appeared to be pious, sedate folk living in peaceful villages. But as John Demos says in the following selection, Puritan New England "also had its share of discordant change, of inner stress and turmoil, and even of deadly violence." The Puritans believed, for instance, that Satan could seize people, especially women, and force them to practice witchcraft, which was a capital crime: those found guilty were hanged. As for the Native Americans in New England, as we have seen, the

Puritans practiced a policy of killing the Indians off or driving them west or into Canada, where they formed alliances with the French.

The English had come to the New World to settle; the French had come not to settle, but to make money, by creating a fur-trading empire in Canada. Instead of exterminating the Indians, the French learned their language, traded, formed alliances, and even intermarried with them and sought to convert them to the Catholic faith. As imperial England and imperial France clashed on the American continent, the French army and its Indian allies fought a series of wars with the English army in America in which, as Demos says, the American colonials were "a junior partner." The recent motion picture, The Last of the Mohicans, starring Daniel Day-Lewis and Madeleine Stowe, vividly illustrates this imperial conflict and the secondary role of the American militia in it. The film also shows how colonial civilians were often victims of the warfare between the two European nations.

The citizens of colonial Deerfield were such victims. In Demos's skilled hands, the massacre of the town is an action-packed thriller, made all the more immediate because it is told in the present tense. When the French and Indian forces attack the little town, ordinary folk are slain, mutilated, or captured. One captive, the daughter of the town minister, does an incredible thing in the view of the survivors: she elects to remain with the Indians, marry a brave, and live out her life with them. Unfortunately, the author does not tell us why she found Indian life more attractive than Puritan life in Deerfield, Massachusetts. Perhaps she felt safer with the Indians: they would never have executed her on a charge of witchcraft. Perhaps, too, she found the Indians' spiritual views, which stressed the harmony of human beings with the sun, the moon, mother earth, and other living creatures, more meaningful and comforting to her than the implacable doctrines of Puritan theology.

GLOSSARY

GARRISON   Hired soldiers who manned a stockade.

NEW FRANCE   France's fur-trading colony in Canada.

STOCKADE   A fortified area inside a high palisade fence.

WILLIAMS, EUNICE   The daughter of Deerfield's minister who was taken captive during the Deerfield raid. To the bafflement of her father and the other white survivors of the attack, she elected to live with the Indians, married a warrior, and raised a family.

WILLIAMS, JOHN   Puritan minister of Deerfield who was captured during the Indian attack and subsequently returned to safety. He wrote a book about his experiences called The Redeemed Captive Returning to Zion.

Our traditional picture of colonial New England is essentially a still life. Peaceful little villages. Solid, strait-laced, steadily productive people. A landscape serene, if not bountiful. A history of purposeful, and largely successful, endeavor.

And yet, as historians are learning with ever-greater clarity, this picture is seriously at odds with the facts. New England had its solidity and purposefulness, to be sure. But it also had its share of discordant change, of inner stress and turmoil, and even of deadly violence. New England was recurrently a place of war, especially during the hundred years preceding the Revolution. The French to the north in Canada and the various Indian tribes on every side made determined, altogether formidable enemies. The roster of combat was long indeed: King Philip's War (1675–76), King William's War (1689–97), Queen Anne's War (1702–13), Father Rasle's War (1724–26), King George's War (1744–48), and the French and Indian War (1754–63). Most of these were intercolonial, even international, conflicts, in which New England joined as a very junior partner. But there were numerous other skirmishes, entirely local and so obscure as not to have earned a name. All of them exacted a cost, in time, in money, in worry — and in blood.

Much of the actual fighting was small-scale, hit-and-run, more a matter of improvisation than of formal strategy and tactics. Losses in any single encounter might be only a few, but they did add up. Occasionally the scale widened, and entire towns became targets. Lancaster and Haverhill, Massachusetts; Salmon Fall and Oyster River, New Hampshire; York and Wells, Maine: Each suffered days of wholesale attack. And Deerfield, Massachusetts —

From *American Heritage*, February/March 1993, pp. 82–89. Adapted from *The Unredeemed Captive: A Family Story from Early America* by John Demos. © 1994 by John Demos. Reprinted by permission of Alfred A. Knopf, Inc.

above all, Deerfield — scene of the region's single, most notorious "massacre."

The year is 1704, the season winter, the context another European war with a "colonial" dimension. New France (Canada) versus New England. (New York and the colonies farther south are, at least temporarily, on the sidelines.) The French and their Indian allies have already engineered a series of devastating raids along the "eastern frontier" — the Maine and New Hampshire coasts. The English have counterattacked against half a dozen Abenaki Indian villages. And now, in Montreal, the French governor is secretly planning a new thrust "over the ice" toward "a little village of about forty households," a place misnamed in the French records "Guerrefille." (An ironic twist just there: Deerfield becomes "War-girl.")

Deerfield is not unready. Like other outlying towns, it has labored to protect itself: with a "stockade" (a fortified area, at its center, inside a high palisade fence), a "garrison" of hired soldiers, a "watch" to patrol the streets at night, and "scouts" to prowl the woods nearby. Indeed, many families are living inside the stockade. Conditions are crowded and uncomfortable, to say the least, but few doubt the need for special measures. The town minister, Rev. John Williams, conducts an extraordinary day of "fasting and prayer" in the local church — "possessed," as he reportedly is, "that the town would in a little time be destroyed."

The attack forces — French led, largely Indian in rank and file — set out in early February. Steadily they move southward, on frozen rivers and lakes, with one hard leg across the Green Mountains. They have snowshoes, sleds to carry their supplies, and dogs to pull the sleds. The lower part of their route follows the Connecticut River valley till it reaches a point near what would later become Brattleboro, Vermont. Here they will strike off into the woods to the south, leaving dogs and sleds for their return. They are barely a day's march — twenty miles —

from their objective. The rest they will cover as quickly and quietly as possible. Surprise is their most potent weapon. The people of Deerfield, though generally apprehensive, know nothing of this specific threat. On the evening of February 28, the town goes to sleep in the usual way.

Midnight. Across the river to the west the attackers are making their final preparations: loading weapons, putting on war paint, reviewing plans. The layout of Deerfield is apparently known to them from visits made in previous years by Indian hunters and traders. Presently a scout is sent "to discover the posture of the town, who observing the watch walking in the street," returns to his comrades and "puts them to a stand." (Our source for the details of this sequence was a contemporary historian, writing some years after the fact.) Another check, a short while later, brings a different result. The village lies "all . . . still and quiet"; the watch evidently has fallen asleep. It is now about four o'clock in the morning, time for the attackers to move.

Over the river, on the ice. Across a mile of meadowland, ghostly and white. Past the darkened houses at the north end of the street. Right up to the stockade. The snow has piled hugely here; the drifts make walkways to the top of the fence. A vanguard of some forty men climbs quickly over and drops down on the inside. A gate is opened to admit the rest. The watch awakens, fires a warning shot, cries, "Arm!" Too late. The attackers separate into smaller parties and "immediately set upon breaking open doors and windows."

The townspeople come to life with a rush. Some find opportunities to escape by jumping from windows or roof lines. Several manage to flee the stockade altogether and make their way to neighboring villages. In half a dozen households the men leave families behind in order to rally outside as a counterforce. In others there is a frantic attempt to hide.

The minister's house is a special target, singled out "in the beginning of the onset"; later John Williams will remember (and write about) his experience in de-

tail. Roused "out of sleep . . . by their violent endeavors to break open doors and windows with axes and hatchets," he leaps from the bed, runs to the front door, sees "the enemy making their entrance," awakens a pair of soldiers lodged upstairs, and returns to his bedside "for my arms." There is hardly time, for the "enemy immediately brake into the room, I judge to the number of twenty, with painted faces and hideous acclamations." They are "all of them Indians"; no Frenchmen in sight as yet. The minister does manage to cock his pistol and "put it to the breast of the first Indian who came up." Fortunately — for both of them — it misfires. Thereupon Williams is "seized by 3 Indians, who disarmed me, and bound me naked, as I was in my shirt"; in this posture he will remain "for near the space of an hour."

With their chief prize secured, the invaders turn to "rifling the house, entering in great numbers into every room." There is killing work too: "some were so cruel and barbarous as to take and carry to the door two of my children and murder them [six-year-old John, Jr., and six-week-old Jerusha], as also a Negro woman [a family slave named Parthena]." After "insulting over me a while, holding up hatchets over my head, [and] threatening to burn all I had," the Indians allow their captive to dress. They also permit Mrs. Williams "to dress herself and our children."

By this time the sun is "about an hour high" (perhaps 7:00 A.M.). The sequence described by John Williams has been experienced, with some variations, in households throughout the stockade: killings (especially of infants and others considered too frail to survive the rigors of life in the wilderness); "fireing houses"; "killing cattle, hogs, sheep & sacking and wasting all that came before them." In short, a village-size holocaust. When John Williams and his family are finally taken outside, they see "many of the houses . . . in flames"; later, in recalling the moment, he asks, "Who can tell what sorrows pierced our souls?"

The Williamses know they are destined "for a march . . . into a strange land," as prisoners. And prisoners are being herded together — in the meeting-house and in a home nearby — from all over town. However, one household — that of the militia leader, Sgt. Benoni Stebbins — has mounted a remarkable resistance. Its occupants are well armed and fiercely determined; moreover, the walls of this house, "being filled up with brick," effectively repel incoming fire. The battle (as described in a subsequent report by local militia officers) continues here for more than two hours. The attackers fall back, then surge forward in an unsuccessful attempt "to fire the house." Again they retreat — this time to the shelter of the meetinghouse — while maintaining their fusillade all the while. The defenders return bullet for bullet, "accepting of no quarter, though offered," and "causing several of the enemy to fall," among them "one Frenchman, a gentleman to appearance," and "3 or 4 Indians," including a "captain" who had helped seize John Williams.

In the meantime, some of the attackers with their captives begin to leave the stockade. Heading north, they retrace their steps toward the river. Then a stunning intervention: A band of Englishmen arrives from the villages below (where an orange glow on the horizon "gave notice . . . before we had news from the distressed people" themselves). "Being a little above forty in number," they have rushed on horseback to bring relief. They stop just long enough to pick up "fifteen of Deerfield men." And this combined force proceeds to the stockade, to deliver a surprise of its own: "when we entered at one gate, the enemy fled out the other." Now comes a flat-out chase — pell-mell across the meadow — the erstwhile attackers put to rout. The Englishmen warm, literally, to the fight, stripping off garments as they run. (Later the same soldiers will claim reimbursement for their losses — and record details of the battle.) They inflict heavy casualties: "we saw at the time many dead bodies, and . . . afterwards . . . manifest prints in the snow, where other dead bodies were drawn to a hole in the river."

They make, in sum, a highly successful counterattack. But one that is "pursued too far, imprudently."

For across the river the French commanders hear the tumult and swiftly regroup their own forces. The riverbank affords an excellent cover for a new stand; soon a "numerous company . . . [of] fresh hands" is in place there, concealed and waiting. On the Englishmen come, ignoring the orders of the officer "who had led them [and] called for a retreat." On and on — the river is just ahead, and the captives are waiting on the other side — into the teeth of the withering "ambuscade." Back across the meadow one more time, pursued and pursuers reversing roles. The English are hard pressed, "our breath being spent, theirs in full strength." Their retreat is as orderly as they can make it, "facing and firing, so that those that first failed might be defended"; even so, "many were slain and others wounded." Eventually the survivors regain the stockade and clamber inside, at which "the enemy drew off." They will appear no more.

It is now about 9:00 A.M. A numbness settles over the village. The fires are burning down. There is blood on the snow in the street. The survivors of the "meadow fight" crouch warily behind the palisades. The townspeople who had escaped start to filter back in through the south gate. Time to look after their wounded and count their dead.

Viewed from close up, the carnage is appalling. Death — by gunshot, by hatchet, by knife, by war club, grisly beyond words. And the torn bodies on the ground are not the whole of it [;] when the survivors poke through the rubble, they find more. Casualty lists have entries like this: "Mary, Mercy, and Mehitable Nims [ages, five, five, and seven, respectively] supposed to be burnt in the cellar." Indeed, several cellar hideouts have turned into death-traps; in one house ten people lie "smothered" that way.

And then the wounded. One man shot through the arm. Another with a bullet in his thigh. Another with a shattered foot. Yet another who was briefly captured by the Indians, and "when I was in their hands, they cut off the forefinger of my right hand" (a traditional Indian practice with captives). A young woman wounded in the Stebbins house. A second with an ankle broken while jumping from an upper-story window.

There are, too, the lucky ones, quite a number who *might* have been killed or injured (or captured) but managed somehow to escape. The people who ran out in the first moments and fled the town unobserved. A young couple and their infant son whose "small house" was so small that the snow had covered it completely. A woman who lay hidden beneath an overturned tub. A boy who dived under a pile of flax. Some of this is remembered only by "tradition," not hard evidence, but is too compelling to overlook. Here is another instance, passed through generations of the descendants of Mary Catlin: "The captives were taken to a house . . . and a Frenchman was brought in [wounded] and laid on the floor; he was in great distress and called for water; Mrs. Catlin fed him with water. Some one said to her, 'How can you do that for your enemy?' She replied, 'If thine enemy hunger, feed him; if he thirst give him water to drink.' The Frenchman was taken and carried away, and the captives marched off. Some thought the kindness shown to the Frenchman was the reason of Mrs. Catlin's being left . . . " (Mary Catlin was indeed "left," the only one of her large family not killed or captured. And this is as plausible an explanation of her survival as any.)

Thus Deerfield in the immediate aftermath: the living and the dead, the wounded and the escaped. Tradition also tells of a mass burial in the southeast corner of the town cemetery. Another "sorrowful" task for the survivors.

Soon groups of armed men begin arriving from the towns to the south. All day and through the evening they come; by midnight there are "near about 80." Together they debate the obvious question, the only one that matters right now: "Should they follow the retreating enemy in order to retake their captive "friends"? Some are for it, but eventually counterarguments prevail. They have no snow-shoes, "the snow being at least 3 foot deep." The enemy has "treble our number, if not more." Following "in their path . . . we should too much expose our men." Moreover, the captives themselves will be endangered, "Mr. Williams's family especially, whom the enemy would kill, if we come on."

The day after, "Connecticut men begin to come in"; by nightfall their number has swelled to fully 250. There is more debate on whether to counterattack. However, the "aforesaid objections" remain — plus one more. The weather has turned unseasonably warm, "with rain," and the snowpack is going to slush. They "judge it impossible to travel [except] . . . to uttermost disadvantage." Under the circumstances they could hardly hope "to offend the enemy or rescue our captives, which was the end we aimed at in all." And so they "desist" once again. They give what further help they can to "the remaining inhabitants" — help with the burials and with rounding up the surviving cattle. They prepare a report for the colony leaders in Boston, including a detailed count of casualties: 48 dead, 112 taken captive. (Another 140 remain "alive at home.") They leave a "garrison of 30 men or upwards" in the town. And the rest return to their home villages.

Meanwhile, the "march" of the captives, and their captors, is well under way: through the wilderness on to Canada. There is extreme privation and suffering on both sides. The French and Indians are carrying wounded comrades. The captives include many who are physically weak and emotionally stricken: young children, old people, pregnant women, lone survivors of otherwise shattered families. Food is short, the weather inclement, the route tortuous.

The captors, fearing a possible English pursuit, push forward as rapidly as possible. Any who cannot keep up must be killed and left by the trail "for meat to the fowls of the air and beasts of the earth." Among the first to suffer this fate is the minister's wife. Still convalescent following a recent pregnancy, she nearly

The burning of Deerfield, Massachusetts. "Viewed close up," writes John Demos, "the carnage is appalling." (North Wind Picture Archives)

drowns in a river crossing, after which, according to John Williams, "the cruel and bloodthirsty savage who took her, slew her with his hatchet at one stroke." In the succeeding days another seventeen of the captives will be similarly "dispatched."

Later in the journey the French and the Indians separate. And later still the Indians, who now hold all the captives, subdivide into small "bands." At one critical juncture Reverend Williams is marked for

execution by revenge-minded kinsmen of the "captain" killed at Deerfield; a rival chief's intervention saves him. His five surviving children are scattered among different "masters" and, surprisingly, are "looked after with a great deal of tenderness."

There are two additional deaths — from starvation — as the various bands move farther north, but sooner or later ninety-two captives reach Canada. Some, like John Williams, are ransomed "out of the hands of Indians" by French officials; others are taken to Indian "forts" and encampments throughout the St. Lawrence River Valley.

Almost immediately their relatives and friends in New England begin efforts to secure their release. But the process is complicated, and progress is painfully slow. Eventually some fifty-three will be returned home, with John Williams as one of the last among them. His subsequent account of his experiences, published under the imposing title *The Redeemed Captive Returning to Zion,* will make him famous throughout the Colonies.

His daughter Eunice will become equally famous, but for a different reason: she declines to return and spends the rest of her long life among the Indians. She forgets her English and adjusts completely to Indian ways; she marries a local "brave" and raises a family. Another fifteen or so of her fellow captives will make a similar choice, and still others stay on with the French Canadians. These are the captives *un*redeemed: a source of sorrow, and of outrage, for the New Englanders.

In fact, efforts to bring them back will continue for decades. "Friends" traveling back and forth quite unofficially, and full-fledged "ambassadors" sent from one royal governor to the other, seek repeatedly to force a change. In some cases there are direct — even affectionate — contacts between the parties themselves. Eunice Williams pays four separate visits to her New England relatives. Each time they greet her with great excitement and high hopes for her permanent "return," but there is no sign that she even considers the possibility. She acknowledges the claims of her blood, but other, stronger claims draw her back to Canada. She has become an Indian in all *but* blood, and she prefers to remain that way. She will become the last surviving member of the entire "massacre" cohort.

The destruction of Deerfield came nearer the beginning than the end of the Anglo-French struggle for control of North America. And was barely a curtain raiser in the long, sorry drama of "white" versus "red." But it left special, and enduring, memories. Well into the nineteenth century New England boys played a game called Deerfield Massacre, complete with mock scalpings and captive taking. A curious bond grew between Deerfield and the descendants of those same Canadian Indians who had formed the attack party, with visits back and forth on both sides. And particular "massacre" memorabilia have been carefully — almost lovingly — preserved to the present day.

Indeed, Deerfield today recalls both sides of its former frontier experience. It remains an exquisitely tranquil — and beautiful — village, its main street lined with stately old houses (twelve of them open to the public). But its most celebrated single artifact is an ancient wooden door, hacked full of hatchet holes on that bitter night in the winter of 1704.

QUESTIONS TO CONSIDER

1   How was the Deerfield Massacre symbolic of the struggle between England and France for supremacy in North America? Why did the Indians side with the French and not the English?

2   Was Deerfield an isolated, defenseless town? What political and military objectives did the French and Indians hope to gain by raiding a community like Deerfield? Was the raid a success or a failure for the French and Indian forces?

3   Who was John Williams and what was his status in the community? What "terrible insults" did he suffer at the hands of his Indian captors? Why did the Indians take captives?

4   According to the author, Eunice Williams became as famous as her father? Why so? Why would she make the decision that earned her fame? Why would fifteen of her "fellow captives" do what she did?

TRANSFORMATIONS

5

The Transformation of European Society

GARY B. NASH

In all, Americans lived for 169 years under British rule. To place the colonial era in chronological perspective, this is the number of years that elapsed between John Quincy Adams's election to the presidency in 1824 and Bill Clinton's inauguration as president in 1993. In this selection, Gary Nash examines some of the momentous economic, social, and religious changes that occurred in North America during the last decades of British rule. In 1650, as Nash points out elsewhere, the population of the English colonies ran to about fifty thousand — "about the same as the daytime population of a large university campus today." But by 1750, thanks to a continuous stream of immigration from Europe and Africa, the colonial population had leaped to 1,125,000, including 240,000 blacks. As Nash says, this remarkable growth, unparalleled anywhere in the world at that time, encouraged Benjamin Franklin to speculate that one day the population of colonial America would surpass that of England itself.

By the eighteenth century, as Nash says, the colonists had transformed the European attitudes and social structures they had brought with them into something uniquely American. This "transformation of European society" had much to do with the abundance and availability of land in North America, which allowed quite ordinary people to acquire real estate and aspire to fortunes and higher stations in life. As Nash points out, two different forms of agricultural society emerged in eighteenth-century English America. There was the farming and artisan society of the North, where slaves were few and most free men — those who were not indentured servants — could boast of owning at least a fifty-acre farm. Here the Protestant work ethic, which celebrated hard work, thrift, and individual economic enterprise, took hold. In the South, by contrast, a slave-based, planter-dominated society emerged. "But," Nash warns us, "the usual picture of a Southern plantation society made up of immensely wealthy men exploiting the labor of huge gangs of black slaves is badly overdrawn." He observes that perhaps 40 percent of southern white men were non-slaveholding farm workers or tenant farmers — those who rented or leased their land. And many more were independent small farmers, often called yeomen, who raised the same crops as the planters did. Only about 5 percent of southern white landowners were wealthy planters — those who owned twenty or more slaves and sizable plantations. Even so — and this is a crucial point — owning slaves was a potent status symbol, and the slave-holding planter was the role model in the South, the "ideal" to which other white men aspired. And planters and yeomen alike "were as avid in the pursuit of wealth and material comfort" as were their neighbors in the North.

The remarkable growth of the English colonies, as Nash says, had dramatic consequences. First, it destroyed "the utopian dream" of the seventeenth-century colonists that communities should consist of people who worked for the common good, not simply for individual success. Driven by the Protestant work ethic and apparently unlimited opportunity, eighteenth-century colonists celebrated the individual pursuit of wealth, the idea of every man for himself. As a result, Nash says, "the individual replaced the community as the conceptual unit of thought." Thus was born the "democratic personality, brash, assertive, individualistic, and competitive." And that personality would shape the entire course of American history and thought.

Second, Nash says, economic and population growth — and the emphasis on aggressive individualism — altered the very structure of colonial society. The traditional notion of a God-ordained "hierarchy in human affairs" gave way to a more fluid social structure and the ideal of egalitarianism, that is, of "the equality of all men." As Nash points out, most Americans "below the elite free whites" believed that they were creating a society free of class rule. But this, as Nash says, was the ideal, not the reality, of eighteenth-century colonial America. In reality, the abundance of opportunity allowed the rich to get richer at the expense of the poor and led to a concentration of wealth in the hands of the few. Such "aggrandizement of wealth" was to haunt America's capitalist system for generations to come.

In the last section of his essay, Nash analyzes the great religious and social upheaval in the 1730s and 1740s known as the Great Awakening, which he sees as a cultural crisis that resulted from decades of economic and social change and from the fear that American churches, as William McLoughlin put it, "no longer met the spiritual needs of the people." The Awakening was thus a rebellion against religious authority and dogma. As another historian said, it was "a search for new sources of authority, new principles of action, new foundations of hope." It unleashed "the greatest flow of religious energy since the Puritan movement" in Europe in the six-

teenth and seventeenth centuries and transformed the structure and attitudes of colonial religion into something uniquely American. Among the "middling sort," or middle class, the Awakening represented something more. It represented "a groundswell of individualism" and skepticism of authority that anticipated the American Revolution.

GLOSSARY

DAVENPORT, JAMES   Itinerant preacher during the Great Awakening.

EDWARDS, JONATHAN   Massachusetts Congregational minister who rejected the new religious ideas of "easy salvation for all" and preached traditional Calvinist doctrine — the sovereignty of God, the innate depravity of people, the notion of the elect, and predestination.

EGALITARIANISM   The doctrine of "the equality of all men."

FREEHOLDER   One who owned a landed estate for life.

GREAT AWAKENING   Protestant revivals that swept the colonies from 1725 to 1770. The movement was more than just a religious one. It was "a profound cultural crisis that had been building for several generations," a crisis that demanded "a thorough reconsideration of the Christian ethic" as it had come to be known in 1730s America. The movement meant different things to different classes of people, but on the whole "it produced the greatest flow of religious energy since the Puritan movement a century before."

INNER LIGHT   The Quaker belief that one can find spiritual understanding and guidance through the light within one's self, which the Holy Spirit provides.

ITINERANT PREACHER   One who traveled from place to place, spreading the word of God.

PLANTER   Wealthy southerner who owned a sizable plantation and twenty or more slaves.

WHITEFIELD, GEORGE   English Methodist leader who helped ignite the Great Awakening in America.

YEOMAN FARMER   Small farmer, or lesser freeholder.

☆

LAND, GROWTH, AND CHANGING VALUES

Out of the combination of fertile land, a pool of bound laborers, white, black, and red, and the ambition of thousands of small farmers and artisans who labored independently, two variants of agricultural society emerged in eighteenth-century North America. In the North, small communities made up of farmers and artisans dotted the landscape. New Englanders engaged in mixed farming, which included farming the forests for timber used in barrels and ships, and farming the offshore waters for fish that provided one of the staples in the diet of the fast-growing slave population of the West Indies. The Middle Colonies specialized in producing corn, wheat, beef, and pork. By mid-eighteenth century they were provisioning not only the West Indies but also parts of Spain, Portugal, and England. Slaves were few in number in most of the Northern communities, rarely representing more than 5 percent of the population. A large percentage of free men owned land, and, though differences in ability and circumstances led gradually to greater social and economic stratification, the truly rich and abjectly poor were few in number and the gap between them was small in comparison to European society. Most men lived to acquire a farm of at least fifty acres. They extracted from the soil a modest income that allowed for security from want and provided a small inheritance for their children.

In the Southern colonies, where tobacco, rice, indigo, and timber products predominated, many yeomen farmers also struggled independently, although they were more frequently dispersed across the land than clustered in villages. These men have been far less noticed by historians than the plantation owners with slaves and indentured servants who lived along the rivers and streams that flowed from the Piedmont through the coastal plain to the ocean. But the usual picture of a Southern plantation society made up of immensely wealthy men exploiting the labor of huge gangs of black slaves is badly overdrawn. Perhaps as many as 40 percent of the Southern white males worked as tenant farmers or agricultural laborers, and of the remaining men who owned land, about two out of every three in the Chesapeake region worked farms of two hundred acres or less. In North Carolina farms were even smaller and men of real wealth rarer. In South Carolina the opposite was true; slaveholding was more widespread, plantations tended to be larger, and planters of substantial wealth represented a larger proportion of the population. As early as 1726 in St. George's Parish, 87 of 108 families held slaves. . . .

On the whole, probably not more than 5 percent of the white landowners were wealthy enough by the mid-eighteenth century to possess a plantation worth £1,000 — not too different from the North. Similarly, those owning large numbers of slaves were not as numerous as we commonly think. The number of Southern slaves increased rapidly in the eighteenth century, rising from about 20,000 in 1700 to 240,000 in 1750. But a majority of white adult males held no slaves at all at mid-century, and those who operated plantations with more than twenty slaves probably did not exceed 10 percent of the white taxables. South Carolina excepted, the South throughout the pre-Revolutionary period was dominated numerically by small landowners whose holdings, if perhaps twice the size of the average New England farm, were not more than half again as large as the typical farm in Pennsylvania, New Jersey, or New York.

Nonetheless, the ideal in the South, if not the reality, was the large plantation where black slaves would make the earth yield up profits sufficient to

From Gary B. Nash, *Red, White, and Black: The Peoples of Early North America* (3rd ed.), copyright © 1992, 144–161, 208–225. Reprinted by permission of Prentice-Hall, Englewood Cliffs, New Jersey.

support the leisured life. Statistically speaking, not many white colonists in the South achieved the dream. But that is what people worked for, and they came to identify the quest for material comfort with the exploitation of African slave labor in an era when the Northern colonists were beginning to phase out white bound labor and turning to a market economy where both goods and labor were freely exchanged.

The Protestant work ethic, which purportedly propelled people upward by inculcating a life of frugality, industriousness, and highly rationalized economic activity, perhaps operated less compellingly in the psyches of Southern colonists than in their Northern counterparts. But the abundant, fertile land of the South and the wider availability of slaves after 1690 provided all the incentive necessary for an aggressive, competitive society to develop. Much folklore about Southern cavaliers reposing under magnolia trees has been handed down in the history books, but in the eighteenth century European colonizers in the South were as avid in the pursuit of wealth and material comfort as European colonizers in the North. If the warm climate of the South bred languor, it was also true that farmers in the South had no long frozen winters when there was little to do but mend harnesses and chop wood. The typical New England farm produced just one crop each year, but a South Carolina rice or indigo plantation produced two. Moreover, the restraints of a New England community orientation and the Puritan bias against the accumulation of wealth which was not disposed of in socially useful ways never hindered entrepreneurial activity in the South. Organized religion was only shallowly rooted in most of the Southern colonies, and the community orientation never took hold because communities themselves were few and far between.

Paradoxically, one of the effects of the growth and success of the colonies in eighteenth-century British America was to shatter the utopian dream of the first generation that communities could be built where men and women worked for the commonweal, not only for themselves. The Puritan work ethic and an atmosphere of seemingly limitless opportunity encouraged men to work arduously at their callings. That was to the good. And their labors had generally been rewarded with success. So was that. But living where the ratio of people to land was so favorable compared to the societies from which they came, many colonists developed an aggressive outlook that patterned their behavior. What was to hold a man back in these uncharted expanses of land and unclaimed river valleys, as soon as the Indians were gone? In Europe, the absence of uncultivated lands ripe for exploitation and the grinding poverty that enshrouded the lives of the great mass of people produced in the peasant consciousness a very low level of expectations. "The frontier zone between possibility and impossibility barely moved in any significant direction, from the fifteenth to the eighteenth century," writes Fernand Braudel. But it moved in North America. The new concept was of a society where anything was possible. A competitive, entrepreneurial spirit began to take hold.

Religion and commitment to community, which acted as brakes on competitive, individualistic behavior, were by no means dead in the eighteenth century. But in general, piety, in terms of defining one's life as a preparation for the afterlife, declined greatly. Even in the seventeenth century Roger Williams had deplored the "depraved appetite after the great vanities, dreams, and shadows of this vanishing life, great portions of land, land in this wilderness, as if men were in as great necessity and danger for want of great portions of land, as poor, hungry seamen have, after a sick and stormy, a long and starving passage." In the eighteenth century land became ever more regarded not simply as a source of livelihood but a commodity to be bought and sold speculatively as a means of building a fortune. It was Franklin's little how-to-do-it best-seller, *The Way to Wealth,* that caught the spirit of the aggressive entrepreneurial eighteenth century. The brakes on economic ambition had been suddenly removed, and with the decline of fervid Puritanism in the eighteenth century, there was little left to restrain predatory instincts in those who were eager to pit themselves against their fellows in the pursuit of material gain. "Every man is for himself," lamented a prominent Philadelphian in 1706, only a generation after Penn had planted the seed of his "holy experiment." Two generations later the lieutenant-governor of New York, who had grown up in the colony, put it more explicitly: "The only principle of life propagated among the young people," wrote Cadwallader Colden, "is to get money and men are only esteemed according to what they are worth — that is the money they are possessed of." A contemporary in Rhode Island echoed the thought when he wrote "A Man who has Money here, no matter how he came by it, he is Everything, and wanting [lacking] that he's a meer Nothing, let his Conduct be ever so ereproachable."

As these acquisitive values took hold, the individual replaced the community as the conceptual unit of thought. The advice of the ancestors, such as the Puritan minister John Cotton, to "goe forth, every man that goeth, with a public spirit, looking not on your owne things only," or Winthrop's maxim that "the care of the publick must oversway all private respects," carried less and less weight in eighteenth-century society. The conquest of the wilderness and its inhabitants had proceeded far enough, men had shown enough adaptability and endurance for a hundred years, and the future possibilities seemed so great that a mental set developed in which colonial Americans appeared bent upon proving wrong the Elizabethan poet, John Donne, who counseled that no man could survive as an island unto himself. Having gained something, the typical colonist wanted more. A French visitor, who took up residence in New York, described this psychological reorientation:

An European, when he first arrives, seems limited in his intentions, as well as in his views; but he very suddenly al-

In eighteenth-century British America, "the individual replaced the community as the conceptual unit of thought." When a European first arrived, wrote a New York resident, "he no sooner breathes our air than he forms schemes, and embarks in designs he never would have thought of in his own country." This portrait by John Singleton Copley captures the individualistic spirit of eighteenth-century colonial America. (Courtesy of the Museum of Fine Arts, Boston)

ters his scale. . . . He no sooner breathes our air than he forms schemes, and embarks in designs he never would have thought of in his own country. . . . He begins to feel the effects of a sort of resurrection; hitherto he had not lived, but simply vegetated; he now feels himself a man, because he is treated as such; . . . he begins to forget his former servitude and dependence. . . .

Paradoxically, this transformation of attitudes, while it helped promote phenomenal growth and unleashed economic energies, led toward material success that contained within it the seeds of social strain. The demand for land east of the Appalachian Mountain barrier grew rapidly after 1740, as the population rose rapidly through immigration and natural increase. Especially in New England, ungranted land in the coastal region was a thing of the past, and the division and redivision of original land grants among sons and grandsons had progressed as far as it could go without splitting farms into unviably small economic units. New land — on the Maine frontier, in western Massachusetts and Connecticut, across the Appalachians in Pennsylvania, Virginia, Maryland, and the Carolinas — was the obvious solution to the problem of overcrowding. With the saturation of the Eastern coastal plain making the lands of the interior more attractive, land companies were formed in the mid-eighteenth century. They laid claim, however flimsy, to the valuable Western lands, their investors understanding the enormous appreciation in value that would occur as the next generation came of age and sought *lebensraum* to the west.★ But before a westward movement could begin, interior Indian peoples, as well as the French and Spanish, had to be overcome. . . .

☆

CHANGING SOCIAL STRUCTURE

Population growth and economic development, carried on for a century and a half by aggressive and opportunistic individuals, changed both the structure of colonial society and the attitudes of the people toward social structure — but changed them in opposite directions. Seventeenth-century Europeans on both sides of the Atlantic accepted the naturalness of hierarchy in human affairs, the inevitability of poverty, and the right of those in the upper stratum

of society to rule those below them. The belief was general that social gradations and internal subordination were not only sanctioned by God but were also essential to the maintenance of social stability and cohesion. Therefore care was taken to differentiate individuals by dress, by titles, in social etiquette, and even in penalties imposed in criminal proceedings. Puritans, for example, did not simply file into church on Sunday mornings and occupy the pews in random fashion. Instead, each seat was assigned according to the social rank of the person in the community. "Dooming the seats," as the assignment process was aptly called, was the responsibility of a church committee, which used every available yardstick of social respectability — age, parentage, social position, service to the community, and wealth — in drawing up a seating plan for the congregation. Puritans never entered their church without being reminded where they stood in the ranks of the community.

In spite of the philosophical commitment to hierarchy, the early European immigrants in North America were notably undifferentiated in their social makeup. Immigrant society was strongly lower-middle class in its composition, and the wide availability of land, combined with the lack of opportunities to amass great fortunes (when one had only his own labor and that of his wife, children, and a servant or two) kept the spectrum of wealth relatively narrow throughout most of the seventeenth century. Even in the cities, where the redistribution of wealth proceeded the fastest, the dawn of the eighteenth century witnessed a colonial society that was overwhelmingly middle class in character. In the Hudson River Valley and in the Southern colonies a handful of large plantation owners had made their mark, but the largest slave owners in Virginia at the beginning of the eighteenth century still owned fewer than one hundred slaves and not more than a handful of men had as much as £2,000 to leave to their heirs. As late as 1722 one of Philadelphia's richest merchants died with personal possessions worth just over £1,000 — a sizeable estate but unimpressive by European standards.

★*Lebensraum* means territorial expansion to extend trade — Ed.

In the eighteenth century, and especially in the half-century before the Revolution, the customary commitment to hierarchy and deference waned at the same time that stratification in society was increasing. Social attitudes and social structure were moving in opposite directions. Below the elite free whites developed the ideal of egalitarianism. The middling sort of people, wrote a Philadelphian in 1756, "enjoy and are fond of freedom, and the meanest among them thinks he has a right to civility from the greatest." Such comments were common. The Frenchman, Crèvecoeur, was surprised to see hired workers who "must be at your table and feed . . . on the best you have," and the schoolteacher Philip Fithian wrote of "labourers at the tables and in the parlours of their betters enjoying the advantage, and honour of their society and conversation."

Europeans judged what they saw against what they had known at home and thus sometimes exaggerated the degree of egalitarianism that they thought they saw. But it was true that most American colonists believed they were creating a society where a wealthy aristocracy did not dominate and no masses of poor whites were ground into the dust. The ideal was a rough economic equality where each person would have enough and a social equality "in which invidious discriminations would be abolished." When Benjamin Franklin toured the English countryside in 1772 he was appalled at what he saw and raised thanks that America was different. He described "landlords, great noblemen, and gentlemen, extremely opulent, living in the highest affluence and magnificence" alongside "the bulk of the people, tenants, extremely poor, living in the most sordid wretchedness, in dirty hovels of mud and straw, and clothed only in rags." Franklin could only shake his head and take solace in the knowledge that North America was different. Ignoring Indians and Africans, he wrote: "I thought often of the happiness of New England, where every Man is a Freeholder, has a Vote in publick Affairs, lives in a tidy, warm House, has plenty of good Food and fewel, with

whole cloaths from Head to Foot, the Manufacture perhaps of his own Family." The German Mittelberger summed up the twin ideals of economic equality and democratic scorn for authorities and authoritarian institutions. Pennsylvania, he said, was "heaven for farmers, paradise for artisans, and hell for officials and preachers."

All these commentators occupied favorable positions in society, which may account for the fact that they were describing not the reality but the ideal of colonial life. The reality, in fact, was that eighteenth-century society, even for white colonists, was moving away from the ideal. As the old deferential attitudes gave way to brash, assertive, individualistic modes of thought and behavior — what would become known as "the democratic personality" — society became more stratified, wealth became less evenly distributed, and impressively rich and truly impoverished classes emerged. Population growth and economic development in the eighteenth century made rich men of those with capital to speculate in land, buy slaves and servants, or participate in trade. The aggrandizement of wealth became clearly apparent in all sections of the country — North and South, rural and urban. In Boston, Newport, New York, Philadelphia, and Charleston stately townhouses rose as testimony to the fortunes being acquired in trade, shipbuilding, and land speculation. Probably the last of these was the most profitable of all. "It is almost a proverb," wrote a Philadelphian in 1767, "that Every great fortune made here within these 50 years has been by land." By the late colonial period, it was not unusual to find merchant-land speculators with estates valued at £10,000–£20,000. Even in the rural areas of the North, wealthy farmers amassed estates worth £4,000–£5,000. In the South, plantation magnates built even larger fortunes, for the rapid importation of African slaves after 1720 accelerated the rate at which profits could be extracted from the cultivation of tobacco or rice. By the eve of the Revolution, the great planters of the Chesapeake region, men such as Charles Carroll,

Robert "King" Carter, and William Byrd, had achieved spectacular affluence. Their estates, valued at £100,000 or more, were equivalent in purchasing power to a fortune of about six million dollars in 1990. It was not unusual to see 300 to 400 slaves toiling on such plantations, whereas in the late seventeenth century the largest slaveholder on the continent had no more than 50 bound laborers.

While the rapid increase in population and large-scale capital investment in land and slaves enabled a small number of men to accumulate fortunes that would have been noteworthy even in English society, the development of colonial society also created conditions in which a growing number of persons were finding it difficult to keep bread on the table and wood in the fireplace. This was especially true in the cities, where the social stratification proceeded most rapidly. All the major cities built almshouses and workhouses in the second quarter of the century to provide for those who could not care for themselves — the aged, indigent, sick, insane, and orphaned. Between 1725 and 1760, however, the poor in the cities increased more rapidly than the urban population as a whole, and after about 1750 poverty was no longer confined to the old or physically depleted. . . .

Inexorably the expanding economy and the individualistic values incorporated in the society tended to favor the aggressive and able in their drive toward material success. The greater the opportunities — a primary characteristic of a democratic society — the greater the gulf became between the rich and the poor. The growth of cultural and political egalitarianism was accompanied by, and indirectly sanctioned, the decline of economic equality. An open society with ample opportunities in the eighteenth century for entrepreneurship, and with relatively few restraints imposed by government, led, paradoxically, to a concentration of economic power in the hands of a thin upper layer of society. Becoming a society in which the individual and not the common weal

was the central concern, the white population of colonial North America was transforming what they thought to be uniquely American into what resembled more and more the European conditions they had fled.

The differing abilities of men to manipulate their economic environment, capitalize on the freedom to exploit white and black labor, and obtain title to Indian land were eventually recorded on the tax lists of the community where each man's wealth was set alongside that of his neighbors. Colonial historians have scrutinized those tax lists that have survived and have found that population growth and economic development led toward a less even distribution of wealth and an increase in the proportion of those without property in virtually every community. The change occurred slowly in rural areas and proceeded more rapidly in the seaboard centers of commercial activity.

In the rural town of Northampton, Massachusetts, for example, the upper 10 percent of property owners controlled 25 percent of the taxable wealth in 1676 and slowly increased their control of the community's assets to 34 percent in 1759. At the same time the proportion of the community's taxable property owned by the bottom third of the society remained steady at about 10 percent. . . .

In the cities the rate of change was far greater. Boston's upper tenth in 1687 held 46 percent of the taxable property while the lowest 30 percent had a meager 2.6 percent of the wealth. Four generations later, in 1771, the top tenth had 63 percent of the wealth; the lowest three-tenths had virtually nothing — a mere tenth of one percent of the community's taxable resources. Economic polarization in Boston, where the population was static after 1735 and economic recession hit hard at many elements of the community, was duplicated in vigorously expanding Philadelphia. In 1693, little more than a decade after settlement, the wealthiest tenth laid claim to 46 percent of the city's wealth. Three quarters of a century later, in 1772, they possessed 71 percent of the taxable wealth. As in Boston, these gains were not made at the expense of those in the bottom third of society, who possessed only a meager 2.2 percent of the wealth in 1693, but were accomplished at the expense of those in the middling elements of society.

If poverty touched the lives of a growing part of the urban laboring class, it was the usual condition on the frontier. Here the gap between rich and poor hardly existed because the rich were nowhere to be found. In its social order the frontier of the mid-eighteenth century was even cruder than rural society on the edge of the continent a century before. Whether in the towns of western Massachusetts and Connecticut, founded in the second and third quarters of the eighteenth century by the sons of Yankee farmers; or the lands along the Mohawk River in New York and the Susquehannah River in Pennsylvania, which represented the hopes of the German and Scots-Irish immigrants; or the backcountry of Maryland, Virginia, and the Carolinas, which sponged up some 250,000 souls in the late colonial period, frontier society was composed of small farmers and rural artisans who all stood roughly on the same plane. They purchased land cheaply, often for as little as four shillings an acre, and struggled to carve farms from the wilderness. Many hoped to get enough land under cultivation within a few years to produce surplus crops for market. But with only the help of one's sons and a few farm animals this often took most of a man's life. Others struggled only to make enough improvements on a piece of land so that other settlers pushing westward on the next wave of settlement would find it attractive enough to pay a price that rewarded one's labor.

On the New England frontier, where people pushed westward in groups, they founded new towns and churches as they went, quickly reproducing the institutions of eastern society. While poor, these simple villagers and farmers lived a life where institutional ligaments had not been altogether severed. But southward from New York on the east side of the Appalachian slopes frontier society existed in what many observers took to be a semibarbarous state. William Byrd described one of the largest plantations on the Virginia frontier in 1733 as "a poor dirty hovel, with hardly anything in it but children that wallowed about like so many pigs." Charles Woodmason, an itinerant Anglican minister who spent three years tramping from settlement to settlement in the Carolina backcountry in the 1760s, was appalled at what he found. "For thro' want of Ministers to marry and thro' the licentiousness of the People, many hundreds live in Concubinage — swopping their Wives as Cattel, and living in a State of Nature, more irregularly and unchastely than the Indians." As an English Anglican, Woodmason carried with him all the prejudices that were usually harbored against the Presbyterian Scots-Irish, the main inhabitants of the region. But there is little reason to doubt that the crudeness of life he described actually existed. After preaching at Flat Creek to "a vast Body of people . . . Such a Medley! such a mixed Multitude of all Classes and Complexions," he paled at their afterservice "Revelling Drinking Singing Dancing and Whoring" and threw up his hands that "most of the Company were drunk before I quitted the Spot — They were as rude in their Manners as the Common Savages, and hardly a degree removed from them." Some of what he saw made him close his eyes in horror, but he kept them open long enough to observe the young women who "have a most uncommon Practise. . . . They draw their Shift as tight as possible to the Body, and pin it close, to shew the roundness of their Breasts, and . . . their Petticoat close to their Hips to shew the fineness of their Limbs — so that they might as well be in Puri Naturalibus — Indeed Nakedness is not censurable or indecent here, and they expose themselves often quite Naked, without Ceremony — Rubbing themselves and their Hair with Bears Oil and tying it up behind in a Bunch like the Indians — being hardly one degree removed from them."

☆

THE GREAT AWAKENING

Nowhere did the line between social and economic change on the one hand and religion on the other crumble more swiftly than in the experiential and ideological upheaval called the Great Awakening. More than a solely religious movement, this period of sustained religious enthusiasm must be seen as a profound cultural crisis that had been building for several generations.

At its core the Great Awakening was "a search for new sources of authority, new principles of action, new foundations of hope" among people who had come to believe that the colonial churches "no longer met the spiritual needs of the people." The Awakeners preached that the old sources of authority were too effete to solve the problems of the day, too encrusted with tradition, hypocrisy, and intellectualism to bring hope and faith to a generation that was witnessing the rapid transformation of the world of their fathers. A new wellspring of authority was needed, and that source, the evangelists preached, was the individual himself. Like the Quaker "inner light," which dwelled in every man and woman, the "new light" within the awakened would enable them to achieve grace through the conversion experience. When enough people were "born again," as the evangelists of the Great Awakening phrased it, a new sense of community would be forged, a new brotherhood of man achieved, and the city on the hill restored. The Awakening, in its way, was a "revitalization movement," similar to those that would occur periodically in Indian societies, as attempts were made to reject corrosive new ways and return to the traditions of the past.

The Awakening had its first stirrings in the colonies in the 1720s in New Jersey and Pennsylva-

The Great Awakening erupted in full force when the English evangelist George Whitefield barnstormed the coast of North America, evoking an unprecedented mass response. This painting shows his spellbinding effect on congregations. (By courtesy of the National Portrait Gallery, London)

nia and then in the 1730s in Jonathan Edwards' church in Northampton, Massachusetts. But it was not until 1739, with the arrival of George Whitefield from England, that it struck with full force. Whitefield was a master of open-air preaching and had trekked across the English countryside for several years preaching the word of God. A diminutive man with a magnificent voice, he began a barnstorminig trip along the coast of North America in 1739 that evoked a mass response of a sort never witnessed before in the colonies. Thousands turned out to see him, and with each success his fame grew. Especially in the cities, which were the crucibles of social change, his effect was extraordinary, as people fought for places in the churches to hear him or congregated by the thousands in open fields to receive his message.

Some of Whitefield's appeal can be attributed to his genius for dramatic performances, his perfection of the art of advanced publicity, and his ability to simplify theological doctrine and focus the attention of masses of people on one facet of religious life — the conversion experience. In his electrifying performances, where written sermons were cast away, where spastic body movements and magnificent voice control replaced dry, logical, rigidly structured sermons, thousands experienced the desire to "fly to Christ." But it was the message as well as the medium that explains why people flocked to hear Whitefield. He frontally assaulted traditional sources of authority, called upon people to become the instruments of their own salvation, and implicitly attacked the upper-class notion that the simple folk had no minds of their own.

When Whitefield began his American tour in 1739, the social dynamite buried deep in his message was not yet clearly perceived by the elite. After all, his preaching produced thousands of conversions and filled the churches that had been languishing for more than a generation. Whitefield magnified the importance of religion in almost everyone who heard him, so it is no wonder that he was welcomed as "an angel of God, or as Elias, or John the Baptist risen from the dead." But Whitefield's popularity soon waned among the gentry because he was followed by itinerant Awakeners whose social radicalism was far less muted and because of the effects the evangelists' message had on the lower orders. Roaming preachers like Gilbert Tennant infused evangelical preaching with a radical egalitarianism that left many former supporters of Whitefield sputtering. Tennant attacked the established clergy as unregenerate and encouraged people to forsake their ministers. "The sapless Discourses of such dead Drones" were worthless, he proclaimed. James Davenport,

another itinerant preacher, told huge crowds that they should drink rat poison rather than listen to the corrupt clergy. Even more dangerous, Davenport indicted the rich and powerful, criticized the growing gap between rich and poor, and exhorted ordinary people to resist those who exploited and deceived them. Only then, he cried, would the Lamb Jesus return to earth.

Crowds followed Davenport through the towns, singing and clapping so that "they look'd more like a Company of *Bacchanalians* after a mad Frolick, than sober Christians who had been worshipping God," as one distressed Boston newspaper complained. Respectable people were convinced that revivalism had gotten out of hand and that social control of the lowest layers of society was crumbling. Revivalism had started out as a return to religion among backsliding Christians but now was turning into a social experience that profoundly threatened the established culture, which stressed order, discipline, and submissiveness from laboring people. The fear of the Awakeners' attacks on genteel literate culture, on wealth and ostentatious living, was epitomized in New London, Connecticut in 1743 when Davenport scandalized the gentry by inducing a huge crowd

to burn "sundry good and useful treatises, books of practical godliness, the works of able divines," as well as "hoop petticoats, silk gowns, short cloaks, cambrick caps, red heeled shoes, fans, necklaces, gloves, and other such apparell." While psalms and hymns were sung over the pile, the preacher added his own pants, "a pair of old, wore out, plush breeches." This, commented one critic, would have obliged him "to strut about bare-arsed" had not the fire been extinguished.

By 1742 New England and the middle colonies were being criss-crossed by a procession of itinerant gospelers and haranguers, all of them labeled social incendiaries by the established clergy. Of all the signs of social leveling that conservatives saw springing from evangelicalism, the one they feared the most was the practice of public lay exhorting. Within the established churches there was no place for lay persons to compete with the qualified ministry in preaching the word of God. Nor was there room for "self-initiated associations of the people meeting outside of regularly constituted religious or political meetings," for to do so was to relocate authority collectively in the mass of common people. Lay exhorting shattered the monopoly of the educated clergy on religious discourse, put all people on a plane in the area of religion, gave new importance to the oral culture of common people, whose spontaneous outpourings contrasted sharply with the literary culture of the gentry, established among them the notion that their destinies and their souls were in their own hands instead of the hands of the elite clergy, and turned the world upside down in allowing those who had traditionally been consigned to the bottom of society to assume roles customarily reserved for educated, adult men. In lay exhorting, class lines were crossed and sexual and racial roles were defied, as ordinary men, women, and even children, servants, and slaves rose before throngs to testify emotionally to their own conversion and exhort others to a state of religious ecstasy by preaching extemporaneously the Lord's truth.

The Great Awakening thus represented far more than a religious earthquake. Through it, ordinary people haltingly enunciated a distinctive popular ideology that challenged inherited cultural norms. To some extent, as many historians have noted, the Awakening represented a groundswell of individualism, a kind of protodemocratic spirit that anticipated the Revolution. This was true, especially among the middling people of colonial society for whom the revival years involved an expansion of political consciousness and a new feeling of self-importance, as they partook of spontaneous meetings, assumed new power in ecclesiastical affairs, and were encouraged by the evangelists to adopt a skeptical attitude toward dogma and authority. But among the lowliest

members of society, including impoverished city dwellers, servants, slaves, and those who struggled to gain a foothold on the treacherous slopes of economic security, the Awakening experience implied not a movement forward toward democratic bourgeois revolution but backwards to an earlier age when it was conceived that individuals acted not for themselves, always striving to get ahead at the expense of their neighbors, but pulled together as a community. Hence the dispossessed harked to the anti-entrepreneurial, communalistic tone permeating the exhortations of the radical evangelists such as Tennant, who preached that in any truly Christian community "mutual *Love* is the *Band* and *Cement*. . . . For men, by the Neglect of its Exercise, and much more by its Contrary, will be tempted, against the *Law of Nature,* to seek a *single* and independent State, in order to secure their Ease and Safety."

The radical Awakeners were not preaching class revolt or the end to wealth-producing commerce. What they urged was "a thorough reconsideration of the Christian ethic as it had come to be understood in the America of the 1730s." Nor were those who harked to the Awakeners inspired to foment social revolution, for in fact the seeds of overt political radicalism were still in the germinative stage. But the multitudes who were moved by the message of the revivalists, in the North in the 1740s and in the South during the next decade, began to believe that it was justifiable in some circumstances to take matters into their own hands. This is why Jonathan Edwards, a highly intellectual, latter-day Puritan minister, was seen by the commercial elite and their clerical allies as "the grand leveler of Christian history," even though sedition and leveling were not what he had in mind. The Great Awakening produced the greatest flow of religious energy since the Puritan movement a century before, but this outpouring was intimately connected with the tensions in colonial society that had grown from generations of social and economic change.

1   To what conditions does Gary Nash ascribe the growth of individualism in eighteenth-century America? What emphasis does he place on land and its availability?

2   Gary Nash says that in the eighteenth century, American social structure and ideas about social structure changed in opposite directions. How did they change and why? How did seventeenth- and eighteenth-century American social and economic conditions compare with those of Europe and why?

3   How did social conditions vary from one region to another? What influences led to these variations?

4   According to Gary Nash, how did social and economic conditions and religion influence each other in the seventeenth and eighteenth centuries?

5   What does Gary Nash think the Great Awakening reveals about the tensions in eighteenth-century American society? Did the experience mean the same thing to all parts of society? What implications would the Great Awakening have for subsequent American history?

6

Meet Dr. Franklin

RICHARD B. MORRIS

Benjamin Franklin, who called himself "the printer of Philadelphia," was one of the most remarkable human beings colonial America ever produced. As Richard B. Morris says, Franklin was America's first pragmatist: he believed that "what was moral was what worked and what worked was moral." He also celebrated the Protestant work ethic in his bestselling Poor Richard's Almanack, *the advice in which became the maxims of Franklin's generation: "Early to bed, and early to rise, makes a man healthy, wealthy, and wise." "He that riseth late must trot all day, and shall scarce overtake his business at night." "Sloth makes all things difficult, but industry all easy." "Laziness travels so slowly, that poverty soon overtakes him." "Women and Wine, Game and Deceit, Make the Wealth Small and his Wants Great." Franklin not only personified the frugality, hard work, restlessness, and occasional irreverence of colonial Americans but came to symbolize their growing sense of nationality as well.*

In his long lifetime, Franklin tried his hand at virtually every trade and profession young America had to offer — among other things, he was a farmer, a printer, a scientist, an author, a philosopher, a statesman, a diplomat, and a connoisseur of women. In the last capacity, he composed an article on the cultivation of a mistress and became a legendary womanizer. According to one anecdote, he fathered so many children that a colleague was moved to quip that it was not Washington but Benjamin Franklin who was "the real father of our country." Franklin would have appreciated the anecdote, for he had a consummate sense of humor. But above all, he had an unflagging love for liberty and the natural rights of people.

Still, Franklin was a complex and often contradictory person. As Morris demonstrates in his lively and candid portrait, Franklin went through identity crises such as anyone else, indulged in literary pranks, and had ambivalent attitudes toward women. Although he abhorred violence, he was a devious individual who rebelled against convention and authority and in time became a leading American revolutionary. At the same time, Franklin regarded himself as truly a citizen of the world who hoped one day "that not only the love of liberty, but a thorough knowledge of the rights of man, may pervade all the nations of the earth, so that a philosopher may set his foot anywhere on its surface, and say, 'This is my country.'"

On the issue of slavery and race, however, Franklin was not always enlightened. In the 1730s, he held a low opinion of black people's intellectual abilities and even traded in slaves at his Philadelphia printing shop, either selling them for others or buying them as an investment. He once advertised that he had for sale "a breeding Negro woman about twenty years of age. Can do any household work." He also owned a slave couple, who worked with white servants in his home. By 1751, however, he had come to regard slavery as an economically unsound labor system. Twenty-one years later, a visit to an African American school was a revelation for him. What he saw convinced him that the schoolchildren were the equal of their white peers in intellectual capacity. That same year, Franklin publicly condemned the slave trade as "a detestable commerce" and damned slavery as a crime against humanity. After the Revolution, at the age of eighty-one, Franklin became the president of the Pennsylvania Society for the Abolition of Slavery. His evolution from slave trader to prominent American abolitionist demonstrated that people can become enlightened and can grow out of their prejudices.

GLOSSARY

BRILLON, MME   One of Franklin's French mistresses.

CARROLL, JOHN   Franklin had him appointed as the first Roman Catholic bishop in the United States.

DEISTS   Eighteenth-century rationalists who rejected formal religion and the idea of "supernatural revelation." Deists argued that God created all nature, then allowed it to operate by natural laws.

GRAND OHIO COMPANY   Land-speculating operation with which Franklin was associated.

HELVÉTIUS, MME   Widow with whom Franklin carried on a long flirtation.

HUTCHINSON-OLIVER LETTERS   A series of injudicious epistles sent to English authorities by the Massachusetts Bay governor and lieutenant governor. The letters recommended that England severely restrict liberties in the Bay colony.

LOCKE, JOHN (1632–1704)   Preeminent English philosopher of the Enlightenment who contended that all human beings were innately good and equal and were entitled to "life, health, liberty, and possessions."

PENNSYLVANIA ABOLITION SOCIETY   America's first antislavery society; Franklin became its president.

PLAN OF UNION OR ALBANY
PLAN   Franklin's 1751 plan to unite the colonies.

POLLY BAKER STORY   One of Franklin's "outrageous" inventions that illustrated his "liberal sexual code."

POOR RICHARD   Fictional character in Franklin's immensely popular almanac who offered aphorisms and proverbs for Franklin's colonial readers.

Deceptively simple and disarmingly candid, but in reality a man of enormous complexity, [Benjamin] Franklin wore many masks, and from his own time to this day each beholder has chosen the mask that suited his fancy. To D. H. Lawrence, Franklin typified the hypocritical and bankrupt morality of the do-gooder American with his stress upon an old-fashioned Puritan ethic that glorified work, frugality, and temperance — in short, a "snuff-coloured little man!" of whom "the immortal soul part was a sort of cheap insurance policy." Lawrence resented being shoved into "a barbed wired paddock" and made to "grow potatoes or Chicagoes." Revealing in this castigation much about himself and little insight into Franklin, Lawrence could not end his diatribe against the most cosmopolitan of all Americans without hurling a barbed shaft at "clever America" lying "on her muck-heaps of gold." F. Scott Fitzgerald quickly fired off a broadside of his own. In *The Great Gatsby,* that literary darling of the Jazz Age, he indicted *Poor Richard* as midwife to a generation of bootleggers.

If Lawrence and Fitzgerald were put off by Franklin's commonsense materialism which verged on crassness or if Max Weber saw Franklin as embodying all that was despicable in both the American character and the capitalist system, if they and other critics considered him as little more than a methodical shopkeeper, they signally failed to understand him. They failed to perceive how Franklin's materialism was transmuted into benevolent and humanitarian ends, how that shopkeeper's mind was enkindled by a ranging imagination that set no bounds to his intellectual interests and that continually fed an extraordinarily inventive and creative spark. They failed to explain how the popularizer of an American code of hard work, frugality, and moral restraint had

From pp. 6–30 in *Seven Who Shaped Our Destiny* by Richard B. Morris. Copyright © 1973 by Richard B. Morris. Reprinted by permission of the author.

Joseph Duplessis painted Franklin from life in 1787 and later made this copy from it. Franklin was a complex, contradictory individual, now witty and self-confident, now deceitful and given to literary pranks. Even so, he succeeded in everything he tried, from publishing a Philadelphia newspaper and Poor Richard's Almanack *to charming the women of Paris. (New York Public Library)*

penniless waif who arrived in Philadelphia disheveled and friendless, walking up Market Street munching a great puffy roll, had by grit and ability propelled himself to the top. Not only did the young printer's apprentice manage the speedy acquisition of a fortune, but he went on to achieve distinction in many different fields, and greatness in a few of them. In an age when the mastery of more than one discipline was possible, Franklin surpassed all his contemporaries as a well rounded citizen of the world. Endowed with a physique so strong that as a young man he could carry a large form of type in each hand, "when others carried but one in both hands," a superb athlete and a proficient swimmer, Franklin proved to be a talented printer, an enterprising newspaper editor and publisher, a tireless promoter of cultural institutes, America's first great scientist whose volume on electricity turned out to be the most influential book to come out of America in the eighteenth century, and second to none as a statesman. Eldest of the Founding Fathers by a whole generation, he was in some respects the most radical, the most devious, and the most complicated.

From the available evidence, mainly provided by the subject himself, Franklin underwent two separate identity crises, when, as modern-day psychoanalysts suggest, the subject struggles for a new self and a new conception of his place in the world. In adolescence Franklin experienced a psychological crisis of the kind that Erik Erikson has so perceptively attributed to personages as disparate as Martin Luther and Mahatma Gandhi. Again, Franklin, the middle-aged man seeking a new image of himself, seems the prototype of Jung's classic case. As regards the first crisis, Franklin's autobiography reveals a sixteen-year-old rebelling against sibling rivalry and the authority of his household, using a variety of devices to maintain his individuality and sense of self-importance.

Born in Boston in 1706, the tenth son of Josiah and Abiah Folger Franklin, and the youngest son of the youngest son for five generations, Franklin could very easily have developed an inferiority complex as one of the youngest of thirteen children sitting

no conscientious scruples about enjoying high living, a liberal sexual code for himself, and bawdy humor. They failed to explain how so prudent and methodical a man could have got caught up in a revolution in no small part of his own making.

Franklin would have been the first to concede that he had in his autobiography created a character gratifying to his own vanity. "Most people dislike vanity in others, whatever share they have of it themselves," he observed, "but I give it fair quarter wherever I meet it." Begun in 1771, when the author had completed a half-dozen careers and stood on the threshold of his most dramatic role, his autobiography constitutes the most dazzling success story of American history. The

around his father's table at one time. Everything about the home reduced Franklin's stature in his own eyes. When his father tried to make a tallow chandler and soap boiler out of him, he made it clear that his father's trade was not to his liking. His father then apprenticed the twelve-year-old lad to his brother James, who had started a Boston newspaper, the *New England Courant,* in 1721. For the next few years Benjamin was involved in one or another kind of rebellion.

Take the matter of food. Benjamin, an omnivorous reader, devoured a book recommending a vegetarian diet. Since his brother James boarded both himself and his apprentices at another establishment, Franklin's refusal to eat meat or fish proved an embarrassment to his elder brother and a nuisance to the housekeeper. Franklin, to save arguments which he abhorred, worked out a deal with his brother, who agreed to remit to him half the money he paid out for him for board if he would board himself. Concentrating on a frugal meatless diet, which he dispatched quickly, Franklin, eating by himself, had more time to continue his studies. While eating one of his hastily prepared meals he first feasted on Locke's treatise *On Human Understanding.*

A trivial episode, indeed, but this piece of self flagellation forecast a lifelong pattern of pervasive traits. Benjamin Franklin did not like to hurt anyone, even nonhuman creatures. He avoided hostilities. Rather than insisting upon getting the menu he preferred, he withdrew from the table of battle and arranged to feed himself. This noncombative nature, masking a steely determination, explains much of Franklin's relation with others thereafter. Even his abandonment of the faddish vegetarian diet provides insights into the evolving Franklin with his pride in rational decision. On his voyage from Boston to Philadelphia, he tells us, his ship became becalmed off Block Island, where the crew spent their idle moments catching cod. When the fish were opened, he saw that smaller fish came out of the stomachs of the larger cod. "Then, thought I," he confessed in his autobiogra-

phy, "If you eat one another, I don't see why we mayn't eat you." With that, he proceeded to enjoy a hearty codfish repast and to return at once to a normal flesh-eating diet. With a flash of self-revelation, he comments, "So convenient a thing it is to be a *reasonable creature,* since it enables one to find or make a reason for everything one has a mind to do."

Franklin's rebellion against authority and convention soon assumed a more meaningful dimension. When, in 1722, his brother James was jailed for a month for printing critical remarks in his newspaper about the authorities, the sixteen-year-old apprentice pounced on the chance to achieve something on his own. He published the paper for his brother, running his own name on the masthead to circumvent the government. Continually quarreling with his overbearing brother, Franklin determined to quit his job, leave his family and Boston, and establish himself by his own efforts unaided. The youthful rebel set forth on his well-publicized journey to Philadelphia, arriving in that bustling town in October, 1723, when he was little more than seventeen years of age.

To carve out a niche for himself in the printing trade, Franklin had to keep a checkrein on his rebellious disposition. For weeks he bore without ill temper the badgering of his master Keimer. When the blow-up came, Franklin, rather than stay and quarrel, packed up and lit out. Once more he was on his own. "Of all the things I hate altercation," he wrote years later to one of his fellow commissioners in Paris with whom he was continually at odds. He would write sharp retorts and then not mail the letters. An operator or negotiator *par excellence,* Franklin revealed in his youthful rebellion against family and employers the defensive techniques he so skillfully utilized to avoid combat. Yet there was little about Franklin's behavior which we associate with neurotics. He was a happy extrovert, who enjoyed the company of women, and was gregarious and self-assured, a striking contrast to Isaac Newton, a tortured introvert who remained a bachelor all his life. Suffice it to say that Franklin never suffered the kind of nervous breakdown that Newton experienced at the height of his powers, and as a result his effectiveness remained undiminished until a very advanced age.

If Franklin early showed an inclination to back away from a quarrel, to avoid a head-on collision, if his modesty and candor concealed a comprehension of his own importance and a persistent deviousness, such traits may go far to explain the curious satisfaction he took in perpetrating hoaxes on an unsuspecting and gullible public. The clandestine side of Franklin, a manifestation of his unwillingness to engage in direct confrontation, hugely benefited by his sense of humor and satirical talents. An inveterate literary prankster from his precocious teens until his death, Franklin perpetrated one literary hoax after another. In 1730, when he became the sole owner of a printing shop and proprietor of the *Pennsylvania Gazette,* which his quondam boss Keimer had launched a few years earlier, Franklin's paper reported a witch trial at Mount Holly, New Jersey, for which there is no authority in fact.

Franklin's greatest hoax was probably written in 1746 and perpetrated the following year, when the story ran in London's *General Advertiser.* Quickly it was reprinted throughout England, Scotland, and Ireland, and in turn picked up by the Boston and New York papers. This was his report of a speech of Polly Baker before a Massachusetts court, in defense of an alleged prosecution for the fifth time for having a bastard child. "Can it be crime (in the nature of things I mean) to add to the number of the King's subjects, in a new country that really wants people?" she pleaded. "I own it, I should think it as praiseworthy, rather than a punishable action." Denying that she had ever turned down a marriage proposal, and asserting that she was betrayed by the man who first made her such an offer, she compared her role with that of the great number of bachelors in the new country who had "never sincerely and honourably courted a woman in their lives" and insisted that, far from sinning, she had obeyed the "great

command of Nature, and of Nature's God, *Encrease and Multiply.*" Her compassionate judges remitted her punishment, and, according to this account, one of them married her the very next day.

How so obviously concocted a morality tale as that one could have gained such wide credence seems incredible on its face. Yet the French sage, the Abbé Raynal, picked it up for his *Histoire Philosophique et Politique,* published in 1770. Some seven years later, while visiting Franklin at Passy, Raynal was to be disabused. "When I was young and printed a newspaper," Franklin confessed, "it sometimes happened, when I was short of material to fill my sheet, that I amused myself by making up stories, and that of Polly Baker is one of the number."

When some years later Franklin's severe critic John Adams listed Polly Baker's speech as one of Franklin's many "outrages to morality and decorum," he was censoring not only Franklin's liberal sexual code but the latter's ability to throw off bad habits in old age. Franklin's penchant for pseudonymous writing was one side of his devious nature and evidenced his desire to avoid direct confrontation. He continued in later life to write a prodigious number of letters under assumed names which appeared in the American, English, and French press, some still undetected. His sly "Edict by the King of Prussia," appearing in an English newspaper in 1773, was a parody, in which Frederick the Great threatened reprisals against England for failing to emancipate the colonists from Germany that originally settled the island. As commissioner in Paris Franklin reputedly wrote a vitriolic hoax, *The Sale of the Hessians,* in which a Count de Schaumbergh expressed delight that 1605 of his Hessians had been killed in America, 150 more than Lord North had reported to him. This was a windfall, since he was entitled to a sum of money for every fatality suffered by the mercenaries he had sold to George III. In the midst of delicate negotiations with the British to end the war of the American Revolution, the irrepressible Franklin fabricated a hoax about the scalping of Americans by Indians in the pay of the British, and then printed it in the guise of a *Supplement to the Boston Independent Chronicle*. Gruesome propaganda indeed, but Franklin justified his deception to the censorious Adams by remarking that he believed the number of persons actually scalped "in this murdering war by the Indians to exceed what is mentioned in invoice."

The image of himself Franklin chose to leave us in his unfinished autobiography was of a man on the make, who insincerely exploited popular morality to keep his printing presses running. Yet he himself, perhaps tongue in cheek, would have said that the morality of *Poor Richard* was foreshadowed by the plan of conduct Franklin had put down on paper on a return voyage in 1726 to Philadelphia from London, where he had spent almost two years in an effort to be able to buy equipment to set himself up as a printer. Later in life Franklin praised the plan as "the more remarkable, as being formed when I was so young, and yet being pretty faithfully adhered to quite through to old Age." The plan stressed the practice of extreme frugality until he had paid his debts, as well as truthfulness, industry, and the avoidance of speaking ill of others.

Franklin, the sixteen-year-old apprentice, absorbed the literary styles of his brother James and other New England satirists running their pieces in the *Courant,* and he clearly used the *Spectator* as his literary model. He produced the Silence Dogood letters, thirteen in a row, until, he admitted, "my small fund of sense for such performances was pretty well exhausted." Until then even his own brother was not aware of the identity of the author. Typical was No. 6, which criticized pride in apparel, singling out such outlandish fashions as hoop petticoats, "monstrous topsy-turvy *Mortar-Pieces* . . . neither fit for the Church, the Hall, or the Kitchen," and looming more "like Engines of War for bombarding the Town, than Ornaments of the Fair Sex."

If the Dogood letters satisfied Franklin's itch for authorship, *Poor Richard* brought him fame and fortune. Lacking originality, drawing upon a wide range of proverbs and aphorisms, notably found in a half-dozen contemporary English anthologies, Franklin skillfully selected, edited, and simplified. For example, James Howell's *Lexicon Tetraglotton* (London, 1660), says: "The greatest talkers are the least doers." *Poor Richard* in 1733 made it: "Great talkers, little doers." Or Thomas Fuller's *Gnomolonia* (London, 1732): "The way to be safe is never to be secure"; this becomes in *Poor Richard*, 1748: "He that's secure is not safe." Every so often one of the aphorisms seems to reflect Franklin's own views. Thus, *Poor Richard* in 1747 counseled: "Strive to be the *greatest* Man in your Country, and you may be disappointed; Strive to be the *best,* and you may succeed: He may well win the race that runs by himself." Again, two years later, *Poor Richard* extols Martin Luther for being "remarkably *temperate* in meat and drink," perhaps a throwback to Franklin's own adolescent dietary obsessions, with an added comment, *"There was never any* industrious *man who was not a* temperate *man."* To the first American pragmatist what was moral was what worked and what worked was moral.

If there was any priggish streak in the literary Franklin it was abundantly redeemed by his bawdy sense of humor and his taste for earthy language. Thus, to *Poor Richard,* foretelling the weather by astrology was "as easy as pissing abed." "He that lives upon Hope dies farting." The bawdy note of reportage guaranteed a good circulation of Franklin's *Gazette.* Thus in 1731:

We are credibly inform'd, that the young Woman who not long since petitioned the Governor, and the Assembly to be divorced from her Husband, and at times, industriously solicited most of the Magistrates on that Account, has at last concluded to cohabit with him again. It is said the Report of the Physicians (who in Form examined his *Abilities,* and allowed him to be in every respect *sufficient*) gave her but small Satisfaction; Whether any Experiments *more satisfactory* have been try'd, we cannot say; but it

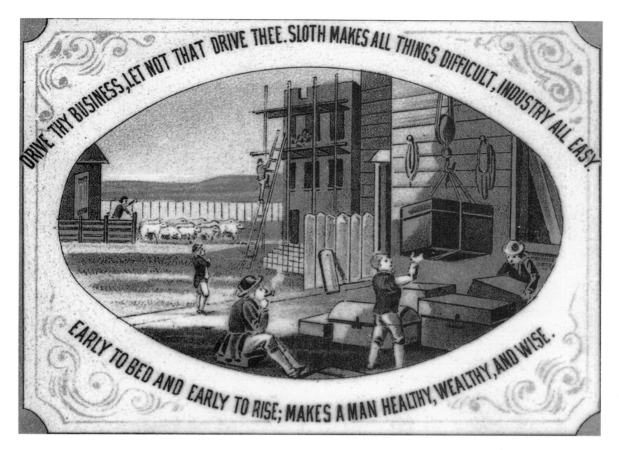

DRIVE THY BUSINESS, LET NOT THAT DRIVE THEE. SLOTH MAKES ALL THINGS DIFFICULT, INDUSTRY ALL EASY. EARLY TO BED AND EARLY TO RISE; MAKES A MAN HEALTHY, WEALTHY, AND WISE.

Poor Richard, *which brought Franklin fame and fortune, offered readers a broad range of aphorisms and proverbs. The ones shown here are fairly tame. Others reflected Franklin's bawdy sense of humor and taste for pungent language. (Corbis-Bettmann)*

seems she now declares it as her Opinion, That *George is as good as de best.*

Franklin's ambivalent views of women indubitably reflected his own personal relations with the other sex. In his younger days he took sex hungrily, secretly, and without love. One of his women — just which one nobody knows for sure — bore him a son in 1730 or 1731. It was rumored that the child's mother was a maidservant of Franklin's named Barbara, an accusation first printed in 1764 by a political

foe of Franklin's, reputedly Hugh Williamson. Whether it was this sudden responsibility or just the boredom of sowing his wild oats, Franklin came to realize that "a single man resembles the odd half of a pair of scissors." Having unsuccessfully sought a match with a woman who would bring him money, Franklin turned his thoughts back to Deborah Read, the girl he had first courted in Philadelphia and then jilted. Rebounding from that humiliation, Deborah married a potter named Rogers who quickly deserted her. Then she did not even bother to have the marriage annulled, relying instead on the rumor that her husband had left behind him a wife in England. Franklin, so he tells us in his autobiography, conveniently overlooked "these difficulties," and "took her to wife, September 1st, 1730." The illegitimate child, William, whether born before or after Franklin's common-law marriage to Deborah, became part of the household, a convenient arrangement for Franklin while a constant reminder to Deborah of her spouse's less than romantic feeling about her. Soon there arose between Deborah and William a coldness bordering on hostility.

The married Franklin's literary allusions to women could be both amicable and patronizing; he could treat them as equals but show downright hostility at times. He portrayed the widow Silence Dogood as frugal, industrious, prosaic, and earthy, but somehow retaining her femininity. Such inferiority as women appeared to have must be attributed to their inferior education. While believing in the moral equality of the sexes, Franklin did not encourage women to enter unconventional fields of activity. He stuffed his *Almanack* with female stereotypes, perhaps charging off his own grievances to the sex in general. He frequently jabbed at "domineering women," with Richard Saunders the prototype of all henpecked husbands and Bridget, his "shrewish, clacking" wife. Scolding, gossipy women and talkative old maids are frequent targets of Franklin's jibes. A woman's role in life, he tells us, is to be a wife and have babies, but a man has a more versatile role and therefore commands a higher value.

Franklin's bagatelles "On Perfumes" and "On Marriages," frequently, if furtively, printed and kept under wraps for years by the Department of State, attained a clandestine fame, but few in the nineteenth century dared to print either. With the sexual revolution of the twentieth century and the penchant for scatological vocabulary, Franklin's letter on marriage and mistresses attained respectability and wide circulation. In essence, Franklin, in a letter dated June 25, 1745, commended marriage as the state in which a man was "most likely to find solid Happiness." However, those wishing to avoid matrimony without foregoing sex were advised to choose *"old Women to young ones."* Among the virtues of older women he listed their more agreeable conversation, their continued amiability to counteract the "Diminution of Beauty," the absence of a "hazard of Children," their greater prudence and discretion in conducting extra-marital affairs, and the superiority of techniques of older women. "As in the dark all Cats are grey, the Pleasure of corporal Enjoyment with an old Woman is at least equal, and frequently superior, every Knack being by Practice capable of Improvement." Furthermore, who could doubt the advantages of making an old woman *"happy"* against debauching a virgin and contributing to her ruin. Finally, old women are *"so gratefull!!"*

How much this advice reflected Franklin's own marriage of convenience remains for speculation. *Poor Richard* is constantly chiding cuckolds and scolding wives, and suggesting that marital infidelity is the course of things. "Let thy maidservant be faithful, strong, and homely." "She that paints her Face, thinks of her Tail." "Three things are men most liable to be cheated in, a Horse, a Wig, and a Wife." Or consider poor Lubin lying on his deathbed, both he and his wife despairing, he fearing death, she, "that he may live." Or the metaphor of women as books and men the readers. "Are Women Books? says Hodge, then would mine were an *Almanack,* to change her every Year."

Enough examples, perhaps, have been chosen to show that Franklin's early view of women was based on a combination of gross and illicit sexual experiences and a less than satisfying marriage with a wife neither glamorous nor intellectually compatible.

Abruptly, at the age of forty-two, Franklin retired from active participation in his printing business. He explained the action quite simply; "I flattered myself that, by the sufficient tho' moderate fortune I had acquir'd, I had secured leisure during the rest of my life for philosophical studies and amusements."

These words masked the middle-age identity crisis that he was now undergoing. Seeking to project himself on a larger stage, he did not completely cut his ties to a less glamorous past, including a wife who was a social liability, but conveniently eluded it. Now he could lay aside the tools of his trade and the garments of a petit bourgeois and enter the circles of gentility. Gone were the days he would sup on an anchovy, a slice of bread and butter, and a half-pint of ale shared with a companion. His long bouts with the gout in later life attest to his penchant for high living, for Madeira, champagne, Parmesan cheese, and other continental delicacies. Sage, philanthropist, statesman, he became, as one critic has remarked, "an intellectual transvestite," affecting a personality switch that was virtually completed before he left on his first mission (second trip) to England in 1757. Not that Franklin was a purely parochial figure at the time of his retirement from business. Already he had shown that passion for improvement which was to mark his entire career. Already he had achieved some local reputation in public office, notably in the Pennsylvania Assembly. Already he had displayed his inventive techniques, most notably his invention of the Pennsylvania fireplace, and had begun his inquiries into the natural sciences.

Now, on retirement from private affairs, he stood on the threshold of fame. In the subsequent decade he plunged into his scientific investigations and into provincial politics with equal zest. Dispatched to England in 1757 to present the case of the Pennsylvania Assembly against the proprietor, he spent five of the happiest years of his life residing at the Craven Street residence of Mrs. Margaret Stevenson. Mrs. Stevenson, and especially her daughter Mary, provided for him a pleasant and stimulating home away from home. Reluctantly he returned to Philadelphia at the end of his five-year stay, so enraptured of England that he even contemplated settling there, "provided we can persuade the good Woman to cross the Seas." Once more, in 1764, he was sent abroad, where he stayed to participate in all the agitation associated with the Grenville revenue measures. Snugly content in the Stevenson ménage, Franklin corresponded perfunctorily with his wife back in Philadelphia. Knowing that Deborah was unwilling to risk a sea voyage to join him in London, Franklin did not insist. And although he wrote his wife affectionate letters and sent her gifts, he never saw her again. She died of a stroke in December, 1774, without benefit of Franklin's presence.

It was in France after the American Revolution had broken out that Franklin achieved more completely that new identity which was the quest of his later years. There the mellow septuagenarian, diplomat, and peacemaker carried out a game with the ladies of the salon, playing a part, ironic, detached but romantic, enjoying an *amitié amoureuse* with his impressionable and neurotic neighbor, Mme. Brillon in Passy, flirting in Paris with the romantically minded Comtesse d'Houdetot, and then in the rustic retreat of Auteuil falling in love with the widow of Helvétius, whom he was prepared to marry had she been so inclined. In the unreal world of the salon Franklin relished the role of "papa." Still he avoided combat or confrontation even in his flirtation. Where he scented rejection, he turned witty, ironic, and verbally sexual.

He found time, while engaged in the weighty affairs of peacemaking during the summer of '82, to draw up a treaty of "eternal peace, friendship, and love" between himself and Madame Brillon. Like a good draftsman, Franklin was careful to preserve his freedom of action, in this case toward other females, while at the same time insisting on his right to behave without inhibitions toward his amiable neighbor. Some months before he had written her:

I often pass before your house. It appears desolate to me. Formerly I broke the Commandment by coveting it along with my neighbor's wife. Now I do not covet it any more, so I am less a sinner. But as to his wife I always find these Commandments inconvenient and I am sorry that they were ever made. If in your travels you happen to see the

Holy Father, ask him to repeal them, as things given only to the Jews and too uncomfortable for good Christians.

Franklin met Mme. Brillon in 1777, and found her a beautiful woman in her early thirties, an accomplished musician, married to a rich and tolerant man, twenty-four years her senior. To Mme Brillon Franklin was a father figure, while to Franklin she combined the qualities of daughter and mistress. Part tease, part prude, Mme. Brillon once remarked: "Do you know, my dear papa, that people have criticized the sweet habit I have taken of sitting on your lap, and your habit of soliciting from me what I always refuse?" In turn, Franklin reminded her of a game of chess he had played in her bathroom while she soaked in the tub.

If Franklin was perhaps most passionately fond of Brillon, other ladies of the salon set managed to catch his eye, among them the pockmarked, cross-eyed Comtesse d'Houdetot, who made up in sex appeal what she lacked in looks. Unlike Rousseau, who cherished for the Comtesse an unrequited passion, which he widely publicized in his posthumous *La Nouvelle Héloise,* Franklin's relations with her never seemed to border on close intimacy. Contrariwise, Franklin carried on a long flirtation with the widowed Mme Helvétius. Abigail Adams, John's strait-laced wife, was shocked at the open intimacies between the pair. Franklin complained that since he had given Madame "so many of his days," she appeared "very ungrateful in not giving him one of her nights." Whether in desperation or because he really felt the need to rebuild some kind of family life, he proposed to her. When she turned him down, he wrote a bagatelle, recounting a conversation with Madame's husband in the Elysian Fields, as well as his own encounter with his deceased wife Deborah. He then dashed into print with the piece, an odd thing to do if he were deadly serious about the proposal. As Sainte-Beuve remarked of this episode, Franklin never allowed himself to be carried away by feeling, whether in his youth or in old age, whether in love or in religion. His romantic posture was almost ritualistic. He almost seemed relieved at the chance to convert an emotional rebuff into a literary exercise.

Franklin's casual attitude toward sexual morality was shared by his son and grandson. Himself illegitimate, William, who sought to efface the cloud over his origin by becoming an arrant social climber and most respectable Tory, also sired an illegitimate son, William Temple Franklin, whose mother remains as much a mystery as William's own. Temple, engaged at Franklin's behest by the American peace commissioners as secretary in Paris, had an affair with Blanchette Caillot, a married woman by whom he had a child and whom he abandoned on his return to America.

If Temple was a playboy, that charge could never fairly be leveled at his grandfather. The Old Doctor, an irrepressible activist and dogooder, embodied in his own career that blend of practicality and idealism which has characterized Americans ever since. Convinced from early youth of the values of self-improvement and self-education, Franklin on his return to Philadelphia from his first trip to England organized the Junto, a society half debating, half social, attesting both to the sponsor's belief in the potentialities of continued adult education and to his craving for intellectual companionship not provided in his own home. Then came the subscription library, still flourishing in Philadelphia. Franklin's plans for an academy, drawn up in 1743, reached fruition a decade later, and were a positive outgrowth of his conviction that an English rather than a classical education was more suitable to modern man and that most colleges stuffed the heads of students with irrelevant book knowledge. Then, too, the Pennsylvania Hospital project drew upon his seemingly inexhaustible fund of energy, hospitalization being defended by him as more economical than home care. So did his organization of a local fire company, and his program for a tax-supported permanent watch, and for lighting, paving, sweeping, draining, and deicing the streets of Philadelphia. Convinced of the virtues of thrift and industry, Franklin could be expected to take a dim view of poor relief, and questioned "whether the laws peculiar to England which compel the rich to maintain the poor have not given the latter a dependence that very much lessens the care of providing against the wants of old age." Truly, this revolutionary, if he returned to us today, might well be aghast at the largess of the modern welfare state with its indifference to the work ethos.

Franklin evolved what he called his "moral algebra" to explain his code of ethics, a system which clearly anticipated Jeremy Bentham. In a letter to Joseph Priestley written in 1772 he outlined his method of marshaling all the considerations pro and con for a contemplated decision, setting them down in parallel columns, and then pausing for a few days before entering "short hints" for or against the measure. Subtracting liability from assets, one would come up with a moral or political credit or debit. Franklin never narrowed down the springs of human conduct to pain and pleasure, as did Bentham, but assumed a more complex set of motives. Franklin's moral algebra stemmed in part from his bookkeeping mentality and also in part from his desire to reduce life to an orderly system.

That the oldest of American Revolutionaries should be committed to controlled, orderly change takes on larger significance when one seeks explanations as to why the American Revolution did not pursue the violent, even chaotic, course of the French. Nowhere is this better illustrated than in Franklin's evolving view about the Negro and slavery, in neither of which subjects did he show any active interest until well after middle life (after due allowance for the fact that as printer he published a few antislavery tracts in his earlier years). By shrewd calculation he demonstrated that the labor of a slave in America was dearer than that of an iron or wool worker in England. Embodying these calculations in what turned out to be a seminal paper on American demography, written when he was forty-five, Frank-

lin did not let himself get actively drawn into the Negro question for another twenty years, and then he agreed to serve as a trustee for an English fund to convert Negros. As a Deist he could hardly have been passionately aroused by the prospect of saving souls, but may have consented to serve because of the degree of respectable public exposure involved. Earlier, in 1764, he was prepared to concede that some Negroes had "a strong sense of justice and honour," but it was not until 1772, when he was sixty-six years old, that he became aroused about the slave trade, that "detestable commerce." By the next year he was on record sympathizing with the movement to abolish slavery, and in 1787 he became president of the Pennsylvania Abolition Society, the oldest society of its kind in the world. He soon proposed a program for the education of free blacks in trades and other employment to avoid "poverty, idleness, and many vicious habits."

Franklin's last public act before his death was the signing of a memorial to Congress from his own Abolition Society asking for justice for the blacks and an end in the "traffic in the persons of our fellowmen." When Southern congressmen denounced the measure he sent to the press one of the last writings to come from his pen, a fictional account of an observation by an official of Algiers in 1687 denying a petition of an extremist sect opposing the enslaving of Christians. Accordingly, the divan resolved, in Franklin's tongue-in-cheek reporting, "The doctrine that plundering and enslaving the Christians is unjust, is, at best, problematical; but that it is the interest of the state to continue the practice, is clear: therefore let the petition be rejected."

A man of the Enlightenment, Franklin had faith in the power and beneficence of science. In moments snatched from public affairs during the latter 1740's and early 1750's — moments when public alarms interrupted his research at the most creative instant — he plunged into scientific experimentation. While his lightning kite and rod quickly made him an international celebrity, Franklin was no mere dilettante gadgeteer. His conception of electricity as a flow with negative and positive forces opened the door to further theoretical development in the field of electromagnetism. His pamphlet on electricity, published originally in 1751, went through ten editions, including revisions, in four languages before the American Revolution. Honors from British scientists were heaped upon him, and when he arrived in England in 1757 and again in 1764, and in France in 1776, he came each time with an enlarged international reputation as a scientist whom Chatham compared in Parliament to "our Boyle" and "our Newton."

Pathbreaking as Franklin's work on electricity proved to be, his range of scientific interest extended far beyond theoretical physics. He pioneered in locating the Gulf Stream, in discovering that northeast storms come from the southwest, in making measurements of heat absorption with regard to color, and in investigating the conductivity of different substances with regard to heat. A variety of inventions attested to his utilitarian bent — the Franklin stove, the lightning rod, the flexible metal catheter, bifocal glasses, the glass harmonica, the smokeless chimney. Indefatigable in his expenditure of his spare time on useful ends, he made observations on the nature of communication between insects, contributed importantly to our knowledge of the causes of the common cold, advocated scientific ventilation, and even tried electric shock treatment to treat palsy on a number of occasions.

To the last Franklin stoutly defended scientific experimentation which promised no immediate practical consequences. Watching the first balloon ascension in Paris, he parried the question, "What good is it?" with a characteristic retort, "What good is a newborn baby?"

Committed as he was to discovering truth through scientific inquiry, Franklin could be expected to be impatient with formal theology. While not denigrating faith, he regretted that it had not been "more productive of Good Works than I have generally seen it." He suggested that, Chinese style, laymen leave praying to the men who were paid to pray for them. At the age of twenty-two he articulated a simple creed, positing a deistic Christian God, with infinite power which He would abstain from wielding in arbitrary fashion. His deistic views remained unchanged when, a month before his death, Ezra Stiles asked him his opinion of the divinity of Jesus. Confessing doubts, Franklin refused to dogmatize or to busy himself with the problem at so late a date, since, he remarked, "I expect soon an opportunity of knowing the truth with less trouble."

Unlike the philosophers who spread toleration but were intolerant of Roman Catholicism, Franklin tolerated and even encouraged any and all sects. He contributed to the support of various Protestant churches and the Jewish synagogue in Philadelphia, and, exploiting his friendship with the papal nuncio in Paris, he had his friend John Carroll made the first bishop of the Catholic Church in the new United States. He declared himself ready to welcome a Muslim preacher sent by the grand mufti in Constantinople, but that exotic spectacle was spared Protestant America of his day.

Although he fancied the garb of a Quaker, a subtle form of reverse ostentation that ill-accorded with his preachments about humility, Franklin was no pacifist. During King George's War he urged the need of preparedness upon his city and province, praising "that *Zeal* for the *Publick Good,* that *military prowess, and* that *undaunted Spirit,"* which in past ages had distinguished the British nation. Like most of the Founding Fathers he could boast a military experience regardless of its brevity, and in Franklin's case it lasted some six weeks. Following Braddock's disastrous defeat in December, 1755, Franklin as a civilian committeeman marched into the interior at the head of an armed force, directing an improvised relief program for the frontier refugees who had crowded into Bethlehem and seeing about the fortifying of the Lehigh gap. Back in Philadelphia he organized a defense force known as the "Associators," of which he was elected colonel. As in his other projects, he entered into these military arrangements with gusto, all to the annoyance of the proprietor, who regarded Franklin as a dangerous political rival and who regularly vetoed all tax bills which included military levies on the proprietary estate of the Penn family.

Once again, almost a decade later, he took command of a military force — this time to face down a frontier band known as the Paxton Boys who in 1764 set out on a lawless march to Philadelphia to confront the government with a demand for protection against the Indians. Franklin issued a blazing pamphlet denouncing the Paxton Boys for their attacks on peaceful Indians and organized and led a force to Germantown, where he confronted the remonstrants and issued a firm warning. The Paxton Boys veered off, and order was finally restored. "For about forty-eight hours," Franklin remarked, "I was a very great man, as I had been once some years before in a time of public danger."

Franklin's brief exposure as a military figure, combined with his leadership of the antiproprietary party, and his general prominence and popularity had by now made him anathema to proprietors and conservatives alike. Standing out against the Establishment, Franklin was heartened by the enemies he had made. A thorough democrat, Franklin had little use for proprietary privileges or a titled aristocracy. In his Silence Dogood letters written as far back as 1723 he had pointed out that "Adam was never called *Master* Adam; we never read of Noah *Esquire,* Lot *Knight* and *Baronet,* nor the *Right Honourable* Abraham Viscount Mesopotamia, Baron of Carian; no, no, they were plain Men." Again, *Poor Richard* engaged in an amusing genealogical computation to prove that over the centuries it was impossible to preserve blood free of mixtures, and "that the Pretension of such Purity of Blood in ancient Families is a mere Joke." With perhaps pardonable inconsistency Franklin took the trouble to trace his own family back to stout English gentry, but his basic an-

tiaristocratic convictions stood the test of time. When, in the post-Revolutionary years, the patrician-sounding Society of the Cincinnati was founded in America, Franklin in France scoffed at the Cincinnati as "hereditary knights" and egged on Mirabeau to publish an indictment of the Order which set off an international clamor against its hereditary character.

For courts and lawyers, defenders of property and the status quo, Franklin reserved some of his most vitriolic humor. His *Gazette* consistently held up to ridicule the snobbery of using law French in the courts, excessive legal fees and court costs, and the prolixity and perils of litigation. For the lawyers who "can, with Ease, Twist Words and Meanings as you please," *Poor Richard* shows no tolerance. Predictably, Franklin took the side of the debtor against the creditor, the paper-money man against the hard-currency man.

Franklin's support of paper money did not hurt him in the least. As a matter of fact, the Assembly gave him the printing contract in 1731 for the £40,000 in bills of credit that it authorized that year. This incident could be multiplied many times. Franklin ever had an eye for the main chance. Whether as a poor printer, a rising politician, or an established statesman-scientist, he was regarded by unfriendly critics as a man on the make of dubious integrity. One of the improvements Franklin introduced as deputy postmaster general of the colonies was to make the carrying of newspapers a source of revenue and to compel his riders to take all the papers that were offered. On its face a revenue producer and a safeguard against monopoly, the ruling could hardly damage Franklin, publisher or partner of seven or eight newspapers, a chain stretching from New York to Antigua, and even including a German-language paper in Pennsylvania.

Accumulating a tidy capital, Franklin invested in Philadelphia town lots, and then, as the speculative bug bit him, plunged into Nova Scotian and western land ventures. His secretive nature seemed ideally suited to such investments, in which he followed a rule he laid down in 1753: "Great designs should not be made publick till they are ripe for execution, lest obstacles are thrown in the way." The climax of Franklin's land speculations came in 1769 when he joined forces with Samuel Wharton to advance in England the interests of the Grand Ohio Company, which was more British than colonial in composition. This grand alliance of speculators and big-time politicians succeeded in winning from the Privy Council of July 1, 1772, a favorable recommendation supporting their fantastic dream of a colony called Vandalia, to be fitted together from pieces of the present-day states of Pennsylvania, Maryland, West Virginia, and Kentucky. There Franklin's love of order would replace that frontier anarchy which he abhorred.

Standing on the brink of a stunning success, the Vandalia speculators were now put in jeopardy by Franklin's rash indiscretion in turning over to his radical friends in Massachusetts some embarrassing letters of Governor Thomas Hutchinson which had been given to him in confidence. Indignant at Franklin's disloyalty, the Crown officers refused to complete the papers confirming the grant to the Grand Ohio Company. With his usual deviousness, Franklin, in concert with the banker Thomas Walpole, publicly resigned from the company. In reality Walpole and Franklin had a private understanding by which the latter would retain his two shares out of the total of seventy-two shares of stock in the company. As late as April 11, 1775, Franklin, Walpole and others signed a power of attorney authorizing William Trent to act on their behalf with respect to the grant, hardly necessary if Franklin was indeed out of the picture. In the summer of 1778 Franklin had a change of heart and decided to get back his original letter of resignation. When Walpole complied, Franklin added thereto a memorandum asserting: "I am still to be considered as an Associate, and was called upon for my Payments as before. My right to two shares, or two Parts of 72, in that Purchase still

continues . . . and I hope, that when the Trouble of America is over, my Posterity may reap the Benefits of them." Franklin's posterity, it should be pointed out, stood a much better chance were England to retain the Old Northwest and the Crown validate the Grand Ohio claim than were title thereto to pass to the new United States, whose claim to that region Franklin would be expected by Congress to press at the peacemaking. Such an impropriety on Franklin's part was compounded by his casual attitude about his carrying on a correspondence with a British subject in wartime while officially an American commissioner to France.

Franklin's critics denounced his penchant for nepotism, his padding the postmastership payroll with his relatives, the pressure he exercised on his fellow peace commissioners to have the unqualified Temple Franklin appointed as secretary to the Commission, and his willingness to have his grandnephew Jonathan Williams set up as a shipping agent at Nantes. Franklin's conduct of his office in France continued to supply grounds for ugly charges. What is significant is not that Franklin was guilty as charged but rather that the suspicion of conflict of interest would not die down despite his own disclaimer. At best, Franklin in France was untidy and careless in running his office. What can be said about a statesman whose entourage numbered a secretary who was a spy in British pay, a maître d'hôtel who was a thief, and a grandson who was a playboy! Only a genius could surmount these irregularities and achieve a stunning triumph. And Franklin had genius.

Because of Franklin's prominence in the Revolutionary movement it is often forgotten that in the generation prior to the final break with England he was America's most notable imperial statesman, and that the zigzag course he was to pursue owed more to events than to logic. As early as 1751 he had proposed an intercolonial union to be established by voluntary action on the part of the colonies. Three years later, at Albany, where he presented his grand design of continental union, he included therein a provision for having the plan imposed by parliamentary authority. A thorough realist, Franklin by now saw no hope of achieving union through voluntary action of the colonies, and, significantly, every delegate to the Albany Congress save five voted in favor of that provision. Twenty years later a number of these very same men, chief of them Franklin himself, were to deny Parliament's authority either to tax or to legislate for the colonies.

Franklin's Plan of Union conferred executive power, including the veto, upon a royally appointed president general, as well as the power to make war and peace and Indian treaties with the advice and consent of the grand council. That body was to be chosen triennially by the assemblies of the colonies in numbers proportionate to the taxes paid into the general treasury. Conferring the power of election upon the assemblies rather than the more aristocratic and prerogative-minded governor's councils constituted a notable democratic innovation, as was his proposal for a central treasury for the united colonies and a union treasury for each colony.

Each intensely jealous of its own prerogatives, the colonial assemblies proved cool to the plan while the Privy Council was frigid. As Franklin remarked years later, "the Crown disapproved it as having too much weight in the democratic part of the constitution, and every assembly as having allowed too much to the prerogative; so it was totally rejected." In short, the thinking of the men who met at Albany in 1754 was too bold for that day. In evolving his Plan of Union Franklin had shown himself to be an imperial-minded thinker who placed the unity and effective administration of the English-speaking world above the rights and rivalries of the separate parts. Had Franklin's Plan of Union been put in operation it would very likely have obviated the necessity for any Parliamentary enactment of taxes for the military defense and administration of the colonies.

If Britain did not come up with a plan of union of her own soon enough to save her own empire, the Americans did not forget that momentous failure of statesmanship. Franklin's plan constituted the basic core of that federal system that came into effect with the First Continental Congress and, as proposed in modified form by Franklin in 1775, provided a scheme of confederation pointing toward national sovereignty. While the Articles of Confederation drew upon notions embodied in the Albany Plan, such as investing the federal government with authority over the West, it rejected Franklin's proposal to make representation in Congress proportional to population, a notion which found recognition in the federal Constitution. Writing in 1789, Franklin was justified in his retrospective judgment about his Albany Plan of Union. His was a reasonable speculation that had his plan been adopted "the different parts of the empire might still have remained in peace and union."

Franklin's pride in the Empire survived his letdown in 1754. In April, 1761, he issued his famous Canada pamphlet, "The Interest of Great Britain," wherein he argued the case for a plan which would secure for Great Britain Canada and the trans-Appalachian West rather than the French West Indian islands, arguments upon which Lord Shelburne drew heavily in supporting the Preliminary Articles of Peace of 1762 that his sponsor Lord Bute had negotiated with France.

For Franklin, 1765 may be considered the critical year of his political career. Thereafter he abandoned his role as imperial statesman and moved steadily on a course toward revolution. Some would make Franklin out as a conspirator motivated by personal pique, and while one must concede that Franklin's reticence and deviousness endowed him with the ideal temperament for conspiracy and that his public humiliation at the hands of Crown officials provided him with all the motivation that most men would need, one must remember that, above all, Franklin was an empiricist. If one course would not work, he would try another. Thus, Franklin as agent for Pennsylvania's Assembly in London not only approved the Stamp Act in advance, but proposed many of the stamp collectors to the British government. To John Hughes, one of his unfortunate nominees who secured the unhappy job for his own province, Franklin counseled "coolness and steadiness," adding

... a firm Loyalty to the Crown and faithful Adherence to the Government of this Nation, which it is the Safety as well as Honour of the Colonies to be connected with, will always be the wisest Course for you and I to take, whatever may be the Madness of the Populace or their blind Leaders, who can only bring themselves and Country into Trouble and draw on greater Burthens by Acts of rebellious Tendency.

But Franklin was a fast learner. If the violence and virtual unanimity of the opposition in the colonies to the Stamp Act took him by surprise, Franklin quickly adjusted to the new realities. In an examination before the House of Commons in February, 1766, he made clear the depth of American opposition to the new tax, warned that the colonies would refuse to pay any future internal levy, and intimated that "in time" the colonists might move to the more radical position that Parliament had no right to levy external taxes upon them either. Henceforth Franklin was the colonists' leading advocate abroad of their rights to self-government, a position grounded not only on his own eminence but on his agency of the four colonies of Pennsylvania, New Jersey, Massachusetts, and Georgia. If he now counseled peaceful protest, it was because he felt that violent confrontations would give the British government a pretext for increasing the military forces and placing the colonies under even more serious repression. A permissive parent even by today's lax standards, Franklin drew an interesting analogy between governing a family and governing an empire. In one of his last nostalgic invocations of imperial greatness, Franklin wrote:

Those men make a mighty Noise about the importance of keeping up our Authority over the Colonies. They govern and regulate too much. Like some unthinking Parents, who are every Moment exerting their Authority, in obliging their Children to make Bows, and interrupting the Course of their innocent Amusements, attending constantly to their own Prerogative, but forgetting Tenderness due to their Offspring. The true Act of governing the Colonies lies in a Nut-Shell. It is only letting them alone.

A hostile contemporary, the Tory Peter Oliver, denounced Franklin as "*the instar omnium* of Rebellion" and the man who "set this whole Kingdom in a flame." This is a grotesque distortion of Franklin's role. While he was now on record opposing the whole Grenville-Townshend North program as impractical and unrealistic, the fact is that his influence in government circles declined as his reputation in radical Whig intellectual circles and in the American colonies burgeoned. It must be remembered that, almost down to the outbreak of hostilities, he still clung to his post of absentee deputy postmaster general of the colonies, with all the perquisites thereto attached. All that dramatically changed in the years 1773–74, a final turning point in Franklin's political career.

Franklin had got his hands on a series of indiscreet letters written by Thomas Hutchinson and Andrew Oliver, the governor and lieutenant governor of Massachusetts Bay respectively, and addressed to Thomas Whately, a member of the Grenville and North ministries. The letters, which urged that the liberties of the province be restricted, were given to Franklin to show him that false advice from America went far toward explaining the obnoxious acts of the British government. Tongue-in-cheek, Franklin sent the letters on to Thomas Cushing, speaker of the Massachusetts House of Representatives, with an injunction that they were not to be copied or published but merely shown in the original to individuals in the province. But in June, 1773, the irrepressible Samuel

Adams read the letters before a secret session of the House and later had the letters copied and printed.

The publication of the Hutchinson-Oliver letters, ostensibly against Franklin's wishes, caused an international scandal which for the moment did Franklin's reputation no good. Summoned before the Privy Council, he was excoriated by Solicitor General Alexander Wedderburn. The only way Franklin could have obtained the letters, Wedderburn charged, was by stealing them from the persons who stole them, and, according to one account, he added, "I hope, my lords, you will mark and brand the man" who "has forfeited all the respect of societies and of men." Henceforth, he concluded, "Men will watch him with a jealous eye; they will hide their papers from him, and lock up their escritoires. He will henceforth esteem it a libel to be called a man of letters; *homo trium literarum!*" Of course, everyone in the audience knew Latin and recognized the three-lettered word Wedderburn referred to as *fur,* or thief.

Discounting Wedderburn's animosity, the solicitor general may have accurately captured the mental frame of mind of Franklin at this time when he remarked that "Dr. Franklin's mind may have been so possessed with the idea of a Great American Republic, that he may easily slide into the language of the minister of a foreign independent state," who, "just before the breaking out of war . . . may bribe a villain to steal or betray any state papers." There was one punishment the Crown could inflict upon its stalwart antagonist, and that was to strip him of his office as deputy postmaster general. That was done at once. Imperturbable as was his wont, Franklin remained silent throughout the entire castigation, but inwardly he seethed at both the humiliation and the monetary loss which the job, along with his now collapsed Vandalia scheme, would cost him. He never forgot the scorching rebuke. He himself had once revealingly remarked that he "never forgave contempt." "Costs me nothing to be civil to inferi-

ors; a good deal to be submissive to superiors." It is reported that on the occasion of the signing of the treaty of alliance with France he donned the suit of figured blue velvet that he had worn on that less triumphal occasion and, according to an unsubstantiated legend, wore it again at the signing of the preliminary Peace Treaty by which Great Britain recognized the independence of the United States.

Believing he could help best by aiding Pitt in his fruitless efforts at conciliation, Franklin stayed on in England for another year. On March 20, 1775, he sailed for America, convinced that England had lost her colonies forever. On May 6, 1775, the day following his return to Philadelphia, he was chosen a member of the Second Continental Congress. There he would rekindle old associations and meet for the first time some of the younger patriots who were to lead the nation along the path to independence.

An apocryphal story is told of Franklin's journey from Nantes to Paris, to which he was to be dispatched by Congress. At one of the inns in which he stayed, he was informed that the Tory-minded Gibbon, the first volume of whose *History* had been published in the spring of that year, was also stopping. Franklin sent his compliments, requesting the pleasure of spending the evening with the historian. In answer he received a card stating that notwithstanding Gibbon's regard for the character of Dr. Franklin as a man and a philosopher, he could not reconcile it with his duty to his king to have any conversation with a rebellious subject. In reply Franklin wrote a note declaring that "though Mr. Gibbon's principles had compelled him to withhold the pleasure of his conversation, Dr. Franklin had still such respect for the character of Mr. Gibbon, as a gentleman and a historian, that when, in the course of his writing a history of the *decline and fall* of empires, the *decline and fall* of the British Empire should come to be his subject, as he expects it soon would, Dr. Franklin would be happy to furnish him with ample materials which were in his possession."

QUESTIONS TO CONSIDER

1   In what ways was Benjamin Franklin a representative man of his time, a man who reflected and helped to shape the values of his culture?

2   Morris says that Franklin was an enormously complicated man who wore many masks, which disguised the real Franklin from his contemporaries as well as from future scholars and biographers. What were these masks, and how successful is Morris in uncovering the man behind them?

3   How does the available evidence support or detract from Morris's thesis that Franklin underwent two separate identity crises? What do you think are the strengths and weaknesses of trying to apply twentieth-century psychoanalytic theories to eighteenth-century lives?

4   Morris calls Franklin "the first American pragmatist," a person who defined morality by what worked and concluded that what worked must be moral. In what sense does Franklin embody the seventeenth-century Puritan ethic described by Degler in selection 3? In what important ways did Franklin alter the ethic?

5   In what ways, if any, would you consider Franklin a revolutionary? Do you agree with Morris that if Franklin "returned to us today" he would be "aghast at the largess of the modern welfare state with its indifference to the work ethos"?

IV

"When in the Course of Human Events . . ."

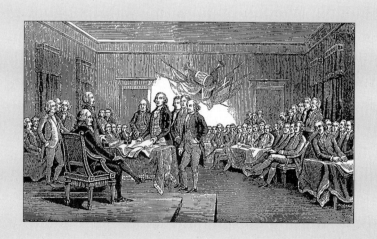

7

Sam Adams, Firebrand of the Revolution

ALEXANDER WINSTON

Until 1765, Benjamin Franklin remained an ardent defender of the British Empire. Most other colonists shared his pride in the empire and saw no reason to break away from it. But after 1765 — and the date is significant, as we shall see — Franklin and many others marched steadily down the path toward revolution. By 1775, as one historian has noted, the relationship between the America colonials and their English rulers had become "so strained, so poisoned, so characterized by suspicion and resentment that the once seemingly unbreakable bonds of empire were on the verge of dissolution." That same year, in fact, Minutemen at Lexington and Concord fired the opening shots of the war that resulted in American independence.

What were the causes of the American Revolution? What had so poisoned American-English relations that armed conflict broke out? Most experts agree that the roots of the Revolution are to be found in the previous century, when American colonists began developing their own institutions and ideas — particularly ideas about constitutions, taxation, and representation — that significantly diverged from those in England. This "first American revolution," as Clinton Rossiter called it, took place during a period of "salutary neglect," when the British imperial government allowed the colonies to develop without rigid and consistent government control. After 1763, however, all that changed. Reacting to new circumstances inside England and to the enormous cost of a recent war with France (the French and Indian War) for supremacy in North America, the imperial government abandoned salutary neglect and attempted to do what it had every legal right to do: rule the empire, including the North American colonies, forcefully and consistently for the benefit of the mother country. Among other measures, the Stamp Act of 1765 reflected the new imperial approach: it taxed newspapers, pamphlets, and other printed documents in the colonies for the purpose of making the colonies pay a third of the cost of England's protecting them. Unaccustomed to such interference from faraway London, colonial Americans protested, first with restraint, then with rising anger and bitterness, every new measure imposed on them from abroad. By 1775, a sizable and outspoken group of colonists had become profoundly disillusioned with imperial rule, and in 1776 they struck for independence.

In the following selection, Alexander Winston, a specialist in Revolutionary history, tells the story of the coming of the Revolution through the life and deeds of Sam Adams, leader of Boston's hot-headed radicals and one of the foremost opponents to perceived British tyranny in all the colonies. Winston's biographical approach personalized events; it elicits from cold fact the warmth of a living man of action, a true agitator who was in the thick of colonial resistance to the hated Stamp Act, the Townshend Acts, and the Five Intolerable Acts and who led his "boys" in the Boston Tea Party, in which he was "in his glory." As an energetic member of the Continental Congresses, Winston tells us, "Sam was ready for independence when most Congress members still clung to compromise." When the break for independence finally came, no one had worked harder for it than the firebrand from Boston. In summing up Sam's significance, John Randolph of Roanoke called him "The Father of the Revolution."

GLOSSARY

BERNARD, FRANCIS   Tory governor of Massachusetts who opposed the boycotts against the Townshend Acts and begged the British for military protection, which made him overnight the most hated man in Massachusetts. The English recalled him, leaving Thomas Hutchinson as acting governor.

BOSTON MASSACRE (1770)   An angry Boston mob converged on the Customs House and taunted the nine English guards, throwing snowballs and brickbats at them. The guards panicked and fired their muskets into the crowd, killing five citizens.

BOSTON TEA PARTY (1773)   When Parliament allowed the East India Company to dump its stockpile of tea on the American colonies, Adams signaled his "boys," and a band of them disguised as Mohawk Indians boarded the ship and dumped the entire cargo into the bay. Parliament retaliated by closing Boston's port and ordering

other harsh changes, all of which became known as the Intolerable Acts.

CONTINENTAL CONGRESS (1774)   Delegates from all colonies except Georgia attended this assembly in Philadelphia in 1774. Sam and John Adams were among the Massachusetts delegates. The Congress pledged not to obey the Intolerable Acts and, while promising obedience to the king, denied Parliament's right to tax the colonies.

FRENCH AND INDIAN WAR (ALSO CALLED THE GREAT WAR FOR THE EMPIRE)   Anglo-French and Iroquois war (1754–1763) fought for control of North America. In the treaty ending the war, the French ceded Canada to Great Britain, along with all other French possessions east of the Mississippi except New Orleans.

GAGE, GENERAL THOMAS   Commander-in-chief of English forces in America who, as part of

England's retaliation for the Boston Tea Party, replaced Hutchinson as governor of Massachusetts. Not long after, four regiments of redcoats encamped on the Boston Common.

HUTCHINSON, THOMAS   Conservative, pro-English lieutenant governor and then acting governor of Massachusetts whom Adams smeared by reading to the Massachusetts House passages of Hutchinson's letters out of context.

STAMP ACT (1765)   Enacted by the English Parliament, the measure levied fees on all legal documents, customs papers, newssheets, and pamphlets that were disseminated in the colonies. The purpose of the act was to raise money with which to pay for the recent French and Indian War, which had benefited the colonists, and to pay for the expense of protecting them with English troops.

TORIES   Colonists who supported the English government and wished to retain a colonial relationship with the mother country.

TOWNSHEND ACTS (1767)   Parliamentary law, named after the English chancellor of the exchequer, that imposed new taxes on glass, tea, printer's supplies, and paper in the colonies; the taxes were to help pay for the defense of the North American colonies. Sam Adams and his fellow patriots resisted the acts by boycotting the importation of the taxed items.

Members of the British Parliament who voted approval of the Stamp Act late one night in 1765 and went yawning off to bed had never heard, it would seem, of Boston's "Man of the Town Meeting," Samuel Adams. It was a fatal lapse. From that moment until the Declaration of Independence, Sam Adams pounced on Britain every time she moved to impose her will on the colonies. He made politics his only profession and rebellion his only business. He drove two royal governors out of Massachusetts and goaded the British government into open war. New England Tories branded him the "grand Incendiary," the "all-in-all" of colonial turmoil, and neatly capsuled Boston resistance as "Adams' conspiracy." In the opinion of his astute cousin John Adams, Sam was "born and tempered a wedge of steel to split the knot of *lignum vitae* that tied America to England."

"Born and tempered," as Cousin John put it, was more than rhetorical flourish. Sam's father — also named Samuel — made an avocation of politics, and was suspected of republican leanings. The boy got a taste for public affairs almost with his milk; while he was but a toddler his father was deep in the Caucus Club, the same radical brotherhood that Sam was to use with such adroitness. Sam senior clashed with the royal governors, and in 1741 saw his Land Bank venture — an effort to aid debtors by putting negotiable paper money into circulation — outlawed by Parliament. Father and son shared the bitter conviction that Britain's colonial policy was both arbitrary and unjust.

From his parents Sam also inherited a strenuous Calvinism that was to make his vision of the conflict with Britain resemble a huge and murky illustration for *Paradise Lost*. The American patriots, Sam was sure, were children of light who fought England's

Alexander Winston, "Sam Adams, Firebrand of the American Revolution," *American Heritage,* vol. 13, no. 3 (Apr. 1967), pp. 61–64, 105–108. Reprinted by permission of *American Heritage* Magazine, a division of Forbes, Inc. Copyright © Forbes, Inc., 1967.

Samuel Adams, engraved from the portrait by John Singleton Copley in 1773. "He made politics his only profession," writes Alexander Winston, "and rebellion his only business." (North Wind Picture Archives)

sons of Belial in a struggle decisive for the future of mankind. Everyone knew where God stood on that. Sam saw England through a glass, darkly: her government venal, her manners effeminate and corrupt, her religion popish. In saving the colonies from her tyranny Sam hoped to save their manly virtues as well, and make of Boston a "Christian Sparta" — chaste, austere, godly. By 1765 three dominant strains were firmly fixed in his character: puritanism, political acumen, and hatred of British rule. He laced them together tight as a bull whip and, as Parliament was to discover, twice as deadly.

Any calm appraisal of his life up to that point, however, would surely have rated him among those least likely to succeed. After Harvard (M.A., 1743) he had dabbled at the study of law and later spent a few fruitless months as apprentice in a counting-house. His father loaned him a thousand pounds to make a try at business — any business. The money ran through his fingers like water. Appointed Boston's tax collector in 1756, he combined soft-heartedness and negligence so ably that he ended at least four thousand pounds in arrears and faced court action. The prosperous little malt works that his father had left the family fell to ruins. The sheriff threatened to sell his house for debts. When the Stamp Act was passed in 1765, Sam was forty-two; he looked prematurely old, his hands trembled, his head shook with a palsied tremor.

But while his private affairs were in a perpetual state of collapse, Sam was making himself the gray eminence of Boston politics. The base of his power was the Caucus Club, a judicious mixture of shipyard laborers ("mechanics") and uptown intellectuals. They met in a garret to drink punch, turn the air blue with pipe smoke, and plot the next political move. Their decisions were passed quietly along to other radical cells — the Merchants' Club (which met in the more genteel Boston Coffee House), the contentious Monday Night Club, the Masons, the Sons of Liberty. With tactics mapped out and support solidified, the action was rammed — or finessed, if need be — through town meeting. Nothing was left to chance; Sam and his tight coterie of patriots simply outworked, outmaneuvered, and, on occasion, outlasted the opposition.

At first rumor of the Stamp Act, Sam cried that "a deep-laid and desperate plan of imperial despotism has been laid, and partly executed, for the extinction of all civil liberty." But Parliament considered its act perfectly just. England's recent conquest of Canada [in the French and Indian War] which had removed an armed threat to the colonies from the French, had also run up a burdensome debt. Obviously the colonies, who had benefited most from the costly Canadian expedition, should not mind paying part of the bill. Passed in the spring of 1765, the Stamp Act required that after November 1 of that year validating stamps be bought from government offices and affixed to all legal documents, customs papers, newssheets, and pamphlets. To enforce the act Parliament decreed that offenders be tried in admiralty courts, where there were no juries, and pay their fines in silver coin, which was hard to get.

Sam rolled out his artillery months before the act

went into effect. The instructions from the Boston town meeting to its representatives in the Massachusetts House constituted one of the first formal protests made in the colonies against the act, and one of the first appeals for united resistance. Sam declared that since the act imposed taxation by a body in which the taxed were not represented it flouted the Massachusetts charter, violated the established rights of British subjects, and was therefore null and void.

On the morning of August 14, 1765, the effigy of old Andrew Oliver, Boston distributor of stamps, hung from the Liberty Tree, a great oak in Hanover Square. Sam inspected the stuffed figure with care and wondered aloud how it got there. That night a mob knocked down the frame of the stamp office and built a fire of the debris in front of Oliver's house. After burning the decapitated effigy, they made the real Oliver swear to resign at the Liberty Tree — which he did, finally, under the added humiliation of a driving December rainstorm.

Sam was pleased. The event, he announced, "ought to be for ever remembered in America," for on that day "the People shouted; and their shout was heard to the distant end of this Continent." Two weeks later rioters racked and gutted the mansion of Lieutenant Governor Thomas Hutchinson, emptying his wine cellar and scattering his papers in the street.

On November 1, 1765, the day the Stamp Act went into effect, church bells tolled as for the dead. Flags hung at half-mast; from the harbor rolled the dull boom of minute guns. For the next six weeks the people of Boston refused to buy stamps. Port business came to a halt, law courts tried no cases. Sam had warned the farmers: "If our Trade may be taxed why not our Lands? Why not the Produce of our Lands and in short everything we possess or make use of?" He doubly damned the stamp revenue by prophesying that it would be used to fasten an episcopacy on puritan New England. In the provincial House, to which he had been elected in September, Sam had a gallery installed to bring waverers under the accusing eye of his patriots. He and his colleague James Otis published a black list of those House members whose antagonism to the act lacked proper vigor. Frightened stamp officials fled for protection to Castle William in the harbor. Enforcement collapsed, and early in the next year Parliament repealed the act. But Sam did not join in Boston's celebration. Why rejoice, he grimly demanded, when Parliament has only granted us our just due?

The defeat of the Stamp Act suggested that no one in the colonies could hatch and execute a scheme with half Sam's cunning. His strategy was to let Britain make all the moves and then give her a bloody nose. "It is a good maxim in Politicks as well as War," he counselled, "to put and keep the enemy in the wrong." Britain soon obliged again. In May, 1767, Parliament launched a series of colonial bills named for their sponsor, Charles Townshend, Chancellor of the Exchequer. The Townshend Acts placed import duties on painters' colors, glass, lead, paper, and tea. At the same time they set up Commissioners of Customs with broad powers, authorized search warrants, and specified that the revenue would be used to pay Crown officials previously salaried (and therefore in part controlled) by the colonies.

Sam worked hard at nonimportation as the chief weapon against the Townshend Acts. By 1769 all the colonies had joined in the boycott. Sam revelled in their unity: "The *tighter* the cord of unconstitutional power is drawn round this bundle of arrows, the *firmer* it will be."

To enforce the boycott in Boston, gangs ranged outside the homes of Tory merchants by night, and small boys pelted their customers with dirt and dung by day. One shopkeeper, more obstinate than the rest, was ridden out of town to the gallows and loosed only when he swore never to return. Tories slept with loaded pistols by their beds. Governor Francis Bernard pleaded for military protection, and in September of 1768 two regiments of soldiers sailed in from Halifax. They set up guardposts, and levelled a pair of cannon at the town hall.

Overnight Governor Bernard became the most hated man in Massachusetts. The House demanded his removal; at Harvard, students slashed his portrait. Sam denounced him as "a Scourge to this Province, a curse to North America, and a Plague on the whole Empire." Recalled to England, Bernard sailed at the end of July, 1769, leaving Hutchinson to act as governor in his place. Despite Sam's outraged cry that Boston was now an occupied town, the troops remained, and he began sending a periodic *Journal of Events* to other colonies, accusing the redcoats of beating defenseless boys and raping women.

Early in March, 1770, a soldier was injured in a scuffle with dockmen. One morning soon after, the town was plastered with forged notices, allegedly signed by redcoats, promising a broad-scale attack on the townspeople. That night, March 5, as a bright moon shone on the late snow, a crowd gathered in front of the Custom House. It began to taunt the nine-man guard; snowballs and brickbats flew, the guard fired, and five citizens were left dead or dying. [The colonists called it "The Boston Massacre."]

The town was in a frenzy of anger. On the following afternoon an immense rally of excited citizens massed in and around Old South Church. Hutchinson told a committee of protest that he was willing to send the one offending regiment to the fort at Castle William but that he had no military authority to send the other as well. At dusk Sam came to the State House to deliver his ultimatum: "If you . . . have the power to remove *one* regiment you have the power to remove *both*. It is at your peril if you refuse. The meeting is composed of three thousand people. They are become impatient. A thousand men are already arrived from the neighborhood, and the whole country is in motion. Night is approaching. An immediate answer is expected. Both regiments or none!" Hutchinson caved in and ordered the two regiments out of town.

Sam relished his moment of triumph. "If Fancy deceive me not," he reported, "I observ'd his Knees to tremble. I thought I saw his face grow pale (and I enjoy'd the Sight)." Copley's fine portrait . . . catches

Sam at the moment of confrontation: broad fore-head, heavy eyebrows, steady blue-gray eyes, nose like the prow of a ship, stubborn mouth, a chin you could plow with.

Sam wanted the soldiers who had fired the fatal shots to be tried immediately, while indignation still flamed white-hot, but the judges put it off for six months. He acquiesced when two patriots, his cousin John and Josiah Quincy, volunteered to be defense attorneys, sure that they would not press too hard on prosecution witnesses. The two proved more honorable than he had counted on; they argued their case ably and the sentence was light — a pair of soldiers were branded on the thumb. Sam was disgusted. He retried the case in the Boston *Gazette,* over the signature "Vindex," the avenger. . . .

After that, to Sam's chagrin, things quieted down. The blood of the "massacre" had washed away with the melting snow. In England a liberal government had assumed power and in April it repealed the Townshend Acts, except for the duty on tea. A majority of the colonists were tired of agitation, and the radical patriots temporarily lost control of the Massachusetts House. John Hancock courted the royalists; John Adams shook the dust of politics from his shoes and went back to pastoral Braintree. James Otis, who had been bludgeoned in a brawl, sank into recurrent fits of dementia.

Only Sam never let up. "Where there is a Spark of patriotick fire," he vowed, "we will enkindle it." Between August, 1770, and December, 1772, he wrote more than forty articles for the *Gazette*. Night after night, a lamp burned late in the study off his bedroom. Friends, passing in the small hours, could look up at the yellow square of window light and comfort themselves that Sam Adams was busily at work against the Tories. Sam alternately stated the fundamentals of colonial liberty (based on the charter, British law, and, finally, natural right) and whiplashed the British for transgressing it. His style in this period was at times severely reasoned, more often impassioned; the content was unfailingly polemical, partisan, and, on occasion, willfully inaccurate. As the conflict with Britain deepened, his accusations became more violent. "Every dip of his pen," Governor Bernard had once said, "stung like a horned snake." As clerk of the House (to which office he had been elected in 1765) Sam poured out a stream of remonstrances, resolves, and letters to the colony's London agents; but beyond their effect as propaganda he expected them to do little good. When his daughter expressed awe that a petition to the King might be touched by the royal hand, he growled that it would more likely be spurned by the royal foot.

In November, 1772, Sam managed to set up a Boston Committee of Correspondence to link the Massachusetts towns. Within a few months other towns had followed suit, and he had a taut organization poised to act at his command. A discerning Tory declared it the "foulest, subtlest, and most venomous serpent ever issued from the egg of sedition."

In fact, everything Sam did for a decade smacked of sedition. As early as 1768 Hutchinson had secretly sent depositions to England to see if there might be grounds for his arrest. Parliament dusted off a neglected statute of Henry VIII that would bring all treasonable cases to London for trial. Tories were sure that Sam would now end on the gibbet, where he belonged. They gloated that he "shuddered at the sight of hemp." A Londoner wrote jubilantly to Hutchinson: "The talk is strong of bringing them over and trying them by impeachment. Do you write me word of their being seized, and I will send you an account of their being hanged." But the British solicitor general took a long look at the evidence and decided that it was not sufficient — yet.

Meanwhile Sam was out to ruin Hutchinson, and didn't care how he did it. To beat the devil any stick would do. The chance came in 1772 when Ben Franklin, then in London as an agent for the Massachusetts House, laid hands on a bundle of letters written by Hutchinson and Andrew Oliver to correspondents in England. Franklin sent them to Boston with instructions to share them among the trusted inner circle of patriots and return them uncopied and unpublished. Whether he meant these instructions to be strictly obeyed, or issued them for his self-protection, we do not know. The patriots brooded over the letters for several months; then Sam announced that "a most shocking scene would soon open," and that a vicious plot against American liberties would be disclosed.

Expectation of horrifying news was raised to a fever pitch. In June, 1773, Sam ordered the House galleries cleared. He told the members in grave tones that he had letters vital to their concern, but that they must first swear neither to copy them nor make them public. At this Hancock rose to say that someone unknown to him had thrust copies of letters into his hand on the street. Might they be the same as those held by Mr. Adams? If so, were the letters not already abroad? Yes, to be sure, they were the same; obviously they were abroad. The House decided that the letters should no longer be concealed.

Hutchinson's correspondence was really fairly mild, and said little that he had not already stated openly, but Sam managed to put it in the worst possible light. When the letters were published, passages had been slyly snipped from the context, and an outraged commentary had been so mixed with the text that the unwary reader was easily led to see an evil purpose when none was intended. Other letters in the packet were more damaging than Hutchinson's, but he was neatly smeared with their brush. He suffered great discredit even in the rural villages, where most of his conservative support lay. The House petitioned the King, asking that Hutchinson be removed from office.

Now the storm was gathering. Alone of the revenue acts, the duty on tea remained. For years Boston matrons had boycotted the rich English brew, and instead had concocted somewhat unsavory beverages of catnip and mint. Prompted by the desperate straits of the East India Company, Parliament tried in 1773 to help the company unload its

embarrassing stockpile of tea on the colonies. Boston patriots decided that the flesh should not be so tempted. While ships bearing 342 chests of tea lay at the wharfs, Sam gave the signal and a band of his mechanics disguised as Mohawk Indians whooped off toward the harbor. As every schoolboy knows, they dumped the whole cargo into Massachusetts Bay [in what became know as "the Boston Tea Party"]. "Sam Adams is in his glory," said Hutchinson; and he was.

Parliament retaliated in a rage. In March, 1774, it ordered the port of Boston clamped shut. It decreed that after August 1 the Provincial Council, which formerly had been elected by the House, would be named by the governor, as would the higher judges. The royal sheriff would select all juries; town meetings throughout the province would assemble only with the governor's consent, and discuss only what he authorized. General Thomas Gage, commander in chief of His Majesty's forces in America, supplanted Hutchinson as governor. By June, four regiments of redcoats were encamped on the Common. This was the showdown; it was knuckle under or risk war.

Sam knew that to pit Boston (population 17,000) against British power was to place the mouse beneath the lion's paw. "I wish we could arouse the continent," he had written to a fellow patriot the year before. Now, in the spring of 1774, the continent was awakening: a Continental Congress was in the making. How could this matter be discussed and delegates elected before Gage got wind of it and prorogued the Massachusetts legislature? He already had moved the House temporarily from troublesome Boston to the Tory stronghold of Salem; the town swarmed with redcoats.

For ten days the House dispatched routine business with disarming amiability while Sam lined up votes behind the scenes. On June 17, when all was ready, he suddenly ordered the doors of the meeting hall locked. Sensing a plot, one Tory member slipped past the doorkeeper and hurried away to alert

Gage. Sam put the key in his pocket and presented a slate of delegates (of which he was one) to attend the Congress, set for Philadelphia in September. Gage scratched off a hurried order to dissolve the House, but the messenger beat on the door in vain. Inside, the House leisurely elected the delegates and assessed the towns for their expenses.

For the first time in his life Sam Adams was to leave the shores of Massachusetts Bay. He still lived in the crumbling ancestral home on Purchase Street, with land running down to the harbor, where he had a small dock. The household consisted of his second wife, Elizabeth Wells Adams (his first wife had died in 1757), a son and a daughter by his earlier marriage, a servant girl, and a shaggy dog famed for biting redcoats. Elizabeth Adams was devoted and above all frugal, for since their marriage his only earnings had been the meager allowance granted him as clerk of the House of Representatives. Fortunately he had few personal wants, and would live on bread and milk and dress in threadbare clothes, if the cause of liberty were thereby served. "He says he never looked forward in his Life," recorded Cousin John, with Yankee amazement at such carelessness, "never planned, laid a scheme, or formed a design of laying up any Thing for himself or others after him."

Friends put together the money to outfit him for the journey to Philadelphia. He was resplendent in new suit, wig, hose, shoes, and cocked hat; he swung a gold-topped cane, and in his pocket there was a much-needed purse of money. On August 10, 1774, the delegation — John Adams, Sam Adams, Thomas Cushing, and Robert Treat Paine — rolled out of Boston in full array — coach, coachmen, and mounted servants.

They were received with great honor along the route, but friendly patriots in Philadelphia advised them that the other colonies were suspicious of Boston's hot-headed radicals. John Adams summed up their warning: "You must not utter the word independence, not give the least hint or insinuation of the idea, either in Congress, or any private conversa-

tion; if you do, you are undone, for independence is as unpopular in all the Middle and South as the Stamp Act itself. No man dares speak of it. . . ."

During the seven-week session the Massachusetts delegation stayed discreetly in the background. When Sam urged that an Anglican clergyman be permitted to open the sessions with prayer, southerners decided that the dour Calvinist might have some good in him after all. But he was bold in opposing any concessions to Britain: "I should advise persisting in our struggle for liberty, though it was revealed from heaven that nine hundred and ninety-nine should perish, and only one of a thousand survive and retain his liberty. One such freeman must possess more virtue and enjoy more happiness than a thousand slaves; and let him propagate his like, and transmit to them what he hath so nobly preserved."

From 1774 to 1781 Sam Adams' public life was bound up with successive Congresses. He brought to them the same stubborn energy and forehandedness that had worked so well in Boston. "He was constantly holding caucuses of distinguished men," Jefferson recalled, ". . . at which the generality of the measures pursued were previously determined on, and at which the parts were assigned to the different actors who afterwards appeared in them." His name bobs up almost daily in the congressional journal. Joseph Galloway, leader of the conciliatory wing in the Congress, recognized him as one to keep a wary eye on, "a man who, though by no means remarkable for brilliant abilities, yet is equal to most men in popular intrigue and the management of a faction. He eats little, drinks little, sleeps little, thinks much, and is most decisive and indefatigable in the pursuit of his objects. It was this man, who, by his superior application, managed at once the faction in Congress at Philadelphia and the factions in New England."

Sam was ready for independence when most Congress members still clung to compromise. Philadelphia Quakers were for leaving the issue to Providence; he tartly replied that Providence had already decided for liberty. To James Warren in Plymouth he wrote during the spring of 1776: "The Child Independence is now struggling for Birth. I trust that in a short time it will be brought forth, and, in Spite of Pharaoh, all America will hail the dignified Stranger."

In July he signed the Declaration of Independence, and with that stroke of the pen signed away his real vocation. Success put him out of business. America no longer needed an agitator; now it had to defeat an army in the field and build a new nation.

Sam admitted that he was unfit for "founding Empires," and in various ways he proved it. In Congress he favored a citizen militia until forced to concede that the war could be fought only with a more permanent army and a unified command. Frankly critical of Washington's Fabian tactics, Sam was widely accused of involvement in a cabal to replace him, but there is no evidence to support the charge. He disapproved of any social gaiety in so grave an hour, and had Congress pass rules forbidding members to attend balls or entertainments. They voted the rules, and diligently ignored them. His weakness for government by committee led the French minister to lament over the man "whose obstinate, resolute character was so useful to the Revolution at its origin, but who shows himself so ill-suited to the conduct of affairs in an organized government."

Yet Sam worked with his old doggedness through the dark years of war. Jefferson considered him "more than any other member, the *fountain* of our more important measures." At the low ebb of American fortunes in October, 1777, he was one of only twenty members who stuck with Congress. "Though the smallest," Sam remarked, "it was the truest Congress we ever had." He was on the committee that framed the Articles of Confederation in 1777. Four years later, when Congress celebrated their ratification with a keg of wine and some biscuits, Sam alone remained of the original drafters. In April, 1781, he went home and never crossed the borders of Massachusetts again.

He returned, like Ulysses, to find his hall full of strangers — the young, the new postwar merchants:

unfamiliar faces, other times. John Hancock, who had been elected first governor of independent Massachusetts, led Boston on a merry romp of feasts and revels; it was far from the "Christian Sparta" of which Sam still dreamed. The old radical was elected to the state Senate and became its president, but he was no longer invincible. In 1783 and again in 1787 he lost the race for the rather empty and unsalaried office of lieutenant governor; in 1788 a youngster defeated him for the first Congress under the federal Constitution. But in 1789, when he teamed with Hancock to become lieutenant governor, some enthusiasts wrote his name on their ballots in gold. At Hancock's death in 1793 he succeeded to the governor's chair, and was re-elected by solid majorities for three more one-year terms.

Changing times even forced the revolutionary into the camp of reaction. As president of the Senate, which under the state constitution required its members to have an estate of four hundred pounds, he headed a body designed to check the democratic excesses of the House. Some Bostonians thought the town's growth warranted a change to representative government; Sam reported for his committee that the town-meeting system had no defects in it. Debtors in the western counties who in 1786, under a Revolutionary War veteran named Daniel Shays, resorted to mob violence discovered in the former rebel an implacable foe. He branded them "banditti" and urged the execution of their leaders. Popular opinion was more merciful; Hancock commuted the death penalty. As governor, Sam vetoed a bill to permit stage performances, and Bostonians howled that he was robbing them of their natural rights. Toward the dispossessed Tories, others softened, but Sam's hatred burned with its old fierceness. He would not have a British subject left on American soil nor, indeed, admitted by naturalization.

But Sam had not really changed at all, and that was his misfortune. He earned the lasting enmity of Federalists by his opposition to the new federal Constitution proposed in 1787. Shocked to discover that it would set up "a National Government instead of a Federal Union of Sovereign States," he declared himself "open & decided" against it. But he also insisted that the state convention called in 1788 to ratify the federal Constitution give the document the careful paragraph-by-paragraph discussion that it deserved. Antifederalists who wanted a quick vote while their hostile majority was intact pleaded financial inability to stay for a long session. Sam dryly remarked that if they were so pressed he would dig up funds for their living expenses.

Very likely some of the fight went out of him with the death of his doctor-son while the convention was going on. According to one story, the Federalists finally swung him around by a shrewd move. They staged a meeting of Sam's beloved mechanics at the Green Dragon Inn, where resolutions were passed urging ratification. Daniel Webster wrote a dramatized account of how Paul Revere brought Sam the news:

"'How many mechanics,' said Mr. Adams, 'were at the Green Dragon when the resolutions were passed?'

"'More, sir,' was the reply, 'than the Green Dragon could hold.'

"'And where were the rest, Mr. Revere?'

"'In the streets, sir.'

"'And how many were in the streets?'

"'More, sir, than there are stars in the sky.'"

Sam, Webster tells us, thought that over a while. To him, the voice of the common man was as close to the voice of God as one could get. "Well," he mused, "if they must have it, they must have it."

He retired from public life in 1797, and lived six years more in a yellow frame house on Winter Street. Its parlor was hung with engravings of the great champions of liberty. He liked to sit on the doorstep or wander in the little garden, talking about old times. Death came on October 2, 1803, when he was 81 years of age.

The Federalist regime in Massachusetts was embarrassed about full burial honors for its political foe. The

governor was absent; no subordinate dared risk a misstep, and the first suggestion was a modest cortege of school children. Aroused at this, friends rallied a fitting processional of state and town officials, dressed out with a muster of cadets. But eulogies delivered in the Massachusetts House were whittled down for public consumption. In Congress no member from Sam's state rose to memorialize him. It fell to Virginia's John Randolph of Roanoke to remind the House that a great patriot had died. With these small honors "The Father of the Revolution" went to his last sleep in the soil of a free and independent America.

QUESTIONS TO CONSIDER

1 Discuss Adams's personality and character traits. In light of his career as an anti-English agitator, is it significant that Adams lived in Boston? Could he have met with similar success had he been from another colonial city, such as Philadelphia, New York, or Richmond?

2 What was the French and Indian War? How did it set the stage for the coming of the Revolution? Do you think that the Stamp Act and Townshend Acts were justifiable? What, after all, was the English Parliament attempting to do through such enactments? Why did Adams rebel against them? Why was the Boston Tea Party such a powerful symbol?

3 How would you assess the role that Adams played in the coming of the Revolution? Does his career demonstrate that an individual can affect the course of historical events — that people, not abstract forces, make history?

4 Describe Adams's activities in the Continental Congresses. At what point, according to the author, did Adams "sign away his real vocation"? Why did he argue that he was not fit "for founding Empires"? Why did he oppose the new federal Constitution of 1787?

8

Thomas Jefferson and the Meanings of Liberty

Douglas L. Wilson

The United States was conceived in idealism and in paradox. America joined the family of nations dedicated to the proposition that "all men are created equal," that all are endowed with the unalienable rights of life, liberty, and the pursuit of happiness, and that they have a natural right to rebel when those rights are denied. So said Thomas Jefferson in the American Declaration of Independence, summing up truths that Americans had learned in the eighteenth-century Enlightenment, or Age of Reason, a time of momentous intellectual and scientific advancements that began in Europe and spread to America. Enlightenment thinkers in Europe stressed a belief in natural law, human progress, and government as a rational instrument, ideas that profoundly influenced Jefferson, Benjamin Franklin, and most other American patriots. The ringing prologue of Jefferson's Declaration, in fact, drew much of its inspiration from English philosopher John Locke, who had held that all human beings were innately equal and good and were entitled to "life, liberty, and possessions."

Yet in 1776, enlightened America held some 500,000 Africans in chains. Jefferson himself and George Washington, the commander of the patriot army, were large slaveholders. Indeed, slavery existed in all thirteen states and was an indispensable labor force for the patriot cause. Even so, many northerners, in a burst of revolutionary idealism, moved to abolish the institution in their states. Vermont was the first to do so, in 1777. Massachusetts outlawed it by a judicial decision six years later. New Hampshire removed it by "constitutional interpretation," and Pennsylvania, Rhode Island, and Connecticut all adopted gradual emancipation programs. When New York and New Jersey finally freed their slaves, the institution of bondage became peculiar to the South — hence the term peculiar institution.

The story was dramatically different in the South. True, some individual masters, swept up in the spirit of the Revolution, voluntarily manumitted their slaves. But most southern planters and political leaders refused to follow the lead of the northern states. Because those states had so few slaves in relation to their white population, white southerners liked to ask what the northerners had to lose in adopting emancipation. Southern whites did not see how they could abolish slavery, not with their heavy concentration of slaves (in some places they outnumbered whites) and their correspondingly large investments. For white southerners of the Revolutionary generation, however, slavery was more than a labor system, more even than a means of race control in a region brimming with blacks. It was the foundation of an entire patrician way of life, so interwoven with the fabric of southern society — as a potent status symbol, as personal wealth, as inheritances and dowries — that it did not seem possible to remove it.

And what of Jefferson, perhaps the most enlightened southerner of his day? In Jefferson, we meet an American anomaly: the antislavery slaveholder. Jefferson truly hated slavery; he damned it as "this blot in our country," this "great political and moral evil," and he devised a specific plan to get rid of it in Virginia — by gradual emancipation and colonization of the freed blacks outside the state. Yet Virginia never adopted his plan, and Jefferson himself was so much a part of his slave-holding culture — and so much in debt — that he felt unable to free his own slaves while he was alive (he did, however, provide for the liberation of five of his skilled slaves upon his death). It is not unfair to point out that Jefferson's illustrious political career — among other things, he was Revolutionary governor of Virginia, United States minister to France, Washington's secretary of state, and the third president of the United States — was made possible by slave labor.

In this selection, a distinguished Jefferson scholar reflects on this "many-sided and multi-talented man," especially on his contradictions concerning slavery and race. In doing so, Douglas Wilson raises a crucial point about the perils of presentism — that is, of intruding today's values and attitudes upon the past. To do that, he warns, risks distorting history. What annoys him is that too many Americans today seem unable to discuss the past in its own terms, unable "to make appropriate allowances for prevailing historical conditions." As an example of presentism, Wilson discusses the story of Jefferson's alleged liaison with his house slave, Sally Hemings. The author denies the story as wholly out of character for Jefferson. But even if it were true, does it matter? This leads Wilson to a profound question that all of us ought to ponder. "How should we remember the leading figures of our history?" he asks. "By their greatest achievements and most important contributions or by their personal failures and peccadilloes?" Wilson emphatically sides with the first position.

Of Jefferson's many achievements, Wilson contends that his "pre-eminent contribution to the world was the Declaration of Independence." In discussing that contri-

bution, Wilson confronts even worse examples of presentism: the view of Jefferson as a ranting hypocrite for trumpeting liberty and equality, yet failing to free his own slaves, and as an inveterate racist for his observations about the traits of black people in his Notes on the State of Virginia. Frankly, those observations are offensive to read today. Yet Wilson reminds us that they were speculative, "a suspicion only," and maintains that Jefferson would have readily discarded them had he encountered an outspoken, literate African American such as Frederick Douglass (whom we will meet in later selections). Addressing the question of why Jefferson did not free his slaves, Wilson observes that the great Virginian faced formidable obstacles in the context of his time and place. Then Wilson turns the whole question around. Instead of asking why Jefferson continued to hold slaves, the question ought to be, "How did a man who was born into a slaveholding society, whose family and admired friends owned slaves, who inherited a fortune that was dependent on slaves and slave labor, decide at an early age that slavery was morally wrong and forcefully declare that it ought to be abolished?"

As for the Declaration of Independence, Wilson makes a convincing case that Jefferson meant to include both blacks and women in his philosophical conception of equality. The author goes on to establish a powerful connection between Jefferson's Declaration and Lincoln's address at Gettysburg during the Civil War. The Gettysburg Address, Wilson points out, "invested Jefferson's eighteenth-century notion of equality with an essentially new meaning and projected it onto the future of the nation." As a result, Americans today have a different view of the prologue of the Declaration than did Jefferson's generation.

This is a powerful, thought-provoking essay. Now that you are aware of the problem of presentism, how would you evaluate the other readings in Portrait of America? Do they judge the past through the lens of the present, or do they assess historical figures and societies on their own terms, within the context of their times?

GLOSSARY

HEMINGS, SALLY Jefferson's mulatto house slave, by whom he supposedly fathered seven children.

MONTICELLO Jefferson's Virginia estate.

NOTES ON THE STATE OF VIRGINIA (1785) Jefferson's only published book, in which he made observations about the racial traits of blacks and also offered a plan of gradual emancipation and colonization; later, Henry Clay and Abraham Lincoln (in his pre–Civil War career) would endorse that approach.

PRESENTISM The imposition of present-day values and assumptions on individuals and societies of the past.

SOCIAL DARWINISM A belief, based on Charles Darwin's theories of biological evolution, that only the fittest individuals and societies survive.

"Today, makes yesterday mean." Emily Dickinson's gnomic utterance contains at least one undoubted truth — that the perspectives of the present invariably color the meanings we ascribe to the past. Nothing confirms this so readily as the changing reputations of historical figures, whose status often appears indexed to present-day preoccupations. It may be inevitable that every age should refashion its historical heroes in a contemporary idiom, but doing so carries with it an obvious and inherent danger. In imposing Today's meanings on Yesterday, we run the risk of distorting it — whether willfully, to suit our own purposes, or unintentionally, by unwarranted assumptions and because of meager information. In this way we lose track of what might be considered the obverse of Emily Dickinson's remark: that Yesterday has meanings of its own that are prior to and necessarily independent of Today's.

Thomas Jefferson is one of the few historical Americans who need no introduction. Even the most abbreviated knowledge of American history, at home or abroad, includes the author of the Declaration of Independence. Identified around the world with democracy and human rights, Jefferson's name and words have been invoked for two hundred years in the cause of freedom and political reform. But here in his own country, where the name synonymous with democracy is exhibited everywhere — on counties, cities, schools, streets, and every imaginable form of institution, business, and product — it sometimes seems that the man himself is receding from view, and that what is commonly thought and said about him gets harder and harder to reconcile with the great national hero. With the . . . two hundred and fiftieth anniversary of his birth, in 1743, it seems appropriate to note some of the ways in which Thomas Jefferson is remembered by the American

Thomas Jefferson, in an oil painting done in 1805 by Rembrandt Peale. Jefferson was tall and slender, with a freckled face, gray eyes, and short, powdered, red hair. The color of his hair inspired one correspondent to salute him as "You red-headed son of a bitch." Despite his aristocratic upbringing, he was largely indifferent about his clothes, which rarely fit him. A Federalist senator once mistook Jefferson for a servant, observing with a sniff that his shirt was dirty. (New York Historical Society)

public and to examine the historical lens through which the man and his contributions are seen.

Only a generation ago Jefferson was still considered to be and treated as an object of veneration, so closely identified with the spirit of America as to constitute a problem for the historian. In 1960 Merrill D. Peterson confronted this problem in one of the most revealing works of Jefferson scholarship, *The Jefferson Image in the American Mind,* which surveys what Jefferson has meant to succeeding genera-

Originally published in the November 1992 issue of *The Atlantic Monthly.* Reprinted by permission from *The Atlantic Monthly.*

tions of Americans. "Where the object is Jefferson," Peterson wrote,

the historian's obligation to historical truth is compromised, in some degree, by his sense of obligation to the Jefferson symbol. Jefferson occupies such an important place in the symbolical architecture of this nation that the search for the elusive *himself* from the vaunted summit, Objectivity, must not be allowed to empty the symbol of meaning for "Jefferson's children."

It is a measure of the change that has occurred in the past thirty years that the one thing Jefferson's children nowadays are most likely to associate with him, apart from his authorship of the Declaration of Independence, is a sexual liaison with one of his slaves, Sally Hemings. College teachers are often dismayed to discover that many if not most of their students now regard this as an accepted fact. But this is not all. In the prevailing ethos of the sexual revolution, Jefferson's supposed liaison is widely received with equanimity and seems to earn him nothing more reproachful than a knowing smile. For most, such a liaison is apparently not objectionable, and for some, its presumed reality actually seems to work in his favor, showing him to have been not a stuffy moralist but a man who cleverly managed to appear respectable while secretly carrying on an illicit relationship. In effect, something that before the 1960s would have been universally considered a shameful blot on Jefferson's character has become almost an asset. Confirming this state of affairs is the case of a prominent black civil-rights leader who complained not long ago that Jefferson's alleged relationship with Hemings is not forthrightly acknowledged by the proprietors of Monticello, Jefferson's residence, and who frankly confessed that this liaison had for him a positive effect in showing that, though a slaveholder, Jefferson was well disposed toward black people. Although the charge that Jefferson had fathered several children by one of his slaves was first made public in his lifetime, by a vindictive journalist and

office-seeker, James Callender, it was believed mainly by those who disparaged Jefferson for political reasons and was not credited by Jefferson scholars or the public at large. But that began to change in 1974, when Fawn M. Brodie published a widely read book on Jefferson in which she attempted to establish the truth of Callender's charge as a prime biographical fact. Brodie's thesis about Jefferson and Hemings is an embellished and controversial reading of the evidence, but what is more significant in the present context is that her story was well geared to the dispositions of her audience. She insisted that her object was not to pillory Jefferson or to make him out as a moral monster but merely to depict him as a man. If, as a widower, he fell in love with a beautiful slave girl and took her as a mistress when she was fourteen years old, it was "not scandalous debauchery with an innocent slave victim," she assured us, "but rather a serious passion that brought Jefferson and the slave woman much private happiness over a period lasting thirty-eight years." Brodie's benign version of the story has proved persuasive, and where previous versions had depicted such behavior as scandalous, hypocritical, or shameful, Jefferson and Hemings are represented as a pair of happy lovers, bravely defying the conventions of a sexually puritanical and racist society.

Compelling as this picture has proved to the American public, most Jefferson scholars and historians have remained unpersuaded. It is true that Jefferson was extremely protective of his personal life and went to considerable lengths to keep it private, but it does not follow, as Brodie would have us believe, that he must therefore have had something to hide. In accounting for Jefferson's behavior in the context of his own time, rather than ours, it is difficult for knowledgeable authorities to reconcile a liaison with Hemings with much else that is known about him. Jefferson implicitly denied the charge, and such evidence as exists about the paternity of Heming's children points not to Jefferson but to his nephews. It is, of course, impossible to prove a negative, but the real problem with Brodie's interpretation is that it doesn't fit Jefferson. If he did take advantage of Hemings and father her children over a period of twenty years, he was acting completely out of character and violating his own standards of honor and decency. For a man who took questions of morality and honor very seriously, such a hypocritical liaison would have been a constant source of shame and guilt. For his close-knit family, who worshipped him and lived too near to him to have been ignorant of such an arrangement, it would have been a moral tragedy of no small dimensions.

But haunted as he was by other troubles and difficulties, there is no sign of this sort of shame or guilt in Jefferson's life. That is why Brodie must present Jefferson and Hemings as a happy couple and their supposed life together as giving satisfaction and lasting pleasure. And whereas there are grounds for suspecting a liaison, such as the terms of Jefferson's will and the testimony of Hemings's son Madison, there are no grounds whatever for believing in what Brodie called the "private happiness" enjoyed by Jefferson and Hemings. That is pure speculation. Because Brodie's thesis deals in such unwarranted assumptions, the great Jefferson biographer Dumas Malone regarded it as "without historical foundation." But what makes it possible for the American public to take the Sally Hemings story to heart, even more than the suspicious circumstances, seems to be a prevailing presentism.

"Presentism" is the term that historians use for applying contemporary or otherwise inappropriate standards to the past. An awkward term at best, it nevertheless names a malaise that currently plagues American discussions of anything and everything concerning the past: the widespread inability to make appropriate allowances for prevailing historical conditions. The issue of presentism is hardly new, but it has perhaps been amplified of late by the debunking and revisionist spirit of the times and the effect this has had on public perceptions. As the un-

critically positive and unabashedly patriotic approach that for so long characterized the teaching of American history in the public schools has abated, the emphasis has steadily shifted to the problems and failures of the past. The saga of the glories of the old West has thus given way to a saga of exploitation and greed. Pride in conquering the wilderness has yielded to the shame of despoiling the land and dispossessing the indigenous peoples. What seems to have happened is that a laudably corrective trend has predominated to such an extent that the emphasis seems somehow reversed, and parents complain that they scarcely recognize the history their children are taught.

With a built-in emphasis on what had previously been ignored or suppressed, it is hardly surprising that almost all the revisionist news, at least where traditional American heroes are concerned, is bad. A question that was once reasonably clear has become a muddle: How should we remember the leading figures of our history? By their greatest achievements and most important contributions or by their personal failures and peccadilloes? Can one category cancel out the other? In a sense these reversals of fortune are inevitable, inasmuch as nothing ever keeps its place in a world of incessant change. It is perhaps an instance of what the historian Henry Adams called the law of acceleration — the tendency of change to come faster and faster — that John F. Kennedy and Martin Luther King Jr., whose murders elevated them to martyrdom, should both come in for reappraisal while their memories and legacies are still fresh. Do the revelations about such things as Kennedy's womanizing, his not-so-heroic war record, and his non-authorship of a book for which he accepted the Pulitzer Prize detract from his positive accomplishments as President? Do the revelations about King's philandering and his plagiarism as a graduate student have any bearing on his conspicuous achievements as a civil-rights leader? Or is this a case of asking the question backward? Is it perhaps more appropriate and revealing to ask, Are the significant contributions of Kennedy and King, which affected the lives of millions of Americans, in any way diminished by subsequent revelations about their shortcomings and failings in other areas?

In this climate the difficulties of judging a figure like Thomas Jefferson by an appropriate standard are considerably compounded. One who writes voluminously over a long time may easily have his own words quoted against him or cited to prove that he held views later modified or abandoned. Jefferson was pre-eminently such a person. On this point Merrill D. Peterson has observed,

His speculative and practical sides were frequently confused. Few men took into account that Jefferson's private self, as expressed in his letters, might not coincide with his public self. Or that his opinion at one time might not represent his opinion under different circumstances. Or that a man of his intellectual temperament did not often bother to qualify felicitous generalizations.

In some ways that are little recognized, Jefferson is surprisingly modern and accessible to the present age. His pronounced notions about health, for example, which seemed somewhat odd to previous generations, appear nowadays in an entirely different light. He believed strongly that regular exercise was essential to physical and mental well-being. As a college student, he developed a regimen of daily running to keep himself fit, and he came to believe in later life that walking was the most salutary form of exercise for the ordinary person. On the subject of diet he also held strong views, which minimized meat and animal products and emphasized instead the prime importance of vegetables. For our own time, at least, Jefferson turns out to have been something of a health-food prophet.

Whether his leading ideas on politics and government will prove as resilient remains to be seen. In spite of his great reputation as a statesman, many of these have proved as counter to the prevailing currents of American history as his prejudice against large cities and manufacturing. He could never reconcile himself, for example, to the Supreme Court's deciding the constitutionality of laws and acts of the executive — a development he regarded as unwarranted and disastrous. His preference for a small central government and his insistence on the prerogatives of the states have been strongly rebuffed, if not virtually obliterated, by decisive turns in our national development. Although history cannot be reversed, the relative size and power of the central government is once more (or still) at issue, as is the proper scope and authority of the Supreme Court. Even Jefferson's views on the disadvantages of large cities have today a resonance that was unheard or unheeded by previous generations.

Because he was attracted to laborsaving devices and was an ingenious adopter and adapter of new gadgets, Jefferson has gained a reputation as an inventor, but aside from a few items — an innovative moldboard for a plough, a revolving book stand — he probably invented little. Though he used and enthusiastically promoted the polygraph, a machine for making simultaneous copies of a written document, he did not invent it, and could not even keep his own in repair. But the fact that Jefferson is perceived as an inventor tells us something about the way he is valued. Abraham Lincoln was much interested in inventions and even went so far as to have one of his own patented, but this fact has made little impression on his admirers and is entirely absent from the legend.

President Kennedy paid a famous tribute to the multiplicity of Jefferson's talents, but they have always been regarded as astonishing. James Parton, one of Jefferson's nineteenth-century biographers, gave his dazzling range of abilities a dramatic accent when he characterized his subject as a man who "could calculate an eclipse, survey an estate, tie an artery, plan an edifice, try a cause, break a horse, dance a minuet, and play the violin." And Parton was describing a young Jefferson who had not yet written the Declaration. When the world's leading scientist and explorer, Alexander von Humboldt, came to visit Jefferson in Washington in 1804, he came to see not the President of the United States so much as the president of the American Philosophical Society and the author of *Notes on the State of Virginia* (1785). Had he visited the President at his home in Virginia, he would have seen what was perhaps the finest private library in America, which later became the foundation of the Library of Congress.

Not all of Jefferson's extraordinary talents are fully recognized by the public at large. One that is not is his great achievement as an architect. Self-taught from books and, until he went abroad, almost without worthy architectural models to observe, Jefferson managed to design a number of memorable structures. The residence of his that crowns (and names) a small mountain in the Virginia Piedmont has become one of the most familiar objects in American iconography. And Jefferson can claim credit for not just one Monticello but two: the domed structure represented on the back of the nickel is his second version of the house, which superseded the first one on the same site, and is dramatically different.

Part of the evidence for Jefferson's distinction as an architect is found in his beautifully detailed drawings, some of which reveal fanciful structures that were never built. But his most original and most imaginative design, and the one recognized by professional architects as among the greatest of all American architectural achievements, is his "academical village" — the campus of the University of Virginia. In forming his conception Jefferson effectively reinvented the idea of the university, from the innovative curriculum to the unique arrangement and design of the buildings. Here those seeking his monument have only to look about them.

Although he was a many-sided and multi-talented man who left a lasting imprint on a number of endeavors, there seems to be little doubt that Jefferson's pre-eminent contribution to the world was the Declaration of Independence — particularly its enduring affirmations of liberty and equality. In the prologue of the Declaration these affirmations were made the axioms from which the rights of revolution and self-government could confidently be deduced. The idea of individual liberty was not, of course, original with Jefferson, or exclusively an American invention. It was fostered in Western Europe by philosophers, religious dissidents, and political rebels, but it took root tenaciously among transplanted Europeans in the New World and, with the founding of the American republic, received its most durable expression in the Declaration of Independence. To the Declaration's studious and deeply learned author, many of what had passed in the history of the world for the prerogatives of governmental power were arbitrary and intolerable restraints on individual freedom. In fact, it is not too much to say that Jefferson's reigning political passion was a hatred of tyranny. And although his fear of the tyrannous abuse of power has sometimes been judged excessive, it is hard to argue that tyranny has ever been, or is even now, in short supply.

If it is possible to reduce so complex an issue to its simplest terms, one might venture that for Jefferson the paramount political issue in the American Revolution was what he called liberty and what we now call personal freedom, or choice. It was and remains the virtual sine qua non of American culture, something that Americans from the first have been strongly conscious of and willing to fight for. But what has become the most familiar and the most quoted phrase in the Declaration — "all men are created equal" — is about something else. It is an intriguing fact that although Americans generally understand that the prologue to the Declaration is their charter of freedom, even more indelibly impressed upon their imagination is its affirmation of the ideal of human equality.

How could the man who wrote, that "all men are created equal" own slaves? This, in essence, is the question most persistently asked of those who write about Thomas Jefferson, and by all indications it is

Isaac Jefferson, born in 1775, was a skilled slave on Jefferson's Monticello plantation. This daguerreotype was taken by John Plumbe circa 1845. (Tracy W. McGregor Library, Special Collections Department, University of Virginia Library)

the thing that contemporary Americans find most vexing about him. In a recent series of some two dozen radio talk shows, I was asked this question on virtually every program, either by the host or by a caller. Most often, those who point to this problem admire Jefferson, and they appear as reluctant to give up their admiration as they would be to give up the principle of equality itself. But they are genuinely baffled by the seeming contradiction.

The question carries a silent assumption that because he practiced slaveholding, Jefferson must have somehow believed in it, and must therefore have been a hypocrite. My belief is that this way of asking the question, as in the cases of Kennedy and King, is essentially backward, and reflects the pervasive presentism of our time. Consider, for example, how dif-

ferent the question appears when inverted and framed in more historical terms: How did a man who was born into a slaveholding society, whose family and admired friends owned slaves, who inherited a fortune that was dependent on slaves and slave labor, decide at an early age that slavery was morally wrong and forcefully declare that it ought to be abolished?

Though stating the same case, these are obviously different questions, focusing on different things, but one is framed in a historical context and the other ignores historical circumstances. The rephrased question reveals that what is truly remarkable is that Jefferson went against his society and his own self-interest to denounce slavery and urge its abolition. And, crucially, there is no hidden assumption that he must in some way have believed in or tacitly accepted the morality of slavery.

But when the question is explained in this way, another invariably follows: If Jefferson came to believe that holding slaves was wrong, why did he continue to hold them? This question, because of its underlying assumptions, is both harder and easier than the first. It is harder because we are at such a great remove from the conditions of eighteenth-century Virginia that no satisfactory explanation can be given in a nutshell. To come to terms with the tangle of legal restrictions and other obstacles faced by the eighteenth-century Virginia slaveholder who might have wished freedom for his slaves, together with the extraordinary difficulties of finding them viable places of residence and means of livelihood, requires a short course in early American history. But the question is easier in that there is no doubt that these obstacles to emancipation in Jefferson's Virginia were formidable, and the risk was demonstrably great that emancipated slaves would enjoy little, if any, real freedom and would, unless they could pass as white, be more likely to come to grief in a hostile environment. In short, the master whose concern extended beyond his own morality to the well-being of his slaves was caught on the horns of a

Twenty-nine slaves are listed on this roll of Jefferson's slaves at Monticello in 1774. In fact, Jefferson owned a total of 180 slaves and three large plantations, in addition to several smaller land holdings. The slaves listed on the roll without a footnote designation were under the age of ten. (Massachusetts Historical Society)

dilemma. Thus the question of why Jefferson didn't free his slaves only serves to illustrate how presentism involves us in mistaken assumptions about historical conditions — in this case that an eighteenth-century slaveholder wanting to get out from under the moral stigma of slavery and improve the lot of his slaves had only to set them free.

The inevitable question about slavery and equality partly reflects the fact that most Americans are only vaguely familiar with the historical Jefferson, but delving into his writings and attempting to come to terms with the character of his thought, though illu-

minating, can create further consternation. The college student confronting Jefferson's one published book, *Notes on the State of Virginia,* is nowadays unprepared for and often appalled at what the author of the Declaration of Independence had to say about race. Thirty years ago college students were shocked to find Jefferson referring to the slave population as "blacks," a term that to them suggested racial insensitivity. But to those born after the civil-rights acts of the 1960s, it comes as a shock to discover that Jefferson, while firmly in favor of general emancipation, held out no hope for racial integration. Believing that an amalgamation of the races was not desirable and would not work, he advocated a plan of gradual emancipation and resettlement. Present-day students are even more shocked to find Jefferson concluding, albeit as "a suspicion only," that the blacks he had observed were "inferior to the whites in the endowments both of body and mind." Even his positive finding that blacks appeared to be superior to whites in musical ability rankles, for it comes through to students of the current generation as an early version of a familiar stereotype.

At a time like the present, when relations between the races are in the forefront of public discussion and desegregation is the law of the land, it is not surprising that college students should be sensitive to discrepancies between what they understand to be the prevailing ideals of their country and the views of its most prominent Founding Father. National ideals, however, spring not only from the beliefs and aspirations of founders but also, as this essay attempts to show, from the experience and efforts of subsequent generations. Though he foresaw that slavery could not prevail ("Nothing is more certainly written in the book of fate than that these people are to be free"), Jefferson can hardly be counted bigoted or backward for seriously doubting that a racially integrated society of white Europeans and black Africans was truly feasible. As the Harvard historian Bernard Bailyn has written, "It took a vast leap of the imagination in the eighteenth century to consider integrating into the political community the existing slave population, whose very 'nature' was the subject of puzzled inquiry and who had hitherto been politically non-existent." Interestingly, the reasons that Jefferson gave for doubting the possibility of integration — "deep rooted prejudices entertained by the whites; ten thousand recollections, by the blacks, of the injuries they have sustained; new provocations; [and] the real distinctions which nature has made" — are the same reasons often cited by black separatists, who entertain the same misgivings.

But if Jefferson's being a separatist can be accounted for, what can be said about his invidious comparison of the natural endowments of blacks with those of whites, or with those of American Indians, whom he found to be on a par with whites? His own testimony suggests an answer, for he admitted that his acquaintance with blacks did not extend to the African continent and embraced only black people who had been born in and forced to live under the degrading conditions of slavery. "It will be right to make great allowances for the difference of condition, of education, of conversation, of the sphere in which they move," Jefferson wrote, but it is evident in the hindsight of two hundred years that his estimate of the capabilities of blacks failed to make sufficient allowances, particularly for the things he himself named. It is perhaps poetic justice that posterity should be liable to the same kind of mistake in judging him.

But if Jefferson's beliefs add up to a kind of racism, we must specify two important qualifications. First, that Jefferson offered his conclusions as a hypothesis only, acknowledging that his own experience was not a sufficient basis on which to judge an entire race. Had he lived long enough to meet the ex-slave Frederick Douglass or hear the searing eloquence of his oratory, he would have recognized intellectual gifts in a black man that were superior to those of most whites. Douglass's oratory brings us to the second qualification, which is a telling one. Attacking the justifications for slavery in 1854, Douglass observed,

Ignorance and depravity, and the inability to rise from degradation to civilization and respectability, are the most usual allegations against the oppressed. The evils most fostered by slavery and oppression are precisely those which slaveholders and oppressors would transfer from their system to the inherent character of their victims. Thus the very crimes of slavery become slavery's best defence. By making the enslaved a character fit only for slavery, they excuse themselves for refusing to make the slave a freeman.

Although we may find Jefferson guilty of failing to make adequate allowance for the conditions in which blacks were forced to live, Jefferson did not take the next step of concluding that blacks were fit only for slavery. This rationalization of slavery was indeed the common coin of slaveholders and other whites who condoned or tolerated the "peculiar" institution, but it formed no part of Jefferson's thinking. In fact, he took the opposite position: that having imposed the depredations of slavery on blacks, white Americans should not only emancipate them but also educate and train them to be self-sufficient, provide them with necessary materials, and establish a colony in which they could live as free and independent people.

But if going back to original sources and historical contexts is essential in discerning the meanings that Today has imposed on Yesterday, it is equally important in determining how Yesterday's meanings have colored Today's. The concept of equality that is universally recognized in our own time as a fundamental principle of American society only had its beginnings in the eighteenth century; it did not emerge full-blown from the Declaration of Independence.

Whenever he sent correspondents a copy of the Declaration, Jefferson transcribed the text in such a way as to show what the Continental Congress had added to his draft and what it had cut out. The process of congressional emendation was clearly a painful memory for him, and the deletion about which he probably felt the most regret was also the most radical of the passages, for it undertook to blame the King of England directly for the African slave trade. It begins,

He has waged cruel war against human nature itself, violating it's most sacred rights of life and liberty in the persons of a distant people who never offended him, captivating & carrying them into slavery in another hemisphere, or to incur miserable death in their transportation thither. . . . Determined to keep open a market where MEN should be bought & sold, he has prostituted his negative for suppressing every legislative attempt to prohibit or to restrain this execrable commerce.

Had this passage been ratified as part of the official Declaration, then a question often raised in the nineteenth century — Did Jefferson mean to include blacks in the language of the Declaration? — would have been susceptible of a clear-cut and demonstrable answer. For, as the political scientist Jean Yarbrough has recently pointed out, this passage says unmistakably that the Africans captured into slavery were not a separate category of beings but men, with the sacred rights of life and liberty that are said in the prologue of the Declaration to be the natural endowments of all men. It is precisely in having these same rights that the prologue asserts that all men are created equal.

This deleted passage also provides an answer to a question often raised in the twentieth century: Did Jefferson mean to include women in the phrase "all men are created equal"? Implicit in the passage is that "men" is being used in the broader sense of "mankind," for those who were cruelly transported to be "bought & sold" on the slave market were certainly female as well as male.

That blacks and women were meant to be included in the affirmations of Jefferson's Declaration at a time when they enjoyed nothing remotely like political and social equality underscores a source of continuing confusion for contemporary Americans — the difference between a philosophical conception of natural rights and a working system of laws and societal values which allows for the fullest expression of those rights. In our own time the stubbornly persistent disparity between these two is often a source of cynicism and despair, but a Jeffersonian perspective would put more emphasis on the considerable progress made in closing the gap. Jefferson himself was sustained by a profound belief in progress. His unshakable conviction that the world was steadily advancing, not only in the material but also in the moral sphere, is abundantly evident in his writings. Though sometimes criticized as being naive in this regard, he was fully aware that his belief embraced the prospect of recurrent political and social transformations. Writing from retirement at the age of seventy-three, he told a correspondent that "laws and institutions must go hand in hand with the progress of the human mind."

As that becomes more developed, more enlightened, as new discoveries are made, new truths disclosed, and manners and opinions change with the change of circumstances, institutions must advance also, and keep pace with the times. We might as well require a man to wear still the coat which fitted him when a boy, as civilized society to remain ever under the regimen of their barbarous ancestors.

One way of looking at American history from Jefferson's day down to our own is as the series of changes and adjustments in our laws and institutions necessitated by the ideals implicit in Jefferson's Declaration. Sometimes the effect of these ideals has been simply to prevent other, incompatible ideals from gaining ascendancy, as in the case of Social Darwinism, whose notions of the natural inferiority of certain racial and social groups were impeded by the prevalence and familiarity of the Declaration's precepts. But without doubt the most important event in the development of the American ideal of equality, after Jefferson's Declaration, was Abraham Lincoln's address at Gettysburg. Without any warrant from the founders themselves or from subsequent interpreters or historians, Lincoln declared that not only the essential meaning of the Civil War but also the national purpose itself was epitomized in Jefferson's phrase "all men are created equal."

As Garry Wills has cogently argued, Lincoln at Gettysburg was practicing not presentism but futurism. In the most stunning act of statesmanship in our history, he invested Jefferson's eighteenth-century notion of equality with an essentially new meaning and projected it onto the future of the nation. Transfigured in the context of civil war, and transformed by Lincoln into a larger and more consequential ideal, Jefferson's formulation would never be the same. Thanks in large part to Lincoln, Americans no longer understand the prologue of the Declaration as a philosophical expression of natural rights, but rather take it to be a statement about the social and political conditions that ought to prevail.

Jefferson's Declaration is thus remarkable not only for its durability — its ability to remain meaningful and relevant — but also for its adaptability to changing conditions. At a time when natural rights are widely proclaimed a nullity, the language of the Declaration is universally understood as affirming human rights, and is resorted to even by those who do not consciously associate their ideas or aspirations with Jefferson. When the black separatist Malcolm X underwent a change of heart about white people and publicly renounced the "sweeping indictments of one race," he told an audience in Chicago, "I am not a racist and do not subscribe to any of the tenets of racism. In all honesty and sincerity it can be stated that I wish nothing but freedom, justice, and equality; life, liberty, and the pursuit of happiness — for all people." Simply to name the most basic American ideals is to invoke the words of Jefferson.

QUESTIONS TO CONSIDER

1   Compare Thomas Jefferson and the Benjamin Franklin you met in selection 6. In what ways were they both representative of their time? Are there ways in which they were not?

2   How did the story of Jefferson and Sally Hemings first surface? What was the purpose of its publication? This story has been treated and interpreted in very different ways at different times. What do the varying interpretations say about the periods in which they originated?

3   Wilson says that one should not ask why Jefferson, author of the Declaration of Independence, did not free his slaves but rather how Jefferson, member of a slaveholding society, came to hate slavery. Do you agree with Wilson's point of view? During the Revolution and influenced especially by the Declaration of Independence, a number of southern slaveholders as well as the northern states did in fact free their slaves in the name of the liberty for which the American Revolution was being fought. So why did Jefferson not free his own? Is this question necessarily presentist?

4   The anthology entitles this selection "Thomas Jefferson and the Meanings of Liberty." What are the different meanings of liberty embodied in the Declaration of Independence? Which were most current in the eighteenth century? Which are most current today, and why have they changed?

5   Douglas Wilson raises the question of whether figures from the past should be remembered for their "greatest achievements" or for their "personal failures." What are the good sides and bad sides of revisionism that often stress the faults of great figures? What does this trend in historical writing say about the present?

V

BIRTH OF THE REPUBLIC

9

Sunrise at Philadelphia

BRIAN MCGINTY

Once the Revolution began, Americans set about creating the political machinery neces-sary to sustain an independent nation. The Second Continental Congress, called in 1775, continued as an emergency, all-purpose central government until 1781, when the Articles of Confederation were finally ratified and a new one-house Congress was elected to function as the national government. Wary of central authority because of the British experience, Americans now had precisely the kind of government most of them wanted: an impotent Congress that lacked the authority to tax, regulate commerce, or enforce its own ordinances and resolutions. Subordinate to the states, which supplied it with funds as they chose, Congress was powerless to run the country. Indeed, its delegates wandered from Princeton to Annapolis to Trenton to New York, endlessly discussing where they should settle.

Patriots such as James Madison of Virginia, Alexander Hamilton of New York, and the venerable George Washington fretted in their correspondence about the near paralysis of the central government and the unstable conditions that plagued the land. "An opin-ion begins to prevail, that a General Convention for revising the Articles of Confedera-tion would be expedient," John Jay wrote Washington in March 1787. Washington agreed that the "fabrick" was "tottering." When Massachusetts farmers rose in rebellion under Daniel Shays, Washington was horror stricken. "Are your people getting mad?. . . What is the cause of all this? When and how is it to end?. . . What, gracious God, is man! that there should be such inconsistency and perfidiousness in his conduct?. . . We are fast verging to anarchy and confusion!"

Many of his colleagues agreed. There followed a series of maneuvers and meetings that culminated in the great convention of 1787, a gathering of fifty-five notables sent to

Philadelphia to overhaul the feeble Articles of Confederation. Without authority, they proceeded to draft an entirely new constitution that scrapped the Articles, created a new government, and undoubtedly saved the country and America's experiment in popular government. As James MacGregor Burns has noted, it was a convention of "the well-bred, the well-fed, the well-read, and the well-wed." Most delegates were wealthy, formally educated, and youngish (their average age was the early forties), and more than a third of them were slave owners. The poor, the uneducated, the backcountry farmers, and women, blacks, and Indians were not represented. Throughout their deliberations, moreover, they compromised on the volatile slavery issue. "For these white men," wrote one scholar, "the black man was always a brooding and unsettling presence (the black woman, even more than the white woman, was beyond the pale, beyond calculation)." For most of the framers of the Constitution, order and national strength were more important than the inalienable rights of blacks or women. Like their countrymen, most could simultaneously love liberty, recognize the injustice of slavery, yet tolerate bondage as a necessary evil.

As we enter our third century under the Constitution, we need more than ever to remember that the framers were not saints but human beings — paradoxical, complex, unpredictable, and motivated by selfishness as well as high idealism. Yet, as Brian McGinty shows in his account of "the miracle of Philadelphia," the founders were able to rise above petty self-interest to fashion what remains the oldest written national constitution, which in turn created one of the oldest and most successful federal systems in history. McGinty tells the full story of the great convention; he describes the remarkable personalities gathered there, the debates and the compromises that shaped the new Constitution, the battle for ratification, and the forging of the Bill of Rights in the form of the first ten amendments.

GLOSSARY

ARTICLES OF CONFEDERATION (1781–1789)   First American union, in which a weak central government was subordinate to the states; it consisted of a one-house Congress that exercised all judicial, executive, and legislative functions but that lacked the power to tax or regulate currency.

THE FEDERALIST (OR *FEDERALIST* PAPERS)   Eighty-five letters written by Alexander Hamilton, James Madison, and John Jay defending the Constitution during the ratification process.

HENRY, PATRICK   Fiery opponent of the Constitution in Virginia.

MADISON, JAMES   Convention delegate from Virginia; planter, slaveholder, and brilliant political theorist who was responsible for much of the substance of the new Constitution.

MORRIS, GOUVERNEUR   Convention delegate from Pennsylvania who assumed the chief responsibility for drafting the new Constitution; the preamble, which began, "We the people," was his inspiration and was one of the single most important acts of the Constitutional Convention.

NECESSARY AND PROPER

CLAUSE   Provision in the Constitution empowering Congress to enact all laws that were "necessary and proper" for executing its enumerated powers; the clause would later become one of the chief building blocks of a strong central government.

NEW JERSEY PLAN   Proposed by William

Paterson, it called for a one-house legislature comprised of members chosen by the state legislatures.

SHERMAN, ROGER   Convention delegate from

Connecticut who proposed the first major compromise: it called for a lower house of Congress in which representation was based on population, and an upper house in which the states would be represented equally.

SUPREME LAW OF THE LAND

CLAUSE   Provision in the Constitution designating it and the national laws made under it as the supreme law of the land.

THREE-FIFTHS CLAUSE   By this provision in

the Constitution, each slave was counted as three-fifths of a person when it came to apportioning representation in the lower house on the basis of population; the clause gave the white South disproportionate power in the House of Representatives (the slaves, while counted thus, had no political rights whatever).

VIRGINIA PLAN   Proposed by Edmund

Randolph, it called for a national executive with veto power, a national judiciary, and a two-house legislature, with the lower house "elected by the people and the upper chosen by the lower."

As Benjamin Franklin looked over the roster of delegates at the start of the Constitutional Convention, he confessed that he was well pleased. "We have here at present," Franklin wrote a friend, "what the French call *une assemblée des notables,* a convention composed of some of the principal people from the several states of our Confederation." [Thomas] Jefferson, examining the same roster in Paris, proclaimed the convention "an assembly of demi-gods."

Most prominent among the "demi-gods" was George Washington. Early on the morning of May 9, 1787, he had left Mount Vernon in his carriage. Washington was no stranger to the road from the Potomac to Philadelphia, for he had traveled it often during the days of the First and Second Continental Congresses, oftener still while he was leading the military struggle for independence. He would have liked to travel with Martha this time, but the mistress of the plantation on the Potomac had "become too domestic and too attentive to her two little grandchildren to leave home." The retired general's progress was impeded more than a little by the joyful greetings he received at every town and stage stop along the way. When he arrived in Philadelphia on May 13, the biggest celebration of all began. Senior officers of the Continental Army greeted him on the outskirts of the city, and citizens on horseback formed an escort. Guns fired a salute and the bells of Christ Church pealed as the great man rode into the city.

Washington had reflected carefully before deciding to attend the Philadelphia convention. He was fifty-five years old now, and his once-powerful physique was wracked with rheumatism. He was far from certain that the Philadelphia convention would

From "Sunrise at Philadelphia" by Brian McGinty, *American History Illustrated* (Summer 1987), excerpted from pp. 22–47. Reprinted through the courtesy of Cowles Magazines, Inc., publisher of *American History Illustrated.*

find a solution to the nation's political problems and had little wish to risk his reputation in an effort that might be doomed to failure. More important, when he had resigned his military commission in December 1783 he had clearly stated his intention of spending the rest of his days in private life. But his friends had urged him to reconsider his decision and lend his commanding influence and prestige to the Philadelphia assembly.

Despite his lingering doubts about the convention's ultimate outcome, Washington had no reservations about its purpose. "The discerning part of the community," he wrote a friend, "have long since seen the necessity of giving adequate powers to Congress for national purposes; and the ignorant and designing must yield to it ere long." What most troubled the Virginian was the realization that his failure to go to Philadelphia might be interpreted as a rejection of the convention. And so he decided, more out of a sense of duty than with any enthusiasm, to make the long trip to Philadelphia. Although Washington arrived there the day before the assembly was set to convene, he found that some delegates were already in the city. The Pennsylvania delegates, who all lived in Philadelphia, were there, of course, headed by the venerable Dr. Benjamin Franklin. Franklin received Washington in the courtyard of his home just off Market Street above Third, after which the general repaired to the luxurious home of Robert Morris on Market just east of Sixth, where he was to be a guest during the convention.

Franklin was eighty-one years old and beset by infirmities (gout and gall stones) that made it all but impossible for him to walk. But his mind was bright and alert, and he continued to play an active role in the affairs of his city and state. He had returned in 1785 from Paris, where he had been American minister to France, to enjoy comforts of a well-earned retirement, but relented when members of the Supreme Executive Council of Pennsylvania asked him to accept the post of president, an office that corresponded to the position of governor in other states. By late

March, on the motion of Robert Morris, Franklin had accepted a commission to attend the upcoming convention as a Pennsylvania delegate. . . .

Although Washington was the most celebrated of the Virginia delegates, he was not the first to arrive in Philadelphia. Thirty-six-year-old James Madison of Montpelier in the Old Dominion's Orange County arrived in Philadelphia on May 3, 1787, from New York, where he had been serving in Congress. A slight man, barely five feet, six inches tall, Madison was shy and bookish. What he lacked in force and dynamism, the little Virginian more than made up in thought and scholarship. After graduating from the College of New Jersey (later Princeton), he had returned to his home state to take an active interest in public affairs. He served in the Virginia House of Delegates and Council of State before accepting election to Congress, where he served twice (in 1780–83 and again in 1786–88). A close friend of Thomas Jefferson, Madison came to the convention with well-developed ideas about democratic processes and republican institutions. . . .

In all, seventy-four delegates were selected to attend the convention, and fifty-five actually appeared in Philadelphia. Although not all of the fifty-five would attend all of the sessions, it was a sizable group—large enough to give the spacious, panelled assembly room on the east side of the ground floor of the Pennsylvania State House (the same room in which the Declaration of Independence had been signed in 1776) an air of excitement when the convention was in session.

In some ways the convention was as notable for the men who were not there as for those who were. The absence of John Adams and Thomas Jefferson was sharply felt, for both of these veterans of 1776 were widely regarded as American giants. Important diplomatic assignments kept them away from Philadelphia: Jefferson was American minister in Paris, while Adams filled the same post in London. Both were apprised of

A view of the Pennsylvania State House (Independence Hall), where the delegates to the Constitutional Convention assembled in May 1787. During these meetings, the United States government, as we know it, took shape. In the tower of the State House hung the Liberty Bell, which tolled the news of the signing of the Declaration of Independence and of American victories in the Revolution. An impassioned motto girdled the bell: "Proclaim Liberty throughout the land, and to all the inhabitants thereof." But given all the inhabitants excluded from the blessings of liberty, the motto seems more than a little ironic. (By permission of the Houghton Library, Harvard University)

developments in the Pennsylvania city by faithful correspondents on the scene. Adams's intellectual presence was strongly felt at the convention, for he had recently published *A Defence of the Constitutions of Government of the United States of America,* a treatise that explained and analyzed the constitutional structures of a half-dozen American states. Jefferson exchanged letters with James Madison and, at the younger man's request, sent him books on constitutional theory and history, for Madison was particularly interested in the histories of ancient confederacies. . . .

George Washington's presence in Philadelphia was enough to reassure all those who worried about the absence of Adams, Jefferson, [Richard Henry] Lee, [Patrick] Henry, and [John] Jay. When the hero of the Revolution entered Philadelphia at the head of a parade of cheering well-wishers, nearly everyone in the city was able to breathe more easily. If anyone could guarantee the results of the Philadelphia assembly, surely the Squire of Mount Vernon could. New York's Henry Knox wrote the Marquis de Lafayette: "General Washington's attendance at the convention adds, in my opinion, new lustre to his character. Secure as he was in his fame, he has again committed it to the mercy of events." "This great patriot," said the *Pennsylvania Herald,* "will never think his duty performed, while anything remains to be done."

It is not surprising that so many of the delegates (more than half) were lawyers, for members of the legal profession had long led the struggle for independence. Nor was it remarkable that many were present or former public officials. Fully four-fifths of the delegates were serving in or had been members of Congress, while even more had been involved, at one time or another, in colonial, state, and local governments. Many had helped draft their states' constitutions, and about half were veterans of military service. There were merchants, farmers, and one or two men who described themselves as "bankers" in the group. Three of the delegates were physicians, and one, Franklin, was a printer.

On the whole, the delegates were remarkably young: The average age was forty-three. Jonathan Dayton of New Jersey, at twenty-six, was the youngest; Franklin, at eighty-one, the oldest. Many had humble origins. Franklin had once been an indentured servant, and [Roger] Sherman of Connecticut had begun his working life as a cobbler's apprentice. But most delegates had acquired comfortable positions in life. A few ranked among the richest men in the country.

In a letter to Jefferson, Franklin expressed cautious optimism about the convention. The delegates were men of character and ability, Franklin said, "so that I hope Good from their meeting. Indeed," he added, "if it does not do good it must do Harm, as it will show that we have not Wisdom enough among us to govern ourselves; and will strengthen the opinion of some Political writers, that popular Governments cannot long support themselves.". . .

George Washington appeared regularly in the State House (the historic building would not be known as Independence Hall until the nineteenth century) at the appointed time each day, waiting patiently for the stragglers to appear and be recorded as present. When on May 25, the delegates of seven states were at last in their chairs, the convention was ready to begin.

First, a presiding officer had to be selected. Nobody in attendance had any doubt that the honor would be conferred on Washington; the only uncertainty was who would nominate him. Benjamin Franklin had planned to do so, but it was raining on May 25 and he was not well enough to make the trip from his home to the State House in poor weather. The motion was made in his stead by Robert Morris (Pennsylvania) and seconded by John Rutledge (South Carolina). Without discussion, the question was put to a vote, and Washington was unanimously elected president of the convention. Morris and Rutledge escorted the Virginian to the President's Chair. The chair belonged to the Pennsylvania Assembly and had been used by all the presidents of the Continental Congress when it had met in Philadelphia. Surmounting its back was the carved and gilded image of a sun that, before the assembly was concluded, would become a symbol for the convention and its work.

Second, rules for the convention's proceedings had to be adopted. One rule . . . was readily approved. It provided that "no copy be taken of any entry on the journal during the sitting of the House without the leave of the House. That members only be permitted to inspect the journal. That nothing spoken in the House be printed, or otherwise published, or communicated without leave.". . .

To impress on the delegates the seriousness with which the rule of secrecy was to be enforced, armed sentries were posted in the hall beyond the assembly chamber and on the street outside the State House. . . .

The delegates, on the whole, were scrupulous in their observance of the "rule of secrecy"; so scrupulous, in fact, that for nearly a generation after the convention the positions taken during the debates were still largely unknown to the public. Washington even refused to write about the debates in his diary. A few delegates kept private records that found their way into print long after the events at Philadelphia had become history. The best record was kept by James Madison. "I chose a seat," the Virginian later explained, "in front of the presiding member, with the other members on my right hand and left hand. In this favorable position for hearing all that passed I noted in terms legible and abbreviations and marks intelligible to [no one but] myself what was read from the Chair or spoken by the members; and losing not a moment unnecessarily between the adjournment and reassembling of the Convention I was enabled to write out my daily notes during the session or within a few finishing days after its close. . . . I was not absent a single day, nor more than a casual fraction of any hour in any day, so that I could not have lost a single speech, unless a very short one." Published in 1840, Madison's notes form the single best record of the convention's proceedings.

The Virginia delegates came to the convention's first deliberative session on May 29 equipped with a comprehensive plan for a new charter of government. Although the "Virginia Plan" had been discussed at length by members of that state's delegation, it bore the mark of Madison's careful thought and planning on every page. Edmund Randolph, who, as governor of the state, was titular leader of the Virginia delegation, presented the plan to the convention. The Virginia Plan proclaimed that it was designed to "correct and enlarge" the Articles of Confederation, but it was actually a blueprint for a whole new structure of government. Under it, the "national legislature" would consist of not one, but two houses, with the lower elected by the people and the upper chosen by the lower. There would be a "national executive," with veto power over legislative acts, and a "national judi-

ciary," with authority to decide cases involving "national peace or harmony."

The Virginia plan was a tempting subject for debate, but the convention's leaders believed more fundamental questions had to be decided first—questions upon which all other as yet undecided questions depended.

First among these threshold questions was whether the convention ought to content itself with revising the Articles of Confederation or propose an entirely new government with truly national purposes and powers. Delegates from at least four of the states had been sent to Philadelphia with strict instructions to consider revisions of the Articles and nothing else; and Congress, in its resolution approving the convention, had purported to limit the convention to revising the old charter.

Next the delegates resolved to organize into a Committee of the Whole. The purpose of this parliamentary maneuver was to keep discussions informal and to allow the representatives to change their votes until near the end of the convention. The device promoted open minds and frank speech.

As discussion began, South Carolina's Charles Pinckney expressed concern that, if the convention proposed a national government, the states might cease to exist. But Edmund Randolph (Virginia) assured him that a national government would not prevent the states from continuing to exercise authority in their proper spheres. John Dickinson (Delaware) and Elbridge Gerry (Massachusetts) admitted that the Articles of Confederation were defective, but they thought that the convention should correct their defects, not toss them aside.

Gouverneur Morris (Pennsylvania) expressed his belief that a national government was essential to the future of the country. "We had better take a supreme government now," Morris warned his fellow-delegates, "than a despot twenty years hence—for come he must." Agreeing with Morris, George Mason (Virginia) argued that the country needed a government that could govern directly, without the intervention of the states.

On May 30, on the motion of Gouverneur Morris, the convention decided, by a vote of six states to one, that "a *national* government ought to be established consisting of a *supreme* Legislative, Executive and Judiciary." Almost before they knew it, the delegates had decided what was to be the single most important issue of the convention. From that day forward, the convention would be irrevocably dedicated to the construction of a national government for the United States.

On May 31 the Committee of the Whole (the convention delegates) proceeded to consider other potentially explosive questions: whether the "national legislature" should have two houses or one; whether either or both houses should be elected by the people; and how the national government should function in terms of the citizens and the states. . . . Surprisingly, the delegates quickly agreed that there should be two houses in the legislature, that the lower house should be popularly elected, and that the legislature should have broad powers "to legislate in all cases to which the separate States are incompetent."

After deliberating for two weeks, the Committee of the Whole presented its recommendations to the convention. The proposed form of government followed the terms of the "Virginia Plan" closely—too closely, some delegates thought. Elbridge Gerry (Massachusetts) protested that some decisions might have been made too hastily, "that it was necessary to consider what the people would approve." Taking his cue from Gerry, William Paterson (New Jersey) proposed an alternative to the "Virginia Plan." Introduced on June 15, Paterson's "New Jersey Plan" suggested an entirely different frame of government: a unicameral legislature with members chosen by the state legislatures but with powers to "pass Acts for the regulation of trade and commerce." . . .

The delegates now decided to refer both the New Jersey Plan and the Virginia Plan to the Committee of the Whole for discussion.

The debates were now becoming contentious. The large states, led in size by Virginia, believed it was essential to do away with the old principle embodied in the Articles of Confederation of "one state, one vote." Under this rule, voters in the large states were effectively disfranchised by those in the small states. For their part, the small states insisted they could never consent to any rule that would deprive them of an equal voice in the federal government. If such a resolution were passed, Delaware's George Read announced, he would have no choice but to leave the convention, for his credentials forbade him to consent to such a measure.

Washington had been pleased when, in the early days of the convention, the delegates quickly and readily reached agreement on difficult questions. Now, it seemed, they were arguing about every issue that came before them. Discouraged, he wrote home for additional clothing, explaining that he saw "no end to my staying here." The sweltering heat (some Philadelphians thought the summer of 1787 was the worst since 1750) added to the bad humor of the delegates. Franklin, noting the rancor of the debates, suggested the representatives invite clergymen to attend their sessions and offer daily prayers. Roger Sherman (Connecticut) seconded the motion, but Alexander Hamilton (New York) doubted the wisdom of calling for "foreign aid." Many different faiths were represented among the delegates, and it would have been difficult to meet the demands of them all. Besides, a call for prayer might signal to the public outside the hall that all was not well inside. After some discussion, Franklin's proposal was dropped.

Sensing that the convention was approaching an impasse, Roger Sherman (Connecticut) rose to propose the convention's first important compromise. Representation in the lower house, Sherman suggested, should be based on population, while representation in the upper house should be equal. Sherman's proposal was ingenious. Its chief virtue was that it satisfied neither the large states nor the small states. Hamilton called it a "motley measure," and Madison said it was a "novelty & a compound." Because it met the demands of neither interest, however, it was acceptable to both. On July 16, by a vote of five states in favor, four states against, and one (Massachusetts) evenly divided, the "Connecticut Compromise" was passed. Another major hurdle to agreement had been overcome.

But many difficult questions still remained to be resolved. After spirited debate, the convention decided that each state would be allotted two representatives (senators) in the upper house of the national legislature and that the senators would vote "per capita," that is, individually. Additional debate prompted the delegates to decide that the "national executive" (the president) would be chosen neither by the national legislature nor by the people directly, but by a body of men (the electoral college) specially chosen for the purpose. George Mason (Virginia) proposed that membership in the national legislature be limited to "citizens of the United States," and no one objected.

By July 26, the convention felt it had made enough progress on the broad questions that faced it to safely proceed to more particular issues. To this end, it referred the proposed Constitution to a Committee of Detail with instructions to report back on August 6 with specific proposals to implement the convention's broad intentions. Its five members, John Rutledge (South Carolina), Edmund Randolph (Virginia), James Wilson (Pennsylvania), Oliver Ellsworth (Connecticut), and Nathaniel Gorham (Massachusetts) represented all sections of the country; the committee constituted a kind of "miniature convention."

From July 26 to August 6, the committee proposed, debated, revised, and, finally, resolved a host of important questions. It spelled out the powers of the national legislature, including a power that the Articles of Confederation had never given the old Congress: "to lay and collect taxes, duties, imposts and excises." The committee proposed to grant the national legislature the power to make all laws that should be "necessary and proper" for carrying out its specific powers. The "necessary and proper" clause would later become one of the chief building blocks of a strong central government. The committee decided the Supreme Court should have jurisdiction to decide all "Cases arising under the Laws passed by the general Legislature." And, significantly, the Committee of Detail provided that acts of the national legislature, treaties, and "this Constitution" should all be the "supreme Law of the Land."

With the basic structure of the proposed government now agreed upon, the convention appointed a Committee of Style and Arrangement to draft the Constitution. Some of the best penmen of the convention were appointed to the committee—James Madison (Virginia), Alexander Hamilton (New York), William Samuel Johnson (Connecticut), and Rufus King (Massachusetts). But the chief responsibility for drafting the document fell to the talented Gouverneur Morris (Pennsylvania). Years later, Morris would write that the Constitution "was written by the fingers, which write this letter." Madison, who was responsible for much of the substance of the document, admitted "the finish given to the style and arrangement of the Constitution fairly belongs to the pen of Mr. Morris."

Morris worked quickly and apparently with inspiration. One of the last sections he composed was the Preamble. As originally drafted by the Committee of Detail, the Preamble had stated:

"We the People of the States of New-Hampshire, Massachusetts, Rhode-Island and Providence Plantations, Connecticut, New-York, New-Jersey, Pennsylvania, Delaware, Maryland, Virginia, North Carolina, South-Carolina, and Georgia, do ordain, declare, and establish the following Constitution for the Government of Ourselves and our Posterity."

The Committee of Style and Arrangement re-wrote the same passage to read:

"We the People of the United States, in Order to form a more perfect Union, to establish Justice, insure domestic Tranquility, provide for the common defence, promote the general Welfare, and secure the Blessings of Liberty to ourselves and our Posterity, do ordain and establish this Constitution for the United States of America."

The change from "We the People" of named states to "We the People of the United States" did not seem particularly significant to the delegates when they read and considered Morris's draft. To history, however, it became one of the single most important acts of the Constitutional Convention. It would signify that the Union was the product, not of thirteen states, but of more than three million citizens. It was not a compact between sovereign governments, but a contract to which the citizens were parties.

When the Committee of Style presented its draft to the convention, there was a flurry of last-minute objections. Some delegates thought that Congress's right to overrule presidential vetoes should be by a vote of two-thirds rather than three-fourths of both houses. Others thought the document ought to guarantee the right of trial by jury in all civil cases. George Mason (Virginia) demanded that a bill of rights (similar to the precedent-setting Bill of Rights he drafted for the Virginia Constitution in 1776) be appended to the Constitution. But the hour was late, and the delegates were opposed to making major revisions. All states on the convention floor (including Mason's own Virginia) voted "no" to adopting a bill of rights.

Some delegates left the convention before the final copy of the Constitution was prepared. Others remained in Philadelphia, but only to express their opposition to the final version of the charter. George Mason, obstinate on the point of a bill of rights, announced that he "would sooner chop off his right hand than put it to the Constitution." Another Vir-

ginian, Edmund Randolph, who had first proposed the "Virginia Plan" that had formed the basis for many of the Constitution's major provisions, now doubted whether the people of his state would approve the document, and announced that he could not sign it. Elbridge Gerry (Massachusetts) thought that members of the Senate would hold their offices too long, that Massachusetts would not be fairly represented in the House of Representatives, and that a Supreme Court without juries would be a "Star-Chamber as to civil cases." He announced that he would not sign.

Word was circulating in Philadelphia that Pennsylvania's Benjamin Franklin also objected to the Constitution, but the philosopher-statesman soon put an end to such speculation. On Monday morning, September 17, after the secretary of the convention read a newly engrossed copy of the document, Franklin asked for permission to present a speech he had written. Because it was painful for him to stand, he asked James Wilson to read it for him:

"I confess that there are several parts of this constitution which I do not at present approve, but I am not sure I shall never approve them: For having lived long, I have experienced many instances of being obliged by better information or fuller consideration, to change opinions even on important subjects, which I once thought right, but found to be otherwise.... Thus I consent, Sir, to this Constitution because I expect no better, and because I am not sure, that it is not the best."

Before the Constitution could be signed, Nathaniel Gorham (Massachusetts) proposed that one final change be made in the document. Where the charter provided that each member of the House of Representatives would represent 40,000 citizens, Gorham suggested that the number be changed to 30,000. Several of the delegates felt that 40,000 was too large a constituency to be represented by one man. Rufus King (Massachusetts), Daniel Carroll (Maryland), and, finally, George Washington announced their agreement with Gorham. Although Washington had previously maintained a rigorous silence on disputed questions, he felt that he should express his opinion on this matter. He hoped that grounds for objection to the Constitution would, wherever possible, be eliminated. He believed that 40,000 was too large a constituency, and, although the hour was late, he still favored the change. Without objection, the word "forty" was erased and the word "thirty" written in its place on the engrossed copy.

The question now arose as to the manner in which the Constitution should be signed. Quorums in all of the represented states (although not all of the delegates in those states) were in favor of submitting the document to ratification. Most delegates wished to present the document to the public in the most favorable light possible and, to that end, hoped to give the impression of unanimity. Accordingly, Franklin moved that the signature clause be made to read: "Done in Convention by the Unanimous Consent of the States present." The motion was passed by a vote of eleven states to one. (South Carolina was divided on the issue. Charles Pinckney and Pierce Butler thought the clause too ambiguous.)

That same day, September 17, nearly four months after the convention began, the engrossed copy of the Constitution was signed. Proceeding in the traditional order of states from north to south, the delegates walked to the front of the room, bent over the table in front of the President's Chair and, with quill pen dipped in iron gall ink, signed their names on the last of the four pages of parchment. There were thirty-eight delegates and thirty-nine signatures (George Read of Delaware, who had overcome his earlier opposition to the document, signed both for himself and for John Dickinson, who was feeling ill and had gone home to Wilmington). Only three members present—Edmund Randolph (Virginia), George Mason (Virginia), and Elbridge Gerry (Massachusetts)—abstained. Thirteen members had left the convention before the final day.

Appropriately, Benjamin Franklin had a few last words. While the other delegates signed their names, the old patriot looked thoughtfully toward the President's Chair. He told a few delegates near him that painters had found it difficult "to distinguish in their art a rising from a setting sun. I have," said he, "often and often in the course of the Session, and the vicissitudes of my hopes and fears as to its issue, looked at that behind the President without being able to tell whether it was rising or setting: But now at length I have the happiness to know that it is a rising and not a setting Sun."

After the Constitution was signed and the last gavel fell, the delegates filed out of the State House, then proceeded to the City Tavern on Second Street near Walnut. The City Tavern was one of old Philadelphia's most enjoyable gathering places and had been a favorite haunt of the delegates during the convention. The members shared a last dinner together, complete with toasts and speeches, then bade each other a fond farewell. George Washington's mind was still excited when he returned to his room at Robert Morris's house. Washington tended to some business matters and then, in the words of his diary, "retired to meditate on the momentous work which had been executed."

The newspapers were full of news from the convention. The delegates' self-imposed "rule of secrecy" had heightened the air of mystery surrounding the meeting, and now it seemed as if the public could not hear enough about what had happened during the convention. In Philadelphia on September 19, the *Pennsylvania Packet and Daily Advertiser* published the full text of the Constitution. Just under the newspaper's masthead, in boldface type, were the words of the Preamble, beginning with the soon-to-be memorable phrase: "We, the People of the United States." Within weeks, the Constitution was reprinted in newspapers, pamphlets, and booklets all over the country. . . .

Article VII of the Constitution prescribed the process by which the charter was to be ratified. When conventions in at least nine states had approved the document, the Constitution would be "established" between the ratifying states. Until ratifying conventions had assembled, deliberated, and expressed their approval, however, the document would be nothing more than a hope for a better future. . . .

When Congress received the document, some of its members were baffled. The Articles of Confederation, from which Congress derived its authority, did not authorize it to do away with the Confederation and replace it with a *national government*. Those members of Congress who had also attended the Philadelphia assembly argued strongly that Congress should follow the wishes of the convention and submit the Constitution to state ratifying conventions. Richard Henry Lee, a Congressman from Virginia, objected. Lee thought the "Federalists" (as proponents of the Constitution were now being called) were trying "to push the business on with dispatch . . . that it might be adopted before it had stood the test of reflection and due examination." But a majority of Congress favored the document, paving the way for passage of a resolution referring the Constitution to the legislatures, by them to be "submitted to a convention of Delegates chosen in each state by the people thereof in conformity to the resolves of the Convention. . . ."

[Meanwhile], proponents and opponents of the Constitution began to argue their cases. James Madison [noted:] "The advocates for it come forward more promptly than the adversaries. . . . The sea coast seems everywhere fond of it."

Indeed, many were "fond" of the Constitution — but hardly anyone entertained the notion that it was "perfect." The charter was the work of different men with various ideas, the product of a long string of concessions and compromises. To be sure, it called for the establishment of some notable features: three autonomous branches of government, each invested with power and authority to check the excesses of the others; a Congress consisting of two houses with specifically enumerated powers; a na-

tional judiciary; and a strong executive. And it provided the framework for a federal government that combined national supremacy with state autonomy and made both subservient to the popular will.

But the document was not free of anomalies. For instance, members of the House of Representatives were to be apportioned among the states "according to their respective numbers," but the "numbers" were to be calculated in a curious way: all "free persons" were to be counted, as were persons "bound to service for a term of years," but "Indians not taxed" were to be excluded, and only three-fifths of "all other persons" were to be counted. The delegates knew, of course, that the words "all other persons" referred to slaves and that, by allowing the southern states to count three-fifths of their slaves, the document gave tacit recognition to slavery. But the Constitution by no means approved slavery; indeed, many delegates believed the institution should be abolished throughout the country. The document did require enforcement of fugitive slave laws, but it also empowered Congress to forbid the importation of new slaves into the country after the year 1808. In its curious and conflicting references to slavery, the Constitution was reflecting the concessions and compromises by which it was produced.

In many ways, the charter was a hodgepodge. And yet it was bound together by common values: dedication to the ideals of American independence and liberty, and a conviction that a strong federal government was the best way to safeguard those ideals. . . .

By the end of October, however, Madison could see that the tide of opinion in the country was beginning to turn away from the Constitution. In Virginia, Richard Henry Lee and Patrick Henry announced their intention to work against ratification. In Massachusetts, James Winthrop (writing under the pseudonym of "Agrippa") published letters that charged that the Constitution gave too much power to the central government and not enough to the states. In New York, Melancton Smith published an *Address to the People of the State of New York* in which he warned that the Constitution would create an "aristocratic tyranny." Meanwhile, in Pennsylvania, Samuel Bryan published a broadside predicting that, under the Constitution, the United States would be "melted down into one empire" with a government "devoid of all responsibility or accountability to the great body of the people."

Richard Henry Lee's views were recorded in his *Letters from the Federal Farmer*. Forgetting for the moment his own privileged background, Lee said that the Constitution was the work of "the artful and ever active aristocracy." He agreed with George Mason that the Constitution should include a bill of rights. He also thought that it should provide for a council to assist and advise the president and guarantee the right of jury trial. "If our countrymen are so soon changed," Lee charged, "and the language of 1774 is become odious to them, it will be in vain to use the language of freedom, or attempt to rouse them to free inquiries."

Patrick Henry warned Virginians who lived in the region called Kentucky (it would not become a state until 1792) that the Constitution favored the eastern part of the country at the expense of the west and that it would inevitably lead to loss of navigation rights on the Mississippi. Henry was angered by the Preamble's reference to "We the People" and challenged the right of the Philadelphia delegates to use such an all-encompassing term. "[W]ho authorized them to speak the language of *We the people*," Henry demanded, "instead of, *We the states*? States are the characteristics and the soul of a confederation. If the states be not the agents of this compact, it must be one great consolidated national government, of the people of all the states."

In New York on September 27 the newspapers began to publish a series of articles attacking the Constitution and the Philadelphia convention. Signed with the pseudonym "Cato," the letters were widely supposed to have been written by New York's staunchly antifederalist governor, George Clinton. Other letters, similar in tone and content, appeared under the names of "Sydney" and "Brutus" and were widely recognized as pseudonyms for Clinton's supporters. Alarmed by the vigor of the "anti-Federalist" letters, Alexander Hamilton decided to mount a reply.

Hamilton had been the only New Yorker to sign the Constitution. He now tried to use the influence he had with other New York politicians. Hamilton was one of the state's most brilliant lawyers and effective writers. His home and law office on Wall Street were not far from the residences of John Jay and James Madison. The three soon joined forces to answer the attacks of "Cato," "Sydney," and "Brutus" with a series of letters [to various newspapers] signed with the name of "Publius.". . .

There were eighty-five letters from "Publius" — fifty-five written by Hamilton, twenty-nine by Madison, and five by Jay. Never one to lose the opportunity to publicize his views, Hamilton arranged with a printing firm to publish the letters in book form, and on May 28, 1788, a two-volume edition bearing the title of *The Federalist* was issued by J. and A. McLean in New York. . . . The book was both a reasoned defense of the Constitution and a ringing call for its ratification. "The establishment of a Constitution," Hamilton wrote in his last *Federalist* paper, "in time of profound peace, by the voluntary consent of a whole people, is a prodigy, to the completion of which I look forward with trembling anxiety.". . .

The demand for a bill of rights had become a clarion call of the antifederalists. In his speeches and letters, George Mason, who had written the Virginia Bill of Rights, argued that the people needed protection against a strong and powerful central government and that they could secure that protection only by specifically limiting the government's powers. Supporting Mason, Richard Henry Lee complained of the Constitution's lack of provisions to protect "those essential rights of mankind without which liberty cannot exist."

Prominent supporters of the Constitution generally opposed a bill of rights. Hamilton thought such a declaration not only unnecessary, but "dangerous." Under the Constitution, the federal government would have only the powers that the people granted it. Therefore, Hamilton argued, the government could have no power to abridge the people's rights unless they *gave* it that power. He pointed out that the Constitution already contained many provisions guaranteeing basic civil rights: protection of the writ of *habeas corpus,* a prohibition against bills of attainder and *ex post facto* laws, strict proof requirements in all prosecutions for treason, and a guarantee of the right of trial by jury in all criminal cases except impeachments. A bill of rights, Hamilton said, would inevitably "contain various exceptions to powers which are not granted; and on this very account would afford a colourable pretext to claim more than were granted. For why declare that things shall not be done which there is no power to do?"

South Carolina's Charles Cotesworth Pinckney pointed out that bills of rights "generally begin with declaring that all men are by nature born free." "Now, we should make that declaration with a very bad grace," Pinckney said, "when a large part of our property consists in men who are actually born slaves." Connecticut's Roger Sherman said, "No bill of rights ever yet bound the supreme power longer than the honeymoon of a new married couple, unless the rulers were interested in preserving the rights." And Pennsylvania's James Wilson sneered: "Enumerate all the rights of men? I am sure that no gentlemen in the late Convention would have attempted such a thing."

James Madison at first agreed with Hamilton that a bill of rights was unnecessary and potentially dangerous. But, by the fall of 1788, he had become convinced that such a declaration was not only desirable but essential to ratification of the Constitution. On October 17, 1788, Madison expressed his belief that an enumeration of the "fundamental maxims of free Government" would be "a good ground for an appeal to the sense of community" and "counteract the impulses of interest and passion." Madison pledged that, if the new Constitution went into effect, he would do everything in his power to see that it was amended in such a way as to protect basic human rights from federal infringement. . . .

[The ratification process began in Delaware, whose convention voted unanimously to endorse the new Constitution. The conventions of several other states did likewise. New Hampshire was the ninth and deciding state to ratify. The federalists found themselves hard-pressed in Virginia, where Patrick Henry and other antifederalists resisted tenaciously. "Whither is the spirit of America gone?" Patrick Henry cried. "Sir, the American spirit, assisted by the ropes and chains of consolidation, is about to convert this country into a powerful and mighty empire." Virginia narrowly approved the Constitution, as did New York. North Carolina was the twelfth state to ratify, but tiny Rhode Island, the only state that had refused to send a delegation to Philadelphia, held out until May, 1790, when it finally approved the Constitution and joined the new Union. Meanwhile, Congress had adopted] an "ordinance" setting March 4, 1789, as the date and New York City as the place for the first meeting of the first Congress under the Constitution. Members of the electoral college were chosen, and on February 4 they cast their ballots. To nobody's surprise, their unanimous choice as the first president under the Constitution was George Washington.

James Madison attended the new Congress as a member of the House of Representatives from Orange County, Virginia. He was denied a Senate seat by a vindictive Patrick Henry, who declared him "unworthy of the confidence of the people." In the House, Madison took responsibility for introducing the Bill of Rights that Henry, George Mason, and other antifederalists had demanded. . . . [This took the form of seventeen amendments to the new Constitution; Congress approved most of them and sent them to the states for ratification. By the end of 1791, the requisite three-fourths of the states had approved ten of the amendments, which afterward became known as the American "Bill of Rights."] Now United States citizens everywhere could be sure that their most valued civic rights — freedom of speech and of the press, freedom of assembly and of religion, freedom from unreasonable searches and seizures, the right to bear arms, the privilege against self-incrimination, the right to due process of law, the right to trial by jury, and the right to representation by counsel — would be protected from federal abridgment.

The process was complete. . . . The United States had become a nation.

QUESTIONS TO CONSIDER

1   James Madison was not destined to be a happy president (1809–1817), but he was a brilliant statesman and the true father of the Constitution. In what ways did he shape the drafting and passage of the Constitution? How did he overcome his own prejudices and the pressures exerted on him by his fellow Virginians in order to ensure the final success of the document?

2   Why did the delegates to the Constitutional Convention, instead of revising the Articles of Confederation as they were charged to do, scrap that document and devise an entirely new plan of government? What might have been the consequences had they kept the Articles of Confederation?

3   The framers of the Constitution were all well-to-do, socially prominent Americans. Did they produce a document that was fundamentally democratic or undemocratic? How did they feel about the will of the majority? What steps did they take to control that majority?

4   In many ways, as author McGinty says, the Constitution was a hodgepodge, a collection of ideas based on northern or southern biases, agricultural or commercial interests, federalist or antifederalist sentiments. What kinds of compromises did the representatives of these divergent interests finally accept?

5   How did the framers deal with the issue of slavery? Where, in particular, did they find it an embarrassment? Wherein did they sow the seeds of future discord?

6   The Constitution nearly failed the battle for ratification. What was the most significant area of dissension? What forms of suasion and compromise did both federalists and antifederalists employ?

IO

George Washington and the Use of Power

EDMUND S. MORGAN

In polls taken in 1948, 1962, and 1982, American historians and presidential scholars ranked George Washington as the second-best president in American history (the first in all three surveys was Abraham Lincoln). More than any other statesman, specialists contend, Washington defined the presidency and set the standard for executive leadership. "It is no exaggeration to say that but for George Washington, the office of president might not exist," one historian maintains. Washington was so respected in his day, so much above factional bickering and regional jealousies, that he was probably the only leader behind whom the country could unite. "One of the problems with Washington," says writer Garry Wills, "is that we think of him in the wrong company, as a peer of Franklin and Jefferson, when he belongs in the select company of Caesar, Napoleon and Cromwell as a charismatic nation-builder who personified an epoch."

Not that Washington was a saint. As historian Edmund S. Morgan makes clear, the first president had human flaws — among them, an aloofness that made him a hard man to know. Uncomfortable among learned men, he developed the habit of listening carefully to what was being said, pondering it, but rarely expressing his own opinion. His reticence struck some as arrogance, what an Englishman described as "repulsive coldness." His formidable size contributed to his seeming aloofness: standing a "ramrod straight" six-feet, three inches, which made him a giant in his day, he looked down at everybody. A man of robust health and energy, he nevertheless suffered from chronic dental problems and had to wear false teeth made of ivory and wood.

Adapting himself to the slave-owning world in which he was born and raised, Washington became a wealthy Virginia planter who owned as many as 317 slaves and shared the racial prejudice of most whites of his time. He even brought slave "servants" to the

131

president's house in Philadelphia. He said he regretted that slavery existed and wished it could be abolished but was unable to do anything about it beyond providing for the manumission of his own slaves upon his death.

In The First of Men *(1988), the best biography of Washington yet written, historian John E. Ferling reveals that Washington had a complex and contradictory character. He suffered from low self-esteem, struggled all his life to overcome feelings of worthlessness, and had a pathological need for the admiration and affirmation of other people. Yet, as Ferling reminds us, Washington was also a man of extraordinary personal courage. He demonstrated a rare ability for self-criticism, strove hard to better himself, proved to be an excellent organizer, and gave his family "tender love and abiding steadfastness." But his most significant trait, Edmund Morgan believes, was his understanding of the use of power, both as commander in chief of the Continental Army and as president of his infant nation. When it came to understanding power, Morgan contends, Washington was unsurpassed among his contemporaries.*

GLOSSARY

CORNWALLIS, LORD   Commander of the British forces in the southern colonies who surrendered to Washington in the Battle of Yorktown (1781), which ended the fighting in the Revolution.

HAMILTON, ALEXANDER   Washington's aide-de-camp during the Revolution and the nation's first secretary of the treasury, he served in the latter capacity under both Washington and second president John Adams.

JAY'S TREATY (1795)   Treaty that provided, among other things, that Great Britain would evacuate its posts in the Northwest Territory and that commissions would resolve boundary disputes.

PINCKNEY'S TREATY (1795)   Treaty with Spain that established the United States' southern boundary at the 31st parallel and that granted Americans free navigation rights on the Mississippi River.

☆

1

When a crowd of American farmers opened fire on the regular troops of the British army some 200 years ago, the action must have seemed foolhardy to any impartial observer. Such an observer might have been a little surprised at the events that immediately followed, when the farmers put the regulars to rout, chased them from Concord to Boston, and laid siege to that town. But however impressive this performance, it did not alter the fact that the British army was probably the most powerful in the world, having succeeded scarcely a dozen years before in defeating the armies of France, England's only serious rival. For a handful of colonists, unorganized, without any regular source of arms or ammunition, with no army and no navy, to take on the world's greatest power in open war must still have looked like a foolhardy enterprise.

Somehow or other it proved not to be. Yet it remains something of a puzzle that the farmers were able to bring it off. With the benefit of hindsight we can offer a number of explanations. For one thing, the generals whom the British sent to put down the rebels proved to be somewhat less than brilliant in using the immense force at their disposal. For another thing, the colonists got a great deal of assistance from England's old enemy, France. But perhaps most important, the American Revolution seems to have elicited from those who participated in it a response that no other event or situation in American history has been able to do.

It was not that extraordinarily large numbers of people were ready to sacrifice their lives or their fortunes for the common good. That has often happened in times of crisis. And the revolution did not in fact induce this kind of sacrifice very widely. It was always difficult to fill up enlistments in the Continental Army. What was extraordinary about the revolution was the talent it generated, the number of men of genius who stepped out of farmyards and plantations, out of countinghouses and courtrooms, to play a leading role in winning the war and then in building a national government. Prominent among them was George Washington, who more than any other single man was responsible for bringing success to this seemingly foolhardy enterprise. Since there was nothing in his previous career to suggest that he could play so large a role, it may be worth asking what there was in him that enabled him to do what he did.

This is not an easy task, for George Washington is and was a hard man to know. Part of the difficulty in approaching him comes from the heroic image in which we have cast him and which already enveloped him in his own lifetime. But it is not simply the plaster image that stands between him and us. We have other national heroes who also became legendary figures in their own lifetimes, a Benjamin Franklin, an Andrew Jackson, an Abraham Lincoln; and yet with them we find no great difficulty in pushing past the image to find the man. In their letters and other writings, in the countless anecdotes they inspired, we can meet them on familiar terms and feel comfortable in their company.

But not George Washington. The familiar anecdotes about Washington tell us to keep our distance. The most arresting one is told about a gathering at the time of the Constitutional Convention in 1787. One evening during the sessions of the convention a group of Washington's old friends from wartime days were remarking on the extraordinarily reserved and remote manner he maintained, even among his most intimate acquaintances. One of them, Gouverneur Morris, who was always full of boldness and wit, had the nerve to disagree with the rest about Washington's aloofness. He could be as familiar with Washington, he said, as with any of his other friends. Alexander Hamilton called his bluff by offering to provide a dinner with the best of wine for a dozen of them if Morris would, at the next reception Washington gave, simply walk up to him, gently slap him on the shoulder, and say, "My dear general, how happy I am to see you look so well." On the appointed evening a substantial number were already present when Morris arrived, walked up to Washington, bowed, shook hands, and then placed his left hand on Washington's shoulder and said, "My dear General, I am very happy to see you look so well." The response was immediate and icy. Washington reached up and removed the hand, stepped back, and fixed his eyes in silence on Morris, until Morris retreated abashed into the crowd. The company looked on in dismay, and no one ever tried it again.

It seems today a rather extravagant reaction on the part of our national hero, a bit of overkill. It makes us almost as embarrassed for Washington as for poor Morris. Yet it may serve as an appropriate starting

133

"Washington's genius," says Edmund S. Morgan, "lay in his understanding of power, both military and political. . . . But he accepted the premises of a Republican government as an Oliver Cromwell never did . . . [and] he never sought power on any other terms than those on which he had initially accepted it, as servant of the people." (The Metropolitan Museum of Art, Bequest of Charles Allen Munn, 1924)

place for our inquiry, because Washington's dignity and reserve, the aloofness that separated him from his contemporaries and still separates him from us, were, I believe, an integral part of the genius that enabled him to defeat the armies of Great Britain and to establish the United States as an independent world power.

Washington's genius lay in his understanding of power, both military power and political power, an understanding unmatched by that of any of his contemporaries. At a time when the United States needed nothing quite so much as military power but had very little, this hitherto obscure Virginia planter knew how to make the best possible use of what

there was. And after securing independence, when the United States was trying to establish itself in a war-torn world, he knew how to deal with foreign countries to the maximum advantage of his own. He was not a bookish man. He contributed nothing to the formal political thought of the American Revolution, nor did he produce any treatises on military strategy or tactics. But he did understand power in every form.

At the simplest level Washington's understanding of power showed itself in the ability to take command. Some men have the quality; others do not. Washington had it, and in exercising it he nourished the aloofness that became his most conspicuous trait. That aloofness was deliberate, as it may be in many men who have the gift of command. In Washington it may have grown around a nucleus of inborn native reserve, but Washington purposely cultivated it. We should not mistake it for arrogance. Washington did crave honor and pursued it relentlessly, but he did not deceive himself with that spurious substitute for honor which is arrogance. His aloofness had nothing to do with arrogance. It had to do with command.

He explained the matter in a letter to a fledgling colonel in the Continental Army in 1775: "Be easy and condescending in your deportment to your officers," he wrote, "but not too familiar, lest you subject yourself to a want of that respect, which is necessary to support a proper command."

Washington practiced what he preached, and as his talents for command developed there were fewer and fewer persons with whom he could allow himself to be familiar. As commander in chief and later as president, he could scarcely afford it with anyone. The remoteness that still surrounds him was a necessary adjunct of the power he was called upon to exercise.

But Washington's understanding of power went far beyond mere posture. Although he had not had a great deal of military experience before he took charge of the Continental Army in 1775, his participation in the French and Indian War from 1754 to

1758 had exposed him to the geographical conditions of warfare on the American continent and the way in which they must affect the exercise of military power. As commander of the revolutionary army he was quick to perceive the significance of geographical factors that his opponents seem never to have grasped. At the outset of the war, when the British almost caught him in the Battle of Long Island, he learned the danger of allowing his forces to be bottled up in any location where their retreat might be cut off. Having learned that lesson, he did not make the same mistake again. Though he was not always able to prevent his subordinates from making it, his constant alertness to it enabled him to keep his precarious army in existence. In September 1777, for example, he sent a letter on the subject to Brigadier General Thomas Nelson in Virginia. In the light of future events it was a remarkable letter. Nelson had proposed to station his forces at Hampton and Yorktown, which lay at the end of the peninsula between the James and the York rivers. Here, of course, they would be in a position to observe the movement of any British troops into the area by sea. But the location, Washington perceived at once, was one where they could be trapped, and he quickly warned Nelson against it. The troops, he said,

by being upon a [narrow] neck of land would be in danger of being cut off. The Enemy might very easily throw up a few Ships into York and James's river, as far as Queens Creek; and land a body of men there, who by throwing up a few Redoubts, would intercept their retreat and oblige them to surrender at discretion.

Four years later Lord Cornwallis made the mistake that Washington warned Nelson against, and Washington pounced. It was almost like taking candy from a child. For Cornwallis it was the world turned upside down, but for Washington it was a lesson learned long before in the geography of power.

Of course, if the British navy had been on hand in sufficient strength Cornwallis might have escaped by sea. But Washington did not move until he had the French navy to dominate the seas nearby. He had realized early in the war that without local naval superiority to stand off the British warships, he could not capture a British army at any point on the coast. Washington understood this better than his more experienced French helpers. The Comte de Grasse, in command of the French navy, seems to have missed the whole point of the Yorktown strategy, complaining to Washington that he would prefer to cruise off New York where he might encounter the main British fleet, rather than be an idle spectator in the Chesapeake. Washington knew, however, that even with de Grasse on hand, he was not strong enough to attack the main British force in New York. But by picking off Cornwallis at Yorktown he could deal the British a crippling blow.

Washington's appreciation of geographical factors made him not only wary of being trapped like Cornwallis but also averse to defending any particular point, including cities. The British armies were much more powerful than his and capable of taking any place they wanted. It was therefore not worthwhile to erect elaborate stationary defenses. When General Howe was approaching Philadelphia and Congress wanted Washington to divert troops to the preparation of fortifications for the city's defense, he refused. If he could defeat Howe in the field, he said, the defenses would be unnecessary. If he could not, then the time and labor spent on them would be lost, for the fortifications would sooner or later fall to Howe's superior forces and could then be used against the Americans. It was imperative, he believed, to keep his small force concentrated and mobile, so that he could strike effectively when opportunity presented. "It would give me infinite pleasure," he assured the Congress, "to afford protection to every individual and to every Spot of Ground on the whole of the United States." But that was not the way wars were won. Wars were won by destroying or disarming the enemy, not by trying to spare civilians from occupation. And Washington was bent on winning.

Washington, in other words, was or became a good field general. But his understanding of military power did not stop at the ability to command troops and deploy them effectively. He also understood that the power he could wield in battle depended on the willingness of the civil government to supply him with men and money. He understood the political basis of military power, and he also understood that in the new United States this was a very precarious basis. His army was the creature of a Congress that never quite dared to act like a government. Congress declared independence. It authorized the creation of the army. It even authorized the creation of a navy. But it did not attempt to levy taxes to pay for these things. Instead, it recommended to the states that they make contributions, specifying the amount for each state. Whether a state followed the recommendation depended on public opinion. And public opinion was as fickle then as now. Rumors of peace and of British surrender came with every skirmish, and each one produced a debilitating effect on the willingness of taxpayers in the different states to advance money for a war that might soon be over.

Men were almost as hard to get as the money to pay and clothe and feed them. As a result Washington was never able to build an army strong enough to face the British on even terms. At the outset of the war he had hoped to enlist soldiers for the duration. Instead, Congress provided for enlistments of a year only. It took almost that long to collect and build a disciplined fighting force, even from men who already knew how to fire a gun. By the time he had them trained, their terms would be up, and off they would go, frequently taking with them the guns he had issued them. In their place would often come raw militia on even shorter terms, men who were not used to obeying commands and who did not take kindly to them, men who were ready to head for home and tend the crops the moment they were offended by some officer's efforts to bring them in line. In 1780, after the war had dragged on for five years, Washington was still trying to get Congress to place the army on a more lasting basis. If they had done so at the beginning, he reminded them, his forces would

not have been the greatest part of the War inferior to the enemy, indebted for our safety to their inactivity, enduring frequently the mortification of seeing inviting opportunities to ruin them, pass unimproved for want of a force which the Country was completely able to afford.

Although Washington's complaints to Congress were fruitless, he never appealed over the heads of Congress to their constituents. He refrained from doing so in part because the very effort to explain the situation to the public would also have explained it to the enemy. He did not dare to advertise the weakness of his force, when the only thing between him and defeat was the fact that the enemy did not realize how weak he was. But his restraint was also based on principle. In spite of the imperious manner with which he bolstered his ability to command, Washington was a republican. He had been fully persuaded that the king of England and the minions surrounding him were conspiring to destroy the liberties of Americans. More than that, he was persuaded that kings in general were a bad lot. He welcomed Thomas Paine's devastating attack not only on George III but on monarchy itself. He never doubted that the United States must be a republic. And the principles of republican liberty as he saw them dictated that the military must be forever subordinate to the civil power. Although he could lament the short-sightedness exhibited by Congress and the state legislatures, he never even suggested that he and his army should be anything but their servants.

Washington realized that he could have commanded an immense popular following in defiance of the do-nothing Congress and that he could have counted on the backing of his officers and troops in such an adventure. But he accepted the premises of republican government as an Oliver Cromwell never did. Although it meant submitting to a body that became increasingly incompetent, irresponsible, and corrupt, he never sought power on any other terms than those on which he had initially accepted it, as servant of the people. And when his men grew exasperated with the failure of the government to feed, arm, or pay them, he stood between them and Congress and thwarted every threat against the civil power. Enlisted men mounted mutinies, and he faced them down with his steely authority. Some of his officers conspired to seize power, and he nipped the movement in the bud.

Washington was fighting not simply for independence but for an independent republic. He was fighting a people's war, and he knew that he would lose what he was fighting for if he tried to take more power than the people would freely give. One of the difficulties of republican government, as he explained later to uncomprehending foreigners, was that the people must always feel an evil before they can see it. "This," he admitted, "is productive of errors and temporary evils, but generally these evils are of a nature to work their own cure." In the end, he believed the people would do the right thing.

Washington's patience in waiting for the people to do the right thing is the more remarkable because he knew that the ineffectiveness of Congress not only prolonged the war needlessly but also exposed the country to needless perils. Because Congress lacked the nerve to vote him the needed men and money, he had to rely on assistance from the French in order to bring the war to a successful conclusion. And reliance on the French could have meant the loss of the very independence Americans were fighting for. Once French forces were engaged on the American continent, Washington feared that they would wish to invade and occupy Canada. Ostensibly the United States would be the sole beneficiary of such a move, for the French agreed to forgo any territorial claims on the continent in their treaty of alliance with the United States. But Washington had no illusions about the binding power of treaties.

Unfortunately Congress did have illusions. At the beginning of the war Americans had hoped that Canada would join them in rebellion against England, and Washington himself thought it highly desirable to eliminate this bastion of British power. He had sent an expedition to effect the liberation of the province, but the inhabitants had not responded in the manner hoped for, and the expedition was a disaster. With the arrival of French troops, congressmen developed an enthusiasm for trying again with French forces. The population of Canada was mainly French, and it was plausible to suppose that they would welcome their countrymen more warmly than they had the Americans. But Washington was alarmed. He would not have been in a position to refuse if the French had decided to employ their troops in this way, but he did not want Congress encouraging them to do so. He wrote out all the tactical reasons he could think of against the expedition and sent them in an official communication to Congress. Then he wrote out a private, confidential letter to Henry Laurens, the president of Congress, explaining his real objection. The letter remains one of the more striking examples of the quick perception of political realities that lay behind Washington's understanding of power.

The expedition, he explained to Laurens, would mean

the introduction of a large body of French troops into Canada, and putting them in possession of the capital of that Province, attached to them by all the ties of blood, habits, manners, religion and former connexions of government. I fear this would be too great a temptation to be resisted by any power actuated by the common maxims of national policy.

He went on to outline all the economic and political benefits that France would gain by holding on to the province in violation of the treaty. It would not be difficult to find a plausible pretext. The United States had borrowed funds from France on a large scale; and the United States government, if one could dignify Congress by that name, had no power to tax its citizens in order to repay the debt. The United States could scarcely object if France retained Canada as security for the payment. "Resentment, reproaches, and submission" would be the only recourse left to the United States. And Washington went on to read a gentle lecture to the gullible members of Congress: "Men are very apt," he said,

to run into extremes; hatred to England may carry some into an excess of Confidence in France; especially when motives of gratitude are thrown into the scale. Men of this description would be unwilling to suppose France capable of acting so ungenerous a part. I am heartily disposed to entertain the most favourable sentiments of our new ally and to cherish them in others to a reasonable degree; but it is a maxim founded on the universal experience of mankind, that no nation is to be trusted farther than it is bound by its interest; and no prudent statesman or politician will venture to depart from it.

☆

2

With the victory at Yorktown and the peace that followed, the United States had no further need of the military wisdom of which it had made such poor use. But Washington as a civilian was no less cogent in his understanding of power than he had been as commander in chief. His response to the postwar vicissitudes of the nation matched that of the most constructive political thinkers on the scene, and his influence may have been greater than theirs because of the enormous prestige he now carried.

The ineffectiveness of Congress that had hampered Washington's prosecution of the war continued to threaten the viability of the new republic in peacetime. Having submitted to the military loss of her mainland colonies, England set about to regain them by economic warfare, or so it seemed. In the early years of peace English merchants, offering liberal credits, sent shiploads of goods to their old customers in America, and Americans rang up a huge debt. But when Americans tried to ship their own goods to their old prewar markets in the British West Indies and elsewhere, England closed the ports to them. Before the Americans could gain new outlets for their produce many found themselves bankrupt. Washington's reaction was that power should be met with power. If England barred American ships, Americans should bar English ships until England relented. But for some states to do so and others not would defeat the strategy, and Congress had no authority to regulate trade for the whole nation. Washington supported every move to give it such authority, but at the same time he despaired of putting power in the hands of men who had demonstrated again and again their timidity in using it. What was the use of giving them more powers, he asked, when "the members seem to be so much afraid of exerting those which they already have, that no opportunity is slipped of surrendering them, or referring the exercise of them, to the States individually?"

Washington had been convinced, long before the war ended, that the national government as it operated under the Articles of Confederation was not adequate to carry out its functions; and he feared it had in effect written its own death warrant by failing to exercise what powers it had. "Extensive powers not exercised," he once observed, ". . . have I believe scarcely ever failed to ruin the possessor." But he hoped against hope that this would not be the case with the United States. When the inhabitants of western Massachusetts rose in arms against their own elected government in Shays' Rebellion, and neither the state nor the national government seemed ready to do anything about it, it looked as though the case was hopeless. Henry Lee urged Washington to use his influence to quiet the troubles, but Washington snapped back, "Influence is no Government. . . . If they have *real* grievances, redress them. . . . If they have not, employ the force of government against them at once." It was mortifying to see the new American republic exhibiting the weakness that doctrinaire European political philosophers had always attributed to republics. "How melancholy is the reflection," Washington wrote to James Madison,

that in so short a space, we should have made such large strides towards fulfilling the predictions of our transatlantic foe! 'Leave them to themselves, and their government will soon dissolve.'. . . What stronger evidence can be given of the want of energy in our governments than these disorders? If there exists not a power to check them, what security has a man for life, liberty, or property?

But the weakness of the American republic did not diminish Washington's republican ardor. He was outraged by the very idea of rebellion against a republican government, but he was also outraged by the reaction of Americans who talked without horror of substituting a monarch for the ineffective Congress. And after the Massachusetts government finally succeeded in putting down the rebels, he objected to the fact that they had been disfranchised. To deprive them of political rights was as much an abuse of power as the failure to use power effectively against them in the first place.

When Washington became the first president of the United States, he brought to the office a determination to establish what he called "a national character," by which he meant something like national reputation. It was essential, in his view, that the country gain a reputation that would oblige other countries to respect it. "We are a young Nation," he had written in 1783, "and have a character to establish. It behooves us therefore to set out right for first impressions will be lasting, indeed are all in all." And in the years that followed the winning of independence, as the power of Congress continued to wane, his great worry had been that the failure of the states to support the union would "destroy our National character, and render us as contemptible in the eyes

of Europe as we have it in our power to be respectable." With an effective national government in operation at last, it became possible to establish a proper national character, a reputation that would command respect both at home and abroad. And in his conduct of the presidency Washington bent his every effort toward that end.

He recognized that he was on trial, that the character of the government and the respect accorded it would be measured by the respect that he himself demanded and commanded. As president of a republic he aimed at an elegant simplicity in his style of living, sumptuous enough to escape any imputation of ostentatious poverty, but restrained enough to avoid outright splendor. At the same time he cultivated his characteristic aloofness, even to the point where his critics charged that his condescension smacked of monarchy.

Washington identified the national interest so closely and so personally with the new national government that he could scarcely recognize the validity of any kind of dissent. It is all too easy at the present day to see his impatience with public criticism as intolerance bordering on paranoia. But Washington had borne the brunt of a war that was needlessly prolonged because of the supineness of the central government. He had watched the nation approach the point of dissolution in the 1780s, a development that threatened everything he had fought for. And in the 1790s it was by no means clear that the new government was there to stay. If he greeted criticism with distrust, it was because domestic dissent might belie the character he was seeking to establish for his government, might return the nation to the impotence of the 1780s, might signal to the watching world the predicted collapse of the republic.

In spite of his determination to establish a strong character for the nation, Washington had no yearning for personal power, nor did he want any military adventures of the kind that so often infatuate men who are obsessed with power for its own sake. He did want the United States to grow in strength, for strength must be the ultimate basis of respect. And strength, he was sure, would not come to the United States by going to war. He had had ample experience that war was the way to poverty, and poverty meant impotence. The way for the country to grow strong, he believed, was to eschew internal dissension and steer clear of the quarrels which he saw were about to envelop the nations of Europe. The United States was encumbered with a French alliance, but as Washington read the terms of it, it did not require the United States to become involved in any quarrel that France might have with other countries, including England. And although he was grateful for the assistance received from France in the winning of American independence, he did not think that gratitude had a place in the determination of national policy. As he had pointed out some years earlier to Henry Laurens, the nation, like other nations, should not be counted on to act beyond its own interest. France in helping Americans during the Revolution had acted out of self-interest — her interest to have England weakened by loss of the colonies. Now, as Washington saw it, the main interest of the United States was to recover from the economic exhaustion incurred, however needlessly, in the Revolutionary War. The means of recovery, he thought, lay in exploiting the American land to produce as much as possible for sale to nations less fruitfully engaged in quarreling with one another.

Washington had no difficulty in persuading the new Congress or the advisers whom he appointed to his cabinet that a policy of neutrality was the way to let the United States develop its powers. But his advisers never understood the operation of the policy as well as Washington did. Jefferson was bent on making a weapon of neutrality, on wringing concessions, especially from England, in return for American neutrality. Hamilton, on the other hand, was highly conciliatory in trying to restore commercial relations with England, and went almost past the limits of neutrality in his obsession with the ideological dangers presented by the French Revolution. Although Washington was closer to Hamilton than to Jefferson, neither of the two men fully grasped the sophistication of their chief's policy for the nation.

Washington realized that the people of the United States would benefit from high prices for their agricultural exports while European farmers were distracted by war. But other than this benefit, he did not propose to take advantage of the distress of any country in order to wring concessions from it, because he was convinced that benefits thus obtained would not last. In 1791, when he was about to appoint Gouverneur Morris (he of the slap on the back) as minister to France, he warned him against seeking to obtain favorable treaties from countries in distress, "for unless," he said, "treaties are mutually beneficial to the Parties, it is in vain to hope for a continuance of them beyond the moment when the one which conceives itself to be over-reached is in a situation to break off the connexion." A treaty had to match the powers and interests of the parties making it. Otherwise it would be indeed a scrap of paper. Washington signed two treaties as president of the United States. The first one, Jay's Treaty with England, was extremely unpopular; and Washington himself did not think well of it. But he signed it because he thought that commercial relations with England would be worse with no treaty than with this one. The popular outcry against it did not move him and indeed struck him as senseless, because he believed that the United States in 1795 was not sufficiently powerful and England was not sufficiently weak to have negotiated a better treaty. And even if Jay had been able to get a better treaty, Washington thought there was no reason to suppose that it would have been better kept than the peace treaty, in which England had agreed to give up her posts in the Northwest Territory. The fact that England had not yet given up the posts and the fact that Jay had not secured any further agreement for her to give them up was no surprise to Washington. The American negotiators at the peace conference had got more from England than America's bargaining powers really entitled her to. England's retention of the northwest posts was therefore to be expected and was no reason for rejecting Jay's treaty if it might improve the commercial situation of the United States in any way.

Washington could afford to be equally calm about Pinckney's Treaty with Spain. That treaty was almost as popular with the American people as Jay's had been unpopular, and it had generally been hailed as a triumph because it secured the American right to navigate the Mississippi. Yet it merely obtained what Washington was certain the United States would get anyhow. After the Revolutionary War settlers had poured into the western country in such numbers that by 1795 Spain could not safely have denied them the right to export their produce down the Mississippi. What prompted the concession was not Pinckney's negotiating skill but the expanding American strength in the west and the strong character that Washington had conferred on the national government. Treaties, in Washington's view, were not important. What was important was power.

Washington was not a man of many talents. He had none of the range of the brilliant men around him, the intellectual curiosity of a Jefferson, the fiscal genius of a Hamilton. But in his understanding of power he left them all behind, as he did the British generals who opposed him and the French who assisted him. When he retired from the presidency after eight years, he had placed the United States on the way to achieving the power that he had aspired to for it. In the years that have followed, that power has grown until there are those who wonder whether it has been a good thing for the world. But at the time it looked like a very good thing indeed. And for better or for worse, it was the work of George Washington, the man who still keeps us all at a distance.

QUESTIONS TO CONSIDER

1   Contrast the image of George Washington with the reality of the man. In what ways does Morgan's biographical portrait demythologize Washington and restore his humanity?

2   How much credit should we give to individuals, particularly to one man — George Washington — for achieving what at first must have seemed impossible: the defeat of the most powerful army in the world, winning independence from England, and establishing a viable national government in the former colonies?

3   Do you agree with Morgan that Washington was a genius in his understanding of the use of power? On that score, how does he compare with such modern presidents as George Bush and Bill Clinton?

4   In what ways did Washington, as president, help to establish the national reputation of the new Republic? What were his greatest fears for the new nation?

5   Washington's goal as president was to make the new Republic strong. Today the United States is the most powerful country in the world. If Washington could speak to us now, what advice do you think he might offer?

VI

PATTERNS OF SOCIETY

11

The Personal Side of a Developing People

JACK LARKIN

The study of everyday life is one of the most fascinating new fields of American history. Like biography, it is firmly grounded in specific experience; it allows us to see ordinary people of the past going about the daily business of living, and it invites us to compare their patterns of behavior with our own. By allowing us to reach back and touch the people of a bygone time, and be touched by them, the new social history does much to preserve the human continuum.

The following essay focuses on broad patterns of social behavior in the young Republic. The difference between that America and ours can be astounding but so can the similarities, and you will want to note those as you read. In his narrative, Jack Larkin, chief historian of Old Sturbridge Village in Massachusetts, relies on contemporary observers of the young nation to answer several fascinating questions: What were people then really like? What did they eat and drink? What did they wear? What did they do for amusement? How did they occupy their leisure time? How did they deal with tension and stress? How did they make love?

The picture that emerges is of a vibrant, busy, contentious people who grew taller than the average European, who spat tobacco, wore dour expressions, slept in bug-ridden beds, dumped their sewage in the streets, pursued the pleasures of the flesh more than we might have imagined, and drank too much liquor. Indeed, as Larkin reports, their per capita annual consumption is estimated "at the equivalent of three and one-half gallons of pure two-hundred-proof alcohol," which prompted one historian to term it the era of "the alcoholic Republic."

Larkin also discusses customs of courtship and marriage, sexual attitudes, and instances of premarital intercourse in the era of the young Republic. As Larkin points out, Americans of the early nineteenth century "were remarkably straitlaced about sexual matters in public and eager to insist upon the 'purity' of their manners." But their actual practices were a different matter. "Bundling," the custom of allowing a premarital couple to sleep together (they were supposed to keep their clothes on), was still being practiced. Moreover, pregnancy was a frequent "prelude to marriage." In the early colonial period, 20 percent of the native-born brides were with child. In rural New England in the last decades of the eighteenth century, the figure had risen to 30 percent. As Larkin points out, "the frequency of sexual intercourse before marriage was surely higher, since some couples would have escaped early pregnancy." For "reining in the passions," health specialists such as Sylvester Graham preached sexual restraint and prescribed a strict regimen of diet and exercise to control "animal lusts." What was more, there appeared in the 1830s a new theory of female sexuality, which held that "carnal passion" was not natural in a woman. In her role as mother and "guardian of the home," the theory went, she had no interest in sex beyond bearing children. Although Larkin does not say so, this new theory of female sexuality was linked to the concomitant doctrine of "sexual spheres," which arose to justify and perpetuate the practice of segregating women in the sphere of the home and men in politics and wage-earning (this is discussed in detail in selection 22, "Women and Their Families on the Overland Trails"). Why do you suppose such theories emerged? As you study "the personal side of a developing people," note the significance of patterns of regional, ethnic, and class distinctiveness in the young Republic.

GLOSSARY

BUNDLING   The custom of allowing a premarital couple to sleep "on the same bed without undressing."

CHAMBER POTS   Saved early Americans a trip to the outhouse on cold, dark nights.

CHAMBER SETS   Matching basin and ewer (a pitcher with a wide spout) for private bathing, a cup for brushing the teeth, and a chamber pot with cover to minimize odor and spillage.

CLAPP, SUMNER G.   Minister who led a temperance campaign in Enfield, Massachusetts.

DRAMMING   Ritual of downing a glass of hard cider twice a day.

GRAHAM, SYLVESTER   Author and lecturer who preached sexual restraint and a strict regimen of diet and exercise to control physical passions; his call for dietary reform, for eating bread and water in place of animal flesh, coffee, and tea, spawned a dietary movement, the adherents to which called themselves Grahamites. The graham cracker is named after him.

HALL, MARGARET   Prominent Scottish visitor to America whose letters home complained about the bugs and filth she saw there.

MILLER–WEAVER FEUD   Protracted quarrel between two bellicose families in York, Pennsylvania.

☆
DOUR VISAGES

Contemporary observers of early-nineteenth-century America left a fragmentary but nonetheless fascinating and revealing picture of the manner in which rich and poor, Southerner and Northerner, farmer and city dweller, freeman and slave presented themselves to the world. To begin with, a wide variety of characteristic facial expressions, gestures, and ways of carrying the body reflected the extraordinary regional and social diversity of the young republic.

When two farmers met in early-nineteenth-century New England, wrote Francis Underwood, of Enfield, Massachusetts, the author of a pioneering 1893 study of small-town life, "their greeting might seem to a stranger gruff or surly, since the facial muscles were so inexpressive, while, in fact, they were on excellent terms." In courtship and marriage, countrymen and women were equally constrained, with couples "wearing all unconsciously the masks which custom had prescribed; and the onlookers who did not know the secret would think them cold and indifferent."

Underwood noted a pervasive physical as well as emotional constraint among the people of Enfield; it was rooted, he thought, not only in the self-denying ethic of their Calvinist tradition but in the nature of their work. The great physical demands of unmechanized agriculture gave New England men, like other rural Americans, a distinctively ponderous gait and posture. Despite their strength and endurance, farmers were "heavy, awkward and slouching in movement" and walked with a "slow inclination from side to side."

Yankee visages were captured by itinerant New England portraitists during the early nineteenth century, as rural storekeepers, physicians, and master craftsmen became the first more or less ordinary Americans to have their portraits done. The portraits caught their caution and immobility of expression as well as recording their angular, long-jawed features, thus creating good collective likenesses of whole communities.

The Yankees, however, were not the stiffest Americans. Even by their own impassive standards, New Englanders found New York Dutchmen and Pennsylvania German farmers "clumsy and chill" or "dull and stolid." But the "wild Irish" stood out in America for precisely the opposite reason. They were not "chill" or "stolid" enough, but loud and expansive. Their expressiveness made Anglo-Americans uncomfortable.

The seemingly uncontrolled physical energy of American blacks left many whites ill at ease. Of the slaves celebrating at a plantation ball, it was "impossible to describe the things these people did with their bodies," Frances Kemble Butler, an English-born actress who married a Georgia slave owner, observed, "and above all with their faces. . . ." Blacks' expressions and gestures, their preference for rhythmic rather than rigid bodily motion, their alternations of energy and rest made no cultural sense to observers who saw only "antics and frolics," "laziness," or "savagery." Sometimes perceived as obsequious, childlike, and dependent, or sullen and inexpressive, slaves also wore masks — not "all unconsciously" as Northern farm folk did, but as part of their self-protective strategies for controlling what masters, mistresses, and other whites could know about their feelings and motivations.

American city dwellers, whose daily routines were driven by the quicker pace of commerce, were easy to distinguish from "heavy and slouching" farmers attuned to slow seasonal rhythms. New Yorkers, in particular, had already acquired their own characteristic body language. The clerks and commercial men

Country revelers at a quilting "frolic" in the days of the early Republic. This 1813 painting, by German-born John Lewis Krimmel, is conspicuous for its fine detail and racial contrasts. Notice how well dressed the newly arrived whites are in comparison with the fiddler. Krimmel's comic portrayal marked the start of an al- *most constant popular association of blacks with music and music making. It also contributed to the development of degrading racial stereotypes: note that both the fiddler and the serving girl have toothy grins and oversized red lips. (Courtesy The Henry Francis duPont Winterthur Museum)*

who crowded Broadway, intent on their business, had a universal "contraction of the brow, knitting of the eyebrows, and compression of the lips . . . and a hurried walk." It was a popular American saying in the 1830s, reported Frederick Marryat, an Englishman who traveled extensively in the period, that "a New York merchant always walks as if he had a good dinner before him, and a bailiff behind him."

Northern and Southern farmers and city merchants alike, to say nothing of Irishmen and blacks, fell well short of the standard of genteel "bodily carriage" enshrined in both English and American etiquette books and the instructions of dancing masters: "flexibility in the arms . . . erectness in the spinal column . . . easy carriage of the head." It was the ideal of the British aristocracy, and Southern planters came closest to it, expressing the power of their class in the way they stood and moved. Slave owners accustomed to command, imbued with an ethic of honor and pride, at ease in the saddle, carried themselves more gracefully than men hardened by toil or preoccupied with commerce. Visiting Washington in 1835, the Englishwoman Harriet Martineau contrasted not the politics but the postures of Northern and Southern congressmen. She marked the confident bearing, the "ease and frank courtesy . . . with an occasional touch of arrogance" of the slaveholders alongside the "cautious . . . and too deferential air of the members of the North." She could recognize a New Englander "in the open air," she claimed, "by his deprecatory walk."

Local inhabitants' faces became more open, travelers observed, as one went west. Nathaniel Hawthorne found a dramatic contrast in public appearances only a few days' travel west of Boston. "The people out here," in New York State just west of the Berkshires, he confided to his notebook in 1839, "show out their character much more strongly than they do with us," in his native eastern Massachusetts. He compared the "quiet, silent, dull decency . . . in our public assemblages" with Westerners' wider gamut of expressiveness, "mirth, anger, eccentricity, all showing themselves freely." Westerners in general, the clergyman and publicist Henry Ward Beecher observed, had "far more freedom of manners, and more frankness and spontaneous geniality" than did the city or country people of the New England and Middle Atlantic states, as did the "odd mortals that wander in from the western border," that Martineau observed in Washington's political population.

☆

A Pungent Folk

Early-nineteenth-century Americans lived in a world of dirt, insects, and pungent smells. Farmyards were strewn with animal wastes, and farmers wore manure-spattered boots and trousers everywhere. Men's and women's working clothes alike were often stiff with dirt and dried sweat, and men's shirts were often stained with "yellow rivulets" of tobacco juice. The locations of privies were all too obvious on warm or windy days. Unemptied chamber pots advertised their presence. Wet baby "napkins," today's diapers, were not immediately washed but simply put by the fire to dry. Vats of "chamber lye" — highly concentrated urine used for cleaning type or degreasing wool — perfumed all printing offices and many households. "The breath of that fiery barroom," as Underwood described a country tavern, "was overpowering. The odors of the hostlers' boots, redolent of fish-oil and tallow, and of buffalo-robes and horse-blankets, the latter reminiscent of equine ammonia, almost got the better of the all-pervading fumes of spirits and tobacco."

Densely populated, but poorly cleaned and drained, America's cities were often far more noisome than its farmyards. Horse manure thickly covered city streets, and few neighborhoods were free from the spreading stench of tanneries and slaughterhouses. New York City accumulated so much refuse that it was generally believed the actual surfaces of the streets had not been seen for decades. During her stay in Cincinnati, the English writer Frances Trollope followed the practice of the vast majority of American city housewives when she threw her household "slops" — refuse food and dirty dishwater — out into the street. An irate neighbor soon informed her that municipal ordinances forbade "throwing such things at the sides of the streets" as she had done; "they must just all be cast right into the middle and the pigs soon takes them off." In most cities hundreds, sometimes thousands, of free-roaming pigs scavenged the garbage; one exception was Charleston, South Carolina, where buzzards patrolled the streets. By converting garbage into pork, pigs kept city streets cleaner than they would otherwise have been, but the pigs themselves befouled the streets and those who ate their meat — primarily poor families — ran greater than usual risks of infection.

☆

PRIVY MATTERS

The most visible symbols of early American sanitation were privies or "necessary houses." But Americans did not always use them; many rural householders simply took to the closest available patch of woods or brush. However, in more densely settled communities and in regions with cold winters, privies were in widespread use. They were not usually put in out-of-the-way locations. The fashion of some Northern farm families, according to Robert B. Thomas's *Farmer's Almanack* in 1826, had long been to have their "necessary planted in a garden or other conspicuous place." Other countryfolk went even further in turning human wastes to agricultural account and built their outhouses "within the territory of a hog yard, that the swine may root and ruminate and devour the nastiness thereof." Thomas was a long-standing critic of primitive manners in the countryside and roundly condemned these traditional sanitary arrangements as demonstrating a "want of taste, decency, and propriety." The better arranged necessaries of the prosperous emptied into vaults that could be opened and cleaned out. The dripping horse-drawn carts of the "nocturnal goldfinders," who emptied the vaults and took their loads out for burial or water disposal — "night soil" was almost never used as manure — were a familiar part of nighttime traffic on city streets.

The humblest pieces of American household furniture were the chamber pots that allowed people to avoid dark and often cold nighttime journeys outdoors. Kept under beds or in corners of rooms, "chambers" were used primarily upon retiring and arising. Collecting, emptying, and cleaning them remained an unspoken, daily part of every housewife's routine.

Nineteenth-century inventory takers became considerably more reticent about naming chamber pots than their predecessors, usually lumping them with miscellaneous "crockery," but most households probably had a couple of chamber pots; genteel families reached the optimum of one for each bedchamber. English-made ceramic pots had become cheap enough by 1820 that few American families within the reach of commerce needed to go without one. "Without a pot to piss in" was a vulgar tag of long standing for extreme poverty; those poorest households without one, perhaps more common in the warm South, used the outdoors at all times and seasons.

The most decorous way for householders to deal with chamber-pot wastes accumulated during the night was to throw them down the privy hole. But more casual and unsavory methods of disposal were still in wide use. Farm families often dumped their chamber pots out the most convenient door or window. In densely settled communities like York, Pennsylvania, the results could be more serious. In 1801, the York diarist Lewis Miller drew and then described an event in North George Street when "Mr. Day an English man [as the German-American Miller was quick to point out] had a bad practice by pouring out of the upper window his filthiness . . . one day came the discharge . . . on a man and wife going to a wedding, her silk dress was fouled."

☆

LETTING THE BEDBUGS BITE

Sleeping accommodations in American country taverns were often dirty and insect-ridden. The eighteenth-century observer of American life Isaac Weld saw "filthy beds swarming with bugs" in 1794; in 1840 [English novelist] Charles Dickens noted "a sort of game not on the bill of fare." Complaints increased in intensity as travelers went south or west. Tavern beds were uniquely vulnerable to infestation by whatever insect guests travelers brought with them. The bedding of most American households was surely less foul. Yet it was dirty enough. New England farmers were still too often "tormented all night by bed bugs," complained *The Farmer's Almanack* in 1837, and books of domestic advice contained extensive instructions on removing them from feather beds and straw ticks.

Journeying between Washington and New Orleans in 1828, Margaret Hall, a well-to-do and cultivated Scottish woman, became far more familiar with intimate insect life than she had ever been in the genteel houses of London or Edinburgh. Her letters home, never intended for publication, gave a graphic and unsparing account of American sanitary conditions. After sleeping in a succession of beds with the "usual complement of fleas and bugs," she and her party had themselves become infested: "We bring them along with us in our clothes and when I undress I find them crawling on my skin, nasty wretches." New and distasteful to her, such discoveries were commonplace among the ordinary folk with whom she lodged. The American children she saw on her Southern journey were "kept in such a state of filth," with clothes "dirty and slovenly to a degree," but this was "nothing in comparison with their heads . . . [which] are absolutely crawling!" In New Orleans she observed women picking through children's heads for lice, "catching them according to the method depicted in an engraving of a similar proceeding in the streets of Naples."

☆

BIRTH OF THE BATH

Americans were not "clean and decent" by today's standards, and it was virtually impossible that they should be. The furnishings and use of rooms in most American houses made more than the most elementary washing difficult. In a New England farmer's household, wrote Underwood, each household member would "go down to the 'sink' in the lean-to, next to the kitchen, fortunate if he had not to break ice in order to wash his face and hands, or more fortunate if a little warm water was poured into his basin from the kettle swung over the kitchen fire." Even in the comfortable household of the prominent minister Lyman Beecher in Litchfield, Connecticut, around 1815, all family members washed in the kitchen, using a stone sink and "a couple of basins."

Southerners washing in their detached kitchens or, like Westerners in warm weather, washed outside, "at the doors . . . or at the wells" of their houses. Using basins and sinks outdoors or in full view of others, most Americans found anything more than "washing the face and hands once a-day," usually in cold water, difficult, even unthinkable. Most men and women also washed without soap, reserving it for laundering clothes; instead they used a brisk rubbing with a coarse towel to scrub the dirt off their skins.

Gradually the practice of complete bathing spread beyond the topmost levels of American society and into smaller towns and villages. This became possible as families moved washing equipment out of kitchens and into bedchambers, from shared space to space that could be made private. As more prosperous households furnished one or two of their chambers with washing equipment — a washstand, a basin, and a ewer, or large-mouthed pitcher — family members could shut the chamber door, undress, and wash themselves completely. The daughters of the Larcom family, living in Lowell, Massachusetts, in the late 1830s, began to bathe in a bedchamber in this way; Lucy Larcom described how her oldest sister started to take "a full cold bath every morning before she went to her work . . . in a room without a fire," and the other young Larcoms "did the same whenever we could be resolute enough." By the 1830s better city hotels and even some country taverns were providing individual basins and pitchers in their rooms.

At a far remove from "primitive manners" and "bad practices" was the genteel ideal of domestic sanitation embodied in the "chamber sets" — matching basin and ewer for private bathing, a cup for brushing the teeth, and a chamber pot with cover to minimize odor and spillage — that American stores were beginning to stock. By 1840 a significant minority of American households owned chamber sets and washstands to hold them in their bedchambers. For a handful there was the very faint dawning of an entirely new age of sanitary arrangements. In 1829 the new Tremont House hotel in Boston offered its patrons indoor plumbing: eight chambers with bathtubs and eight "water closets." In New York City and Philadelphia, which had developed rudimentary public water systems, a few wealthy households had water taps and, more rarely, water closets by the 1830s. For all others flush toilets and bathtubs remained far in the future.

The American people moved very slowly toward cleanliness. In "the backcountry at the present day," commented the fastidious author of the *Lady's Book* in 1836, custom still "requires that everyone should wash at the pump in the yard, or at the sink in the kitchen." Writing in 1846, the physician and health reformer William Alcott rejoiced that to "wash the surface of the whole body in water daily" had now been accepted as a genteel standard of personal cleanliness. But, he added, there were "multitudes who pass for models of neatness and cleanliness, who do not perform this work for themselves half a dozen times — nay once — a year." As the better-off became cleaner than ever before, the poor stayed dirty.

☆

Besotted Era

In the early part of the century America was a bawdy, hard-edged, and violent land. We drank more than we ever had before or ever would again. We smoked and chewed tobacco like addicts and fought and quarreled on the flimsiest pretexts. The tavern was the most important gateway to the primarily male world of drink and disorder: in sight of the village church in most American communities, observed Daniel Drake, a Cincinnati physician who wrote a reminiscence of his Kentucky boyhood, stood the village tavern, and the two structures "did in fact represent two great opposing principles."

The great majority of American men in every region were taverngoers. The printed street directories of American cities listed tavernkeepers in staggering numbers, and even the best-churched parts of New England could show more "licensed houses" than meetinghouses. In 1827 the fast-growing city of Rochester, New York, with a population of approximately eight thousand, had nearly one hundred establishments licensed to sell liquor, or one for every eighty inhabitants.

America's most important centers of male sociability, taverns were often the scene of excited gaming and vicious fights and always of hard drinking, heavy smoking, and an enormous amount of alcohol-stimulated talk. City men came to their neighborhood taverns daily, and "tavern haunting, tippling, and gaming," as Samuel Goodrich, a New England historian and publisher, remembered, "were the chief resources of men in the dead and dreary winter months" in the countryside.

City taverns catered to clienteles of different classes: sordid sailors' grog-shops near the waterfront were rife with brawling and prostitution; neighborhood taverns and liquor-selling groceries were visited by craftsmen and clerks; well-appointed and relatively decorous places were favored by substantial merchants. Taverns on busy highways often specialized in teamsters or stage passengers, while country inns took their patrons as they came.

Taverns accommodated women as travelers, but their barroom clienteles were almost exclusively male. Apart from the dockside dives frequented by prostitutes, or the liquor-selling groceries of poor city neighborhoods, women rarely drank in public.

Gambling was a substantial preoccupation for many male citizens of the early republic. Men played billiards at tavern tables for money stakes. They threw dice in "hazard," slamming the dice boxes down so hard and so often that tavern tables wore the characteristic scars of their play. Even more often Americans sat down to cards, playing brag, similar to modern-day poker, or an elaborate table game called faro. Outdoors they wagered with each other on horse races or bet on cockfights and wrestling matches.

Drink permeated and propelled the social world of early-nineteenth-century America — first as an unquestioned presence and later as a serious and divisive problem. "Liquor at that time," recalled the builder and architect Elbridge Boyden, "was used as commonly as the food we ate." Before 1820 the vast majority of Americans considered alcohol an essential stimulant to exertion as well as a symbol of hospitality and fellowship. Like the Kentuckians with whom Daniel Drake grew up, they "regarded it as a duty to their families and visitors ... to keep the bottle well replenished." Weddings, funerals, frolics, even a casual "gathering of two or three neighbors for an evening's social chat" required the obligatory "spirituous liquor" — rum, whiskey, or gin — "at all seasons and on all occasions."

Northern householders drank hard cider as their common table beverage, and all ages drank it freely. Dramming — taking a fortifying glass in the forenoon and again in the afternoon — was part of the daily regimen of many men. Clergymen took sustaining libations between services, lawyers before going to court, and physicians at their patients' bedsides. To raise a barn or get through a long day's haying without fortifying drink seemed a virtual impossibility. Slaves enjoyed hard drinking at festival times and at Saturday-night barbecues as much as any of their countrymen. But of all Americans they probably drank the least on a daily basis because their masters could usually control their access to liquor.

In Parma, Ohio, in the mid–1820s, Lyndon Freeman, a farmer, and his brothers were used to seeing men "in their cups" and passed them by without comment. But one dark and rainy night they discovered something far more shocking, "nothing less than a *woman beastly drunk* ... with a flask of whiskey by her side." American women drank as well as men, but usually much less heavily. They were more likely to make themselves "tipsy" with hard cider and alcohol-containing patent medicines than to become inebriated with rum or whiskey. Temperance advocates in the late 1820s estimated that men consumed fifteen times the volume of distilled spirits that women did; this may have been a considerable exaggeration, but there was a great difference in drinking habits between the sexes. Americans traditionally found drunkenness tolerable and forgivable in men but deeply shameful in women.

By almost any standard, Americans drank not only nearly universally but in large quantities. Their yearly consumption at the time of the Revolution has been estimated at the equivalent of three and one-half gallons of pure two-hundred-proof alcohol for each person. After 1790 American men began to drink even more. By the late 1820s their imbibing had risen to an all-time high of almost four gallons per capita.

Along with drinking went fighting. Americans fought often and with great relish. York, Pennsylvania, for example, was a peaceable place as American communities went, but the Miller and Weaver families had a long-running quarrel. It had begun in 1800 when the Millers found young George Weaver stealing apples in their yard and punished him by "throwing him over the fence," injuring him painfully. Over the years hostilities broke out periodically. Lewis Miller remembered walking down the street as a teenaged boy and meeting Mrs. Weaver, who drenched him with the bucket of water she was carrying. He retaliated by "turning about and giving her a kick, laughing at her, this is for your politeness." Other York households had their quarrels too; in "a general fight on Beaver Street," Mistress Hess and Mistress Forsch tore each

LIFE IN AN AMERICAN HOTEL?

This British cartoon suggests the American propensity to violence in a hard-edged, hard-drinking era, when people fought often and with relish. Perhaps the irritable fellow with the gun spent a sleepless night battling the hotel's bed bugs. (Punch, June 28, 1856)

other's caps from their heads. Their husbands and then the neighbors interfered, and "all of them had a knock down."

When Peter Lung's wife, Abigail, refused "to get up and dig some potatoes" for supper from the yard of their small house, the Hartford, Connecticut, laborer recalled in his confession, he "kicked her on the side . . . then gave her a violent push" and went out to dig the potatoes himself. He returned and "again kicked her against the shoulder and neck." Both had been drinking, and loud arguments and blows within the Lung household, as in many others, were routine. But this time the outcome was not. Alice Lung was dead the next day, and Peter Lung was arrested, tried, and hanged for murder in 1815.

In the most isolated, least literate and commercialized parts of the United States, it was "by no means uncommon," wrote Isaac Weld, "to meet with those who have lost an eye in a combat, and there are men who pride themselves upon the dexterity with

which they can scoop one out. This is called *gouging*."

☆

PUBLIC PUNISHMENT

The penal codes of the American states were far less bloodthirsty than those of England. Capital punishment was not often imposed on whites for crimes other than murder. Yet at the beginning of the nineteenth century many criminal offenses were punished by the public infliction of pain and suffering. "The whipping post and stocks stood on the green near the meetinghouse" in most of the towns of New England and near courthouses everywhere. In Massachusetts before 1805 a counterfeiter was liable to have an ear cut off, and a forger to have one cropped or partially amputated, after spending an hour in the pillory. A criminal convicted of manslaughter was set up on the gallows to have his forehead branded with a letter M. In most jurisdictions town officials flogged petty thieves as punishment for their crime. In New Haven, Connecticut, around 1810, Charles Fowler, a local historian, recalled seeing the "admiring students of [Yale] college" gathered around to watch petty criminals receive "five or ten lashes . . . with a rawhide whip."

Throughout the United States public hangings brought enormous crowds to the seats of justice and sometimes seemed like brutal festivals. Thousands of spectators arrived to pack the streets of courthouse towns. On the day of a hanging near Mount Holly, New Jersey, in the 1820s, the scene was that of a holiday: "around the place in every direction were the assembled multitudes — some in tents, and by-wagons, engaged in gambling and other vices of the sort, in open day." In order to accommodate the throngs, hangings were usually held not in the public square but on the outskirts of town. The gallows erected on a hill or set up at the bottom of a natural amphitheater allowed onlookers an unobstructed

153

view. A reprieve or stay of execution might disappoint a crowd intent on witnessing the deadly drama and provoke a riot, as it did in Pembroke, New Hampshire, in 1834.

☆

RISE OF
RESPECTABILITY

At a drunkard's funeral in Enfield, Massachusetts, in the 1830s — the man had strayed out of the road while walking home and fallen over a cliff, "his stiffened fingers still grasping the handle of the jug" — Rev. Sumner G. Clapp, the Congregationalist minister of Enfield, mounted a log by the woodpile and preached the town's first temperance sermon before a crowd full of hardened drinkers. In this way Clapp began a campaign to "civilize" the manners of his parishioners, and "before many years there was a great change in the town; the incorrigible were removed by death, and others took warning." Drinking declined sharply, and along with it went "a general reform in conduct."

Although it remained a powerful force in many parts of the United States, the American way of drunkenness began to lose ground as early as the mid–1820s. The powerful upsurge in liquor consumption had provoked a powerful reaction, an unprecedented attack on all forms of drink that gathered momentum in the Northeast. Some New England clergymen had been campaigning in their own communities as early as 1810, but their concerns took on organized impetus with the founding of the American Temperance Society in 1826. Energized in part by a concern for social order, in part by evangelical piety, temperance reformers popularized a radically new way of looking at alcohol. The "good creature" became "demon rum"; prominent physicians and writers on physiology, like Benjamin Rush, told Americans that alcohol, traditionally considered healthy and fortifying, was actually a physical

and moral poison. National and state societies distributed anti-liquor tracts, at first calling for moderation in drink but increasingly demanding total abstinence from alcohol.

To a surprising degree these aggressive temperance campaigns worked. By 1840 the consumption of alcohol had declined by more than two-thirds, from close to four gallons per person each year to less than one and one-half. Country storekeepers gave up the sale of spirits, local authorities limited the number of tavern licenses, and farmers even abandoned hard cider and cut down their apple orchards. The shift to temperance was a striking transformation in the everyday habits of an enormous number of Americans. "A great, though silent change," in Horace Greeley's words, had been "wrought in public sentiment." . . .

Closely linked as they were to drink, such diversions as gambling, racing, and blood sports also fell to the same forces of change. In the central Massachusetts region that George Davis, a lawyer in Sturbridge, knew well, until 1820 or so gaming had "continued to prevail, more and more extensively." After that "a blessed change had succeeded," overturning the scenes of high-stakes dice and card games that he knew in his young manhood. Impelled by a new perception of its "pernicious effects," local leaders gave it up and placed "men of respectable standing" firmly in opposition. Racecourses were abandoned and "planted to corn." Likewise, "bearbaiting, cock-fighting, and other cruel amusements" began to dwindle in the Northern countryside. Elsewhere the rude life of the tavern and "cruel amusements" remained widespread, but some of their excesses of "sin and shame" did diminish gradually.

Over the first four decades of the nineteenth century the American people increasingly made churchgoing an obligatory ritual. The proportion of families affiliated with a local church or Methodist circuit rose dramatically, particularly after 1820, and there were fewer stretches of the wholly pagan, unchurched territory that travelers had noted around

1800. "Since 1830," maintained Emerson Davis in his retrospect of America, *The Half Century,* "... the friends of the Sabbath have been gaining ground. ... In 1800, good men slumbered over the desecration of the Sabbath. They have since awoke...." The number of Sunday mails declined, and the campaign to eliminate the delivery of mail on the Sabbath entirely grew stronger. "In the smaller cities and towns," wrote Mrs. Trollope in 1832, worship and "prayer meetings" had come to "take the place of almost all other amusements." There were still communities near the edge of settlement where a traveler would "rarely find either churches or chapels, prayer or preacher," but it was the working-class neighborhoods of America's larger cities that were increasingly the chief strongholds of "Sunday dissipation" and "Sabbath-breaking."

Whipping and the pillory, with their attentive audiences, began to disappear from the statute book, to be replaced by terms of imprisonment in another new American institution, the state penitentiary. Beginning with Pennsylvania's abolition of flogging in 1790 and Massachusetts's elimination of mutilating punishments in 1805, several American states gradually accepted John Hancock's view of 1796 that "mutilating or lacerating the body" was less an effective punishment than "an indignity to human nature." Connecticut's town constables whipped petty criminals for the last time in 1828.

Slaveholding states were far slower to change their provisions for public punishment. The whipping and mutilation of blacks may have become a little less ferocious over the decades, but the whip remained the essential instrument of punishment and discipline. "The secret of our success," thought a slave owner, looking back after emancipation, had been "the great motive power contained in that little instrument." Delaware achieved notoriety by keeping flogging on the books for whites and blacks alike through most of the twentieth century.

Although there were important stirrings of sentiment against capital punishment, all American states continued to execute convicted murderers before the mid–1840s. Public hangings never lost their drawing power. But a number of American public officials began to abandon the long-standing view of executions as instructive communal rituals. They saw the crowd's holiday mood and eager participation as sharing too much in the condemned killer's own brutality. Starting with Pennsylvania, New York, and Massachusetts in the mid-1830s, several state legislatures voted to take executions away from the crowd, out of the public realm. Sheriffs began to carry out death sentences behind the walls of the jailyard, before a small assembly of representative onlookers. Other states clung much longer to tradition and continued public executions into the twentieth century.

☆

SEX LIFE
OF THE NATIVES

Early-nineteenth-century Americans were more licentious than we ordinarily imagine them to be.

"On the 20th day of July" in 1830, Harriet Winter, a young woman working as a domestic in Joseph Dunham's household in Brimfield, Massachusetts, "was gathering raspberries" in a field west of the house. "Near the close of day," Charles Phelps, a farm laborer then living in the town, "came to the field where she was," and in the gathering dusk they made love — and, Justice of the Peace Asa Lincoln added in his account, "it was the Sabbath." American communities did not usually document their inhabitants' amorous rendezvous, and Harriet's tryst with Charles was a commonplace event in early-nineteenth-century America. It escaped historical oblivion because she was unlucky, less in becoming pregnant than in Charles's refusal to marry her. Asa Lincoln did not approve of Sabbath evening indiscretions, but he was not pursuing Harriet for immorality. He was concerned instead with economic responsibility for the child. Thus he interrogated Harriet about the baby's father — while she was in labor, as was the long-customary practice — in order to force Charles to contribute to the maintenance of the child, who was going to be "born a bastard and chargeable to the town."

Some foreign travelers found that the Americans they met were reluctant to admit that such things happened in the United States. They were remarkably straitlaced about sexual matters in public and eager to insist upon the "purity" of their manners. But to take such protestations at face value, the unusually candid Englishman Frederick Marryat thought, would be "to suppose that human nature is not the same everywhere."

The well-organized birth and marriage records of a number of American communities reveal that in late-eighteenth-century America pregnancy was frequently the prelude to marriage. The proportion of brides who were pregnant at the time of their weddings had been rising since the late seventeenth century and peaked in the turbulent decades during and after the Revolution. In the 1780s and 1790s nearly one-third of rural New England's brides were already with child. The frequency of sexual intercourse before marriage was surely higher, since some couples would have escaped early pregnancy. For many couples sexual relations were part of serious courtship. Premarital pregnancies in late-eighteenth century Dedham, Massachusetts, observed the local historian Erastus Worthington in 1828, were occasioned by "the custom then prevalent of females admitting young men to their beds, who sought their company in marriage."

Pregnancies usually simply accelerated a marriage that would have taken place in any case, but community and parental pressure worked strongly to assure it. Most rural communities simply accepted the "early" pregnancies that marked so many marriages, although in Hingham, Massachusetts, tax records suggest that the families of well-to-do brides were considerably less generous to couples who had had "early babies" than to those who had avoided pregnancy.

"Bundling very much abounds," wrote the anonymous author of "A New Bundling Song," still circulating in Boston in 1812, "in many parts in country towns." Noah Webster's first Dictionary of the American Language defined it as the custom that allowed couples "to sleep on the same bed without undressing" — with, a later commentator added, "the shared understanding that innocent endearments should not be exceeded." Folklore and local tradition, from Maine south to New York, had American mothers tucking bundling couples into bed with special chastity-protecting garments for the young woman or a "bundling board" to separate them.

In actuality, if bundling had been intended to allow courting couples privacy and emotional intimacy but not sexual contact, it clearly failed. Couples may have begun with bundling, but as courtship advanced, they clearly pushed beyond its restraints, like the "bundling maid" in "A New Bundling Song" who would "sometimes say when she lies down/She can't be cumbered with a gown."

Young black men and women shared American whites' freedom in courtship and sexuality and sometimes exceeded it. Echoing the cultural traditions of West Africa, and reflecting the fact that their marriages were not given legal status and security, slave communities were somewhat more tolerant and accepting of sex before marriage.

Gradations of color and facial features among the slaves were testimony that "thousands," as the abolitionist and former slave Frederick Douglass wrote, were "ushered into the world annually, who, like myself, owe the existence to white fathers, and those fathers most frequently their own masters." Sex crossed the boundaries of race and servitude more often than slavery's defenders wanted to admit, if less frequently than the most outspoken abolitionists claimed. Slave women had little protection from whatever sexual demands masters or overseers might make, so that rapes, short liaisons, and long-term "concubinage" all were part of plantation life.

As Nathaniel Hawthorne stood talking with a group of men on the porch of a tavern in Augusta, Maine, in 1836, a young man "in a laborer's dress" came up and asked if anyone knew the whereabouts of Mary Ann Russell. "Do you want to use her?" asked one of the bystanders. Mary Ann was, in fact, the young laborer's wife, but she had left him and their child in Portland to become "one of a knot of whores." A few years earlier the young men of York, Pennsylvania, made up a party for "overturning and pulling to the ground" Eve Geese's "shameful house" of prostitution in Queen Street. The frightened women fled out the back door as the chimney collapsed around them; the apprentices and young journeymen — many of whom had surely been previous customers — were treated by local officials "to wine, for the good work."

From medium-sized towns like Augusta and York to great cities, poor American women were sometimes pulled into a darker, harsher sexual world, one of vulnerability, exploitation, and commerce. Many prostitutes took up their trade out of poverty and domestic disaster. A young widow or a country girl arrived in the city and, thrown on her own resources, often faced desperate economic choices because most women's work paid too poorly to provide decent food, clothing, and shelter, while other women sought excitement and independence from their families.

As cities grew, and changes in transportation involved more men in long-distance travel, prostitution became more visible. Men of all ages, married and unmarried, from city lawyers to visiting country storekeepers to sailors on the docks, turned to brothels for sexual release, but most of the customers were young men, living away from home and unlikely to marry until their late twenties. Sexual commerce in New York City was elaborately graded by price and the economic status of clients, from the "parlor houses" situated not far from the city's best hotels on Broadway to the more numerous and moderately priced houses that drew artisans and clerks, and finally to the broken and dissipated women who haunted dockside grogshops in the Five Points neighborhood.

From New Orleans to Boston, city theaters were important sexual marketplaces. Men often bought tickets less to see the performance than to make assignations with the prostitutes, who sat by custom in the topmost gallery of seats. The women usually received free admission from theater managers, who claimed that they could not stay in business without the male theatergoers drawn by the "guilty third tier."

Most Americans — and the American common law — still did not regard abortion as a crime until the fetus had "quickened" or began to move perceptibly in the womb. Books of medical advice actually contained prescriptions for bringing on delayed menstrual periods, which would also produce an abortion if the woman happened to be pregnant. They suggested heavy doses of purgatives that created violent cramps, powerful douches, or extreme kinds of physical activity, like the "violent exercise, raising great weights ... strokes on the belly ... [and] falls" noted in William Buchan's *Domestic Medicine,* a manual read widely through the 1820s. Women's folklore echoed most of these prescriptions and added others, particularly the use of two American herbal preparations — savin, or the extract of juniper berries, and Seneca snakeroot — as abortion-producing drugs. They were dangerous procedures but sometimes effective.

☆

REINING IN
THE PASSIONS

Starting at the turn of the nineteenth century, the sexual lives of many Americans began to change, shaped by a growing insistence on control: reining in the passions in courtship, limiting family size, and even redefining male and female sexual desire.

Bundling was already on the wane in rural America before 1800; by the 1820s it was written about as a rare and antique custom. It had ceased, thought an elderly man from East Haddam, Connecticut, "as a consequence of education and refinement." Decade by decade the proportion of young women who had conceived a child before marriage declined. In most of the towns of New England the rate had dropped from nearly one pregnant bride in three to one in five or six by 1840; in some places prenuptial pregnancy dropped to 5 percent. For many young Americans this marked the acceptance of new limits on sexual behavior, imposed not by their parents or other authorities in their communities but by themselves.

These young men and women were not more closely supervised by their parents than earlier generations had been; in fact, they had more mobility and greater freedom. The couples that courted in the new style put a far greater emphasis on control of the passions. For some of them — young Northern merchants and professional men and their intended brides — revealing love letters have survived for the years after 1820. Their intimate correspondence reveals that they did not give up sexual expression but gave it new boundaries, reserving sexual intercourse for marriage. Many of them were marrying later than their parents, often living through long engagements while the husband-to-be strove to establish his place in the world. They chose not to risk a pregnancy that would precipitate them into an early marriage.

Many American husbands and wives were also breaking with tradition as they began to limit the size of their families. Clearly, married couples were renegotiating the terms of their sexual lives together, but they remained resolutely silent about how they did it. In the first two decades of the nineteenth century, they almost certainly set about avoiding childbirth through abstinence, coitus interruptus, or male withdrawal, and perhaps sometimes abortion. These contraceptive techniques had long been traditional in preindustrial Europe, although previously little used in America.

As they entered the 1830s, Americans had their first opportunity to learn, at least in print, about more effective or less self-denying forms of birth control. They could read reasonably inexpensive editions of the first works on contraception published in the United States: Robert Dale Owen's *Moral Physiology* of 1831 and Dr. Charles Knowlton's *The Fruits of Philosophy* of 1832. Both authors frankly described the full range of contraceptive techniques, although they solemnly rejected physical intervention in the sexual act and recommended only douching after intercourse and coitus interruptus. Official opinion, legal and religious, was deeply hostile. Knowlton, who had trained as a physician in rural Massachusetts, was prosecuted in three different counties for obscenity, convicted once, and imprisoned for three months.

But both works found substantial numbers of Americans eager to read them. By 1839 each book had gone through nine editions, putting a combined total of twenty to thirty thousand copies in circulation. An American physician could write in 1850 that contraception had "been of late years so much talked of." Greater knowledge about contraception surely played a part in the continuing decline of the American birthrate after 1830.

New ways of thinking about sexuality emerged that stressed control and channeling of the passions. Into the 1820s almost all Americans would have subscribed to the commonplace notion that sex, within proper social confines, was enjoyable and healthy and that prolonged sexual abstinence could be injurious to health. They also would have assumed that women had powerful sexual drives.

Starting with his "Lecture to Young Men on Chastity" in 1832, Sylvester Graham articulated very different counsels about health and sex. Sexual indulgence, he argued, was not only morally suspect but psychologically and physiologically risky. The sexual overstimulation involved in young men's lives produced anxiety and nervous disorders, "a shocking state of debility and excessive irritability." The remedy was diet, exercise, and a regular routine that pulled the mind away from animal lusts. Medical writings that discussed the evils of masturbation, or "solitary vice," began to appear. Popular books of advice, like William Alcott's *Young Man's Guide,* gave similar warnings. They tried to persuade young men that their health could be ruined, and their prospects for success darkened, by consorting with prostitutes or becoming sexually entangled before marriage.

A new belief about women's sexual nature appeared, one that elevated them above "carnal passion." Many American men and women came to believe during the nineteenth century that in their true and proper nature as mothers and guardians of the home, women were far less interested in sex than men were. Women who defined themselves as passionless were in a strong position to control or deny men's sexual demands either during courtship or in limiting their childbearing within marriage.

Graham went considerably farther than this, advising restraint not only in early life and courtship but in marriage itself. It was far healthier, he maintained, for couples to have sexual relations "very seldom."

Neither contraception nor the new style of courtship had become anything like universal by 1840. Prenuptial pregnancy rates had fallen, but they remained high enough to indicate that many couples simply continued in familiar ways. American husbands and wives in the cities and the Northern countryside were limiting the number of their children, but it was clear that those living on the farms of the West or in the slave quarters had not yet begun to. There is strong evidence that many American women felt far from passionless, although others restrained or renounced their sexuality. For many

people in the United States, there had been a profound change. Reining in the passions had become part of everyday life.

☆

SMOKING AND SPITTING

"Everyone smokes and some chew in America," wrote Isaac Weld in 1795. Americans turned tobacco, a new and controversial stimulant at the time of colonial settlement, into a crucially important staple crop and made its heavy use a commonplace — and a never-ending source of surprise and indignation to visitors. Tobacco use spread in the United States because it was comparatively cheap, a home-grown product free from the heavy import duties levied on it by European governments. A number of slave rations described in plantation documents included "one hand of tobacco per month." Through the eighteenth century most American smokers used clay pipes, which are abundant in colonial archeological sites, although some men and women dipped snuff or inhaled powdered tobacco.

Where the smokers of early colonial America "drank" or gulped smoke through the short, thick stems of their seventeenth-century pipes, those of 1800 inhaled it more slowly and gradually; from the early seventeenth to the late eighteenth century, pipe stems became steadily longer and narrower, increasingly distancing smokers from their burning tobacco.

In the 1790s cigars, or "segars," were introduced from the Caribbean. Prosperous men widely took them up; they were the most expensive way to consume tobacco, and it was a sign of financial security to puff away on "long-nines" or "principe cigars at three cents each" while the poor used clay pipes and much cheaper "cut plug" tobacco. After 1800 in American streets, barrooms, stores, public conveyances, and even private homes it became nearly impossible to avoid tobacco chewers.

Chewing extended tobacco use, particularly into workplaces; men who smoked pipes at home or in the tavern barroom could chew while working in barns or workshops where smoking carried the danger of fire.

"In all the public places of America," wrote Charles Dickens, multitudes of men engaged in "the odious practice of chewing and expectorating," a recreation practiced by all ranks of American society. Chewing stimulated salivation and gave rise to a public environment of frequent and copious spitting, where men every few minutes were "squirting a mouthful of saliva through the room."

Spittoons were provided in the more meticulous establishments, but men often ignored them. The floors of American public buildings were not pleasant to contemplate. A courtroom in New York City in 1833 was decorated by a "mass of abomination" contributed to by "judges, counsel, jury, witnesses, officers, and audience." The floor of the Virginia House of Burgesses in 1827 was "actually flooded with their horrible spitting," and even the aisle of a Connecticut meetinghouse was black with the "ejection after ejection, incessant from twenty mouths," of the men singing in the choir. In order to drink, an American man might remove his quid, put it in a pocket or hold it in his hand, take his glassful, and then restore it to his mouth. Women's dresses might even be in danger at fashionable balls. "One night as I was walking upstairs to valse," reported Margaret Hall of a dance in Washington in 1828, "my partner began clearing his throat. This I thought ominous. However, I said to myself, 'surely he will turn his head to the other side.' The gentleman, however, had no such thought but deliberately shot across me. I had not courage enough to examine whether the result landed in the flounce of my dress."

The segar and the quid were almost entirely male appurtenances, but as the nineteenth century began, many rural and lower-class urban women were smoking pipes or dipping snuff. During his boyhood in New Hampshire, Horace Greeley remembered,

"it was often my filial duty to fill and light my mother's pipe."

After 1820 or so tobacco use among women in the North began to decline. Northern women remembered or depicted with pipe or snuffbox were almost all elderly. More and more Americans adopted a genteel standard that saw tobacco use and womanliness — delicate and nurturing — as antithetical, and young women avoided it as a pollutant. For them, tobacco use marked off male from female territory with increasing sharpness.

In the households of small Southern and Western farmers, however, smoking and snuff taking remained common. When women visited "among the country people" of North Carolina, Frances Kemble Butler reported in 1837, the "proffer of the snuffbox, and its passing from hand to hand, is the usual civility." By the late 1830s visiting New Englanders were profoundly shocked when they saw the women of Methodist congregations in Illinois, including nursing mothers, taking out their pipes for a smoke between worship services.

☆

FROM DEFERENCE
TO EQUALITY

The Americans of 1820 would have been more recognizable to us in the informal and egalitarian way they treated one another. The traditional signs of deference before social superiors — the deep bow, the "courtesy," the doffed cap, lowered head, and averted eyes — had been a part of social relationships in colonial America. In the 1780s, wrote the American poetess Lydia Huntley Sigourney in 1824, there were still "individuals . . . in every grade of society" who had grown up "when a bow was not an offense to fashion nor . . . a relic of monarchy." But in the early nineteenth century such signals of subordination rapidly fell away. It was a natural consequence of the Revolution, she maintained, which, "in giv-

ing us liberty, obliterated almost every vestige of politeness of the 'old school.'" Shaking hands became
the accustomed American greeting between men, a
gesture whose symmetry and mutuality signified
equality. Frederick Marryat found in 1835 that it was
"invariably the custom to shake hands" when he was
introduced to Americans and that he could not carefully grade the acknowledgment he would give to
new acquaintances according to their signs of wealth
and breeding. He found instead that he had to "go
on shaking hands here, there and everywhere, and
with everybody." Americans were not blind to in-
equalities of economic and social power, but they
less and less gave them overt physical expression.
Bred in a society where such distinctions were far
more clearly spelled out, Marryat was somewhat dis-
oriented in the United States; "it is impossible to
know who is who," he claimed, "in this land of
equality."

Well-born British travelers encountered not just
confusion but conflict when they failed to receive
the signs of respect they expected. Margaret Hall's
letters home during her Southern travels outlined a
true comedy of manners. At every stage stop in the
Carolinas, Georgia, and Alabama, she demanded that
country tavernkeepers and their households give her
deferential service and well-prepared meals; she received instead rancid bacon and "such an absence of
all kindness of feeling, such unbending frigid heart-
lessness." But she and her family had a far greater
share than they realized in creating this chilly reception. Squeezed between the pride and poise of the
great planters and the social debasement of the slaves,
small Southern farmers often displayed a prickly insolence, a considered lack of response, to those who
too obviously considered themselves their betters.
Greatly to their discomfort and incomprehension,
the Halls were experiencing what a British traveler
more sympathetic to American ways, Patrick
Shirreff, called "the democratic rudeness which assumed or presumptuous superiority seldom fails to
experience."

☆

LAND OF ABUNDANCE

In the seventeenth century white American colonials
were no taller than their European counterparts, but
by the time of the Revolution they were close to
their late-twentieth-century average height for men
of slightly over five feet eight inches. The citizens of
the early republic towered over most Europeans.
Americans' early achievement of modern stature —
by a full century and more — was a striking consequence of American abundance. Americans were
taller because they were better nourished than the
great majority of the world's peoples.

Yet not all Americans participated equally in the nation's abundance. Differences in stature between whites
and blacks, and between city and country dwellers,
echoed those between Europeans and Americans.
Enslaved blacks were a full inch shorter than whites.
But they remained a full inch taller than European
peasants and laborers and were taller still than their fellow slaves eating the scanty diets afforded by the more
savagely oppressive plantation system of the West Indies. And by 1820 those who lived in the expanding
cities of the United States — even excluding immigrants, whose heights would have reflected European,
not American, conditions — were noticeably shorter
than the people of the countryside, suggesting an increasing concentration of poverty and poorer diets in
urban places.

Across the United States almost all country households ate the two great American staples: corn and
"the eternal pork," as one surfeited traveler called it,
"which makes its appearance on every American
table, high and low, rich and poor." Families in the
cattle-raising, dairying country of New England,
New York, and northern Ohio ate butter, cheese,
and salted beef as well as pork and made their bread
from wheat flour or rye and Indian corn. In Pennsylvania, as well as Maryland, Delaware, and Virginia,
Americans ate the same breadstuffs as their Northern

neighbors, but their consumption of cheese and beef declined every mile southward in favor of pork.

Farther to the south, and in the West, corn and corn-fed pork were truly "eternal"; where reliance on them reached its peak in the Southern uplands, they were still the only crops many small farmers raised. Most Southern and Western families built their diets around smoked and salted bacon, rather than the Northerners' salt pork, and, instead of wheat or rye bread, made cornpone or hoecake, a coarse, strong bread, and hominy, pounded Indian corn boiled together with milk.

Before 1800, game — venison, possum, raccoon, and wild fowl — was for many American households "a substantial portion of the supply of food at certain seasons of the year," although only on the frontier was it a regular part of the diet. In the West and South this continued to be true, but in the Northeast game became increasingly rare as forests gave way to open farmland, where wild animals could not live.

Through the first half of the eighteenth century, Americans had been primarily concerned with obtaining a sufficiency of meat and bread for their families; they paid relatively little attention to foodstuffs other than these two "staffs of life," but since that time the daily fare of many households had grown substantially more diverse. . . .

Important patterns of regional, class, and ethnic distinctiveness remain in American everyday life. But they are far less powerful, and less central to understanding American experience, than they once were. Through the rest of the nineteenth century and into the twentieth, the United States became ever more diverse, with new waves of Eastern and Southern European immigrants joining the older Americans of Northern European stock. Yet the new arrivals — and even more, their descendants — have experienced the attractiveness and reshaping power of a national culture formed by department stores, newspapers, radios, movies, and universal public education. America, the developing nation, developed into us. And perhaps our manners and morals, to some future observer, will seem as idiosyncratic and astonishing as this portrait of our earlier self.

QUESTIONS TO CONSIDER

1 Compare Larkin's description of American urban conditions, crime, disorder, and drunkenness with the conditions Page Smith found in seventeenth-century London (selection 2). Were these Americans worse or better off than their English forbears? How did the American legal response to crime and disorder compare with the earlier British model?

2 Bacterial pollution from animal and human wastes, offal, open drains, and contaminated water were major threats to American health in the early nineteenth century. Are we more fortunate nearly two centuries later, or have we found new ways to poison our environment? Which era do you think is the more deadly?

3 Larkin is a social and cultural historian. What sources has he used to compile his vivid account of everyday life among ordinary Americans in the early nineteenth century? What are the advantages of using these sources? Potential disadvantages?

4 Larkin points out that American women drank less than a third as much as American men at the turn of the nineteenth century and that alcohol consumption by slaves was also limited. A few decades later, women spearheaded the temperance movement in communities all over the country. What issues of social control do you suppose were in operation throughout this period?

5 In what personal ways are these ordinary nineteenth-century Americans different from us today? How are they the same? What distinctively American traits does Larkin suggest were born in this era?

12

Beyond Mother's Knee:
The Struggle to Educate Women

ELAINE KENDALL

White men of the early Republic were enterprising builders of farms and plantations, merchant shops and law firms, hard at work making their fortunes in a bustling, materialistic society. For white men, the opportunities for individual advancement and self-fulfillment were increasingly plentiful. But it was not so for white women, who, like African Americans, were excluded from the Revolutionary promise of freedom and equality. Although men like Alexander Hamilton, Benjamin Franklin, and John Jay worried about the discrepancy between the idealism of the Declaration of Independence and the reality of slavery, no statesmen of note thought to extend the equality doctrine to white women. Though not slaves in a legal sense, they were certainly not free. Women in the young Republic could not vote or hold political office. Unmarried women and widows could own landed property, but few occupations were open to them. Indeed, custom held that the only proper sphere for women was in the home. According to the women's magazines and religious journals, which reflected the pervasive attitudes of a male-dominated world, the ideal woman was not only domesticated, but pious, pure, submissive, and unopinionated. Once a woman married, she was expected to be "with child" within a year, since child rearing, along with duty to her husband, was her main purpose in life. A married woman soon discovered that the law treated her like a child. She could not own property or sue in court without her husband. If a married woman did work outside the home, her husband legally commanded her wages. He was also the sole guardian of their children. If he died without a will and there were children, the woman was entitled to only one-third of her husband's estate. In certain cases, she could keep only her dowry — the property she had brought to the marriage. If she wedded again (and widows usually did remarry in order to survive), she had to surrender her property to her new husband. If the woman was an African American, she faced a double wall of discrimination — one because she was a woman, the other because she was black. The underlying assumption behind the whole range of discrimination against the so-called "fairer sex" was that women were inferior to men.

Educational restrictions hampered women further. After the Revolution, an enlightened community here and there in New England did admit girls to elementary schools for a couple of hours in the morning or in the evening, and southern planters who hired tutors for their sons might also engage dancing and singing instructors for their daughters. But before 1820 that was about all the education a women could expect beyond what she learned on her own. "As a result," says biographer Norman Risjold, "adult women received politeness from menfolk, but rarely intellectual companionship or conversation."

As Elaine Kendall says in the sparkling composition that follows, an intrepid band of pioneering female educators set out to change all that: Catherine and Harriet Beecher established a female academy in Hartford; Emma Willard set up one of the first and most influential schools of higher education for women in Troy, New York; Mary Lyon founded Mount Holyoke Seminary for Women; aggressive if not always responsible "professors" opened "adventure" schools, independent commercial operations that admitted girls as well as boys; and the Quakers and Moravians established sectarian schools for girls. But the pioneers in female education in the early Republic faced a wall of opposition from male chauvinists. "If all our girls become philosophers," asked the male critics, "who will darn our stockings and cook the meals?" Said another: "Women are born for a life of uniformity and dependence. Were it in your power to give them genius, it would be almost always a useless and very often a dangerous present. It would, in general, make them regret the station which Providence has assigned them." The nineteenth-century female educators, Kendall reminds us, had "to live with this attitude and work within and around it." How they did so and still managed to advance the cause of women's education — the first feminist victory — is brilliantly described in Kendall's narrative. As you read her story, ask yourself how much things have changed in the education and treatment of women today.

GLOSSARY

ADVENTURE SCHOOLS Private commercial enterprises run by a single "professor" or an occasional husband-and-wife team; although intended for boys, they welcomed girls as well because the purpose of the schools was not to educate, but to make money. Many of those who administered such schools were academic frauds who left town when the money dried up.

BEECHER, CATHERINE AND HARRIET
Established an early female academy in Hartford, Connecticut. Harriet later married Calvin Stowe and went on to write *Uncle Tom's Cabin* in response to the 1850 fugitive slave law.

DAME SCHOOLS   These were really no more than a daycare center run by a solitary female teacher. The curriculum depended on the "dame" in charge, but rarely exceeded the teaching of the alphabet and instruction in domestic skills.

LYON, MARY   Founder of Mount Holyoke Seminary (now Mount Holyoke College for Women) in Holyoke, Massachusetts, in 1837.

MOTHER'S KNEE   Term for the "education" that young children, particularly girls, received while sitting in their mother's lap. Until the nineteenth century, this was the prevailing form of education for girls. The mothers simply passed on to their daughters what they had been taught, mostly about domestic responsibilities.

WILLARD, EMMA   Established one of the first and most influential schools of higher education for American women, in Troy, New York, in 1821.

"Could I have died a martyr in the cause, and thus ensured its success, I could have blessed the faggot and hugged the stake." The cause was state support for female education, the would-be Saint Joan was Emma Willard, and the rhetorical standards of the 1820's were lofty and impassioned. The most militant feminists rarely scale such heights today. For one thing, dogged effort has finally reduced the supply of grand injustices; and today's preference for less florid metaphor has deprived the movement of such dramatic images. Comparatively speaking, the rest of the struggle is a downhill run, leading straight to twenty-four-hour daycare centers, revised and updated forms of marriage, free access to the executive suite, and rows of "Ms's" on Senate office doors. Glorying in our headway, we easily forget that leverage comes with literacy, and literacy for women is a relative novelty.

Long before the Revolution, American males already had Harvard, Yale, and Princeton, as well as a full range of other education institutions — grammar schools, academies, seminaries, and numerous smaller colleges. American girls had only their mother's knee. By 1818, the year in which Emma Willard first introduced her *Plan for the Improvement of Female Education,* the gap was almost as wide as ever. Public schooling was a local option, quite whimsically interpreted. The towns could provide as much or as little as they wished, extending or restricting attendance as they saw fit. Ms. Willard presented her novel proposals to the New York State legislature, which dealt with the question by putting it repeatedly at the bottom of the agenda until the session was safely over. Lavish tributes to Mother's Knee filled the halls of Albany. In the opinion of the senators, M.'s K. not only outshone our men's colleges but also Oxford, Cambridge, and

Elaine Kendall, "Beyond Mother's Knee," *American Heritage*, vol. 24, no. 4 (June 1973), 12–16, 73–78. Reprinted by permission of *American Heritage* magazine, a division of Forbes, Inc. Copyright © Forbes, Inc., 1973.

Emma Willard (1787–1876), pioneer woman educator who wrote Plan for the Improvement of Female Education *(1818) and "presented her novel proposals to the New York State legislature." In 1821, she established one of the first and most influential schools of higher education for women in Troy, New York. (Archive Photos)*

Heidelberg as an institution of female edification. Despite the support of De Witt Clinton, John Adams, and Thomas Jefferson, it was three more years — when a building and grounds were offered independently by the town of Troy — before the Willard Seminary actually got under way. The academy still flourishes and claims to "mark the beginning of higher education for women in the United States." Since that is not precisely the same as being the first such school and the rival contenders have either vanished or metamorphosed into other sorts of institutions entirely, there is no reason to dispute it. The pre-Revolutionary South did have a few early convents, including one at New Orleans that was established by the

Ursuline order in 1727 and taught religion, needlework, and something of what was called basic skills. Other religious groups, particularly the Moravians and Quakers, supported female seminaries during the eighteenth century, but these places did not really attempt to offer advanced education — a commodity for which there was little market in an era when girls were unwelcome in elementary schools. A few New England clergymen opened small academies for girls during the first decade of the nineteenth century, but these noble and well-intentioned efforts were ephemeral, never outlasting their founders. Until Emma Willard succeeded in extracting that bit of real estate from Troy, public and private support for such ventures was virtually nonexistent.

Some few ambitious and determined girls did succeed in learning to read and write in colonial America, but hardly ever at public expense and certainly not in comfort. Their number was pitifully small, and those who gained more than the rudiments of literacy would hardly have crowded a saltbox parlor. . . .

As the grip of Puritanism gradually relaxed, the image of a learned female improved infinitesimally. She was no longer regarded as a disorderly person or a heretic but merely as a nuisance to her husband, family, and friends. A sensible woman soon found ways to conceal her little store of knowledge or, if hints of it should accidentally slip out, to disparage or apologize for it. Abigail Adams, whose wistful letters show a continuing interest in women's education, described her own with a demurely rhymed disclaimer:

> The little learning I have gained
> Is all from simple nature drained.

In fact, the wife of John Adams was entirely self-educated. She disciplined herself to plod doggedly through works of ancient history whenever her household duties permitted, being careful to do so in the privacy of her boudoir. In her letters she deplored the fact that it was still customary to "ridicule female learning" and even in the "best families" to deny girls more than the barest rudiments.

The prevailing colonial feeling toward female education was still so unanimously negative that it was not always thought necessary to mention it. Sometimes this turned out to be a boon. A few villages, in their haste to establish schools for boys, neglected to specify that only males would be admitted. From the beginning they wrote their charters rather carelessly, using the loose generic term "children." This loophole was nearly always blocked as soon as the risks became apparent, but in the interim period of grace girls were occasionally able to pick up a few crumbs of knowledge. They did so by sitting outside the schoolhouse or on its steps, eavesdropping on the boys' recitations. More rarely, girls were tolerated in the rear of the schoolhouse behind a curtain, in a kind of makeshift seraglio. This Levantine arrangement, however, was soon abandoned as inappropriate to the time and place, and the attendance requirements were made unambiguous. New England winters and Cape Cod architecture being what they are, the amount of learning that one could have acquired by these systems was necessarily scanty. Still it was judged excessive. The female scholars in the yard and on the stairs seemed to suffer disproportionately from pleurisy and other respiratory ailments. Further proof of the divine attitude toward the educating of women was not sought. Girls were excluded for their own good, as well as to ensure the future of the Colonies.

After the Revolution the atmosphere in the New England states did become considerably more lenient. Here and there a town council might vote to allow girls inside the school building from five to seven in the morning, from six to eight at night, or, in a few very liberal communities, during the few weeks in summer when the boys were at work in the fields or shipyards. This was a giant step forward and would have been epochal if teachers had always appeared at these awkward times. Unfortunately the girls often had to muddle through on their own without benefit

of faculty. The enlightened trend, moreover, was far from general. In 1792 the town of Wellesley, Massachusetts, voted "not to be at any expense for schooling girls," and similarly worded bylaws were quite usual throughout the northern states until the 1820's. In the southern Colonies, where distances between the great estates delayed the beginnings of any public schooling even longer, wealthy planters often imported tutors to instruct their sons in academic subjects. If they could afford the additional luxury, they might also engage singing and dancing masters for the daughters, who were not expected to share their brothers' more arduous lessons. In a pleasant little memoir of the South, *Colonial Days and Dames,* Anne Wharton, a descendant of Thomas Jefferson, noted that "very little from books was thought necessary for a girl. She was trained to domestic matters . . . the accomplishments of the day . . . to play upon the harpsichord or spinet, and to work impossible dragons and roses upon canvas."

Although the odds against a girl's gaining more than the sketchiest training during this era seem to have been overwhelming, there were some remarkable exceptions. The undiscouraged few included Emma Willard herself; Catherine and Harriet Beecher, the clergyman's daughters, who established an early academy at Hartford; and Mary Lyon, who founded the college that began in 1837 as Mount Holyoke Seminary. Usually, however, the tentative and halfhearted experiments permitted by the New England towns served only to give aid and comfort to the opposition. They seemed to show that the female mind was not inclined to scholarship and the female body was not strong enough to withstand exposure — *literal* exposure, in many cases — to it. By 1830 or so primary education had been grudgingly extended to girls almost everywhere, but it was nearly impossible to find anyone who dared champion any further risks. Boston had actually opened a girls' high school in 1826 only to abolish it two years later. . . .

Public schools obviously were not the only route to learning or most female American children up through colonial times would have been doomed to total ignorance. Fathers, especially clergymen fathers, would often drill their daughters in the Bible and sometimes teach them to read and do simple sums as well. Nothing that enhanced an understanding of the Scriptures could be entirely bad, and arithmetic was considered useful in case a woman were to find herself the sole support of her children. Brothers would sometimes lend or hand down their old school books, and fond uncles might help a favorite and clever niece with her sums. The boys' tutor was often amenable to a pretty sister's pleas for lessons. For those girls not fortunate enough to be the daughters of foresighted New England parsons or wealthy tobacco and cotton factors, most colonial towns provided dame schools. These catered to boys as well as to girls of various ages. They offered a supplement to the curriculum at Mother's Knee, but only just. Because these schools were kept by women who had acquired their own learning haphazardly, the education they offered was motley at best. The solitary teacher could impart no more than she herself knew, and that rarely exceeded the alphabet, the shorter catechism, sewing, knitting, some numbers, and perhaps a recipe for baked beans and brown bread. The actual academic function of these early American institutions seems to have been somewhat exaggerated and romanticized by historians. Dame schools were really no more than small businesses, managed by impoverished women who looked after neighborhood children and saw to it that idle little hands did not make work for the devil. The fees (tuition is too grand a word) were tiny, with threepence a week per child about par. That sum could hardly have paid for a single hornbook for the entire class. The dame school itself was an English idea, transplanted almost intact to the Colonies. Several seem to have been under way by the end of the seventeenth century. . . .

As the country became more affluent, schoolkeeping gradually began to attract more ambitious types. Older girls were still being excluded from the town seminaries and in many places from the grammar schools as well. A great many people quickly realized that there was money to be made by teaching the children of the new middle class and that they could sell their services for far more than pennies. No special accreditation or qualification was required, and there was no competition from the state. Toward the end of the eighteenth century and at the beginning of the nineteenth, platoons of self-styled professors invaded American towns and cities, promising to instruct both sexes and all ages in every known art, science, air, and grace. These projects were popularly known as adventure schools, a phrase that has a pleasant modern ring to it, suggesting open classrooms, free electives, and individual attention.

That, however, is deceptive. The people who ran such schools were usually adventurers in the not very admirable sense of the word: unscrupulous, self-serving, and of doubtful origins and attainments. Many simply equipped themselves with false diplomas and titles from foreign universities and set up shop. The schools continued to operate only as long as they turned a profit. When enrollment dropped, interest waned, or fraud became obvious, the establishment would simply fold and the proprietors move to another town for a fresh start. The newer territories were particularly alluring to the worst of these entrepreneurs, since their reputations could neither precede nor follow them there. A new name, a new prospectus, an ad in the gazette, and they were in business again until scandal or mismanagement obliged them to move on. Such "schools" were not devised for the particular benefit of girls; but because they were independent commercial enterprises, no solvent person was turned away. Thousands of young women did take advantage of the new opportunity and were, in many cases, taken advantage of in return. For boys the adventure schools were an alternative to the strict classicism and religiosity of the academies and seminaries, but for girls they were the only educational possibility between the dame school and marriage.

There was little effort to devise a planned or coherent course of study, though elaborately decorated certificates were awarded upon completion of a series of lessons. The scholar could buy whatever he or she fancied from a mind-bending list. One could take needlework at one place, languages at another, dancing or "ouranology" at a third. (It was a pompous era, and no one was fonder of polysyllables than the professors. Ouranology was skywatching, but is sounded impressive.) There were no minimum of maximum course requirements, though the schoolmasters naturally made every effort to stock the same subjects offered by the competition, in order to reduce the incidence of school-hopping. . . .

Many of the adventure schools hedged their financial risks by functioning as a combination store and educational institution, selling fancywork, "very good Orange-Oyl," sweetmeats, sewing notions, painted china, and candles along with lessons in dancing, foreign languages, geography, penmanship, and spelling. Usually they were mama-and-papa affairs, with the wife instructing girls in "curious works" and the husband concentrating upon "higher studies." Curious works covered a great deal of ground — the making of artificial fruits and flowers, the "raising of paste," enamelling, japanning, quilting, fancy embroidery, and in at least one recorded case "flowering on catgut," an intriguing accomplishment that has passed into total oblivion, leaving no surviving examples.

The adventure schools advertised heavily in newspapers and journals of the period, often in terms indicating that teaching was not an especially prestigious profession. One Thomas Carroll took several columns in a May, 1765, issue of the New York *Mercury* to announce a curriculum that would have taxed the entire faculty of Harvard and then proceeded to explain that he "was not under the necessity of coming here to teach, he had views of living more happy, but some unforeseen, and unexpected events have happened since his arrival here . . . ,"

thus reducing this Renaissance paragon to school-keeping and his lady to teaching French knots and quilting.

While they lasted adventure schools attempted to offer something for everyone, including adults, and came in all forms, sizes, and price ranges. They met anywhere and everywhere: "at the Back of Mr. Benson's Brew-House," in rented halls, in borrowed parlors, at inns, and from time to time in barns or open fields. The adventurer was usually available for private lessons as well, making house calls "with the utmost discretion," especially in the case of questionable studies like dancing or French verbs. The entire physical plant usually fitted into a carpetbag. . . .

The pretentious and empty promises of the adventure schools eventually aroused considerable criticism. Americans may not yet have appreciated the value of female education, but they seem always to have known the value of a dollar. It was not long before the public realized that flowering on catgut was not so useful an accomplishment for their daughters as ciphering or reading. The more marginal operators began to melt away, and those schoolmasters who hung on were obliged to devote more attention to practical subjects and eliminate many of the patent absurdities. . . .

Certain religious groups, particularly the Moravians and the Quakers, had always eschewed frippery and pioneered in the more realistic education of women. Friends' schools were organized as soon as the size and prosperity of the settlements permitted them. This training emphasized housewifery but did include the fundamentals of literacy. Many of the earliest eighteenth-century Quaker primary schools were co-educational, though access to them was limited to the immediate community. Because these were concentrated in the Philadelphia area, girls born in Pennsylvania had a much better chance of acquiring some education than their contemporaries elsewhere. The Moravians (who also settled in the southeastern states) quickly recognized the general lack of facilities in the rest of the Colonies and offered boarding arrangements in a few of their schools. The student body soon included intrepid and homesick girls from New England and even the West Indies. These institutions were purposeful and rather solemn, the antithesis of superficiality. The Moravians insisted upon communal household chores as well as domestic skills, and in the eighteenth century these obligations could be onerous; dusting, sweeping, spinning, carding, and weaving came before embroidery and hemstitching. These homely lessons were enlivened by rhymes celebrating the pleasure of honest work. Examples survive in the seminary archives and supply a hint of the uplifting atmosphere:

> I've spun seven cuts, dear companions allow
> That I am yet little, and know not right how;
>
> Mine twenty and four, which I finished with joy,
> And my hands and my feet did willing employ.

Though the teaching sisters in these sectarian schools seem to have been kind and patient, the life was rigorous and strictly ordered, a distinct and not always popular alternative to pleasant afternoons with easygoing adventure masters. In an era when education for women was still widely regarded as a luxury for the upper classes, the appeal of the pioneering religious seminaries tended to be somewhat narrow. If a family happened to be sufficiently well-off to think of educating their girls, the tendency was to make fine ladies of them. As a result there were many young women who could carry a tune but not a number, who could model a passable wax apple but couldn't read a recipe, who had memorized the language of flowers but had only the vaguest grasp of English grammar. There seemed to be no middle ground between the austerities of the religious schools and the hollow frivolities offered by commercial ventures. Alternatives did not really exist until the 1820's, when the earliest tentative attempts were made to found independent academies and seminaries.

Catherine and Harriet Beecher, who were among the first to open a school designed to bridge the gulf, believed almost as strongly as the Moravians in the importance of domestic economy. They were, however, obliged by public demand to include a long list of dainty accomplishments in their Hartford curriculum. Many girls continued to regard the new secular seminaries as they had the adventure schools — as rival shops where they could browse or buy at will, dropping in and out at any time they chose. To the despair of the well-intentioned founders few students ever stayed to complete the course at any one place. Parents judged a school as if it were a buffet table, evaluating it by the number and variety of subjects displayed. In writing later of the difficult beginnings of the Hartford Seminary, Catherine Beecher said that "all was perpetual haste, imperfection, irregularity, and the merely mechanical commitment of words to memory, without any chance for imparting clear and connected ideas in a single branch of knowledge. The review of those days is like the memory of a troubled and distracting dream."

Public opinion about the education of girls continued to be sharply (if never clearly) divided until after the Civil War. Those who pioneered in the field were at the mercy of socially ambitious and ambivalent parents, confused and unevenly prepared students, and constantly shifting social attitudes. In sudden and disconcerting switches "the friends" of women's education often turned out to be less than whole-hearted in their advocacy. Benjamin Rush, whose *Thoughts Upon Female Education,* written in 1787, influenced and inspired Emma Willard, Mary Lyon, and the Beecher sisters, later admitted that his thoughtful considerations had finally left him "not enthusiastical upon the subject." Even at his best, Rush sounds no more than tepid; American ladies, he wrote, "should be qualified to a certain degree by a peculiar and suitable education to concur in instructing their sons in the principles of liberty and government." During her long editorship of *Godey's Lady's Book* Sarah Josepha Hale welcomed every new female seminary and academy but faithfully reminded her readers that the sanctity of the home came first: ". . . on what does social well-being rest but in our homes . . . ?" "Oh, spare our homes!" was a constant refrain, this chorus coming from the September, 1856, issue. *Godey's Lady's Book* reflects the pervasive nineteenth-century fear that the educated woman might be a threat to the established and symbiotic pattern of American family life. The totally ignorant woman, on the other hand, was something of an embarrassment to the new nation. The country was inundated by visiting European journalists during this period, and they invariably commented upon the dullness of our social life and the disappointing vacuity of the sweet-faced girls and handsome matrons they met. Though Americans themselves seemed to feel safer with a bore than with a bluestocking, they were forced to give the matter some worried thought.

"If all our girls become philosophers," the critics asked, "who will darn our stockings and cook the meals?" It was widely, if somewhat irrationally, assumed that a maiden who had learned continental stichery upon fine lawn might heave to and sew up a shirt if necessary, but few men believed that a woman who had once tasted the heady delights of Shakespeare's plays would ever have dinner ready on time — or at all.

The founders of female seminaries were obliged to cater to this unease by modifying their plans and their pronouncements accordingly. The solid academic subjects were so generally thought irrelevant for "housewives and helpmates" that it was usually necessary to disguise them as something more palatable. The Beechers taught their girls chemistry at Hartford but were careful to assure parents and prospective husbands that its principles were applicable in the kitchen. The study of mathematics could be justified by its usefulness in running a household. Eventually the educators grew more daring, recommending geology as a means toward understanding the Deluge and other Biblical mysteries and suggesting geography and even history as suitable because these studies would "enlarge women's sphere of thought, rendering them more interesting as companions to men of science." There is, however, little evidence that many were converted to this extreme point of view. The average nineteenth-century American man was not at all keen on chat with an interesting companion, preferring a wife like the one in the popular jingle *"who never learnt the art of schooling/Untamed with the itch of ruling."* The cliché of the period was "woman's sphere." The phrase was so frequently repeated that it acquires almost physical qualities. Woman's Sphere — the nineteenth-century woman was fixed and sealed within it like a model ship inside a bottle. To tamper with the arrangement was to risk ruining a complex and fragile structure that had been painstakingly assembled over the course of two centuries. Just one ill-considered jolt might make matchwood of the entire apparatus.

In 1812 the anonymous author of *Sketches of the History, Genius, and Disposition of the Fair Sex* wrote that women are "born for a life of uniformity and dependence. . . . Were it in your power to give them genius, it would be almost always a useless and very often a dangerous present. It would, in general, make them regret the station which Providence has assigned them, or have recourse to unjustifiable ways to get from it." The writer identified himself only as a "friend of the sex" (not actually specifying which one).

This century's feminists may rage at and revel in such quotes, but the nineteenth-century educators were forced to live with this attitude and work within and around it. In order to gain any public or private support for women's secondary schools they had to prove that a woman would not desert her husband and children as soon as she could write a legible sentence or recite a theorem. That fear was genuine, and the old arguments resurfaced again and again. What about Saint Paul's injunction? What about the sanctity of the home? What about the health of the future mothers of the race? What about supper?

Advocates of secondary education for women, therefore, became consummate politicians, theologians, hygienists, and, when necessary, apologists. "It is desirable," wrote Mary Lyon in 1834 of her Mount Holyoke Female Seminary project, "that the plans relating to the subject should not seem to originate with us but with benevolent *gentlemen*. If the object should excite attention there is danger that many good men will fear the effect on society of so much female influence and what they will call female greatness." New and subtle counterarguments were presented with great delicacy. God had entrusted the tender minds of children to women; therefore women were morally obliged to teach. The home would be a holier place if the chatelaine understood religious principles and could explain them. The founders of Abbot Academy proclaimed that "to form the immortal mind to habits suited to an immortal being, and to instill principles of conduct and form the character for an immortal destiny, shall be subordinate to no other care." All that harping on immortality went down smoothly in the evangelistic atmosphere of the 1820's. A thick coating of religion was applied to every new educational venture. The parents of prospective students were assured that their daughters would not only study religion in class but would have twice-daily periods of silent meditation, frequent revival meetings, and a Sunday that included all of these. In reading the early seminary catalogues, one finds it hard to see where secular studies could have fit in at all. To the religious guarantees were appended promises of careful attention to health. The educators lost no time in adding the new science of calisthenics to their curricula. They had the medical records of their students compared to that of the public at large and published the gratifying results in newspapers and magazines. Domestic work was also to be required of girls who attended the new seminaries, partly for economy's sake but mainly so that they would not forget their ultimate destiny.

All of this was calming and persuasive, but nothing was so effective as simple economics. By the 1830's most states had begun a program of primary public education. As the West followed suit the need for teachers became acute and desperate. Men were not attracted to the profession because the pay was wretched, the living conditions were lonely, and the status of a schoolmaster was negligible if not downright laughable. Saint Paul was revised, updated, and finally reversed. He had not, after all, envisioned the one-room schoolhouses of the American prairies, the wages of three dollars a month, or the practice of "boarding around."

Within an astonishingly short time fears for female health subsided. The first women teachers proved amazingly durable, able to withstand every rigor of frontier life. In a letter to her former headmistress one alumna of the Hartford Seminary described accommodations out west:

I board where there are eight children, and the parents, and only two rooms in the house. I must do as the family do about washing, as there is but one basin, and no place to go to wash but out the door. I have not enjoyed the luxury of either lamp or candle, their only light being a cup of grease with a rag for a wick. Evening is my only time to write, but this kind of light makes such a disagreeable smoke and smell, I cannot bear it, and do without light, except the fire. I occupy a room with three of the children and a niece who boards here. The other room serves as a kitchen, parlor, and bedroom for the rest of the family. . . .

Other graduates were just as stoical and often no more comfortable:

I board with a physician, and the house has only two rooms. One serves as kitchen, eating, and sitting room; the other, where I lodge, serves also as the doctor's office, and there is no time, night or day, when I am not liable to interruption.

"Long before the Revolution," writes Elaine Kendall, American men attended Harvard, Princeton, and Yale, as well as "grammar schools, academies, seminaries, and numerous smaller colleges."

As illustrated here, girls in early America had only one place to learn: at their mother's knee.

My school embraces both sexes, and all ages from five to seventeen, and not one can read intelligibly. They have no idea of the proprieties of the schoolroom or of study. . . . My furniture consists now of . . . benches, a single board put up against the side of the room for a writing desk, a few bricks for andirons, and a stick of wood for shovel and tongs.

These letters were collected by Catherine Beecher in her book *True Remedy for the Wrongs of Women,* which advanced the cause of women's education by showing the worthwhile uses to which to could be put. Delighted with the early results, several states quickly set up committees to consider training women teachers on a larger scale. Their findings were favorable, though couched in oddly ambiguous language. New York's group reported that women seemed to be "endued with peculiar faculties" for the occupation. "While man's nature is rough, stern, impatient, ambitious, hers is gentle, tender, enduring, unaspiring." That was most encouraging, but the gentlemen also generously acknowledged that "the habits of female teachers are better and their morals purer; they are much more apt to be content with, and continue in, the occupation of teaching." A Michigan report stated in 1842 that "an elementary school, where the rudiments of an English education only are taught, such as reading, spelling, writing, and the outlines barely of geography, arithmetic, and grammar, requires a female of practical common sense with amiable and winning manners, a patient spirit, and a tolerable knowledge of the springs of human action. A female thus qualified, carrying with her into the schoolroom the gentle influences of her sex, will do more to inculcate right morals and prepare the youthful intellect for the severer discipline of its after years, than the most accomplished and learned male teacher." Far from objecting to these rather condescending statements, the founders of the struggling seminaries were more than happy to hear them. Even the miserable wages offered to teachers could be regarded as an advantage, since they provided the single most effective argument for more female academies. "But where are we to raise such an army of teachers as are required for this great work?" asked Catherine Beecher in the same book that contained the letters from her ex-students. "Not from the sex which finds it so much more honorable, easy, and lucrative, to enter the many roads to wealth and honor open in this land.... It is WOMAN who is to come [forth] at this emergency, and meet the demand — woman, whom experience and testimony have shown to be the best, as well as the cheapest guardian and teacher of childhood, in the school as well as the nursery."

Teaching became a woman's profession by default and by rationalization. Clergymen and theologians suddenly had nothing but praise for women teachers. God must have meant them to teach because he made them so good at it. They would work for a half or a third of the salary demanded by a man. What, after all, was a schoolroom but an extension of the home, woman's natural sphere? And if females had to have schools of their own to prepare them for this holy mission, then so be it. Future American generations must not be allowed to suffer for want of instruction when a Troy, Hartford, or Mount Holyoke girl asked no more than three dollars a month, safe escort to the boondocks, and a candle of her own.

QUESTIONS TO CONSIDER

1   What was the prevailing opinion toward educating women in the colonial period? How did females get around the restrictions? Did things improve for women after the Revolution? If so, how? What difficulties did Emma Willard encounter in trying to establish a female academy? What was its significance? Were there other "undiscouraged women" in the early Republic who beat the odds against "a girl's gaining more than the sketchiest training"?

2   Why did men of the early Republic want to keep women "ignorant" and out of schools? What did men fear? What excuses did they make for opposing the education of women? Compare the opportunities for women to gain an education in those early years with the opportunities today. Have men's attitudes toward an educated woman changed?

3   What were dame schools? What sort of education did they offer women? Describe how the "adventure" schools operated and what they promised. What happened to them?

4   How did the nineteenth-century women's educators "work within and around" the hostile attitudes against educating women — in short, how did they manipulate the male-dominated system in order to beat it?

5   There are many parallels between the subjugation of white women and the subjugation of African Americans in the period we are studying. Can you name some of those parallels? What does the subjugation of white women and black tell you about the nature of American society in this period?

VII

THE NATION TAKES SHAPE

13

The Louisiana Purchase:
A Dangerous Precedent

WALTER LaFEBER

Students of the past have long debated what determines the course of history. There are those who maintain that great "forces" shape the direction and composition of human societies; some even argue that people, individuals, are not important. There are others, however, who focus on the human side of the past, examining how the interaction of people and events dictates the course of subsequent events. From this view, human beings are not mere cogs in the engines of history; they can and do make a difference. Portrait of America *stresses the latter view of history. In the next two selections, the authors describe in human terms some major political and judicial developments in the young Republic, from the dawn of the nineteenth century to the turbulent 1820s.*

Let us pick up political events where Edmund S. Morgan leaves off in his assessment of George Washington in selection 10. When John Adams replaced Washington as president in 1796, Federalist leaders were extremely apprehensive about the French Revolution and the anarchy and violence that seemed to characterize it. Might the French virus spread to America as it appeared to be spreading across Europe? Might a conspiracy already be under way in the United States to fan the flames of revolution, to unleash the American mob on Federalist leaders, to destroy the order and stability they had worked so hard to establish? Since 1793, when a Frenchman, Citizen Genêt, had tried to enlist American men and privateers for the French cause, the Federalists had feared revolution in their midst. Champions of a strong government to maintain order, apostles of elitist rule and the sancity of private property, the Federalists soon equated the Republicans under Madison and Jefferson with revolution, chaos, and destruction. After all, did the Republicans not support the French? Did they not defend the mob here at home? Did they not call for more democracy in government (although many of their leaders paradoxically were southern slave owners)?

The harried Federalists barely fought off a Republican attempt to seize the government in 1796, when Adams defeated Jefferson by only three votes in the electoral college. Then, as though the Republican threat were not bad enough, trouble broke out with revolutionary France. In the notorious XYZ affair, French agents tried to extract a bribe from American representatives sent to negotiate about deteriorating Franco-American relations. Many Americans thought the nation's honor had been besmirched and demanded a war of revenge. In response, the Federalists undertook an undeclared sea war against France that lasted from 1798 to 1800. Using the war as a pretext to consolidate their power, bridle the Republicans, and prevent revolution in the United States, the Federalists passed the Alien and Sedition Acts. These, they declared, were necessary for the nation's security in the war with France.

The Alien Act severely restricted the rights and political influence of immigrants, who usually joined the Republicans after they were naturalized and who might be carrying the French virus. The Sedition Act made hostile criticism of Federalist policies punishable by fine and imprisonment. The Republicans, decrying such government censorship, launched a counterattack against Federalist "despotism." The Federalists were so discredited by the Alien and Sedition laws, and so divided by an irreconcilable feud between Adams and Hamilton, that the Republicans were able to win the government in 1801. Their victory marked the decline and eventually the end of the Federalist party as a national political organization.

Jefferson liked to describe his rise to power as "the revolution of 1800." But was it really a revolution? True, the Republicans allowed the hated Alien and Sedition Acts to expire in 1801, reduced the residence requirement for naturalized citizenship from fourteen years to five so that America could again function as an "asylum" for "oppressed humanity," inaugurated a new fiscal policy of government frugality and efficiency, and strove to retire the national debt of $83 million in sixteen years. Jefferson also repudiated the idea of government by and for a political elite. Yet he and his top administrators were as educated, talented, and upper class as their Federalist predecessors. Moreover, while Jefferson embraced the laissez-faire principle that that government is best which governs least, he found that reversing all Federalist commitments could cause confusion and consternation across the land. Therefore, he and his followers permitted the United States Bank to continue operating (it closed in 1811 when its charter ran out), and they maintained Federalist measures for refunding the national debt, stimulating American shipping, and assuming the states' Revolutionary War debts. Nor did Jefferson's "revolution of 1800" change the condition of America's enslaved blacks. As president, the author of the Declaration of Independence carefully avoided the subject of bondage.

"What is practicable," Jefferson said, "must often control what is pure theory." As Washington's secretary of state, Jefferson had demanded a strict construction of the Constitution, arguing that what was not specifically delegated to the federal government was reserved to the states. By that argument, he had opposed Secretary of the Treasury Alexander Hamilton's sweeping economic schemes. But when he became president and saw a chance to double the size of the United States by purchasing the Louisiana Territory, Jefferson abandoned strict construction and embraced the Federalist doctrine of "loose construction," for that was the only way he could justify the annexation of territory. In the next selection, distinguished historian Walter LaFeber discusses the intriguing case of Jefferson and the Louisiana Purchase, pointing out how the Federalists and the Jeffersonian Republicans switched roles when it came to interpreting the president's constitutional authority. As LaFeber sees it, Jefferson and his supporters set "a dangerous precedent" in the Louisiana Purchase: they transformed the Constitution into "an instrument for imperial expansion," he argues, and made it possible for the president and Congress to stretch and even violate the Constitution if they considered it to be in the national interest. As Jefferson proved, any president could stretch the Constitution in order to pursue an expansionist foreign policy — especially if his party controlled Congress. Indeed, as LaFeber says, later presidents did exactly that.

In selection 8, we saw Jefferson in a different light, as reluctant slaveholder, philosopher of liberty, and author of the Declaration of Independence. In this selection, we see a pragmatic politician who abandoned his own political philosophy and party doctrine in order to gain a practical objective — to annex Louisiana and thereby enlarge "the empire of liberty." How do you reconcile the Jefferson who wrote the Declaration of Independence and who demanded a strict construction of the Constitution with the Jefferson who used party politics to force through Congress a measure of questionable constitutional legality? What does this tell you about the nature of American politics? About Jefferson himself? In selection 8, Douglas Wilson argued that Jefferson intended to include blacks in the proposition that all men were created equal and entitled to the unalienable rights of life, liberty, and the pursuit of happiness. Yet in the debates over Louisiana, Jefferson opposed a proposed ban on slavery in the new territory, arguing that Creoles — Louisianans of French ancestry — were incapable of self-government, and permitting only white men of his own choosing to govern there. How do you account for this apparent inconsistency?

GLOSSARY

ADAMS, JOHN QUINCY Newly elected member of Congress from Massachusetts who favored the Louisiana treaty but was appalled that Jefferson interpreted the Constitution so broadly as to let himself rule the Louisiana Territory as a colony.

BRECKINRIDGE, JOHN Kentucky senator who had helped Jefferson write the Kentucky resolutions and who longed to control the Mississippi River.

GALLATIN, ALBERT Jefferson's secretary of the treasury, who advised the president that the United States, as an "aspect of its sovereignty," had the right to annex territory.

HILLHOUSE, JAMES Senator from Connecticut who proposed that slavery be banned in the Louisiana Territory, thus precipitating a debate that anticipated arguments that would later threaten to disrupt the Union.

KENTUCKY RESOLUTIONS Written by Jefferson and John C. Breckinridge of Kentucky, these state resolutions denounced the Federalists for expanding federal power beyond constitutional limits and argued that the states should have the authority to decide the constitutionality of federal acts.

LINCOLN, LEVI Jefferson's attorney general, who tried to get around constitutional objections to the Louisiana Purchase by saying that the French defined the territory as an extension of the state of Georgia or of the Mississippi Territory.

LIVINGSTON, ROBERT R. United States minister to France who, with James Monroe, negotiated the treaty that purchased Louisiana for the United States.

RANDOLPH, JOHN Virginia member of Congress who broke with Jefferson when the president violated his own constitutional doctrine.

Thomas Jefferson was one of the greatest expansionists in an American history full of ardent expansionists. But then, he believed the success of America's great experiment in democracy demanded an expanding territory. In the Virginian's mind, the republic must be controlled by ambitious, independent, property-holding farmers, who would form the incorruptible bedrock of democracy. As he wrote in 1785 in his *Notes on the State of Virginia,* "Those who labour in the earth are the chosen people.... Corruption of [their] morals ... is a phenomenon of which no age nor nation has furnished an example." Americans who worked the land would never become dependent on factory wages. "Dependence begets subservience and venality," Jefferson warned in *Notes,* "and prepares fit tools for the designs of ambition."

But Jefferson's virtuous farmers needed land, and their population was growing at an astonishing rate. Jefferson and his close friend and Virginia neighbor, James Madison, had studied the birthrate carefully. The two men rightly perceived that Americans were nearly doubling their population every 25 to 27 years. Moreover, the number of immigrants seemed to be increasing so quickly that as early as 1785 Jefferson had actually suggested restricting their numbers. Virginia provided a striking example of how fast land was being peopled. The region on the state's western frontier had filled with settlers so quickly that in 1792 it became the state of Kentucky. Unless something was done, Jefferson declared, Virginia would within the next century be burdened with "nearly the state of population in the British islands." Given Jefferson's convictions about the corruption to be found in Britain's cities, the analogy was damning.

During his first term as President (1801–1805), Jefferson had the chance to obtain that "extension of

Walter LaFeber, "A Dangerous Precedent," *Constitution,* vol. 5, no. 3 (Fall 1993), 4–7, 74–80. Reprinted by permission of the author.

territory which the rapid increase of our numbers will call for" by purchasing Louisiana, an area larger than Western Europe. In a single step he could double the size of the United States and open the possibility of an "empire for liberty," as he later described it, of mind-boggling proportions.

The President was playing for large stakes. Louisiana stretched from the Mississippi westward to the Rocky Mountains, and from Canada's Lake of the Woods southward to the Gulf of Mexico. If annexed, these 825,000 square miles would give the new nation access to one of the world's potentially richest trading areas. The Missouri, Kansas, Arkansas and Red rivers and their tributaries could act as giant funnels carrying goods into the Mississippi and then down to New Orleans. Even in the 1790s, with access to the Mississippi only from the east, the hundreds of thousands of Americans settled along the river depended on it and on the port of New Orleans for access to both world markets and imported staples for everyday living. "The Mississippi is to them everything," Secretary of State James Madison observed privately in November 1802. "It is the Hudson, the Delaware, the Potomac, and all the navigable rivers of the Atlantic formed into one stream."

Louisiana had long been a focus for imperial ambitions. The French had largely controlled the region until 1763 when, after losing the so-called Seven Years War, they were forced to cede it to Spain. But in 1799 Napoleon Bonaparte became head of the French government, and the next year he seized the opportunity to retake the territory. In exchange for his promise to make the Spanish royal family rulers of Tuscany, Spain handed over Louisiana. Though Bonaparte never bothered to carry out his end of the bargain, he set in motion plans for a New World colonial empire that would make Louisiana the food source for the rich French sugar island of Saint Domingue (Haiti) in the Caribbean.

Jefferson and Madison reacted with alarm. A decaying Spanish empire along the western American border was little threat. But Napoleon was something else. He would dam up American expansionism and perhaps attract settlements east of the Mississippi away from the United States. In 1801, after hearing rumors of Napoleon's bargain with Spain, Jefferson ordered Robert R. Livingston to Paris as the new U.S. minister. He instructed Livingston to talk Napoleon out of occupying Louisiana or, if that was impossible, to buy New Orleans. By 1802 both Jefferson and Livingston began to mention the possibility of acquiring not just the port, but also its vast interior.

Jefferson told Livingston that if France insisted on occupying New Orleans, he would consider an Anglo-American alliance against France. That threat was probably empty. But others were not. In February the Senate authorized Jefferson to create an 80,000-man army to defend the Mississippi. Although the House adjourned before acting on the measure, the President had already begun strengthening forts along the river. He sent three artillery and four infantry companies into position north of New Orleans. The commander of these forces, William C.C. Claiborne, assured him that these troops could seize New Orleans if they attacked before French forces arrived to strengthen the Spanish garrison.

But just as war with Napoleon loomed in the early months of 1803, Jefferson faced a crisis of quite another kind. He knew that the Constitution had no provision giving him the power to take New Orleans — let alone an area such as Louisiana that would double the nation's size — and he believed he could take no action not explicitly authorized by the Constitution.

This conviction was no mere infatuation with theory. As George Washington's secretary of state from 1790 until 1793, Jefferson had fought Secretary of the Treasury Alexander Hamilton's attempt to interpret the Constitution's phrases in broad terms. Beaten by Hamilton over such critical issues as whether the Constitution permitted the United

States to create a national bank, or the federal government to assume state debts, Jefferson resigned from the cabinet. He retired to Monticello and — even as Vice-President under the Federalist President John Adams — organized the Republican Party to take power and, as he saw it, restore the Constitution's true meaning. "The powers not delegated to the United States," he wrote in a debate with Hamilton in 1790 and 1791, "are reserved to the States respectively, or to the people." He warned, in words that were later to cause him anguish, that "to take a single step beyond the boundaries thus specially drawn around the powers of Congress is to take possession of a boundless field of power, no longer susceptible of any definition."

In 1798 Jefferson's fears seemed to come true. Enmeshed in undeclared war with France on the high seas, the Federalists tried to force Americans to cooperate with Adams's war plans by passing the Alien and Sedition Acts. These measures gave President John Adams the power to arrest and imprison his critics. Jeffersonians believed the acts were aimed at them — and with good reason: the 14 indictments and 10 convictions that occurred under the act were against members of the Republican Party. In secret, Jefferson and Madison helped the Virginia and Kentucky legislatures draft resolutions that condemned the Federalists for enlarging central government — especially presidential — powers beyond the limits set by the Constitution. The resolutions argued that a state should have the power to decide whether federal governmental acts were constitutional or not. Demanding that Congress support a strict construction of the 1787 document, Jefferson won what he called "the revolution of 1800," which threw Adams and the Hamiltonians out of office. The "sum of good government," he observed in his 1801 inaugural address, was small and limited government.

Thus Jefferson's dilemma in January and February 1803. As he and his closest advisers agreed, nothing in the Constitution explicitly permitted the

This painting shows Americans James Monroe and Robert Livingston and the French finance minister signing the Louisiana Purchase treaty in 1803. The transaction enlarged the size of the United States by "about 140 per cent," adding nearly 100,000 inhabitants — half of them white, the rest mostly Indian and African-American — to the national realm. (The Granger Collection, New York)

government to annex and govern new territory — let alone a territory so immense that it would transform the nation's political balance. Reading that power into the Constitution's general wording, Jefferson warned, could so twist and distort the document that American liberty would be threatened. "Our peculiar security is in possession of a written Constitution," he wrote privately to a close friend.

"Let us not make it a blank paper by construction." By no means, however, was he willing to turn away Louisiana.

In January 1803, Jefferson discussed these difficulties with Attorney General Levi Lincoln and the brilliant young secretary of the treasury, Albert Gallatin. Lincoln suggested that Jefferson have the French, if they sold any part of the territory, designate it as an extension of the Mississippi Territory or the state of Georgia. Gallatin retorted that if the central government lacked the constitutional power to annex new territory, then so did the states. By mid-January he had given Jefferson his rather Hamiltonian view of the matter: "1st. That the United States as a nation have an inherent right to acquire territory. 2nd. That whenever that acquisition is by treaty, the same constituted authorities in whom the treaty-making power is vested [that is, in the President and the Senate] have a constitutional right to sanction the acquisition. 3rd. That whenever the territory has been acquired, Congress have the power either of admitting into the Union as a new State, or of annexing to a State with the consent of that State, or of making regulations for the government of such territory."

In acquiring a territorial empire over the next century, Americans were to follow precisely these principles. But Gallatin's views did little to quell Jefferson's uneasiness, which reached a climax on July 3 when he learned that the two U.S. diplomats in Paris, Robert R. Livingston and James Monroe, had signed a treaty in which Napoleon sold Louisiana to the United States for $11,250,000. A separate agreement stipulated that the United States would assume $3,750,000 more for claims of U.S. citizens against France. The two diplomats also agreed that for 12 years French and Spanish ships would receive special tariff rates over other foreign ships and merchandise in New Orleans. The inhabitants of the vast territory, moreover, were to receive full constitutional rights as soon as possible.

These last provisions were to bedevil Jefferson. Giving French and Spanish traders preferences in New Orleans violated the Constitution's provisions that duties be levied uniformly throughout the nation. Granting full constitutional rights to the many non-Americans, especially nonwhites, in this vast area went against Jefferson's better judgment — not to mention the devout wishes of conservative and increasingly agitated New Englanders.

On July 16, Jefferson placed the agreements before his cabinet (or "executive council" as it was then known) and suggested that Congress "be obliged to ask from the people an amendment to the Constitution authorizing their receiving the province into the Union, and providing for its government." Gallatin, Madison, Lincoln, Secretary of War Henry Dearborn and Secretary of the Navy Robert Smith vigorously disagreed. They did not share the President's constitutional sensitivities.

The council pointed out a more immediate danger: the treaty provided for an exchange of ratifications within six months of the signing on April 30, 1803. No constitutional amendment could be passed by the necessary two-thirds vote in both houses of Congress and the three fourths of the states in the time remaining. But if there were any delay, Napoleon could renounce the agreement and recommence his empire building along the Mississippi. The advisers urged that Jefferson call a special session of Congress in October and rush the treaty and conventions through without mentioning the amendment.

Jefferson's friends warned him that if he so much as hinted at the need for an amendment, the treaty's enemies — most notably, New England Federalists whose fear of a vast western empire beyond their control was matched only by their hatred of Jefferson — would delay and probably kill the agreements. The President realized this. Nevertheless, that summer he tried to write at least two drafts of an amendment. He admitted to his close friend, Senator John Breckinridge of Kentucky, that in agreeing to the purchase he had gone far beyond what the Constitution permitted. Breckinridge, who had written the

Kentucky Resolutions with Jefferson just four years earlier, disagreed. He had long nurtured the ambition to control New Orleans and the trans-Mississippi — an ambition that in the 1790s had led him to plot secretly (and in some Easterners' eyes, treasonously) with a French agent to gain control of the river without the knowledge or approval of the Washington administration. In any case, the President's desire for empire was becoming overwhelming. "I infer," he wrote Madison later in August, "that the less we say about constitutional difficulties respecting Louisiana the better, and that what is necessary for surmounting them must be done sub silentio."

Jefferson found these "constitutional difficulties" distinctly less important after he received two letters. In the first, which arrived from Paris on August 17, Livingston warned that Napoleon now regretted having signed the treaty. The French leader was searching for any excuse ("the slightest alteration" made by the United States, in the envoy's words) to avoid carrying it out. If Congress did not act within the six-month limit, the First Consul would renounce the deal. The second letter carried a long-expected message from the Spanish minister in Washington, Marquis de Casa Yrujo. It reached Jefferson on September 12. The king of Spain, Yrujo wrote, was shocked that Napoleon had sold Louisiana. The French leader had no right to do so. The President now had to fear that either his majesty or Napoleon might use this message as an excuse to reclaim New Orleans and the interior.

Livingston's note decided Jefferson, and Yrujo's protest reinforced his determination. The President concluded that although it would be advisable to push for an amendment, it could be done only after Congress had acted on the agreements and the territory was safely in hand. In the meantime, he told Gallatin, Congress should approve the documents "without talking."

Jefferson needed two thirds of the Senate to ratify his treaty and a simple majority of the House to carry the agreements into effect. In the Senate, where his forces were led by the loyal Breckinridge, his party held 25 seats to the Federalists' nine; in the House the numbers were also overwhelming — 103 to 39. Jefferson, however, left nothing to chance. Regularly working 10 to 13 hours a day to ensure that his wishes were carried out, he became the most powerful party leader in the republic's short history. Such a regimen left, according to this remarkably organized man, "an interval of 4 hours for riding, dining, and a little unbending." Even then he used the dinner hour several times a week to invite congressional members, stoke them with excellent food and wine and, as Jefferson delicately put it, exchange information for the sake of the "public interest."

Many New England Federalists feared the idea of annexing a vast territory whose people would over time develop immense political power — and, no doubt, be forever grateful to Jeffersonians. A Boston Federalist newspaper sniffed that Louisiana was nothing more than "a great waste, a wilderness unpeopled with any beings except wolves and wandering Indians. . . . We are to give money of which we have too little for land of which we already have too much." Senator William Plumer, a Federalist from New Hampshire, warned that New England would not "tamely shrink into a state of insignificance."

On October 17, 1803, Jefferson told the Congress he had summoned into session that he was sending it the treaty and the accompanying agreements. Nothing was said about a constitutional amendment. The measures were being whipped through after only three days of debate when a crisis developed. Senate Federalists demanded that Jefferson send the documents proving that Napoleon had rightfully obtained Louisiana from Spain and so had the power to sell the territory. This demand presented a problem: the documents did not exist. Republicans nevertheless closed ranks and "with unblushing front" (as Plumer sarcastically commented) voted down the resolution on the grounds that such information was not needed. The agreements were then rammed through, 24 to 7.

"The Senate," Plumer complained, "have taken less time to deliberate on this most important treaty than they allowed themselves on the most trivial Indian contract."

Next the papers went to the House for legislation that would authorize monetary payments to carry out the agreements. Again the Federalists demanded documents, particularly a deed of cession from Spain to France. The request touched a nerve. Seven years earlier, Madison, then the Jeffersonian leader in a Federalist-dominated House of Representatives, had tried to kill the Jay treaty with Great Britain by demanding all appropriate documents. President Washington had refused on the grounds that the House was obliged to carry out treaties that, under the Constitution, only the Senate had to ratify. Madison protested, but he was beaten in a showdown vote that had large implications for the constitutional role the House was to play in future U.S. foreign policy. Now, in 1803, the roles were reversed. As the Federalists demanded the deed, Samuel Mitchill of New York rose to reply on behalf of the Jeffersonians that if the President had thought the House needed to see any more papers, he certainly would have sent them. After that disingenuous response, the House voted down the Federalist demand by two votes.

In his pioneering analysis of how rapidly presidential power grew during the Jeffersonian years, Abraham Sofaer argues that the Virginian set a precedent in refusing to acknowledge the Federalists' call for the documents. President Washington had taken the position that, yes, papers that Congress had requested did exist, but, no, he did not have to send certain confidential papers to Congress. The Jeffersonians had responded vigorously that such official information could be demanded and used by the people's representatives in the legislature. In 1803, however, (and again during the treason trial of former Vice-President Aaron Burr in 1807) Jefferson took the position that it was unnecessary to tell the Congress (or the court) that such papers even existed. Instead, he labeled the documents "private" or

"confidential" and kept them out of sight. The people's representatives in Congress apparently had a limited right to know, and the limits were determined by the President.

This embarrassment eased in December 1803 when Jefferson learned that Napoleon had finally pressured Spain into giving him official possession of Louisiana. In January 1804, the forces Jefferson had dispatched under Claiborne's command a year earlier controlled the region. The Stars and Stripes replaced the French Tricolor over New Orleans.

One major obstacle remained, however. Jefferson had to create, and Congress approve, a government for this vast territory. The region held fewer than 100,000 inhabitants, and Jefferson believed, rightly as it turned out, that only half of those were white and that the remainder were largely Indian and African-American. The President indicated from the start of the debate that he thought only whites could govern the territory. But even some of them were suspect. New Orleans had attracted renegades and runaways, like former New York district attorney, Edward Livingston, who had moved to New Orleans after he was suspected of having illegally siphoned money from his office. Roman Catholic groups, long protected by Spain, were fearful and suspicious of Jefferson's intentions. As for the large population of Creoles (those with French ancestry born in Louisiana), the President believed they were "as yet as incapable of self-government as children." When a Creole delegation traveled to Washington to demonstrate its ability to lobby, it was turned away.

Congress divided the region into two districts: Orleans (the future state of Louisiana) and Louisiana. Late in 1803 the President sent Congress a bill for governing the area during the next year. This measure gave the inhabitants guarantees for their "liberty, property, and religion," which the treaty had obligated him to grant. There was, however, no self-government, no indication that, to repeat one of Jefferson's earlier principles, governments derived "their just powers from the consent of the gov-

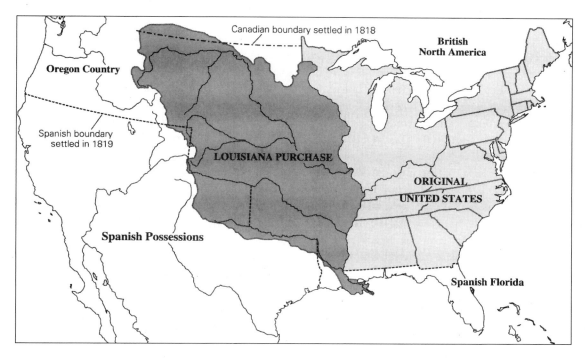

Map of the Louisiana Purchase

erned." Military officers, chosen by the President, were to rule in the iron-handed manner of the former Spanish governor. They were responsible to no local authorities, but only to the President in the faraway city of Washington. Senator John Quincy Adams, who had just won election from Massachusetts, supported the annexation, but he was appalled that the Constitution was being interpreted as giving the President authority to rule the territory as a colony. When Adams moved that a constitutional amendment be considered to make such rule legitimate, no senator seconded his proposal. Jefferson's governing bill passed the Senate 26 to 6.

The House's view of Jefferson's constitutional powers was revealed when angry Federalists attacked the treaty provision that gave French and Spanish merchants trade preferences in New Orleans. Joseph H. Nicholson of Maryland replied for the Jeffersoni-

ans that the whole of Louisiana "is in the nature of a colony whose commerce may be regulated without any reference to the Constitution" and its provision that duties be uniformly imposed throughout the Union. Madison, with his sensitivity to such issues, excused the Jeffersonians' tough approach by granting that while "Republican theory" would not immediately govern the newly annexed people, "it may fairly be expected that every blessing of liberty will be extended to them as fast as they shall be prepared and disposed to receive it." The secretary of state was known for choosing his words carefully.

From January through March 1804, Congress discussed Jefferson's plans for a more permanent government, which would last until both sections of Louisiana had enough white settlers to be entrusted with regular territorial government. Few problems arose in the debates until Senator James Hillhouse of

185

Connecticut proposed that slavery be prohibited from both parts of the purchase. A struggle erupted in the Senate that previewed some of the arguments that later threatened to splinter the Union. When one slave-state senator tried to stop the uproar by saying, "I am unwilling to think let alone speak on this subject," another grimly warned that "if we leave it, it will follow us." Jefferson notably refused to support Hillhouse, and Senator James Jackson of Georgia led the opposition to the Connecticut senator by declaring that Louisiana could "not be cultivated" without slavery. He urged that the people on the scene (many of whom owned slaves) be allowed to decide. "You cannot prevent slavery.... Men will be governed by their interest not the law." In the end, though, Congress again broadly construed its power by recognizing slavery where it existed in the purchase, while allowing a previous act to stand that stringently limited the slave trade. Provisions were added to prevent Orleans, a center of the foreign slave trade, from becoming a state until after the 1810 census. This delay not only appeased New England Federalists but also prevented Orleans' entry as a state until after 1808 when, as the Constitution provided, the foreign trade in slaves was to end.

The final bill gave the President the power to appoint governors over Orleans and Louisiana who, with a small legislative body they were to choose, would rule autocratically. The rights of the inhabitants were not "self-evident," as Jefferson had once described them, but were granted by the will of the central government. The law became effective October 1, 1804.

In less than one year Jefferson had enlarged the central government's constitutional powers more broadly than had Washington and Adams in 12 years. He had set a dangerous precedent, moreover, by arguing that when time was of the essence, the President and Congress could ignore, perhaps violate, the Constitution if they considered it to be in the national interest. Critics called Jefferson's government in Louisiana "about as despotic as that of

Turkey in Asia." The President and his supporters responded that such a government was, unfortunately, necessary to ensure that the vast territory would remain orderly until enough white Americans could populate the region. The new states would then prosper as a part of the Union with rights equal to those of the older parts.

Critics were not reassured. "We rush like a comet into infinite space," Fisher Ames of Massachusetts warned. "In our wild career we may jostle some other world out of its orbit, but we shall, in every event, quench the light of our own." John Randolph of Virginia had a less apocalyptic response to Jefferson's actions. He had helped the President push the Louisiana legislation through the House. But by 1806 he had turned against his fellow Virginian for having overthrown Republican constitutional doctrine. There were only "two parties in all States," Randolph concluded, "the *ins* and the *outs*." The ins construed governmental power broadly for the gain of their own "patronage and wealth," while the outs tried to limit such power. "But let the *outs* get in . . . and you will find their Constitutional scruples and arguments vanish like dew before the morning sun."

As the ins, Jefferson and his supporters realized larger objectives than "patronage and wealth." They succeeded in transforming the Constitution into an instrument for imperial expansion, which made it possible for Jefferson to resolve the crisis in his great democratic experiment.

But the transformation of the Constitution for the sake of "enlarging the empire of liberty" had a price. The President, as Jefferson had demonstrated, could find in the Constitution virtually any power he needed to carry out the most expansive foreign policy, especially if his party commanded a majority in Congress. Loose construction was given the seal of bipartisanship as the Republicans, now the ins, out-Hamiltoned Hamilton in construing the 1787 document broadly. Such loose construction would be used by others, among them President James K. Polk from 1845 to '46 as he maneuvered Mexico into a war in order to annex California, President William McKinley between 1898 and 1901 when he expanded U.S. power into the Philippines and landed troops in China, and President Harry S Truman when he claimed the authority to wage war in Korea. Jefferson's experiment in democracy cast long shadows.

QUESTIONS TO CONSIDER

1   Why was Louisiana such an attractive prize to so many? Why was Jefferson in particular tempted by it? Who was generally opposed to the acquisition of the Louisiana Territory and why?

2   Describe the constitutional questions raised by the acquisition of Louisiana. What was Jefferson's decision, and how did it compare with the position he took during his constitutional debates with Alexander Hamilton and the Federalists in the 1790s? How do you reconcile this portrait of the political Jefferson with the one drawn by Douglas Wilson in selection 8? How do you think Jefferson compares with the President Washington of selection 10?

3   What kind of government did Jefferson recommend for the Louisiana Territory and why? What social and political ironies are there in this choice?

4   What position did Jefferson take on slavery in the new territory, and how does it jibe with his feelings on slavery as portrayed by Douglas Wilson in selection 8? How did Congress deal with this issue?

5   In what ways does LaFeber find the Louisiana Purchase "a dangerous precedent"? Do you agree? What might have happened if we had not bought Louisiana?

14

The Great Chief Justice

BRIAN MCGINTY

As the court of last appeal in all matters involving the Constitution, the United States Supreme Court may be the most powerful branch of the federal government. It has the authority to uphold or strike down federal and state legislation, overturn decisions by lower courts, and determine the rights of individuals. Consequently, as in the modern struggle over abortion, the Court often stands at the center of national controversy.

You may be surprised to read in this selection that the Court was not always supreme, that in the first decade of its existence it was a maligned junior branch of the federal government, ignored by lawyers and scorned by politicians. How did it change into the powerful national tribunal we know today? As Brian McGinty points out, Chief Justice John Marshall made the nation's high tribunal a court that is supreme in fact as well as in name. During his thirty-four years on the bench (from 1801 to 1835), Marshall, a dedicated Federalist, also read the basic tenets of federalism into American constitutional law: the supremacy of the nation over the states, the sanctity of contracts, the protection of property rights, and the superiority of business over agriculture.

If you fear you are about to read a dull and dreary essay on constitutional law, don't despair. McGinty's warm portrait of the chief justice personalizes the major currents of the period and captures Marshall the human being in vivid scenes. We see him doing his own shopping for groceries, frequenting taverns and grog shops (he loves wine so much that a colleague quips, "the Chief was brought up on Federalism and Madeira"), and carrying a turkey for a young man who is too embarrassed to do so in public. Marshall clashes repeatedly with Jefferson over fundamental political and constitutional issues;

later, Marshall tangles with Andrew Jackson in defending the treaty rights of the Chero-kee Indians, a subject to be treated in more detail in selection 21.

It was Marshall's Court decisions, however, that had the biggest influence on his country. As McGinty says, Marshall's ruling in Marbury v. *Madison, which estab-lished the principle of judicial review, was perhaps the most important decision ever to come from the United States Supreme Court. Judicial review empowered the Supreme Court to interpret the meaning of the Constitution and so to define the authority of the national government and the states. The system of judicial review helped ensure the flex-ibility of the Constitution — so much so that a document originally designed for a small, scattered, largely agrarian population on the East Coast could endure for two centuries, during which the United States became a transcontinental, then a transpacific urban and industrial nation. That the Constitution has been able to grow and change with the country owes much to John Marshall.*

GLOSSARY

BURR, AARON First United States citizen to be tried for treason; Marshall helped acquit him in his trial before the Supreme Court.

FEDERALISTS Those such as Washington, Hamilton, and Marshall who favored a strong federal government and a stable, well-ordered society run by the great landowners and merchants.

GIBBONS v. *OGDEN* (1824) Case in which Marshall upheld federal jurisdiction over interstate commerce.

MARBURY v. *MADISON* (1803) Case in which Marshall established the principle of judicial review, which empowered the Supreme Court to interpret the Constitution and thus to define the authority of the national government and the states.

MCCULLOCH v. *MARYLAND* (1819) Case in which Marshall ruled that the first United States Bank was constitutional and that the state of Maryland could not tax it.

STORY, JOSEPH Associate justice on the Marshall Court and the chief justice's personal friend.

WORCESTER v. *GEORGIA* (1832) Marshall decision forbidding the state of Georgia to violate the treaty rights of the Cherokees.

WYTHE, GEORGE Professor at the College of William and Mary in Virginia who was a mentor to Marshall, Jefferson, and Henry Clay (to be treated in a later selection); he was the first law professor in the United States.

He was a tall man with long legs, gangling arms, and a round, friendly face. He had a thick head of dark hair and strong, black eyes — "penetrating eyes," a friend called them, "beaming with intelligence and good nature." He was born in a log cabin in western Virginia and never wholly lost his rough frontier manners. Yet John Marshall became a lawyer, a member of Congress, a diplomat, an advisor to presidents, and the most influential and respected judge in the history of the United States. "If American law were to be represented by a single figure," Supreme Court Justice Oliver Wendell Holmes, Jr., once said, "sceptic and worshipper alike would agree without dispute that the figure could be but one alone, and that one John Marshall."

To understand Marshall's preeminence in American legal history it is necessary to understand the marvelous rebirth the United States Supreme Court experienced after he became its chief justice in 1801. During all of the previous eleven years of its existence, the highest judicial court in the federal system had been weak and ineffectual — ignored by most of the nation's lawyers and judges and scorned by its principal politicians. Under Marshall's leadership, the court became a strong and vital participant in national affairs. During his more than thirty-four years as chief justice of the United States, Marshall welded the Supreme Court into an effective and cohesive whole. With the support of his colleagues on the high bench, he declared acts of Congress and of the president unconstitutional, struck down laws that infringed on federal prerogatives, and gave force and dignity to basic guarantees of life and liberty and property. Without John Marshall, the Supreme Court might never have been anything but an inconsequential junior partner of the executive and

From "The Great Chief Justice" by Brian McGinty, *American History Illustrated* (September 1988), pp. 8–14, 46–47. Reprinted by permission of Cowles Magazines, publisher of *American History Illustrated.*

legislative branches of the national government. Under his guidance and inspiration, it became what the Constitution intended it to be — a court system in fact as well as in name.

Born on September 4, 1755, in Fauquier County, Virginia, John Marshall was the oldest of fifteen children born to Thomas Marshall and Mary Randolph Keith. On his mother's side, the young Virginian was distantly related to Thomas Jefferson, the gentlemanly squire of Monticello and author of the Declaration of Independence. Aside from this kinship, there was little similarity between Marshall and Jefferson. A son of the frontier, Marshall was a backwoodsman at heart, more comfortable in the company of farmers than intellectuals or scholars. Jefferson was a polished aristocrat who liked to relax in the library of his mansion near Charlottesville and meditate on the subtleties of philosophy and political theory.

The contrast between the two men was most clearly drawn in their opposing political beliefs. An advocate of limiting the powers of central government, Thomas Jefferson thought of himself first and foremost as a Virginian (his epitaph did not even mention the fact that he had once been president of the United States). Marshall, in contrast, had, even as a young man, come to transcend his state roots, to look to Congress rather than the Virginia legislature as his government, to think of himself first, last, and always as an American. Throughout their careers, their contrasting philosophies would place the two men at odds.

Marshall's national outlook was furthered by his father's close association with George Washington and his own unflinching admiration for the nation's first president. Thomas Marshall had been a schoolmate of Washington and, as a young man, helped him survey the Fairfax estates in northern Virginia. John Marshall served under Washington during the bitter winter at Valley Forge and later became one of the planter-turned-statesman's most loyal supporters.

Years after the Revolution was over, Marshall attributed his political views to his experiences as a

Chester Harding's 1829 portrait of John Marshall. The chief justice, writes Brian McGinty, "was a tall man with long legs, gangling arms, and a round, friendly face. He had a thick head of dark hair and strong, black eyes — 'penetrating eyes,' a friend called them, 'beaming with intelligence and good nature.'" (Washington and Lee University, Virginia)

ent states who were risking life and everything valuable in a common cause believed by all to be most precious; and where I was confirmed in the habit of considering America as my country, and Congress as my government."

After Washington's death, Marshall became the great man's biographer, penning a long and admiring account of Washington's life as a farmer, soldier, and statesman, expounding the Federalist philosophy represented by Washington and attacking those who stood in opposition to it. Jefferson, who detested Federalism as much as he disliked Marshall, was incensed by the biography, which he branded a "five-volume libel."

Frontiersman though he was, Marshall was no bumpkin. His father had personally attended to his earliest schooling, teaching him to read and write and giving him a taste for history and poetry (by the age of twelve he had already transcribed the whole of Alexander Pope's *Essay on Man*). When he was fourteen, Marshall was sent to a school a hundred miles from home, where future president James Monroe was one of his classmates. After a year, he returned home to be tutored by a Scottish pastor who had come to live in the Marshall house. The future lawyer read Horace and Livy, pored through the English dictionary, and scraped at least a passing acquaintance with the "Bible of the Common Law," William Blackstone's celebrated *Commentaries on the Laws of England*.

In 1779, during a lull in the Revolution, young Marshall attended lectures at the College of William and Mary in Williamsburg. He remained at the college only a few weeks, but the impression made on him by his professor there, George Wythe, was lasting. A lawyer, judge, and signer of the Declaration of Independence, Wythe is best remembered today as the first professor of law at any institution of higher learning in the United States. As a teacher, he was a seminal influence in the development of American law, counting among his

foot soldier in the great conflict, recalling that he grew up "at a time when a love of union and resistance to the claims of Great Britain were the inseparable inmates of the same bosom — when patriotism and a strong fellow feeling with our suffering fellow citizens of Boston were identical; — when the maxim 'united we stand, divided we fall' was the maxim of every orthodox American . . ." "I had imbibed these sentiments so thoughroughly (sic) that they constituted a part of my being," wrote Marshall. "I carried them with me into the army where I found myself associated with brave men from differ-

many distinguished students Thomas Jefferson, John Breckinridge, and Henry Clay.

Marshall did not remain long at William and Mary. It was the nearly universal custom then for budding lawyers to "read law" in the office of an older lawyer or judge or, failing that, to appeal to the greatest teacher of all — experience — for instruction. In August 1780, a few weeks before his twenty-fifth birthday, Marshall appeared at the Fauquier County Courthouse where, armed with a license signed by Governor Thomas Jefferson of Virginia, he was promptly admitted to the bar.

His first cases were not important, but he handled them well and made a favorable impression on his neighbors; so favorable that they sent him to Richmond in 1782 as a member of the Virginia House of Delegates. Though he retained a farm in Fauquier County all his life, Richmond became Marshall's home after his election to the legislature. The general courts of Virginia held their sessions in the new capital, and the commonwealth's most distinguished lawyers crowded its bar. When Marshall's fortunes improved, he built a comfortable brick house on the outskirts of the city, in which he and his beloved wife Polly raised five sons and one daughter (four other offspring died during childhood).

Marshall's skill as a lawyer earned him an enthusiastic coterie of admirers and his honest country manners an even warmer circle of friends. He liked to frequent the city's taverns and grog shops, more for conviviality than for refreshment, and he was an enthusiastic member of the Barbecue Club, which met each Saturday to eat, drink, "josh," and play quoits.

Marshall liked to do his own shopping for groceries. Each morning he marched through the streets with a basket under his arm, collecting fresh fruits, vegetables, and poultry for the Marshall family larder. Years after his death, Richmonders were fond of recalling the day when a stranger came into the city in search of a lawyer and found Marshall in front of the Eagle Hotel, holding a hat filled with cherries and speaking casually with the hotel proprietor. After Marshall went on his way, the stranger approached the proprietor and asked if he could direct him to the best lawyer in Richmond. The proprietor replied quite readily that the best lawyer was John Marshall, the tall man with the hat full of cherries who had just walked down the street.

But the stranger could not believe that a man who walked through town so casually could be a really "proper barrister" and chose instead to hire a lawyer who wore a black suit and powdered wig. On the day set for the stranger's trial, several cases were scheduled to be argued. In the first that was called, the visitor was surprised to see that John Marshall and his own lawyer were to speak on opposite sides. As he listened to the arguments, he quickly realized that he had made a serious mistake. At the first recess, he approached Marshall and confessed that he had come to Richmond with a hundred dollars to hire the best lawyer in the city, but he had chosen the wrong one and now had only five dollars left. Would Marshall agree to represent him for such a small fee? Smiling good-naturedly, Marshall accepted the five dollars, then proceeded to make a brilliant legal argument that quickly won the stranger's case.

Marshall was not an eloquent man; not eloquent, that is, in the sense that his great contemporary, Patrick Henry, a spellbinding courtroom orator, was eloquent. Marshall was an effective enough speaker; but, more importantly, he was a rigorously logical thinker. He had the ability to reduce complex issues to bare essentials and easily and effortlessly apply abstract principles to resolve them.

Thomas Jefferson (himself a brilliant lawyer) was awed, even intimidated, by Marshall's powers of persuasion. "When conversing with Marshall," Jefferson once said, "I never admit anything. So sure as you admit any position to be good, no matter how remote from the conclusion he seeks to establish, you are gone. . . . Why, if he were to ask me if it were daylight or not, I'd reply, 'Sir, I don't know, I can't tell.'"

Though Marshall's legal prowess and genial manner won him many friends in Richmond, his political views did little to endear him to the Old Dominion's political establishment. While Jefferson and his followers preached the virtues of agrarian democracy, viewing with alarm every step by which the fledgling national government extended its powers through the young nation, Marshall clearly allied himself with Washington, Alexander Hamilton, and John Adams and the Federalist policies they espoused.

Marshall was not a delegate to the convention that met in Philadelphia in 1787 to draft a constitution for the United States, but he took a prominent part in efforts to secure ratification of the Constitution, thereby winning the special admiration of George Washington. After taking office as president, Washington offered Marshall the post of attorney general. Marshall declined the appointment, as he did a later offer of the prestigious post of American minister to France, explaining that he preferred to stay in Richmond with his family and law practice.

He did agree, however, to go to Paris in 1798 as one of three envoys from President John Adams to the government of revolutionary France. He did this, in part, because he was assured that his duties in Paris would be temporary only, in part because he believed he could perform a real service for his country, helping to preserve peaceful relations between it and France during a time of unusual diplomatic tension.

After Marshall joined his colleagues Elbridge Gerry and Charles Pinckney in Paris, he was outraged to learn that the French government expected to be paid before it would receive the American emissaries. Marshall recognized the French request as a solicitation for a bribe (the recipients of the payments were mysteriously identified as "X," "Y," and "Z"), and he refused to consider it.

Thomas Jefferson, who was smitten with the ardor and ideals of the French Revolution, suspected that Marshall and his Federalist "cronies" were planning war with France to promote the interests of their friends in England. But the American people believed otherwise. When they received news of the "XYZ Affair," they were outraged. "Millions for defense," the newspapers thundered, "but not one cent for tribute!" When Marshall returned home in the summer of 1798, he was welcomed as a hero. In the elections of the following fall, he was sent to Congress as a Federalist representative from Richmond.

Jefferson was not pleased. He declined to attend a dinner honoring Marshall in Philadelphia and wrote worried letters to his friends. Though he deprecated his fellow Virginian's popularity, alternatively attributing it to his "lax, lounging manners" and his "profound hypocrisy," Jefferson knew that Marshall was a potentially dangerous adversary. A half-dozen years before the Richmonder's triumphal return from Paris, Jefferson had written James Madison a cutting letter about Marshall that included words he would one day rue: "I think nothing better could be done than to make him a judge."

In Congress, Marshall vigorously supported the Federalist policies of President John Adams. Adams took note of the Virginian's ability in 1800 when he appointed him to the important post of secretary of state, a position that not only charged him with conduct of the country's foreign affairs but also left him in effective charge of the government during Adam's frequent absences in Massachusetts.

John Marshall's future in government seemed rosy and secure in 1800. But the elections in November of that year changed all that, sweeping Adams and the Federalists from power and replacing them with Jefferson and the Democratic Republicans.

After the election, but before Adam's term as president expired, ailing Supreme Court Chief Justice Oliver Ellsworth submitted his resignation. Casting about for a successor to Ellsworth, Adams sent John Jay's name to the Senate, only to have Jay demand that it be withdrawn. The thought of leaving the appointment of a new chief justice to Jefferson was abhorrent to Adams, and the president was growing anxious. He summoned Marshall to his office to confer about the problem.

"Who shall I nominate now?" Adams asked dejectedly. Marshall answered that he did not know. He had previously suggested that Associate Justice William Paterson be elevated to the chief justiceship, but Adams had opposed Paterson then and Marshall supposed that he still did. The president pondered for a moment, then turned to Marshall and announced: "I believe I shall nominate you!"

Adams's statement astounded Marshall. Only two years before, Marshall had declined the president's offer of an associate justiceship, explaining that he still hoped to return to his law practice in Richmond. "I had never before heard myself named for the office," Marshall recalled later, "and had not even thought of it. I was pleased as well as surprized (sic), and bowed my head in silence."

Marshall's nomination was sent to the Senate and promptly confirmed, and on February 4, 1801, he took his seat as the nation's fourth Chief Justice. As subsequent events would prove, it was one of the most important dates in American history.

With Thomas Jefferson in the Executive Mansion and John Marshall in the Chief Justice's chair, it was inevitable that the Supreme Court and the executive branch of the government should come into conflict. Marshall believed firmly in a strong national government and was willing to do all he could to strengthen federal institutions. Jefferson believed as firmly in state sovereignty and the necessity for maintaining constant vigilance against federal "usurpations." In legal matters, Jefferson believed that the Constitution should be interpreted strictly, so as to reduce rather than expand federal power.

Marshall, in contrast, believed that the Constitution should be construed fairly so as to carry out the intentions of its framers. Any law or executive act that violated the terms of the Constitution was, in Marshall's view, a nullity, of no force or effect; and it was the peculiar prerogative of the courts, as custodians of the laws of the land, to strike down any law that offended the Supreme Law of the Land.

Jefferson did not question the authority of the courts to decide whether a law or executive act violated the Constitution, but he believed that the other branches of the government also had a duty and a right to decide constitutional questions. In a controversy between the Supreme Court and the president, for example, the Supreme Court could order the president to do whatever the Court thought the Constitution required him to do; but the president could decide for himself whether the Supreme Court's order was proper and whether or not it should be obeyed.

As he took up the duties of the chief justiceship, Marshall contemplated his role with uncertainty. The Supreme Court in 1801 was certainly not the kind of strong, vital institution that might have been expected to provide direction in national affairs. There were six justices when Marshall joined the Court, but none (save the Chief Justice himself) was particularly distinguished. One or two men of national prominence had accepted appointment to the Court in the first eleven years of its existence, but none had remained there long. John Jay, the first Chief Justice, had resigned his seat in 1795 to become governor of New York. During the two years that John Rutledge was an associate justice, he had regarded the Court's business as so trifling that he did not bother to attend a single session, and he finally resigned to become chief justice of South Carolina. The Court itself had counted for so little when the new capitol at Washington was being planned that the architects had made no provision for either a courtroom or judges' chambers, and the justices (to everyone's embarrassment) found that they had to meet in a dingy basement room originally designed for the clerk of the Senate.

How could Chief Justice Marshall use his new office to further the legal principles in which he believed so strongly? How could he strengthen the weak and undeveloped federal judiciary when most of the nation's lawyers and judges regarded that judiciary as superfluous and unnecessary? How could he implement his view of the Supreme Court as the final arbiter of constitutional questions when the President of the United States — his old nemesis, Thomas Jefferson — disagreed with that view so sharply? It was not an easy task, but John Marshall was a resourceful man, and he found a way to accomplish it.

His opportunity came in 1803 in the case of *Marbury* v. *Madison*. William Marbury was one of several minor federal judges who had been appointed during the closing days of John Adams's administration. When Jefferson's secretary of state, James Madison, refused to deliver the commissions of their offices, the judges sued Madison to compel delivery. In 1789, Congress had passed a law granting the Supreme Court authority to issue writs of mandamus, that is, legally enforceable orders compelling public officials to do their legal duties. Following the mandate of Congress, Marbury and the other appointees filed a petition for writ of mandamus in the Supreme Court.

Marshall pondered the possibilities of the case. He was sure that Marbury and his colleagues were entitled to their commissions, and he was just as sure that Jefferson and Madison had no intention of letting them have them. He could order Madison to deliver the commissions, but the secretary of state would certainly defy the order; and, as a practical matter, the Court could not compel obedience to any order that the president refused to acknowledge. Such an impasse would weaken, not strengthen, the federal union, and it would engender unprecedented controversy. No, there must be a better way. . . .

All eyes and ears in the capitol were trained on the lanky Chief Justice as he took his seat at the head of the high bench on February 24, 1803, and began to read the Supreme Court's opinion in *Marbury* v. *Madison*.

The evidence, Marshall said, clearly showed that Marbury and the other judges were entitled to their commissions. The commissions had been signed and sealed before John Adams left office and were, for all legal purposes, complete and effective. To withhold them, as Jefferson and Madison insisted on doing, was an illegal act. But the Supreme Court would not order the secretary of state to deliver the commissions because the law authorizing it to issue writs of mandamus was unconstitutional: the Constitution does not authorize the Supreme Court to issue writs of mandamus; in fact, it prohibits it from doing so. And any law that violates the Constitution is void. Since the law purporting to authorize the Supreme Court to act was unconstitutional, the Court would not — indeed, it could not — order Madison to do his legal duty.

If historians and constitutional lawyers were asked to name the single most important case ever decided in the United States Supreme Court, there is little doubt that the case would be *Marbury* v. *Madison*. Though the dispute that gave rise to the decision was in itself insignificant, John Marshall used it as a springboard to a great constitutional pronouncement. The rule of the case — that the courts of the United States have the right to declare laws unconstitutional — was immediately recognized as the cornerstone of American constitutional law, and it has remained so ever since.

More than a half-century would pass before the Supreme Court would again declare an act of Congress unconstitutional, but its authority to do so would never again be seriously doubted. Marshall had made a bold stroke, and he had done so in such a way that neither Congress, nor the president, nor any other public official had any power to resist it. By denying relief to Marbury, he had made the Supreme Court's order marvelously self-enforcing!

Predictably, Thomas Jefferson was angry. If the Supreme Court could not issue writs of mandamus, Jefferson asked, why did Marshall spend so much time discussing Marbury's entitlement to a commission?

And why did the Chief Justice lecture Madison that withholding the commission was an illegal act?

The president thought for a time that he might have the Chief Justice and his allies on the bench impeached. After a mentally unstable federal judge in New Hampshire was removed from office, Jefferson's supporters in the House of Representatives brought a bill of impeachment against Marshall's colleague on the Supreme Court, Associate Justice Samuel Chase. Chase was a Federalist who had occasionally badgered witnesses and made intemperate speeches, but no one seriously contended that he had committed an impeachable offense (which the Constitution defines as "treason, bribery, or other high crimes and misdemeanors"). So the Senate, three quarters of whose members were Jeffersonians, refused to remove Chase from office. Marshall breathed a deep sigh of relief. Had the associate justice been impeached, the chief had no doubt that he himself would have been Jefferson's next target.

Though he never again had occasion to strike down an act of Congress, Marshall delivered opinions in many cases of national significance; and, in his capacity as circuit judge (all Supreme Court justices "rode circuit" in the early years of the nineteenth century), he presided over important, sometimes controversial, trials. He was the presiding judge when Jefferson's political arch rival, Aaron Burr, was charged with treason in 1807. Interpreting the constitutional provision defining treason against the United States, Marshall helped to acquit Burr, though he did so with obvious distaste. The Burr prosecution, Marshall said, was "the most unpleasant case which has been brought before a judge in this or perhaps any other country which affected to be governed by law."

On the high bench, Marshall presided over scores of precedent-setting cases. In *Fletcher* v. *Peck* (1810) and *Dartmouth College* v. *Woodward* (1819), he construed the contracts clause of the Constitution so as to afford important protection for the country's growing business community. In *McCulloch* v. *Mary-land* (1819), he upheld the constitutionality of the first Bank of the United States and struck down the Maryland law that purported to tax it. In *Gibbons* v. *Ogden* (1824), he upheld federal jurisdiction over interstate commerce and lectured those (mainly Jeffersonians) who persistently sought to enlarge state powers at the expense of legitimate federal authority.

Though Marshall's opinions always commanded respect, they were frequently unpopular. When, in *Worcester* v. *Georgia* (1832), he upheld the treaty rights of the Cherokee Indians against encroachments by the State of Georgia, he incurred the wrath of President Andrew Jackson. "John Marshall has made his decision," "Old Hickory" snapped contemptuously. "Now let him enforce it!" Marshall knew, of course, that he could not enforce the decision; that he could not enforce any decision that did not have the moral respect and acquiescence of the public and the officials they elected. And so he bowed his head in sadness and hoped that officials other than Andrew Jackson would one day show greater respect for the nation's legal principles and institutions.

Despite the controversy that some of his decisions inspired, the Chief Justice remained personally popular; and, during the whole of his more than thirty-four years as head of the federal judiciary, the Court grew steadily in authority and respect.

Well into his seventies, Marshall continued to ride circuit in Virginia and North Carolina, to travel each year to his farm in Fauquier County, to attend to his shopping duties in Richmond, and to preside over the high court each winter and spring in Washington. On one of his visits to a neighborhood market in Richmond, the Chief Justice happened on a young man who had been sent to fetch a turkey for his mother. The youth wanted to comply with his mother's request, but thought it was undignified to carry a turkey in the streets "like a servant." Marshall offered to carry it for him. When the jurist got as far as his own home, he turned to the young man and said, "This is where I live. Your house is not far off; can't you carry the turkey the balance of the way?" The young man's face turned crimson as he suddenly realized that his benefactor was none other than the Chief Justice of the United States.

Joseph Story, who served as an associate justice of the Supreme Court for more than twenty years of Marshall's term as chief justice, spent many hours with the Virginian in and out of Washington. Wherever Story observed Marshall, he was impressed by his modesty and geniality. "Meet him in a stagecoach, as a stranger, and travel with him a whole day," Story said, "and you would only be struck with his readiness to administer to the accommodations of others, and his anxiety to appropriate the least to himself. Be with him, the unknown guest at an inn, and he seemed adjusted to the very scene, partaking of the warm welcome of its comforts, wherever found; and if not found, resigning himself without complaint to its meanest arrangements. You would never suspect, in either case, that he was a great man; far less that he was the Chief Justice of the United States."

In his youth, Marshall had been fond of corn whiskey. As he grew older, he lost his appetite for spirits but not for wine. He formulated a "rule" under which the Supreme Court judges abstained from wine except in wet weather, but Story said he was liberal in allowing "exceptions." "It does sometimes happen," Story once said, "the Chief Justice will say to me, when the cloth is removed, 'Brother Story, step to the window and see if it does not look like rain.' And if I tell him that the sun is shining brightly, Judge Marshall will sometimes reply, 'All the better; for our jurisdiction extends over so large a territory that it must be raining somewhere.'" "You know," Story added, "that the Chief was brought up upon Federalism and Madeira, and he is not the man to outgrow his early prejudices."

In Richmond, Marshall held regular dinners for local lawyers, swapped stories with old friends, and tossed quoits with his neighbors in the Barbecue Club. An artist named Chester Harding remembered seeing the chief justice at a session of the Barbecue Club in 1829. Harding said Marshall was "the best pitcher of the party, and could throw heavier quoits than any other member of the club." "There were several ties," he added, "and, before long, I saw the great Chief Justice of the United States, down on his knees, measuring the contested distance with a straw, with as much earnestness as if it had been a point of law; and if he proved to be in the right, the woods would ring with his triumphant shout."

In 1830, a young Pennsylvania congressman and future president of the United States commented on Marshall's enduring popularity among his neighbors. "His decisions upon constitutional questions have ever been hostile to the opinions of a vast majority of the people in his own State," James Buchanan said, "and yet with what respect and veneration has he been viewed by Virginia? Is there a Virginian whose heart does not beat with honest pride when the just fame of the Chief Justice is the subject of conversation? They consider him, as he truly is, one of the great and best men which this country has ever produced."

Marshall was nearly eighty years old when he died in Philadelphia on July 6, 1835. His body was brought back to Virginia for burial, where it was met by the longest procession the city of Richmond had ever seen.

In the contrast between proponents of strong and weak national government, Marshall had been one of the foremost and clearest advocates of strength. The struggle — between union and disunion, between federation and confederation, between the belief that the Constitution created a nation and the theory that it aligned the states in a loose league — was not finally resolved until 1865. But the struggle *was* resolved. "Time has been on Marshall's side," Oliver Wendell Holmes, Jr., said in 1901. "The theory for which Hamilton argued, and he decided, and Webster spoke, and Grant fought, is now our cornerstone."

Justice Story thought that Marshall's appointment to the Supreme Court contributed more "to the preservation of the true principles of the Constitution than any other circumstances in our domestic history." "He was a great man," Story said. "I go farther; and insist, that he would have been deemed a great man in any age, and of all ages. He was one of those, to whom centuries alone give birth."

John Adams and Thomas Jefferson both lived long and distinguished lives, but neither ever gave an inch in their differences of opinion over Marshall. Jefferson went to his grave bemoaning the "cunning and sophistry" of his fellow Virginian. Adams died secure in the belief that his decision to make Marshall chief justice had been both wise and provident. Years later, Adams called Marshall's appointment "the pride of my life." Time has accorded Thomas Jefferson a great place in the affections of the American people, but, in the controversy over John Marshall, the judgment of history has come down with quiet strength on the side of John Adams.

QUESTIONS TO CONSIDER

1   John Marshall and Thomas Jefferson were both Virginians; they were also distant relatives. How did they turn out to be so different? How has McGinty's article altered or expanded your view of the Thomas Jefferson you met in selections 8 and 13?

2   *Marbury* v. *Madison* was a case of small immediate significance in 1803, a legal squabble over a few petty government appointments. How did it turn out to have such enormous consequences for America's governmental structure? What implications did Marshall's legal actions have for the Supreme Court's future, particularly when the Court was pitted against a popular president?

3   In *Marbury* v. *Madison* and in a few other cases, Chief Justice Marshall, a staunch Federalist, wrote decisions unfavorable to his party's interests. What elements in his character caused him to ignore party politics? Discuss the precedents that may have been set by his actions.

4   McGinty's biography alternates episodes from Marshall's famous legal career with anecdotes from his private life. Do you find this technique distracting, or does it help you to understand Marshall more fully? What sort of man do the personal anecdotes reveal? Are these traits evident in Marshall's long career as chief justice?

5   We live today under a strong central government that owes much to legal decisions written by Chief Justice Marshall more than 150 years ago. Discuss the ways in which the United States today is a "Federalist" rather than a "Republican" nation.

WOE IF IT COMES
WITH STORM
AND BLOOD AND FIRE

The Fires of Jubilee: Nat Turner's Fierce Rebellion

STEPHEN B. OATES

While John Marshall was sitting on the bench, handing down judicial rulings aimed at stabilizing the Republic, there was another America, a black America, struggling on the underside of society to gain its freedom, its wholeness and humanity. Let us pick up the story of that struggle with the outbreak of the Revolution. The labor of slaves, as we have seen, was indispensable to the American cause. Hoping to disrupt the American war effort, the British invited the slaves to desert their American masters and join the British side, ultimately promising freedom if they did so. This promise horrified the American patriots. "Hell itself," one cried, "could not have vomited anything more black than this design of emancipating our slaves."

The Americans had reason to be worried, for their slaves went over to the British in ever increasing numbers. That blacks fought against the Revolution challenges the traditional notions of freedom and oppression in the Revolutionary era. From the view of fleeing slaves, the redcoats were the liberators, the American patriots the oppressors. To forestall mass slave defections, the Americans started recruiting blacks as soldiers too; some states even offered freedom in exchange for military service (South Carolina, however, offered white volunteers a bounty in slaves, in the form of one adult black to each private, three adult blacks and a child to each colonel). Altogether some five thousand blacks served the American cause. But approximately 100,000 blacks, a fifth of the slave population in revolutionary America, were "loyalists," who sided with the British. When the war ended, General Washington, angry because some of his own slaves had fled, demanded that the defeated British return the black loyalists to their American masters. The British, however, asserted that the blacks had been emancipated in accordance with royal policy. In the end, the British did give up blacks who had been seized by royal forces and refugees who had come to British lines after the war had ended. Other black loyalists wound up in slavery in the British West Indies; three thousand more were colonized in Nova Scotia, where they braved discrimination and established a community that still exists.

The black patriots, by contrast, gained a measure of freedom when the northern states abolished slavery. New Jersey even allowed them to vote — for a while. But most "free" blacks in the North languished in the twilight zone between bondage and full liberty. As Leon Litwack observes in North of Slavery (1961), "Until the post-Civil War era, in fact, most northern whites would maintain a careful distinction between granting Negroes legal protection — a theoretical right to life, liberty, and property — and political and social equality. No statute or court decision could immediately erase from the public mind, North or South, that long and firmly held conviction that the African race was inferior and therefore incapable of being assimilated politically, socially, and most certainly physically with the dominant and superior white society." As a contemporary said of northern blacks, "Chains of a stronger kind still manacled their limbs, from which no legislative act could free them; a mental and moral subordination and inferiority, to which . . . custom has here subjected all the sons and daughters of Africa."

There were northern blacks, of course, who overcame the obstacles against them and managed to lead prominent and influential lives. Phillis Wheatley of Boston was an internationally known poet, whose Poems on Various Subjects, Religious and Moral, was the first book published by a black woman in American and only the second by an American woman. Prince Hall, one of several thousand blacks who fought for America in the Revolution, formed the first black Masonic lodge. And Benjamin Banneker, born a free black in slave-holding Maryland, became a well-known astronomer and the most famous African American in the young Republic.

In the South, meanwhile, slavery took even deeper root with the invention of the cotton gin in 1793, and blacks on the booming plantations sank into bleak despair. Here "the human cattle moved," recalled Frederick Douglass, a former slave, "hurried on by no hope of reward, no sense of gratitude . . . no prospect of bettering their condition; nothing, save the dread and terror of the slave-driver's lash. So goes one day, and so comes and goes another." Yet, as Vincent Harding observes, the slaves were anything but passive drones, submitting to their lot without complaint. They resisted bondage every way they could: they ran away, faked illness, broke hoes, and resorted to other forms of sabotage. Inspired by the charismatic Toussaint L'Ouverture and the great slave rebellion he led on Santo Domingo in the Caribbean, southern blacks also plotted insurrection, something their masters most feared from them. In 1800 Gabriel Prosser plotted an insurrection in Richmond, but the authorities found out about it and hanged the conspirators. The same thing happened in Charleston in 1821 when house slaves told authorities that Denmark Vesey, a free black man, was plotting a giant slave rebellion. Vesey and his followers were all hanged.

Then in 1831, in an obscure county in southern Virginia, the worst fears of southern whites became a brutal reality when Nat Turner staged the bloodiest slave rebellion in southern history. It made him the most famous slave insurgent America had ever known, the victim of a violent system who struck back with retributive violence. His rebellion illustrates a profound truth. As black historian Lerone Bennett says, "Nat Turner reminds us that oppression is a kind of violence which pays in coins of its own minting. He reminds us that the first and greatest of all gospels in this: that individuals and systems always reap what they sow."

The following article attempts to transport you back into Nat Turner's time so that you might suffer with him and see the world through his eyes. That way you might gain melancholy insight into what it was like to be a slave. You might understand why Turner finally chose the sword as his instrument of liberation, and why he set out to fulfill the injunction in Exodus that "thou shalt give life for life, eye for eye, tooth for tooth, hand for hand, foot for foot, burning for burning." By placing Turner and his revolt in proper historical context, the article seeks to convey how the insurrection shocked the slave South to its foundations, exacerbated sectional tensions, and pointed the way toward civil war thirty years later.

GLOSSARY

BLUNT, SIMON   The last plantation attacked by Nat Turner's insurgents. Blunt's own slaves helped him repel Nat's attack.

FLOYD, JOHN   Governor of Virginia at the time of Nat Turner's insurrection and one of the first Virginians to blame Nat's rebellion on northern abolitionists.

FRANCIS, WILL   One of Nat Turner's confederates, a violent and angry slave who did much of the killing, only to be killed instead when Turner's force attacked Simon Blunt's plantation.

GRAY, THOMAS   Jerusalem lawyer and slaveholder who interrogated Nat Turner in his prison cell and published his "confession," which detailed the genesis and execution of the insurrection.

MOORE, PUTNAM   When Thomas Moore died, his nine-year old son, Putnam, became Nat Turner's legal owner.

MOORE, THOMAS   Nat Turner's third owner. Moore beat him in 1828 when Turner announced that the slaves ought to be free and would be "one day or other."

SOUTHAMPTON COUNTY   Obscure Virginia county on the North Carolina border where Nat Turner lived all his life and launched his insurrection.

TRAVIS, JOSEPH AND SALLY   After Thomas Moore's death, his widow, Sally, married Joseph Travis and took Putnam and the Moore slaves, including Nat Turner, to live at the Travis homestead. The Travis family was the first to die in Turner's insurrection.

TURNER, BENJAMIN   Nat's first owner and the source of his last name. All slaves had to take the last names of their owners; when they were sold, they had to assume the last names of their new owners. It is a measure of the respect Nat Turner commanded that he retained his initial last name despite being sold to Thomas Moore.

WHITEHEAD, MARGARET   The only white person Nat Turner himself killed during the revolt.

Some seventy miles below Richmond, in the southeastern part of Virginia along the North Carolina border, lay a little-known backwater called Southampton County. It was a rolling, densely forested area, with farms, plantations, and crossroad villages carved out of the woods. In 1831 most of the farms and smaller plantations were hardly distinguishable from one another — the houses were charmless, two-story rectangles, surrounded by haystacks and corn and cotton patches. Around the "big house" were various satellite sheds, a one-room kitchen, a barn, and maybe some slave cabins. Out in back were pungent outhouses poised on the edge of a slope or a steep ravine. A typical homestead had a menagerie of dogs, chickens, hogs, cows, mules, and maybe a couple of horses. And it had an apple orchard, too, for the succulent fruit not only commanded a fair price at market, but was the source of Southampton's most cherished product — an apple brandy potent enough to make a sailor reel. Not a homestead was complete without a brandy still, and the county's most popular citizens were those with well-stocked cellars.

The county seat or "county town" was Jerusalem, a smoky cluster of buildings where pigs rooted in the streets and old-timers spat tobacco juice in the shade of the courthouse. Consisting of some two thousand souls, Jerusalem lay on the forested bank of the Nottoway River some fifty or sixty miles from Norfolk and the Atlantic Ocean. To the west of Jerusalem was Bethlehem Crossroads and to the southwest a loose cluster of homesteads called Cross Keys. Such villages were the nerve centers of Southampton's social life — here on Sundays and holidays white families gathered to hear preaching, dance to fiddles, enjoy a communal barbecue, joke, gossip, cheer on a

Stephen B. Oates, "The Fires of Jubilee: Nat Turner's Fierce Rebellion," adapted from Stephen B. Oates, *The Fires of Jubilee: Nat Turner's Fierce Rebellion* (New York: Harper & Row, 1975). Reprinted by permission of HarperCollins Publishers.

shooting match or a horse race, get drunk, talk about the weather or argue about politics in their distinct Virginia accent ("hoose" for house). Most political discussions focused on local issues, for Southampton had no newspapers of its own and people here lived in considerable isolation from the outside world. What news they received came mainly from travelers and express riders, who brought mail in from Petersburg, Norfolk, and Murfreesboro down in North Carolina.

Although Southampton was a remote, generally lackluster neighborhood, it did have a planter class and in that respect was no different from most other Southern tidewater communities. If you had to own at least 20 slaves to rank as a planter, then 96 of Southampton's 734 slaveholders — about 13 percent — could claim that coveted distinction. Some fifteen men, with names like Newsom, Worrell, and Briggs, owned fifty slaves or more — which theoretically classified them as aristocrats. And Thomas Ridley, old man Urquhart, and John Kelly possessed large plantations with 145 to 179 Negroes apiece, which, in terms of slave wealth, placed *them* among the Old South's elite. Evidently these backwater squires had inherited or married into most of their possessions and had bought the rest. Some enterprising fellows had even constructed homes that were impressive by Southampton standards — with columned front porches and imported finery — and now found themselves hard-pressed to meet their mortgage payments. Still, Southampton's large planters lacked the tradition and prestige — and the majestic, landscaped mansions — that characterized Virginia's established gentry, especially the patricians along the great tidewater rivers in the more eastern and northeastern counties.

As was true of the rest of Dixie, most of Southampton's slaveowners resided on modest farms, some fighting to climb up the social and economic scale, others scratching out a hardscrabble existence from their crops and livestock. What is more, over one-third of Southampton's white families owned no slaves, none at all, and the average for the entire county was ten or eleven per slaveowning family. Many small slaveholders could not afford overseers and worked alongside their Negroes in the orchards and cotton patches. Though Virginia was no longer in a depression in 1831, the state had suffered over the past decade, as soil exhaustion and ruinous farm prices — particularly in the early 1820s — had plagued farmers and planters alike. In Southampton, assessed land values had declined sharply during the last twenty years, and a number of whites had moved on to new cotton lands in Georgia and Alabama, so that the county's population was now almost 60 percent black, with some 6,500 whites and 9,500 Negroes residing there. While most of the blacks were still enslaved, an unusual number — some 1,745, in fact — were "free persons of color." Only three counties in all of tidewater Virginia had more free Negroes than that.

By Southern white standards, enlightened benevolence did exist in Southampton County — and it existed in the rest of the state as well. Virginians liked to boast that slavery was not so harsh in the Old Dominion as it was on the brutal cotton plantations in the Deep South. Sure, Virginians conceded, there might be occasional mistreatment in the form of a sadistic overseer or a licentious poor white who hankered after slave girls, but respectable Virginians convinced themselves that all was sweetness and sunshine in their master-slave relations. Why, on Sundays Virginia masters even took their darkies to white churches, where they got to sit at the back or up in the balcony, murmuring a rehearsed *"Amen"* from time to time. After church, the slaves often gathered in a field — a shack or a shed — to conduct their own praise meetings, to shout and sing in an arcane language that aroused little interest among picnicking whites, who dismissed the noise as innocuous "nigger gabble."

Southampton whites, too, were pretty lax toward their slaves, allowing them to gather for religious

Deep in the woods near Cabin Pond, Nat and his confederates, all field slaves, work out their plans for rebellion. From an old print published by J. D. Torrey, New York. (Culver Pictures)

purposes, visit other farms, and even travel to Jerusalem on market Saturdays to see relatives and friends. After all, what was there to worry about? Southampton's slaves were well treated, whites said, and apart from a few solitary incidents the county had never had any severe slave troubles. True, the Negroes did get a bit carried away in their praise meetings these days, with much too much clapping and singing. And true, some white evangelists were coming in from outside the county and "ranting" about equality at local revivals. But generally things were quiet and unchanged in this tidewater neighborhood, where time seemed to stand as still as a windless summer day.

But all was not so serene as whites liked to believe. For a storm was brewing in Southampton's backwoods, in the slave cabins northwest of Cross

Keys. It blew up with shattering suddenness, an explosion of black rage that struck Southampton County like a tornado roaring out of the Southern night. In the early morning hours of August 22, 1831, a band of slave insurgents, led by a black mystic called Nat Turner, burst out of the forests with guns and axes, plunging southeastern Virginia — and much of the rest of the South — into convulsions of fear and racial violence. It turned out to be the bloodiest slave revolt in Southern history, one that was to have a profound and irrevocable impact on the destinies of Southern whites and blacks alike.

Afterward, white authorities described him as a small man with "distinct African features." Though his shoulders were broad from work in the fields, he was short, slender, and a little knock-kneed, with thin hair, a complexion like black pearl, and large, deep-set eyes. He wore a mustache and cultivated a tuft of whiskers under his lower lip. Before that fateful August day whites who knew Nat Turner thought him harmless, even though he was intelligent and did gabble on about strange religious powers. Among the slaves, though, he enjoyed a powerful influence as an exhorter and self-proclaimed prophet.

He was born in 1800, the property of Benjamin Turner of Southampton County and the son of two strong-minded parents. Tradition has it that his African-born mother threatened to kill him rather than see him grow up in bondage. His father eventually escaped to the North, but not before he had helped inculcate an enormous sense of self-importance in his son. Both parents praised Nat for his brilliance and extraordinary imagination; his mother even claimed that he could recall episodes that happened before his birth — a power that others insisted only the Almighty could have given him. His mother and father both told him that he was intended for some great purpose, that he would surely become a prophet. Nat was also influenced by his grandmother, who along with his white masters taught him to pray and to take pride in his superior intelligence. He learned to read and write with great ease, prompting those who knew him to remark that he had too much sense to be raised in bondage — he "would never be of any service to any one as a slave," one of them said.

In 1810 Benjamin Turner died, and Nat became the property of Turner's oldest son Samuel. Under Samuel Turner's permissive supervision Nat exploited every opportunity to improve his knowledge: he studied white children's school books and experimented in making paper and gunpowder. But it was religion that interested him the most. He attended Negro religious meetings, where the slaves cried out in ecstasy and sang hymns that expressed their longing for a better life. He listened transfixed as black exhorters preached from the Bible with stabbing gestures, singing out in a rhythmic language that was charged with emotion and vivid imagery. He studied the Bible, too, practically memorizing the books of the Old Testament, and grew to manhood with the words of the prophets roaring in his ears.

Evidently Nat came of age a bit confused if not resentful. Both whites and blacks had said he was too intelligent to be raised a slave; yet here he was, fully grown and still in bondage. Obviously he felt betrayed by false hopes. Obviously he thought he should be liberated like the large number of free blacks who lived in Southampton County and who were not nearly so gifted as he. Still enslaved as a man, he zealously cultivated his image as a prophet, aloof, austere, and mystical. As he said later in an oral autobiographical sketch, "Having soon discovered to be great, I must appear so, and therefore studiously avoided mixing in society, and wrapped myself in mystery, devoting myself to fasting and prayer."

Remote, introspective, Turner had religious fantasies in which the Holy Spirit seemed to speak to him as it had to the prophets of old. "Seek ye the kingdom of Heaven," the Spirit told him, "and all things shall be added unto you." Convinced that he

"was ordained for some great purpose in the hands of the Almighty," Turner told his fellow slaves about his communion with the Spirit. "And they believed," Turner recalled, "and said my wisdom came from God." Pleased with their response, he began to prepare them for some unnamed mission. He also started preaching at black religious gatherings and soon rose to prominence as a leading exhorter in the slave church. Although never ordained and never officially a member of any church, he was accepted as a Baptist preacher in the slave community, and once he even baptized a white man in a swampy pond. There can be little doubt that the slave church nourished Turner's self-esteem and his desire for independence, for it was not only a center for underground slave plottings against the master class, but a focal point for an entire alternate culture — a subterranean culture that the slaves sought to construct beyond the white man's control. Moreover, Turner's status as a slave preacher gave him considerable freedom of movement, so that he came to know most of Southampton County intimately.

Sometime around 1821 Turner disappeared. His master had put him under an overseer, who may have whipped him, and he fled for his freedom as his father had done. But thirty days later he voluntarily returned. The other slaves were astonished. No fugitive ever came back on his own. "And the negroes found fault, and murmured against me," Turner recounted later, "saying that if they had my sense they would not serve any master in the world." But in his mind Turner did not serve any earthly master. His master was Jehovah — the angry and vengeful God of ancient Israel — and it was Jehovah, he insisted, who had chastened him and brought him back to bondage.

At about this time Nat married. Evidently his wife was a young slave named Cherry who lived on Samuel Turner's place. But in 1822 Samuel Turner died, and they were sold to different masters — Cherry to Giles Reese and Nat to Thomas Moore. Although they were not far apart and still saw each other from time to time, their separation was nevertheless a painful example of the wretched privations that slavery placed on black people, even here in mellowed Southampton County.

As a perceptive man with a prodigious knowledge of the Bible, Turner was more than aware of the hypocrisies and contradictions loose in this Christian area, where whites gloried in the teachings of Jesus and yet discriminated against the "free coloreds" and kept the other blacks in chains. Here slave owners bragged about their benevolence (in Virginia they took care of their "niggers") and yet broke up families, sold Negroes off to whip-happy slave traders when money was scarce, and denied intelligent and skilled blacks something even the most debauched and useless poor white enjoyed: freedom. Increasingly embittered about his condition and that of his people, his imagination fired to incandescence by prolonged fasting and Old Testament prayers, Turner began to have apocalyptic visions and bloody fantasies in the fields and woods southwest of Jerusalem. "I saw white spirits and black spirits engaged in battle," he declared later, "and the sun was darkened — the thunder rolled in the heavens, and blood flowed in streams — and I heard a voice saying, 'Such is your luck, such you are called to see, and let it come rough or smooth, you must surely bare it.'" He was awestruck, he recalled, but what did the voice mean? What must he bare? He withdrew from his fellow slaves and prayed for a revelation; and one day when he was plowing in the field, he thought the Spirit called out, "Behold me as I stand in the Heavens," and Turner looked up and saw forms of men there in a variety of attitudes, "and there were lights in the sky to which the children of darkness gave other names than what they really were — for they were the lights of the Saviour's hands, stretched forth from east to west, even as they extended on the cross on Calvary for the redemption of sinners."

Certain that Judgment Day was fast approaching, Turner strove to attain "true holiness" and "the true knowledge of faith." And once he had them, once he was "made perfect," then the Spirit showed him other miracles. While working in the field, he said, he discovered drops of blood on the corn. In the woods he found leaves with hieroglyphic characters and numbers etched on them; other leaves contained forms of men — some drawn in blood — like the figures in the sky. He told his fellow slaves about these signs — they were simply astounded — and claimed that the Spirit had endowed him with a special knowledge of the seasons, the rotation of the planets, and the operation of the tides. He acquired an even greater reputation among the county's slaves, many of whom thought he could control the weather and heal disease. He told his followers that clearly something large was about to happen, that he was soon to fulfill "the great promise that had been made to me."

But he still did not know what his mission was. Then on May 12, 1828, "I heard a loud noise in the heavens," Turner remembered, "and the Spirit instantly appeared to me and said the Serpent was loosened, and Christ had laid down the yoke he had borne for the sins of men, and that I should take it on and fight against the Serpent." Now at last it was clear. By signs in the heavens Jehovah would show him when to commence the great work, whereupon "I should arise and prepare myself, and slay my enemies with their own weapons." Until then he should keep his lips sealed.

But his work was too momentous for him to remain entirely silent. He announced to Thomas Moore that the slaves ought to be free and would be "one day or other." Moore, of course, regarded this as dangerous talk from a slave and gave Turner a thrashing.

In 1829 a convention met in Virginia to draft a new state constitution, and there was talk among the slaves — who communicated along a slave grapevine — that they might be liberated. Their hopes were crushed, though, when the convention emphatically

207

rejected emancipation and restricted suffrage to whites only. There was also a strong backlash against antislavery publications thought to be infiltrating from the North, one of which — David Walker's *Appeal* — actually called on the slaves to revolt. In reaction the Virginia legislature enacted a law against teaching slaves to read and write. True, it was not yet rigorously enforced, but from the blacks' viewpoint slavery seemed more entrenched in "enlightened" Virginia than ever.

There is no evidence that Turner ever read antislavery publications, but he was certainly sensitive to the despair of his people. Still, Jehovah gave him no further signs, and he was carried along in the ebb and flow of ordinary life. Moore had died in 1828, and Turner had become the legal property of Moore's nine-year-old son — something that must have humiliated him. In 1829 a local wheelwright, Joseph Travis, married Moore's widow and soon moved into her house near the Cross Keys, a village located southwest of Jerusalem. Still known as Nat Turner even though he had changed owners several times, Nat considered Travis "a kind master" and later said that Travis "placed the greatest confidence in me."

In February, 1831, there was an eclipse of the sun. The sign Turner had been waiting for — could there be any doubt? Removing the seal from his lips, he gathered around him four slaves in whom he had complete trust — Hark, Henry, Nelson, and Sam — and confided what he was called to do. They would commence "the work of death" on July 4, whose connotation Turner clearly understood. But they formed and rejected so many plans that his mind was affected. He was seized with dread. He fell sick, and Independence Day came and passed.

On August 13 there was another sign. Because of some atmospheric disturbance the sun grew so dim that it could be looked at directly. Then it seemed to change colors — now pale green, now blue, now white — and there was much excitement and consternation in many parts of the eastern United States. By afternoon the sun was like an immense ball of polished silver, and the air was moist and hazy. Then a black spot could be seen, apparently on the sun's surface — a phenomenon that greatly aroused the slaves in southeastern Virginia. For Turner the black spot was unmistakable proof that God wanted him to move. With awakened resolution he told his men that "as the black spot passed over the sun, so shall the blacks pass over the earth."

It was Sunday, August 21, deep in the woods near the Travis house at a place called Cabin Pond. Around a crackling fire Turner's confederates feasted on roast pig and apple brandy. With them were two new recruits — Jack, one of Hark's cronies, and Will, a powerful man who intended to gain his freedom or die in the attempt. Around midafternoon Turner himself made a dramatic appearance, and in the glare of pine-knot torches they finally made their plans. They would rise that night and "kill all the white people." It was a propitious time to begin, because many whites of the militia were away at a camp meeting. The revolt would be so swift and so terrible that the whites would be too panic-stricken to fight back. Until they had sufficient recruits and equipment, the insurgents would annihilate everybody in their path — women and children included. When one of the slaves complained about their small number (there were only seven of them, after all), Turner was quick to reassure him. He had deliberately avoided an extensive plot involving a lot of slaves. He knew that blacks had "frequently attempted similar things," but their plans had "leaked out." Turner intended for his revolt to happen completely without warning. The "march of destruction," he explained, "should be the first news of the insurrection," whereupon slaves and free blacks alike would rise up and join him. He did not say what their ultimate objective was, but possibly he wanted to fight his way into the Great Dismal Swamp some twenty miles to the east. This immense, snake-filled quagmire had long been a haven for fugitives, and Turner may have planned to establish a slave stronghold there from which to launch punitive raids against Virginia and North Carolina. On the other hand, he may well have had nothing in mind beyond the extermination of every white on the ten-mile route to Jerusalem. There are indications that he thought God would guide him after the revolt began, just as He had directed Gideon against the Midianites. Certainly Turner's command of unremitting carnage was that of the Almighty, who had said through his prophet Ezekiel: "Slay utterly old and young, both maids and little children, and women. . . ."

The slaves talked and schemed through the evening. Night came on. Around two in the morning of August 22 they left the woods, by-passed Giles Reese's farm, where Cherry lived, and headed for the Travis homestead, the first target in their crusade.

All was still at the Travis house. In the darkness the insurgents gathered about the cider press, and all drank except Turner, who never touched liquor. Then they moved across the yard with their axes. Hark placed a ladder against the house, and Turner, armed with a hatchet, climbed up and disappeared through a second-story window. In a moment he unbarred the door, and the slaves spread through the house without a sound. The others wanted Turner the prophet, Turner the black messiah, to strike the first blow and kill Joseph Travis. With Will close behind, Turner entered Travis' bedroom and made his way to the white man's bed. Turner swung his hatchet—a wild blow that glanced off Travis' head and brought him out of bed yelling for his wife. But with a sure killer's instinct Will moved in and hacked Travis to death with his axe. In minutes Will and the others had slaughtered the four whites they found in the house, including Mrs. Travis and young Putnam Moore, Turner's legal owner. With Putnam's death Turner felt that at last, after thirty years in bondage, he was free.

The rebels gathered up a handful of old muskets and followed "General Nat" out to the barn. There Turner paraded his men about, leading them through every military maneuver he knew. Not all of them, however, were proud of their work. Jack sank to his knees with his head in his hands and said he was sick. But Hark made him get up and forced him along as they set out across the field to the next farm. Along the way somebody remembered the Travis baby. Will and Henry returned and killed it in its cradle.

And so it went throughout that malignant night, as the rebels took farm after farm by surprise. They used no firearms, in order not to arouse the countryside, instead stabbing and decapitating their victims. Although they confiscated horses, weapons, and brandy, they took only what was necessary to continue the struggle, and they committed no rapes. They even spared a few homesteads, one because Turner believed the poor white inhabitants "thought no better of themselves than they did of negroes." By dawn on Monday there were fifteen insurgents—nine on horses—and they were armed with a motley assortment of guns, clubs, swords, and axes. Turner himself now carried a light dress sword, but for some mysterious reason (a fatal irresolution? the dread again?) he had killed nobody yet.

At Elizabeth Turner's place, which the slaves stormed at sunrise, the prophet tried once again to kill. They broke into the house, and there, in the middle of the room, too frightened to move or cry out, stood Mrs. Turner and a neighbor named Mrs. Newsome. Nat knew Elizabeth Turner very well, for she was the widow of his second master, Samuel Turner. While Will attacked her with his axe the prophet took Mrs. Newsome's hand and hit her over the head with his sword. But evidently he could not bring himself to kill her. Finally Will moved him aside and chopped her to death as methodically as though he were cutting wood.

With the sun low in the east, Turner sent a group on foot to another farm while he and Will led the horsemen at a gallop to Caty Whitehead's place. They surrounded the house in a rush, but not before several people fled into the garden. Turner chased after somebody, but it turned out to be a slave girl, as terrified as the whites, and he let her go. All around him, all over the Whitehead farm, there were scenes of unspeakable violence. He saw Will drag Mrs. Whitehead kicking and screaming out of the house and almost sever her head from her body. Running around the house, Turner came upon young Margaret Whitehead hiding under a cellar cap between two chimneys. She ran crying for her life, and Turner set out after her — a wild chase against the hot August sun. He overtook the girl in a field and hit her again and again with his sword, but she would not die. In desperation he picked up a fence rail and beat her to death. Finally he had killed someone. He was to kill no one else.

After the Whitehead massacre the insurgents united briefly and then divided again, those on foot moving in one direction and Turner and the mounted slaves in another. The riders moved across the fields, kicking their horses and mules faster and faster, until at last they raced down the lane to Richard Porter's house, scattering dogs and chickens as they went. But the Porters had fled — forewarned by their own slaves that a revolt was under way. Turner knew that the alarm was spreading now, knew that the militia would soon be mobilizing, so he set out alone to retrieve the other column. While he was gone Will took the cavalry and raided Nathaniel Francis' homestead. Young Francis was Will's owner, but he could not have been a harsh master: several free blacks voluntarily lived on his farm. Francis was not home, and his pregnant young wife survived Will's onslaught only because a slave concealed her in the attic. After killing the overseer and Francis' two nephews Will and his men raced on to another farm, and another, and then overran John Barrow's place on the Barrow Road. Old man Barrow fought back manfully while his wife escaped in the woods, but the insurgents overwhelmed him and slit his throat. As a tribute to his courage they wrapped his body in a quilt and left a plug of tobacco on his chest.

Meanwhile Turner rode chaotically around the countryside, chasing after one column and then the other, almost always reaching the farms after his scattered troops had done the killing and gone. Eventually he found both columns waiting for him at another pillaged homestead, took charge again, and sent them down the Barrow Road, which intersected the main highway to Jerusalem. They were forty strong now and all mounted. Many of the new recruits had joined up eager "to kill all the white people." But others had been forced to come along as though they were hostages. A Negro later testified that several slaves — among them three teen-age boys — "were constantly guarded by negroes with guns who were ordered to shoot them if they attempted to escape."

On the Barrow Road, Turner's strategy was to put his twenty most dependable men in front and send them galloping down on the homesteads before anybody could escape. But the cry of insurrection had preceded them, and many families had already escaped to nearby Jerusalem, throwing the village into pandemonium. By midmorning church bells were tolling the terrible news — *insurrection, insurrection* — and shouting men were riding through the countryside in a desperate effort to get the militia together before the slaves overran Jerusalem itself.

As Turner's column moved relentlessly toward Jerusalem one Levi Waller, having heard that the blacks had risen, summoned his children from a nearby schoolhouse (some of the other children came running too) and tried to load his guns. But before he could do so, Turner's advance horsemen swept into his yard, a whirlwind of axes and swords, and chased Waller into some tall weeds. Waller managed to escape, but not before he saw the blacks cut down his wife and children. One small girl also escaped by crawling up a dirt chimney, scarcely daring to breathe as the insurgents decapitated the other children — ten in all — and threw their bodies in a pile.

Turner had stationed himself at the rear of his little army and did not participate in these or any other killings along the Barrow Road. He never explained why. He had been fasting for several days and may well have been too weak to try any more killing himself. Or maybe as God's prophet he preferred to let Will and the eight or nine other lieutenants do the slaughtering. All he said about it afterward was that he "sometimes got in sight in time to see the work of death completed" and that he paused to view the bodies "in silent satisfaction" before riding on.

Around noon on Monday the insurgents reached the Jerusalem highway, and Turner soon joined them. Behind them lay a zigzag path of unredeemable destruction: some fifteen homesteads sacked and approximately sixty whites slain. By now the rebels amounted to fifty or sixty — including three or four free blacks. But even at its zenith Turner's army showed signs of disintegration. A few reluctant slaves had already escaped or deserted. And many others were roaring drunk, so drunk they could scarcely ride their horses, let alone do any fighting. To make matters worse, many of the confiscated muskets were broken or too rusty to fire.

Turner resolved to march on Jerusalem at once and seize all the guns and powder he could find there. But a half mile up the road he stopped at the Parker farm, because some of his men had relatives and friends there. When the insurgents did not return, Turner went after them — and found his men not in the slave quarters but down in Parker's brandy cellar. He ordered them back to the highway at once.

On the way back they met a party of armed men — whites. There were about eighteen of them, as far as Turner could make out. They had already routed his small guard at the gate and were now advancing toward the Parker house. With renewed zeal Turner rallied his remaining troops and ordered an attack.

Yelling at the top of their lungs, wielding axes, clubs, and gun butts, the Negroes drove the whites back into Parker's cornfield. But their advantage was short-lived. White reinforcements arrived, and more were on the way from nearby Jerusalem. Regrouping in the cornfield, the whites counterattacked, throwing the rebels back in confusion. In the fighting some of Turner's best men fell wounded, though none of them died. Several insurgents, too drunk to fight any more, fled pell-mell into the woods.

If Turner had often seemed irresolute earlier in the revolt, he was now undaunted. Even though his force was considerably reduced, he still wanted to storm Jerusalem. He led his men away from the main highway, which was blocked with militia, and took them along a back road, planning to cross the Cypress Bridge and strike the village from the rear. But the bridge was crawling with armed whites. In desperation the blacks set out to find reinforcements: they fell back to the south and then veered north again, picking up new recruits as they moved. They raided a few more farms, too, only to find them deserted, and finally encamped for the night near the slave quarters on Ridley's plantation.

All Monday night news of the revolt spread beyond Southampton County as express riders carried the alarm up to Petersburg and from there to the capitol in Richmond, Governor John Floyd, fearing a statewide uprising, alerted the militia and sent cavalry, infantry, and artillery units to the stricken county. Federal troops from Fortress Monroe were on the way, too, and other volunteers and militia outfits were marching from contiguous counties in Virginia and North Carolina. Soon over three thousand armed whites were in Southampton County, and hundreds more were mobilizing.

With whites swarming the countryside, Turner and his lieutenants did not know what to do. During the night an alarm had stampeded their new recruits, so that by Tuesday morning they had only twenty men left. Frantically they set out for Dr. Simon

On October 30, 1831, a Sunday, a white named Benjamin Phipps accidentally discovered Nat Turner in his hideout near *Cabin Pond. Since the white man had a loaded shotgun, Turner had no choice but to throw down his sword. (Brown Brothers)*

Blunt's farm to get volunteers — and rode straight into an ambush. Whites barricaded in the house opened fire on them at pointblank range, killing one or more insurgents and capturing several others — among them Hark Travis. Blunt's own slaves, armed with farm tools, helped in the defense and captured a few rebels themselves.

Repulsed at Blunt's farm, Turner led a handful of the faithful back toward the Cross Keys, still hoping to gather reinforcements. But the signs were truly ominous, for armed whites were everywhere. At last the militia overtook Turner's little band and in a final, desperate skirmish killed Will and scattered the rest. Turner himself, alone and in deep anguish, es-

caped to the vicinity of the Travis farm and hid in a hole under some fence rails.

By Tuesday evening a full-scale manhunt was under way in southeastern Virginia and North Carolina as armed whites prowled the woods and swamps in search of fugitive rebels and alleged collaborators. They chased the blacks down with howling dogs, killing those who resisted — and many of them resisted zealously — and dragging others back to Jerusalem to stand trial in the county court. One free black insurgent committed suicide rather than be taken by white men. Within a week nearly all the bona fide rebels except Turner had either been executed or imprisoned, but not before white vigilantes — and some militiamen — had perpetrated barbarities on more than a score of innocent blacks. Outraged by the atrocities committed on whites, vigilantes rounded up Negroes in the Cross Keys and decapitated them. Another vigilante gang in North Carolina not only beheaded several blacks but placed their skulls on poles, where they remained for days. In all directions whites took Negroes from their shacks and tortured, shot, and burned them to death and then mutilated their corpses in ways that witnesses refused to describe. No one knows how many innocent Negroes died in this reign of terror — at least a hundred twenty, probably more. Finally the militia commander of Southampton County issued a proclamation that any further outrages would be dealt with according to the articles of war. Many whites publicly regretted these atrocities but argued that they were the inevitable results of slave insurrection. Another revolt, they said, would end with the extermination of every black in the region.

Although Turner's uprising ended on Tuesday, August 24, reports of additional insurrections swept over the South long afterward, and dozens of communities from Virginia to Alabama were seized with hysteria. In North Carolina rumors flew that slave armies had been seen on the highways, that one — maybe led by Turner himself — had burned Wilmington, butchered all the inhabitants, and was now marching on the state capital. The hysteria was even worse in Virginia, where reports of concerted slave rebellions and demands for men and guns swamped the governor's office. For a time it seemed that thousands of slaves had risen, that Virginia and perhaps the entire South would soon be ablaze. But Governor Floyd kept his head, examined the reports carefully, and concluded that no such widespread insurrection had taken place. Actually no additional uprisings had happened anywhere. Out of blind panic whites in many parts of the South had mobilized the militia, chased after imaginary insurgents, and jailed or executed still more innocent blacks.

Working in cooperation with other political and military authorities in Virginia and North Carolina, Floyd did all he could to quell the excitement, to reassure the public that the slaves were quiet now. Still, the governor did not think the Turner revolt was the work of a solitary fanatic. Behind it, he believed, was a conspiracy of Yankee agitators and black preachers — especially black preachers. "The whole of that massacre in Southampton is the work of these Preachers," he declared, and demanded that they be suppressed.

Meanwhile the "great bandit chieftain," as the newspapers called him, was still at large. For more than two months Turner managed to elude white patrols, hiding out most of the time near Cabin Pond where the revolt had begun. Hunted by a host of aroused whites (there were various rewards totalling eleven hundred dollars on his head), Turner considered giving himself up and once got within two miles of Jerusalem before turning back. Finally on Sunday, October 30, a white named Benjamin Phipps accidentally discovered him in another hideout near Cabin Pond. Since the man had a loaded shotgun, Turner had no choice but to throw down his sword.

The next day, with lynch mobs crying for his head, a white guard hurried Turner up to Jerusalem to stand trial. By now he was resigned to his fate as the will of Almighty God and was entirely fearless and unrepentant. When a couple of court justices examined him that day, he stated emphatically that *he* had conceived and directed the slaughter of all those white people (even though he had killed only Margaret Whitehead) and announced that God had endowed him with extraordinary powers. The justices ordered this "fanatic" locked up in the same small wooden jail where the other captured rebels had been incarcerated.

On November 1 one Thomas Gray, an elderly Jerusalem lawyer and slaveholder, came to interrogate Turner as he lay in his cell "clothed with rags and covered with chains." In Gray's opinion the public was anxious to learn the facts about the insurrection — for whites in Southampton could not fathom why their salves would revolt. What Gray wanted was to take down and publish a confession from Turner that would tell the public the truth about why the rebellion had happened. It appears that Gray had already gathered a wealth of information about the outbreak from other prisoners, some of whom he had defended as a court-appointed counsel. Evidently he had also written unsigned newspaper accounts of the affair, reporting in one that whites had located Turner's wife and lashed her until she surrendered his papers (remarkable papers, papers with hieroglyphics on them and sketches of the Crucifixion and the sun). According to Gray and to other sources as well, Turner over a period of three days gave him a voluntary and authentic confession about the genesis and execution of the revolt, recounting his religious visions in graphic detail and contending again that he was a prophet of Almighty God. "Do you not find yourself mistaken now?" Gray asked. Turner replied testily, "Was not Christ crucified?" Turner insisted that the uprising was local in origin but warned that other slaves might see signs and act as he had done. By the end of the confession Turner was in high spirits, perfectly "willing to suffer the fate that awaits me." Although Gray considered him "a gloomy fanatic," he thought Turner was one of the most articulate men he had ever met. And Turner could be frightening. When, in a burst of enthusiasm, he spoke of the killings and raised his manacled hands toward heaven, "I looked on him," Gray said, "and my blood curdled in my veins."

On November 5, with William C. Parker acting as his counsel, Turner came to trial in Jerusalem. The court, of course, found him guilty of committing insurrection and sentenced him to hang. Turner, though, insisted that he was not guilty because he did not feel so. On November 11 he went to his death in resolute silence. In addition to Turner, the county court tried some forty-eight other Negroes on various charges of conspiracy, insurrection, and treason. In all, eighteen blacks — including one woman — were convicted and hanged. Ten others were convicted and "transported" — presumably out of the United States.

But the consequences of the Turner revolt did not end with public hangings in Jerusalem. For southern whites the uprising seemed a monstrous climax to a whole decade of ominous events, a decade of abominable tariffs and economic panics, of obstreperous antislavery activities, and of growing slave unrest and insurrection plots, beginning with the Denmark Vesey conspiracy in Charleston in 1822 and culminating now in the worst insurrection Southerners had ever known. Desperately needing to blame somebody besides themselves for Nat Turner, Southerners linked the revolt to some sinister Yankee-abolitionist plot to destroy their cherished way of life. Southern zealots declared that the antislavery movement, gathering momentum in the North throughout the 1820's, had now burst into a full-blown crusade against the South. In January, 1831, William Lloyd Garrison had started publishing *The Liberator* in Boston, demanding in bold, strident language that the slaves be immediately and unconditionally emancipated. If Garrison's rhetoric shocked Southerners, even more disturbing was the fact that about eight months after the appearance of *The Liberator* Nat Turner embarked on his bloody crusade — something southern politicians and newspapers refused to accept as mere coincidence. They charged that Garrison was behind the insurrection, that it was his "bloodthirsty" invective that had incited Turner to violence. Never mind that there was no evidence that Turner had ever heard of *The Liberator;* never mind that Garrison categorically denied any connection with the revolt, saying that he and his abolitionist followers were Christian pacifists who wanted to free the slaves through moral suasion. From 1831 on, northern abolitionism and slave rebellion were inextricably associated in the southern mind.

But if Virginians blamed the insurrection on northern abolitionism, many of them defended emancipation itself as the only way to prevent further violence. In fact, for several months in late 1831 and early 1832 Virginians engaged in a momentous public debate over the feasibility of manumission. Out of the western part of the state, where antislavery and anti-Negro sentiment had long been smoldering, came petitions demanding that Virginia eradicate the "accursed," "evil" slave system and colonize all blacks at state expense. Only by removing the entire black population, the petitions argued, could future revolts be avoided. Newspapers also discussed the idea of emancipation and colonization, prompting one to announce that "Nat Turner and the blood of his innocent victims have conquered the silence of fifty years." The debate moved into the Virginia legislature, too, and early in 1832 proslavery and antislavery orators harangued one another in an unprecedented legislative struggle over emancipation. In the end most delegates concluded that colonization was too costly and too complicated to carry out. And since they were not about to manumit the blacks and leave them as free men in a white man's country, they rejected emancipation. Indeed, they went on to revise and implement the slave codes in order to restrict blacks so stringently that they could never mount another revolt. The modified codes not only strengthened the patrol and militia systems, but sharply curtailed the rights of free blacks and all but eliminated slave schools, slave religious meetings, and slave preachers. For Turner had taught white Virginians a hard lesson about what might happen if they gave slaves enough education and religion to think for themselves.

In the wake of the Turner revolt, the rise of the abolitionists, and the Virginia debates over slavery, the other southern states also expanded their patrol and militia systems and increased the severity of their slave codes. What followed was the Great Reaction of the 1830's and 1840's, during which the South, threatened it seemed by internal and external enemies, became a closed, martial society determined to preserve its slave-based civilization at whatever cost. If Southerners had once apologized for slavery as a necessary evil, they now trumpeted that institution as a positive good — "the greatest of all the great blessings," as James H. Hammond phrased it, "which a kind providence has bestowed." Southern postmasters set about confiscating abolitionist literature, lest these "incendiary" tracts invite the slaves to violence. Some states actually passed sedition laws and other restrictive measures that prohibited Negroes and whites alike from criticizing slavery. And slave owners all across the South tightened up slave discipline, refusing to let blacks visit other plantations and threatening to hang any slave who even looked rebellious. By the 1840's the Old South had devised such an oppressive slave system that organized insurrection was all but impossible.

Even so, southern whites in the ante-bellum period never escaped the haunting fear that somewhere, maybe even in their own slave quarters, another Nat Turner was plotting to rise up and slit their throats. They never forgot him. His name became for them a symbol of terror and violent retribution.

But for ante-bellum blacks — and for their descendants — the name of Nat Turner took on a profoundly different connotation. He became a legendary black hero who broke his chains and murdered white people because slavery had murdered Negroes. Turner, said an elderly black man in Southampton County only a few years ago, was "God's man. He was a man for war, and for legal rights, and for freedom."

QUESTIONS TO CONSIDER

1   Why did Nat Turner decide to strike back at the slave system with retributive violence? Was he abused as a slave? What role did the Old Testament, the slave church, the slave underground, and extensive fasting play in the genesis of Turner's insurrection? Do you believe that he actually heard wind voices in the trees, saw angels in the sky, and heard the call of Jehovah?

2   Why did Turner command great respect in the slave community? Why did he exclude privileged house slaves from his plot? Who were his confederates and why did they agree to follow him? When did he finally decide to move? What do you think was Turner's ultimate objective?

3   The details of the revolt — women hacked to death with axes, children decapitated — are grisly indeed. But the slave system was a brutal system that daily maimed and murdered its victims. In light of that, do you think Turner's actions were justifiable?

4   Why did most African Americans in Southampton County refuse to join Turner's revolt? Why do you think it failed? Or, to put it another way, how did Nat and his followers, hopelessly outnumbered and facing the tremendous firepower of the slave system, manage to get as far as they did?

5   Why did the Virginia legislature debate and then decide against abolishing slavery in that state? Who or what did the governor and other white leaders blame for the insurrection? How could they not put the blame on the cruelties of the slave system? In what ways do you think that the southern reaction to the insurrection fueled sectional tensions and precipitated the Civil War?

16

William Lloyd Garrison and the Abolitionist Crusade

RALPH KORNGOLD

As we saw in the previous selection, southern whites blamed Nat Turner's insurrection on William Lloyd Garrison, insisting that Nat had somehow acquired a copy of the Liberator, *Garrison's spirited abolitionist newspaper published in Boston. In the southern perception of events, the paper had driven Nat mad and caused him to revolt. Nothing was further from the truth — there is no evidence that Nat had ever even heard of the* Liberator; *and Garrison himself said that Nat Turner had plenty of his own reasons to revolt. But southerners, unable to blame the insurrection on their own system, desperately needed a scapegoat. And so they pointed fingers at Garrison and his fellow northern abolitionists.*

The following selection will introduce you to Garrison and the northern antislavery crusade. Garrison, however, was hardly the first abolitionist. Thomas Jefferson had hated slavery and advocated eradicating it by a gradual emancipation program. And southern and northern Quakers had opposed the institution since the colonial period. But in the 1820s — a decade of religious and political ferment — the antislavery movement truly took shape. Groups of Quakers and free blacks collected antislavery petitions and sent them to Congress, where intimidated southerners had them tabled, and Benjamin Lundy, a Baltimore Quaker, not only started publishing The Genius of Universal Emancipation *but organized antislavery societies in the South itself. At this time, most antislavery whites (a distinct minority of the population) were both gradualists and colonizationists such as Henry Clay. But by the 1830s, some had emphatically changed their minds. They renounced colonization, demanded immediate emancipation, organized a national antislavery society, and started an abolitionist crusade that would haunt the American conscience and arouse latent racism everywhere in the land.*

The best-known leader of the crusade was William Lloyd Garrison. A shy, intense, bespectacled young man who came from a broken home (his father had run away), he was raised by his mother as an ardent Baptist; later, he became a radical Christian perfectionist. Initially, Garrison too was a gradualist and a colonizer. But in 1829, after he went to work for Lundy's paper, Garrison renounced colonization and came out for immediate emancipation. Ralph Korngold speculates that Garrison was influenced by the abolitionist writings of James Duncan and the Reverend George Bourne, who denounced slavery as a sin and demanded that blacks be freed at once.

At any rate, in the columns of Lundy's paper, Garrison conducted a stunning moral attack against slavery and anybody who condoned or perpetuated it. For example, when he learned that a ship belonging to Francis Todd of Newburyport, Massachusetts (Garrison's hometown), was taking a cargo of slaves from Baltimore to New Orleans, Garrison castigated Todd as a highway robber and a murderer. The man, a highly respected citizen and a church deacon, slapped Garrison with a $5,000 libel suit. The court decided against Garrison and fined him $50, but he couldn't pay and had to go to jail. Korngold's narrative opens with Garrison in prison. It follows his career as he founded his antislavery newspaper, the Liberator, *and launched his moral crusade against slavery, that "sum of villanies."*

Garrison's method, as Korngold explains, was to overcome slavery by nonviolent "moral suasion" — that is, by arousing the conscience of the nation in favor of immediate emancipation. Korngold says it would be more accurate to call Garrison's method "moral pressure." *By immediate emancipation, however, Garrison did not mean that slaves should be "let loose to roam as vagrants" or that they should be "instantly invested with all political rights and privileges." What he wanted was to break the chains on African Americans, guarantee them the protection of the law, preserve their families, and place them under "benevolent supervision" until they learned religion and became "economically secure," whereupon they were to be assimilated into American society.*

While Garrison doubted that slavery could ever be abolished by peaceful means, Korngold argues, he nevertheless thought the effort should be made. And that effort had an enormous influence on the country (see selection 18 for Henry Clay's response to the abolitionist movement). As you read Korngold's portrait, note how the South reacted to Garrison's attack and to Walker's Appeal, *a pamphlet by Boston free black David Walker. Note, too, that Garrison also championed the rights of free blacks. And yet he refused to speak out against the exploitation of northern workers as a class and thus lost an important potential ally.*

GLOSSARY

ABOLITIONIST   A person who wanted to free the slaves immediately or gradually. Garrison became the leader of the "immediate" abolitionists.

ALCOTT, A. BRONSON   Samuel May's brother-in-law, "mystic," teacher, and abolitionist.

ALCOTT, LOUISA MAY   Bronson Alcott's daughter and popular novelist (Little Women).

AMERICAN COLONIZATION SOCIETY   A private, philanthropic organization founded in 1816 for the purpose of repatriating "free persons of color" on a voluntary basis outside the United States. While not an abolitionist enterprise, the society did hope to induce the southern states to abolish their institutions of slavery by promising to remove their liberated blacks to other lands.

BEECHER, LYMAN   Well-known Calvinist minister who was preaching in Litchfield, Connecticut, in 1831; the next year, he became president of Lane Theological Seminary in Cincinnati, Ohio; his daughter, Harriet Beecher Stowe, wrote Uncle Tom's Cabin (1852).

BIRNEY, JAMES G.   Kentucky slave owner and Alabama solicitor general who freed his slaves, relocated in the North, joined the abolitionist movement, and became the presidential candidate of the Liberty party in 1840 and 1844 (see selection 18).

CLAY, CASSIUS M.   Kentucky slave owner who was converted to abolition by William Lloyd Garrison; Clay established an antislavery paper in

Lexington called the True American, which urged gradual emancipation; a mob suppressed it in 1845.

COLONIZATIONIST   A follower of the American Colonization Society (above).

KNAPP, ISAAC   Garrison's partner at the Liberator.

LIBERATOR   Garrison's abolitionist newspaper, first published on January 1, 1831, in Boston; although it never had a circulation of more than three thousand, the Liberator was nevertheless the most famous abolitionist newspaper of the antebellum era.

MAY, SAMUEL J.   Unitarian minister who, like Garrison, had first been a colonizationist; Garrison converted him to immediate abolitionism.

OTIS, HARRISON   Boston mayor in 1831; southern governors demanded that he shut down Garrison's "incendiary" paper.

SEWALL, SAMUEL E.   May's cousin and a Boston lawyer who actually importuned Garrison to tone down his violent language; nevertheless, he became a Garrison disciple.

TURNER, NAT   Slave mystic and preacher who led the 1831 slave rebellion in Virginia, the bloodiest insurrection in southern history.

WALKER, DAVID   Boston free black whose pamphlet, Walker's Appeal (1829), urged the slaves to revolt.

☆

1

While in prison Garrison had prepared three lectures. The first contrasted the program of the Colonization Society with his own; the second gave a vivid description of the slavery system; the third showed the extent to which the North shared responsibility for the "peculiar institution." After his release he left Baltimore for the North, intending to make a lecture tour of several months' duration and then launch an antislavery weekly in Washington. If he later chose Boston, it was because Lundy moved the *Genius* to the National Capital. Garrison had become convinced the North needed enlightenment even more than the South. In the first issue of his new paper he was to write:

"During my recent tour for the purpose of exciting the minds of the people by a series of discourses on the subject of slavery, every place that I visited gave fresh evidence of the fact, that a greater revolution in public sentiment was to be effected in the free States — *and particularly in New England* — than at the South. I found contempt more bitter, opposition more active, detraction more relentless, prejudice more stubborn, and apathy more frozen, than among slaveowners themselves."

He delivered his lectures in Philadelphia, where he was the guest of James and Lucretia Mott, whose influence was to be largely responsible for his abandonment of religious orthodoxy. "If my mind has since become liberalized in any degree (and I think it has burst every sectarian trammel)," he wrote, "if theological dogmas which I once regarded as essential to Christianity, I now repudiate as absurd and pernicious, — I am largely indebted to them for the changes." When he reached Massachusetts he decided that his native Newburyport should be the first to hear his message. But he had reckoned without Mr. [Francis] Todd, whose influence was sufficiently great to have the trustees of the Presbyterian Church intervene when the minister offered Garrison the use of the church auditorium. The pastor of the Second Congregational Church came to the rescue and he was able to deliver his first lecture. Then again Todd intervened. Garrison made no further attempt to enlighten his native town, and left for Boston.

☆

2

In Boston Garrison took lodgings as usual at Parson Collier's, and then called on the Reverend Lyman Beecher, hoping to enlist his moral support. Dr. Beecher, however, was not the man to identify himself with an unpopular cause. ("True wisdom," he said in one of his Seminary lectures, "consists in advocating a cause only so far as the community will sustain the reformer.") He now excused himself, saying: "I have too many irons in the fire already."

"Then," replied the young zealot, "you had better let them all burn than to neglect your duty to the slave."

Dr. Beecher did not think so. "Your zeal," he said, "is commendable, but you are misguided. If you will give up your fanatical notions and be guided by us [the clergy] we will make you the Wilberforce of America."

When not looking for a hall in which to deliver his message Garrison wrote letters to public men imploring them to declare themselves for immediate emancipation. He wrote to [William Ellery] Channing, to [Daniel] Webster and to several others, but received no reply. His search for a meeting place likewise remained unrewarded. Finally he inserted the following advertisement in the Boston *Courier:*

From pages 42–64 in *Two Friends of Man* by Ralph Korngold, published by Little, Brown & Co., 1950. Reprinted by special permission of Mrs. Ralph Korngold.

WANTED — For three evenings, a Hall or meetinghouse (the latter would be preferred), in which to vindicate the rights of TWO MILLIONS of American citizens who are now groaning in servile chains in this boasted land of liberty; and also to propose just, benevolent, and constitutional measures for their relief. As the addresses will be gratuitous, and as the cause is of public benefit, I cannot consent to remunerate any society for the use of its building. If this application fails, I propose to address the citizens of Boston in the open air, on the Common.

WM. Lloyd Garrison

No. 30, Federal Street, Oct. 11, 1830

The advertisement attracted the attention of sexagenarian Abner Kneeland, founder of the First Society of Free Enquirers. Kneeland was an atheist, and his society made war on religion. A few years later he was to be indicted for having published in his paper, the Boston *Enquirer,* a "scandalous, injurious, obscene, blasphemous and profane libel of and concerning God." His society was the lessee of Julian Hall, on the northwest corner of Milk and Congress Streets. He had no sooner read Garrison's advertisement than he offered him the use of the hall.

It was only a couple of years since Garrison had written about "the depravity and wickedness of those . . . who reject the gospel of Jesus Christ," but he now saw no reason why he should "reject the cooperation of those who . . . make no pretense to evangelical piety" when "the religious portion of the community are indifferent to the cries of suffering humanity."

☆

3

The hall was filled. Dr. Beecher and other notables were present. Three men were there who were destined to become Garrison's staunch friends and sup-

porters. They had come together and were seated side by side. The eldest was Samuel J. May, a Unitarian minister from Brooklyn, Connecticut, who was visiting his father, Colonel Joseph May, a prosperous Boston merchant. His friends called him "God's chore boy," for while far less combative than Garrison, he was just as ready to rush to the succor of anyone in need of assistance. Sitting beside him was his brother-in-law, Bronson Alcott, whose daughter Louisa May Alcott was to become a popular novelist. He was a philosopher and a mystic who combined great profundity with great extravagance of thought. The Sage of Concord has called him "the most refined and the most advanced soul we have ever had in New England," and "the most remarkable and the highest genius of his time." Along with gems of thought worthy of Aristotle, Alcott propounded such absurdities as that the atmosphere surrounding the earth was the accumulated exhalation of mankind, and that the weather was fair or foul depending on whether good or evil thought predominated! He would say in all seriousness to a friend: "Men must have behaved well today to have such fine sunshine." The third man was May's cousin, Samuel E. Sewall, a Boston attorney and a direct descendant of the judge of that name who a hundred and thirty years before had written the first antislavery pamphlet in America.

When the speaker had finished, May turned to his two companions and said: "That is a providential man; he is a prophet; he will shake our nation to its center, but he will shake slavery out of it. We ought to know him, we ought to help him. Come, let us go and give him our hands." When they had done so, May said to the young lecturer: "Mr. Garrison, I am not sure that I can endorse all you have said this evening. Much of it requires careful consideration. But I am prepared to embrace you. I am sure you are called to a great work, and I mean to help you."

Alcott suggested that all come home with him. They accepted and remained in animated conversation until after midnight. Garrison told his new friends of his plan to launch an antislavery paper in Boston, which he intended to call the *Liberator*. Sewall thought the name too provoking and suggested the *Safety Lamp*. Garrison would not hear of it. "Provoking!" That was exactly what he meant it to be. Slavery in the United States had now lasted over two hundred years. During nearly three quarters of that time the Quakers had agitated against it in their inoffensive, conciliatory fashion. What had been accomplished? There were now more than four times as many slaves as when they began their propaganda. New Slave States had been added to the Union. The slave laws were more oppressive than ever. He meant to agitate. He meant to call hard names. He meant to make it impossible for any man to confess without shame that he was the owner of slaves. He was prepared for any sacrifice: "A few white victims must be sacrificed to open the eyes of this nation and show the tyranny of our laws. I expect and am willing to be persecuted, imprisoned and bound for advocating African rights; and I should deserve to be a slave myself if I shrunk from that duty or danger."

May was so fascinated by the young man's enthusiasm that the following morning, immediately after breakfast, he called on him at his boardinghouse and remained until two in the afternoon. Before the week was over he and Sewall had made arrangements for Garrison to repeat his lectures at Athenaeum Hall.

The Sunday following, May occupied the pulpit at "Church Green," in Summer Street. So filled was he with Garrison's message that he interpolated his sermon with frequent references to slavery and finished with an appeal to the congregation to help abolish the institution before it destroyed the Republic. He was aware of the mounting uneasiness among his listeners, and having pronounced the benediction, said: "Every one present must be conscious that the closing remarks of my sermon have caused an unusual emotion throughout the church. I am glad.... I have been prompted to speak thus by the words I have heard during the past week from a

young man hitherto unknown, but who is, I believe, called of God to do a greater work for the good of our country than has been done by any one since the Revolution. I mean William Lloyd Garrison. He is going to repeat his lectures the coming week. I advise, I exhort, I entreat — would that I could compel! — you to go and hear him."

The following day May's father, Colonel Joseph May, was walking down State Street when a friend rushed up to him and impulsively grasped his hand.

"Colonel," he said, "you have my sympathy. I cannot tell you how much I pity you."

The old man looked at him astounded. "Sympathy? Pity? For what?"

The other appeared embarrassed. "Well," he said, "I hear your son went mad at 'Church Green' yesterday."

☆

4

In a small chamber, friendless and unseen,
    Toiled o'er his types one poor, unlearned young man;
The place was dark, unfurnitured and mean,
    Yet there the freedom of a race began.

Help came but slowly; surely, no man yet
    Put lever to the heavy world with less;
What need of help? He knew how types were set,
    He had a dauntless spirit and a press.

James Russell Lowell, the author of these lines, has availed himself of the usual poetic license. The room on the third floor of Merchants' Hall, in Boston, where on January 1, 1831, Garrison launched the *Liberator,* was not particularly small, being eighteen feet square, and not one, but two unlearned young men "toiled over the types," for he and Isaac Knapp of Newburyport had joined forces. Later they were aided by a Negro apprentice. The windows were

William Lloyd Garrison, celebrated abolitionist and editor of the controversial Liberator. *"I will be as harsh as truth, and as uncompromising as justice," wrote Garrison in his manifesto in the first issue of the* Liberator. *On the subject of slavery, "I do not wish to think, or speak, or write, with moderation. . . . I am in earnest — I will not equivocate — I will not excuse — I will not retreat a single inch —* AND I WILL BE HEARD." *(Department of Special Collections, Wichita State University Library)*

grimy and spattered with printer's ink, as were the dingy walls. There was a press, picked up at a bargain, a couple of composing stands with worn secondhand type, a few chairs and a long table covered with exchanges, at which the editor attended to his correspondence. In a corner of the room was a mattress on which the two friends slept, for they could not afford the luxury of a boardinghouse. They lived on bread, milk and a little fruit, sharing the first two with a cat

who, when Garrison sat down to write, would jump on the table and rub her fur caressingly against his bald forehead. Although the paper advocated temperance as well as abolition, Knapp found it impossible to wean himself from his craving for strong drink, a weakness which eventually led to his undoing.

In the literature of social protest few lines are more stirring than the following paragraph from Garrison's salutatory to the public in the first number of the *Liberator*:

"I am aware that many object to the severity of my language; but is there not cause for severity? I *will* be as harsh as truth, and as uncompromising as justice. On this subject, I do not wish to think, or speak, or write, with moderation. No! No! Tell a man whose house is on fire to give a moderate alarm; tell him to moderately rescue his wife from the hands of the ravisher; tell the mother to gradually extricate her babe from the fire into which it has fallen — but urge me not to use moderation in a cause like the present. I am in earnest — I will not equivocate — I will not excuse — I will not retreat a single inch — AND I WILL BE HEARD."

The last statement proved prophetic. The *Liberator* never paid expenses, never had over three thousand subscribers, but its message became known from coast to coast and across the Atlantic. The paper had a fertilizing influence that caused the sprouting of various forms of opposition to slavery, of most of which Garrison disapproved, but for all of which he was directly or indirectly responsible. There were to be Abolitionists who formed political parties and others who abstained from voting; those who were orthodox churchmen and those who set out to destroy organized religion; those who believed in nonresistance and those who advocated armed intervention; those who wished to arouse the slaves to revolt and those who opposed this; those determined to remain within constitutional limits and those who scoffed at the Constitution. The Liberty Party, the Free-Soil Movement, the Republican Party — all, to a greater extent than their leaders cared to acknowledge, owed their existence to Garrison. He was the sower who went forth to sow and whose seed fell onto fertile ground, blossoming forth in a variety of shapes. He was the spiritual father of innumerable children, most of whom disowned him. He shamed a reluctant nation into doing what it did not wish to do, and the nation has never forgiven him. In 1853, [abolitionist] Wendell Phillips said:

"The community has come to hate its reproving Nathan so bitterly, that even those whom the relenting part of it is beginning to regard as standard-bearers of the antislavery host think it unwise to avow any connection or sympathy with him. I refer to some of the leaders of the political movement against slavery.... They are willing to confess privately, that our movement produced theirs, and that its continued existence is the very breath of their life. But, at the same time, they would fain walk on the road without being soiled by too close contact with the rough pioneers who threw it up.... If you tell me that they cherished all these principles in their own breasts before Mr. Garrison appeared, I can only say, if the antislavery movement did not give them their ideas, it surely gave them the courage to utter them."

☆

5

"Why so hot my little man?" wrote Ralph Waldo Emerson; and at another time: "There is a sublime prudence which, believing in a vast future, sure of more to come than is yet seen, postpones always the present hour to the whole life." But now see Emerson, returning from Boston in 1850, a copy of the [new] Fugitive Slave Law in his pocket, writing in his Journal: "This filthy enactment was made in the nineteenth century — I will not obey it — by God!" What has become of the "sublime prudence"? To refuse to obey the Fugitive Slave Law meant to incur a thousand dollar fine and be liable to pay another

thousand to the claimant of the fugitive, not to speak of a possible six months in jail. Was it that Emerson had come to agree with Whittier that a civilized man could no more obey the Fugitive Slave Law, even when a Lincoln set out to enforce it, than he could become a cannibal?

Garrison never worried about keeping cool. He agreed with Burke that "To speak of atrocious crimes in mild language is treason to virtue," with Luther that "Those things that are softly dealt with, in a corrupt age, give people but little concern, and are presently forgotten." Samuel J. May once said to him: "O, my friend, do try to moderate your indignation, and keep more cool; why, you are all on fire." His friend replied: "Brother May, I have need to be *all on fire,* for I have mountains of ice about me to melt."

Was the method effective? That it made it well-nigh impossible to spread the gospel of emancipation in the South admits of no doubt. But except among Southern Quakers such propaganda had born no fruit. Indeed, while at one time the slaveholders had been willing to concede that slavery was an evil and a curse, foisted upon the South by the mother country, after years of propaganda by Quakers and others they had arrived at the conclusion that it was the best of all possible labor systems, far superior to that prevailing in the North. This change of outlook was clearly perceptible at the time of the Missouri Compromise, long before the appearance of the *Liberator.* It was due to the fact that the invention of the cotton gin had made slavery far more profitable.

When Garrison began publication of his paper nearly all opposition to slavery had disappeared, North as well as South. Albert Bushnell Hart, in a profound study of the subject, wrote: "When Jackson became President in 1829, anti-slavery seemed, after fifty years of effort, to have spent its force. The voice of the churches was no longer heard in protest; the abolitionist societies were dying out; there was hardly an abolitionist militant in the field.... In Congress there was only one antislavery man and his efforts were without avail." But in 1839 the managers of the Massachusetts Anti-Slavery Society were able to declare: "Ten years ago a solitary individual stood up as the advocate of immediate and unconditional emancipation. Now, that individual sees about him hundreds of thousands of persons, of both sexes, members of every sect and party, from the most elevated to the humblest rank of life. In 1829 not an Anti-Slavery Society of a genuine stamp was in existence. In 1839 there are nearly two thousand such societies swarming and multiplying in all parts of the free States. In 1829 there was but one Anti-Slavery periodical in the land. In 1839 there are fourteen. In 1829 there was scarcely a newspaper of any religious or political party which was willing to disturb the 'delicate' question of slavery. In 1839 there are multitudes of journals that either openly advocate the doctrine of immediate and unconditional emancipation, or permit its free discussion in their columns. Then scarcely a church made slaveholding a bar to communion. Now, multitudes refuse to hear a slaveholder preach, or to recognize one as a brother. Then, no one petitioned Congress to abolish slavery in the District of Columbia. Now, in one day, a single member of the House of Representatives (John Quincy Adams) has presented one hundred and seventy-six such petitions in detail; while no less than seven hundred thousand persons have memorialized Congress on that and kindred subjects."

Garrison was to say: "In seizing the trump of God, I had indeed to blow a 'jarring blast' — but it was necessary to wake up a nation then slumbering in the lap of moral death. . . . What else but the *Liberator* primarily, (and of course instrumentally,) has effected this change? Greater success than I have had, no man could reasonably desire, or humbly expect."

When in 1837 Dr. William Ellery Channing complimented James G. Birney on the reasonableness and moderation of his antislavery paper, in contrast with the *Liberator,* which he accused of being "blemished by a spirit of intolerance, sweeping censure and rash, injurious judgment," the for-

mer Kentucky slaveholder and Solicitor General of Alabama replied: "Our country was asleep, whilst slavery was preparing to pour its 'leprous distilment' into her ears. So deep was becoming her sleep that nothing but a rude and almost ruffian-like shake could rouse her to a contemplation of her danger. If she is saved, it is because she has been thus treated." He left no doubt about whom he had in mind when he said on another occasion: "My antislavery trumpet would never have roused the country — Garrison alone could do it."

Another former Kentucky slaveholder, the famous Cassius Marcellus Clay, who while a student at Yale heard Garrison speak and became a convert, wrote: "There is one saying of his [Garrison's] traducers, and the traducers of those who act with him, . . . that 'they have set back the cause of emancipation by agitation'! Nothing is more false. The cause of emancipation advances only with agitation: let that cease and despotism is complete."

☆

6

Garrison did not expect to convert the slaveholders. He considered such an attempt a waste of time. In 1837 he wrote to Elizabeth Pease: "I have relinquished the expectation that they [the slaveholders] will ever, by mere moral suasion, consent to emancipate their victims." In 1840 he wrote to Elizabeth's brother Joseph: "There is not any instance recorded either in sacred or profane history, in which the oppressors and enslavers of mankind, except in individual cases, have been induced, by mere moral suasion, to surrender their despotic power, and let the oppressed go free; but in nearly every instance, from the time that Pharaoh and his hosts were drowned in the Red Sea, down to the present day, they have persisted in their evil course until sudden destruction came upon them, or they were compelled to surrender their ill-gotten power in some other manner."

Others were of the same opinion. Cassius M. Clay wrote: "The slaveholders have just as much intention of yielding up their slaves as the sum of the kings of the earth have of laying down, for the benefit of the people, their sceptres." In August, 1855, Abraham Lincoln was to write to George Robertson of Kentucky that the Tsar of Russia would abdicate and free his serfs sooner than American slaveholders would voluntarily give up their slaves. "Experience has demonstrated, I think, that there is no peaceful extinction of slavery in prospect for us."

Garrison feared, like Lincoln, that slavery would never be abolished except by force of arms, but he believed there was one other method worth trying. When Jesus of Nazareth called the Pharisees "fools," "hypocrites," "devourers of widows' houses," "serpents," "generation of vipers" — and asked, "How can ye escape the damnation of hell?" — he was obviously not using moral *suasion,* but moral *pressure.* This was the method Garrison had decided to adopt. Shortly after he founded the *Liberator,* he told Samuel J. May: "Until the term 'slaveholder' sends as deep a feeling of horror to the hearts of those who hear it applied to any one as the term, 'robber,' 'pirate,' 'murderer' do, we must use and multiply epithets when condemning the sins of him who is guilty of 'the sum of all villainies.'" He hoped to arouse such a feeling of abhorrence and storm of disapproval in the North (and in fact throughout the civilized world) that the South would be forced to yield. That the method offered some hope of success was acknowledged by General Duff Green, who wrote: "We believe that we have most to fear from the organized action upon the conscience and fears of the slaveholders themselves.... It is only by alarming the consciences of the weak and feeble, and diffusing among our own people a morbid sensibility on the question of slavery, that the abolitionists can accomplish their object."

The method did not succeed any more than it had succeeded in Christ's time; but who will say that it was not worth trying? Nor can it be said that it pro-duced no results. If Garrison failed to shame and intimidate the South, he yet succeeded in arousing such an aversion to, and fear of, slavery in the North that war seemed preferable to allowing it to spread. Archibald H. Grimké has well said: "The public sentiment which Lincoln obeyed, [Garrison and] Phillips created."

☆

7

About a year before the appearance of the *Liberator,* David Walker, a Boston Negro who made a living as an old-clothes man, published a pamphlet entitled *Walker's Appeal.* He boldly called upon the slaves to revolt. "If you commence," he wrote, "make sure work — do not trifle, for they will not trifle with you — they want us for their slaves, and think nothing of murdering us in order to subject us to that wretched condition — therefore, if there is an attempt made by us, kill or be killed." There were three editions of the pamphlet, copies of which found their way into the Slave States. The consternation these produced in the South bordered on the ridiculous and was eloquent testimony of the fear that lurked under the South's brave exterior. Governors sent special messages to Legislatures. Repressive laws were hastily passed. Incoming ships and trains were searched. Colored seamen were taken from Northern ships entering Southern ports and imprisoned. "How much is it to be regretted," declared *Niles' Weekly Register,* "that a negro dealer in old clothes, should thus excite two states to legislative action." Walker, however, died in June, 1830, and the South breathed a sigh of relief.

Then, in January, 1831, again in the city of Boston, appeared the *Liberator,* and in an early issue of the paper a poem from the editor's pen warning of the danger of a slave uprising if emancipation were delayed. One stanza read:

Woe if it come with storm, and blood, and fire,
When midnight darkness veils the earth and sky!
   Woe to the innocent babe — the guilty sire —
Mother and daughter — friends of kindred tie!
   Stranger and citizen alike shall die!
Red-handed slaughter his revenge shall feed,
   And Havoc yell his ominous death-cry;
   And wild Despair in vain for mercy plead —
   While Hell itself shall shrink, and sicken at the
      deed!

The slave uprising in the French colony of San Domingo towards the close of the eighteenth century proved there were reasons for the warning. Garrison, however, did not advise the slaves to revolt. He had condemned *Walker's Appeal* in the *Genius,* and the last stanza of his poem read:

Not by the sword shall your deliverance be;
   Not by the shedding of your masters' blood,
Not by rebellion — or foul treachery,
   Upspringing suddenly, like swelling flood:
Revenge and rapine ne'er did bring forth good.
   God's *time is best!* — nor will it long delay:
Even now your barren cause begins to bud,
   And glorious shall the fruit be! — Watch and
      pray,
For, lo! the kindling dawn, that ushers in the day!

Shortly after the appearance of this poem, on August 22, 1831, there took place in Southampton County, Virginia, the most sanguinary slave uprising in the annals of American slavery. A Negro mystic named Nat Turner, a slave belonging to a small planter, gathered a band of followers variously estimated at from forty to two hundred, and after killing his master and the latter's family, moved from plantation to plantation, slaughtering between fifty and sixty persons, men, women and children. Bands of white men and the state militia finally subdued the rebels, but not without committing outrages upon innocent Negroes surpassing in cruelty anything of which Turner had been guilty. Finally, the Negro leader and nineteen of his followers were hanged. The uprising was responsible for a sensational debate in the Virginia Legislature during which slavery was condemned in language as violent as any Garrison had ever used. For a while indeed it seemed that what years of propaganda by the Quakers had failed to accomplish would come as a result of Turner's bloodletting. Governor John Floyd of Virginia noted in his diary: "Before I leave this Government I will have contrived to have a law passed gradually abolishing slavery in this state." But the people and the authorities eventually got over their fright and began looking about for a scapegoat. Walker was read, but there was Garrison and his paper. Turner and his confederates had denied that they had read either *Walker's Appeal* or the *Liberator,* and no evidence to the contrary was introduced; but Governor Floyd wrote to Governor James Hamilton of South Carolina that black preachers had read from the pulpit the inflammatory writings of Walker and Garrison, which may or may not have been true. Anyway, Harrison Gray Otis, Mayor of Boston, received letters from the Governors of Virginia and Georgia "severally remonstrating against an incendiary newspaper published in Boston, and, as they alleged, thrown broadcast among their plantations, inciting to insurrection and its horrid results."

Mayor Otis was puzzled. Although the *Liberator* had now been published in Boston for nearly a year, he had never seen a copy or even heard of the paper's existence. "It appeared on enquiry," he wrote, "that no member of the city government, nor any person of my acquaintance, had ever heard of the publication. Some time afterward, it was reported to me by the city officers that they had ferreted out the paper and its editor; that his office was an obscure hole, his only visible auxiliary a negro boy, and his supporters a very few insignificant persons of all colors. This information, with the consent of the aldermen, I communicated to the above-named governors, with an assurance of my belief that the new fanaticism had not made, nor was likely to make, proselytes among the respectable classes of our people. In this, however, I was mistaken."

Neither the Mayor of Boston nor the Governor of Massachusetts felt he possessed the power to stop publication of the *Liberator,* though both regretted that shortcoming in the law. The South was indignant. The Columbia (South Carolina) *Telescope* believed the matter called for armed intervention. "They [the people of Massachusetts] permit a battery to be erected upon their territory, which fires upon us, and we should be justified in invading that territory to silence their guns," the editor declared. A Vigilance Committee in Columbia offered a reward of fifteen hundred dollars for the arrest and conviction of any person "distributing or circulating the *Liberator* or any other publication of a seditious nature." Georgetown, District of Columbia, passed a law forbidding any colored person to take the *Liberator* from the post-office on pain of twenty dollars' fine and thirty days' imprisonment. In Raleigh, North Carolina, the grand jury found a true bill against Garrison and Knapp in the hope of extraditing them. A correspondent in the *Washington National Intelligence* proposed that the President of the United States or the Governor of Virginia demand Garrison's extradition, and in case of refusal by the Governor of Massachusetts "the people of the South offer an adequate reward to any person who will deliver him dead or alive, into the hands of the authorities of any State South of the Potomac." He did not have long to wait. On November 30, 1831, the Senate and the House of Representatives of Georgia appropriated five thousand dollars to be paid by the Governor "to any person or persons who shall arrest, bring to trial and prosecute to conviction, under the laws of the State, the editor or publisher of a certain paper called the *Liberator,* published in the town of Boston and State of Massachusetts."

Garrison was not in the least intimidated and wrote defiantly: "A price upon the head of a citizen of Massachusetts — for what? For daring to give his

opinion of the moral aspect of slavery! ... Know this, ye Senatorial Patrons of kidnappers! that we despise your threats as much as we deplore your infatuation; nay, more — know that a hundred men stand ready to fill our place as soon as it is made vacant by violence."

☆

8

On his last visit to the United States, General Lafayette expressed his astonishment at the increase in racial prejudice. He recalled that in Washington's army, white and black had fought side by side and had messed together in harmony. Now, however, in the Free as well as in the Slave States, free Negroes were despised, persecuted, deprived of most of the prerogatives of the free man, permitted to earn a living only at the most menial and ill-paid employments.

A glance at some of the laws governing the free people of color leaves no doubt concerning the tenuous nature of the freedom they enjoyed. In Maryland a Justice of the Peace could order a free Negro's ears cropped for striking a white man even in self-defense. A free Negro entering that State incurred a penalty of fifty dollars for every week spent within its borders, and if unable to pay was sold into slavery. In Georgia the penalty for teaching a free Negro to read or write was five hundred dollars if the offender was white, if colored he was fined and flogged at the discretion of the court. In Virginia and South Carolina any Justice of the Peace could disband a school where free Negroes or their offspring were taught to read or write, fine the teacher five hundred dollars and have twenty lashes administered to each pupil. In Louisiana a fine of like amount awaited the zealous Christian who taught a free Negro in Sunday School. In Mississippi and the District of Columbia a Negro unable to prove his legal right to freedom could be sold into slavery. In South Carolina a Negro who "entertained" a runaway slave by giving him as much as a crust of bread was fined fifty dollars, and if unable to pay was sold. In several Slave States free Negroes were not permitted to assemble for religious purposes unless white people were present, and they were forbidden to preach. In Ohio a white man who hired a Negro or mulatto even for a day made himself liable for his future support. In the Free States, Negro children could not attend public school and little or no provision was made for their instruction. In several Free and of course in all the Slave States, free people of color were denied the right of suffrage.

Custom solidified this edifice of injustice. It made it well-nigh impossible for an artisan, mechanic or shopkeeper to employ a colored apprentice. In the North as well as in the South, Negroes were required to travel in the steerage of a boat or on the outside of a stagecoach, when they were not barred altogether. When a convention of colored people in Philadelphia made a brave attempt to establish a manual labor school for Negroes in New Haven, Connecticut, the Mayor called a mass meeting of the citizens, and such a hue and cry arose that the plan had to be abandoned. When Noyes Academy, in Canaan, New Hampshire, admitted a few colored students, three hundred citizens with a hundred yoke of oxen dragged the building from its foundation and deposited it outside the town. In church, Negroes had to sit in separate pews — which in the Baptist Church at Hartford, Connecticut, were boarded up and provided with peepholes. When in Houghton, Massachusetts, a colored man acquired a white man's pew, the church authorities had the floor removed in that part of the edifice. . . .

☆

9

Garrison championed the free people of color as fervently as the slaves. "This then is my consolation," he wrote on one occasion: "if I cannot do much in this quarter towards abolishing slavery, I may be able to elevate our free colored population in the scale of society." Speaking before a colored convention in Philadelphia he said with feeling: "I never rise to address a colored audience without feeling ashamed of my color; ashamed of being identified with a race of men who have done you so much injustice and yet retain so large a portion of your brethren in servitude."

No matter how pressing his work, he would lay it aside when invited to address a colored audience. He did not flatter his listeners, but urged them to be worthy of liberty, to be temperate, industrious and to surpass the white man in virtue, which, he assured them, was no difficult task. They must not resort to violence, but should incessantly petition to be permitted to vote, to send their children to public school and to exercise every other right of the freeman. "If your petition is denied seven times, send it seven times seven."

His influence was great among them. Once in Boston, when he had addressed them on temperance, they immediately formed a temperance society, which within a few days counted one hundred and fifty members. "Such acts as these, brethren, give me strength and boldness in your cause," he assured them. Henry E. Benson, in a letter to Isaac Knapp, described a scene that took place in Providence, Rhode Island, after Garrison had addressed a colored audience. "After the meeting," he wrote, "the poor creatures wept and sobbed like children — they gathered round him anxious to express their gratitude for what he had done for them, and tell him how well they loved him."

So persistent was he in their defense that some believed him to be colored, and when he advocated the repeal of the Massachusetts law against intermarriage, the rumor spread that he meant to marry a Negress. No resentment at the rumor is noticeable in this mild denial he published in the *Liberator:* "We declare that our heart is neither affected *by,* nor pledged *to,* any lady, black or white, bond or free."

☆

10

If "the style is the man," then one might have expected Garrison in his maturity to have been a scowling, brusque, bitter, opinionated individual. Such in fact was the mental image formed by many. The reality confounded Buffon's maxim. Josiah Copley, editor of a religious paper in Pittsburgh, Pennsylvania, happening to be in Boston in 1832, called on Garrison after some hesitation. "I never was more astonished," he wrote. "All my preconceptions were at fault. My ideal of the man was that of a stout, rugged, dark-visaged desperado — something like we picture a pirate. He was a quiet, gentle and I might say handsome man — a gentleman indeed, in every sense of the word."

William H. Herndon, Lincoln's law partner, who visited Garrison in the latter's old age, wrote: "I had imagined him a shriveled, cold, selfish, haughty man, one who was weak and fanatically blind to the charities and equities of life, at once whining and insulting, mean and miserable, but I was pleasantly disappointed. I found him warm, generous, approachable, communicative; he has some mirth, some wit, and a deep abiding faith in coming universal charity. I was better and more warmly received by him than by any man in Boston."

Harriet Martineau, famous British authoress, who met Garrison in 1835, declared: "His aspect put to flight in an instant what prejudices his slanderers had raised in me. I was wholly taken by surprise. It was a countenance glowing with health and wholly expressive of purity, animation and gentleness. I did not now wonder at the citizen who, seeing a print of Garrison at a shop window without a name to it, went in and bought it and framed it as the most saintlike of countenances. The end of the story is, that when the citizen found whose portrait he had been hanging in his parlor, he took the print out of the frame and huddled it away."

Helen Eliza Benson Garrison not only shared her husband's commitment to reform but provided him with the refuge of a stable personal life. "By her unwearied attentions to my want, her sympathetic regards, her perfect equanimity of mind," Garrison said, "she is no trifling support to abolitionism, inasmuch as she lightens my labors, and enables me to find exquisite delight in the family circle, as an off-set to public adversity." (The Bettmann Archive)

The preponderance of opinion is that his conversation was the very opposite of his writing — mild, tolerant, disarming. Miss Martineau wrote: "Garrison had a good deal of a Quaker air; and his speech is deliberate like a Quaker's but gentle as a woman's. . . . Every conversation I had with him confirmed my opinion that sagacity is the most striking attribute of his conversation. It has none of the severity, the harshness, the bad taste of his writing; it is as gladsome as his countenance, and as gentle as his voice."

Harriet Beecher Stowe, who had confided to one of Garrison's sons that she was "dreadfully afraid" of his father, having made the editor's acquaintance, wrote to him: "You have a remarkable tact at conversation."

Ralph Waldo Emerson, who for a long time had been prejudiced against him, in 1844 wrote in his Journal: "The haters of Garrison have lived to rejoice in that grand world movement which, every age or two, casts out so masterly an agent for good. I cannot speak of the gentleman without respect."

☆

11

In the first number of the *Liberator,* where appeared Garrison's immortal challenge to the slaveholders, one may read these lines from the editor's pen:

"An attempt has been made — it is still making — we regret to say, with considerable success — to inflame the minds of our working classes against the more opulent, and to persuade them that they are contemned and oppressed by a wealthy aristocracy. That public grievances exist, is unquestionably true; but they are not confined to any one class of society. Every profession is interested in their removal — the rich as well as the poor. It is in the highest degree criminal, therefore, to exasperate our mechanics to deeds of violence, or to array them under a party banner; for it is not true, that, at any time, they have been the objects of reproach. . . . We are the friends of reform; but that is not reform, which, in curing one evil, threatens to inflict a thousand others."

The reason for this outburst was an attempt by Seth Luther and others to organize a Working Men's Party and to form labor unions.

In the fifth number of the paper a correspondent pointed out to Garrison that he was wrong in trying to discourage labor's attempts to organize:

"Although you do not appear to have perceived it, I think there is a very intimate connexion be-

tween the interests of the working men's party and your own. . . . In the history of the origin of slavery is to be found the explanation of the evils we deplore and seek to remove, as well as those you have attacked. . . . We seek to enlighten our brethren in the knowledge of their rights and duties. . . . It is a duty owed by working men to themselves and the world to exert their power through the ballot-box."

Garrison replied: "There is a prevalent opinion that . . . the poor and vulgar are taught to consider the opulent as their natural enemies. Where is the evidence that our wealthy citizens, as a body, are hostile to the interests of the laboring classes? It is not in their commercial enterprises, which whiten the ocean with canvas and give employment to a useful and numerous class of men. It is not found in the manufacturing establishments, which multiply labor and cheapen the necessities of the poor. It is not found in the luxuries of their tables, or the adornments of their dwellings, for which they must pay in proportion to their extravagance. . . . Perhaps it would be the truth to affirm, that mechanics are more inimical to the success of each other, more unjust toward each other, than the rich are toward them."

Yet in 1831, and for a long time thereafter, the hours of labor in New England factories were from five in the morning until seven-thirty in the evening — the working day being thirteen and one half hours. The two half hours allowed for breakfast and midday dinner were as tiring as any, since the workers had to hurry home, bolt their food and hasten back to the factory to escape a fine. In 1849 a report submitted to the American Medical Association by one of its members contained the statement that "there is not a State's prison, or house of correction in New England, where the hours of labor are so long, the hours for meals so short, or the ventilation so much neglected, as in all the cotton mills with which I am acquainted." In Boston Irish workmen were forced to labor fifteen hours a day, including Sunday. The death rate among them was so appalling that it was claimed the Irish lived on an average only fourteen years after reaching Boston. The Cochee Manufacturing Company required its workers to sign an agreement to "conform in all respects to the regulations which are now, or may be hereafter adopted . . . and to work for such wages as the company may see fit to pay." Workers were commonly required to buy at the company store and were usually in debt to their employers. If they attempted to leave their employment without paying what they owed they were imprisoned. In 1831 there were over fifteen hundred people imprisoned for debt in Boston alone, more than half of whom owed less than twenty dollars. It may therefore be said that a system of veritable peonage prevailed.

Strikes were frequent, but prior to 1860 not a single strike was won in Massachusetts, and not until 1874 did that State have any legal restriction on the number of hours adult wageworkers could be required to work. Employers in other parts of the country often gave working conditions in New England as an excuse for not improving labor's lot.

In view of all this, how could a man ready for almost any sacrifice for the sake of the Negro have remained indifferent to the lot of white wageworkers?

Garrison was an individualist. In his opinion, if a man was not a chattel, he was master of his own fate. If he was poor the fault was his. In the days of handicraft, poverty had indeed usually been the result of shiftlessness; but the poverty of the factory worker was more often due to the greed of the employer. The handicraftsman, having finished his apprenticeship, looked forward to being his own master. If he worked long hours he was buoyed up by the hope of getting ahead in the world. But later, only the exceptional man could hope to become a factory owner or even a foreman. Garrison, grown to maturity in a transition period, failed to grasp that the average wageworker's only hope of improving his lot was to unite with his fellows.

When Garrison wrote "Mechanics are more inimical to the success of each other, more unjust toward each other than the rich are towards them," he failed to comprehend that fear was at the bottom of this. Yankee workmen feared the competition of Irish immigrants and sometimes rioted against them. White workmen were hostile to Negroes for the same reason and opposed emancipation fearing it would result in hordes of Negroes from the South invading the North and lowering their standard of living, already sufficiently low. Southern leaders shrewdly exploited this fear. In 1843, Henry Clay wrote to the Reverend Calvin Colton, urging him to prepare a popular tract whose "great aim and object . . . should be to arouse the laboring classes of the free States against abolition. The slaves, being free, would be dispersed throughout the Union; they would enter into competition with the free laborer; with the American, the Irish, the German; reduce his wages; be confounded with him, and affect his moral and social standing. And as the ultras go for both abolition and amalgamation, show that their object is to unite in marriage the laboring white man and the laboring black man, and to reduce the white laboring man to the despised and degraded condition of the black man."

The situation required shrewd and careful handling. Most of all it required a thorough understanding of the problem. Garrison lacked that understanding, and antagonized his natural allies. As a result American wageworkers remained indifferent, if not hostile, to Abolition. Some regarded it as a plot of the employers to lower wages. Others saw it as a scheme of professional philanthropists. The editor of the *Chronicle,* a Massachusetts weekly devoted to the interests of labor, wrote: "Philanthropists may speak of negro slavery, but it would be well first to emancipate the slaves at home. Let us not stretch our ears to catch the sound of the lash on the flesh of our oppressed black, while the oppressed in our midst are crying in thunder tones, and calling upon us for assistance."

QUESTIONS TO CONSIDER

1   Garrison always insisted that he was a Christian pacifist who expected to abolish slavery through nonviolent methods. How, then, can you explain his words in 1850 that in order to achieve black emancipation "a few white victims must be sacrificed to open the eyes of this nation and show the tyranny of our laws"?

2   When Samuel May spoke from the pulpit at "Church Green" in Boston in 1830, condemning slavery and exhorting the congregation to help destroy the institution before the institution destroyed the nation, his amazed audience thought he had lost his mind. What conclusions can you draw from this incident about the attitudes of northern whites toward African Americans, slavery, and abolitionists?

3   Analyze the effectiveness of Garrison's method of achieving the abolition of slavery. Would a cooler, more moderate approach than his have made more headway, especially in the South? In what national context did Garrison propose his radical objective of immediate emancipation? How did that context affect his choice of tactics?

4   Compare the treatment of free blacks in the North and in the South. Was racial prejudice, like the institution of slavery, confined below the Mason-Dixon Line?

5   Southern proslavery apologists frequently pointed to the evils of what they called "wage slavery" among the northern working classes. They accused abolitionists of hypocrisy in ignoring the harsh "slavery" in their own backyards while condemning the South's more "benevolent" institution of black slavery. How valid were these accusations when leveled at Garrison?

IX

FREEDOM'S FERMENT: THE AGE OF JACKSON

17

The Jacksonian Revolution

ROBERT V. REMINI

The age of Jackson was a turbulent era — a period of boom and bust, of great population shifts into the cities and out to the frontier, of institutionalized violence and racial antagonisms, of utopian communities, reform movements, the abolitionist crusade, and the "great southern reaction" in defense of slavery. It was also a time of graft and corruption, of machine politics and ruthless political bosses. But above all, it was an age of the self-made man, a time when privilege and elitist rule gave way to the vestiges of popular democracy — at least for white males. Between the 1820s and the 1840s, America witnessed the rise of universal manhood suffrage for whites, long ballots, national nominating conventions, and grassroots political parties.

The man who gave the age its name was a self-made planter and slaveholder of considerable wealth. Like most aristocrats from the Tennessee country of his day, Andrew Jackson could not spell, he lacked education and culture, but he did aspire to wealth and military glory, both of which he won. Despite his harsh, gaunt features, he looked like a gentleman and a soldier, and in calm moods he could be gentle, even grave.

In politics, however, Jackson was an "aggressive, dynamic, charismatic, and intimidating individual," as Robert V. Remini describes him. He became a symbol of "the common man," Remini says, because he was devoted to liberty and democracy and had a powerful faith in "the people." In Remini's view, Jackson's ascension to the presidency in 1828 launched a genuine revolution against the "gentry republic" founded by the signers in which the rich and powerful ruled. The Jacksonian revolution, Remini argues, moved America toward a more democratic system in which the government was responsive to the popular will. In Remini's view, Jackson himself played a major role in the shift toward democracy — that is, toward a system of true majority rule, not just rule

236

by a propertied elite. He set out to make the president and every other federal official answerable to the people. Thus, he favored abolishing the electoral college and rotating every elected office. He even challenged the role of the Supreme Court as the final arbiter in interpreting the Constitution, a subject covered in selection 14. In Remini's view, Jackson also inaugurated the history of powerful executive leadership in this country. He used his veto power more than all his predecessors combined and asserted the right of the chief executive to initiate legislation, which altered the president's relationship with Congress and made the president the head of state. Surprisingly enough, Remini does not mention Jackson's crucial role in solving the nullification crisis of 1832, which Remini heralds elsewhere as the single most important achievement of Jackson's presidency. That event is discussed in the portrait of Henry Clay (selection 18).

As Remini explains in an afterword, his view of Jackson is a revival of a once popular interpretation that had fallen into disfavor. The author of a recent three-volume biography of Jackson and perhaps the country's leading Jackson scholar, Remini disputes those who have dismissed Jackson as an opportunist and a fraud masquerading as a man of the people. Remini even defends Jackson's Indian removal policy, which so offends many modern Americans. That policy is discussed in selection 21.

Remini's interpretation is provocative. Do you agree that a slave owner could really be a man of the people? As you ponder that question, remember Professor Wilson's warning about presentism. Jackson himself would have answered the question with a resounding yes on two counts. First, the Jacksonian revolution ushered in universal white manhood suffrage in most states and created a true mass electorate. Second, "the people" in Jackson's day was a political concept that included all those who could vote. That meant white men almost exclusively. Women, slaves, and free blacks outside New England were all denied the electoral franchise and were excluded from the idea of "the people." They had no will to which Jackson or any other government official could be responsive.

Because Remini makes much of the transition from Washington's generation to Jackson's, you may want to compare the records and outlooks of the two presidents (for an analysis of Washington, see selection 10). But Remini's essay is best studied and discussed in conjunction with the next selection, a portrait of Jackson's great adversary, Whig leader Henry Clay.

GLOSSARY

BENSON, LEE   Quantifying historian who dismissed as "claptrap" Jacksonian rhetoric about "the people" and democracy.

CALHOUN, JOHN C.   South Carolina planter and Jackson's first vice president, he later broke with Jackson and helped form the rival Whig party.

CLAY, HENRY   Kentucky planter and one of the great leaders of the rival Whig party (see selection 18).

DEMOCRATIC PARTY   New political organization, formed around the Jackson presidency, that opposed a strong central government and a broad interpretation of the Constitution; Jackson himself and many Democrats were against government-financed internal improvements.

DUANE, WILLIAM   Jackson's secretary of the treasury; Old Hickory fired him when he refused to transfer federal deposits from the National Bank.

HOFSTADTER, RICHARD   Historian whose book *The American Political Tradition* (1948) argues that the typical Jacksonian was "an expectant capitalist," a "man on the make."

INTERNAL IMPROVEMENTS   Roads, railroads, and canals financed by the federal government or the states.

OLIGARCHY   System of government in which a dominant class rules.

PROGRESSIVE HISTORIANS   Those in the early part of the twentieth century who dubbed the Jacksonian revolution an age of egalitarianism that produced the rise of the common man, first in the western states, then in the older ones in the East.

SCHLESINGER, ARTHUR M., JR.   Historian who argued in 1945 that the Jacksonian revolution was an effort on the part of the "less fortunate," urban working classes and yeoman farmers, to challenge the power of the wealthy business community.

SECOND NATIONAL BANK (SECOND BANK OF THE UNITED STATES)   Founded in 1816 by congressional charter to run twenty years, the bank was supposed to stabilize the national economy by issuing sound paper money, serving as a depository for federal funds, and establishing branches across the country; Jackson vetoed the bank recharter bill.

SPOILS SYSTEM   Pejorative term for Jackson's principle of rotation in office.

"TIPPECANOE AND TYLER TOO"   Campaign slogan for Whig candidates William Henry ("Tippecanoe") Harrison and John Tyler in the "log cabin" presidential campaign of 1840.

TOCQUEVILLE, ALEXIS DE   French aristocrat who visited the United States in 1831 and wrote the classic *Democracy in America* on the basis of his observations; he praised "the general equality of condition among the people" in America but feared that industrialization would create a new class of dependent workers and a new ruling aristocracy.

VAN BUREN, MARTIN ("LITTLE VAN")   New Yorker who advocated the two-party system, served as Jackson's second vice president, and succeeded him in the White House in 1837.

WEBSTER, DANIEL   Great Whig leader who represented Massachusetts in the Senate.

WHIG PARTY   Coalition of Jackson haters that favored a strong central government and federally financed international improvements (treated in detail in selection 18).

☆

A New Generation of Political Leaders

"What?" cried the outraged North Carolina lady when she heard the dreadful news. "Jackson up for president? Jackson? Andrew Jackson? The Jackson that used to live in Salisbury? Why, when he was here, he was such a rake that my husband would not bring him into the house! It is true, he might have taken him out to the stable to weigh horses for a race, and might drink a glass of whiskey with him there. Well, if Andrew Jackson can be president, anybody can!"

Indeed. After forty years of constitutional government headed by presidents George Washington, John Adams, Thomas Jefferson, James Madison, James Monroe, and John Quincy Adams, the thought of Gen. Andrew Jackson of Tennessee — "Old Hickory" to his devoted soldiers — succeeding such distinguished statesmen came as a shock to some Americans in 1828. And little did they know at the time that Old Hickory would be followed in succession by the little Magician, Tippecanoe and Tyler, too, Young Hickory, and then Old Rough and Ready.

What had happened to the American political process? How could it come about that the Washingtons, Jeffersons, and Madisons of the world could be replaced by the Van Burens, Harrisons, Tylers, and Taylors? What a mockery of the political system bequeathed by the Founding Fathers!

The years from roughly 1828 to 1848 are known today as the Age of Jackson or the Jacksonian era. To many contemporaries, they initiated a "revolution,"

a shocking overthrow of the noble republican standards of the founders by the "common people," who in 1828 preferred as president a crude frontiersman like Andrew Jackson to a statesman of proven ability with a record of outstanding public service like John Quincy Adams.

Over the forty years following the establishment of the American nation under the Constitution, the United States had experienced many profound changes in virtually all phases of life. Following the War of 1812, the industrial revolution took hold and within thirty years all the essential elements for the creation of an industrial society in American were solidly in place. At the same time, a transportation revolution got underway with the building of canals, bridges, and turnpikes, reaching a climax of sorts in the 1820s with the coming of the railroads. The standard of living was also improved by numerous new inventions. Finally, many of the older eastern states began to imitate newer western states by democratizing their institutions, for example, amending their constitutions to eliminate property qualifications for voting and holding office, thereby establishing universal white manhood suffrage.

The arrival of many thousands of new voters at the polls in the early nineteenth century radically changed American politics. In the past, only the wealthy and better educated were actively involved in government. Moreover, political parties were frowned upon by many of the Founding Fathers. Parties stood for factions or cliques by which greedy and ambitious men, who had no interest in serving the public good, could advance their private and selfish purposes. John Adams spoke for many when he declared that the "division of the republic into two great parties . . . is to be dreaded as the greatest political evil under our Constitution."

But times had changed. An entirely new generation of politicians appeared at the outbreak of the War of 1812, men like Henry Clay, John C. Calhoun, Martin Van Buren, and Daniel Webster, who regarded political parties more favorably. Indeed, the

This article appeared in the January 1988 issue and is reprinted with permission from *The World & I,* a publication of The Washington Times Corporation, copyright © 1988.

party structure that had emerged before the end of President Washington's administration had been their corridor to power, since none of them could offer to their constituents a public record to match what the founders had achieved.

None had fought in the revolution. None had signed the Declaration or participated in the debates leading to the writing and adoption of the Constitution. Some of them — Martin Van Buren is probably the best example — actually considered parties to be beneficial to the body politic, indeed essential to the proper working of a democratic society. Through the party system, Van Buren argued, the American people could more effectively express their will and take measures to ensure that that will was implemented by their representatives. "We must always have party distinctions," he wrote, "and the old ones are the best. . . . Political combinations between the inhabitants of the different states are unavoidable and the most natural and beneficial to the country is that between the planters of the South and the plain Republicans of the North."

In supporting Andrew Jackson for the presidency in 1828 and trying to win support from both planters and plain Republicans, Van Buren affirmed his belief in the American need for a two-party system. Jackson's election, he told Thomas Ritchie, editor of the Richmond *Enquirer,* "as the result of his military services without reference to party, and, as far as he alone is concerned, scarcely to principle, would be one thing. His election as the result of combined and concerted effort of a political party, holding in the main, to certain tenets and opposed to certain prevailing principles, might be another and far different thing."

Van Buren eventually formed an alliance with John C. Calhoun and a number of other southern politicians, and led the way in structuring a political organization around the presidential candidacy of Andrew Jackson. That organization ultimately came to be called the Democratic Party. Its leaders, including Jackson, Van Buren, Calhoun, and Thomas

Hart Benton, claimed to follow the republican doctrines of Thomas Jefferson. Thus they opposed both a strong central government and a broad interpretation of the Constitution, and they regarded the states, whose rights must be defended by all who cared about preserving individual liberty, as a wholesome counterweight to the national government. Many of them opposed the idea of the federal government sponsoring public works, arguing that internal improvements dangerously inflated the power of the central government and jeopardized liberty. As president, Andrew Jackson vetoed the Maysville road bill and contended that the national government should avoid internal improvements as a general practice, except for those essential to the national defense.

The political philosophy these Democrats espoused was fundamentally conservative. It advocated economy in operating the government because a tight budget limited government activity, and Jackson swore that if ever elected president he would liquidate the national debt. True to his word, he labored throughout his administration to cut expenditures by vetoing several appropriations bills he tagged as exorbitant, and he finally succeeded in obliterating the national debt altogether in January 1835 — a short-lived accomplishment.

The organization of the Democratic Party in its initial stages included a central committee, state committees, and a national newspaper located in Washington, D.C., the *United States Telegraph,* which could speak authoritatively to the party faithful. In time it was said that the Democratic organization included "a chain of newspaper posts, from the New England States to Louisiana, and branching off through Lexington to the Western States." The supporters of Jackson's election were accused by their opponents of attempting to regulate "the popular election by means of organized clubs in the States, and organized presses everywhere."

Democrats took particular delight in celebrating the candidacy of Andrew Jackson. They found that

When Jackson set out for his inauguration in Washington, D.C., large crowds turned out to see "the man of the people." This prompted an old Federalist to cry, "The reign of KING MOB seemed triumphant." But a westerner thought it "a proud day for the people. General Jackson is their own President." (New York Historical Society)

Old Hickory's personality and military accomplishments made him an attractive and viable candidate for the ordinary voter. Indeed his career and personality stirred the imagination of Democratic leaders around the country and they devised new methods, or improved old ones, to get across the message that Andrew Jackson was a "man of the people." "The Constitution and liberty of the country were in imminent peril, and he has preserved them both!" his supporters boasted. "We can sustain our republican principles . . . by calling to the presidential chair . . . ANDREW JACKSON."

Jackson became a symbol of the best in American life — a self-made man, among other things — and party leaders adopted the hickory leaf as their symbol. Hickory brooms, hickory canes, hickory sticks shot up everywhere — on steeples, poles, steamboats, and stage coaches, and in the hands of all who could wave them to salute the Old Hero of New Orleans. "In every village, as well as upon the corners of many city streets," hickory poles were erected. "Many of these poles were standing as late as 1845," recorded one contemporary, "rotten mementoes [*sic*] of the delirium of 1828." The opponents of the Democratic Party were outraged by this crude lowering of the political process. "Planting hickory trees!" snorted the Washington *National Journal* on May 24, 1828. "Odds nuts and drumsticks! What have hickory trees to do with republicanism and the great contest?"

The Democrats devised other gimmicks to generate excitement for their ticket. "Jackson meetings"

241

were held in every county where a Democratic organization existed. Such meetings were not new, of course. What was new was their audience. "If we go into one of these meetings," declared one newspaper, "of whom do we find them composed? Do we see there the solid, substantial, moral and reflecting yeomanry of the country? No. . . . They comprise a large portion of the dissolute, the noisy, the discontented, and designing of society." The Democratic press retorted with the claim that these so-called dissolute were actually the "bone and muscle of American society. They are the People. The real People who understand that Gen. Jackson is one of them and will defend their interests and rights."

The Jacksonians were also very fond of parades and barbecues. In Baltimore a grand barbecue was scheduled to commemorate the successful defense of the city when the British attacked during the War of 1812. But the Democrats expropriated the occasion and converted it into a Jackson rally. One parade started with dozens of Democrats marching to the beat of a fife and drum corps and wearing no other insignia save "a twig of the sacred [hickory] tree in their hats." Trailing these faithful Jacksonians came "gigantic hickory poles," still live and crowned with green foliage, being carted in "on eight wheels for the purpose of being planted by the democracy on the eve of the election." These poles were drawn by eight horses, all decorated with "ribbons and mottoes." Perched in the branches of each tree were a dozen Democrats, waving flags and shouting, "Hurrah for Jackson!"

"Van Buren has learned you know that the *Hurra Boys* were for Jackson," commented one critic, "and to my regret they constitute a powerful host." Indeed they did. The number of voters in the election of 1828 rose to 1,155,340, a jump of more than 800,000 over the previous presidential election of 1824.

The Hurra Boys brought out the voters in 1828, but at considerable cost. The election set a low mark for vulgarity, gimmickry, and nonsensical hijinks. Jackson's mother was accused of being a prostitute brought to America to service British soldiers, and his wife was denounced as an "adulteress" and bigamist. "Ought a convicted adulteress and her paramour husband to be placed in the highest offices of this free and Christian land?" asked one editor. But the Democrats were no better, accusing John Quincy Adams of pimping for the czar of Russia.

The tone and style of this election outraged many voters who feared for the future of American politics. With so many fresh faces crowding to the polls, the old republican system was yielding to a new democratic style and that evolution seemed fraught with all the dangers warned against by the Founding Fathers. Jackson's subsequent victory at the polls gave some Americans nightmares of worse things to come.

At his inauguration people came from five hundred miles away to see General Jackson, wrote Daniel Webster, "and they really seem to think that the country is rescued from some dreadful danger!" They nearly wrecked the White House in their exuberance. Their behavior shocked Joseph Story, an associate justice of the Supreme Court, and sent him scurrying home. "The reign of KING MOB seemed triumphant," he wailed. But a western newspaper disagreed. "It was a proud day for the people," reported the *Argus of Western America*. "General Jackson is *their own* President."

Jackson himself was fiercely committed to democracy. And by democracy he meant majoritarian rule. "The people are the government," he wrote, "administering it by their agents; they are the Government, the sovereign power." In his first message to Congress as president, written in December 1829, Jackson announced: "The majority is to govern." To the people belonged the right of "electing their Chief Executive." He therefore asked Congress to adopt an amendment that would abolish the College of Electors. He wanted all "intermediary" agencies standing between the people and their government swept away, whether erected by the Founding Fathers or not. "The people are sovereign," he reiterated. "Their will is absolute."

So committed was Jackson to the principle of popular self-rule that he told historian-politician George Bancroft that "every officer should in his turn pass before the people, for their approval or rejection." And he included federal judges in this sweeping generalization, even justices of the Supreme Court. Accordingly, he introduced the principle of rotation, which limited government appointments to four years. Officeholders should be regularly rotated back home and replaced by new men, he said. "The duties of all public officers are . . . so plain and simple that men of intelligence may readily qualify themselves for their performance." Otherwise abuse may occur. Anyone who has held office "a few years, believes he has a life estate in it, a vested right, & if it has been held 20 years or upwards, not only a vested right, but that it ought to descend to his children, & if no children than the next of kin — This is not the principles of our government. It is rotation in office that will perpetuate our liberty." Unfortunately, hack politicians equated rotation with patronage and Jackson's enemies quickly dubbed his principle "the spoils system."

But it was never meant to be a spoils system. Jackson wanted *every* office of government, from the highest to the lowest, within the reach of the electorate, arguing that "where the people are everything . . . there and there only is liberty." Perhaps his position was best articulated by Alexis de Tocqueville, the French visitor in the 1830s whose *Democracy in America* remains one of the most profound observations about American life in print. "The people reign in the American political world," declared Tocqueville, "as the Deity does in the universe. They are the cause and aim of all things; everything comes from them, and everything is absorbed in them." The "constant celebration" of the people, therefore, is what Jackson and the Democratic Party provided the nation during his eight years in office. It is what Jacksonian Democracy was all about.

As president, Jackson inaugurated a number of important changes in the operation of government. For example, he vetoed congressional legislation more

According to Professor Remini, Jackson "was fiercely committed to democracy. And by democracy he meant majoritarian rule." Jackson himself wrote, "The people are the government, administering it by their agents; they are the Government, the sovereign power." Oil on Canvas by Ralph E.W. Earl, circa 1834. (Courtesy, Tennessee State Museum, Tennessee Historical Society Collection)

times than all his predecessors combined, and for reasons other than a bill's presumed lack of constitutionality. More importantly, by the creative use of his veto power be successfully claimed for the chief executive the right to participate in the legislative process. He put Congress on notice that they must consider his views on all issues *before* enacting them into law or run the risk of a veto. In effect he assumed the right to initiate legislation, and this essentially altered the relationship between the executive and the Congress. Instead of a separate and equal branch of the government, the president, according to Jackson, was the head of state, the first among equals.

Jackson also took a dim view of the claim that the Supreme Court exercised the final and absolute right to determine the meaning of the Constitution. When the court decided in *McCulloch vs. Maryland* that the law establishing a national bank was constitutional, Jackson disagreed. In his veto of a bill to recharter the Second National Bank in 1832, he claimed among other things that the bill lacked authority under the Constitution, despite what the high court had decided. Both the House and Senate, as well as the president, he continued, must decide for themselves what is and what is not constitutional before taking action on any bill. The representatives of Congress ought not to vote for a bill, and the president ought not to sign it, if they, in their own good judgment, believe it unconstitutional. "It is as much the duty of the House of Representatives, of the Senate, and of the President to decide upon the constitutionality of any bill or resolution which may be presented to them for passage or approval as it is of the supreme judges when it may be brought before them for judicial decision." Jackson did not deny the right of the Supreme Court to judge the constitutionality of a bill. What he denied was the presumption that the Court was the final or exclusive interpreter of the Constitution. All three branches should rule on the question of constitutionality, Jackson argued. In this way the equality and independence of each branch of government is maintained. "The authority of the Supreme Court," he declared, "must not, therefore, be permitted to control the Congress, or the Executive when acting in their legislative capacities, but to have only such influence as the force of their reasoning may deserve." What bothered Jackson was the presumption that four men could dictate what 15 million people may or may not do under their constitutional form. To Jackson's mind that was not democratic but oligarchic. But that was precisely the intention of the Founding Fathers: to provide a balanced mix of democratic, oligarchic, and monarchial forms in the Constitution.

Of course Jackson was merely expressing his own opinion about the right of all three branches to pass on the constitutionality of all legislation, an opinion the American people ultimately rejected. The great fear in a

democratic system — one the Founding Fathers knew perfectly well — was the danger of the majority tyrannizing the minority. Jackson would take his chances. He believed the American people were virtuous and would always act appropriately. "I for one do not despair of the republic," he wrote. "I have great confidence in the virtue of a great majority of the people, and I cannot fear the result. The republic is safe, the main pillars [of] virtue, religion and morality will be fostered by a majority of the people." But not everyone shared Jackson's optimism about the goodness of the electorate. And in time — particularly with the passage of the Fourteenth Admendment — it fell to the courts to guard and maintain the rights of the minority.

Jackson summed up his assertion of presidential rights by declaring that he alone — not Congress, as was usually assumed — was the sole representative of the American people and responsible to them. After defeating Henry Clay in the 1832 election, he decided to kill the Second National Bank by removing federal deposits because, as he said, he had received a "mandate" from the people to do so. The Senate objected and formally censured him, but Jackson, in response, merely issued another statement on presidential rights and the democratic system that had evolved over the last few years.

By law, only the secretary of the treasury was authorized to remove the deposits, so Jackson informed his secretary, William Duane, to carry out his order. Duane refused pointblank. And he also refused to resign as he had promised if he and the president could not agree upon a common course of action with respect to the deposits. Thereupon, Jackson sacked him. This was the first time a cabinet officer had been fired, and there was some question whether the president had this authority. After all, the cabinet positions were created by Congress and appointment required the consent of the Senate. Did that not imply that removal also required senatorial consent — particularly the treasury secretary, since he handled public funds that were controlled by Congress? The law creating the Treasury Department never called in an "executive" department, and it required its secretary to report to the Congress, not the president. None of this made a particle of difference to Andrew Jackson. All department heads were *his* appointees and they would obey *him* or pack their bags. The summary dismissal of Duane was seen by Jackson's opponents as a presidential grab for the purse strings of the nation. And in fact presidential control over all executive functions gave the chief executive increased authority over the collection and distribution of public funds.

☆

THE JACKSONIAN REVOLUTION

By the close of 1833 many feared that Andrew Jackson was leading the country to disaster. Henry Clay regularly pilloried the president on the Senate floor. On one occasion he accused Jackson of "open, palpable and daring usurpation" of all the powers of government. "We are in the midst of a revolution," Clay thundered, "hitherto bloodless, but rapidly tending towards a total change of the pure republican character of the Government."

A "revolution" — that was how the opposition Whig Party characterized Jackson's presidency. The nation was moving steadily away from its "pure republican character" into something approaching despotism. What the nation was witnessing, cried Clay, was "the concentration of all power in the hands of one man." Thereafter Whig newspapers reprinted a cartoon showing Jackson as "King Andrew the First." Clad in robes befitting an emperor, he was shown wearing a crown and holding a scepter in one hand and a scroll in the other on which was written the word "veto."

Democrats, naturally, read the "revolution" differently. They saw it as the steady progress of the country from the gentry republic originally established by the Founding Fathers to a more democratic system that mandated broader representation in government and a greater responsiveness to popular will.

Andrew Jackson did not take kindly to Clay's verbal mauling. "Oh, if I live to get these robes of office

off me," he snorted at one point, "I will bring the rascal to a dear account." He later likened the senator to "a drunken man in a brothel," reckless, destructive, and "full of fury."

Other senators expressed their opposition to this "imperial" president and seconded Clay's complaints. John C. Calhoun, who by this time had deserted to the enemy camp, adopted the Kentuckian's "leading ideas of revolution" and charged that "a great effort is now making to choke and stifle the voice of American liberty." And he condemned Jackson's insistence on taking refuge in democratic claims. The president "tells us again and again with the greatest emphasis," he continued, "that he is the immediate representative of the American people! What effrontery! What boldness of assertion! Why, he never received a vote from the American people. He was elected by electors . . . who are elected by Legislatures chosen by the people."

Sen. Daniel Webster and other Whigs chimed in. "Again and again we hear it said," rumbled Webster, "that the President is responsible to the American people! . . . And this is thought enough for a limited, restrained, republican government! . . . I hold this, Sir, to be a mere assumption, and dangerous assumption." And connected with this "airy and unreal responsibility to the people," he continued, "is another sentiment . . . and that is, that the President is the direct representative of the American people." The sweep of his language electrified the Senate. And "if he may be allowed to consider himself as the sole representative of all the American people," Webster concluded, "then I say, Sir, that the government . . . has already a master. I deny the sentiment, and therefore protest against the language; neither the sentiment nor the language is to be found in the Constitution of this Country."

Jackson's novel concept that the president served as the people's tribune found immediate acceptance by the electorate, despite the warnings of the Whigs. In effect, he altered the essential character of the presidency. He had become the head of government, the one person who would formulate national policy and direct public affairs. Sighed Senator Benjamin W. Leigh of Virginia: "Until the President developed the faculties of the Executive power, all men thought it inferior to the legislature — he manifestly thinks it superior: and in his hands [it] ... has proved far stronger than the representatives of the States."

☆

JACKSON INTERPRETED

From Jackson's own time to the present, disagreement and controversy over the significance of his presidency has prevailed. In the twentieth century the disagreements intensified among historians. Confusion over the meaning of Jacksonian Democracy, varying regional support for democratic change, and the social and economic status of the Democrats and Whigs have clouded the efforts of scholars to reach reliable conclusions about the Old Hero and the era that bears his name.

Andrew Jackson himself will always remain a controversial figure among historians. That he can still generate such intense partisan feeling is evidence of his remarkable personality. He was an aggressive, dynamic, charismatic, and intimidating individual. And although modern scholars and students of history either admire or dislike him intensely, his rating as president in polls conducted among historians over the past thirty years varies from great to near great. He carries an enormous burden in winning any popularity contest because of his insistence on removing the eastern Indians west of the Mississippi River and on waging a long and vicious war against the Second National Bank of the United States.

His first biographer, James Parton, wrote a three-volume *Life of Andrew Jackson* (1859, 1860), and came away with mixed feelings about the man and his democracy. At times Parton railed against the mindless mob "who could be wheedled, and flattered, and drilled," but at other times he extolled democracy as the mark of an enlightened society. What troubled Parton particularly was the spoils sys-

tem. Rotation, he wrote, is "an evil so great and so difficult to remedy, that if all his other public acts had been perfectly wise and right, this single feature of his administration would suffice to render it deplorable rather than amiable."

William Graham Sumner's *Andrew Jackson* (1882) was relentlessly critical of his subject, deploring in particular Jackson's flawed moral charter and emotional excesses. Sumner and other early historians, such as Herman von Holst and James Schouler, constituted what one student of the Jacksonian age called a "liberal patrician" or "Whig" school of history. These individuals came from European middle- or upper middle-class families with excellent backgrounds of education and public service. Because their class had been ousted from political power, these historians were biased against Jacksonian Democracy, and their books reflect their prejudice.

The interpretation of Old Hickory and his adherents took a sharp about-face with the appearance in 1893 of the vastly influential article by Frederick Jackson Turner, "The Significance of the Frontier in American History." Turner argued that American democracy emerged from the wilderness, noting that universal white manhood suffrage guaranteed by the new western states became something of a model for the older, eastern states. Naturally Jackson and his followers were seen as the personification of this frontier democracy. The thesis was advanced and sometimes amplified by Charles A. Beard, Vernon L. Parrington, and other western and southern historians of the early twentieth century who were caught up in the reform movement of the Progressive era. They dubbed the Jacksonian revolution an age of egalitarianism that produced the rise of the common man. Jackson himself was applauded as a man of the people. Thus the liberal patrician school of historiography gave way to the Progressive school.

This interpretation dovetailed rather well with the views of Tocqueville. During his visit, Tocqueville encountered a widespread belief in egalitarianism but worried that majoritarian rule could endanger minority rights. There are so many sharp and accurate insights into American society and institutions in *Democracy in America* that it ought to be the first book anyone reads in attempting to understand the antebellum period of American history. Among other things, he catches the American just as he is emerging from his European and colonial past and acquiring many of the characteristics of what are generally regarded as typically American today.

Tocqueville's democratic liberalism, augmented by the works of the Progressive historians — especially Turner, Beard and Parrington — dominated historical thought about the American past for the next fifty years or more. Almost all the Progressive historians stressed the role of geographic sections in the nation, and Turner at one point even denied any class influence in the formation of frontier democracy. The only important negative voice concerning Jackson during this period came from Thomas P. Abernethy, whose *From Frontier to Plantation in Tennessee: A Study in Frontier Democracy* (1932) insisted that Jackson himself was a frontier aristocrat, an opportunist, and a land speculator who strongly opposed the democratic forces in his own state of Tennessee.

The virtual shattering of the Progressive school's interpretation of Jacksonian Democracy came with the publication of one of the most important historical monographs ever written concerning American history: *The Age of Jackson* (1945), by Arthur M. Schlesinger, Jr. The classic work virtually rivals in importance the frontier thesis of Frederick Jackson Turner. It is a landmark study and represents the beginning of modern scholarship on Jackson and his era.

Schlesinger argued that class distinctions rather than sectional differences best explain the phenomenon of Jacksonian Democracy. He interpreted Jackson's actions and those of his followers as an effort of the less fortunate in American society to combat the power and influence of the business community. The working classes in urban centers as well as the yeoman farmers, he argued, were the true wellsprings of the Jacksonian movement. Jacksonian

Democracy evolved from the conflict between classes and best expressed its goals and purposes in the problems and needs facing urban laborers. Schlesinger singled out the bank war as the most telling example of the conflict and as the fundamental key to a fuller understanding of the meaning of Jacksonian Democracy. What attracted many historians to this path-breaking study, besides its graceful and majestic style, was Schlesinger's perceptive definition of Jacksonian Democracy and a precise explanation of its origins.

The reaction to Schlesinger's work was immediate and dramatic. It swept the historical profession like a tornado, eliciting both prodigious praise and, within a relatively short time, fierce denunciations. Bray Hammond, in a series of articles as well as his *Banks and Politics in America from the Revolution to the Civil War* (1957), and Richard Hofstadter, in his *The American Political Tradition and the Men Who Made It* (1948), contended that the Jacksonians were not the champions of urban workers or small farmers but rather ambitious and ruthless entrepreneurs principally concerned with advancing their own economic and political advantage. They were "men on the make" and frequently captains of great wealth. According to Hofstadter, the Jacksonians were not so much hostile to business as they were hostile to being excluded from entering the confined arena of capitalists. Where Schlesinger had emphasized conflict in explaining the Jacksonian era, Hofstadter insisted that consensus best characterized the period. The entrepreneurial thesis, as it was called, found strong support among many young scholars who constituted the Columbia University school of historians. In a series of articles and books produced by these critics, Jackson himself was described as an inconsistent opportunist, a strikebreaker, a shady land speculator, and a political fraud. Marvin Meyers, in his *The Jackson Persuasion* (1957), provides a slight variation on the entrepreneurial thesis by arguing that Jacksonians did indeed keep their eyes on the main chance but yearned for the virtues of a past agrarian republic. They hungered after the rewards

247

of capitalism but looked back reverentially on the blessings of a simpler agrarian society.

A major redirection of Jacksonian scholarship came with the publication of Lee Benson's *The Concept of Jacksonian Democracy: New York as a Test Case* (1961). This work suggested a whole new approach to the investigation of the Jacksonian age by employing the techniques of quantification to uncover solid, factual data upon which to base an analysis. Moreover, Benson emphasized social questions and found that such things as ethnicity and religion were far more important than economics in determining how a person voted or which party won his allegiance. He dismissed Jacksonian rhetoric about democracy and the rights of the people as "claptrap" and contended that local issues in elections meant more to the voters than national issues. Andrew Jackson himself was dismissed as unimportant in understanding the structure and meaning of politics in this period. In time, some college textbooks virtually eliminated Jackson from any discussion of this period except to mention that he opposed social reforms and that his removal of the Indians was one of the most heinous acts in American history. . . .

[In more recent years] Jackson has been somewhat restored to his former importance, if not his former heroic stature. My own three-volume life of Old Hickory, *Andrew Jackson and the Course of American Empire, 1767–1821; Andrew Jackson and the Course of American Freedom, 1822–1832; Andrew Jackson and the Course of American Democracy, 1833–1845* (1977, 1981, 1984) highlights Schlesinger's findings and Jackson's faith and commitment to liberty and democracy. I contend that Jackson was in fact a man of the people, just as the Progressive historians had argued, and that he actively attempted to advance democracy by insisting that all branches of government, including the courts, reflect the popular will. I also tried to show that, for a number of reasons, the president's policy of Indian removal was initiated to spare the Indian from certain extinction. And Francis Paul Prucha has argued persuasively that Indian removal was probably the only policy possible under the circumstances.

The study of the Jacksonian era is essential for any serious examination of the evolution of the American presidency. This has been widely recognized since the avalanche of articles and books triggered by the appearance of Schlesinger's monumental work. Jackson himself has never lost his ability to excite the most intense passions and interest among students of American history. No doubt scholars and popular writers will continue to debate his role as a national hero and as an architect of American political institutions.

QUESTIONS TO CONSIDER

1   The first decades of the nineteenth century were a dynamic period for the young Republic. What kinds of changes were occurring in American life?

2   Americans today often express pride at the thought that any American can become president, but in 1828 many Americans were worried by precisely the same notion. Why? How had the founders conceived of republicanism, and what were their fears of majority rule? Were those fears entirely unjustified?

3   What were the basic tenets of the new Democratic party and its leader, Andrew Jackson? What did Jackson give as the principles behind his most important policies? How did his opponents view those policies, their purposes and consequences?

4   Robert Remini says that Jackson "altered the essential character of the presidency." What had been its character, according to Remini, and how and why did Jackson transform it?

5   Andrew Jackson has been interpreted in very different, even conflicting, ways by different historians at different times. What are some of the most influential interpretations and their authors? What is it in Jackson that has elicited such varying responses? What can these varying interpretations tell you about the historians and the periods that shaped those historians?

18

Henry Clay, the American System, and the Sectional Controversy

STEPHEN B. OATES

This selection presents another view of the Jacksonian era, from the perspective of a man who fought against both Andrew Jackson and the abolitionists, particularly the political wing of the movement. Indeed, Henry Clay was Jackson's arch rival on the political battleground of the 1830s, which saw a major new party, the Whigs, organize under the leadership of Clay, John C. Calhoun, and Daniel Webster. A coalition of Jackson haters, the Whigs favored an active federal role in stimulating economic and industrial growth (the Jacksonians, by contrast, preferred a policy of laissez faire, or minimal government interference in economic affairs). On the platform, Whig campaigners such as young Abraham Lincoln of Illinois championed the Whig principles of national order and unity and called for a strong federal government with responsibility to provide a prosperous, stable economy that allowed everyone an opportunity to get ahead. Unlike Jackson, the Whigs favored internal improvements — roads, railroads, and canals — financed by the federal government, federal subsidies to help the states build their own canals and turnpikes, and state banks to ensure financial growth and stability. Lincoln summed up the Whig creed when he said, "The legitimate object of government is 'to do for the people what needs to be done, but which they can not, by individual effort, do at all, or do so well, for themselves.'"

Henry Clay, whom Lincoln idolized, was the most glamorous of the three Whig leaders, all of whom served in the Senate. His nickname, "Prince Hal," fit him to the dot. Charming, debonair, arrogant, and exceedingly ambitious, Clay considered himself the best politician in the land and viewed the presidency as his almost by divine right.

He tried five times to reach the White House but never made it, to his bafflement and despair. As historian Holman Hamilton has said, Clay was "one of the most spectacular victims of what became an American tradition." Hamilton explains: "From Clay's day well into the 20th century, only one sitting senator was elected president of the United States, and not a single chief executive was chosen wholly because of an outstanding congressional career." Had Clay had an outstanding military career, or any military career at all, he would probably have won the White House.

Henry Clay was a household name in his day, yet few Americans in the 1990s would be able to state with precision who he was or what he did beyond negotiating certain compromises over slavery. In point of fact, Clay's illustrious political career spanned the entire first half of the nineteenth century, and he left an indelible mark on the America of those years. He coined the term self-made man to describe an ambitious individual such as himself—the ultimate go-ahead American. And his rise to national prominence was meteoric. He became a United States senator at age twenty-nine, speaker of the House of Representatives at thirty-three. Within a few years, "Harry of the West," another of his nicknames, was one of the most powerful men in Washington, a nationalist with a sweeping vision of a powerful, productive, and unified America. He helped lead America into the ill-starred War of 1812 with England and went on to serve for twenty years in the Senate. At a time when political debates were major theater, Clay was one of America's greatest orators—people flocked to Washington just to watch him perform.

As the selection that follows shows, Clay did indeed help forge several significant compromises to save the Union. But his great plan for national growth and unity—the celebrated American System—never became a reality in his day because of the inflammable slavery issue. An antislavery slaveholder like Jefferson, his hero, Clay genuinely hated the institution and searched desperately and in vain for some way to solve the slavery problem. His solution, gradual emancipation and the voluntary repatriation of free blacks to Africa, resurrected Jefferson's old scheme and brought Clay into a dramatic collision with the abolitionists, black and white alike. As we shall see, Clay's solution proved unworkable. At one point, gazing into the future, he saw the country in flames, torn apart by civil war, and he begged his countrymen to find some way to avert such a disaster.

Reading the life of Henry Clay will introduce you to some of the most important themes, events, and historical figures in the first fifty years of the new century. This portrait attempts to personalize the historical record, to thrust a face and a personality into the vortex of events. It focuses on the human side of the past, showing how the interaction of individuals and events dictates the course of history.

GLOSSARY

ALABAMA LETTERS Clay's public statements during the 1844 presidential canvass favoring Texas annexation so long as it did not provoke a war with Mexico.

AMERICAN COLONIZATION SOCIETY Private philanthropic organization, cofounded by Clay, that sought financial aid from governments and citizens alike for the voluntary repatriation of free blacks to the African colony of Liberia.

AMERICAN SYSTEM Economic program championed by Clay that called for a protective tariff, a national bank, and internal improvements.

ASHLAND Clay's Kentucky plantation and his proudest possession.

COMPROMISE OF 1820 (Also known as the FIRST MISSOURI COMPROMISE) Admitted Missouri as a slave state and Maine as a free state and drew an imaginary line that divided the rest of the Louisiana Purchase into slave and free territory.

COMPROMISE OF 1850 Warded off a powerful disunion movement over the issue of slavery in the territories. The compromise, the work of Clay and Stephen A. Douglas of Illinois, among others, admitted California as a free state, organized the territories of New Mexico and Utah without congressional conditions on slavery, outlawed the slave trade in the national capital, and created a stringent new fugitive slave law.

DOUGLASS, FREDERICK A former slave and editor of a black newspaper in Rochester, New York, Douglass was one of the great leaders and orators of the abolitionist movement.

GREAT SOUTHERN REACTION To counteract the abolitionist argument that slavery was a sin, southerners defended slavery as "a positive good."

LIBERTY PARTY Antislavery third party that ran James G. Birney for the presidency in 1840 and again in 1844. The party advocated that the federal government abolish slavery in all areas under its jurisdiction — namely, Washington, D.C., and the territories — and that it outlaw the interstate slave trade.

MISSOURI COMPROMISE (FIRST) See COMPROMISE OF 1820.

MISSOURI COMPROMISE (SECOND) Engineered by Clay, this "sleight-of-hand solution" allowed Missouri to retain a Negro exclusion clause in its constitution so long as the legislature pledged never to restrict persons who were or might become United States citizens.

NULLIFICATION Doctrine formulated by John C. Calhoun that the states were supreme in the American confederation and that each state had the power to nullify within its borders any federal measure it disliked.

POLK, JAMES K. Expansionist Democrat who became president in 1844 and led the country to war with Mexico in 1846.

SLAVE TRADE (INTERNATIONAL) Outlawed by Congress in 1808.

WARHAWKS Hotspurs such as Clay, mainly from the South and West, who advocated a second war with England. They got their wish in the War of 1812.

Had we attended one of his speeches in the United States Senate in the 1830s, we would have found the galleries crowded with people who had come out to enjoy the show. In his day, political oratory was a form of theater, and he excelled at it. Always elegantly dressed, he spoke with impeccable elocution and theatrical gestures, his gray-blue eyes glittering with amused contempt for the inferior mortals sitting around him. He was tall and slender, with a receding hairline, a long nose, and a mouth so wide that he could never learn to spit. Nicknamed "Prince Hal," he exuded a charm and physical magnetism that few could resist. In the galleries women would smile, bewitched, when he made a point with a graceful sweep of his arm, his head held high, his whole body moving to the rhythms of his voice. He was a master of the bon mot and the satiric jest, and he even used his snuff box to dramatic effect. As ambitious as he was arrogant, he was certain that his destiny was to become president of the United States and to forge the nation into a great world power.

When he spoke of his early years, Henry Clay spun a myth of himself as a poor, orphaned, uneducated "mill boy from the Slashes." Thus he wove his story into his mythic vision of America as a land of limitless opportunity where even the lowest-born had the right to rise, to go as far as his talent and toil would take him. In reality, Clay was the scion of tobacco planters of Tidewater Virginia. At the time he was born, on April 12, 1777, his preacher father owned twenty-one slaves and a four-hundred-acre homestead in an area in Hanover County called The Slashes. Henry's father died when he was four, leaving his mother to raise him and his four brothers and three sisters. The boy loved his mother deeply,

would always think of her with warmth in his heart. His formal education was about average for children of his time, consisting of three years before the master of the neighborhood log school. Inspired by Patrick Henry, he developed a passion for public speaking and practiced it wherever he could, haranguing livestock in the barn or assemblies of trees in the forest.

In 1791 his mother married a kindly man named Henry Watkins, who moved the family to his home in Richmond. Taking a particular interest in young Henry, Watkins found him employment in a retail store and then in the clerk's office in the High Court Chancery. When the family migrated to Kentucky, Clay remained in Richmond, where he had fallen under the spell of the chancellor, a bald, erudite gentleman of the Enlightenment named George Wythe.

As it happened, Wythe had been Thomas Jefferson's mentor, had taught him law, the classics, and an adamant hatred of slavery. Like Wythe, Jefferson had denounced human bondage as a "blot" on Virginia, a "great political and moral evil" that should be gradually abolished. Now Clay too became Wythe's protégé; he too damned slavery as "the greatest of human evils" and embraced the "sacred cause" of gradual emancipation, turning to Jefferson's own *Notes on Virginia,* published in 1785, for a plan to bring that about. Jefferson called for the state of Virginia to free all its slaves who were born after the scheme was adopted; first they were to live with their parents as charges of the state, which was to provide for their education in the arts, the sciences, and the practical aspects of farming; they were to be freed at a prescribed age — eighteen for females, twenty-one for males — and then colonized outside Virginia so as to avoid race-mixing, a prospect that filled Jefferson with loathing. Jefferson hoped that the other slave states would follow Virginia's example and that bondage would ultimately disappear in America, thus consummating the promise of the Revolution.

It was a vain hope. In 1796 the Virginia legislature emphatically rejected a variation of Jefferson's plan;

An earlier version of this essay, entitled "Harry of the West," appeared in the October–November 1991 issue of *Timeline,* a publication of the Ohio Historical Society.

Henry Clay coined the term "self-made man" to describe ambitious gentlemen like himself. He created his own nirvana at Ashland, his plantation near Lexington. It featured immaculate grounds, tree-lined paths, and rolling bluegrass meadows where blooded cattle and horses grazed. Ashland was hardly nirvana for Clay's slaves, who resided in rude cabins not shown here and whose labor made it possible for him to pursue a political career. (Ohio Historical Society)

it did so because slavery was the cornerstone of Virginia's entire way of life: it was a potent status symbol, a valuable labor system, and an indispensable means of race control in a white man's country. Even so, Wythe still hoped that somehow, someday, slavery could be removed from the commonwealth, and he passed that hope on to Clay, who echoed his mentor's impassioned rhetoric about the Rights of Man.

Under Wythe's influence, Clay had decided to become a lawyer. He studied one year with the attorney general of the commonwealth and at age twenty was admitted to the Virginia bar. By then he stood well over six feet, with a slender, loose-jointed frame, prematurely white hair, and a wide and win-

ning smile. He could have remained in Richmond, where he had friends and connections. But he decided that the new state of Kentucky offered better opportunities for a young lawyer on the rise. In late 1797 Clay turned up in Lexington, "the Athens of the West," owning only his clothes, the horse he was riding, and an ambition to get ahead that burned in him like a furnace.

No sooner had he arrived in Kentucky, a slave state, than he plunged into an abolition movement, aligning himself with a group of reformers who called for a new state constitution that would allow for general, gradual emancipation similar to Jefferson's plan. Just turned twenty-one, a member of the Lexington bar for only one month, Clay published in the *Kentucky Gazette* a ringing appeal to Kentuckians to rid themselves of the curse of slavery. "Can any humane man be happy and contented when he sees near thirty thousand of his fellow beings around him, deprived of all rights which make life desirable, transferred like cattle from the possession of one to another?" Borrowing an argument from Jefferson, Clay pointed out that blacks were not the only victims of bondage. "All America acknowledges the existence of slavery to be an evil, which while it deprives the slave of the best gift of heaven, in the end injures the master too, by laying waste his lands, enabling him to live indolently, and thus contracting all the vices generated by a state of idleness. If it be this enormous evil," said Clay, "the sooner we attempt its destruction the better."

But the vast majority of white Kentuckians, from wealthy planters to nonslaveholding farmers, objected to emancipation in any form, lest it result in racial violence and amalgamation, that bugaboo of white supremacists everywhere in the Republic. In 1799 Kentucky voters sent an overwhelming number of anti-emancipation delegates to a state constitutional convention, which went on to draft a new charter that incorporated the proslavery provisions of the old, thus smashing the hopes of Clay and the

253

other reformers that Kentucky might lead the way in removing slavery from America.

Clay always insisted that this was one of his bitterest disappointments. Yet he considered himself a realist. There was no point, he decided, in crusading for an unpopular cause, so he accepted the will of the majority and proceeded to blend into his Kentucky environment. In 1799, the same year Kentucky turned back the gradual-emancipation movement, Clay bought a slave, married the eighteen-year-old daughter of Lexington's most prosperous businessman and speculator, and started building what became a lucrative law practice.

Clay was living in the age of the go-ahead man, a time when an entire generation of white American males reached out and seized the future as if by divine right. Clay came to personify the acquisitive spirit of the era and even coined the term "self-made man" to describe an individual like himself — the ultimate go-ahead American. His rise to wealth and power was so meteoric that it earned him another of his nicknames: he was the Star of the West, a man who reflected perfectly the heady optimism of his young section.

By age twenty-eight, Clay had risen to the top of the legal profession in Kentucky and was serving in the state legislature as a Jeffersonian and a spokesman for the lawyer aristocracy centered in Lexington. Suave as he was, he could be touchy about his honor. When a Federalist adversary called him a liar, Clay challenged him to a duel with pistols at ten paces; both were wounded in the ensuing faceoff, which got them censured by the Kentucky legislature. The episode, however, scarcely hurt Clay in his spectacular rise to power. At age twenty-nine, he became a United States senator when the Kentucky legislature chose him to fill out the term of John Adair, who had resigned. One of Clay's first speeches was an impassioned denunciation of the international slave trade, whose atrocities appalled him. Later he called it "the most abominable traffic that ever disgraced the annals of the human race." No politician was happier than he when Congress, following President Jefferson's lead, outlawed the "infamous commerce" in 1808.

Back in Kentucky, Clay acquired a plantation near Lexington, named it Ashland, built a brick mansion on it, and bought additional slaves to work his fields — all before he turned thirty. He could be seen at Olympian Springs, a fashionable resort near Lexington, where wealthy members of the master class met for mint juleps, billiards, and cards as well as medicinal baths. He soon ruled over an impressive personal empire comprising six hundred acres on the home plantation, a second farm, a house in Lexington, and additional land in Missouri.

Ashland was his proudest possession. Here he created his own nirvana, with immaculate grounds and tree-lined paths, flourishing fields of corn, hemp, and rye, and rolling bluegrass meadows, landscaped with clusters of trees like a park, where his blooded cattle and horses grazed. He kept buying slaves, too, rooting himself ever deeper into the very system he abhorred. Eventually he owned sixty of his "fellow human beings," a number that ranked him in the middle of the planter class, considerably behind Jefferson, who held some two hundred slaves when he left the presidency, and Washington, who owned more than three hundred when he died.

To justify being a slaveowner, Clay resorted to the Jeffersonian rationalization that slave labor was "a necessary evil" and that he was at least a "kind" master. There was, of course, no such thing as a kind slavemaster — the ownership of another human being was in itself a cruel act, a violent act. Over the years Clay did manumit several of his slaves who gave him faithful service. But like every other master, he knew that the whip made the slave system work, and his overseer used it to keep Clay's "people" in line. Perhaps that is why Kentucky slaves sang a work song about him:

> Heave away! Heave away!
> I'd rather co't a yeller gal,

Dan work for Henry Clay
Heave away, yaller gal, I want to go.

Actually, several of his slaves did leave, demonstrating with their feet what they thought of their treatment under Clay. At least one of his slaves, a woman named Black Lottie, sued for her freedom while the Clays were living in Washington, D.C. To forestall further defections, Clay dealt harshly with Black Lottie: he had her jailed while successfully contesting the suit, then dragged her back into a life she hated. When another house servant, a mulatto boy, took flight from Clay's wife, Clay offered a $50 reward for his capture and made a remark that betrayed his true feelings about kindness to slaves. "We have spoiled him," Clay said, "by good treatment."

At least one of Clay's slaves, a man who escaped to Canada, accused him in the abolitionist press of being heartless and cruel. The man claimed that Clay had once had him stripped and whipped with 150 lashes on his naked back for a trifling offense. Clay's overseer testified that the slave in question had been insolent and violent, which presumably, at least in the overseer's eyes, justified such brutal punishment.

Claiming to be a kind participant in a brutal system was not Clay's only contradiction when it came to slavery. While he damned the international slave trade in some of his most memorable utterances, he no longer condemned the *domestic* slave trade in Kentucky, despite its cruel breakup of families, its brutal coffles, rancid jails, and demeaning auctions. In private conversation Clay said that internal slave traders performed a service for Kentucky: they acted "as scavengers for the public" by "carrying off the vicious and incorrigible [slaves] to another country where new characters may be formed with better habit and propensities."

Meanwhile, Clay continued to prosper politically. Deciding to forego the Senate so that he could be "an immediate representative of the people," he ran for the national House of Representatives in 1811 and won easily. On his first day there, he was elected Speaker of the House, a remarkable achievement for a man of only thirty-three. He was now Harry of the West, the spokesman for his entire section, which, in addition to Kentucky, included the new free state of Ohio and the free territories of the Old Northwest. In Congress, Clay articulated the West's militant nationalism. He led the Warhawks in clamoring for another war against England, boasting that the Kentucky militia alone could seize Upper Canada; he helped push President Madison into the War of 1812 and stood resolutely by him throughout the vicissitudes of that unpopular conflict.

By now, Clay had earned a reputation as a bon vivant with a love for his glass and a singular passion for cards. His love for gambling became legendary. In Washington he won $1,500 in a single night, only to lose $600 in another. In one marathon match, he won $40,000 from a friend, but because Clay was a gentleman, he settled for the man's $500 note. A few nights later, Clay lost $60,000 to the same friend, who returned the favor by asking only that Clay hand back the $500 note.

In 1814 Clay was one of three U.S. commissioners sent to Ghent, Belgium, to negotiate a peace treaty with Britain. He saved the Mississippi River for the United States when he blocked a move by fellow commissioner John Quincy Adams to give England free access to the Mississippi in exchange for fisheries in Newfoundland. Working by day and gambling and drinking by night, Clay seemed never to sleep. Such debauchery shocked Adams, a prudish man who always rose early and read five chapters of his Bible before breakfast. When Adams awoke in his room, he noted with disgust, the company in Clay's quarters was often just departing. There was gossip that Clay sought the pleasures of women, too, in Ghent as well as in America. But such stories were unsubstantiated. From all appearances, he remained loyal to his wife, Lucretia, throughout their married life.

As postwar Speaker of the House, Clay became one of the most powerful men in Washington, a brilliant parliamentarian and mesmerizing orator who helped raise legislative leadership to supremacy in national affairs. In a day of rampant localism, Clay had an international vision, a dream of the United States as the world's foremost power. His vision, fueled by his ambition, made him aspire to the presidency with palpable self-confidence. Certain that he had never met his superior, he thought himself the best man to lead America into a golden new age of prosperity and world prominence.

With fellow congressman John C. Calhoun, who was then in his nationalist phase, Clay devised the celebrated American System to implement his vision. It called for a tariff to protect America's infant industries, a national bank to stimulate and stabilize the country financially, and internal improvements to promote the general welfare. In the long run, Clay and his supporters hoped to unify the country by establishing a mutually supporting and balanced economy of manufacturing, commerce, and agriculture. In this scheme of things, each of the three great sections was to produce what suited it best: the South was to concentrate on staples like cotton and rice, the West on livestock and grain, and the Northeast on manufactures. Clay conceded that the system was founded on sectional interests, yet he believed that the whole — national interest — would exceed the sum of its parts.

On paper it was a brilliant idea. In reality it was doomed by the combustible slavery issue, which split Clay's own section, bitterly divided the country into slave and free states, and eventually blew them apart. Clay was aware of the danger: the Missouri crisis of 1819–21 revealed to him and his generation the grim possibility of sectional war over slavery. The crisis came about when Missouri sought to enter the Union as a slave state. At that time the free states had a majority in the House of Representatives and a margin of one state in the Senate. The admission of Alabama, due to take place in December 1819, would tie the score. If Missouri entered the Union as a slave state, it would not only give the South a one-

state margin in the Senate but open a gateway for proslavery expansion into the West.

To prevent that, Senator James Tallmadge, Jr., of New York proposed an amendment to the Missouri enabling bill that prohibited white settlers from taking any more slaves into Missouri and decreed that all henceforth born there would be freed at age twenty-five, which was a variation on Jefferson's plan. The Tallmadge Amendment provoked riotous debates in Congress, with both sides threatening war. "If you persist, the Union will be dissolved," a Georgia senator told Tallmadge. "You have kindled a fire which seas of blood can only extinguish." Retorted Tallmadge, "If a dissolution of the Union must take place, let it be so! If civil war . . . must come, I can only say, let it come!"

Contrary to legend, Clay did not put forth the compromise that averted a blowup in 1820. In fact, he sided with the South, contending that slavery was a state institution and that Congress had no constitutional authority to prohibit bondage in Missouri after it had become a state. With the fate of his American System hanging in the balance, he complained that "it is a most unhappy question, awakening sectional feelings, and exasperating them to the highest degree. The words, civil war, and disunion, are uttered almost without emotion." When a compromise package finally emerged, Clay threw his enormous influence behind it, thus ensuring its passage. The Compromise of 1820 admitted Maine as a free state and Missouri as a slave state, thus maintaining an equilibrium of power between North and South in the Senate. It also divided the rest of the Louisiana Purchase Territory at the latitude of 36° 30′ north, excluding slavery above that line and endorsing the principle of congressional nonintervention south of it. In practice, this meant that slavery could and did expand there.

It was the second Missouri Compromise for which Clay was responsible and for which he became famous. When Missouri adopted a constitution that excluded free blacks from entering the state, antislavery northerners leaped on the offending passage as a violation of the privileges and immunities clause of the federal Constitution and demanded that Missouri delete the restriction or be kept out of the Union. This in turn only provoked southerners into renewed threats of secession and war. "Unhappy subject!" Clay exclaimed. Yet his sympathies again were Southern. Indeed, it seemed to him that free-state forces were ganging up on Missouri and the South since few places in the country allowed free blacks equal privileges and immunities with whites. To make matters worse, he had resigned as speaker, leaving the House rudderless in the currents of the controversy. When nobody else would do so, the go-ahead man himself took charge and promoted compromise with all his powers of persuasion: "he begs, instructs, adjures, supplicates, & beseeches us to have mercy on the people of Missouri," reported one northern congressman. Clay wanted mercy for the *white* people of Missouri; he had no interest whatever in the rights of black Americans there. In the end, Congress approved his compromise, which allowed Missouri to retain its exclusion clause as long as the legislature pledged never to restrict persons who were or might become U.S. citizens. It was, as one writer has pointed out, "a sleight-of-hand solution, upholding the supremacy of the federal Constitution in the face of the Missouri provision that flagrantly violated it." Yet it avoided apparent catastrophe and won Clay kudos throughout the country as a man for whom Union was his motto, conciliation his maxim.

Clay hoped that the slavery issue was now "happily settled" and that "mutual forbearance and mutual toleration" would restore "concord and harmony" to the country. But in truth he worried about the future of the Union, worried that slavery and its concomitant problem — the presence of blacks in a white man's country — would continue to inflame and divide white Americans. To Clay, it seemed clear that both slaves and free blacks had to be removed if the nation was ever to be united under the banners of his American System.

The slavery issue haunted him. Despite his own status as a slaveowner, Clay hated the peculiar institution, consistently calling it the "greatest of human evils" and a "great stain upon the American name," and he hoped that all the southern states would one day eradicate it by schemes of gradual emancipation. The problem, of course, was how to persuade them to do so, especially in view of what had happened to gradual emancipation in Kentucky. The more he thought about that, the more Clay believed that emancipation had failed there for want of a program of colonization that would ease white racial fears by resettling the liberated blacks outside the country. Had not Jefferson warned that emancipation without colonization was unacceptable to whites? For Clay the key to emancipation was to establish a successful colonization scheme first, as an inducement to the states to act. They might be willing to rid themselves of slavery, he reasoned, if they could count on a flourishing colonization operation to siphon off liberated blacks.

Throughout the next three decades, Clay held up the American Colonization Society, a private, "philanthropic" organization he had co-founded in 1816, as the instrument for the nation's salvation. It became his panacea, a cure-all that would save the nation from the horrors of sectional war over slavery. Sponsored at its inception by such prominent figures as James Madison, John Marshall, Daniel Webster, Andrew Jackson, and Francis Scott Key, the society sought financial aid from governments and citizens alike for the voluntary repatriation of free blacks in Liberia. The society's leading spokesman and its third president, Clay rehearsed again and again what he deemed to be the manifold benefits of deporting "free persons of color."

First, colonization would remove "the most vicious," "degraded," and "contaminated" class in America, whose wretched condition was the inevitable consequence of liberating members of an inferior race and allowing them to remain among the

superior white race, with its "unconquerable prejudices."

Second, there was "a peculiar, moral fitness in
restoring blacks to the land of their fathers," Clay argued. If through such black "missionaries" Americans could give heathen Africa "the blessings of our
arts, our civilization and our religion, may we not
hope that America will extinguish a great portion of
that moral debt which she has contracted to that unfortunate continent?" Clay seemed blissfully unaware
of the contradiction involved in this point, never explaining how a "vicious," "degraded" people were
supposed to civilize a "pagan" continent. Nor was
his disparaging description of free blacks likely to
draw many of them to his voluntary program. He
was directing his arguments exclusively at white
Americans, especially skeptical slaveholders, who
tended to view colonization as abolitionism in
disguise.

Clay assured them that the society entertained "no
purpose, on its own authority or by its own means,
to attempt emancipation partial or general." Nor did
it desire that the national government remove slavery, for the society acknowledged that only the states
where it existed had the power to do that. The goal
of the society, Clay explained, was to point the way,
to demonstrate to the slave states that colonization
was practicable, in hopes that they would incorporate the society's plan into their own schemes of
gradual emancipation. Clay contended that if the
southern states freed and transported only the annual
increase of blacks within their borders, the value of
slave labor would one day diminish to the point
where it would succumb to superior white labor,
and the states would thus "rid themselves of a universally acknowledged curse."

For all the zeal and sincerity Clay brought to his
arguments, they seemed to have been devised in
never-never land. In the end, they failed to win over
a single slave state, not even Kentucky. In truth,
many slaveowners called Clay a traitor to his region
for even suggesting gradual emancipation by the

states. The society also offended genuine abolitionists
like William Lloyd Garrison. Calling it "malignant,"
"sinful," and "inhumane," "the foulest conspiracy in
the history of the world," Garrison led the New
England Antislavery Society in a successful campaign
against it in his region. But the main reason the colonization society failed was because the vast majority
of free blacks opposed it and refused to participate in
its voluntary program. No matter how badly America treated them, as black spokesman Frederick Douglass said, it was their country too: they had roots
here, families here, and most had no intention of
leaving. In the thirty-six years Clay was associated
with the society, it persuaded only 6,792 black volunteers to relocate in Liberia. Thus the society never
had a viable operation to offer the slave states as an
entice-ment to emancipation. Instead of dying out,
as Clay hoped, slavery became more entrenched in
the South than ever.

Frustrated in his efforts to remove slavery, Clay
also suffered a string of personal and political defeats
that scarred him deeply. His wife bore him eleven
children, five sons and six daughters, but all his
daughters died, the last in 1835. Clay was incon-
solable. "Alas! my dear wife, the great Destroyer has
come and taken away from us our dear, dear, only
daughter!" Lucretia said he never recovered from the
loss. His sons were a source of sorrow, too. His eldest, Theodore, suffered brain damage in an accident, became mentally deranged, and had to be institutionalized. Another son, Thomas, almost cost Clay
his cherished plantation. When Thomas's Lexington
manufacturing firm collapsed, Clay had to sell off his
additional property and mortgage Ashland itself to
pay his son's debts. Later, thanks to the generosity of
friends throughout the country, Clay was able to re-
purchase the mortgage.

Meanwhile, Clay found himself on a political roller
coaster. In 1824 he made his first bid for the presidency, but ran last in a controversial, four-man race
that put pious John Quincy Adams in the White
House. It was a galling setback for a man of Clay's

enormous ambitions. He spent four miserable years as Adams's secretary of state, the dullest position he ever held, and then had to sit on the sidelines while Andrew Jackson, a military man Clay despised, beat Adams for the presidency in 1828. Three years later, to put Clay into a more advantageous position for seeking the presidency, the Kentucky legislature again sent him to the United States Senate, where he served on and off for the next twenty years, always with his eye on the other end of Pennsylvania Avenue.

As senator, Clay employed all his prodigious skills to get his American System established, only to see Jackson destroy the second Bank of the United States, which Clay had sought to recharter, and South Carolina almost detonate a civil war by nullifying Clay's protective tariff of 1832 as well as the tariff of 1828. The slavery issue was involved, too, since the nullifiers, led by eagle-eyed John C. Calhoun, hoped to legitimize nullification as a shield against federal tampering with the peculiar institution in the southern states. Clay saw slavery involved in another way, since he considered it a wasteful labor system that retarded economic development, and blamed it for the economic ills then plaguing South Carolina.

Once again, slavery and sectionalism were playing havoc with Clay's dream of a united American empire. Thundering defiance, South Carolina raised twenty-five thousand volunteers and prepared for war. When Jackson threatened to hang Calhoun and vowed to hurl a federal army into South Carolina to uphold national authority, Clay was appalled. Once again he stepped in to mediate, forging a compromise tariff acceptable to South Carolina. The nation had another reprieve, and Clay had a new nickname: the Great Pacificator. The nullification crisis, however, had shaken him profoundly: he had peered into the future and grimaced at what he saw. "We want no war," he pleaded with his countrymen, "above all no civil war, no family strife. We want no sacked cities, no desolated fields, no smoking ruins, no streams of American blood shed by American arms!"

By 1832 Clay was trapped in a monstrous contradiction: he was promoting a program of nationalism based on sectional interests at a time when sectionalism threatened the nation's very existence. Yet he fought doggedly on. From the Senate, he dueled and harassed Jackson, calling King Andrew a menace to the country. Supremely confident, Clay ran against Jackson in the 1832 presidential election, but he was no match for the popular president and suffered a disastrous defeat. Clay plunged into gloom. What was wrong with the country that it would not, could not, see that he was its president of destiny? He helped found the Whig party, a coalition of Jackson haters, and employed it to promote his programs and his ambitions. But the Jacksonians remained so powerful that Clay did not even offer himself as candidate in the presidential canvass of 1838, which put Jackson's successor, Martin Van Buren, in the White House.

Enduring four years of Little Van was almost more than Clay could bear. In his eyes the country desperately needed him as president, needed Harry of the West to heal its divisions and restore its prosperity after the disastrous 1837 panic. To make matters worse, the abolitionists had launched a crusade that further polarized the country. Demanding that the slaves be emancipated "immediately" and assimilated into America's social order, they held rallies across the North, bombarded the South with abolitionist literature, and inundated Congress with petitions. Soon they invaded politics, too, organizing the Liberty party and promoting antislavery men for state and national office.

Clay was horrified. He thought the abolitionists "rash and impolitic," not to say dangerous. Yet the stridency of the Great Southern Reaction distressed him, too. To counter the abolitionist attack, southern spokesmen argued that slavery was a "positive good" ordained by God from the beginning of time. Gone was the Jeffersonian argument that slavery was "a necessary evil." Now proslavery apologists proclaimed it "the greatest of all blessings" and the *sine qua non* of southern patriotism. In 1837, on the floor of the Senate, speaking in his rapid-fire fashion, John C. Calhoun warned that overturning slavery in the South would result in a war of extermination between the races, and he insisted that the abolitionists be silenced.

In the ensuing war of words over slavery, Clay tried to stand in the middle. In the Senate he expressed "the strongest disapprobation of the course of the northern abolitionists, who were intermeddling with a subject that no way concerned them." Yet he emphatically disagreed with Calhoun, too. *"I consider slavery as a curse,"* Clay told the Senate, "a curse to the master, a wrong, a grievous wrong to the slave. In the abstract it is ALL WRONG; and no possible contingency can make it right."

Clay succeeded only in provoking both sides, as proslavery men damned him as an abolitionist, and the abolitionists castigated him as a canting hypocrite. How, they demanded, could a man who held slaves, represented a slave state, and advocated colonization be a true friend of liberty? In his newspaper, *The North Star,* Frederick Douglass declared Clay's "the most helpless, illogical, and cowardly apologies" for the wrong of slavery Douglass had ever heard. "You are at this moment," Douglass told Clay, "the robber of nearly fifty human beings, of their liberty, compelling them to live in ignorance." If the senator meant what he said about the crime of bondage, Douglass said, then he should emancipate his human property and enlist in the abolitionist cause. "Let me ask if you think that God will hold you guiltless in the great day of account, if you die with the blood of these fifty slaves clinging to your garments[?]"

Stung by such criticism, Clay struck back in self-defense. He told one abolitionist, "Excuse me, Mr. Mendenhall, for saying that my slaves are as well fed and clad, look as sleek and hearty, and are quite as civil and respectful in their demeanor, and as little disposed to wound the feelings of any one, as you are." Yet, Clay perceived what the controversy cost him politically. "The Abolitionists are denouncing me as a slaveholder," he wrote in 1838, "and slaveholders as an Abolitionist, whilst they both unite on Mr. Van Buren."

Convinced that he had to make a choice, Clay sided with his fellow slaveholders. In an 1839 speech in the Senate, he not only defended slavery but accused the abolitionists of promoting amalgamation ("revolting admixture, alike offensive to God and man") and trying to foment civil war. The speech so excited Calhoun that he leaped to his feet and happily proclaimed it "the finishing stroke" to the abolitionists in American politics. It was a premature benediction, since the Liberty party ran James G. Birney for president in the election of 1840. Alas for Clay, he lost the Whig party nomination to war hero William Henry Harrison, who went on to win the presidency that year. Clay could hardly believe that the Whigs preferred a political tyro like Harrison to himself. When Harrison died, Clay felt even more cheated since Vice-President John Tyler of Virginia, a cranky, old-school Democrat, now succeeded to the presidency. After Tyler vetoed Clay's attempts to recharter the national bank and raise the tariff, the go-ahead man was so disillusioned that he resigned from the Senate, said he was "retiring" from politics, and went home to his stock farming, his family, and his slaves.

He soon came out of retirement, thanks to a ground swell of popular support for him as president. The fact was, Harry of the West towered over his lackluster rivals, so much so that by 1843 more than two hundred Whig newspapers and seventeen Whig conventions or Whig-dominated legislatures had announced for him. When he spoke at a barbecue in Dayton, Ohio, more than 100,000 people turned out for the event, in what was perhaps the largest political gathering the Republic had witnessed thus far. It was clear to party bigwigs that, lacking another military man to run in the 1844 presidential contest, Clay was the only potential winner they had. When the Whig national convention nominated him by acclamation, Clay had never seemed so close to the White House and the consummation of his dreams.

His victory seemed assured when the Democrats nominated James K. Polk, the first dark-horse candidate in American presidential history. The Democrats thereupon endorsed the annexation of slaveholding Texas, an explosive issue that Clay's forces had hoped to keep out of the campaign. Clay had gone on record as opposing annexation, on the grounds that "annexation and war with Mexico are identical." What America needed, he said, was "union, peace, and patience." Now the Democrats shrewdly linked Texas annexation to Oregon and the popular notion that America had a God-given right to rule the continent. Sensing that they had Clay on the run, the Democrats grew malicious. They attacked him as a duelist, a rake, and an abolitionist who opposed Texas annexation because he wanted to free the blacks. This in turn aroused zealots of the Liberty party. Fearful that antislavery voters would go for Clay, they pummelled him as a "man-stealer" under the sway of the Slave Power.

The Texas question proved Clay's downfall. Convinced that his southern support was slipping away, he resorted to a desperate ploy, asserting in a series of labored public statements — the "Alabama letters" — that he had no personal objection to annexation, indeed that he would like to have Texas, slavery and all, if it could be done "without dishonor" and "without war." The Alabama letters may have won Clay some support in the South, but they cost him pivotal New York State, where antislavery Whigs went for Birney and threw the state and the election itself to Polk. Clay lost by only 38,000 popular votes out of a total of 2,700,000 cast. It was the most painful setback of his political life. Blaming it on fraud, slander, and abolitionism, he declared himself "forever off the public stage."

The annexation of Texas led to exactly what Clay had feared — war with Mexico. That war hurt him personally, for it took his favorite son, Henry Clay, Jr., who fell at Buena Vista. It also made a military hero of Zachary Taylor, who won the Whig nomination and the presidency in 1848. Clay was thoroughly disgusted that the party had again passed over him in favor of a man utterly devoid of political experience. Clay was certain that had he been the nominee, *he* would have been sitting in the White House in Taylor's place. This overlooked a crucial fact. Clay lacked the one thing — military glory — that had ensured the victory of the Whig party's only two elected presidents. Had he possessed a military record, he would doubtless have won the presidency long before.

In 1849 the Kentucky legislature again elected Clay to the Senate. Seventy-two now, he was tired and in poor health; the bons mots and repartee no longer came so quickly as they once had. What was more, he had a haunting fear that he had failed in politics, having been unable to win the presidency, the pinnacle of his ambition, or to unite the country behind his American System. What he had was a reputation as the Great Compromiser — "I go for honorable compromise whenever it can be made," he said. "Life itself is but a compromise." And now, in the winter of 1849–50, the country needed him again as sectional mediator, for the Mexican War had thrust the slavery question back into the center of American politics, precipitating a desperate power struggle between free and slave states for control of the territories and ultimately of the nation itself.

At issue now was the status of slavery in the newly acquired territories of the Southwest. If northern free-soilers demanded that Congress ban slavery there, southern militants like Calhoun argued that Congress had a constitutional obligation to safeguard slave property in all federal territories. To make matters worse that fateful winter, California had drawn up a constitution prohibiting slavery and was ready for admission as a free state, with New Mexico not far behind. The California and New Mexico questions rocked Congress to its foundations. Two new free states would alter the balance of power against the South, perhaps forever, and southerners swore they would sunder the Union before they would let

Clay stood in the center of the impassioned debates in the Senate over the Compromise of 1850. In his major speech, Clay begged his colleagues to pause "at the edge of the precipice" of civil war.

Too sick to continue, he had to escape to the seashore, leaving others to negotiate the final compromise. (Ohio Historical Society)

that happen. "Slavery here is the all-engrossing theme," Clay wrote a friend; "and my hopes and my fears alternately prevail as to any settlement of the vexed question."

Frail and weak, racked by a persistent cough, Clay labored once again to avert catastrophe. In January 1850 he introduced in the Senate eight separate measures designed to settle all current disputes in the vexed slavery question. Among other things, his measures called for California to enter the Union as a free state, for New Mexico and Utah territories to be organized without congressional conditions on slavery (Clay assumed that Mexican law, which had abolished it, would continue in both territories), for the slave trade to be outlawed in the District of Columbia, and for a stringent new fugitive slave law to be enacted as a sop to southerners. At one point in his speech, Clay mentioned a "precious relic" he had recently received — it was a fragment that had been taken from the coffin of George Washington. Holding it aloft, Clay said that the "venerated" father of the country was warning Congress from Mount Vernon not to destroy his handiwork. In his major speech in February, Clay beseeched his colleagues to pause "at the edge of the precipice, before the fearful and disastrous leap is taken into the yawning abyss below." If the Union were dissolved, he fervently prayed that he might not live "to behold the sad and heart-rending spectacle."

But his separate compromise measures ran into seemingly insurmountable opposition from both sides. Frustrated in his initial efforts, Clay tried a new tack. In May he offered all of his proposals in a single omnibus bill, only to see it sink in a vortex of acrimonious speeches, amendments, and shouts to adjourn. It was too much for him. Lacking the strength or the will to continue, he left for Rhode Island, to rest and recuperate on the seashore before returning to Washington. It remained for Senator Stephen A. Douglas of Illinois, in a remarkable display of legislative skill, to guide Clay's measures one by one into law. In Washington crowds shouted "The Union is saved!" and drank toasts of champagne and whiskey. President Millard Fillmore went so far as to pronounce the Compromise of 1850 "a final settlement" of all sectional disputes. But events were to prove how wrong he was. The compromise contained a fatal measure, the draconian fugitive slave law, which inflamed sectional passions anew and took the country another step toward the very precipice Clay had hoped to avoid.

In late 1851, back in Washington after a long stay at Ashland, Clay tried to resume his duties, but he was suffering from insomnia and coughing worse than ever. When a friend urged him not to be despondent, Clay showed a flash of his old go-ahead spirit. "Sir," he said with eyes blazing, "there is no such word in my vocabulary." By June 1852, too sick to go home, he lay dying in a bed in the Na-

tional Hotel, his son Thomas at his side. At one point he called out, "My mother, mother, mother!" On June 29 he murmured, "I believe, my son, I am going," and asked Thomas to button his shirt collar. He caught Thomas's hand, held it tight, and then let go.

Clay's will provided for the gradual liberation and colonization of all children born after January 1, 1850, to the thirty-five slaves he held when he died. In the end, the act was all Clay accomplished in removing slavery from his troubled country, which continued its headlong rush toward its own destruction. Ironically, the Union disintegrated over the election of a Republican president who deeply admired Clay, who hated slavery as Clay had hated it, and who found only in "the sad spectacle" of civil war a means of vanquishing it.

QUESTIONS TO CONSIDER

1   Describe the development over time of Henry Clay's feelings about slavery. What was his youthful judgment on the South's peculiar institution and under what influences did it form? How and why did his early position change? Can these early tensions be seen throughout his life?

2   What solution to the slavery problem did Henry Clay eventually put forward? To whom was he most indebted for his plan? What were the methods and purpose of the American Colonization Society? It was supported by many prominent Americans, so why did it fail?

3   What were the basic tenets and purpose of Henry Clay's American System? How did the particular political climate of the country at that time doom its fulfillment during Clay's life?

4   Describe the basic issues and outcomes of the Missouri Compromise and the Compromise of 1850. Why were these crises so explosive? What role

did Henry Clay play in them and what did he hope to accomplish? Did he succeed?

5   Although Henry Clay was an enormously popular and widely admired figure, he was forever disappointed in his highest political ambitions. What reasons for this can you find in the political climate of the time? How did Clay contribute to his own disappointment with the particular positions he took? In his role as "the Great Compromiser" how effective was he in easing sectional tensions and averting disunion?

The Growth of Technology

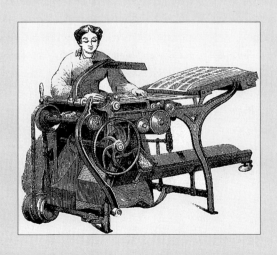

19

The Lords and the
Mill Girls

MAURY KLEIN

One group of Massachusetts businessmen tried to avoid the ugly factory towns and horrible working conditions that Korngold describes in his profile of Garrison (selection 16). They formed the Boston Associates, an organization of financiers who built a model mill town in Massachusetts called Lowell. The story of Lowell — America's first planned industrial community — tells us a great deal about the dreams and realities of a nation already undergoing considerable industrial and urban growth. Maury Klein relates that story with a vivid pen — the landscaped town on the banks of the Concord and Merrimack Rivers that commanded worldwide attention, the healthy farm girls who worked its looms. In 1833, President Andrew Jackson and Vice President Martin Van Buren visited Lowell and watched transfixed as 2,500 mill girls, clad in blue sashes and white dresses, with parasols above their heads, marched by two abreast. "Very pretty women, by the Eternal!" exclaimed the president. Although they loathed Jackson, the members of the Boston Associates were pleased with his observation, for they were proud of their working girls — the showpieces of what they believed was the model of enlightened industrial management.

   To their delight, Lowell became a famous international attraction. English visitors were especially impressed, because female workers in England's coal mines toiled in incredible misery: naked, covered with filth, they had to pull carts of coal on their hands and knees through dark, narrow tunnels. By contrast, as one historian has said, Lowell seemed a "female paradise." Equally impressive was the remarkable productivity of Lowell's "power-driven machinery." Before long, Lowell became (in historian Linda

Evans's words) "the heart of the American textile industry and of the industrial revolution itself."

Lowell's relatively well-disciplined and well-treated work force seemed to demonstrate that industrial capitalism need not be exploitive. Even so, the Lowell system was paternalistic and strict. Sensitive to criticism that it was immoral for women to work, the mill bosses maintained close supervision over their female operatives, imposing curfews and compulsory church attendance. Nevertheless, the mill girls, as they were called, were transformed by their work experience. As Linda Evans says, "Most of these workers saw their mill work as a way to reestablish their value to the family," because they were no longer a burden to their parents (indeed, they could send money home now) and because they could save for their own dowries. "Soon," writes Evans, "it was hard to separate their sense of duty from their sense of independence." They felt a group solidarity, too, and in their boarding houses created "a working-class female culture." They also became aware of themselves as a working class with special problems, for they were powerless and had few options. They could not find other jobs, as could their male counterparts, could not become sailors or dockhands or work on construction gangs. For most of the women, mill work was their only option.

As others have said, their very powerlessness led to the eventual demise of the paternalistic factory system. As more and more textile firms moved to Lowell and other towns, the pressure of competition led to overproduction, to the same cycles of boom and bust that plagued the entire national economy. Thanks to overproduction, many mills fell into decline; wages dropped, and working conditions deteriorated. In a display of solidarity, the mill girls organized a union and went on strikes to protest wage cuts and rising rents. In 1844, organized as the Lowell Female Labor Reform Association, they campaigned for a ten-hour workday and even took their grievances to the state legislature. As Maury Klein points out in the selection that follows, "their efforts were dogged, impressive, and ultimately futile" because they lacked political leverage. The union failed, and the textile bosses eventually replaced most of their once-prized mill girls with another labor force — desperate immigrants, most from Ireland, who worked for lower wages and were far less demanding. By 1860, Lowell had become another grim and crowded mill town, another "squalid slum." As you ponder Lowell's story, consider what it suggests about the nature of American industrialization and about the special problems of women and labor in an industrializing society. Do you agree with Klein, that what happened in Lowell reveals some harsh truths about the incompatibility of democratic ideals and the profit motive?

GLOSSARY

APPLETON, NATHAN   One of the largest stockholders in the Merrimack Manufacturing Company.

BAGLEY, SARAH   One of several women leaders of the Lowell Female Labor Reform Association and the ten-hour workday movement.

BOOTT, KIRK   Planned and supervised the building of the Lowell mill village, which Klein calls "the nation's first planned industrial community."

BOSTON ASSOCIATES   Founders of Lowell and the Merrimack Manufacturing Co., their textile empire eventually comprised eight major firms, twenty mills, and more than six thousand employees.

LOWELL, FRANCIS CABOT   "Farsighted merchant" who formed the Boston Associates and pioneered a unique textile mill at Waltham; after his death, the associates established another mill village on the Merrimack River and named it Lowell.

LOWELL FEMALE LABOR REFORM ASSOCIATION   Formed by the mill girls in 1844 to protest falling wages, this women's labor union campaigned for a ten-hour workday and other reforms during its short existence.

LOWELL OFFERING   Monthly magazine edited and published by the Lowell mill girls.

MERRIMACK MANUFACTURING COMPANY   The new corporation that ran the Lowell mill and turned it into "the largest and most unique mill town in the nation."

WALTHAM SYSTEM   Unique production methods at Francis Lowell's mill.

☆

THE ASSOCIATES

They flocked to the village of Lowell, these visitors from abroad, as if it were a compulsory stop on the grand tour, eager to verify rumors of a utopian system of manufacturers. Their skepticism was natural, based as it was on the European experience where industry had degraded workers and blighted the landscape. In English manufacturing centers such as Manchester, observers had stared into the pits of hell and shrank in horror from the sight. Charles Dickens used this gloomy, putrid cesspool of misery as a model in *Hard Times,* while Alexis de Tocqueville wrinkled his nose at the "heaps of dung, rubble from buildings, putrid, stagnant pools" amid the "huge palaces of industry" that kept "air and light out of the human habitations which they dominate.... A sort of black smoke covers the city.... Under this half daylight 300,000 human beings are ceaselessly at work. A thousand noises disturb this damp, dark labyrinth, but they are not at all the ordinary sounds one hears in great cities."

Was it possible that America could produce an alternative to this hideous scene? It seemed so to the visitors who gaped in wonderment at the village above the confluence of the Concord and Merrimack rivers. What they saw was a planned community with mills five to seven stories high flanked by dormitories for the workers, not jammed together but surrounded by open space filled with trees and flower gardens set against a backdrop of the river and hills beyond. Dwelling

Maury Klein, "The Lords and the Mill Girls," from "From Utopia to Mill Town" by Maury Klein in *American History Illustrated,* October and November 1981. Reprinted by permission of Cowles Magazines, publisher of *American History Illustrated.*

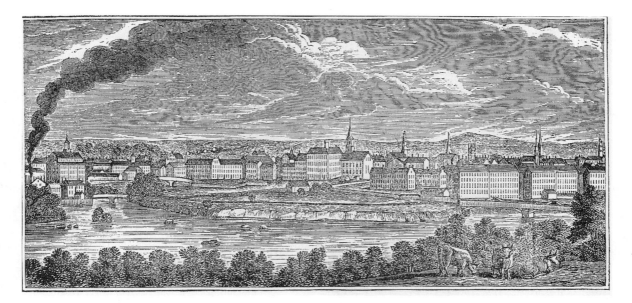

Lowell, Massachusetts, was a model mill town located on the banks of the Concord and Merrimack Rivers. The community attracted worldwide attention because it presented a sharp contrast to the squalor of manufacturing centers in England and Europe. The *buildings stood in groups separated by trees, shrubs, and strips of lawn that were attractively landscaped and reminiscent of a college campus. (Corbis-Bettmann)*

houses, shops, hotels, churches, banks, even a library lined the streets in orderly, uncrowded rows. Taken whole, the scene bore a flavor of meticulous composition, as if a painting had sprung to life.

The contrast between so pristine a vision and the nightmare of Manchester startled the most jaded of foreigners. "It was new and fresh, like a setting at the opera," proclaimed Michel Chevalier, a Frenchman who visited Lowell in 1834. The Reverend William Scoresby, an Englishman, marveled at how the buildings seemed "as fresh-looking as if built within a year." The indefatigable Harriet Martineau agreed, as did J. S. Buckingham, who pronounced Lowell to be "one of the most remarkable places under the sun." Even Dickens, whose tour of America rendered him immune to most of its charms, was moved to lavish praise on the town. "One would

swear," he added "that every 'Bakery,' 'Grocery' and 'Bookbindery' and every other kind of store, took its shutters down for the first time, and started in business yesterday."

If Lowell and its social engineering impressed visitors, the mill workers dazzled them. Here was nothing resembling Europe's *Untermenschen,* that doomed proletariat whose brief, wretched lives were squeezed between child labor and a pauper's grave. These were not men or children or even families as found in the Rhode Island mills. Instead Lowell employed young women, most of them fresh off New England farms, paid them higher wages than females earned anywhere else (but still only half of what men earned), and installed them in dormitories under strict supervision. They were young and industrious, intelligent, and entirely respectable. Like model citizens of a burgeoning republic they saved their money, went to church, and spent their leisure hours in self-improvement.

More than one visitor hurried home to announce the arrival of a new industrial order, one capable of producing goods in abundance without breaking its working class on the rack of poverty. Time proved them wrong, or at best premature. The Lowell experiment lasted barely a generation before sliding back into the grinding bleakness of a conventional mill town. It had survived long enough to tantalize admirers with its unfulfilled promise and to reveal some harsh truths about the incompatibility of certain democratic ideals and the profit motive.

The founding fathers of Lowell were a group known as the Boston Associates, all of whom belonged to that tight knit elite whose dominance of Boston society was exceeded only by their stranglehold on its financial institutions. The seed had been planted by Francis Cabot Lowell, a shrewd, far-sighted merchant who took up the manufacture of cotton cloth late in life. A trip abroad in 1810 introduced him to the cotton mills of Lancashire and to a fellow Boston merchant named Nathan Appleton. Blessed with a superb memory and trained in mathematics, Lowell packed his mind with details about the machinery shown him by unsuspecting mill owners. The Manchester owners jealously hoarded their secrets and patents, but none regarded the wealthy American living abroad for his health as a rival.

Once back in America, Lowell recruited a mechanical genius named Paul Moody to help replicate the machines he had seen in Manchester. After much tinkering they designed a power loom, cottonspinning frame, and some other machines that in fact improved upon the English versions. As a hedge against inexperience Lowell decided to produce only cheap, unbleached cotton sheeting. The choice also enabled him to use unskilled labor, but where was he to find even that? Manchester drew its workers from the poorhouses, a source lacking in America. Both the family system and use of apprentices had been tried in Rhode Island with little success. Most men preferred farming their own land to working in a factory for someone else.

But what about women? They were familiar with spinning and weaving, and would make obedient workers. Rural New England had a surplus of daughters who were considered little more than drains on the family larder. To obtain their services Lowell need only pay decent wages and overcome parental reservations about permitting girls to live away from home. This could be done by providing boarding houses where the girls would be subject to the strict supervision of older women acting as chaperones. There would be religious and moral instruction enough to satisfy the most scrupulous of parents. It was an ingenious concept, one that cloaked economic necessity in the appealing garb of republican ideals.

Lowell added yet another wrinkle. Instead of forming a partnership like most larger businesses, he obtained a charter for a corporation named the Boston Manufacturing Company. Capitalized at $300,000 the firm started with $100,000 subscribed by Lowell and a circle of his caste and kin: Patrick Tracy Jackson and his two brothers, Nathan Appleton, Israel Thorndike and his son, two brothers-in-law, and two other merchants. Jackson agreed to manage the new company, which chose a site at the falls on the Charles River at Waltham. By late 1814 the first large integrated cotton factory in America stood complete, along with its machine shop where Lowell and Moody reinvented the power loom and spinner.

Production began in 1815, just as the war with England drew to a close. The mill not only survived the return of British competition but prospered in spectacular fashion: during the years 1817–1824 dividends averaged more than nineteen percent. Moody's fertile mind devised one new invention after another, including a warp-yarn dresser and double speeder. His innovations made the firm's production methods so unique that they soon became known as the "Waltham system." As Gilman Ostrander observed, "The Waltham method was characterized by an overriding emphasis upon standardization, integration, and mechanization." The shop began to build machinery for sale to other mills. Even more, the company's management techniques became the prototype on which virtually the entire textile industry of New England would later model itself.

Lowell did not live to witness this triumph. He died in 1817 at the age of forty-two, having provided his associates with the ingredients of success. During the next three years they showed their gratitude by constructing two more mills and a bleachery, which exhausted the available water power at Waltham. Eager to expand, the Associates scoured the rivers of New England for new sites. In 1821 Moody found a spot on the Merrimack River at East Chelmsford that seemed ideal. The river fell thirty-two feet in a series of rapids and there were two canals, one belonging to the Pawtucket Canal Company and another connecting to Boston. For about $70,000 the Associates purchased control of the Canal Company and much of the farmland along the banks.

From that transaction arose the largest and most unique mill town in the nation. In this novel enterprise the Associates seemed to depart from all precedent, but in reality they borrowed much from Waltham. A new corporation, the Merrimack Manufacturing Company, was formed with Nathan Appleton and Jackson as its largest stockholders. The circle of inventors was widened to include other members of the Boston elite such as Daniel Webster and the Boott brothers, Kirk and John. Moody took some shares but his ambitions went no further; he was content to remain a mechanic for the rest of his

life. The memory of Francis Cabot Lowell was honored by giving the new village his name.

The task of planning and overseeing construction was entrusted to Kirk Boott. The son of a wealthy Boston Anglophile, Boott's disposition and education straddled the Atlantic. He obtained a commission in the British army and fought under Wellington until the War of 1812 forced his resignation. For several years he studied engineering before returning home in 1817 to take up his father's business. A brilliant, energetic, imperious martinet, Boott leaped at the opportunity to take charge of the new enterprise. As Hannah Josephson observed, he became "its town planner, its architect, its engineer, its agent in charge of production, and the leading citizen of the new community."

The immensity of the challenge appealed to Boott's ordered mind. He recruited an army of 500 Irish laborers, installed them in a tent city, and began transforming a pastoral landscape into a mill town. A dam was put across the river, the old canal was widened, new locks were added, and two more canals were started. The mills bordered the river but not with the monotony of a wall. Three buildings stood parallel to the water and three at right angles in a grouping that reminded some of Harvard College. Trees and shrubs filled the space between them. The boarding houses, semi-detached dwellings two-and-a-half stories high separated by strips of lawn, were set on nearby streets along with the superintendents' houses and long brick tenements for male mechanics and their families. It was a standard of housing unknown to working people anywhere in the country or in Europe. For himself Boott designed a Georgian mansion ornamented with a formidable Ionic portico.

Lowell emerged as the nation's first planned industrial community largely because of Boott's care in realizing the overall concept. At Waltham the boarding houses had evolved piecemeal rather than as an integral part of the design. The Associates took care to avoid competition between the sites by confining

Lowell's production to printed calicoes for the higher priced market. While Waltham remained profitable, it quickly took a back seat to the new works. The machine shop provided a true barometer of change. It not only produced machinery and water wheels for Lowell but also oversaw the construction of mills and housing. Shortly before Lowell began production in 1823, the Associates, in Nathan Appleton's words, "arranged to equalize the interest of all the stockholders in both companies" by formally purchasing Waltham's patterns and patent rights and securing Moody's transfer to Lowell. A year later the entire machine shop was moved to Lowell, leaving Waltham with only a maintenance facility.

The success of the Lowell plant prompted the Associates to unfold ambitious new plans. East Chelmsford offered abundant water power for an expanding industry; the sites were themselves a priceless asset. To use them profitably the Associates revived the old Canal Company under a new name, the Locks and Canals Company, and transferred to it all the land and water rights owned by the Merrimack Company. The latter then bought back its own mill sites and leased the water power it required. Thereafter the Locks and Canals Company sold land to other mill companies, leased water power to them at fixed rates per spindle, and built machinery, mills, and housing for them.

This organizational arrangement was as far advanced for the times as the rest of the Lowell concept. It brought the Associates handsome returns from the mills and enormous profits from the Locks and Canals Company, which averaged twenty-four percent in dividends between 1825 and 1845. As new companies like the Hamilton, Appleton, and Lowell corporations were formed, the Associates dispersed part of their stock among a widening network of fellow Brahmins. New partners entered their exclusive circle, including the Lawrence brothers, Abbott and Amos. Directories of the companies were

so interlocked as to avoid any competition between them. In effect the Associates had created industrial harmony of the sort J. P. Morgan would later promote under the rubric "community of interest."

By 1836 the Associates had invested $6.2 million in eight major firms controlling twenty five-story mills with more than 6,000 employees. Lowell had grown into a town of 18,000 and acquired a city charter. It boasted ten churches, several banks to accommodate the virtue of thrift on the part of the workers, long rows of shops, a brewery, taverns, schools, and other appurtenances of progress. Worldwide attention had transformed it into a showcase. Apart from the influx of foreigners and other dignitaries, it had already been visited by a president the Associates despised (Andrew Jackson), and by a man who would try three times to become president (Henry Clay).

The Associates basked in this attention because they viewed themselves as benevolent, far-seeing men whose sense of duty extended far beyond wealth. To be sure the life blood of the New England economy flowed through their counting houses from their domination of banks, insurance companies, railroads, shipping, and mills elsewhere in New England. Yet such were the rigors of their stern Puritan consciences that for them acquisition was all consuming without being all fulfilling. Duty taught that no fortune was so ample that more was not required. Economist Thorstein Veblen later marveled at the "steadfast cupidity" that drove these men "under pain of moral turpitude, to acquire a 'competence,' and then unremittingly to augment any competence acquired."

Not content with being an economic and social aristocracy, the Associates extended their influence to politics, religion, education, and morality. Lowell fit their *raison d'être* so ideally because it filled their coffers while at the same time reflecting their notion of an orderly, paternal community imbued with the proper values. The operatives knew their place, deferred to the leadership of the Associates, shared their values. . . .

☆

THE MILL GIRLS

In promoting their mills as an industrial utopia [the Associates] were quick to realize that the girls were the prime attraction, the trump card in their game of benevolent paternalism. As early as 1827 Captain Basil Hall, an Englishman, marveled at the girls on their way to work at six in the morning, "nicely dressed, and glittering with bright shawls and showy-colored gowns and gay bonnets . . . with an air of lightness, and an elasticity of step, implying an obvious desire to get to their work."

Observers who went home to rhapsodize about Lowell and its operatives as a model for what the factory system should become trapped themselves in an unwitting irony. While there was much about the Lowell corporations that served later firms as model, the same did not hold true for their labor force. The young women who filled the mills, regarded by many as the heart of the Lowell system, were in fact its most unique element and ultimately its most transient feature. They were of the same stock and shared much the same culture as the men who employed them. This relative homogeneity gave them a kinship of values absent in later generations of workers. Benita Eisler has called them "the last WASP labor force in America."

The women who flocked to Lowell's mills came mostly from New England farms. Some came to augment the incomes of poor families, others to earn money for gowns and finery, to escape the bleak monotony of rural life, or sample the adventure of a fresh start in a new village. Although their motives were mixed, they chose the mills over such alternatives as teaching or domestic service because the pay was better and the work gave them a sense of independence. Lucy Larcom, one of the most talented and articulate of the mill girls, observed that:

Country girls were naturally independent, and the feeling that at this new work the few hours they had of everyday leisure were entirely their own was a satisfaction to them. They preferred it to going out as "hired help." It was like a young man's pleasure in entering upon business for himself.

Leisure hours were a scarce commodity. The mill tower bells tolled the girls to work before the light of day and released them at dusk six days a week, with the Sabbath reserved for solemn observance. The work day averaged twelve-and-a-half hours, depending on the season, and there were only three holidays a year, all unpaid: Fast Day, the Fourth of July, and Thanksgiving. Wages ranged between $2 and $4 a week, about half what men earned. Of this amount $1.25 was deducted for board, to which the company contributed another twenty-five cents. Meager as these sums appear, they exceeded the pay offered by most other mills.

The work rooms were clean and bright for a factory, the walls whitewashed and windows often garnished with potted flowers. But the air was clogged with lint and fumes from the whale-oil lamps hung above every loom. Since threads would snap unless the humidity was kept high, windows were nailed shut even in the summer's heat, and the air was sprayed with water. Delicate lungs were vulnerable to the ravages of tuberculosis and other respiratory ailments. More than one critic attributed the high turnover rate to the number of girls "going home to die."

The machines terrified newcomers with their thunderous clatter that shook the floor. Belts and wheels, pulleys and rollers, spindles and flyers, twisted and whirled, hissing and buzzing, always in motion, a cacophonous jungle alien to rural ears. At first the machines looked too formidable to master. One girl, in the story recalling her first days at Lowell, noted that:

she felt afraid to touch the loom, and she was almost sure she could never learn to weave; the harness puzzled and the reed perplexed her; the shuttle flew out and made a new bump on her head; and the first time she tried to spring the lathe she broke a quarter of the threads. It seemed as if the girls all stared at her, and the overseers watched every motion, and the day appeared as long as a month had at home.... At last it was night.... There was a dull pain in her head, and a sharp pain in her ankles; every bone was aching, and there was in her ears a strange noise, as of crickets, frogs and jews-harps, all mingling together.

Once the novelty wore off, the strangeness of it all gave way to a more serious menace: monotony.

The boarding houses provided welcome havens from such trials. These were dwellings of different sizes, leased to respectable high-toned widows who served as housemothers for fifteen to thirty girls. They kept the place clean and enforced the company rules, which were as strict as any parent might want. Among other things they regulated conduct, imposed a ten o'clock curfew, and required church attendance. The girls were packed six to a bedroom, with three beds. One visitor described the small rooms as "absolutely choked with beds, trunks, band-boxes, clothes, umbrellas and people," with little space for other furniture. The dining room doubled as sitting room, but in early evening it was often besieged by peddlers of all sorts.

This cramped arrangement suited the Associates nicely because it was economical and reinforced a sense of group standards and conformity. Lack of privacy was old hat to most rural girls, though a few complained. Most housemothers set a good table and did not cater to dainty appetites. One girl reported dinner as consisting of "meat and potatoes, with vegetables, tomatoes and pickles, pudding or pie, with bread, butter, coffee or tea." English novelist Anthony Trollope was both impressed and repulsed by the discovery that meat was served twice a day, declaring that for Americans "to live a day without meat would be as great a privation as to pass a night without a bed."

The corporations usually painted each house once a year, an act attributed by some to benevolence and others to a shrewd eye for public relations and property values. Their zeal for cleanliness did not extend to bathing facilities, which were minimal at best. More than one visitor spread tales of dirt and vermin in the boarding houses, but these too were no strangers to rural homes. Like the mills, later boarding houses were built as long dormitory rows unleavened by strips of lawn or shrubbery, but the earlier versions retained a quaint charm for visitors and inhabitants.

Above all the boarding houses were, as Hannah Josephson stressed, "a woman's world." In these cluttered cloisters the operatives chatted, read, sewed, wrote letters, or dreamed about the day when marriage or some better opportunity would take them from the mills. They stayed in Lowell about four years on the average, and most married after leaving. The mill experience was, in Thomas Dublin's phrase, simply "a stage in a woman's life cycle before marriage." For many girls the strangeness of it all was mitigated by the presence of sisters, cousins, or friends who had undertaken the same adventure.

Outside the boarding house the girls strolled and picnicked in the nearby countryside, attended church socials, paid calls, and shopped for the things they had never had. Dozens of shops vied with the savings banks for their hard-earned dollars and won more than their share of them. Those eager to improve their minds, and there were many, patronized the library and the Lyceum, which for fifty cents offered a season ticket for twenty-five lectures by such luminaries as Ralph Waldo Emerson, Horace Mann,

John Quincy Adams, Horace Greeley, Robert Owen, and Edward Everett. Some were ambitious enough to attend evening classes or form study groups of their own in everything from art to German.

Above all the girls read. Their appetite for literature was voracious and often indiscriminate. So strong was this ardor that many slipped their books into the mills, where such distractions were strictly forbidden. It must have pained overseers to confiscate even Bibles from transgressors, but the large number that filled their drawers revealed clearly the Associates' determination to preserve the sharp distinction between the Lord's business and their own.

No one knows how many of the girls were avid readers, but the number probably exceeded the norm for any comparable group. Where so many read, it was inevitable that some would try their hand at writing. By the early 1840s Lowell boasted seven Mutual Self-Improvement Clubs. These were the first women's literary clubs in America, and the members consisted entirely of operatives. From two of these groups emerged a monthly magazine known as the *Lowell Offering* which in its brief life span (1841–1845) achieved a notoriety and reputation far in excess of its literary merits. The banner on its cover described the contents as *A Repository of Original Articles, Written Exclusively by Females Actively Employed in the Mills.*

No other aspect of Lowell rivaled the *Offering* as a symbol for the heights to which an industrial utopia might aspire. Observers at home and abroad were astounded at the spectacle of factory workers — women no less — capable of producing a literary magazine. Even Charles Dickens, that harsh critic of both English industrialism and American foibles, hurried this revelation to his readers:

I am now going to state three facts, which will startle a large class of readers on this side of the Atlantic very much. First, there is a joint-stock piano in a great many of the

Woman factory workers at the Lowell mills were avid readers. They also formed self-improvement clubs and published their own monthly magazine, the Lowell Offering, *The Offering became a symbol for the heights to which an industrial utopia might aspire. As Maury Klein comments, "Observers at home and abroad were astounded at the spectacle of factory workers — women no less — capable of producing a literary magazine." (Lowell Historical Society)*

boarding-houses. Secondly, nearly all these young ladies subscribe to circulating libraries. Thirdly, they have got up among themselves a periodical . . . which is duly printed, published, and sold; and whereof I brought away from

Lowell four hundred good solid pages, which I have read from beginning to end.

As the *Offering*'s fame grew, the Associates were not slow to appreciate its value. Nothing did more to elevate their esteem on both sides of the Atlantic. Contrary to the belief of some, the magazine never became a house organ. Both editors, Harriet Farley and Harriott Curtis, were veterans of the mills who opened their columns to critics and reformers while keeping their own editorial views within more discreet and refined bounds. For their part the Associates were too shrewd not to recognize that the *Offering*'s appeal, its effectiveness as a symbol of republican virtues, lay in its independence. To serve them best it must not smack of self-serving, and it did not.

Although the magazine's prose and poetry seldom rose above mediocre, the material offered revealing insights into every aspect of factory life. Inevitably it attracted authors eager to voice grievances or promote remedies. The editors trod a difficult path between the genteel pretensions of a literary organ and a growing militancy among operatives concerned with gut issues. Few of the girls subscribed to the *Offering* anyway; most of the copies went to patrons in other states or overseas. Small wonder that critics charged the magazine had lost touch with actual conditions in the mills or the real concerns of their operatives.

The *Offering* folded in part because it reflected a system hurrying toward extinction. By the 1840s, when Lowell's reputation as an industrial utopia was still at its peak, significant changes had already taken place. Hard times and swollen ranks of stockholders clamoring for dividends had dulled the Associates' interest in benevolent paternalism. It had always been less a goal than a by-product and not likely to survive a direct conflict with the profit motive. The result was a period of several years during which Lowell coasted on its earlier image while the Associates dismantled utopia in favor of a more cost-efficient system.

The self-esteem of the Associates did not permit them to view their actions in this light, but the operatives felt the change in obvious ways. Their work week increased to seventy-five hours with four annual holidays compared to sixty-nine hours and six holidays for the much maligned British textile workers. To reduce unit costs, girls tended faster machines and were paid lower wages for piecework. That was called speedup; in another practice known as stretchout, girls were given three or four looms where earlier they had tended one or two. Overseers and second hands were offered bonuses for wringing more productivity out of the workers.

At heart the utopian image of Lowell, indeed the system itself, rested on the assumption that grateful, obedient workers would not bite the hand of their masters. When operatives declined to accept this role, factory agents countered with dismissals and blacklists. The result was a growing sense of militancy among the girls and the first stirrings of a labor movement. In 1834 and 1836 there occurred spontaneous "turnouts" or strikes in Lowell, the first protesting wage cuts and the second an increase in the board charge. Neither achieved much, although a large number of girls (800 and 2,500) took part. The Associates showed their mettle in one instance by turning a widow with four children out of her boarding house because her eleven-year-old daughter, a bobbin girl, had followed the others out. "Mrs. Hanson, you could not prevent the older girls from turning out," the corporate agent explained sternly, "but your daughter is a child, and her you could control."

Between 1837 and 1842 a national depression drove wages down and quieted labor unrest at Lowell. When conditions improved and wages still fell, the disturbances began anew. In December 1844 five mill girls met to form the Lowell Female Labor Reform Association; within a year the organization had grown to 600 members in Lowell and had branches elsewhere in New England. Since unions had no legal status or power to bargain directly, LFLRA could only appeal to public opinion and petition the General Court (state legislature) for redress.

For three years the organization dispatched petitions and testified before legislative commissions on behalf of one issue in particular; the ten-hour workday. Led by Sarah Bagley and other women of remarkable energy and intelligence, LFLRA joined hands with workingmen's groups in the push for shorter hours. Their efforts were dogged, impressive, and ultimately futile. As their ranks swelled, they suffered the usual problems of divided aims and disagreement over tactics. More than that, the LFLRA failed in the end simply because it had determination but no leverage. Legislators and other officials did not take them seriously because they were women who had no business being involved in such matters and could not vote anyway. By 1847 LFLRA was little more than a memory. The ten-hour movement lived on, but did not succeed until 1874.

During its brief life LFLRA did much to shatter the image of Lowell as an industrial utopia. The Associates held aloof from controversy and allowed editors, ministers, and distinguished visitors to make their case. There were those who preserved Lowell as a symbol because they wanted to believe, needed to believe in what it represented. After several years of constant labor strife, however, few could overlook the problems pointed up by LFLRA: more work for less pay, deteriorating conditions in the mills and boarding houses, blacklists, and more repressive regulations. Lowell had lost much of what had made it special and was on the verge of becoming another bleak and stifling mill town.

Gradually the river and countryside disappeared behind unbroken walls of factory or dormitory. Nature approached extinction in Lowell, and so did the girls who had always been the core of its system. In 1845 about ninety percent of the operatives were native Americans, mostly farm girls; by 1850 half the mill workers were Irish, part of the flood that migrated after the famine years of 1845–46. The Irish girls were illiterate, docile, and desperate enough to work for low wages. They preferred tenements with their friends and family to boarding houses, which relieved the Associates of that burden. It did not take the Associates long to appreciate the virtues of so helpless and undemanding a work force. In these immigrants they saw great promise for cheap labor comparable to that found in English mill towns like Manchester.

The Associates had lost their bloom as models of propriety and benevolence. Some called them "lords of the loom" and consigned them to the same terrace of Inferno as the South's "lords of the lash." How ironic it was for Nathan Appleton, the most beloved of souls with an unmatched reputation for philanthropy and civic virtue, that his mills were the first to be called "soulless corporations."

So it was that Lowell's utopian vision ended where industrialism began. In time the Irish would rise up in protest as their predecessors had done, but behind them came waves of Dutch, Greek, and French Canadian immigrants to take their places in the mills. The native New England girls continued to flee the mills or shy away from them in droves, until by 1860 they were but a small minority. Their departure marked the emergence of Lowell as a mill town no different than any other mill town. One of the girls, peering from her boarding house window, watched the growing stories of a new mill snuff out her view of the scenery beyond and caught the significance of her loss. In her lament could be found an epitaph for Lowell itself:

Then I began to measure . . . and to calculate how long I would retain this or that beauty. I hoped that the brow of the hill would remain when the structure was complete. But no! I had not calculated wisely. It began to recede from me . . . for the building rose still higher and higher. One hope after another is gone . . . one image after another, that has been beautiful to our eye, and dear to our heart has forever disappeared. How has the scene changed! How is our window darkened!

QUESTIONS TO CONSIDER

1 Thomas Jefferson, an agrarian idealist, hated the idea of America's becoming an industrial nation, basing his feelings on the evils of European cities. How did the city of Lowell, at least in its early years, escape the evils Jefferson believed inherent in urban industrial life?

2 Klein says that what happened at Lowell reveals that the profit motive and certain democratic ideals are incompatible. Do you agree? Was the Lowell experiment doomed from its inception because of conflicting goals?

3 Why did the Boston Associates choose young women from rural parts of New England to be operatives in their Lowell textile mills? What were the advantages of a female labor force?

4 Examine boarding-house life at Lowell from the perspective of the female mill workers. What were the advantages and drawbacks to living in the boarding houses? In what way, if any, was boarding-house life conducive to the development of a positive female subculture?

5 By the 1840s, changes taking place in the Lowell boarding house and in the factories indicated the breakdown of that model factory town. Describe these changes and the reasons for growing labor militancy among the once "docile" female work force.

"Hell in Harness":
The Iron Horse and the Go-Ahead Age

PAGE SMITH

The development of steam power was one of the great technological accomplishments of the late eighteenth and nineteenth centuries. In an age of giant rockets, space shuttles, and satellite probes of other planets, we tend to forget that the "advanced" steam engine, patented by England's James Watts in 1769, fostered myriad technological innovations that came to characterize industrial society.

A significant improvement over an earlier "atmospheric" engine, Watts's machine transformed the textile industry in Europe as well as in America. The steam engine had an equally profound effect on the history of transportation. As train historian David Plowden said in the August/September, 1989 issue of Timeline *magazine, "The railroad builder and the locomotive shattered a fixed distance-time equation for overland travel" that had existed for centuries. Until the advent of the steam engine, people had relied on nature for locomotion—on wind, water, and animals. In the "turnpike and canal eras," which lasted from around 1790 to the 1830s, Americans tried to alter nature by creating roads and waterways, but nature still furnished the power for the boats and barges, wagons and stages. The emergence of the steam-powered locomotive in the 1820s and 1830s was a quantum leap forward. In Plowden's words, "It was a symbol of man's will to rise above nature." Soon a locomotive driven by the steam engine could pull a train of cars at thirty miles per hour, doing so with a chugging roar and puffs of black smoke that would thrill generations of Americans.*

The early railroad promoters, however, found themselves in a bitter struggle with canal and steamboat interests for transportation supremacy. But with the advantages of speed, year-round operation, and location almost anywhere, the railroads were the way of the future. By the 1850s, the age of the iron horse had arrived: thousands of miles of railroad track, shining beneath iron wheels that transported the cargo of a nation, lay across a bustling land. The railroads tied the East to the Middle West; they caused astonishing growth in existing cities such as Chicago that lay along their routes; they spawned foundries, machine shops, new tools, and "a dizzying proliferation of inventions and improvements," as Page Smith says in this selection. Railroads also inspired the American imagination, as poets and storytellers heard America singing in the music of the trains, in the clang of their bells, in the hum of their wheels, and in the throb of their engines. The train even attracted a new breed of artist — the photographer. Railroads were to become America's principal form of transportation, remaining so until the interstate highway system replaced them in the middle of the next century.

Yet, as Smith notes, there was a down side to the railroad boom: along with it came an insatiable American need to "go ahead," to travel faster and make more money regardless of the consequences to human life. In truth, the locomotives smoking up the sky presaged an industrial society with pollutants and destructive forces that would eventually imperil humankind itself. But all that lay in the future. For Americans of the mid-nineteenth century, the train was the supreme example of the illimitable aspiration and resourcefulness of the human spirit.

GLOSSARY

BALTIMORE & OHIO RAILROAD
Established in 1828 by Baltimore merchants to capitalize on the western trade; by 1830, a horse-drawn "train" was operating on thirteen miles of track heading west; the company later switched to the newfangled steam-powered locomotives, designed the passenger car, and went on to become one of the country's leading railroads, with lines that reached clear to St. Louis, Missouri.

DEWITT CLINTON   Built by the Mohawk and Hudson Railroad, this improved steam locomotive made a historic run in 1832, pulling three cars at thirty miles per hour.

COOPER, PETER   Glue maker and inventor who built America's first steam-powered locomotive, a crude little machine that performed erratically; George Johnson and James Milholland produced an improved version called the *Tom Thumb.*

DAVIS, PHINEAS   A watchmaker who built the steam locomotive, the *York,* which won an award from the Baltimore & Ohio Railroad for being "the most improved engine."

GO-AHEAD AGE   "The age of technology wherein any ambitious and dexterous farm boy might dream of becoming as rich as [fur-dealing mogul] John Jacob Astor or Peter Cooper"; the age produced "the disposition to see the world in terms of practical problems to be solved." Americans in the go-ahead age became preeminent problem solvers.

PENNSYLVANIA RAILROAD Led other railroads in building "a 'through line' with a uniform gauge" and "in dressing its train 'captain' or conductor in a uniform."

STEPHENSON, GEORGE British engineer who developed the first passenger railroad locomotive.

TOM THUMB America's first steam-powered locomotive, built by Peter Cooper and improved by George Johnson, a skilled mechanic, and his apprentice, James Milholland; on its maiden run in 1830, the little one-horse engine raced a real horse, attaining a speed of eighteen miles per hour; alas, the locomotive blew its safety valve and lost the race. Nevertheless it inspired confidence in the steam locomotive and dreams of building railroads "with immense stretches of very rough country to pass."

Tracks preceded trains. Enterprising entrepreneurs began laying crude tracks in the 1820s to carry horse-drawn carriages. The advantages were that a horse could pull a much heavier load faster and passengers much more comfortably on tracks than on the commonly rutted and unpaved roads of the time. Rails were usually made of wood with bands of iron on top. In Maryland experiments were conducted with stone "rails" covered with iron. The iron-covered wooden rails proved unsatisfactory as soon as the first steam engines were introduced; they had a tendency to tear loose and curl up, especially at the high rates of speed that the steam engines were soon capable of attaining — as much as fifteen miles an hour.

In England, steam engines at first seemed most promising in carrying passengers over ordinary roads and turnpikes. The Duke of Wellington's barouche was drawn by a steam engine and attained a speed of more than twenty-five miles an hour. English experiments in the use of rails were confined primarily to the hauling of heavy loads by horse or mule and, more and more frequently, by the use of some kind of steam engine.

In America, Peter Cooper, a successful businessman, saw the possibilities of combining rails and steam engines. While Cooper was neither an engineer nor an artisan, he did not hesitate to involve himself in the design of a locomotive, buying up unmounted gun barrels to use as tubes in the engine's boiler. When the locomotive failed to perform satisfactorily, Cooper turned the job of making a better one over to George Johnson, the owner of a machine shop and a skilled mechanic, who set to work with his young apprentice, James Milholland. While Johnson and Milholland were working on an improved version of Cooper's train, the *Stourbridge*

Extracts from *A People's History of the American Revolution*, Vol. IV, *The Nation Comes of Age*, pages 262–282, copyright McGraw-Hill Publishing Company. Used by permission of the publisher.

This is an oil painting of the first railway on the Mohawk and Hudson Road, completed in 1831. Because boilers on the early trains were wood fired, they had to stop frequently for fresh sup- *plies of wood. (Detail of painting by Edward Lamson Henry, Collection of Albany Institute of History and Art, Albany, New York. Gift of Catherine Gensevoort Lansing)*

Lion, imported from England, arrived in New York, followed by several other engines which were eagerly studied; the best features were quickly incorporated into the American machine.

Fourteen miles of railroad had meanwhile been laid between Baltimore and Ellicott's Mills, allowing horse-drawn carriages to make the trip in record time. The run to Ellicott's Mills was made by the horse carriage three times a day at a charge of twenty-five cents.

By May 30, 1830, Cooper's steam engine was ready to be tested. Cooper himself took the throttle of the *Tom Thumb,* with the president and the treasurer of the Baltimore & Ohio Company beside him. The *Tom Thumb* had a fourteen-inch piston stroke, weighed barely a ton, and developed slightly more than one horsepower, but it drew a weight of more than four tons at the rate of fifteen miles an hour. To draw attention to this new machine,

Cooper advertised "a race between a Gray Horse and *Tom Thumb.*" The race took place on August 28, 1830, and a passenger on the coach drawn by the locomotive wrote: "The trip was most interesting. The curves were passed without difficulty, at a speed of fifteen miles an hour. . . . The day was fine, the company in the highest spirits, and some excited gentlemen of the party pulled out memorandum books, and when at the highest speed, which was eighteen miles an hour, wrote their names and some connected sentences, to prove that even at that great velocity it was possible to do so." It was on the way back to Baltimore that the famous race occurred. At first the horse, with quicker acceleration, raced out ahead but as the engine got up steam it overtook and passed the gray. Just at that moment the safety valve on the engine blew open and the train lost pressure and fell behind, despite Peter Cooper's frantic efforts to repair the damage.

George Stephenson, the great British engineer, had been working for almost a decade to perfect a practical engine. He had, in the process, built a dozen locomotives of various types in the well-equipped workshops of the Liverpool and Manchester Railroad and he had the stimulus of half a dozen active competitors. The United States had entered the field late and with far more modest resources, but within two years Cooper had produced the first practical passenger railroad locomotive. Engines designed by Stephenson soon outstripped the *Tom Thumb,* but American railroad building was on its way. When the Baltimore and Ohio offered a four-thousand-dollar reward for the most improved engine, Johnson and Milholland had one waiting. Its most serious rival was one designed and built by Phineas Davis, a watchmaker. Three other engines were also entered, each with important original features and all differing greatly in design. The *York,* built by Davis, won the first prize and Davis became an employee of the Baltimore and Ohio Railroad. It soon seemed as though every ambitious young engineer in the United States who could round up a few financial backers was making a locomotive. A year after the *Tom Thumb* made its historic run, the Mohawk and Hudson Railroad was completed and an engine named the *DeWitt Clinton* drew three cars at speeds that at times reached thirty miles an hour.

The Baltimore and Ohio Railroad Company had been formed on July 4, 1828, and the cornerstone laid by ninety-year-old Charles Carroll of Carrollton. But the course of the railroads, as they were soon called, proved far from smooth. They were opposed by the farmers, through whose lands their right-of-ways must run, in an alliance with the officers and stockholders of canal and highway companies (who rightly saw the railroads as dangerous competition), and by the teamsters (whose jobs were threatened). The engines themselves were so unpredictable that teams of horses had to be kept at way stations to pull broken-down trains to their destination. . . .

By 1832 — two years after *Tom Thumb*'s famous trip — Pennsylvania alone had sixty-seven railroad tracks from a few hundred yards to twenty-two miles in length, many of them constructed of wood. When the Baltimore and Ohio built a passenger carriage with seats on either side of a center aisle, there were strong objections that such an aisle would simply become an extended spittoon, but this seating arrangement soon became standard on most lines. (Davy Crockett was widely reported to have exclaimed at his first sight of a train: "Hell in harness, by the 'tarnal!'")

Locomotives proved easier to build and to improve in efficiency than rails. Many rails were imported from England at an exorbitant cost. The six miles of railroad between Philadelphia and Germantown, for example, cost some thirty thousand dollars per mile and the rails, weighing thirty-nine pounds to the yard, were English-made.

On his way from Quincy to Washington in the fall of 1833 to take his seat in Congress, John Quincy Adams rode on the Amboy railroad from Amboy to Philadelphia. The train consisted of two locomotives, "each drawing an accommodation car, a sort of moving stage, in a square, with open railing, a platform and a row of benches holding forty or fifty persons; then four or five cars in the form of large stage coaches, each in three compartments, with doors of entrance on both sides." Each train ended with a high-piled baggage car, in which the passengers' luggage was covered with an oilcloth. The train sped along at almost thirty miles an hour, but after ten miles it had to stop to allow the wheels to be oiled. Despite this precaution, in another five miles a wheel on one of the cars caught fire and slipped off, killing one passenger and badly maiming another. Of the sixteen passengers in the coach only one escaped injury.

Boilers on the early trains were wood-fired and, like steamboats, trains had to stop frequently to take on fresh supplies of wood. The remarkable thing is that in spite of all these difficulties — the constraints imposed by state legislatures under the control of the canal and highway interests, the scarcity of money, the inadequacy of the rails themselves, the constant litigation, the restrictive municipal ordinances that for a time forbade the building of railroad stations in cities, the disastrous accidents that plagued every line, the barns and fields set afire by sparks that showered from primitive smokestacks — the building of engines and railway tracks went inexorably on.

Boston, which had seen the greater part of the vast commerce with the Mississippi Valley West go to New York with the construction of the Erie Canal, took the lead in developing railroad links with the West, thereby regaining much of its lost financial eminence. New York, anxious to protect the investment of the state and its citizens in the canal, did all it could to impede the development of competing railroads.

By 1850 there were some three thousand miles of track running from Boston to the principal cities of New England and westward to Ohio, representing an investment of seventy million dollars. Of even greater significance was the fact that most of the lines made money. . . .

The railroad mania exceeded, if possible, the earlier canal mania. Canals still continued to be built, of course, and fierce competition developed between canals and railroads, but an extraordinary amount of technical skill and ingenuity was channeled into the development of railroads and the locomotives and the cars that passed over them. Hardly a month passed without some important innovation which, as soon as it had proved itself (and often before), was adopted by other designers and builders. It was as though a particular quality in the American character, until now more or less dormant, had been activated. For forty years — from 1789 to 1830 — the canal, the steamboat, and the bridge had been the primary fields of engineering development. Now, with the "discovery" of the railroad, the machine shop claimed equal importance with the farm or factory and Americans revealed more dramatically than ever before their astonishing facility for marshaling human energies and material resources to meet a particular challenge. Barns became foundries, warehouses were converted into machine shops. New tools were built and old tools improved. Moreover, the primary activity of building locomotives spawned a host of subsidiary and only indirectly related undertakings. Farmers with a bent for mechanics began working on an improved plow. Longer and stronger bridges had to be built to carry heavier and heavier trains, and there were tunnels to be built through mountains that blocked the way. It was clear that principles developed in making locomotives — such elements as pistons and valves — were adaptable to other processes. So there was a dizzying proliferation of inventions and improvements. Dedicated from the first moment to finding labor-saving methods and building labor-saving tools, thereby improving the ratio between work and its monetary return, a new breed of Americans — men like Peter Cooper and Mathias Baldwin and thousands of their less well-known compatriots — ushered in the "go-ahead age," the age of technology wherein any ambitious and dexterous farm boy might dream of becoming as rich as John Jacob Astor or Peter Cooper. A disposition to see the world in terms of practical problems to be solved was both the condition and the consequence of such a habit of mind, and it certainly contributed directly to the optimistic strain in American character. Wherever one looked he or she could see signs of "progress" and improvement in man's long war against nature. Everywhere "nature" was in retreat and civilization in advance. The Indian was nature, the natural man, and he was giving way to the determination of the American to cultivate the land and obey the biblical injunction to make it fruitful and to be fruitful himself, the determination to organize space and apply ideas to landscape with such single-minded zeal and unwearying industry that the landscape must succumb. Philip Hone noted proudly in his diary: "There was never a nation on the face of the earth which equalled this in rapid locomotion." A message had been carried from President Tyler in Washington to New York, a distance of some 225 miles, in twenty-four hours.

In the face of every obstacle the promoters of the railroads pushed ahead, raising their capital primarily by public subscription. A train of seventeen cars ran from Baltimore to Washington in 1835 in two hours and fifteen minutes, carrying relatives of Washington, Adams, Jefferson, and Madison. But antirailroad teamsters still waylaid trains and shot at crews from ambush, and two years later the Depression of 1837 brought railroad building to a virtual halt. It was eleven years before stockholders in the Baltimore and Ohio got any return on their investment and then it was a mere 2 percent. Construction had gone on during that period to connect Baltimore with the Ohio River commerce at the cost of $7,500,000, and only the intervention of the famous British banking house of Alexander Baring made it possible to avoid bankruptcy.

The biggest impediments to the railroads were laws designed to protect the investors in canals. The Chesapeake and Ohio canal, for example, cost $60,000 a mile to build and took twenty-two years to complete, by which time many of the original investors had died. The most notable feature of the canal was a tunnel 3,118 feet long which required the use of headlamps on barges through it, and despite the fact that the Baltimore and Ohio Railroad ran its tracks parallel to the river, the transportation of Cumberland coal down the canal brought in substantial revenues for years, although not enough to pay its enormous costs. Protracted and expensive as its construction was, the canal was by any standard one of the great engineering feats of the century, second only to the Erie Canal. Legislators were under enormous pressure to protect such a huge investment.

A number of states passed laws requiring the railroads, after they had recouped the cost of their construction, to pay all profits above 10 percent to rival

canal companies. Other laws prohibited trains from entering into or passing through the incorporated areas of cities and towns. Some states included in railroad franchises the requirement that railroads sell their tracks and stock to the state after twenty years — at the state's evaluation. Other provisions limited the carrying of freight by train to those times of the year when the canals were frozen. Freight and passenger rates of trains were frequently tied to those of canal transportation to keep the trains from drawing off business. A more practical obstacle was the fact that virtually every railroad company, many of which ran no more than fifty to a hundred miles, had a different gauge, so that freight and passengers had to be unloaded and loaded again at the boundary of every company. Everything in America was bound to have a moral dimension; the railroads must be seen as not merely having a remarkable effect on commerce but as improving morals. In this spirit the Western Railroad Company of Massachusetts sent a circular to all the clergy of the state pointing out "the moral effects of rail-roads" and urging them "to take an early opportunity to deliver a discourse before your congregation, on the moral effect of rail-roads on our wide extended country" — thereby, presumably, encouraging investment.

Since nature and morality (and, indeed, religion) were intertwined, the railroad train must be somehow reconciled with nature. [Ralph Waldo] Emerson, who believed that everything worked for the best, had no trouble in effecting the reconciliation. He was entranced by the technological revolution ushered in by the train. In 1834 he wrote in his journal: "One has dim foresight of the hitherto uncomputed mechanical advantages who rides on the railroad and moreover a practical confirmation of the ideal philosophy that Matter is phenomenal whilst men & trees & barns whiz by you as fast as the leaves of a dictionary. As our teakettle hissed along through a field of mayflowers, we could judge of the sensations of a swallow who skims by trees & bushes with about the same speed. The very permanence of matter seems compromised & oaks, fields, hills, hitherto esteemed symbols of stability do absolutely dance by you." The railroads had introduced a "multitude of picturesque traits into our pastoral scenery," Emerson wrote, "the tunneling of the mountains, the bridging of streams . . . the encounter at short distances along the track of gangs of laborers . . . the character of the work itself which so violates and revolutionizes the primal and immemorial forms of nature; the villages of shanties at the edge of the beautiful lakes . . . the blowing of rocks, explosions all day, with the occasional alarm of a frightful accident." These all served to "keep the senses and the imagination active."

The train, Emerson believed, would complete the conquest of the continent, carrying Americans to every corner and making the United States "Nature's nation." The ambivalence of Emerson's own view of nature is suggested by his remark that "Nature is the noblest engineer, yet uses a grinding economy, working up all that is wasted to-day into to-morrow's creation. . . ." Thus nature was a good Puritan after all, a hard worker who wasted nothing.

In fairness to Emerson it must be said that, visiting the industrial midlands of England, he had second thoughts about the happy union of nature and technology. "A terrible machine has possessed itself of the ground, the air, the men and women, and hardly even thought is free," he wrote. Everything was centered in and conditioned by the omnipresent factory. In 1853, no longer rhapsodic about railroads, he wrote: "The Railroad has proved too strong for all our farmers & has corrupted them like a war, or the incursion of another race — has made them all amateurs, given the young men an air their fathers never had; they look as if they might be railroad agents any day."

By the early 1840s the railroads had an irresistible momentum. Small lines constantly consolidated in an effort to increase their access to capital and improve their service. New lines were established and as soon as they proved themselves (or went bankrupt) they were taken up by larger lines and incorporated into a "system." This process of consolidation was noted by Sidney George Fisher in 1839. "The whole route from Washington to N. York," he wrote, "is now owned by gigantic corporations, who of course manage the lines solely with a view to profit, without reference to the convenience or accommodation of passengers. Heretofore the line on the Chesapeake has been unrivalled for speed, cleanliness, civility of officers & servants, and admirable accommodations of every kind. Secure now from any competition, & sure that all persons must travel by their conveyance, they charge what they please, and the fare & accommodations will I doubt not be as wretched as that of the line to N. York." British capital and the labor of Irish immigrants were two essential ingredients in the extraordinary expansion of the railroads in the decade of the 1840s. The prize was the produce of the Mississippi Valley, the great bulk of which had to be carried down the Mississippi and its tributaries to New Orleans. To carry it by rail to New York and the large East Coast cities and ports would generate enormous profits. The Pennsylvania Railroad took the lead in building a "through line" of uniform gauge (this meant a shift from primarily passenger service to freight and passenger) and in dressing its train "captain" or conductor in a uniform with blue coat and brass buttons. Coal was the principal freight on short hauls within states. Wheat and lumber were common loads on long hauls. Perhaps most important were the changes in the patterns of urban and rural life that the building of innumerable feeder lines brought about. Farmers within a radius of a hundred miles or more of a city could now ship fresh produce — milk, eggs, fruit and vegetables — to city markets. The farmer was thus disposed to specialize, to raise cash crops in sufficient quantity to make it practical to ship them to city markets. Dairy farms and one-crop farms thus began to replace general farming. As the farmer came to depend on distant city markets, he also became vulnerable to the operations of middlemen or wholesalers, who offered the lowest possible price for his produce, and from fluctuations in demand resulting from economic cycles. The farmer thus lost a measure of his cherished independence in return for more hard money. In turn the city, guaranteed a supply of essential foods, was able to grow at an unprecedented rate.

Much of the capital required to build railroads and develop coal mines as ancillary to them came from England. An English family named Morrison started the Hazelton Coal Company at Hazelton, Pennsylvania. Sidney George Fisher's brother Henry was the American representative for the coal company and for the Reading Railroad, which the Morrison family also owned. "The railroad," Sidney wrote, "is excellent, you roll along with great speed and great smoothness, and there is very little jar or noise, the cars are very comfortable, and there is but one source of annoyance, the cinders & smoke from the engine." The mining town of Tamaqua, not far from the Hazelton mine, was "a miserable village, wretched houses & population, produced by and dependent on the Little Schuylkill mines which are all around the town & make the whole place black with coal dust." Hazelton was a pleasant "new town" located in a pine forest under which lay "immense and rich veins of coal." The ground was undermined for miles around with diggings and the Morrisons, Fisher reported, owned "1800 acres of the finest coal land in the state, the buildings, mines, railroad & machinery."

In time the legal impediments to railroad building were struck down by courts or repealed by state legislatures. The emphasis now shifted to providing incentives for building railroads, especially in the Mississippi Valley region, where vast expanses of lands were unsold and unsettled because of their distance from markets. Most settlement took place along rivers and waterways that provided access to markets. Illinois set aside eleven million dollars in 1837, the year of the depression, to build a railroad that would run through the center of the state down to the Ohio River, but the state was in such desperate financial circumstances that it was fourteen years before any substantial progress was made in building the Central Illinois Railroad to link the Great Lakes with the Ohio and the Mississippi, making Chicago the terminus for the proposed route. Irishmen again provided the workers, and the death toll from disease was a heavy one. Cholera was especially deadly in the crowded and unsanitary work camps. "Our laborers," an engineer wrote, "numbered from 5,000 to 8,000 men. We had to recruit in New York and New Orleans paying transportation to Illinois . . . but the men would desert when the cholera epidemics broke out and scatter like frightened sheep. Men at work one day, were in their graves the next. . . . It was dangerous during the summer months to eat beef, butter, or drink milk. Our difficulties were increased by the groggeries and whisky that got in our camps. Drunken frolics ended in riots, when a contractor was murdered and state troops called out. One hundred and fifty laborers left in a body after the riot." . . .

The Central Illinois cost ten million dollars more to build than its projectors had estimated. The state gave the company 2,595,000 acres of land along its right-of-way. Abraham Lincoln was an attorney for the railroad; when he submitted a bill for $2,000 for his services and the railroad protested that that was more than Daniel Webster would have charged, Lincoln raised his fee to $5,000, took the railroad to court, and won his claim. Land through which the railroad passed rose in value from sixteen cents an acre to ten dollars an acre in a five-year period and a decade later to thirty dollars an acre.

The South now lagged behind the North and West in railroad building. All told, the feverish decade of building in the forties resulted in quadrupling the number of miles of railroad. This was all accomplished at enormous cost (the better part of it never recovered) and great loss of life (primarily Irish). When Alexander Mackay visited the United States in 1846 he found "an unbroken line of railway communication extending from Boston ... to beyond Macon in Georgia, a distance of upwards of 1,200 miles." Lines reached out from Philadelphia to Pittsburgh, and the Baltimore and Ohio was pushing through the Cumberland Gap into the Mississippi Valley. Over 5,700 miles of railway had been completed, 2,000 of it within New England and New York state, and more than 4,000 miles of additional railway were under construction. In the 1850s the railroad mileage of the nation quadrupled once more.

Of all those who profited from the incredible expansion of the railroads none rose as dizzily as the city of Chicago. As Gustaf Unonius wrote in 1860, "The web of railroads which Chicago has spun around itself during the last ten years is the thing that more than anything else has contributed to its wealth and progress." The first locomotive reached the city in 1851. Seven years later it was the terminus of more than a dozen trunk lines. Three lines ran from Chicago to New York in less than thirty six-hours (it once had taken ten days to make the trip). Daily 120 trains, some of them hauling as many as forty freight cars, arrived and departed from the stations in various parts of the city. "It should be mentioned," Unonius wrote, "that all these railroads, altogether measuring five thousand miles in length, which radiate from Chicago as a central point in that immense iron web, the threads of which cross each other everywhere in the extensive Mississippi Valley, are private undertakings." Private undertakings, as we have noted, with considerable public encouragement.

The passion to "go ahead," the endless emphasis on speed, exacted a heavy price in lives and serious injuries. In 1838 alone 496 persons died and many more were seriously injured in boiler explosions, not to mention those killed or injured in wrecks. Sidney George Fisher noted in his diary that there had been an accident on the North Pennsylvania Railroad in which thirty-nine persons had been killed and seventy-two wounded. One of the cars had caught fire

and seventeen people had been burned to death. "These horrible scenes," he added, "are constantly recurring, and there seems no remedy." And Philip Hone wrote: "I never open a newspaper that does not contain some account of disasters and loss of life on railroads. They do a retail business in human slaughter, whilst the wholesale trade is carried on (especially on Western waters) by the steamboats. This world is going on too fast. Improvements, Politics, Reform, Religion — all fly. Railroads, steamers, packets, race against time and beat it hollow. Flying is dangerous. By and by we shall have balloons and pass over to Europe between sun and sun. Oh, for the good old days of heavy post-coaches and speed at the rate of six miles an hour!"

Captain Marryat ascribed such American "recklessness" to "the insatiate pursuit of gain among a people who consider that time is money, and who are blinded by their eagerness in the race for it.... At present, it certainly is more dangerous to travel one week in America than to cross the Atlantic a dozen times. The number of lives lost in one year by accidents in steamboats, railroads, and coaches was estimated ... at *one thousand seven hundred and fifty!*" To Hone such disasters were "a stigma on our country; for these accidents (as they are called) seldom occur in Europe.... But we have become the most careless, reckless, headlong people on the face of the earth. 'Go ahead' is our maxim and password; and we do go ahead with a vengeance, regardless of the consequences and indifferent about the value of human life." His reflections were prompted by a report of the burning of the *Ben Sherrod*. The boat's crew, according to newspaper reports, was drunk and the wood took fire. "Out of 235 persons, 175 were drowned or burned to death." By the end of the year fifty-five steamboats had blown up, burned, or run aground and sunk on the Mississippi River alone; thirteen sunk on the Ohio and two on the Missouri.

When Marryat ventured by rail around the United States in the 1830s he wrote: "At every fifteen miles of the railroads there are refreshment rooms; the cars stop, all the doors are thrown open, and out rush the passengers, like boys out of school, and crowd around the tables to solace themselves with pies, patties, cakes, hard-boiled eggs, ham, custards, and a variety of railroad luxuries, too numerous to mention. The bell rings for departure, in they all hurry with their hands and mouths full, and off they go again, until the next stopping place induces them to relieve the monotony of the journey by masticating without being hungry." By the time Isabella Bird traveled west twenty years later there were numerous conveniences not available to Marryat. Bird reported that "water-carriers, book, bonbon, and peach vendors" were "forever passing backwards and forewards." Baggage could be checked with metal checks, which was a novelty and a great convenience. Bird also discovered "through tickets," a single long ticket bought at the station of origin, for an entire trip of fifteen hundred miles on a dozen different lines.

Since Americans traveled so perpetually, travelers' accommodations were generally excellent, clean, and comfortable and virtually interchangeable. Marryat observed that "the wayside inns are remarkable for their uniformity; the furniture of the bar-room is invariably the same: a wooden clock, map of the United States, a map of the state, the Declaration of Independence, a looking-glass, with a hair-brush and comb hanging on it, *pro bono publico;* sometimes with the extra embellishment of one or two miserable pictures, such as General Jackson scrambling upon a horse, with fire and steam coming out of his nostrils, going to the battle of New Orleans, etc. etc." . . .

The feverish railroad building of the 1840s and 1850s opened up a large part of the still undeveloped land of the Mississippi Valley and provided a tremendous stimulus to business activity, although it did not prevent the devastating Depression of 1857. Perhaps most important of all, it had tied the Old West or the Near West to the Northeast and thereby laid the foundation for preserving the Union.

One can only attempt to convey the nature of the railroad boom by such phrases as "reckless enthusiasm" and "extravagant passion." The American public, which had so recently fallen in love with canals, now made trains the objects of its collective affection. Canals suddenly seemed hopelessly pokey and out of date although they continued to be an important part of the transportation network. The loss of money and loss of life attendant upon the marvelous new invention seemed to most people an in-no-way unacceptable price to pay for the intoxicating sense of *speed,* of being drawn along as fast as the wind. So began a hundred-year-long love affair between Americans and railroads. If any one invention or device can be said to have had a determining effect on the history of a people, it was certainly the railroad train on the history of the people of the United States. In the beginning everything was [by water]. Water was the element on which Americans moved — lakes, rivers, and canals provided the initial circulatory system of American travel and American commerce. Now it was iron and soon it would be steel. The canal was an adaption of nature to human needs. The train, with its relentless disposition to go straight and level to its destination, was the subjugation of nature, man's greatest triumph over a world of curves and declivities.

QUESTIONS TO CONSIDER

1 Even more than the factory, the railroad is a symbol of mid-nineteenth-century America, for it was the railroad that linked the agricultural heartland to the industrial cities. How did the growth of the railroad change the way farmers farmed? How did it influence changes in industry?

2 What effect do you think fast travel to practically everywhere may have had on family life? What effect would increased mobility via railroad have had on westward expansion? On immigration?

3   Where does the railroad fit into nineteenth-century America's long philosophic love affair with nature? What did people dislike about the railroad?

4   Which technologies in our own day do you think have expanded with the rapidity of railroads in the mid-nineteenth century and with similar effect?

5   It seems ironic that in present-day America trains evoke nostalgia for a way of life that was slower, safer, and more gracious than our own, for safety and graciousness were the very qualities that nineteenth-century people thought the railroads had destroyed. What do you see as the future of railroads in the United States? What advantages do trains have over airplanes and automobiles? What disadvantages? In a world clouded by pollution and threatened with a scarcity of fossil fuels, what role might the railroads play?

BEYOND THE MISSISSIPPI

21

The Trail of Tears

DEE BROWN

One of the most unhappy chapters in American history is the way whites treated Indians. American Indian policy, however, must be seen in the context of the entire European conquest of the New World. That conquest began with Columbus, who gave the people the name Indios and kidnapped ten San Salvador Indians, taking them back to Spain to learn the white man's ways. In the ensuing four centuries, as Dee Brown writes in Bury My Heart at Wounded Knee, "several million Europeans and their descendants undertook to enforce their ways upon the people of the New World," and when these people would not accept European ways, they were fought, enslaved, or exterminated.

Whites in North America joined the conquest in the colonial period, when they drove most of the eastern tribes into the interior. This pattern of "Indian removal" continued through the eighteenth and nineteenth centuries. When Jefferson came to power, his administration began an official United States policy of Indian removal either by treaty or by outright warfare. During the next three decades, most tribes of the Old Northwest were "removed" in that manner to west of the Mississippi. When a thousand hungry Sac and Fox Indians recrossed the river into Illinois in 1832, militia and federal troops repelled the "invasion" in what became known as the Black Hawk War, in which young Abraham Lincoln commanded a militia company. The Sac and Fox retreated across the Mississippi into Wisconsin, but white soldiers pursued and needlessly slaughtered most of them.

The most forceful champion of removal was Andrew Jackson, whom the Indians called Sharp Knife. In their view, Jackson was an incorrigible Indian hater. In his frontier years he had waged war against the tribes in the South — the Cherokees,

Choctaws, Chicasaws, Creeks, and Seminoles, known as the "Five Civilized Tribes," because most had well-devoped agricultural societies. These tribes were still clinging to their tribal lands when Jackson took office. At once, he announced that the tribes must be sent away to "an ample district west of the Mississippi," and Congress responded with the Indian Removal Act, which embodied his recommendations. Under Jackson's orders, federal officials set about "negotiating" treaties with the southern tribes, with the implication that military force would be used if they did not consent to expulsion. In a subsequent act, passed in 1830, Congress guaranteed that all of the United States west of the Mississippi "and not within the states of Missouri and Louisiana or the Territory of Arkansas" would constitute "a permanent Indian frontier."

But settlers moved into Indian country before Washington could put the law into effect. So United States policymakers were obliged to shift the "permanent Indian frontier" from the Mississippi to the 95th meridian, again promising that everything west of this imaginary line would belong to the Indians "for as long as trees grow and water flows." In the late 1830s, United States soldiers rounded up the Cherokees in Georgia and herded them west into Indian country in what ranks among the saddest episodes in the sordid story of white-Indian relations in this country. Nor were the Cherokees the only Indians who were expelled. The other "civilized tribes" also suffered on the Trails of Tears to the new Indian Territory. What happened to the Cherokees is the subject of the next selection, written with sensitivity and insight by Dee Brown, a prolific historian of the West and of Native Americans.

In selection 17, Robert Remini defends Jackson's Indian policy, contending that the Five Civilized Tribes would have been exterminated had he not removed them. Remini is probably right. By this time, as Brown has said elsewhere, the Wampanoag of Massasoit "had vanished, along with the Chesapeakes, the Chicahominys, and the Potomacs of the great Powhatan confederacy. (Only Pocahontas was remembered.) Scattered or reduced to remnants were the Pequots, Montauks, Nanticokes, Madchapungas, Catawbas, Cheraws, Miamis, Hurons, Eries, Mohawks, Senecas, and Mohegans. . . . Their musical names have remained forever fixed on the American land, but their bones are forgotten in a thousand burned villages or lost in forests fast disappearing before the axes of twenty million invaders."

GLOSSARY

BOUDINOT, ELIAS Coleader of a Cherokee delegation that agreed to resettlement in the West, he had established the Cherokees' first tribal newspaper, the *Cherokee Phoenix*.

CROCKETT, DAVY Member of Congress from Tennessee who sympathized with the Cherokees' plight and damned the "cruel, unjust" way they were treated.

RIDGE, MAJOR Coleader of a Cherokee delegation that agreed to resettlement in the West.

ROSS, JOHN Cherokee leader who tried to save the Cherokee nation in Georgia; he protested to the federal government when the state of Georgia annexed all Cherokee lands within its borders.

SCOTT, WINFIELD Commander of the army forces that rounded up the Cherokees and herded them to present-day Oklahoma.

TSALI Aging Smoky Mountain Cherokee who resisted removal by force; Scott had him, his brother, and two of his sons executed by a firing squad.

UTSALA Chief of the Cherokees who avoided removal by hiding in the Smoky Mountains.

In the spring of 1838, Brigadier General Winfield Scott with a regiment of artillery, a regiment of infantry, and six companies of dragoons marched unopposed into the Cherokee country of northern Georgia. On May 10 at New Echota, the capital of what had been one of the greatest Indian nations in eastern America, Scott issued a proclamation:

The President of the United States sent me with a powerful army to cause you, in obedience to the treaty of 1835, to join that part of your people who are already established in prosperity on the other side of the Mississippi.... The emigration must be commenced in haste.... The full moon of May is already on the wane, and before another shall have passed away every Cherokee man, woman and child ... must be in motion to join their brethren in the west.... My troops already occupy many positions ... and thousands and thousands are approaching from every quarter to render resistance and escape alike hopeless.... Will you then by resistance compel us to resort to arms? Or will you by flight seek to hide yourselves in mountains and forests and thus oblige us to hunt you down? Remember that in pursuit it may be impossible to avoid conflicts. The blood of the white man or the blood of the red man may be spilt, and if spilt, however accidentally, it may be impossible for the discreet and humane among you, or among us, to prevent a general war and carnage.

For more than a century the Cherokees had been ceding their land, thousands of acres by thousands of acres. They had lost all of Kentucky and much of Tennessee, but after the last treaty of 1819 they still had remaining about 35,000 square miles of forested mountains, clean, swift-running rivers, and fine meadows. In this country which lay across parts of Georgia, North Carolina, and Tennessee they culti-

From "The Trail of Tears" by Dee Brown in *American History Illustrated*, June 1972. Reprinted by permission of Cowles Magazines, publisher of *American History Illustrated*.

vated fields, planted orchards, fenced pastures, and built roads, houses, and towns. Sequoya had invented a syllabary for the Cherokee language so that thousands of his tribesmen quickly learned to read and write. The Cherokees had adopted the white man's way — his clothing, his constitutional form of government, even his religion. But it had all been for nothing. Now these men who had come across the great ocean many years ago wanted all of the Cherokees' land. In exchange for their 35,000 square miles the tribe was to receive five million dollars and another tract of land somewhere in the wilderness beyond the Mississippi River.

This was a crushing blow to a proud people. "They are extremely proud, despising the lower class of Europeans," said Henry Timberlake, who visited them before the Revolutionary War. William Bartram, the botanist, said the Cherokees were not only a handsome people, tall, graceful, and olive-skinned, but "their countenance and actions exhibit an air of magnanimity, superiority and independence."

Ever since the signing of the treaties of 1819, Major General Andrew Jackson, a man they once believed to be their friend, had been urging Cherokees to move beyond the Mississippi. Indians and white settlers, Jackson told them, could never get along together. Even if the government wanted to protect the Cherokees from harassment, he added, it would be unable to do so. "If you cannot protect us in Georgia," a chief retorted, "how can you protect us from similar evils in the West?"

During the period of polite urging, a few hundred Cherokee families did move west, but the tribe remained united and refused to give up any more territory. In fact, the council leaders passed a law forbidding any chief to sell or trade a single acre of Cherokee land on penalty of death.

In 1828, when Andrew Jackson was running for President, he knew that in order to win he must sweep the frontier states. Free land for the land-hungry settlers became Jackson's major policy. He hammered away at this theme especially hard in Georgia, where waves of settlers from the coastal low-lands were pushing into the highly desirable Cherokee country. He promised the Georgians that if they would help elect him President, he would lend his support to opening up the Cherokee lands for settlement. The Cherokees, of course, were not citizens and could not vote in opposition. To the Cherokees and their friends who protested this promise, Jackson justified his position by saying that the Cherokees had fought on the side of the British during the Revolutionary War. He conveniently forgot that the Cherokees had been his allies during the desperate War of 1812, and had saved the day for him in his decisive victory over the British-backed Creeks at Horseshoe Bend. (One of the Cherokee chiefs who aided Jackson was Junaluska. Said he afterward: "If I had known that Jackson would drive us from our homes I would have killed him that day at the Horseshoe.")

Three weeks after Jackson was elected President, the Georgia legislature passed a law annexing all the Cherokee country within that state's borders. As most of the Cherokee land was in Georgia and three-fourths of the tribe lived there, this meant an end to their independence as a nation. The Georgia legislature also abolished all Cherokee laws and customs and sent surveyors to map out land lots of 160 acres each. The 160-acre lots were to be distributed to white citizens of Georgia through public lotteries.

To add to the pressures on the Cherokees, gold was discovered near Dahlonega in the heart of their country. For many years the Cherokees had concealed the gold deposits, but now the secret was out and a rabble of gold-hungry prospectors descended upon them.

John Ross, the Cherokees' leader, hurried to Washington to protest the Georgia legislature's actions and to plead for justice. In that year Ross was 38 years old; he was well-educated and had been active in Cherokee government matters since he was 19. He was adjutant of the Cherokee regiment that served with Jackson at Horseshoe Bend. His father had been one of a group of Scottish emigrants who settled near the Cherokees and married into the tribe.

In Washington, Ross found sympathizers in Congress, but most of them were anti-Jackson men and the Cherokee case was thus drawn into the whirlpool of politics. When Ross called upon Andrew Jackson to request his aid, the President bluntly told him that "no protection could be afforded the Cherokees" unless they were willing to move west of the Mississippi.

While Ross was vainly seeking help in Washington, alarming messages reached him from Georgia. White citizens of that state were claiming the homes of Cherokees through the land lottery, seizing some of them by force. Joseph Vann, a hard-working half-breed, had carved out an 800-acre plantation at Spring Place and built a fine brick house for his residence. Two men arrived to claim it, dueled for it, and the winner drove Vann and his family into the hills. When John Ross rushed home he found that the same thing had happened to his family. A lottery claimant was living in his beautiful home on the Coosa River, and Ross had to turn north toward Tennessee to find his fleeing wife and children.

During all this turmoil, President Jackson and the governor of Georgia pressed the Cherokee leaders hard in attempts to persuade them to cede all their territory and move to the West. But the chiefs stood firm. Somehow they managed to hold the tribe together, and helped dispossessed families find new homes back in the wilderness areas. John Ross and his family lived in a one-room log cabin across the Tennessee line.

In 1834, the chiefs appealed to Congress with a memorial in which they stated that they would never voluntarily abandon their homeland, but proposed a compromise in which they agreed to cede the state of Georgia a part of their territory provided that they would be protected from invasion in the remainder. Furthermore, at the end of a definite period of years to be fixed by the United States they would be willing to become citizens of the various states in which they resided.

"Cupidity has fastened its eye upon our lands and our homes," they said, "and is seeking by force and by every variety of oppression and wrong to expel us from our lands and our homes and to tear from us all that has become endeared to us. In our distress we have appealed to the judiciary of the United States, where our rights have been solemnly established. We have appealed to the Executive of the United States to protect those rights according to the obligation of treaties and the injunctions of the laws. But this appeal to the Executive has been made in vain."

This new petition to Congress was no more effectual than their appeals to President Jackson. Again they were told that their difficulties could be remedied only by their removal to the west of the Mississippi.

For the first time now, a serious split occurred among the Cherokees. A small group of subchiefs decided that further resistance to the demands of the Georgia and United States governments was futile. It would be better, they believed, to exchange their land and go west rather than risk bloodshed and the possible loss of everything. Leaders of this group were Major Ridge and Elias Boudinot. Ridge had adopted his first name after Andrew Jackson gave him that rank during the War of 1812. Boudinot was Ridge's nephew. Originally known as Buck Watie, he had taken the name of a New England philanthropist who sent him through a mission school in Connecticut. Stand Watie, who later became a Confederate general, was his brother. Upon Boudinot's return from school to Georgia he founded the first tribal newspaper, the *Cherokee Phoenix,* in 1827, but during the turbulence following the Georgia land lotteries he was forced to suspend publication.

And so in February 1835 when John Ross journeyed to Washington to resume his campaign to save the Cherokee nation, a rival delegation headed by Ridge and Boudinot arrived there to seek terms for removal to the West. The pro-removal forces in the government leaped at this opportunity to bypass Ross's authority, and within a few days drafted a preliminary treaty for the Ridge delegation. It was then announced that a council would be held later in the year at New Echota, Georgia, for the purpose of negotiating and agreeing upon final terms.

During the months that followed, bitterness increased between the two Cherokee factions. Ridge's group was a very small minority, but they had the full weight of the United States government behind them, and threats and inducements were used to force a full attendance at the council which was set for December 22, 1835. Handbills were printed in Cherokee and distributed throughout the nation, informing the Indians that those who did not attend would be counted as assenting to any treaty that might be made.

During the seven days which followed the opening of the treaty council, fewer than five hundred Cherokees, or about 2 percent of the tribe, came to New Echota to participate in the discussions. Most of the other Cherokees were busy endorsing a petition to be sent to Congress stating their opposition to the treaty. But on December 29, Ridge, Boudinot and their followers signed away all the lands of the great Cherokee nation. Ironically, thirty years earlier Major Ridge had personally executed a Cherokee chief named Doublehead for committing one of the few capital crimes of the tribe. That crime was the signing of a treaty which gave away Cherokee lands.

Charges of bribery by the Ross forces were denied by government officials, but some years afterward it was discovered that the Secretary of War had sent secret agents into the Cherokee country with authority to expend money to bribe chiefs to support the treaty of cession and removal. And certainly the treaty signers were handsomely rewarded. In an era

when a dollar would buy many times its worth today, Major Ridge was paid $30,000 and his followers received several thousand dollars each. Ostensibly they were being paid for their improved farmlands, but the amounts were far in excess of contemporary land values.

John Ross meanwhile completed gathering signatures of Cherokees who were opposed to the treaty. Early in the following spring, 1836, he took the petition to Washington. More than three-fourths of the tribe, 15,964, had signed in protest against the treaty.

When the governor of Georgia was informed of the overwhelming vote against the treaty, he replied: "Nineteen-twentieths of the Cherokees are too ignorant and depraved to entitle their opinions to any weight or consideration in such matters."

The Cherokees, however, did have friends in Congress. Representative Davy Crockett of Tennessee denounced the treatment of the Cherokees as unjust, dishonest, and cruel. He admitted that he represented a body of frontier constituents who would like to have the Cherokee lands opened for settlement, and he doubted if a single one of them would second what he was saying. Even though his support of the Cherokees might remove him from public life, he added, he could not do otherwise except at the expense of his honor and conscience. Daniel Webster, Henry Clay, Edward Everett, and other great orators of the Congress also spoke for the Cherokees.

When the treaty came to a final decision in the Senate, it passed by only one vote. On May 23, 1836, President Jackson signed the document. According to its terms, the Cherokees were allowed two years from that day in which to leave their homeland forever.

The few Cherokees who had favored the treaty now began making their final preparations for departure. About three hundred left during that year and then early in 1837 Major Ridge and 465 followers departed by boats for the new land in the West.

About 17,000 others, ignoring the treaty, remained steadfast in their homeland with John Ross.

For a while it seemed that Ross might win his long fight, that perhaps the treaty might be declared void. After the Secretary of War, acting under instructions from President Jackson, sent Major William M. Davis to the Cherokee country to expedite removal to the West, Davis submitted a frank report: "That paper called a treaty is no treaty at all," he wrote, "because it is not sanctioned by the great body of the Cherokees and was made without their participation or assent.... The Cherokees are a peaceable, harmless people, but you may drive them to desperation, and this treaty cannot be carried into effect except by the strong arm of force."

In September 1836, Brigadier General Dunlap, who had been sent with a brigade of Tennessee volunteers to force the removal, indignantly disbanded his troops after making a strong speech in favor of the Indians: "I would never dishonor the Tennessee arms in a servile service by aiding to carry into execution at the point of the bayonet a treaty made by a lean minority against the will and authority of the Cherokee people."

Even Inspector General John E. Wool, commanding United States troops in the area, was impressed by the united Cherokee resistance, and warned the Secretary of War not to send any civilians who had any part in the making of the treaty back into the Cherokee country. During the summer of 1837, the Secretary of War sent a confidential agent, John Mason, Jr., to observe and report. "Opposition to the treaty is unanimous and irreconcilable," Mason wrote. "They say it cannot bind them because they did not make it; that it was made by a few unauthorized individuals; that the nation is not party to it."

The inexorable machinery of government was already in motion, however, and when the expiration date of the waiting period, May 23, 1838, came near, Winfield Scott was ordered in with his army to force compliance. As already stated, Scott issued his proclamation on May 10. His soldiers were already building thirteen stockaded forts — six in North Carolina, five in Georgia, one in Tennessee, and one in Alabama. At these points the Cherokees would be concentrated to await transportation to the West. Scott then ordered the roundup started, instructing his officers not to fire on the Cherokees except in case of resistance. "If we get possession of the women and children first," he said, "or first capture the men, the other members of the same family will readily come in."

James Mooney, an ethnologist who afterwards talked with Cherokees who endured this ordeal, said that squads of troops moved into the forested mountains to search out every small cabin and make prisoners of all the occupants however or wherever they might be found. "Families at dinner were startled by the sudden gleam of bayonets in the doorway and rose up to be driven with blows and oaths along the weary miles of trail that led to the stockades. Men were seized in their fields or going along the road, women were taken from their spinning wheels and children from their play. In many cases, on turning for one last look as they crossed a ridge, they saw their homes in flames, fired by the lawless rabble that followed on the heels of the soldiers to loot and pillage. So keen were these outlaws on the scent that in some instances they were driving off the cattle and other stock of the Indians almost before the soldiers had fairly started their owners in the other direction."

Long afterward one of the Georgia militiamen who participated in the roundup said: "I fought through the Civil War and have seen men shot to pieces and slaughtered by thousands, but the Cherokee removal was the cruelest work I ever knew."

Knowing that resistance was futile, most of the Cherokees surrendered quietly. Within a month, thousands were enclosed in the stockades. On June 6 at Ross's Landing near the site of present-day Chattanooga, the first of many departures began. Eight hundred Cherokees were forcibly crowded onto a flotilla of six flatboats lashed to the side of a steamboat. After surviving a passage over rough rapids which smashed the sides of the flatboats, they landed at Decatur, Alabama, boarded a railroad train (which was a new and terrifying experience for most of them), and after reaching Tuscumbia were crowded upon a Tennessee River steamboat again.

Throughout June and July similar shipments of several hundred Cherokees were transported by this long water route — north on the Tennessee River to the Ohio and then down the Mississippi and up the Arkansas to their new homeland. A few managed to escape and make their way back to the Cherokee country, but most of them were eventually recaptured. Along the route of travel of this forced migration, the summer was hot and dry. Drinking water and food were often contaminated. First the young children would die, then the older people, and sometimes as many as half the adults were stricken with dysentery and other ailments. On each boat deaths ran as high as five per day. On one of the first boats to reach Little Rock, Arkansas, at least a hundred had died. A compassionate lieutenant who was with the military escort recorded in his diary for August 1: "My blood chills as I write at the remembrance of the scenes I have gone through."

When John Ross and other Cherokee leaders back in the concentration camps learned of the high mortality among those who had gone ahead, they petitioned General Scott to postpone further departures until autumn. Although only three thousand Cherokees had been removed, Scott agreed to wait until the summer drought was broken, or no later than October. The Cherokees in turn agreed to organize and manage the migration themselves. After a lengthy council, they asked and received permission to travel overland in wagons, hoping that by camping along the way they would not suffer as many deaths as occurred among those who had gone on the river boats.

During this waiting period, Scott's soldiers continued their searches for more than a thousand Cherokees known to be still hiding out in the deep wilderness of the Great Smoky Mountains. These Cherokees had organized themselves under the leadership of a chief named Utsala, and had developed warning systems to prevent captures by the bands of soldiers. Occasionally, however, some of the fugitives were caught and herded back to the nearest stockade.

One of the fugitive families was that of Tsali, an aging Cherokee. With his wife, his brother, three sons and their families, Tsali had built a hideout somewhere on the border between North Carolina and Tennessee. Soldiers surrounded their shelters one day, and the Cherokees surrendered without resistance. As they were being taken back toward Fort Cass (Calhoun, Tennessee) a soldier prodded Tsali's wife sharply with a bayonet, ordering her to walk faster. Angered by the brutality, Tsali grappled with the soldier, tore away his rifle, and bayoneted him to the ground. At the same time, Tsali's brother leaped upon another soldier and bayoneted him. Before the remainder of the military detachment could act, the Cherokees fled, vanishing back into the Smokies where they sought refuge with Chief Utsala. Both bayoneted soldiers died.

Upon learning of the incident, Scott immediately ordered that Tsali must be brought in and punished. Because some of his regiments were being transferred elsewhere for other duties, however, the general realized that his reduced force might be occupied for months in hunting down and capturing the escaped Cherokee. He would have to use guile to accomplish the capture of Tsali.

Scott therefore dispatched a messenger — a white man who had been adopted as a child by the Cherokees — to find Chief Utsala. The messenger was instructed to inform Utsala that if he would surrender Tsali to General Scott, the Army would withdraw from the Smokies and leave the remaining fugitives alone.

Trail of Tears, *an oil painting by Robert Lindneux. The first group of Cherokee started on their journey west on October 1, 1838. When all the groups had reached the new Indian Territory, as Dee Brown indicates, "the Cherokees had lost about four thousand by deaths — or one out of every four members of the tribe — most of the deaths brought about as the direct result of the enforced removal." (Woolaroc Museum, Bartlesville, Oklahoma)*

When Chief Utsala received the message, he was suspicious of Scott's sincerity, but he considered the general's offer as an opportunity to gain time. Perhaps with the passage of time, the few Cherokees remaining in the Smokies might be forgotten and left alone forever. Utsala put the proposition to Tsali: If he went in and surrendered, he would probably be put to death, but his death might insure the freedom of a thousand fugitive Cherokees.

Tsali did not hesitate. He announced that he would go and surrender to General Scott. To make certain that he was treated well, several members of Tsali's band went with him.

When the Cherokees reached Scott's headquarters, the general ordered Tsali, his brother, and three sons arrested, and then condemned them all to be shot to death. To impress upon the tribe their utter helplessness before the might of the government, Scott selected the firing squad from Cherokee prisoners in one of the stockades. At the last moment, the general spared Tsali's youngest son because he was only a child.

(By this sacrifice, however, Tsali and his family gave the Smoky Mountain Cherokees a chance at survival in their homeland. Time was on their side, as Chief Utsala had hoped, and that is why today there is a small Cherokee reservation on the North Carolina slope of the Great Smoky Mountains.)

With the ending of the drought of 1838, John Ross and the 13,000 stockaded Cherokees began preparing for their long overland journey to the West. They assembled several hundred wagons, filled them with blankets, cooking pots, their old people and small children, and moved out in separate contingents along a trail that followed the Hiwassee River. The first party of 1,103 started on October 1.

"At noon all was in readiness for moving," said an observer of the departure. "The teams were stretched out in a line along the road through a heavy forest, groups of persons formed about each wagon. The day was bright and beautiful, but a gloomy thoughtfulness was depicted in the lineaments of every face. In all the bustle of preparation there was a silence and stillness of the voice that betrayed the sadness of the heart. At length the word was given to move on. Going Snake, an aged and respected chief whose head eighty summers had whitened, mounted on his favorite pony and led the way in silence, followed by a number of younger men on horseback. At this very moment a low sound of distant thunder fell upon my ear ... a voice of divine indignation for the wrong of my poor and unhappy countrymen, driven by brutal power from all they loved and cherished in the land of their fathers to gratify the cravings of avarice. The sun was unclouded — no rain fell — the thunder rolled away and seemed hushed in the distance."

Throughout October, eleven wagon trains departed and then on November 4, the last Cherokee exiles moved out for the West. The overland route for these endless lines of wagons, horsemen, and people on foot ran from the mouth of the Hiwassee in Tennessee across the Cumberland plateau to McMinnville and then north to Nashville where they crossed the Cumberland River. From there they followed an old trail to Hopkinsville, Kentucky, and continued northwestward to the Ohio River, crossing into southern Illinois near the mouth of the Cumberland. Moving straight westward they passed through Jonesboro and crossed the Mississippi at Cape Girardeau, Missouri. Some of the first parties turned southward through Arkansas; the later ones continued westward through Springfield, Missouri, and on to Indian Territory.

A New Englander traveling eastward across Kentucky in November and December met several contingents, each a day apart from the others. "Many of the aged Indians were suffering extremely from the fatigue of the journey," he said, "and several were quite ill. Even aged females, apparently nearly ready to drop into the grave, were traveling with heavy burdens attached to their backs — on the sometimes frozen ground and sometimes muddy streets, with no covering for the feet except what nature had given them. ... We learned from the inhabitants on the road where the Indians passed, that they buried fourteen or fifteen at every stopping place, and they make a journey of ten miles per day only on an average. They will not travel on the Sabbath ... they must stop, and not merely stop — they must worship the Great Spirit, too; for they had divine service on the Sabbath — a camp meeting in truth."

Autumn rains softened the roads, and the hundreds of wagons and horses cut them into molasses, slowing movement to a crawl. To add to their difficulties, tollgate operators overcharged them for passage. Their horses were stolen or seized on pretext of unpaid debts, and they had no recourse to the law. With the coming of cold damp weather, measles and whooping cough became epidemic. Supplies had to be dumped to make room for the sick in the jolting wagons.

By the time the last detachments reached the Mississippi at Cape Girardeau it was January, with the river running full of ice so that several thousand had to wait on the east bank almost a month before the channel cleared. James Mooney, who later

301

heard the story from survivors, said that "the lapse of over half a century had not sufficed to wipe out the memory of the miseries of that halt beside the frozen river, with hundreds of sick and dying penned up in wagons or stretched upon the ground, with only a blanket overhead to keep out the January blast."

Meanwhile the parties that had left early in October were beginning to reach Indian Territory. (The first arrived on January 4, 1839.) Each group had lost from thirty to forty members by death. The later detachments suffered much heavier losses, especially toward the end of their journey. Among the victims was the wife of John Ross.

Not until March 1839 did the last of the Cherokees reach their new home in the West. Counts were made of the survivors and balanced against the counts made at the beginning of the removal. As well as could be estimated, the Cherokees had lost about four thousand by deaths — or one out of every four members of the tribe — most of the deaths brought about as the direct result of the enforced removal. From that day to this the Cherokees remember it as "the trail where they cried," or the Trail of Tears.

QUESTIONS TO CONSIDER

1   Discuss Andrew Jackson's position on the Cherokees. Did he accurately reflect white attitudes toward and assumptions about the Indians?

2   How did factionalism within the Cherokee nation help the state of Georgia and the federal government to carry out their policy of Indian removal?

3   On December 29, 1835, a Cherokee treaty council signed away the Cherokees' tribal lands and agreed to the tribe's being moved west of the Mississippi. What methods did the United States government use to obtain this treaty? Discuss the paradox of how a nation such as the United States, founded on democratic principles of government, could justify signing such a fraudulent treaty.

4   The framers of the Constitution were men of property who also held republican ideals (see selection 9). The Boston Associates, who founded Lowell, Massachusetts, were also wealthy men who tried and ultimately failed to combine benevolent and material ideas (see selection 19). How does the experience of Indian removal also illustrate America's conflict between benevolence and greed, idealism and pragmatism?

22

Women and Their Families on the Overland Trails

JOHNNY FARAGHER
AND CHRISTINE STANSELL

After the War of 1812, America turned away from Old World entanglements and sought to extend its "natural sphere of influence" westward. Pioneers moved in sporadic waves out to the Mississippi River and beyond. Jefferson had made this westward movement possible by purchasing the vast Louisiana Territory from France in 1803. He had also begun American dreams of a transcontinental empire when he sent Lewis and Clark out to the Pacific and back. In the next two decades, Americans occupied the fertile Mississippi Valley, creating the new states of Louisiana, Indiana, Mississippi, Illinois, Alabama, and Missouri. At the same time, army explorers and scientists undertook expeditions up the Arkansas and Missouri Rivers, finding that the complex river systems offered tremendous possibilities for commerce and trade. In the Adams-Onís Treaty of 1819, Spain gave the United States its claims to the Oregon country, an expansive region lying north of the Red and Arkansas Rivers and the 42nd parallel. After Mexico revolted against Spain in 1822, the Mexican Republic also ratified the Adams-Onís Treaty, thus clearing the way for an American march to the Pacific.

American fur companies, operating out of St. Louis and Independence, Missouri, had already sent trappers and traders out into the awesome Rocky Mountains. These fabled mountain men blazed trails and explored rich mountain valleys across the Oregon country, reporting back that the region was excellent for settlement. In the 1830s and 1840s, Americans from the fringes of the South and the old northwestern states headed across the trails the mountain men had blazed, establishing American outposts in Oregon and California. Meanwhile, other settlers — most of them from the Border South — migrated into Mexican-held Texas, where they eventually revolted and set up an independent republic.

In the 1840s — an era of unprecedented westward expansion — the United States virtually doubled its territory. It annexed the Republic of Texas, drove the British out of Oregon with threats of violence, and acquired California and the rest of the Southwest in a highly controversial war with Mexico.

The "glacial inexorability" of this westward sweep, as historian T. H. Watkins phrased it, gave birth to a faith called Manifest Destiny, a belief that Americans had a natural, God-given right to expand their superior institutions and way of life across the continent. And woe indeed to anybody — British, Mexican, or Indian — who stood in the way. To clear the way for Anglo-American settlement, the government rescinded the "permanent" frontier it had granted the Indians west of the 95th meridian and in the 1850s adopted a policy of concentration, which forced them into specified areas in various parts of the West. To justify their broken promises and treaties, white Americans contended that they were the dominant race and so were responsible for the Indians — "along with their lands, their forests, and their mineral wealth." God wished the white men to have all the lands of the West, because they knew how to use the soil and the pagan Indians did not.

Still, as historian Bernard De Voto has reminded us, other energies besides Manifest Destiny thrust America westward. Some southerners, for example, desired the empty lands for southern expansion, in order to maintain an equilibrium of power in Washington between slave and free states. Both southern and northern interests sought to control the Middle West for political and economic gain; and American industrial interests exhibited a "blind drive" to establish ports on the West Coast, thereby opening the Pacific Ocean and distant Asia to United States commercial expansion. There was another story in America's inexorable westward march — the story of the people who made the grueling trek across the overland trails to start new lives. The pioneers — men and women alike — are stock figures in frontier mythology. What were they really like? In their discussion of the conditions of life for women and their families on the Oregon and California Trails, Johnny Faragher and Christine Stansell draw on contemporary diaries and letters to take us beyond the stereotypes. In the process, they raise some provocative questions. Did members of a westering family share the same attitudes? Was the women's experience different from the men's? Did the overland emigration alter eastern conventions about family structure and "proper" women's roles? In answering such questions, the authors paint a vivid and realistic portrait of daily life, family roles, work tasks, cultural expectations, and women's ties with one another as the wagons headed toward the Pacific.

GLOSSARY

BEECHER, CATHARINE   A leading advocate of separate spheres of responsibility for men and women.

"CULT OF TRUE WOMANHOOD"   Argued that the true place for the American woman was her home, where she enjoyed "real autonomy and control" in child rearing, household economy, and the moral and religious life of the family.

SEXUAL SPHERES   The doctrine in Jacksonian America that justified segregating women in the home and men in politics and wage earning.

From 1841 until 1867, the year in which the transcontinental railroad was completed, nearly 350,000 North Americans emigrated to the Pacific coast along the western wagon road known variously as the Oregon, the California, or simply the Overland Trail. This migration was essentially a family phenomenon. Although single men constituted the majority of the party which pioneered large-scale emigration on the Overland Trail in 1841, significant numbers of women and children were already present in the wagon trains of the next season. Families made up the preponderant proportion of the migrations throughout the 1840s. In 1849, during the overwhelmingly male Gold Rush, the number dropped precipitously, but after 1851 families once again assumed dominance in the overland migration. The contention that "the family was the one substantial social institution" on the frontier is too sweeping, yet it is undeniable that the white family largely mediated the incorporation of the western territories into the American nation.

The emigrating families were a heterogeneous lot. Some came from farms in the midwest and upper South, many from small midwestern towns, and others from northeastern and midwestern cities. Clerks and shopkeepers as well as farmers outfitted their wagons in Independence, St. Louis, or Westport Landing on the Missouri. Since costs for supplies, travel, and settlement were not negligible, few of the very poor were present, nor were the exceptionally prosperous. The dreams of fortune which lured the wagon trains into new lands were those of modest men whose hopes were pinned to small farms or larger dry-goods stores, more fertile soil or more

This article is reprinted from *Feminist Studies,* Volume 2, Number 2/3 (1975): 150–166 by permission of the publisher, Feminist Studies, Inc., c/o Women's Studies Program, University of Maryland, College Park, MD 20742.

customers, better market prospects and a steadily expanding economy.

For every member of the family, the trip West was exhausting, toilsome, and often grueling. Each year in late spring, westbound emigrants gathered for the journey at spots along the Missouri River and moved out in parties of ten to several hundred wagons. Aggregates of nuclear families, loosely attached by kinship or friendship, traveled together or joined an even larger caravan. Coast-bound families traveled by ox-drawn wagons at the frustratingly slow pace of fifteen to twenty miles per day. They worked their way up the Platte River valley through what is now Kansas and Nebraska, crossing the Rockies at South Pass in southwestern Wyoming by mid-summer. The Platte route was relatively easy going, but from present-day Idaho, where the roads to California and Oregon diverged, to their final destinations, the pioneers faced disastrous conditions: scorching deserts, boggy salt flats, and rugged mountains. By this time, families had been on the road some three months and were only at the midpoint of the journey; the environment, along with the wear of the road, made the last months difficult almost beyond endurance. Finally, in late fall or early winter the pioneers straggled into their promised lands, after six months and over two thousand miles of hardship.

As this journey progressed, bare necessity became the determinant of most of each day's activities. The primary task of surviving and getting to the coast gradually suspended accustomed patterns of dividing work between women and men. All able-bodied adults worked all day in one way or another to keep the family moving. Women's work was no less indispensable than men's; indeed, as the summer wore on, the boundaries dividing the work of the sexes were threatened, blurred, and transgressed.

The vicissitudes of the trail opened new possibilities for expanded work roles for women, and in the cooperative work of the family there existed a basis for a vigorous struggle for female-male equality. But most women did not see the experience in this way. They viewed it as a male enterprise from its very inception. Women experienced the breakdown of the sexual division of labor as a dissolution of their own autonomous "sphere." Bereft of the footing which this independent base gave them, they lacked a cultural rationale for the work they did, and remained estranged from the possibilities of the enlarged scope and power of family life on the trail. Instead, women fought *against* the forces of necessity to hold together the few fragments of female subculture left to them. We have been bequeathed a remarkable record of this struggle in the diaries, journals, and memoirs of emigrating women. In this study, we will examine a particular habit of living, or culture, in conflict with the new material circumstances of the Trail, and the efforts of women to maintain a place, a sphere of their own.

The overland family was not a homogeneous unit, its members imbued with identical aspirations and desires. On the contrary, the period of westward movement was also one of multiplying schisms within those families whose location and social status placed them in the mainstream of national culture. Child-rearing tracts, housekeeping manuals, and etiquette books by the hundreds prescribed and rationalized to these Americans a radical separation of the work responsibilities and social duties of mothers and fathers; popular thought assigned unique personality traits, spiritual capacities, and forms of experience to the respective categories of man, woman, and child. In many families, the tensions inherent in this separatist ideology, often repressed in the everyday routines of the East, erupted under the strain of the overland crossing. The difficulties of the emigrants, while inextricably linked to the duress of the journey itself, also revealed family dynamics which had been submerged in the less eventful life "back home."

A full-blown ideology of "woman's place" was absent in preindustrial America. On farms, in artisan shops, and in town market-places, women and children made essential contributions to family income and subsistence; it was the family which functioned as the basic unit of production in the colony and the young nation. As commercial exchanges displaced the local markets where women had sold surplus dairy products and textiles, and the workplace drifted away from the household, women and children lost their bread-winning prerogatives.

In Jacksonian America, a doctrine of "sexual spheres" arose to facilitate and justify the segregation of women into the home and men into productive work. While the latter attended to politics, economics, and wage-earning, popular thought assigned women the refurbished and newly professionalized tasks of child-rearing and housekeeping. A host of corollaries followed on the heels of these shifts. Men were physically strong, women naturally delicate; men were skilled in practical matters, women in moral and emotional concerns; men were prone to corruption, women to virtue; men belonged in the world, women in the home. For women, the system of sexual spheres represented a decline in social status and isolation from political and economic power. Yet it also provided them with a psychological power base of undeniable importance. The "cult of true womanhood" was more than simply a retreat. Catharine Beecher, one of the chief theorists of "woman's influence," proudly quoted Tocqueville's observation that "in no country has such constant care been taken, as in America, to trace two clearly distinct lines of action for the two sexes, and to make them keep pace with the other, but in two pathways which are always different." Neither Beecher nor her sisters were simply dupes of a masculine imperialism. The supervision of child-rearing, household economy, and the moral and religious life of the family granted women a certain degree of real autonomy and control over their lives as well as those of their husbands and children. . . .

At its very inception, the western emigration sent tremors through the foundations of this carefully compartmentalized family structure. The rationale behind pulling up stakes was nearly always economic advancement; since breadwinning was a masculine concern, the husband and father introduced the idea of going West and made the final decision. Family participation in the intervening time ran the gamut from enthusiastic support to stolid resistance. Many women cooperated with their ambitious spouses: "The motive that induced us to part with pleasant associations and the dear friends of our childhood days, was to obtain from the government of the United States a grant of land that 'Uncle Sam' had promised to give to the head of each family who settled in this new country." Others, however, only acquiesced. "Poor Ma said only this morning, 'Oh, I wish we never had started,'" Lucy Cooke wrote her first day on the trail, "and she looks so sorrowful and dejected. I think if Pa had not passengers to take through she would urge him to return; not that he should be so inclined." Huddled with her children in a cold, damp wagon, trying to calm them despite the ominous chanting of visiting Indians, another woman wondered "what had possessed my husband, anyway, that he should have thought of bringing us away out through this God forsaken country." Similar alienation from the "pioneer spirit" haunted Lavinia Porter's leave-taking:

I never recall that sad parting from my dear sister on the plains of Kansas without the tears flowing fast and free. . . . We were the eldest of a large family, and the bond of affection and love that existed between us was strong indeed . . . as she with the other friends turned to leave me for the ferry which was to take them back to home and civilization, I stood alone on that wild prairie. Looking westward I saw my husband driving slowly over the plain; turning my face once more to the east, my dear sister's footsteps were fast widening the distance between us. For the time I knew not which way to go, nor whom to follow. But in a few moments I rallied my forces . . . and soon overtook the slowly moving oxen who were bearing my husband

and child over the green prairie ... the unbidden tears would flow in spite of my brave resolve to be the courageous and valiant frontierswoman.

Her dazed vacillation soon gave way to a private conviction that the family had made a dire mistake: "I would make a brave effort to be cheerful and patient until the camp work was done. Then starting out ahead of the team and my men folks, when I thought I had gone beyond hearing distance, I would throw myself down on the unfriendly desert and give way like a child to sobs and tears, wishing myself back home with my friends and chiding myself for consenting to take this wild goose chase." Men viewed drudgery, calamity, and privation as trials along the road to prosperity, unfortunate but inevitable corollaries of the rational decision they had made. But to those women who were unable to appropriate the vision of the upwardly mobile pilgrimage, hardship and the loss only testified to the inherent folly of the emigration, "this wild goose chase."

If women were reluctant to accompany their men, however, they were often equally unwilling to let them go alone. In the late 1840s, the conflict between wives and their gold-crazed husbands reveals the determination with which women enforced the cohesion of the nuclear family. In the name of family unity, some obdurate wives simply chose to block-bust the sexually segregated Gold Rush: "My husband grew enthusiastic and wanted to start immediately," one woman recalled, "but I would not be left behind. I thought where he could go I could and where I went I could take my two little toddling babies." Her family departed intact. Other women used their moral authority to smash the enterprise in its planning stages. "We were married to live together," a wife acidly reminded her spouse when he informed her of his intention to join the Rush: "I am willing to go with you to any part of *God's Foot Stool* where you think you can do best, and under these circumstances you have no right to go where I cannot, and if you do you need never return for I

A frontier woman and her children stand at the Grand Canyon in Arizona. Drudgery and deprivation, the fragility of children, and the hostile environment were not the only problems facing women on the westward journey. Many bitterly regretted the loss of the homes, companionship, and responsibilities that had been theirs in the East. Surely, as Stansell and Faragher tell us, "Harriet Ward's cry — 'Oh, shall we ever live like civilized beings again?' — reverberated through the thoughts of many of her sisters." (Keystone-Mast Collection, California Museum of Photography, University of California, Riverside)

shall look upon you as dead." Roundly chastised, the man postponed his journey until the next season, when his family could leave with him. When included in the plans, women seldom wrote of their husbands' decisions to emigrate in their diaries or memoirs. A breadwinner who tried to leave alone, however, threatened the family unity upon which his authority was based; only then did a wife challenge his dominance in worldly affairs.

There was an economic reason for the preponderance of families on the Trail. Women and children, but especially women, formed an essential supplementary work force in the settlements. The ideal wife in the West resembled a hired hand more than a nurturant Christian housekeeper. Narcissa Whitman wrote frankly to aspiring settlers of the functional necessity of women on the new farms: "Let every young man bring a wife, for he will want one after he gets here, if he never did before." In a letter from California, another seasoned woman warned a friend in Missouri that in the West women became "hewers of wood and drawers of water everywhere." Mrs. Whitman's fellow missionary Elkanah Walker was unabashedly practical in beseeching his wife to join him: "I am tired of keeping an old bachelor's hall. I want someone to get me a good supper and let me take my ease and when I am very tired in the morning I want someone to get up and get breakfast and let me lay in bed and take my rest." It would be both simplistic and harsh to argue that men brought their families West or married because of the labor power of women and children; there is no doubt, however, that the new Westerners appreciated the advantages of familial labor. Women were not superfluous; they were workers. The migration of women helped to solve the problem of labor scarcity, not only in the early years of the American settlement on the coast, but throughout the history of the continental frontier.

In the first days of the overland trip, new work requirements were not yet pressing and the division of labor among family members still replicated familiar patterns. Esther Hanna reported in one of her first diary entries that "our men have gone to build a bridge across the stream, which is impassable," while she baked her first bread on the prairie. Elizabeth Smith similarly described her party's day: "rainy . . . Men making rafts. Women cooking and washing.

Children crying." When travel was suspended, "the men were generally busy mending wagons, harnesses, yokes, shoeing the animals etc., and the women washed clothes, boiled a big mess of beans, to warm over for several meals, or perhaps mended clothes." At first, even in emergencies, women and men hardly considered integrating their work. "None but those who have cooked for a family of eight, crossing the plains, have any idea of what it takes," a disgruntled woman recalled: "My sister-in-law was sick, my niece was much younger than I, and consequently I had the management of all the cooking and planning on my young shoulders." To ask a man to help was a possibility she was unable even to consider.

The relegation of women to purely domestic duties, however, soon broke down under the vicissitudes of the Trail. Within the first few weeks, the unladylike task of gathering buffalo dung for fuel (little firewood was available en route) became women's work. As one traveler astutely noted, "force of surroundings was a great leveler"; miles of grass, dust, glare, and mud erased some of the most rudimentary distinctions between female and male responsibilities. By summer, women often helped drive the wagons and the livestock. At one Platte crossing, "the men drawed the wagons over by hand and the women all crossed in safety"; but at the next, calamity struck when the bridge collapsed, "and then commenced the hurry and bustle of repairing; all were at work, even the women and children." Such crises, which compounded daily as the wagons moved past the Platte up the long stretches of desert and coastal mountains, generated equity in work; at times of Indian threats, for example, both women and men made bullets and stood guard. When mountain fever struck the Pengra family as they crossed the Rockies, Charlotte relieved her incapacitated husband of the driving while he took care of the youngest child. Only such severe afflictions forced men to take on traditionally female chores. While women did men's work, there is little evidence that men reciprocated.

Following a few days in the life of an overland woman discloses the magnitude of her work. During the hours her party traveled, Charlotte Pengra walked beside the wagons, driving the cattle and gathering buffalo chips. At night she cooked, baked bread for the next noon meal, and washed clothes. Three successive summer days illustrate how trying these small chores could be. Her train pulled out early on a Monday morning, only to be halted by rain and a flash flood; Mrs. Pengra washed and dried her family's wet clothes in the afternoon while doing her daily baking. On Tuesday the wagons pushed hard to make up for lost time, forcing her to trot all day to keep up. In camp that night there was no time to rest. Before going to bed, she wrote, "Kept busy in preparing tea and doing other things preparatory for the morrow. I baked a cracker pudding, warm biscuits and made tea, and after supper stewed two pans of dried apples, and made two loaves of bread, got my work done up, beds made, and child asleep, and have written in my journal. Pretty tired of course." The same routine devoured the next day and evening: "I have done a washing. Stewed apples, made pies and baked a rice pudding, and mended our wagon cover. Rather tired." And the next: "baked biscuits, stewed berries, fried meat, boiled and mashed potatoes, and made tea for supper, afterward baked bread. Thus you see I have not much rest." Children also burdened women's work and leisure. During one quiet time, Helen Stewart retreated in mild defiance from her small charges to a tent in order to salvage some private time: "It is exceeding hot . . . some of the men is out hunting and some of them sleeping. The children is grumbling and crying and laughing and howling and playing all around." Although children are notably absent in women's journals, they do appear, frightened and imploring, during an Indian scare or a storm, or intrude into a rare and precious moment of relaxation, "grumbling and crying."

Because the rhythm of their chores was out of phase with that of the men, the division of labor could be especially taxing to women. Men's days were toilsome but broken up at regular intervals with periods of rest. Men hitched the teams, drove or walked until noon, relaxed at dinner, traveled until the evening camp, unhitched the oxen, ate supper, and in the evening sat at the campfire, mended equipment, or stood guard. They also provided most of the labor in emergencies, pulling the wagons through mires, across treacherous river crossings, up long grades, and down precipitous slopes. In the pandemonium of a steep descent,

you would see the women and children in advance seeking the best way, some of them slipping down, or holding on to the rocks, now taking an "otter slide," and then a run til some natural obstacle presented itself to stop their accelerated progress and those who get down safely without a hurt or a bruise, are fortunate indeed. Looking back to the train, you would see some of the men holding on to the wagons, others slipping under the oxen's feet, some throwing articles out of the way that had fallen out, and all have enough to do to keep them busily occupied.

Women were responsible for staying out of the way and getting themselves and the children to safety, men for getting the wagons down. Women's work, far less demanding of brute strength and endurance, was nevertheless distributed without significant respite over all waking hours: mealtimes offered no leisure to the cooks. "The plain fact of the matter is," a young woman complained,

we *have no time for sociability*. From the time we get up in the morning, until we are on the road, it is hurry scurry to get breakfast and put away the things that necessarily had to be pulled out last night — while under way there is no room in the wagon for a visitor, nooning is barely long enough to eat a cold bite — and at night all the cooking utensils and provisions are to be gotten about the camp fire, and cooking enough to last until the next night.

After supper, the men gathered together, "lolling and smoking their pipes and guessing, or maybe betting, how many miles we had covered during the day," while the women baked, washed, and put the children to bed before they finally sat down. Charlotte Pengra found "as I was told before I started that there is no rest in such a journey."

Unaccustomed tasks beset the travelers, who were equipped with only the familiar expectation that work was divided along gender lines. The solutions which sexual "spheres" offered were usually irrelevant to the new problems facing families. Women, for example, could not afford to be delicate: their new duties demanded far greater stamina and hardiness than their traditional domestic tasks. With no tradition to deal with the new exigencies of fuel-gathering, cattle-driving, and cooking, families found that "the division of labor in a party . . . was a prolific cause of quarrel." Within the Vincent party, "assignments to duty were not accomplished without grumbling and objection . . . there were occasional angry debates while the various burdens were being adjusted," while in "the camps of others who sometimes jogged along the trail in our company . . . we saw not a little fighting . . . and these bloody fisticuffs were invariably the outcome of disputes over division of labor." At home, these assignments were familiar and accepted, not subject to questioning. New work opened the division of labor to debate and conflict.

By midjourney, most women worked at male tasks. The men still retained dominance within their "sphere," despite the fact that it was no longer exclusively masculine. Like most women, Lavinia Porter was responsible for gathering buffalo chips for fuel. One afternoon, spying a grove of cottonwoods half a mile away, she asked her husband to branch off the trail so that the party could fell trees for firewood, thus easing her work. "But men on the plains I had found were not so accommodating, nor so ready to wait upon women as they were in more civilized communities." Her husband refused and

Porter fought back: "I was feeling somewhat under the weather and unusually tired, and crawling into the wagon told them if they wanted fuel for the evening meal they could get it themselves and cook the meal also, and laying my head down on a pillow, I cried myself to sleep." Later that evening her husband awakened her with a belated dinner he had prepared himself, but despite his conciliatory spirit their relations were strained for weeks: "James and I had gradually grown silent and taciturn and had unwittingly partaken of the gloom and somberness of the dreary landscape." No longer a housewife or a domestic ornament, but a laborer in a male arena, Porter was still subordinate to her husband in practical matters.

Lydia Waters recorded another clash between new work and old consciousness: "I had learned to drive an ox team on the Platte and my driving was admired by an officer and his wife who were going with the mail to Salt Lake City." Pleased with the compliment, she later overheard them "laughing at the thought of a woman driving oxen." By no means did censure come only from men. The officer's wife as well as the officer derided Lydia Waters, while her own mother indirectly reprimanded teenaged Mary Ellen Todd. "All along our journey, I had tried to crack that big whip," Mary Ellen remembered years later:

Now while out at the wagon we kept trying until I was fairly successful. How my heart bounded a few days later when I chanced to hear father say to mother, "Do you know that Mary Ellen is beginning to crack the whip." Then how it fell again when mother replied, "I am afraid it isn't a very lady-like thing for a girl to do." After this, while I felt a secret joy in being able to have a power that set things going, there was also a sense of shame over this new accomplishment.

To understand Mrs. Todd's primness, so incongruous in the rugged setting of the Trail, we must see it in the context of a broader struggle on the part of women to preserve the home in transit. Against the leveling forces of the Plains, women tried to maintain the standards of cleanliness and order that had prevailed in their homes back East.

Our caravan had a good many women and children and although we were probably longer on the journey owing to their presence — they exerted a good influence, as the men did not take such risks with Indians . . . were more alert about the care of teams and seldom had accidents; more attention was paid to cleanliness and sanitation and, lastly, but not of less importance, meals were more regular and better cooked thus preventing much sickness and there was less waste of food.

Sarah Royce remembered that family wagons "were easily distinguished by the greater number of conveniences, and household articles they carried." In the evenings, or when the trains stopped for a day, women had a chance to create with few props a flimsy facsimile of the home.

Even in camp women had little leisure time, but within the "hurry scurry" of work they managed to re-create the routine of the home. Indeed, a female subculture, central to the communities women had left behind, reemerged in these settings. At night, women often clustered together, chatting, working, or commiserating, instead of joining the men: "High teas were not popular, but tatting, knitting, crochetting, exchanging recipes for cooking beans or dried apples or swopping food for the sake of variety kept us in practice of feminine occupations and diversions." Besides using the domestic concerns of the Trail to reconstruct a female sphere, women also consciously invoked fantasy: "Mrs. Fox and her daughter are with us and everything is so still and quiet we can almost imagine ourselves at home again. We took out our Daguerreotypes [photographs] and tried to live over again some of the happy days of 'Auld Lang Syne.'" Sisterly contact kept "feminine occupations" from withering away

from disuse: "In the evening the young ladies came over to our house and we had a concert with both guitars. Indeed it seemed almost like a pleasant evening at home. We could none of us realize that we were almost at the summit of the Rocky Mountains." The hostess added with somewhat strained sanguinity that her young daughter seemed "just as happy sitting on the ground playing her guitar as she was at home, although she does not love it as much as her piano." Although a guitar was no substitute for the more refined instrument, it at least kept the girl "in practice with feminine occupations and diversions": unlike Mary Ellen Todd, no big whip would tempt her to unwomanly pleasure in the power to "set things going."

But books, furniture, knick-knacks, china, the daguerreotypes that Mrs. Fox shared, or the guitars of young musicians — the "various articles of ornament and convenience" — were among the first things discarded on the epic trash heap which trailed over the mountains. On long uphill grades and over sandy deserts, the wagons had to be lightened; any materials not essential to survival were fair game for disposal. Such commodities of woman's sphere, although functionally useless, provided women with a psychological lifeline to their abandoned homes and communities, as well as to elements of their identities which the westward journey threatened to mutilate or entirely extinguish. Losing homely treasures and memorabilia was yet another defeat within an accelerating process of dispossession.

The male-directed venture likewise encroached upon the Sabbath, another female preserve. Through the influence of women's magazines, by mid-century Sunday had become a veritable ladies' day; women zealously exercised their religious influence and moral skill on the day of their families' retirement from the world. Although parties on the Trail often suspended travel on Sundays, the time only provided the opportunity to unload and dry the precious cargo of the wagons — seeds, food, and clothing —

which otherwise would rot from dampness. For women whose creed forbade any worldly activity on the Sabbath, the work was not only irksome and tedious but profane.

This is Sabath it is a beautiful day indeed we do not use it as such for we have not traveled far when we stop in a most lovely place oh it is such a beautiful spot and take everything out of our wagon to air them and it is well we done it as the flower was damp and there was some of the other ones flower was rotten . . . and we baked and boiled and washed oh dear me I did not think we would have abused the sabeth in such a manner. I do not see how we can expect to get along but we did not intend to do so before we started.

Denied a voice in the male sphere that surrounded them, women were also unable to partake of the limited yet meaningful power of women with homes. On almost every Sunday, Helen Stewart lamented the disruption of a familiar and sustaining order of life, symbolized by the household goods strewn about the ground to dry: "We took everything out the wagons and the side of the hill is covered with flower biscut meat rice oat meal clothes and such a quantity of articles of all discertions to many to mention and childre[n] included in the number. And hobos that is neather men nor yet boys being in and out hang about."

The disintegration of the physical base of domesticity was symptomatic of an even more serious disruption in the female subculture. Because the wagon trains so often broke into smaller units, many women were stranded in parties without other women. Since there were usually two or more men in the same family party, some male friendships and bonds remained intact for the duration of the journey. But by midway in the trip, female companionship, so valued by nineteenth-century women, was unavailable to the solitary wife in a party of hired men, husband, and children that had broken away

from a larger train. Emergencies and quarrels, usually between men, broke up the parties. Dr. Powers, a particularly ill-tempered man, decided after many disagreements with others in his train to make the crossing alone with his family. His wife shared neither his misanthropy nor his grim independence. On the day they separated from the others, she wrote in her journal: "The women came over to bid me goodbye, for we were to go alone, all alone. They said there was no color in my face. I felt as if there was none." She perceived the separation as a banishment, almost a death sentence: "There is something peculiar in such a parting on the Plains, one there realizes what a goodbye is. Miss Turner and Mrs. Hendricks were the last to leave, and they bade me adieu the tears running down their sun-burnt cheeks. I felt as though my last friends were leaving me, for what — as I thought then — was a Maniac." Charlotte Pengra likewise left Missouri with her family in a large train. Several weeks out, mechanical problems detained some of the wagons, including those of the other three women. During the month they were separated, Pengra became increasingly dispirited and anxious: "The roads have been good today — I feel lonely and almost disheartened. . . . Can hear the wolves howl very distinctly. Rather ominis, perhaps you think . . . Feel very tired and lonely — our folks not having come — I fear some of them ar sick." Having waited as long as possible for the others, the advance group made a major river crossing. "Then I felt that indeed I had left all my friends," Pengra wrote, "save my husband and his brother, to journey over the dreaded Plains, without one female acquaintance even for a companion — of course I wept and grieved about it but to no purpose."

Others echoed her mourning. "The whipporwills are chirping," Helen Stewart wrote, "they bring me in mind of our old farm in pensillvania the home of my childhood where I have spent the happiest days I will ever see again. . . . I feel rather lonesome today oh solitude solitude how I love it if I had about a dozen of my companions to enjoy it with me." Uprootedness took its toll in debilitation and numbness. After a hard week, men "lolled around in the tents and on their blankets seeming to realize that the 'Sabbath was made for man,'" resting on the palpable achievements of miles covered and rivers crossed. In contrast, the women "could not fully appreciate physical rest, and were rendered more uneasy by the continual passing of emigrant trains all day long. . . . To me, much of the day was spent in meditating over the past and in forebodings for the future."

The ultimate expression of this alienation was the pressure to turn back, to retrace steps to the old life. Occasionally anxiety or bewilderment erupted into open revolt against going on.

This morning our company moved on, except one family. The woman got mad and wouldn't budge or let the children go. He had the cattle hitched on for three hours and coaxed her to go, but she wouldn't stir. I told my husband the circumstances and he and Adam Polk and Mr. Kimball went and each one took a young one and crammed them in the wagon, and the husband drove off and left her sitting. . . . She cut across and overtook her husband. Meantime he sent his boy back to camp after a horse he had left, and when she came up her husband said, "Did you meet John?" "Yes," was the reply, "and I picked up a stone and knocked out his brains." Her husband went back to ascertain the truth and while he was gone she set fire to one of the wagons. . . . He saw the flames and came running and put it out, and then mustered spunk enough to give her a good flogging.

Short of violent resistance, it was always possible that circumstances would force a family to reconsider and turn back. During a cholera scare in 1852, "women cried, begging their men to take them back." When the men reluctantly relented, the writer observed that "they did the hooking up of their oxen in a spiritless sort of way," while "some of the girls and women were laughing." There was lit-

tle lost and much regained for women in a decision to abandon the migration.

Both sexes worked, and both sexes suffered. Yet women lacked a sense of inclusion and a cultural rationale to give meaning to the suffering and the work; no augmented sense of self or role emerged from augmented privation. Both women and men also complained, but women expanded their caviling to a generalized critique of the whole enterprise. Margaret Chambers felt "as if we had left all civilization behind us" after crossing the Missouri, and Harriet Ward's cry from South Pass — "Oh, shall we ever live like civilized beings again?" — reverberated through the thoughts of many of her sisters. Civilization was far more to these women than law, books, and municipal government; it was pianos, church societies, daguerreotypes, mirrors — in short, their homes. At their most hopeful, the exiles perceived the Trail as a hellish but necessary transition to a land where they could renew their domestic mission: "Each advanced step of the slow, plodding cattle carried us farther and farther from civilization into a desolate, barbarous country. . . . But our new home lay beyond all this and was a shining beacon that beckoned us on, inspiring our hearts with hope and courage." At worst, temporary exigencies became in the minds of the dispossessed the omens of an irrevocable exile: "We have been travelling with 25–18–14–129–64–3 wagons — now all alone — how dreary it seems. Can it be that I have left my quiet little home and taken this dreary land of solitude in exchange?"

Only a minority of the women who emigrated over the Overland Trail were from the northeastern middle classes where the cult of true womanhood reached its fullest bloom. Yet their responses to the labor demands of the Trail indicate that "womanliness" had penetrated the values, expectations, and personalities of midwestern farm women as well as New England "ladies." "Women's sphere" provided them with companionship, a sense of selfworth, and most important, independence from men in a patriarchal world. The Trail, in breaking down sexual segregation, offered women the opportunities of socially essential work. Yet this work was performed in a male arena, and many women saw themselves as draftees rather than partners. . . .

Nonetheless, the journals of overland women are irrefutable testimony to the importance of a separate female province. Such theorists as Catharine Beecher were acutely aware of the advantages in keeping life divvied up, in maintaining "two pathways which are always different" for women and men. The women who traveled on the Overland Trail experienced firsthand the tribulations of integration which Beecher and her colleagues could predict in theory.

QUESTIONS TO CONSIDER

1   How did necessity on the Overland Trail open up new work roles for women? Did women tend to regard these new "opportunities" to share in men's work as a gain or as a loss in status?

2   How does the sphere theory, which emerges in Jacksonian America, lead to a decline in woman's social, political, and economic status but a gain in her psychological and emotional status? Was the so-called cult of true womanhood simply a sexist ideology forced on oppressed American females?

3   Contrast the goals of men and women on the trail. Why did women feel particularly alienated by the migration experience?

4   How were women on the trail able to create a positive female subculture? What difficulties did they encounter?

5   Faragher and Stansell remind us that historians have often associated positive work roles for women with the absence of narrow definitions of woman's place. Why is this association inaccurate in describing women's experiences on the Overland Trail?

"To Make Them Stand in Fear": The Slaveowning South

23

Life in a Totalitarian System

JOHN W. BLASSINGAME

Thanks to the influence of the 1939 motion picture Gone with the Wind, *many white Americans still think of the Old South as a romantic land of magnolias and landscaped manors, of cavalier gentlemen and happy darkies, of elegant ladies and breathless belles in crinoline — an ordered, leisurely world in which men and women, blacks and whites, all had their destined place. This view of Dixie is one of America's most enduring myths (*Gone with the Wind *still commands huge audiences when it runs on television). The real world of the Old South was far more complex and cruel.*

Modern historical studies have demonstrated that antebellum Dixie was a rigidly patriarchal, slave-based social order that might have lasted indefinitely had not the Civil War broken out. At no time was slavery on the verge of dying out naturally. Tobacco cultivation may have become unprofitable by the Revolutionary period, but the invention of the cotton gin in 1793 stimulated cotton production immeasurably and created a tremendous demand for slave labor. Thanks to the cotton gin, slavery spread beyond the fertile black belt of Alabama and Mississippi, out to the Kansas-Missouri border, to the fringes of western Arkansas, and to south and east Texas. Although Congress outlawed the foreign slave trade in 1808 (it simply continued as illicit traffic), the number of slaves rose dramatically so that by 1860 there were nearly 4 million in fifteen slave states, including Delaware and Maryland. Slavery remained profitable, too, as evidenced by the fact that in 1860 a prime field hand sold for $1,250 in Virginia and $1,800 on the auction blocks in New Orleans. A "fancy girl" went for as high as $2,500. Still, from the southern white's viewpoint, the profitability of slavery was not the crucial issue. Had slavery proved too costly in its plantation setting, southerners would have found other ways to use slave labor and keep blacks in chains, to maintain white male supremacy in the region.

The slaveholding South was a brutal system that sought to strip black people of all human rights, reducing them to the status of cattle, swine, wagons, and other "property." The slaveholders resorted to a complex "apparatus of control" by which they ruled the region. The symbol of their power was the ubiquitous whip, which, in the words of another historian, was calculated to make the slaves "stand in fear." Yet, as we saw in the portrait of Nat Turner (selection 13), the slaves created survival mechanisms in the form of their families, black religion, and a slave underground, which helped them "keep on keepin' on" in life under the lash. And they resisted, most of them did, by committing acts of terrorism (arson and sabotage) or day-to-day obstructionism, such as "accidently" breaking their hoes. As historian Deborah Gray White has pointed out, pregnant mothers sometimes conspired with midwives to abort their fetuses and even commit infanticide, so that their children would not suffer as they had. The slaves protested, too, in their songs and in their folk tales about how weak, clever animals (the slaves) could outwit larger, menacing animals (the masters).

To understand the antebellum South, one must remember that the region was divided into two distinct classes of white, slaveholders and non-slaveholders, with the latter constituting a majority of the white population. Non-slaveholders included poor whites — "po white trash," "rednecks," or "hillbillies," in the vernacular of the day — who lived on impoverished subsistence farms in the unproductive hill country and pine barrens. The class also included middle-class yeoman farmers who raised crops for market and city-dwelling merchants, artisans, and day-laborers. Since slaveholding was a potent status symbol and a great means of wealth, most of these individuals aspired to own slaves and rise up in the class scale.

Compared to the slaveholders, all non-slaveholding whites were relatively poor. Slaveholders owned more than ninety per cent of the South's agricultural wealth; their average wealth was fourteen times greater than that of non-slaveholders. The planters, those who owned twenty or more slaves, were a minority in the slaveholding class — they numbered only 46,000 in 1860. Yet the planters owned most of the slaves and most of the agricultural wealth of their class and truly ruled the region. By stressing white racial supremacy and black inferiority and by playing on the fears of abolition, the ruling planters and their small slaveholding allies were able to unite poor whites, yeoman farmers and city dwellers behind the slave regime. In short, they successfully divided whites and Negroes.

Despite the cruel nature of the slave system, African Americans, as black historian John W. Blassingame points out in the following selection, found ways to force the system to recognize their humanity, which compelled the planters to make compromises "in order to maintain the facade of absolute control." Blassingame disagrees with those historians who have argued that the slave system was so brutal that it damaged African Americans irreparably, reducing them to infantile or abject docility. Even so, as Blassingame's narrative *shows, the slave system was cruel to the blacks — Blassingames's description of the various forms of punishment is particularly harrowing.*

Slavery left an indelible mark on both races. As African American historian Lerone Bennett Jr. wrote in his Confrontation: Black and White *(1965): "Slavery, in sum, was a seed experience. The significant dimensions of the race problem, the special dynamism that gave [the racial upheavals of the 1960s] their special harshness, are reflections of eddies that lie deep in the mind and deep in the past. The Negro is what he is today because he was once held in slavery by white people. And white people are what they are today because they cannot forget, because Negroes will not let them forget, what they did yesterday."*

GLOSSARY

BLACK AUTOBIOGRAPHERS African Americans who escaped to the North and wrote autobiographies of their experiences as slaves.

BLACK DRIVERS Typically male slaves chosen by the overseer or master to "drive" the slaves in the field. Armed with a whip, he was to see to it that all hands worked diligently. But "caught in the no-man's land between management and labor," the drivers "earned the undying hatred of the slaves for pushing them too hard."

BLACK MAMMY She nursed and looked after the white child in the Big House and often "ran the household, interceded with his parents to protect him, punished him for misbehavior, rocked him to sleep, told him fascinating stories, and in general served as his second, more attentive, more loving mother."

DOMESTIC SERVANTS Also known as house slaves, they worked daily in and around the Big House as maids, servants, butlers, gardeners, and the like. They were "at the beck and call" of their masters night and day.

OVERSEER The administrative assistant to the master on large slaveholding farms and on plantations, he was usually white, and his job was to manage and discipline the slaves.

The behavior of the black slave was intimately bound up with the nature of the antebellum plantation, the behavior of masters, the white man's perceptions and misperceptions, and a multitude of factors which influenced personal relations. In the final analysis, the character of the antebellum plantation was one of the major determinants of the attitudes, perceptions, and behavior of the slave. There was so much variation in plantations, overseers, and masters, however, that the slave had much more freedom from restraint and more independence and autonomy than his institutionally defined role allowed. Consequently, the slave did not have to be infantile or abjectly docile in order to remain alive. . . .

The plantation did, however, give a certain uniform pattern to the slave's life, especially in terms of labor requirements. According to the black autobiographers, most field hands rose before dawn, prepared their meals, fed the livestock, and then rushed

From *The Slave Community: Plantation Life in the Antebellum South* (revised and enlarged edition) by John W. Blassingame. Copyright © 1979 by Oxford University Press, Inc. Used by permission of Oxford University Press, Inc.

As the master or overseer looks on, a slave named Matt receives a brutal whipping from another slave, probably a driver, on a Virginia plantation. Mary Livermore, a white New Englander serving as a tutor there, witnessed the beating. "The swish of a long whip flashed through the air," she said. "The lash sank with a cutting sound into Matt's quivering flesh. Shrieks of torture pierced the skies as blow after blow fell upon the body of the suffering man. I stood immovable, sick and faint." (North Wind Picture Archives)

to the fields before sunrise. Failure to reach the field on time often brought the overseer's lash into play. Depending upon the season or the crop, the laborer would grub and hoe the field, pick worms off the plants, build fences, cut down trees, construct dikes, pull fodder, clear new land, plant rice, sugar, tobacco, cotton, and corn, and then harvest the crop.

Frequently, after working from dawn to sunset, the weary slaves then had to care for the livestock, put away tools, and cook their meals before the horn sounded bedtime in the quarters. During the cotton-picking season, the men sometimes ginned cotton until nine o'clock at night. For the hapless slaves on the sugar plantation, the work of boiling the sugar cane continued far into the night: they often worked eighteen hours a day during the harvest season; some sugar factories ran in shifts seven days and nights each week. The work, while varying in tempo, seemed almost endless. Cotton-planting started the last of March or first of April, cotton-picking lasted from August to Christmas and frequently until January or February. The corn was harvested after cotton-picking ended. During slack periods, the slaves cleared forest land, built fences, repaired the slave cabins, killed hogs, and engaged in a multitude of other tasks.

While the mass of slaves followed this routine, the domestic servants formed part of the plantation elite. They usually ate better food and wore better clothes than the field slaves because they received leftovers from the planter's larder and hand-me-downs from his wardrobe. In spite of this, their position was no sinecure. They ran errands, worked as part-time gardeners, cooked, served meals, cared for the horses, milked the cows, sewed simple clothes, cared for the master's infant, wove, carded and spun wool, did the marketing, churned the milk, dusted the house, swept the yard, arranged the dining room, cut the shrubbery, and performed numerous other tasks. With the exception of the plantation cook, each domestic servant was responsible not for one but for several of these tasks.

At the beck and call of his master day and night, the domestic servant had no regular hours. Added to the long hours was the discomfiture of constantly being under the watchful eyes of the whites and being subject to their every capricious, vengeful, or sadistic whim. Domestic servants frequently had their ears boxed or were flogged for trifling mistakes, ignorance, delinquent work, "insolent" behavior, or simply for being within striking distance when the master was disgruntled. Lewis Clarke, who felt the domestic servants' lot was worse than that of the field slaves, described the problems which beset them:

We were constantly exposed to the whims and passions of every member of the family; from the least to the greatest their anger was wreaked upon us. Nor was our life an easy one, in the hours of our toil or in the amount of labor performed. We were always required to sit up until all the family had retired; then we must be up at early dawn in summer, and before day in winter.

The quantity, quality, and variety of food, clothing, housing, and medical care the slave received rarely satisfied him. The fact that another man determined how much and what kind of food, clothing, and shelter he needed to survive posed a serious problem for him. Equally serious was his dependence on the "average" amount of food and clothing his master decided was sufficient for *all* slaves. Obviously, an allotment of food or clothing sufficient for one man was not necessarily enough for another man. Most of the black autobiographers complained that they had at least one owner who did not give them enough food. Sometimes, even when slaves generally received enough food, provisions ran low. When the slaves did not receive enough to eat, they stole food. . . . Other slaves trapped animals and fished at night and on Sundays in order to augment their meager diet.

The slaves often complained bitterly about what their masters described as "adequate" housing. Most of the autobiographers reported that they lived in crudely built one-room log cabins with dirt floors and too many cracks in them to permit much comfort during the winter months. John Brown complained that in the log cabins: "The wind and rain will come in and the smoke will not go out." Austin Steward felt that the slave cabins were "not as good as many of our stables at the north." Not only were the slave cabins uncomfortable, they were often crowded. Most of the cabins contained at least two families. The 260 slaves on Charles Ball's plantation shared 38 cabins, and average of 6.8 slaves per cabin. The 160 slaves on Louis Hughes's plantation lived in 18 cabins or an average of 8.8 slaves per cabin. Josiah Henson declared that from 10 to 12 people shared each cabin on his plantation. Some lived not in cabins but in sheds. William Green, for example, lived in a long low shed with 29 others. Some slaves, of course, lived in more spacious and comfortable cabins. Henry Watson's owner, for instance, had 27 cabins for his 100 slaves, an average of 3.7 slaves per cabin. Few slaves were as fortunate as Sam Aleckson whose master's slave cabins were not only neat and commodious, but also had flower gardens in front of them. Usually the slaves had to make what furniture and utensils they used. They built tables, beds, and benches and sometimes carved wooden spoons. Generally the cabins contained beds made of straw covered boards, and tables of packing boxes. Some slaves slept on the ground or on mattresses of corn shucks without blankets. . . .

Whatever their treatment of slaves, most planters worked consistently to make them submissive and deferential. While the lash was the linchpin of his regime, the slaveholder adopted several practices to assure the slave's submissiveness. A master started early trying to impress upon the mind of the young black the awesome power of whiteness: he made the slave bow upon meeting him, stand in his presence, and accept floggings from his young children; he flogged the slave for fighting with young whites. The ritual of deference was required at every turn: the slave was flogged for disputing a white man's word, kicked for walking between two whites on a street, and not allowed to call his wife or mother "Mrs." He had to approach the overseer or master with great humility. For example, on Charles Ball's plantation the slaves "were always obliged to approach the door of the mansion, in the most humble and supplicating manner, with our hats in our hands, and the most subdued and beseeching language in our mouths. . . .

Many masters tried first to demonstrate their own authority over the slave and then the superiority of all whites over blacks. They continually told the slave he was unfit for freedom, that every slave who attempted to escape was captured and sold further South, and that the black man must conform to the white man's every wish. The penalties for non-conformity were severe; the lessons uniformly pointed to one idea: the slave was a thing to be used by the "superior" race. Jermain Loguen, for instance, wrote that he "had been taught, in the severest school, that he was a thing for others' uses, and that he must bend his head, body and mind in conformity to that

idea, in the presence of a superior race. . . ." Likewise, Austin Steward had since his childhood "been taught to cower beneath the white man's frown, and bow at his bidding, or suffer all the rigor of the slave laws."

Planters insisted that their slaves show no signs of dissatisfaction. Instead, they were to demonstrate their humility by cheerful performance of their tasks. Elizabeth Keckley's master, for instance, "never liked to see one of his slaves wear a sorrowful face, and those who offended in this particular way were always punished." Anxiously scanning the faces of his slaves, the master made them reflect, in their countenances, what he wanted rather that what they felt. Henry Watson asserted that "the slaveholder watches every move of the slave, and if he is downcast or sad, — in fact, if they are in any mood but laughing and singing, and manifesting symptoms of perfect content at heart, — they were said to have the devil in them. . . ."

Lest the edifice he was building should fall, the master enlisted the aid of some black men to help him control the others. The most diligent slaves were rewarded and pointed to as models for the others to emulate. Black drivers were forced, on pain of punishment themselves, to keep the slaves at their tasks and to flog them for breaking the plantation rules.

Caught in the no-man's-land between management and labor, the driver suffered the consequences: he was almost literally shot at from all sides. When he earned praise from the master for a job well done, he earned the undying hatred of the slaves for pushing them too hard. Demotion and flogging greeted the driver who allowed the slaves to dawdle at their work, who failed to keep order in the quarters, or who could not account for plantation equipment. While drivers tried to walk the tightrope between the masters who gave them material rewards (money, passes, presents) and the slaves who gave them social rewards (love, respect, companionship), most of them failed. Because masters correctly perceived them as being the most loyal of slaves, the bondsmen treated the drivers as spies and collaborators. The driver was the best example in the quarters of the oppressed identifying with the enemy.... From the perspective of the bondsmen, whenever there was a conflict in loyalties the driver acted out his primary role as the master's man. Using the self-serving testimony of a few remarkable drivers, historians have tried to demonstrate that he was the classic man caught in the middle who went to unusual lengths to protect his fellows, that he ranked high in the social order of the quarters, and that he was as rebellious as other slaves. The evidence from the blacks themselves contradicts this portrait.

Since most plantation were small, slave owners did not employ enough drivers for them to represent significant personages in the community of the slaves. Called whipping man, overlooker, whipping boss, foreman, and overseer by the slaves, the driver was generally described by the bondsmen as being as "mean as the devil." Significantly, the more sympathetic (or neutral) assessments of the drivers come from the drivers themselves, their relatives, or their owners. Rare indeed is the testimony of a field hand that drivers tried in any way to protect the bondsmen or hide their indiscretions from owners. The slaves complained instead of the driver's sexual exploitation of black women, his alacrity in meting out punishment, and his favoritism in giving rewards. In slave interviews and autobiographies, the driver appears as the embodiment of cruelty. Henry Cheatam of Mississippi gave a typical description:

Old Miss had a nigger overseer and dat was de meanest devil dat ever lived on de Lord's green earth. I promise myself when I growed up dat I was a-goin' to kill dat nigger if it was de last thing I ever done. Lots of times I'se seen him beat my mammy, and one day I seen him beat my auntie who was big with a child, and dat man dug a round hole in de ground and put her stomach in it, and beat and beat her for a half hour straight till de baby came out right dere in de hole.

Mistis allow such treatment only 'cause a heap of times she didn't know nothin' about it, and de slaves better not tell her, 'cause dat overseer whip 'em if he finds out dat dey done gone and told.... When de slaves would try to run away our overseer would put chains on deir legs with big long spikes between deir feets, so dey couldn't get away.

The key to the slaves' assessment of the driver was whether or not he had the power to flog them. When masters prohibited drivers from flogging, they had to work out a number of compromises in order to get slaves to labor. Without the whip, the driver spurred his fellows on by example and threats to tell the master when they did not labor conscientiously. Though the size of the plantation, the number of slaves, the crop, the presence or absence of owners, managerial style of masters, and the resort to the task system or gang labor all affected the role of the driver in a variety of ways, the presence or absence of the whip in his hands largely determined his relationship with other slaves and his standing in the quarters.

While the drivers provided part of the coercion necessary to keep the plantation machinery humming, the domestic servants often represented an extension of the master's eyes and ears: the plantation's secret police. Flattered and materially rewarded, the domestic servant kept the master informed of activities in the slave quarters. Trained to speak of his good treatment to Northern visitors and sometimes forced to spy on his fellows, the domestic servant was a valuable adjunct to the slaveholder's security and public relations staff.

Ritual deference and obedience to plantation rules could only be enforced by most planters by constant flogging. William Wells Brown spoke for many slaves when he wrote that on his plantation the whip was used "very frequently and freely, and a small offense on the part of the slave furnished an occasion for its use. The slaves were flogged most frequently for running away and for failure to complete the tasks assigned to them. Slaveholders often punished them for visiting their mates, learning to read, arguing or fighting with whites, working too slowly, stealing, fighting or quarreling with other slaves, drunkenness, or for trying to prevent the sale of their relatives. They were occasionally punished for impudence, asking their masters to sell them, claiming they were free men, breaking household articles, or for giving sexual favors to persons other than their masters.

Nowhere does the irrationality of slavery appear as clearly as in the way that slaves were punished. While generally speaking a slaveholder had no desire to punish his slave so severely as to endanger his life, the master was the only a man, subject, like most men, to miscalculations, to anger, to sadism, and to drink. When angry, masters frequently kicked, slapped, cuffed, or boxed the ears of domestic servants, sometimes flogged pregnant women, and often punished slaves so cruelly that it took them weeks to recover. Many slaves reported that they were flogged severely, had iron weights with bells on them placed on their necks, or were shackled. Recalcitrant slaves received more stripes and were treated more cruelly by exasperated planters than were any other blacks. Moses Roper, an incorrigible runaway, regularly received 100 to 200 lashes from his owner. Once his master poured tar on his head and set it afire. On another occasion, after Roper had escaped from leg irons, his master had the nails of his fingers and toes beaten off. Since every white man considered himself the slave's policeman, the black also suffered at the hands of non-slaveholders. Josiah Henson, for example, accidentally pushed a white man who later broke his arm and shoulder blades.

Uncompromisingly harsh, the portrait which the slaves drew of cruel masters was filled with brutality and horror. On the plantations of these masters, strong black men suffered from overwork, abuse, and starvation; and the overseer's horn usually sounded before sleep could chase the fatigue of the last day's labor. Characteristically, stocks closed on hapless women and children, mothers cried for the infants torn cruelly from their arms, and whimpering black women fought vainly to preserve their virtue in the face of the lash or pleaded for mercy while blood flowed from their bare buttocks. A cacophony of horrendous sounds constantly reverberated throughout such plantations: nauseated black men vomited while strung up over slowly burning tobacco leaves, vicious dogs tore black flesh, black men moaned as they were hung up by the thumbs with the whip raising deep welts on their backs and as they were bent over barrels or tied down to stakes while paddles with holes in them broke blisters on their rumps. Frequently, blacks called God's name in vain as they fainted from their mater's hundredth stroke or as they had their brains blown out. The slaves described masters of this stripe as besotted, vicious, deceitful, coarse, licentious, bloodthirsty, heartless, and hypocritical Christians who were pitiless fiends.

The first impulse of the historian is to reject the slave's portrait as too harsh. There is, however, a great deal of evidence in antebellum court records, newspapers, memoirs, and plantation diaries which suggests that this is not the case. However much it is denied by Southern romantics, there were many slaveholders who were moral degenerates and sadists. Quite frequently, even the most cultured of planters were so inured to brutality that they thought little about the punishment meted out to slaves. Floggings of 50 to 75 lashes were not uncommon. On numerous occasions, planters branded, stabbed, tarred and feathered, burned, shackled, tortured, maimed, crippled, mutilated, and castrated their slaves. Thousands of slaves were flogged so severely that they were permanently scarred. In Mississippi a fiendish planter once administered 1000 lashes to a slave. . . .

Most masters were neither pitiless fiends nor saints in their relationships with slaves. Whenever possible, planters hired physicians for slaves when they were ill, gave them what the planter defined as "adequate" food, clothing, and shelter, and flogged them for lying, stealing, fighting, breaking tools, and numerous other "offenses." While ready to give the slave from 10 to 50 lashes for most offenses, the typical planter preferred to punish slaves in other ways (withholding passes, demotion, extra work, humiliation, solitary confinement, etc.) Less violent means of punishment were preferred because they were not morally reprehensible, involved no physical harm to valuable property, and were often more effective in preserving discipline than floggings.

In spite of the institutionally defined roles, the treatment of slaves varied from plantation to plantation. Differences in family life, childhood experiences, and religious beliefs caused the planters to treat their slaves in a great variety of ways. A few masters were so brutal and sadistic that they could crush the slave's every manly instinct. Others were too humane, too lazy, or too stupid to make childlike dependents of their slaves. While the normal planter extracted all of the labor he could from blacks, there were several conflicting forces which made him at the same time callous towards the slave's sufferings and impelled him to recognize their humanity. . . .

One of the key figures in the white child's socialization was the ubiquitous black mammy to whom he frequently turned for love and security. In was the black mammy who often ran the household, interceded with his parents to protect him, punished him for misbehavior, nursed him, rocked him to sleep, told him fascinating stories, and in general served as his second, more attentive, more loving mother. The mammy's influence on her white charge's thought, behavior, language, and personality is inestimable. One Englishman wrote that in the Carolinas: "Each child has its *Momma,* whose gestures and accent it will necessarily copy, for children, we all know, are imitative beings. It is not unusual to hear an elegant lady say, *Richard always grieves when Quasheehan is whipped, because she suckled him.*" Often the child formed a deep and abiding love for his mammy and as an adult deferred to her demands and wishes.

Black childhood playmates had only a little less influence on the white child than the mammy. As a result of enduring friendships formed during their impressionable childhood, many white youngsters intervened to prevent the punishment or sale of their black favorites, demanded of them far less conformity to the slave role, or preferred the company of slaves to that of their white neighbors. William Wells Brown's master held Brown's father in such high esteem that he refused to sell the boy to New Orleans even after he had tried to escape. Similarly, William Green's mother prevented his separation from her by appealing to his young master whom she had nursed. Jacob Stroyer wrote that one intemperate white man terrorized his white neighbors but never abused his forty slaves because of the control his old mammy exercised over him. Rarely could a planter punish a slave with impunity if he were the favorite of his wife and children. The son of John Thompson's master, for instance, threatened to shoot an overseer for flogging the slave fiddler. The regard in which Andrew Jackson was held by his master's sons was so great that they refused to tell their father where he went when he escaped from Kentucky. Even if the slave were not a favorite, a member of the master's family might prevent unusually cruel treatment.

The early association with blacks, and especially his black mammy, had a profound influence on the white Southerner. His constant exposure to the cruelties perpetrated upon slaves led to a sense of detachment which conflicted with his love and respect for his close black associates. Similarly, the demeanor of all slaves toward his parents and his parents' insistence that he demand deference from blacks taught the child to exercise authority. He soon observed that his strict moral code conflicted with the apparently more desirable loose morality, irresponsibility, and happiness of his black associates. He envied the slave his apparent freedom from social restraints and projected all of his own desires to break through these restraints onto the black. Often he internalized the love ideal of the black mammy but later learned that she was a hated, black thing. His intimate relation with the mammy, his observation of the casual sexual contacts among slaves, the idealization of white women and the pursuit of black women by white males, convinced him that sexual joy lay in the arms of a black paramour. The white male frequently resolved his love-hate complex by pursuing the allegedly passionate black woman. At the same time, he exaggerated the sexual prowess and desire of the black male for liaisons with angelic white women and reacted with extreme cruelty to any challenge to his monopoly of white women. . . .

The first duty of the Christian master was to recognize the slave's humanity. This recognition entailed a respect for the feelings of the slave. Southern divines argued that the slave was also created in God's image. The Reverend J. H. Thornwell testified that

the Negro is of one blood with ourselves — that he has sinned as we have, and that he has an equal interest with us in the great redemption. Science, falsely so called, may attempt to exclude him from the brotherhood of humanity . . . but the instinctive impulses of our nature, combined with the plainest declarations of the word of God, lead us to recognize in his form and lineaments — his moral, religious and intellectual nature — the same humanity in which we glory as the image of God. We are not ashamed to call him our brother.

While the Reverend George W. Freeman was not as certain of the link between master and slave, he was more insistent on the necessity of respecting the black's feelings. Freeman exhorted masters, in their relations with slaves, "never forget that, as low as they are in the scale of humanity, they are yet *human beings, and have the feelings of human beings* — feelings too with many of them, as delicate and sensitive as your own, and which demand to be respected, and carefully preserved from outrage.

Ministers quoted the Bible freely to prove the obligations masters had to their slaves. They reminded them that Paul had advised masters to forbear threatening slaves "knowing that your Master also is in Heaven; neither is there respect of persons with him" (Ephesians 6:9). The most frequently quoted Biblical admonition was Colossians 4:1: "Masters, give unto *your* servants that which is just and equal; knowing that ye also have a Master in heaven." How was the master to determine justice and equity? Most Southern divines translated the terms into the Golden Rule. The Reverend T. A. Holmes summed up the general view when he observed: "Equity pleads the right of humanity. . . . and, in the conscientious discharge of duty, prompts the master to such treatment of his servant as would be desired on his part, were their positions reversed." Ministers asserted that cruel treatment of slaves would lead to Divine censure. The Reverend H. N. McTyeire of New Orleans declared, "As you treat your servants on earth, so will your Master in heaven treat you." The Reverend T. A. Holmes was more direct. He cautioned slaveholders that "the exercise of right and authority on the part of the master, with reference only to his interest, uninfluenced by kindness to his servant, must incur the displeasure of Him with whom there is no respect of persons."

According to the ministers, Christian masters had several duties to their slaves. They had to maintain the slaves properly, care for them in old age, require no more than a reasonable amount of labor from them, give them adequate leisure time, and respect their humanity. Many ministers repeated the question John Wesley asked slaveholders in 1774: "Have you tried what mildness and gentleness would do?" Holmes told planters that "the master should be the friend of his servant, and the servant should know it. Friendship implies good will, Kindness, a desire for the welfare of him for whom it is entertained." Freeman was just as insistent on mild treatment. He declared: "It is the duty of masters not only to be merciful to their servants, but to do everything in their power to make their situation comfortable, and to put forth all reasonable effort to render them contented and happy.

In addition to several personal and social forces which prevented planters from practicing the kind of cruelty necessary for the systematic extinction of every trace of manhood in the slave, there were certain features of the plantation that militated against abject docility on the part of the slaves. Although legally the planter had absolute authority over the slave, there were many restraints on his use of that authority. Dependent on the slave's labor for his economic survival, the planter ordinarily could not afford to starve, torture, or work him to death. Whatever the regimen on the plantation, the planter never had a supervisory staff which was large enough to exact the kind of labor that killed men in a few months. Consequently, in spite of the slave's constant labor, there was an absolute limit beyond which he was not pushed. The most important factor in this limitation was the size of most plantations and the consequent insurance of a low level of surveillance of many of the slave's activities. Since more than half of the slaves in 1860 lived on plantations containing twenty or more slaves, it is obvious that only a small minority of planters could personally supervise every detail of the work. Besides, many masters were too lazy, too stupid, or away too often visiting spas during the summer to maintain a strict surveillance over their slaves. The editor of the *Southern Quarterly Review* recognized this when he wrote that as a result of "the apathy of the master; his love of repose; his absence from his estates ... the slave ... acquires a thousand habits and desires all inconsistent with subordination, labour, decency, sobriety, and all virtues of regularity, humility and temperance."

Seeking to ensure regular labor and humility, most planters hired overseers to manage their slaves. The job of the overseer was unbelievably difficult. One overseer indicated this plainly when he complained:

If there ever was or ever will be a calling in life as mean and contemptible as that of an overseer — I would be right down glad to know what it is, and where to be found. ... If there be ... a favorable crop, the *master* makes a splendid crop; if any circumstances be unpropitious and an inferior crop is made, it is the overseer's fault, and if he flogs [the slaves] to keep them at home, or locked up ... he is a brute and a tyrant. If no meat is made, the overseer *would* plant too much cotton. ... If hogs are taken good care of the overseer is wasting corn, and "the most careless and thriftless creature alive." If he does not "turn out" hands in time, he is *lazy*; if he "rousts" them out as your dad and mine had to do, why he is a brute. ...

Planters insisted that the overseer spend all of his time on the plantation, especially if the owner himself did not reside there. George Washington was characteristic in this regard. He informed one of his overseers:

I do in explicit terms, enjoin it upon you to remain constantly at home, unless called off by unavoidable business, or to attend divine worship, and to be constantly with your people when there. There is no other sure way of getting work well done, and quietly, by negroes; for when and overlooker's back is turned, the most of them will slight their work, or be idle altogether; in which case correction cannot retrieve either, but often produces evils which are worse than the disease. Nor is there any other mode than this to prevent thieving and other disorders, the consequence of opportunities.

While constant surveillance of slaves was mandatory for successful management, this was one of the most onerous of the overseer's duties. One overseer complained in May 1858 that his work was so time consuming that "I don't get time scarcely to eat or sleep. I have not been off the plantation since the 3rd of Oct[.] ... The truth is no man can begin to attend to such a business with any set of negros, without the strictest vigilance on his part."

The disciplining of slaves was the major factor in the success or failure of an overseer. Expected to make a large crop while guarding the welfare of the slaves, the overseer often came into conflict with the planter. If the overseer used unusual force in driving the slaves, he incurred the wrath of the owner for damaging his property. On the other hand, if he were easygoing, the planter might dismiss him for making a small crop. In fact, planters often dismissed overseers for cruelty, drunkenness, absenteeism, and lax discipline.

In order for the overseer to retain his job he had to be adept at managing slaves. There were many pitfalls in the endeavor. If on the one hand the overseer became too familiar with the slaves or had sexual relations with the black women, the slaves extracted favors from him and did little work. On the other hand, if the overseer was too cruel and hard driving, the slaves did everything they could to discredit him. It was often impossible for the overseer to find a happy medium between these two extremes. Whenever the slaves were dissatisfied with the overseer, they informed the owner of his transgressions, or ran away to escape heavy work or to avoid punishment. Often the slaves refused to return to work until they had spoken to their masters about their treatment. One harried overseer indicated the impact of this tactic when he complained that "if I donte please every negro on the place they run away rite strate." If the overseer somehow managed to please the master *and* the slaves, he was guaranteed a long tenure on the plantation, For example, John B. Lamar wrote in 1844 that he was anxious to retain his overseer because "the negroes like him too."

As the visible symbol of authority, the overseer was the most frequent target of rebellious slaves disgruntled over their work load, food allotment, or punishment. According to one observer, "An overseer has to plan all the business and be with the negroes all the time. The negroes have great spite and hatred towards them and frequently fight them, when the over-seer pretends to whip them. The negroes think as meanly of the poor white people, as the rich white people do themselves and think anybody that is so poor as to be an overseer mean enough." Hundreds of overseers were beaten, poisoned, stabbed, and shot by rebellious slaves.

The overseer was the weakest link in the chain of plantation management. Whatever his character, it was impossible for the overseer to supervise every detail of the slave's life. Most men were unwilling to lead the kind of solitary life that plantation management demanded. Consequently, most overseers left the plantations periodically at night or on the weekends in order to find some recreation for themselves. Overwhelmed by a multitude of duties, the overseer could not be everywhere at once and consequently could not keep the slaves under constant surveillance. If he happened to be lazy, the level of surveillance was even lower.

As a result of the differences in the characters of overseers and masters, many plantations deviated strikingly from the ideal outlined in the rules of management. According to the investigations of H. Herbemont of South Carolina, "there are very few planters who have anything like a regular system for either the moral or physical government of their slaves." A writer in the *American Farmer* agreed: "There is in fact little or no *'system'* of management in regard to our slaves — they are insubordinate and *unmanageable.*"

Even when attempts were made to govern the slaves in some systematic fashion, the planters realized that since the slaves had not internalized their ideals they had to make several compromises in order to maintain the facade of absolute control. First, they recognized that their slaves differed in temperament and intelligence. For instance, one planter asserted: "In every servants' quarter there are the strong and the weak, the sagacious and the simple." Second, since they differed so much in character, all slaves could not be treated in the same manner. The most strong-willed and shrewdest slaves received better treatment than most others and were given positions of power in the plantation hierarchy. The intractable slave was either sold or never molested. Planters spotted him quickly, and, inevitably, they were forced by him to be wary. There are certainly many masters who were cautious with slaves like Louis Manigault's Jack Savage. According to Manigault, Jack "was the only negro ever in our possession who I considered capable of murdering me or burning my dwelling at night or capable of committing any act."

Planters often maintained the appearance of strict obedience by making it relatively easy for the slave to obey. Regardless of their desires, most masters realized that the slaves, like soldiers, were adept at "goldbricking." Once the slaves decided how much labor they were going to perform, they refused to work any harder. On slaveholder observed: "Experience has long since taught masters, that every attempt to force a slave beyond the limits that he fixes as a sufficient amount of labor to render his master, instead of extorting more work, only tends to make him unprofitable, unmanageable, a vexation and a curse."

It was primarily because the planters recognized that slaves voluntarily limited their work that many of them set the standard of labor so low that every slave could meet it. Even when every allowance is made for different strains of certain crops, it is impossible to explain the variations in labor performed from plantation to plantation without recognition of the slave's role in restricting his output. Examine, for instance, the average amount of cotton picked per day by an adult slave. Between 1825 and 1860 slaves in Mississippi generally picked between 130 and 150 pounds of cotton per day. On Charles Whitmore's delta plantation, however, few slaves picked more than 100 pounds of cotton daily. The slave's limitation on the labor he performed appears clearly in the results of races arranged by planters. In a race on a Mississippi plantation in 1830 fourteen slaves picked an average of 323 pounds of cotton, twice their nor-

mal average. Many planters gave prizes to the best cotton pickers in an effort to speed up the work. While this was often effective, many slaves still refused to exert themselves.

The slaveholder also kept up the pretense of absolute control by refusing to take note of every deviation from the rules. In effect, each planter had to learn to be selectively inattentive to rules infractions. A group of Alabama planters gave sound advice on this point: "Negroes lack the motive of self interest to make them careful and diligent, hence the necessity of great patience in the management of them. Do not, therefore, notice too many small omissions of duty."

The personal relations between master and slaves were strained. Rarely did their interests coincide. Because of this, the master used physical force to make the slave obedient. The personal relations on the plantation, however, were much more complicated than a simple relationship between subordinate and superordinate. In the first place, all masters did not demand ritual deference at all times to bolster their self-esteem. Second, the same obsequious behavior was not demanded of ordinary slaves and those in positions of trust. Sir Charles Lyell observed that the latter group of slaves were "involuntarily treated more as equals by the whites." Even when all slaves had to be deferential, whites did not require them to go through the ritual at all times. For example, Susan Dabney Smedes wrote that during Christmas "there was an affectionate throwing off of the reserve and decorum of every-day life.". . .

The Southern white man's perceptions of slave behavior make one point quite clear: the planter recognized the variability of slave personality in his day-to-day relationships. In reality, he had to make several compromises in order to maintain the facade of absolute control. He often "bought off" the strongest slaves by placing them in the plantation hierarchy, was selectively inattentive to rules infractions, and accepted the slave's definition of how much labor he would perform. There was so little identification with the master's interest in the quarters that he frequently had to resort to coercion and to more and more oppressive laws. There were so many differences among slaveholders and the legal sanctions of slavery were applied in so many different ways that the regimen to which the slave was subjected varied considerably.

QUESTIONS TO CONSIDER

1   How do you feel about Blassingame's portrait of life in slavery? Is he critical enough in describing the brutalities of the slave system, or is he too apologetic? How is the history of the slave system basic to an understanding of current racial difficulties.

2   How did the slaveholding class maintain a facade of absolute control over the slave system? Why did the white masters subject the slaves to terrible forms of punishment? What factors prevented the slaveholding planters from "practicing the kind of cruelty necessary for the extinction of every trace of manhood in the slave"? Compare the realities of slavery to the doctrine of mankind's inalienable rights of life, liberty, and the pursuit of happiness in the Declaration of Independence. How do you think slaveholders could justify violating the Declaration?

3   In what ways did the slaves resist and protest against their enslavement? As was pointed out in the introduction, slave mothers sometimes conspired with midwives to abort their fetuses and even commit infanticide, so that their children would not have to suffer as they had. Do you think this was justifiable?

4   Who were the black drivers and what were their responsibilities and difficulties? How did the other slaves view them? Describe the duties and importance of the black mammy when it came to the white children who were her charges. How could a white child form "a deep and abiding love" for his black mammy and in adulthood embrace the slave system with all its horror and brutality? Who was the overseer and what was his function on the plantation?

5   *Gone with the Wind* and twentieth-century southern apologists characterized the Old South's slave system as "benevolent" and "natural." The slaveowners themselves extolled the "peculiar institution" as the basis for a superior way of life and argued that slavery cared for the wants and needs of their "inferior and incapable black charges." How do you respond to such arguments? Can you name other instances in history in which an institution or a system inflicted such misery on its victims and yet was so self-righteously praised by its practitioners?

24

Let My People Go:
Harriet Tubman and the Underground Railroad

BENJAMIN QUARLES

The fabled Underground Railroad consisted of secret routes that runaway slaves took to the North and freedom. Though one historian has argued that the Underground Railroad was never so highly organized as legend claims, the system did exist, and its conductors, always black, were brave men and women who stole into slave territory and escorted bands of slaves to the North, relying on black and white homesteads, called "stations," to hide and feed them along the way. Harriet Beecher Stowe said that she and her husband hid fugitives in their barn while they were living in Cincinnati, Ohio; and her great novel, Uncle Tom's Cabin, *drew on a real-life story in describing how Eliza Harris and her child escaped north on the Underground Railroad.*

For African Americans of the antebellum period, as Benjamin Quarles says in the following selection, the Underground Railroad was the most effective means of undermining the slave system and the white-coined myth of the slaves as obsequious Sambos who were happy with their lot. But since most of the northern states had black laws that discriminated against African Americans, denying them the right to vote, run for political office, sit on juries, attend public schools, marry whites, work at skilled jobs, and even be buried in white cemeteries, many fugitives went on to Canada, with the full approval of the Canadian government, where they could work as skilled laborers and enjoy a greater degree of freedom then they could in the United States. After the passage of the stringent new federal fugitive slave law in 1850, more runaways than ever sought refuge in Canada.

Harriet Tubman was the Underground Railroad's most famous conductor. Born a slave on Maryland's Eastern Shore, Tubman "stole" herself in 1849 by escaping to Philadelphia. In the years that followed, she slipped back into slaveholding Maryland, rifle in hand, at least fifteen times, and escorted some two hundred slaves, including her own parents, to freedom. In his marvelous book, Pioneers in Protest *(1968), Lerone Bennett, Jr., the author of the previous selection, describes how Tubman operated once she was in slave territory: "She made her way to selected plantations where slaves were informed of her presence by code songs, prayers, or some other stratagem. Selected slaves were then apprised of the rendezvous area and the time of departure. Once the slaves were assembled, Harriet sized them up, searching them closely with her eyes. Satisfied, she placed the group under strict military discipline. During the trip, she was in absolute and total control and no one could question her orders. William Still, the black rebel who operated the key Philadelphia station of the Underground Railroad, said she 'had a very short and pointed rule of law of her own which implied death to anyone who talked of giving out and going back.' Once a slave committed himself to a Tubman escape, he was committed to freedom or death. On several occasions, slaves collapsed and said they were tired, sick, scared. Harriet always cocked her [rifle] and said: 'You go on or die. Dead Negros tell no tales.' Faced with a determined Harriet Tubman, slaves always found new strength and determination. During ten years of guerrilla action, the great commando leader never lost a slave through capture or return."*

Benjamin Quarles, one of our most eminent historians and an African American, offers a warm and sympathetic portrait of the great conductor, gently pulling back the legends that surround her to show us what she was like as a human being. Along the way, Quarles gives us judicious insights into the operations and significance of the Underground Railroad; and he concludes with a profound statement about Harriet Tubman as a symbol for the black struggle today.

GLOSSARY

BROWN, JOHN   Militant white abolitionist who believed that slavery was too entrenched in the American system ever to be removed except by violent means. In 1859, he led a raid against the federal arsenal and armory at Harpers Ferry, Virginia, and seized the guns there. His goal was to destroy slavery by invading the South and inciting a vast slave uprising; or, failing that, by polarizing the sections and provoking a violent upheaval in which slavery would be wiped out. He was captured at Harpers Ferry and hanged.

GARRETT, THOMAS   Delaware abolitionist and leader of the Society of Friends who assisted Harriet Tubman, providing money and shelter as she brought slaves north on the Underground Railroad.

SEWARD, WILLIAM H.   United States senator from New York and a powerful leader of the all-northern Republican party.

STILL, WILLIAM   Prominent free black who headed the General Vigilance Committee of Philadelphia and the Underground Railroad's "key station" in that city. He, too, assisted Harriet Tubman in her slave-liberating operations.

STOWE, HARRIET BEECHER   Author of *Uncle Tom's Cabin* (1852), the most popular novel of the nineteenth century and a passionate indictment of the cruelties of the South's slave system.

TRUTH, SOJOURNER   Like Tubman, "a deeply religious former slave" who was unlettered but eloquent. Truth was "primarily a women's rights activist" in the North.

"I grew up like a neglected weed — ignorant of liberty, having no experience of it." The speaker, a short, spare, black-skinned woman of thirty-five, was being interviewed at her home in St. Catherines, Ontario, in the summer of 1855. "Now, I've been free," she added, "I know what a dreadful condition slavery is." The speaker's interviewer, Benjamin Drew, a Boston school principal and a part-time journalist, made "verbal alterations" (as he put it) in the broken English of Harriet Ross Tubman, but he caught the animated spirit that would give meaning and purpose to a long career then in its budding stages.

A rescuer of slaves, Tubman had achieved nearly mythic status within ten years after her own dash for freedom. Save for the white South, contemporary references to her invariably bore a eulogistic ring. The author and reformer Thomas Wentworth Higginson dubbed her "the greatest heroine of the age," in a letter (June 17, 1859) to his mother. "Her tales of adventure are beyond anything in fiction and her ingenuity and generalship are extraordinary. I have known her for some time — the slaves call her Moses."

A present-day scholar, Larry Gara, holds that "the legendary exploits of Harriet Tubman are undoubtedly exaggerated." But it is equally undeniable that Tubman has resisted being demythologized. One who lived into her early nineties, she proved to be a legend that would not fade in the memory of her contemporaries and a figure who would find a niche in folk literature ("a heroine in homespun") as well as on the pages of the more formally written histories.

From Benjamin Quarles, "Let My People Go: Harriet Tubman and the Underground Railroad," originally titled "Harriet Tubman's Unlikely Leadership," from Leon Litwack and August Meier (eds.), *Black Leaders of the Nineteenth Century* (Urbana: University of Illinois Press, 1988). Copyright © 1988 by the Board of Trustees of the University of Illinois. Used with permission of the University of Illinois Press.

Harriet Tubman (c. 1820–1913), known as "the Moses of her people" because of her heroic work on the Underground Railroad. She liberated some two hundred slaves in Maryland and escorted them north to freedom. (North Wind Picture Archives)

Whence the source of Tubman's imperishable legendary status? As the premiere conductor on a legendary liberty line, the Underground Railroad, Tubman might elude the sniffing dogs of the slave catchers but she could hardly escape the legends that would attach to her name. Tales of derring-do inevitably cluster around those whose operations, by their very nature, have to be clothed in secrecy. Moreover, in the case of the tight-lipped Tubman, legend had to fill in for her ingrained reticence about her activities, a circumstance growing out of her experiences as a slave and as a rescuer of slaves. Even

after the crusade against slavery and its death in the Civil War, Tubman's modesty kept her from recounting her role in either occurrence; a brief, passing mention on a rare occasion was the extent to which she ever unburdened herself as to those bygone days. The Tubman legendry was also stimulated by her illiteracy, hearsay having to fill in for written records.

Contributing significantly to her fame, Tubman's legendary status played an important part in elevating her to a leadership level that she had not sought but did not spurn. Believing that her actions were preordained, she remained indifferent to whatever the sources of her power, whether stemming from her actual accomplishments or from a romancer's exuberance of spirit.

Even shorn of myth the existential Tubman compiled an impressive record, leaving her mark on our national history. This influence may be assessed by noting in turn her interrelationships with other blacks of her own day and time and her interaction with her white contemporaries, closing with a glance at her hold on the American mind since her death in 1913 — an image that has not lost its luster.

Her basic story is readily grasped, furnishing background and providing us a glimpse into the Tubman psyche, her value system, and her vision of the world. Born in 1821 in Dorchester County, not far from the town of Cambridge on Maryland's Eastern Shore, she was one of the eleven children of Harriet Greene and Benjamin Ross, both slaves. Called Araminta as a baby, but later choosing the name of her mother, Harriet was put to work by the time she was five. For seven years she did general housework, including services as child's nurse and maid. Losing her house-slave status while still in her teens, Harriet then labored in the fields, a circumstance that would lead to her famed muscular strength and the physical endurance that belied her spare figure and habitually underfed look.

Two or three years after becoming a fieldhand, Harriet had an experience that marked her for life.

She was struck on the head by a two-pound weight hurled at another slave, whom she was attempting to shield from a wrathful overseer. She never fully recovered from this nearly fatal blow. By swathing her head in a turban she could conceal the deep scar on her skull, but for the rest of her life she was prone to recurring seizures of deep, sudden sleep. She did regain her strength, however, and her capacity for manual labor rivaled that of a man by the time she was twenty.

Harriet's hard life in slavery was lessened a little by her marriage in 1844 to John Tubman. A free black, he lacked his wife's willpower and sense of mission and scoffed at her forebodings. Not fully reciprocating her deep affection for him, he did not join her after she made the dash for freedom; indeed, he soon took another wife. Losing the man, Harriet kept the name, even after taking a second husband in 1869.

One of Harriet Tubman's forebodings, the dread of being sold to the Deep South, took on a new intensity in 1849 upon the death of her master and the rumor that his estate would be broken up and his property dispersed. Impelled to delay no longer, she made her way to free-soil Pennsylvania. Upon her arrival she felt, she said, like she was in heaven.

Tubman's mood of exultation quickly gave way to a resolve to help others become free. As her schemes required money, she moved to Philadelphia and took work in a hotel, the first in a series of part-time jobs. After a year of penny-pinching frugality, she had saved enough to launch the first of her uniformly successful operations, a trip to Baltimore to rescue her sister, Mary Ann Bowley, and her two children.

To give a connected recital of Tubman's subsequent journeys into slavery locales is not possible. Insofar as she could, she operated in secret. Even had she been able to read and write, her sense of taking no unnecessary risks would have inhibited from her keeping a record of her movements. In some ten years of rescue work she made at least fifteen trips southward, personally escorting at least 200 freedom-bound slaves.

Tubman's traits of character and her methods of operation help to explain this extraordinary record. She was courageous, undeterred by the knowledge that there was a price upon her head. Her bravery was matched, moreover, by her coolness in a tight spot, her resourcefulness in a perilous situation. If the fugitives she led lacked her fearlessness, they were silenced by her blunt, no-nonsense manner. The rifle she carried while on rescue trips was not only for protection against slave catchers but also to intimidate any fugitive who became faint of heart and wished to turn back.

Her character molded by a deep reservoir of faith in God, Tubman felt that Divine Providence had willed her freedom and that a guardian angel accompanied her, particularly on her missions of deliverance. Gospel exhortations and spirituals came readily to her lips. When she was referred to as Moses, she did not demur.

If Tubman had complete trust in the Infinite, she also exercised great care in planning operations. She was unsurpassed in the logistics of escape — in anticipating the needs of her fugitive flocks, whether for food or clothes, disguises or forged passes, train tickets or wagons. Every precaution was carefully considered, down to carrying paregoric for fretful babies whose crying might jeopardize the escaping party. Well might she boast that she never lost a passenger.

Tubman was not a one-woman Underground Railroad, however, as this secretive mode of passage required a concerted effort. Her careful planning included full cooperation with others, and she worked hand in hand with two of the most dedicated stationmasters, Thomas Garrett in Wilmington, Delaware, and William Still in Philadelphia. Both assisted her by providing shelter for the fugitives she conducted and by making arrangements, if necessary, for their transportation further north. . . .

To blacks of the antebellum period, North and South, the central theme was the abolition of slavery. Of all the ways to bring this about the most direct, short of insurrection or war, and hence the most satisfying, was the Underground Railroad — the cooperative work of assisting slaves to run away and then assisting them to get a fresh start as free men, women, and children. In matters relating to fugitive slaves, blacks had a personal and vital interest, a particular sense of responsibility toward one another. In the process of striking at slavery, a black Underground Railroad operator was also striking at the conjoined caricature of a free black as a shiftless ne'er-do-well and of the slave as a submissive Sambo.

In the operations of the Underground Railroad the conductors, those who ventured into slave terrain seeking out prospective escapees, were invariably black, and none was better known than Harriet Tubman. To Afro-Americans she personified resistance to slavery as did no other single figure of her generation. She symbolized courage, determination, and strength.

In slave circles her status was unexcelled. The folklorist Harold Courlander points out that in the isolated communities in which many slaves were located Tubman's name was hardly likely to have been a household word, and when some slaves sang "Go Down, Moses," they must have done so "in the belief that Moses simply meant Moses." True enough. Yet Tubman's name was likely to have been an inspiration to thousands she never met, slave communities having their own systems of communication. Thomas Cole, a runaway slave from Huntsville, Alabama, said that during his escape he "was hopin and prayin all de time dat I could meets up wid dat Harriet Tubman woman." Whether in the flesh or as a symbol, Tubman made slave property less secure.

Tubman's sway over the slaves she sought to rescue was unquestionably absolute. In her relationships with those fugitives her unconscious and unstudied inclination toward self-dramatization came into its fullest sway. Communicating with slaves was easy for her. In overcoming the barrier of their mutual illiteracy, Tubman was verbally resourceful to the point of creativity, an unpolished eloquence being second na-

ture to her. She was nothing if not action-bent, but to accomplish the deed she did not scorn the word. Far from empty, her rhetoric came from a well-stocked mind. As a slave she had developed her powers of recall, memorizing recited passages from the Bible. Her visual memory was no less acute, enabling her to interlard her discourses with homely details of earlier sights and scenes. She had the gift of tongue, a trait much admired by slaves and one that made a lasting impression on them.

Tubman had a strong singing voice, adding to her hold on the fugitives. Her repertoire consisted of those spirituals that bore a barely concealed freedom ring, abounding in code words and double meanings, such as "Didn't My Lord Deliver Daniel?" As used by Tubman, whether to announce her presence in some secluded spot or to keep up the group morale at strategically timed intervals while on the road, such songs became part of slave rescue apparatus. To those she escorted to freedom, one spiritual inevitably came to acquire a special significance. It was first sung some forty years before Tubman's birth, and to the runaways it took on the aspects of prophesy now come to pass. Having lodged itself in their hearts, it came readily to their lips:

> Go down, Moses,
> Way down in Egypt land.
> Tell ole Pharaoh
> Let my people go.

Obviously, too, Tubman's profound religious faith impressed the fugitives. Themselves church-oriented, they quickly recognized in her a deeper sense of Christian commitment than was customary and a great trust in Divine Providence. Praying frequently, spontaneously and with obvious conviction and expectation, Tubman seemed to find it easy to communicate with the Deity, and sometimes she seemed as though she had received a direct reply. Hence, although the biblically knowledgeable slaves knew that God was no respecter of persons, they might sometimes have wondered whether this held for Harriet Tubman.

If the slaves and fugitives revered her, the free blacks held her in the highest esteem short of worship. In the South her free black admirers would have to speak her praises privately and in hushed tones, but blacks north of slavery sang her name in full voice, removing any doubt as to their acclaim. The black in the best position to appraise Tubman and her work was the Philadelphia-based William Still, second only to Tubman herself as the leading black figure in the Underground Railroad. As secretary and executive director of the General Vigilance Committee, Still assisted the runaways reaching Philadelphia. Every major northern city had a similar vigilance committee, but the group in Philadelphia had no equal, in large part because of Still's energetic and resourceful leadership. From his many years of working in concert with Tubman, in 1872 Still offered this assessment of her: "A more ordinary specimen of humanity could hardly be found among the most unfortunate-looking farm hands of the South. Yet in point of courage, shrewdness and disinterested exertions to rescue her fellow-men, she was without equal. . . . Her like it is probable was never known before or since."

A similarly belated appraisal came from Frederick Douglass, like Tubman an escaped slave from Maryland. In a letter he told her that he had "wrought in the day" and to public attention and applause, whereas she had "wrought in the night," her witnesses the midnight sky and the silent stars. But, he went on, "excepting John Brown — of sacred memory — I know of no one who has willingly encountered more perils and hardships to serve our enslaved people than you."

In referring to Tubman, her northern-based black contemporaries readily used the term "heroine." When in April 1860 in Troy, New York, she led a group of rescuers that overpowered the officers and assisted Charles Nalle, a fugitive slave, to escape to Canada, *The Weekly Anglo-African* (May 12, 1860)

praised her "intrepidity," capping their assessment with a complimentary comparison: "She acted like a heroine." During the Civil War, when the young schoolteacher Charlotte L. Forten visited Beaufort, South Carolina, she was ecstatic about Tubman, an entry in her diary for January 31, 1863, expressing her admiration: "We spent all our time at Harriet Tubman's. She is a wonderful woman — a real heroine." This theme recurs in a later notation in the diary for the same day: "My own eyes were full as I listened to her — the heroic woman."

Many antebellum blacks linked Tubman's name with that of Sojourner Truth, the two having much in common. Both were deeply religious former slaves. Like Tubman, the unschooled Truth had a rude eloquence, but unlike Tubman, she was a familiar figure on the lecture circuit, her six-foot frame and deep, resonant voice not without their effects on an audience. Primarily a women's rights activist, Truth played only a minor role in the Underground Railroad. Apparently the first time the two reformers met was in Boston in August 1864, Truth then assuring Tubman that President Lincoln was "our friend," in an effort to allay the latter's doubts on that score. . . .

"Not many of us are animated with the idea which seems to have possessed Harriet Tubman throughout her eventful life — to lay out time, talents, and opportunities for God's glory, and the good of our fellow-men," wrote schoolteacher Pauline E. Hopkins in 1902 in *The Colored American Magazine*. It was an evaluation that few blacks of her day would have questioned. Who among them, in a single person, had demonstrated more of a physical courage amounting to bravery, had lived a life more dedicated to the service of others, had exhibited more traits of an impeccable character, or had a deeper faith in the working of a Divine Providence?

An appraisal somewhat less celebratory and expansive characterized the reaction to Tubman by her white reformist allies. While singing her praises, white admirers hardly viewed her in the capacity of a leader or role model. While ever cordial and devoid of the person-to-person tensions so characteristic among black and white co-workers in reform movements, Tubman's experiences across the color line were not free of racial overtones, reflecting something of the prevailing patterns in race relations and attitudes. Her earliest experiences with white people were hardly reassuring. As a slave she had been constantly overworked and often whipped, whether by her master or those to whom she was hired out. She could never forget the angry overseer who had marked her for life, and she would have no fond memories of a kind and indulgent mistress. As she later explained, she had "heard tell" that there were good masters and mistresses but had not come across any of them.

Locating in Philadelphia after her escape, Tubman came in contact with a white population many of whom were in sympathy with runaway slaves and would incur any risk in assisting them. In 1775 the first organized society against slavery was founded there, its lengthy title indicating its broad program: the Pennsylvania Society for Promoting the Abolition of Slavery, the Relief of Free Negroes Unlawfully Held in Bondage, and for Improving the Condition of the African Race. Tubman became acquainted with abolitionist whites through her association with the General Vigilance Committee, which, though headed by William Still, was interracial in composition. White Underground Railroad operators in Pennsylvania and Delaware reflected a strong Quaker influence, as Tubman quickly found out.

The single white with whom Tubman worked most closely was Thomas Garrett of Wilmington, Delaware, a lifelong member of the Society of Friends. A key figure in slave rescue work along the mid-Atlantic corridor, Garrett gave much of his time and means and ran some risks to his personal safety, Delaware being a slave state. He provided shelter for the fugitives Tubman led and furnished her with the money to carry them on to Philadelphia and beyond.

In August 1857, when Tubman's escaping parents were passing through Wilmington, Garrett gave them thirty dollars to pay their way to Canada. In soliciting funds for Tubman's trips, Garrett wrote to such well-wishers as the Edinburgh Anti-Slavery Society (Scotland), telling them of her exploits. "To our brave Harriet he often rendered most efficient help in her journeys back and forth," wrote Tubman's first biographer, Sarah Bradford. In a letter to William Still on the eve of the Civil War (December 1, 1860), Garrett made a typical reference to their co-worker: "I write to let thee know that Harriet Tubman is again in these parts. She arrived last evening from one of her trips of mercy to God's poor, bringing two men with her as far as New Castle. . . ."

Tubman's attitude toward white people was shaped by her contact with reformers like Garrett — men and women who raised money for her and also gave her a kind of affection and a measure of respect. As a rule, the reform-minded whites with whom she became acquainted liked her. The courage and daring of the runaways was a stimulus to the abolitionist crusade, and Tubman personified the heroic slave.

Whites also liked Tubman because in person-to-person contacts she did not make them feel uncomfortable, burdening them with a sense of guilt. Her language and manner were marked by an absence of bitterness. To whites she was nonthreatening, not pushy, not peer-basis-minded, not status conscious, and hence not given to self-pity or bent on upward mobility. In speaking in public she tended to be folksy, anecdotal, and given to reminiscence. "She spoke in a style of quaint simplicity," wrote a reporter in 1859. Tubman was not likely to pose questions a predominantly white audience would find awkward, such as Sojourner Truth's "Is God dead?" or the Frederick Douglass inquiry as to what the Fourth of July might or might not mean to the slaves.

By their financial support the white abolitionists expressed their kindly sentiments toward Tubman. In addition to raising money specifically for her slave rescue work, they assisted her in purchasing a home in Auburn, New York, for her parents. A befriender of Tubman's, Senator William H. Seward of New York, had sold her the home on liberal terms, and to pay for it she received unsolicited donations from other white supporters. At the annual meeting of the Massachusetts Anti-Slavery Society in 1859, its president, Thomas Wentworth Higginson, asked for a collection to assist her in buying the house so that "her father and mother could support themselves, and enable her to resume the practice of her profession!" Higginson's observation was greeted by "laughter and applause."

In private, as in public, Tubman and her white associates apparently had little trouble adjusting to each other. In their homes, as in their public gatherings, Tubman expected to be hospitably received, and to a greater extent than any other antebellum black she was. Unlike some former slaves, the uninhibited Tubman seems not to have felt ill at ease in a white household, however educated or affluent the family might be.

No white reformer held Tubman in higher respect and esteem than John Brown, who made it a point to establish personal contacts with black leaders. He regarded her as a kindred spirit, and she fitted into his plans as the shepherd of the slaves he proposed to run off, by force of arms, if necessary. He was well aware that Tubman was not gun-shy (Who in abolitionist circles had not heard of the long rifle she carried on her slave rescue trips?). Brown was also aware that the Tubman name would help him raise money from her white admirers, particularly those in Massachusetts. During the eighteen months before his raid on Harpers Ferry, Virginia, in October 1859, Brown met with Tubman on some half dozen occasions, one of them lasting nearly a week. His opinion of her fortified, he called her "General" and, according to his confidant and biographer, Franklin B. Sanborn, "she was fully conversant with his plans."

Apparently due to illness, Tubman did not accompany Brown to Harpers Ferry. Immediately after the abortive raid Frederick Douglass fled to Canada to avoid being served an arrest warrant issued against him as a Brown accomplice. No such warrant was issued for Tubman; even had there been legally admissible evidence of her complicity, an arrest warrant would hardly have been practical for someone whose whereabouts were a mystery.

Brown's hanging impelled Tubman to give his life a scriptural interpretation. She promptly confided to Sanborn that she had "been studying and studying upon it, and its clar to me, it wasn't John Brown that died on the gallows. When I think how he gave up his life for our people, and how he never flinched, but was so brave to the end; its clar to me it wasn't mortal man, it was God in him." The hanged Brown never left Tubman's memory. In an interview in 1912, reporter Anne Fitzhugh Miller quoted her as referring to Brown as "my dearest Friend." . . .

[During the Civil War, which she had predicted, Tubman served as a spy and a scout for the Union army, leading expeditions into the Confederate interior to liberate slaves from enemy plantations. Her services at the battlefront drew high praise from the white officers who fought with her. After the war, she devoted herself to charitable work for African Americans and was an outspoken advocate for women's rights. For her, women's liberation and racial liberation were "inseparably linked."]

Tubman's broad appeal, cutting across lines of race and class, age and gender, received public expression upon her death. The *New York Times* carried a two-paragraph obituary (March 14, 1913), and her funeral was attended by the local post of the Grand Army of the Republic. The city of Auburn, after a year's preparation, held a day-long memorial service on June 1914, unveiling a tablet in her honor. On that day many homes flew the Stars and Stripes, thereby demonstrating "that we are not forgetful of those who suffered for the cause of freedom," in the exhortatory accents of Major Charles W. Brister. At the evening exercises held in the city auditorium the featured speaker, Booker T. Washington, eulogized

Tubman as one who "brought the two races together."

Beginning rather then ending with the observance at Auburn, the memorials to Harriet Tubman would continue over the years, taking a variety of forms and expressions. The national sentiment toward her was conveyed by agencies of the federal government. During World War II a liberty ship was christened the *Harriet Tubman,* prompting President Franklin D. Roosevelt to praise the U.S. Maritime Commission for having chosen so appropriate a name. In 1974 the Department of the Interior gave her Auburn home the status of a national historic landmark, and four years later the U.S. Postal Service issued a thirteen-cent Harriet Tubman commemorative stamp, the first in a "Black Heritage U.S.A. Series."

The mounting interest in women's history, a field sorely neglected until recent decades, has aided in keeping Tubman before us. Pointing out (in 1978) that black protest literature had focused largely on males, historian George P. Rawick advanced a corrective suggestion: "Why must we always use Nat as the name for the rebellious slave? Why not Harriet? The women's liberation movement has for some time used a poster that reproduces the image of Harriet Tubman with a long rifle. I think that might be a good symbol for the black struggle." . . .

QUESTIONS TO CONSIDER

1 What were Harriet's experiences in living under the lash in slaveholding Maryland? What factors prompted her to "steal" herself and escape to the North?

2 Why do you think Tubman invaded the South fifteen times to bring at least two hundred of her fellow slaves north to freedom? What was her incentive? Why was she so successful? What were the unique character traits of this extraordinary woman?

3 Quarles points out that Tubman was "not a one-woman Underground Railroad." What does he mean? In what ways was the Underground Railroad a cooperative operation? Name two prominent stationmasters who assisted Tubman in her slave-liberation expeditions. How did her operations and those of the Underground Railroad in general undermine the slave system and strike a blow at the white myth of the happy Sambo?

4 Who do you think is a more appropriate symbol for the rebellious slave, Nat Turner or Harriet Tubman? Explain the reasons for your choice.

5 The last two articles expose slavery as the brutal, totalitarian system that it really was. What facet of that system caused the strongest reaction in you both emotionally and intellectually? Explain your thoughts and feelings in detail.

XIII

THE DEATH OF SLAVERY

25

Why the War Came: The Sectional Struggle over Slavery in the Territories

DAVID HERBERT DONALD

Modern scholarship has thoroughly documented the central role of slavery in the sectional controversy and the outbreak of the Civil War. As James McPherson says in Battle Cry of Freedom: The Civil War Era *(1988), "the greatest danger to American survival at midcentury . . . was sectional conflict between North and South over the future of slavery." Indeed, from the 1840s on, every major sectional conflict involved the complex slavery problem, especially the expansion of slavery into the western territories and any future territories the United States might acquire. By 1848, in the words of Richard H. Sewell, slavery had become "the issue in American politics."*

As we saw in the portrait of Henry Clay (selection 18), the Union almost dissolved over the status of slavery in the territory acquired from Mexico. The Compromise of 1850 averted disaster at that juncture, and many Americans regarded it as "a final settlement" of all sectional hostilities, particularly over slavery in the national lands. That divisive issue did indeed appear to be settled. The new southwestern territories, Utah and New Mexico, had been organized without congressional conditions on slavery, which meant that the two territories could decide the issue as they wished. Utah went on to legalize the institution in 1852, and New Mexico did likewise seven years later (in 1860, however, Utah had only twenty-nine slaves and New Mexico had none). Oregon Territory, on the other hand, had outlawed slavery, and it remained prohibited by the Missouri Compromise line in the vast northern section of the old Louisiana Purchase territory, which included Minnesota Territory and an immense unorganized section.

In 1854, Congress organized that section by creating the new territories of Kansas and Nebraska. Had the Missouri Compromise line remained in effect, slavery would have been prohibited in both territories. But the Kansas-Nebraska Act overturned the Missouri Compromise and decreed that the people of each territory would decide whether to legalize or outlaw slavery. This formula was called popular sovereignty. Until the settlers of the two territories voted on the issue, southerners were free to take their slaves into a vast domain once preserved for freedom. What had caused Congress to enact such a disastrous measure? David Donald argues that southerners on Capitol Hill maneuvered Stephen A. Douglas, chief architect of the measure, into the explicit repeal of the Missouri Compromise line, because they believed that slavery would die out if it could not expand into new territory.

As it turned out, the Kansas-Nebraska Act was a monumental fiasco that reopened the divisive issue of slavery in the territories and inflamed sectional hostilities worse than ever. The measure led to the disintegration of the Whig party, to the emergence of the new all-northern Republican party, dedicated to stopping the spread of slavery, and to civil war on the Kansas prairies. Because slavery was a national problem that affected both sections of the country, armed pioneers from North and South alike poured into Kansas, establishing rival settlements and rival constitutions and governments. Lying in the nation's heartland, Kansas became the battleground for the sectional struggle over the territories and future states, a struggle that would determine whether the free states or the slave states would control the Union. Abraham Lincoln captured the sectional polarization perfectly when he wrote a southerner: "You think slavery is right and ought to be extended; while we think it is wrong and ought to be restricted. That I suppose is the rub." It was the rub indeed. And no event better illustrates that rub than the struggle over Bleeding Kansas. When Americans started killing Americans there over the future of slavery, it was a dress rehearsal for the national cataclysm a few years later.

In the selection that follows, Pulitzer Prize–winning historian David Donald discusses how the combustible issue of slavery in the territories, revived by the Kansas-Nebraska Act, divided the nation into hostile sections. He places special emphasis upon how people's perception of reality dictated the course of the North and South over the territorial issue. The successive clashes set in motion by the Kansas-Nebraska Act, Donald writes, eroded "the traditional bonds of Union" — national political parties, a faith in the Constitution, and nationalistic oratory — and sent the country hurtling toward civil war.

Donald's account is best read with the first half of the next selection on Lincoln. As you reflect on the two readings, consider a couple of crucial questions. Why did the process of compromise break down after 1854? Was the breakup of the Union inevitable?

GLOSSARY

AMERICAN PARTY (OR KNOW NOTHINGS) An anti-Catholic, anti-foreign party that appeared briefly on the national stage in the mid-1850s.

"APPEAL OF THE INDEPENDENT DEMOCRATS IN CONGRESS" Issued by Salmon P. Chase, Joshua R. Giddings, and other antislavery leaders, the appeal denounced the Kansas-Nebraska Act as part of a sinister plot to spread slavery into the territories.

BORDER RUFFIANS Proslavery Missourians who invaded neighboring Kansas, terrorizing free-state communities and voting illegally in Kansas elections; in 1855, they helped elect a proslavery territorial legislature.

BROOKS, PRESTON S. South Carolina member of Congress who in 1856 assaulted Republican senator Charles Sumner in the Senate chamber, beating him brutally with a cane; in a recent speech, Sumner had impugned the honor of Brooks's relative, Senator Andrew Pickens Butler of South Carolina. Brooks then resigned his seat and returned home in triumph. South Carolina gave him a new cane and defiantly sent him back to Congress.

BROWN, JOHN Northern abolitionist who in May 1856 directed the massacre of five proslavery men on Pottawatomie Creek in eastern Kansas. He did so in retaliation for the atrocities of proslavery forces: they had murdered six free-state men in cold blood and had sacked the free-state settlement of Lawrence, killing several others. The Pottawatomie massacre ignited a civil war in Kansas that left two hundred people dead and cost some $2 million in destroyed property.

BUCHANAN, JAMES Democratic president, 1857–1861, who tried to force Congress to admit Kansas as a slave state, a move that further split the national Democratic party.

BUFORD, JEFFERSON Alabamian who led 350 southerners to Kansas to save it for slavery.

DAVIS, JEFFERSON United States senator from Mississippi who demanded a federal slave code that would protect slavery in all the territories.

DOUGLAS, STEPHEN A. United States senator from Illinois and architect of the Kansas-Nebraska Act, who for the rest of the 1850s would defend popular sovereignty as *the* solution to the slavery question in the territories; known as the "Little Giant."

DRED SCOTT DECISION (1857) Handed down by a prosouthern Supreme Court, it held that neither Congress nor the territories (as creatures of Congress) could outlaw slavery, on the ground that this would violate the property rights clause of the United States Constitution. The decision also ruled that blacks could not be United States citizens.

FRÉMONT, JOHN CHARLES The Republican party's first nominee for president, he ran against Democrat James Buchanan in 1856; Frémont lost.

NEW ENGLAND EMIGRANT AID COMPANY Under its auspices, bands of armed northerners went to Kansas to make it a free territory and ultimately a free state.

PIERCE, FRANKLIN Democratic president, 1853–1857, who signed the disastrous Kansas-Nebraska Bill into law.

POPULAR SOVEREIGNTY The doctrine, incorporated in the Kansas-Nebraska Act, that the settlers of a territory would determine the status of slavery there by voting it in or out.

POTTAWATOMIE MASSACRE See *Brown, John.*

SECESSIONISTS Southerners who believed that only by seceding from the Union and forming an independent confederacy could the South preserve its slave-based way of life.

SUMNER, CHARLES Prominent Republican senator from Massachusetts, he was brutally beaten by Preston S. Brooks after delivering a speech on the "crime against Kansas" committed by proslavery forces.

TANEY, ROGER BROOKE   A Maryland Democrat and a former slaveholder, Chief Justice Taney wrote the majority opinion in the *Dred Scott* decision, handed down by the Supreme Court in 1857.

WILMOT PROVISO   Introduced in Congress by David Wilmot of Pennsylvania, the proviso called for the prohibition of slavery in the territory acquired from Mexico in the Mexican-American War (1846–1848); the proviso was adopted in the House, but failed in the Senate.

YANCEY, WILLIAM L.   Best-known of the southern secessionist orators, this Alabama hotspur hated the North and warned that slave insurrections would result if abolitionists there got their way.

What led to the breakdown of the Compromise of 1850 ... was ... the further agitation of the question of slavery in the national territories. This had been a central issue in the crisis of 1849–1850, until the compromise brought about what President [Millard] Fillmore praised as a settlement "in its character final and irrevocable." Finality and irrevocability lasted just long enough to see that amiable mediocrity, Franklin Pierce, installed in the White House in 1853, when the territorial question erupted again. The Kansas-Nebraska Act of 1854, the rise of the Republican party, the Dred Scott decision of 1857, the Lincoln-Douglas debates of 1858, the split between the Northern and Southern wings of the Democratic party, the election of Abraham Lincoln in 1860, and the secession of the Southern states — all directly stemmed from the renewed dispute over the status of slavery in the territories.

☆

I

In order to understand why this issue was, and remained, such a central one, it is necessary to recognize that, to a considerable extent, it was a surrogate. Under the Constitution there was nothing that the federal government could do about matters that most deeply troubled Southerners. Washington could not keep their section from falling behind the free states in wealth and in numbers. The South lost control of the House of Representatives in the 1840s; with the admission of Wisconsin (1848) and California as free states, it no longer had a majority in the Senate; and, after the death of Zachary Taylor, no Southern man could realistically aspire to become President. But the Constitution gave the federal government no au-

From David Herbert Donald, *Liberty and Union* (D.C. Heath 1978). Reprinted by permission of the author.

thority over these matters. The one field of legislation affecting the sectional balance in which the government clearly had power to act was the regulation
of the national territories. Similarly Northerners,
many of whom were deeply troubled by the moral,
economic, and political consequences of slavery, recognized that the Constitution gave the federal government no power over the peculiar institution
within the states where it existed. The national territory constituted one of the few areas where the federal government unquestionably did have authority
to act adversely toward slavery.

But even this perspective on the territorial question is too narrow. When Northern spokesmen
vowed to resist at all costs the further extension of
slavery into the national territories, they were not
merely expressing their general aversion to slavery;
they were voicing a condemnation of the whole
Southern way of life as being fundamentally un-
American. Increasingly, many Northerners viewed
the South, which they considered monolithic, as a
barrier to the achievement of the American ideal of
democratic equality. While the rest of the United
States was making great economic progress, the
South exhibited the symptoms of "premature and
consumptive decline." In contrast to the thrift, industry, and prosperity of the free states stood the
"worn out soil, dilapidated fences and tenements,
and air of general desolation" of the South. Northerners were sturdy, equal, free men; Southern whites
belonged either to a so-called aristocracy or they
were "poor, shiftless, lazy, uninstructed, cowed non-
slaveholders."

In this Northern view, slavery was responsible for
the backwardness of the South. Condemnation of
the peculiar institution did not derive primarily from
the abolitionists' moral abhorrence of slavery. Indeed, David Wilmot explained that he and his fellow
free-soilers had "no squeamish sensitiveness upon the
subject of slavery, no morbid sympathy for the
slave." Northern hostility toward the South and slavery stemmed, instead, from a sense that a distinctive

culture was rising in that region, one that rejected
the basic and hitherto shared American values of individualism and democracy.

Simultaneously, Southerners were developing a
set of stereotypes concerning the North. They
found it hard to distinguish between abolitionists
and free-soilers and viewed all Northerners, with
the exception of a few political allies, as enemies of
the South, bent upon the total destruction of its society. In Southern minds it was the free, not the
slave, states that were losing sight of the basic, cherished American values. The growth of Northern
manufacturing and commerce, the rise in the North
of cities as large and as pestilent as those of Europe,
and the influx of vast numbers of Irish and German
immigrants changed the character of Americans in
the free states. "The high-toned New England spirit
has degenerated into a clannish feeling of profound
Yankeeism," lamented a Tennessee historian. "The
masses of the North are venal, corrupt, covetous,
mean, and selfish." The "Yankee-Union," agreed
another Southerner, had become "vile, rotten, infi-
delic, puritanic, and negro-worshipping." Considering themselves as a permanent, self-conscious minority in the United States, Southerners felt they
were daily threatened by an alien and fundamentally
hostile Northern majority.

It is, on the whole, beside the point that neither of
these opposing stereotypes bore much relationship to
reality. Political democracy was about as prevalent in
one section as in another. Most Southern whites
were sober, hard-working yeoman farmers who had
little or nothing to do with slavery; they were, in
most respects, comparable to the small farmers of the
North and West. There were very few large slaveholders in the South, just as there were very few
wealthy Northern manufacturers; and the great
Southern planters were, like their Northern counterparts, hard-driving, tight-fisted, and usually prosperous businessmen. But, as so often is the case, facts
have less to do with determining the course of history than [people's] perceptions of them.

Even so, the existence of these obverse stereotypes of North and South did not necessarily lead to conflict except for the fact that, ironically, both value systems shared one fundamental belief: that slave society had to expand or perish. The origin of this idea is obscure. Perhaps it stemmed from the American experience that as the fertility of Eastern lands was depleted the center of agricultural production moved steadily West. The accuracy of this belief is debatable. Some historians argue that Southern lands were becoming exhausted, that the best tracts were being engrossed by large planters, and that small farmers had no choice but to emigrate to new territories where, perhaps, they might become great slaveowners. If there were no further slave territories into which they could move, they would be obliged to remain at home, where they would form a discontented element ultimately subversive of the slave-plantation system. Moreover, these historians add, the slave population in the United States was rapidly increasing; by 1890, it was predicted, the South would have ten million slaves. Since these could not all be profitably employed, their value would drastically drop unless they could be taken to new territory.

Other historians question this internal dynamic of slavery expansion. They point to the modern quantitative studies showing that the Southern economy during the 1850s was in very good condition, not merely in the recently opened lands of the lower Mississippi Valley but also in the older seaboard slave states. The rate of economic growth in the South, taken as a whole, was greater during the 1850s than the national average, and that section suffered far less than did the North from the panic of 1857. The per capita income of Southern white farmers (which is, of course, very different from the per capita income of all whites and blacks in the region) was not significantly lower than it was in the North. On the whole, they conclude, slavery was a very profitable institution where it already existed, and there was no special reason why — apart from the generally ex-

pansive temper of all Americans — for economic reasons it had to be extended into additional territory. But, once again, in history fact is often less important than belief.

Certain it is that virtually every Southern spokesman believed that slavery must expand or die. The same arguments for expansion appeared so frequently in the political rhetoric of the period that they became standard fare. Jefferson Davis perhaps best expressed two of the major doctrines. "We of the South," he explained, "are an agricultural people, and we require an extended territory. Slave labor is a wasteful labor, and it therefore requires a still more extended territory than would the same pursuits if they could be prosecuted by the more economical labor of white men." Restriction of slave territory, Davis noted in a secondary argument, would "crowd upon our soil an overgrown black population, until there will not be room in the country for the whites and blacks to subsist in, and in this way [it would] destroy the institution [of slavery] and reduce the whites to the degraded position of the African race."

Acting on such imperatives, Southern leaders had constantly to seek new areas into which slavery might be extended. Southerners were behind the numerous filibustering expeditions in the Caribbean during the 1850s. . . . [Their failure] made Southern leaders the more insistent that slavery must be given a chance in all the territory already part of the United States, since the peculiar institution must expand or die.

Northern free-soilers accepted this premise of slavery expansion but drew from it a conclusion exactly opposite from the Southerners'. If the extension of slavery could be prevented, they concluded, the whole slave system must collapse. Charles Sumner, the Massachusetts antislavery spokesman who succeeded in 1851 to [Daniel] Webster's place in the Senate, was confident that if slavery was restricted to the states where it presently existed it would soon die, "as a poisoned rat dies of rage in its hole." Then,

Sumner predicted, the slaveholding oligarchy that now ruled the South would sink into impotence, and nonslaveholding whites would come to realize that just as a "blade of grass would not grow where the horse of Attila had trod," so could no "true prosperity spring up in the foot-prints of the slave." They would ultimately force "open the gates of Emancipation in the Slave States." Containment, in short, really meant abolition.

☆

II

These rival sectional stereotypes, with their shared conclusion about the importance of the expansion of slavery, are what made the political controversies of the 1850s such intense struggles over what appears to be a very narrow issue. In every instance the pattern was the same: a powerful and growing majority based in the North opposed an entrenched and increasingly unified minority in the South. The consequence of the successive clashes was to weaken, one after another, the traditional bonds of Union.

After the enactment of the Compromise of 1850, the first great territorial question to come before Congress concerned Kansas — a vast area including not merely the present states of Kansas and Nebraska but most of the rest of the Louisiana Purchase west of Iowa. There were pressing reasons for creating a territorial government for this area. Settlers were already pushing into Kansas from Missouri and Iowa, but they could secure no valid titles to their farms until the federal government extinguished the Indian claims and made a land survey. Territorial organization was also necessary before a transcontinental railroad could be built through the region. Ever since the acquisition of California, the need for direct rail connection with the Pacific coast had been obvious. Some preferred a Southern route, and in order to facilitate its construction the Pierce administration in 1853 purchased an additional tract of land, known as

the Gadsden Purchase, from Mexico. Others looked for a railroad connecting Lake Superior with the Oregon country. Stephen A. Douglas, the chairman of the powerful Senate Committee on Territories, was not opposed to either of these plans, but he also wanted a middle route, connecting San Francisco with St. Louis and Chicago. But before Congress could authorize such a road, it had to provide a government for the territory through which it would run.

By the 1850s any proposal to organize a new territory immediately raised the question of the status of slavery in that territory. In the case of Kansas, the answer at first seemed simple and obvious: the Missouri Compromise had excluded slavery from this region. But by this time Southerners, convinced that slavery must expand or die and unable to acquire further foreign soil, were unwilling to abide by that restriction. Perhaps few Southern congressmen, who were better informed than most of their constituents, ever thought Kansas would become a slave state, but they knew that if they accepted a prohibition on slavery they would be assailed at home. In Mississippi, John A. Quitman thundered that the expansion of slavery was a question of conscience, on which no compromise was ever possible.... The South Carolina fire-eater, Robert Barnwell Rhett, declared that Southern rights had to be maintained even if not a single Southern planter ever set foot in the territory. "But the right is important," Rhett insisted, "because it applies to future acquisitions of territory; and by refusing to acknowledge the obligations of the Missouri compromise, you force open the whole question of power." With such war drums beating in the background, Southern votes in 1853 defeated a proposal to organize Kansas as a free territory.

Douglas cared little about slavery one way or the other, but he cared a great deal about the organization of Western territories and the construction of a transcontinental railroad. In 1854, hoping to create a territorial government in Kansas, he sponsored a bill

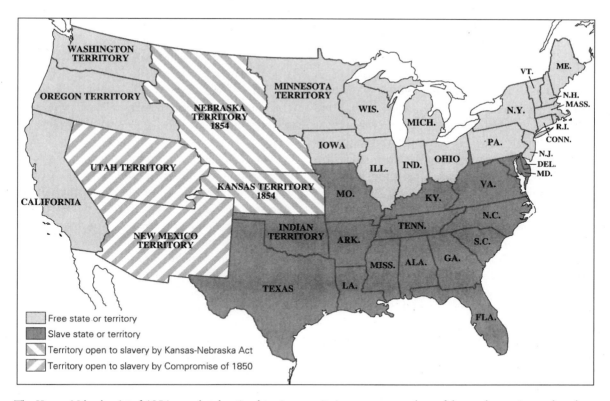

The Kansas-Nebraska Act of 1854 exacerbated sectional tension over slavery in the territories. The measure nullified the Missouri Compromise line, which had prohibited slavery in the old Louisiana Purchase above the latitude of 36° 30'. Two new ter-ritories were now carved out of that northern region, and southerners were free to extend slavery there until such time as the residents voted to outlaw it.

that discreetly failed to mention either slavery or the Missouri Compromise. When Southern senators, whose votes were needed to pass the bill, pointed out that his measure would, because of its silence, leave the Missouri Compromise restriction against slavery in effect, the "Little Giant" discovered that, through "clerical error," an essential section of his bill had been omitted, one that gave the inhabitants of the Kansas territory the power to deal with slavery. Southern congressmen claimed that not even this resort to popular sovereignty was enough, and Douglas further amended his proposal to declare explicitly that the Missouri Compromise was "inopera-

tive" and "void." At the same time he agreed to divide the huge region into two territories, Kansas and Nebraska.

Charged by critics with caving in to proslavery interests, Douglas was, in actuality, attempting to repeat in 1854 the coup he had brought off in the Compromise of 1850. He was willing to add to his bill almost any amendments concerning slavery because he thought them irrelevant and inconsequential. Since, as he believed, "the laws of climate, and of production, and of physical geography have excluded slavery from that country," the wording of the legislation was a "matter of no practical importance." Douglas would, therefore, give the South the language it wanted and the North the substance. To make this compromise palatable, Douglas sought to sweeten it for all parties — just as he had done in 1850 — by sponsoring not one but at least three transcontinental railroad projects, which would give speculators, builders, and politicians in all sections urgent practical reasons for backing his measure.

But the strategy that had succeeded in 1850 failed in 1854. To be sure, Southerners, after an initial period of indifference, came out in support of Douglas's bill and they bullied President Pierce into endorsing it. Following one of the bitterest debates ever to occur in Congress, during which Douglas demonstrated again his superb gifts as a parliamentary tactician, both the Senate and the House passed the bill, and it received the President's signature on May 30. But this time there was no hurrahing that Douglas had saved the Union, no vast public celebration of the new compromise. Instead, when Douglas returned to Illinois at the end of the hard-fought session, he found his way from Washington to Chicago lighted by bonfires where he was being burned in effigy.

Three things had gone wrong with Douglas's calculations. First, the congressional debates on the Kansas-Nebraska bill were so protracted and intricate, so demanding on his time, that he was unable to give sufficient attention to his railroad proposals, which were bottled up in committee, where they died. In 1854, therefore, he could not rally behind his new compromise the powerful influence of America's first big business, the railroad. Second, by permitting Southerners to maneuver him into outright repeal of the Missouri Compromise, Douglas, as many Northerners believed, came close to tampering with the Constitution. Of course, the Missouri Compromise was not part of the written Constitution, but it was an agreement that had almost constitutional status, having been observed loyally for more than three decades and having acquired, as Douglas himself declared in 1849, respect as "a sacred thing which no ruthless hand would ever be

reckless enough to disturb." Third, the congressional maneuvering on the Kansas-Nebraska bill suggested to many Northerners that the great national political parties, which had hitherto served as agents of national unity and sectional conciliation, could instead be exploited to ensure minority rule rather than majority rights. Given a free choice, virtually all Northerners in Congress would have opposed the Kansas-Nebraska bill, but the Pierce administration, using every appeal, from party loyalty to political patronage, applied pressure so intense that a majority of the free-state Democrats voted for it.

To many, this unprecedented misuse of a national party to promote a sectional interest served as a signal that a general political realignment in the United States was long overdue. As early as 1848, early moves in this direction had been made when young Northern Whigs opposed to slavery, disaffected Democratic followers of Martin Van Buren, and former Liberty party men coalesced to form the Free-Soil party. The Compromise of 1850 had weakened traditional parties in the South. . . .

. . . In the years after the passage of the Kansas-Nebraska Act, increasing numbers of Southern Whigs, whose state parties were already in disarray, slipped . . . into the Democratic party. As a consequence, all but one of the slave states voted for James Buchanan, the successful Democratic candidate for President, in 1856. But what the Democratic party gained in the South it lost in the North. Of the 86 Northern Democrats in the House of Representatives, 42 voted, despite all the pressure Pierce could bring to bear, against the Kansas-Nebraska Act. Though many of these remained in the Democratic party, others defected. As a result of these shifts, the center of gravity in the Democratic party shifted sharply to the South after 1854. The party that had once served as a strong bond of national unity now became an equally powerful force for divisive sectionalism.

Meanwhile a major new party opposed to the Democracy was emerging in the North. Early in the debates on Douglas's Kansas bill, antislavery leaders in Congress, including Salmon P. Chase and Joshua R. Giddings of Ohio and Sumner of Massachusetts, issued a widely circulated "Appeal of the Independent Democrats in Congress to the People of the United States," which denounced Douglas's measure "as a gross violation of a sacred pledge; as a criminal betrayal of precious rights; as part and parcel of an atrocious plot to exclude from a vast unoccupied region immigrants from the Old World and free laborers from our own States, and convert it into a dreary region of despotism, inhabited by masters and slaves." Skillfully incorporating two basic free-soil beliefs — that free labor and slave labor could not coexist within the same territory and that slavery blighted the economy wherever it was introduced — the Appeal served as a rallying point, during the protracted debates, for a protest movement throughout the North, in which antislavery Whigs, former members of the Liberty party, and free-soil Democrats joined. Initially given the awkward designation of the "anti-Nebraska" party, the coalition soon accepted the name "Republican."...

... The 1856 presidential election revealed even more decisively the shift in Northern voting patterns. Though Buchanan was elected, he carried only five of the free states and received fewer votes than the combined totals of the American party candidate, Fillmore, and the Republican nominee, the explorer and adventurer John C. Frémont. When voting returns are analyzed on a county-by-county basis, it becomes evident that in most of the free states the Republicans were neither simply former Whigs nor former Democrats masquerading under a new guise; the Republican party was a genuine fusion of free-soil elements from all the earlier parties. The new party was even more strongly sectional than the Democracy, for it had virtually no strength in any slave state. Thus in the North as in the South the party system, once a strong unifying bond for the nation, became a powerful divisive force.

☆

III

Equally ominous was the weakening of the American faith in the Constitution that resulted, though less promptly, from the Kansas-Nebraska Act. Almost immediately it became apparent that Douglas's measure, designed to settle the problems of Kansas, aggravated them. Many of the difficulties in that territory were those of other frontier regions: disputes over land titles, controversies over lucrative governmental contracts for trading with the Indians and carrying the mails, rivalries over the location of county seats, and struggles for the multiplying number of public offices paying generous salaries and profitable fees. But in Kansas these questions took on added significance, because the vehement congressional debates had singled out this territory as the battleground of slavery and freedom. (Everybody conceded that Nebraska would become a free state. Significantly the usual frontier difficulties in that territory received little general attention and were readily settled.)

Since everybody agreed that slavery had to expand or die, and since Kansas was the only national territory into which it could conceivably expand, proslavery and antislavery forces girded up for Armageddon. Throughout the North, organizations such as the New England Emigrant Aid Company recruited quasi-military bands of settlers and sent them to Kansas to help make it a free state. In the South, Jefferson Buford of Alabama sold forty of his slaves to help finance a 350-man expedition designed to save Kansas for slavery. Buford's followers carried Bibles provided by citizens of Montgomery and raised aloft banners that read "The Supremacy of the White Race" and "Kansas, the Outpost." Most of these systematic efforts to colonize Kansas were not successful, and most immigrants to the territory drifted in independently, looking for land and fortune. The Southern contingent of settlers had a ready reserve force in the proslavery inhabitants of Missouri, who were prepared whenever called to pour over the border to cast ballots in territorial elections or to harass free-soilers.

Something close to a state of civil war in Kansas resulted from the frequent conflicts between the free-state settlers and the Southern immigrants reinforced by these Missouri "border ruffians." Both proslavery and free-soil groups held elections for constitutional conventions, and each faction boycotted the election sponsored by its rival. Rival conventions met and drew up constitutions, one guaranteeing slavery in Kansas, the other excluding it; and contending delegations sent to Washington sought congressional approval. A series of territorial governors sent by the federal government could do nothing to bring the opposing sides together.

The danger grew that the usual frontier lawlessness in Kansas might turn into organized blood-letting. On the night of May 24–25, 1856, John Brown, a dedicated, single-minded abolitionist who had emigrated to Kansas after an unsuccessful career in the East as a tanner, sheep raiser, and land speculator, opened hostilities. Without warning, he led a small party, consisting mostly of his own sons, in an attack on the cabins of two Southern families who lived on Pottawatomie Creek and murdered five men, leaving their gashed and mutilated bodies as a warning for other proslavery families to leave Kansas.[*] In revenge, Southern immigrants organized and attacked Brown at Osawatomie, where Brown's son Frederick was killed. Only Brown's departure for the East prevented further slaughter.

At this unpropitious moment, the Supreme Court of the United States decided to risk its prestige and the enormous respect that Americans gave to its exposition of the revered Constitution, in an effort to

Dred Scott in 1858, a year after the Supreme Court decision that bore his name. Originally called Sam, Dred Scott, a slave, sought his freedom on the grounds that he had lived for a time in a free state and a free territory. His case led to one of the most infamous Supreme Court decisions in American judicial history. Bought and freed by a white benefactor in 1857, Scott became a porter at a St. Louis hotel and died in 1858. (Missouri Historical Society)

resolve the snarled question of the status of slavery in the national territories. The events leading up to the Dred Scott decision of 1857 were enormously complex, and no purpose is served by reviewing here the legal intricacies of the case before the Court. At issue was the legal status of Dred Scott, a Missouri slave, who had been taken in the 1830s by his owner, an army surgeon, first to Rock Island, Illinois, a state where slavery was prohibited by the Northwest Ordinance and its own constitution, and subsequently to Fort Snelling in what is now Minnesota, part of the Louisiana Purchase from which slavery had been excluded by the Missouri Compromise. Scott re-

---

[*]Brown instigated the Pottawatomie massacre in retaliation for atrocities committed by proslavery forces in Kansas. See the *John Brown* entry in the glossary. — Ed.

354

turned with his owner to Missouri, but later he sued for his freedom on the ground that he had been resident first of a free state and then of a free territory. After complex and contradictory rulings in the lower courts, his case came before the Supreme Court for the definitive determination of two broad questions: (1) Was a Negro like Scott a citizen of the United States, who was, therefore, entitled to initiate a suit in the federal courts? (2) Was the congressional prohibition of slavery in federal territories, whether in the Missouri Compromise or in subsequent legislation, constitutional?

Initially the justices of the high court planned to avoid these sweeping issues and to deliver a limited opinion, following numerous precedents, declaring that the status of Scott, who continued to be a resident of Missouri, was determined by Missouri state law. Such a decision would have left Scott a slave, but it would have avoided initiating broader controversy. . . .

. . . [But] the aged, high-minded Chief Justice, Roger B. Taney, believed that the American public wished it to settle, once and for all, the critically divisive question of slavery in the territories. In the years since the introduction of the Wilmot Proviso, there had been numerous proposals that the Supreme Court be asked to decide the whole territorial issue. . . .

Consequently, in March 1857, the Court gave such a decision. To be more accurate, it issued nine separate opinions, for each justice made a separate statement. Since these did not all address the same problems, it was not altogether easy to determine just what the Court had decided, but the chief justice seemed to speak for the majority of his brethren on the two essential issues. First he ruled that Scott, as a Negro, was not a citizen of the United States. Neither the Declaration of Independence nor the Constitution, he alleged, was intended to include blacks. The Founding Fathers, claimed Taney with a cheerful disregard of much historical evidence, lived at a period when Negroes were "regarded as beings of an inferior order, and altogether unfit to associate with the white race, . . . and so far inferior that they had no rights which the white man was bound to respect." As a noncitizen, Scott had no right to bring suit in United States courts. Addressing the second major issue, the chief justice announced that when Congress made regulations for governing the territories, its power was restrained by the Fifth Amendment to the Constitution, which prohibits the taking of property without "due process of law." All citizens had an equal right to enter any of the national territories with their property, and slaves were a variety of property. It followed that any congressional enactment — and specifically the Missouri Compromise — that excluded slavery from any national territory was "not warranted by the Constitution" and was "therefore void."

With the advantage of hindsight, it is easy to argue that the Dred Scott decision was of no great practical consequence. Four months after the Court's ruling, Scott's owner manumitted him and his family. The Missouri Compromise, which the Court struck down, had already been repealed in the Kansas-Nebraska Act. The Dred Scott decision did not open vast new areas for the extension of slavery, simply because since 1854 slavery was already permitted in all the territories into which it might conceivably go.

If the practical results of the Dred Scott decision were negligible, its consequences for the American faith in constitutionalism, hitherto one of the strongest bonds of Union, were fateful. As was to be expected, Southerners generally welcomed the decision as a vindication of their rights, and a good many agreed with Jefferson Davis that it meant Congress must enact a slave code that gave positive protection to slavery in all the territories. Southern enthusiasm was tempered, however, by a recognition that most Northerners would not accept the Court's ruling as definitive.

In truth, there was virtually universal condemnation of the decision in the North. Douglas and his Northern Democratic following were hard hit, because the Court appeared to have announced that popular sovereignty was unconstitutional. If Congress could not exclude slavery from a territory, a handful of settlers clearly could not do so either. Attempting to respect the Court, to preserve his doctrine of popular sovereignty, and to keep the Democratic party intact, Douglas devised an elaborate straddle. He conceded the abstract right of the slaveowner to take his chattels into the national territory but pragmatically noted that it was "a barren and worthless right, unless sustained, protected and enforced by appropriate police regulations and local legislation. . . ." Republicans, who had no Southern constituency, did not suffer from the same constraints as Douglas and angrily denounced the Court's "false and wicked judgment," which, as the New York *Tribune* claimed, was "entitled to just as much moral weight as would be the judgment of a majority of those congregated in any Washington bar-room."

☆

IV

At just the time that the great unifying belief in constitutionalism was being eroded, the third great bond of Union, nationalistic oratory, was losing its force. In the South the death of Calhoun removed the last great orator for Union. Though Calhoun was a proponent of nullification and an advocate of Southern sectionalism, he always spoke of the Union with veneration. Even in his final address, explaining why he thought it too late in 1850 for meaningful compromise, he lamented the breaking of national ties.

Calhoun's successors had no such regrets. The most notable of the Southern sectionalist orators was William L. Yancey of Alabama, who was as unswerving in his hatred for the North as he was in his devotion to slavery. With spell-binding rhetoric, Yancey alerted his Southern audiences to the dangers that would result from the success of Northern abo-

litionism. The South, he predicted, would see a repetition of scenes from the Santo Domingo slave rebellion of the 1790s, "where wives were violated upon the bodies of their slaughtered husbands, and the banner of the inhuman fiends was the dead body of an infant, impaled upon a spear, its golden locks dabbled in gore, and its little limbs stiffened by the last agony of suffering nature." Openly an advocate of secession, Yancey explained the purpose of his orations: "All my aims and objects are to cast before the people of the South as great a mass of wrongs committed on them, injuries and insults that have been done, as I possibly can. . . . All united may yet produce spirit enough to lead us forward, to call forth a Lexington, to fight a Bunker's Hill, to drive the [Northern] foe from the city of our rights."

Equally ominous was the disappearance of the oratory of national conciliation in the North. Charles Sumner was not merely Webster's successor in the Senate; he was the new voice of Massachusetts. Drawing upon his Harvard education, his broad reading, and his first-hand knowledge of European developments, Sumner deliberately set about preparing orations that would unite the North in opposition to the South. The very titles of his major addresses indicated his purpose: "Freedom National, Slavery Sectional," "The Barbarism of Slavery," and so on. Because of its consequences, Sumner's most famous oration was "The Crime Against Kansas," delivered in the Senate on May 19–20, 1856, as a commentary on the continuing violence in the Kansas territory. Taking as axiomatic the argument that slavery must expand or die, Sumner claimed that the disturbances in Kansas following the passage of the Kansas-Nebraska Act were evidence of the desperate attempt of Southerners to rape that "virgin territory, compelling it to the hateful embrace of slavery."

In his carefully prepared speech, Sumner attacked Douglas and made offensive personal references to the elderly South Carolina senator, Andrew Pickens Butler, whom he characterized as the Don Quixote of slavery, having "chosen a mistress to whom he has made his vows, and who, though ugly to others, is always lovely to him, though polluted in the sight of the world, is chaste in his sight . . . the harlot, Slavery." Butler was absent from the Senate during Sumner's speech, but his cousin, Representative Preston S. Brooks of South Carolina, seethed over the insult to his family and state. On May 22, before the Senate was called to order, Brooks entered the Senate chamber, approached Sumner, who was seated at his desk writing, and proceeded to punish him by beating him on the head and shoulders with a stout cane. He left Sumner bleeding and insensible in the aisle. It was nearly three years before Sumner recovered from his wounds. During that period, the Massachusetts legislature reelected him to the Senate, where his vacant chair spoke as powerfully for sectionalism as ever Webster had done for Union.

During these years of Sumner's silence, there sounded in the West an even more eloquent voice of sectionalism. [It was the voice of] Abraham Lincoln of Illinois. . . . In a series of nationally publicized debates with Douglas in the 1858 campaign [for the Little Giant's Senate seat, Lincoln] eloquently voiced both the aspirations and the fears of the free-soilers. If, to the present-day reader, the Lincoln-Douglas debates seem to revolve repetitiously around the one limited issue of slavery in the territories, it must be remembered that virtually every political leader in the North and the South agreed that that point was of the utmost importance, since slavery had to grow or it would wither away. After a strenuous campaign, Douglas was reelected to the Senate, but Lincoln emerged as the real victor. Throughout the North, antislavery men now perceived the issues in terms of the stark contrasts Lincoln had presented in the opening address of his campaign:

"A house divided against itself cannot stand."
I believe this government cannot endure, permanently half *slave* and half *free*.

I do not expect the Union to be *dissolved* — I do not expect the house to *fall* — but I *do* expect it will cease to be divided.
It will become *all* one thing, or *all* the other.

With the issue thus baldly stated, the outcome was simply a matter of time. The great forces that had once helped cement American unity — the Constitution, the political parties, the public oratory — now served to divide the people. The United States, it now appeared, was not, and never really had been, a nation; it was merely a loose assemblage of diverse and conflicting groups, interests, and peoples. By the late 1850s these had polarized into two groups, a majority in the North, and a minority in the South. Neither majority nor minority was willing to yield on what both regarded as the vital issue of the expansion of slavery. And the war came.

Donald concedes that this "sketch" is oversimplified. For clarity, he had to "gloss over the fact that neither North nor South was monolithic" and that important groups in both sections dissented from the dominant attitudes. "When a historian speaks of 'the North' or 'the South,'" Donald writes, "he is using a convenient shorthand to refer to the articulate groups who gained control of the political machinery in those sections."

QUESTIONS TO CONSIDER

1   What were the emerging visions that northerners and southerners had of each other in the 1850s? What basic belief about slavery did they share? Why does Donald say that the issue of slavery in the territories was in great part a "surrogate"? Do you agree with the implication that slavery itself was not the major issue dividing North and South? What do you think was the major cause of the Civil War?

2   When Stephen A. Douglas put forth the Kansas-Nebraska Bill in 1854, what was his position on slav-

ery and how did he hope to solve the problem? Why was the Kansas–Nebraska Bill a failure, and how did the failure affect the major political parties? What was its effect on the political process in Kansas?

3   What were the major questions involved in the *Dred Scott* case, and how did the Supreme Court rule on them? What were the consequences of this decision? If Americans were losing their faith in the Constitution as Donald says, why do you think the *Dred Scott* decision caused such a furor?

4   According to Donald, how did the role of oratory change during the 1850s? What do you think is the significance of Brooks's attack against Sumner? If men such as Sumner and Lincoln were upholding sectionalism versus union, why do you think they would soon devote all their energies to prosecuting the Civil War?

5   As the bonds of union snapped, Donald says that the coming of civil war became "simply a matter of time." Do you agree that the Civil War was inevitable and, if you do, when do you think it became so and why?

26

Lincoln's Journey
to Emancipation

STEPHEN B. OATES

Nobody was more upset about the troubles in Kansas than Abraham Lincoln. For him and his Republican colleagues, the Kansas-Nebraska Act, the Kansas civil war, and the Dred Scott decision were all part of an insidious design to spread slavery across the West and ultimately to nationalize that hated institution. From 1854 on, Lincoln was in the thick of the struggle to block slavery expansion, to keep the peculiar institution out of the territories by the force of national law. The first half of the next essay describes Lincoln's battles against both Stephen A. Douglas and proslavery southerners and discusses Lincoln's own solution to slavery before the Civil War, which was a modification of Jefferson's and Clay's plans. You will not only meet an eloquent public Lincoln with a vision of America's historic mission in the world but a private Lincoln troubled by doubts and insecurities, romantic difficulties, and an obsession with death. That same Lincoln, however, was as ambitious as he was deeply principled. He built up a remarkably successful law career, fought Douglas for his seat in the United States Senate, and carried the banner of slave containment all the way to the White House.

The second half of the essay traces Lincoln's evolving emancipation policy during the Civil War. Throughout the first year and a half of the conflict, Lincoln insisted that the North was fighting strictly to save the Union, not to free the slaves. But a combination of problems and pressures caused him to change his mind, and in September 1862, he issued the preliminary Emancipation Proclamation, to take effect on January 1, 1863. The proclamation announced that, after that date, Union military forces would liberate the slaves in the rebellious states.

How Lincoln approached the problem of slavery — and what he did about it — is one of the most written about and least understood facets of his presidency. Indeed, the subject has made Lincoln far more controversial than Andrew Jackson. Ever since he issued his proclamation, legends have flourished about Lincoln as the Great Emancipator — a man who dedicated himself to liberty and equality for all. On the other hand, counterlegends of Lincoln as a Great Racist eventually emerged among white segregationists and among many modern African Americans as well. Which view is correct? Should Lincoln be applauded as a great humanitarian, or was he just another white bigot, as one black historian recently contended? Or, as some of his contemporaries charged, was he an unscrupulous opportunist who sought to eradicate slavery merely for political and military expediency?

Drawing on modern scholarship about Lincoln's life and the times in which he lived, the author of this essay tries to answer the enduring questions about Lincoln and emancipation and to present a realistic portrait of one of the most mythologized human beings in American history. The author concludes that Lincoln truly hated slavery — "If slavery is not wrong," Lincoln thundered "nothing is wrong" — and that he attacked the peculiar institution in part because of deeply held moral principles. In the end, it was this tall and melancholy man who found in a terrible civil war the means of removing the paradox of slavery in "the land of the free."

GLOSSARY

CHANDLER, ZACHARIAH   One of three Republican senators who pressed Lincoln to free the slaves.

CONFISCATION ACT (SECOND)   Provided for the seizure and liberation of all slaves of people who supported or participated in the rebellion; the measure exempted slaveholders in the Confederacy who were loyal to the Union; most slaves would be freed only after case-by-case litigation in the federal courts.

DOUGLASS, FREDERICK   Eminent black abolitionist and editor who pressured Lincoln to free the slaves and enlist black soldiers.

EMANCIPATION PROCLAMATION (JANUARY 1, 1863)   Freed the slaves in the rebel states save for occupied Tennessee and certain areas in Virginia and Louisiana behind Union lines; announced that henceforth Lincoln's military forces would accept black men.

GEORGIA PEN   Slave-trading pen in Washington, D.C., that offended Lincoln.

LINCOLN, MARY TODD   Lincoln's wife and mother of four Lincoln boys, one of whom died in childhood and a second of whom (Willie) died during the Civil War.

REFUGEE SYSTEM   Installed by Lincoln's adjutant general in the Mississippi Valley in 1863; the adjutant enrolled all able-bodied black men in the army and put others to work as laborers in the military or on confiscated farms and plantations for wages.

SPEED, JOSHUA   Lincoln's intimate friend in whom he confided his romantic fears in the 1840s.

SUMNER, CHARLES　A personal friend of Lincoln's and a major Lincoln adviser on foreign affairs; one of three Republican senators who pressed Lincoln to free the slaves.

THIRTEENTH AMENDMENT　Ratified in December 1865, it guaranteed the permanency of Lincoln's Emancipation Proclamation by abolishing slavery everywhere in the country.

☆

1

He comes to us in the mists of legend as a kind of homespun Socrates, brimming with prairie wit and folk wisdom. He is as honest, upright, God-fearing, generous, and patriotic an American as the Almighty ever created. Impervious to material rewards and social station, the Lincoln of mythology is the Great Commoner, a saintly Rail Splitter who spoke in a deep, fatherly voice about the genius of the plain folk. He comes to us, too, as the Great Emancipator who led the North off to Civil War to free the slaves and afterward offered his fellow Southerners a tender and forgiving hand.

There is a counterlegend of Lincoln — one shared ironically enough by many white Southerners and certain black Americans of our time. This is the legend of Lincoln as bigot, as a white racist who championed segregation, opposed civil and political rights for black people, wanted them all thrown out of the country. This Lincoln is the great ancestor of racist James K. Vardaman of Mississippi, of "Bull" Connor of Birmingham, of the white citizens' councils, of the Knights of the Ku Klux Klan.

Neither of these views, of course, reveals much about the man who really lived — legends and politicized interpretations seldom do. The real Lincoln was not a saintly emancipator, and he was not an unswerving racist either. To understand him and the liberation of the slaves, one must eschew artificial, arbitrary categories and focus on the man as he lived, on the flesh-and-blood Lincoln, on that flawed and fatalistic individual who struggled with himself and his countrymen over the profound

Reprinted from *Our Fiery Trial: Abraham Lincoln, John Brown, and the Civil War Era,* by Stephen B. Oates, copyright © 1978 by the University of Massachusetts Press.

moral paradox of slavery in a nation based on the Declaration of Independence. Only by viewing Lincoln scrupulously in the context of his own time can one understand the painful, ironic, and troubled journey that led him to the Emancipation Proclamation and to the Thirteenth Amendment that made it permanent.

☆

2

As a man, Lincoln was complex, many-sided, and richly human. He was almost entirely self-educated, with a talent for expression that in another time and place might have led him into a literary career. He wrote poetry himself and studied Shakespeare, Byron, and Oliver Wendell Holmes, attracted especially to writings with tragic and melancholy themes. He examined the way celebrated orators turned a phrase or employed a figure of speech, admiring great truths greatly told. Though never much at impromptu oratory, he could hold an audience of 15,000 spellbound when reading from a written speech, singing out in a shrill, high-pitched voice that became his trademark.

He was an intense, brooding person, plagued with chronic depression most of his life. "I am now the most miserable man living," he said on one occasion in 1841. "If what I feel were equally distributed to the whole human family, there would not be one cheerful face on the earth." He added, "To remain as I am is impossible; I must die or be better."

At the time he said this, Lincoln had fears of sexual inadequacy, doubting his ability to please or even care for a wife. In 1842 he confided in his closest friend, Joshua Speed, about his troubles, and both confessed that they had fears of "nervous debility" with women. Speed went ahead and married anyway and then wrote Lincoln that their anxieties were groundless. Lincoln rejoiced, "I tell you, Speed, our forebodings, for which you and I are rather peculiar,

are all the worst sort of nonsense." Encouraged by Speed's success, Lincoln finally wedded Mary Todd; and she obviously helped him overcome his doubts, for they developed a strong and lasting physical love for one another.

Still, Lincoln remained a moody, melancholy man, given to long introspections about things like death and mortality. In truth, death was a lifelong obsession with him. His poetry, speeches, and letters are studded with allusions to it. He spoke of the transitory nature of human life, spoke of how all people in this world are fated to die in the end — all are fated to die. He saw himself as only a passing moment in a rushing river of time.

Preoccupied with death, he was also afraid of insanity, afraid (as he phrased it) of "the pangs that kill the mind." In his late thirties, he wrote and rewrote a poem about a boyhood friend, one Matthew Gentry, who became deranged and was locked "in mental night," condemned to a living death, spinning out of control in some inner void. Lincoln retained a morbid fascination with Gentry's condition, writing about how Gentry was more an object of dread than death itself: "A human form with reason fled, while wretched life remains." Yet, Lincoln was fascinated with madness, troubled by it, afraid that what had happened to Gentry could also happen to him — his own reason destroyed, Lincoln spinning in mindless night without the power to know.

Lincoln was a teetotaler because liquor left him "flabby and undone," blurring his mind and threatening his self-control. And he dreaded and avoided anything which threatened that. In one memorable speech, he heralded some great and distant day when all passions would be subdued, when reason would triumph and "*mind, all conquering mind*," would rule the earth.

One side of Lincoln was always supremely logical and analytical. He was intrigued with the clarity of mathematics; and as an attorney he could command a mass of technical data. Yet he was also extremely superstitious, believed in signs and visions, contended that dreams were auguries of approaching triumph or calamity. He was skeptical of organized religion and never joined a church; yet he argued that all human destinies were controlled by an omnipotent God.

It is true that Lincoln told folksy anecdotes to illustrate a point. But humor was also tremendous therapy for his depressions — a device "to whistle down sadness," as a friend put it. Lincoln liked all kinds of jokes, from bawdy tales to pungent rib-ticklers like "Bass-Ackwards," a story he wrote down and handed a bailiff one day. Filled with hilarious spoonerisms, "Bass-Ackwards" is about a fellow who gets thrown from his horse and lands in "a great *tow-curd*," which gives him a "*sick of fitness*." About "*bray dake*," he comes to and dashes home to find "the *door* sick abed, and his *wife* standing open. But thank goodness," the punch line goes, "she is getting right *hat* and *farty* again."

Contrary to legend, Lincoln was anything but a common man. In point of fact, he was one of the most ambitious human beings his friends had ever seen, with an aspiration for high station in life that burned in him like a furnace. Instead of reading with an accomplished attorney, as was customary in those days, he taught himself the law entirely on his own. He was literally a self-made lawyer. Moreover, he entered the Illinois legislature at the age of twenty-five and became a leader of the state Whig party, a tireless party campaigner, and a regular candidate for public office.

As a self-made man, Lincoln felt embarrassed about his log-cabin origins and never liked to talk about them. He seldom discussed his parents either and became permanently estranged from his father, who was all but illiterate. In truth, Lincoln had considerable hostility for his father's intellectual limitations, once remarking that Thomas "never did more in the way of writing than to bunglingly sign his own name." When his father died in a nearby Illinois county in 1851, Lincoln did not attend the funeral.

By the 1850s, Lincoln was one of the most sought-after attorneys in Illinois, with a reputation as a lawyer's lawyer — a knowledgeable jurist who argued appeal cases for other attorneys. He did his most influential legal work in the Supreme Court of Illinois, where he participated in 243 cases and won most of them. He commanded the respect of his colleagues, all of whom called him "Mr. Lincoln" or just "Lincoln." Nobody called him Abe — at least not to his face — because he loathed the nickname. It did not befit a respected professional who'd struggled hard to overcome the limitations of his frontier background. Frankly, Lincoln enjoyed his status as a lawyer and politician, and he liked money, too, and used it to measure his worth. By the mid–1850s, thanks to a combination of talent and sheer hard work, Lincoln was a man of substantial wealth. He had an annual income of around $5,000 — the equivalent of many times that today — and large financial and real-estate investments.

Though a man of status and influence, Lincoln was as honest in real life as in the legend. Even his enemies conceded that he was incorruptible. Moreover, he possessed broad humanitarian views, some of them in advance of his time. Even though he was a teetotaler, he was extremely tolerant of alcoholics, regarding them not as criminals — the way most temperance people did — but as unfortunates who deserved understanding, not vilification. He noted that some of the world's most gifted artists had succumbed to alcoholism, because they were too sensitive to cope with their insights into the human condition. He believed that women, like men, should vote so long as they all paid taxes. And he had no ethnic prejudices. His law partner William Herndon, who cursed the Irish with a flourish, reported that Lincoln was not at all prejudiced against "the foreign element, tolerating — as I never could — even the Irish."

Politically, Lincoln was always a nationalist in outlook, an outlook that began when he was an Indiana farm boy tilling his father's mundane wheat field.

While the plow horse was getting its breath at the end of a furrow, Lincoln would study Parson Weems's eulogistic biography of George Washington, and he would daydream about the Revolution and the origins of the Republic, daydream about Washington and Jefferson as great national statesmen who shaped the course of history. By the time he became a politician, Lincoln idolized the Founding Fathers as apostles of liberty (never mind for now that many of these apostles were also Southern slaveowners). Young Lincoln extolled the founders for beginning an experiment in popular government on this continent, to show a doubting Europe that people could govern themselves without hereditary monarchs and aristocracies. And the foundation of the American experiment was the Declaration of Independence, which in Lincoln's view contained the highest political truths in history: that all men are created equal and are entitled to freedom and the pursuit of happiness. Which for Lincoln meant that men like him were not chained to the condition of their births, that they could better their station in life and harvest the fruits of their own talents and industry. Thus he had a deep, personal reverence for the Declaration and insisted that all his political sentiment flowed from that document.

☆

3

Which brings us to the problem and paradox of slavery in America. Lincoln maintained that he had always hated human bondage, as much as any abolitionist. His family had opposed the peculiar institution, and Lincoln had grown up and entered Illinois politics thinking it wrong. But before 1854 (and the significance of that date will become clear) Lincoln generally kept his own counsel about slavery and abolition. After all, slavery was the most inflammable issue of his generation, and Lincoln observed early on what violent passions Negro bondage — and the

question of race that underlay it — could arouse in white Americans. In his day, as I have said, slavery was a tried and tested means of race control in a South absolutely dedicated to white supremacy. Moreover, the North was also a white supremacist region, where the vast majority of whites opposed emancipation lest it result in a flood of Southern blacks into the free states. And Illinois was no exception, as most whites there were against abolition and were anti-Negro to the core. Lincoln, who had elected to work within the system, was not going to ruin his career by espousing an extremely unpopular cause. To be branded as an abolitionist in central Illinois — his constituency as a legislator and a U.S. congressman — would have been certain political suicide. At the same time, attorney Lincoln conceded that Southern slavery had become a thoroughly entrenched institution, that bondage where it already existed was protected by the Constitution and could not be molested by the national government.

Still, slavery distressed him. He realized how wrong it was that slavery should exist at all in a self-proclaimed free and enlightened Republic. He who cherished the Declaration of Independence understood only too well how bondage mocked and contradicted that noble document. Too, he thought slavery a blight on the American experiment in popular government. It was, he believed, the one retrograde institution that robbed the Republic of its just example in the world, robbed the United States of the hope it should hold out to oppressed people everywhere.

He opposed slavery, too, because he had witnessed some of its evils firsthand. In 1841, on a steamboat journey down the Ohio River, he saw a group of manacled slaves on their way to the cruel cotton plantations of the Deep South. Lincoln was appalled at the sight of those chained Negroes. Fourteen years later he wrote that the spectacle "was a continual torment to me" and that he saw something like it every time he touched a slave border. Slavery, he said, "had the power of making me miserable."

Again, while serving in Congress from 1847 to 1849, he passed slave auction blocks in Washington, D.C. In fact, from the windows of the Capitol, he could observe the infamous "Georgia pen" — "a sort of Negro livery stable," as he described it, "where droves of negroes were collected, temporarily kept, and finally taken to Southern markets, precisely like droves of horses." The spectacle offended him. He agreed with a Whig colleague that the buying and selling of human beings in the United States capital was a national disgrace. Accordingly Lincoln drafted a gradual abolition bill for the District of Columbia. But powerful Southern politicians howled in protest, and his own Whig support fell away. At that, Lincoln dropped his bill and sat in glum silence as Congress rocked with debates — with drunken fights and rumbles of disunion — over the status of slavery out in the territories. Shocked at the behavior of his colleagues, Lincoln confessed that slavery was the one issue that threatened the stability of the Union.

What could be done? Slavery as an institution could not be removed, and yet it should not remain either. Trapped in what seemed an impossible dilemma, Lincoln persuaded himself that if slavery were confined to the South and left alone there, time would somehow solve the problem and slavery would ultimately die out. And he told himself that the Founding Fathers had felt the same way, that they too had expected slavery to perish some day. In Lincoln's interpretation, they had tolerated slavery as a necessary evil, agreeing that it could not be eradicated where it already flourished without causing wide-scale wreckage. But in his view they had taken steps to restrict its growth (had excluded slavery from the old Northwest territories, had outlawed the international slave trade) and so had placed the institution on the road to extinction.

So went Lincoln's argument before 1854. The solution was to bide one's time, trust the future to get rid of slavery and square America with her own ideals. And he convinced himself that when slavery was no longer workable, Southern whites would gradually liberate the blacks on their own. They would do so voluntarily.

To solve the ensuing problem of racial adjustment, Lincoln insisted that the federal government should colonize all blacks in Africa, an idea he got from his political idol, Whig national leader Henry Clay. Said Lincoln in 1852: if the Republic could remove the danger of slavery and restore "a captive people to their long-lost fatherland," and do both so gradually "that neither races nor individuals shall have suffered by the change," then "it will indeed be a glorious consummation."

☆

4

Then came 1854 and the momentous Kansas-Nebraska Act, brainchild of Lincoln's archrival Stephen A. Douglas. The act overturned the old Missouri Compromise line, which excluded slavery from the vast northern area of the old Louisiana Purchase territory. The act then established a new formula for dealing with slavery in the national lands: now Congress would stay out of the matter, and the people of each territory would decide whether to retain or outlaw the institution. Until such time as the citizens of a territory voted on the issue, Southerners were free to take slavery into most western territories, including the new ones of Kansas and Nebraska. These were carved out of the northern section of the old Louisiana Purchase territory. Thanks to the Kansas-Nebraska Act, a northern domain once preserved for freedom now seemed open to proslavery invasion.

At once a storm of free-soil protest broke across the North, and scores of political leaders branded the Kansas-Nebraska Act as part of a sinister Southern plot to extend slave territory and augment Southern political power in Washington. There followed a series of political upheavals. A civil war blazed up in Kansas, as proslavery and free-soil pioneers came into bloody collisions on the prairie there — proof that slavery was far too volatile ever to be solved as a purely local matter. At the same time, the old Whig party disintegrated. In its place emerged the all-Northern Republican party, dedicated to blocking slavery extension and to saving the cherished frontier for free white labor. Then in 1857 came the infamous Dred Scott decision, handed down by the pro-Southern Supreme Court, which ruled that neither Congress nor a territorial government could outlaw slavery, because that would violate Southern property rights. As Lincoln and many others observed, the net effect of the decision was to legalize slavery in all federal territories from Canada to Mexico.

The train of ominous events from Kansas-Nebraska to Dred Scott shook Lincoln to his foundations. In his view, the Southern-controlled Democratic party — the party that dominated the Senate, the Supreme Court, and the presidency — had instituted a revolt against the Founding Fathers and the entire course of the Republic so far as slavery was concerned. Now human bondage was not going to die out. Now it was going to expand and grow and continue indefinitely, as Southerners dragged manacled Negroes across the West, adapting slave labor to whatever conditions they found there, putting the blacks to work in mines and on farms. Now Southerners would create new slave states in the West and make slavery powerful and permanent in America. Now the Republic would never remove the cancer that infected its political system, would never remove the one institution that marred its global image, would never remove a "cruel wrong" that mocked the Declaration of Independence.

Lincoln waded into the middle of the antiextension fight. He campaigned for the national Senate. He joined the Republican party. He thundered against the evil designs of the "Slave Power." He spoke with an urgent sense of mission that gave his speeches a searching eloquence — a mission to save the Republic's noblest ideals, turn back the tide of slavery expansion, restrict the peculiar institution

once again to the South, and place it back on the road to extinction, as Lincoln believed the Founding Fathers had so placed it.

By 1858, Lincoln, like a lot of other Republicans, began to see a grim proslavery conspiracy at work in the United States. The first stage was to betray the founders and send slavery flooding all over the West. At the same time, proslavery theorists were out to undermine the Declaration of Independence, to discredit its equality doctrine as "a self-evident lie" (as many Southern spokesmen were actually saying), and to replace the Declaration with the principles of inequality and human servitude.

The next step in the conspiracy would be to nationalize slavery: the Taney Court, Lincoln feared, would hand down another decision, one declaring that states could not prohibit slavery either. Then the institution would sweep into Illinois, sweep into Indiana and Ohio, sweep into Pennsylvania and New York, sweep into Massachusetts and New England, sweep all over the Northern states, until at last slavery would be nationalized and America would end up a slave house. At that, as George Fitzhugh advocated, the conspirators would enslave all American workers regardless of color. The Northern free-labor system would be expunged, the Declaration of Independence overthrown, self-government abolished, and the conspirators would restore despotism with class rule and an entrenched aristocracy. All the work since the Revolution of 1776 would be obliterated. The world's best hope — America's experiment in popular government — would be destroyed, and mankind would spin backward into feudalism.

For Lincoln and his Republican colleagues, it was imperative that the conspiracy be blocked in its initial stage — the expansion of slavery into the West. In 1858 Lincoln set out after Douglas's Senate seat, inveighing against the Little Giant for his part in the proslavery plot and warning Illinois — and Northerners beyond — that only the Republicans could save their free-labor system and their free government. Now Lincoln openly and fiercely declaimed his antislavery sentiments. He hated the institution. He hated slavery because it degraded blacks and whites alike. Because it prevented the Negro from "eating the bread which his own hand earns." Because it not only contradicted the Declaration, but violated the principles of free labor, self help, social mobility, and economic independence, all of which lay at the center of Republican ideology, of Lincoln's ideology. Yet, while branding slavery as an evil and doing all they could to contain it in the South, Republicans would not, could not, molest the institution in those states where it already existed.

Douglas, fighting for his political life in free-soil Illinois, lashed back at Lincoln with unadulterated race-baiting. Throughout the Great Debates of 1858, Douglas smeared Lincoln and his party as Black Republicans, as a gang of radical abolitionists out to liberate all Southern slaves and bring them stampeding into Illinois and the rest of the North, where they would take away white jobs and copulate with white daughters. Again and again, Douglas accused Lincoln of desiring intermarriage and racial mongrelization.

Lincoln protested emphatically that race was not the issue between him and Douglas. The issue was whether slavery would ultimately triumph or ultimately perish in the United States. But Douglas understood the depth of anti-Negro feeling in Illinois, and he hoped to whip Lincoln by playing on white racial fears.

Forced to take a stand lest Douglas ruin him with his allegations, Lincoln conceded that he was not for Negro political or social equality. He was not for enfranchising Negroes, was not for intermarriage. There was, he said, "a physical difference" between blacks and whites that would "probably" always prevent them from living together in perfect equality. Having confessed his racial views, Lincoln then qualified them: if Negroes were not the equal of Lincoln

and Douglas in moral or intellectual endowment, they *were* equal to Lincoln, Douglas, and "every living man" in their right to liberty, equality of opportunity, and the fruits of their own labor. (Later he insisted that it was bondage that had "clouded" the slaves' intellects and that Negroes were capable of thinking like whites.) Moreover, Lincoln rejected "the counterfeit argument" that just because he did not want a black woman for a slave, he necessarily wanted her for a wife. He could just let her alone. He could let her alone so that she could also enjoy her freedom and "her natural right to eat the bread she earns with her own hands."

Exasperated with Douglas and white Negrophobia in general, Lincoln begged American whites "to discard all this quibbling about this man and the other man — this race and that race and the other race as being inferior," begged them to unite as one people and defend the ideals of the Declaration and its promise of liberty and opportunity for all.

Lincoln lost the 1858 Senate contest to Douglas. But in 1860 he won the Republican nomination for president and stood before the American electorate on the free-soil, free-labor principles of the Republican party. As the Republican standard bearer, Lincoln was uncompromising in his determination to prohibit slavery in the territories by national law and to save the Republic (as he put it) from returning to "class, caste, and despotism." He exhorted his fellow Republicans to stand firm in their duty: to brand slavery as an evil, contain it in the South, look to the future for slavery to die a gradual death, and promise colonization to solve the question of race. Some day, somehow, the American house must be free of slavery. That was the Republican vision, the distant horizon Lincoln saw.

Yet, for the benefit of Southerners, he repeated that he and his party would not harm slavery in the Southern states. The federal government had no constitutional authority in peace time to tamper with a state institution like slavery.

But Southerners refused to believe anything Lincoln said. In Dixie, orators and editors alike castigated him as a black-hearted radical, a "sooty and scoundrelly" abolitionist who wanted to free the slaves at once and mix the races. In Southern eyes, Lincoln was another John Brown, a mobocrat, a Southern hater, a chimpanzee, a lunatic, the "biggest ass in the United States," the evil chief of the North's "Black Republican, free love, free Nigger" party, whose victory would ring the bells of doom for the white man's South. Even if Southerners had to drench the Union in blood, cried an Atlanta man, "the South, the loyal South, the Constitution South, would never submit to such humiliation and degradation as the inauguration of Abraham Lincoln."

After Lincoln's victory and the secession of the seven states of the Deep South, Lincoln beseeched Southerners to understand the Republican position on slavery. In his Inaugural Address of 1861, he assured them once again that the federal government would not free the slaves in the South, that it had no legal right to do so. He even gave his blessings to the original Thirteenth Amendment, just passed by Congress, that would have guaranteed slavery in the Southern states for as long as whites there wanted it. Lincoln endorsed the amendment because he thought it consistent with Republican ideology. Ironically, Southern secession and the outbreak of war prevented that amendment from ever being ratified.

When the rebels opened fire on Fort Sumter, the nation plunged into civil war, a conflict that began as a ninety-day skirmish for both sides, but that swelled instead into a vast and terrible carnage with consequences beyond calculation for those swept up in its flames. Lincoln, falling into a depression that would plague him through his embattled presidency, remarked that the war was the supreme irony of his life: that he who sickened at the sight of blood, who abhorred stridency and physical violence, was caught in a national holocaust, a tornado of blood and wreckage with Lincoln himself whirling in its center.

☆

5

At the outset of the war, Lincoln strove to be consistent with all that he and his party had said about slavery: his purpose in the struggle was strictly to save the Union; it was not to free the slaves. He would crush the rebellion with his armies and restore the national authority in the South with slavery intact. Then Lincoln and his party would resume and implement their policy of slave containment.

There were other reasons for Lincoln's hands-off policy about slavery. Four slave states — Delaware, Maryland, Kentucky, and Missouri — remained in the Union. Should he try to free the slaves, Lincoln feared it would send the crucial border spiraling into the Confederacy, something that would be catastrophic for the Union. A Confederate Maryland would create an impossible situation for Washington, D.C. And a Confederate Missouri and Kentucky would give the rebels potential bases from which to invade Illinois, Indiana, and Ohio. So Lincoln rejected emancipation in part to appease the loyal border.

He was also waging a bipartisan war effort, with Northern Democrats and Republicans alike enlisting in his armies to save the Union. Lincoln encouraged this because he insisted that it would take a united North to win the war. An emancipation policy, he feared, would alienate Northern Democrats, ignite a racial powder keg in the Northern states, and possibly cause a civil war in the rear. Then the Union really would be lost.

But the pressures and problems of civil war caused Lincoln to change his mind, caused him to abandon his hands-off policy and hurl an executive fist at slavery in the rebel states, thus making emancipation a Union war objective. The pressures operating on Lincoln were complex and merit careful discussion.

First, from the summer of 1861 on, several Republican senators — chief among them, Charles

Sumner of Massachusetts, Ben Wade of Ohio, and Zachariah Chandler of Michigan — sequestered themselves with Lincoln and implored and badgered him to free the slaves.[1] Sumner, as Lincoln's personal friend and one of his chief foreign policy advisers, was especially persistent. Before secession, of course, Sumner and his colleagues had all adhered to the Republican position on slavery in the South. But civil war had now removed their constitutional scruples about the peculiar institution. After all, they told Lincoln, the Southern people were in rebellion against the national government; they could not resist that government and yet enjoy the protection of its laws. Now the senators argued that the national government could eradicate slavery by the War Power, and they wanted Lincoln to do it in his capacity as commander-in-chief. If he emancipated the slaves, it would maim and cripple the Confederacy and hasten an end to the rebellion.

Second, they pointed out that slavery had caused the war, was the reason why the Southern states had seceded, and was now the cornerstone of the confederacy. It was absurd, the senators contended, to fight a war without removing the thing that had brought it about. Should the South return to the Union with slavery intact, as Lincoln desired, Southerners would just start another war over slavery, whenever they thought it threatened again, so that the present struggle would have accomplished nothing, nothing at all. If Lincoln really wanted to save the Union, he must tear slavery out root and branch and smash the South's planter class — that mischievous class the senators thought had masterminded secession and fomented war.

---

[1] These "more advanced Republicans," as the *Detroit Post and Tribune* referred to Sumner and his associates, belonged to a powerful minority faction of the party inaccurately categorized as "radicals," a misnomer that has persisted through the years. For a discussion of this point, see my article, "The Slaves Freed," *American Heritage* (December 1980), 74–83.

Sumner, as a major Lincoln adviser on foreign affairs, also linked emancipation to foreign policy. On several occasions in 1861 and 1862, Britain seemed on the verge of recognizing the Confederacy as an independent nation — a move that would be calamitous for the Union. As a member of the family of nations, the Confederacy could form alliances and seek mediation and perhaps armed intervention in the American conflict. But, Sumner argued, if Lincoln made the obliteration of slavery a Union war aim, Britain would balk at recognition and intervention. Why so? Because she was proud of her antislavery tradition, Sumner contended, and would refrain from helping the South protect human bondage from Lincoln's armies. And whatever powerful Britain did, the rest of Europe was sure to follow.

Also, as Sumner kept reminding everyone, emancipation would break the chains of several million oppressed human beings and right America at last with her own ideals. Lincoln could no longer wait for the future to remove slavery. He must do it. The war, monstrous and terrible though it was, had given Lincoln the opportunity to do it.

Black and white abolitionists belabored that point too. They wrote Lincoln, petitioned him, and addressed him from the stump and in their newspapers. Foremost in that effort was Frederick Douglass, the most eminent African American of his generation, a handsome, eloquent man who had escaped from slavery in Maryland and become a self-made man like Lincoln, raising himself to prominence as an editor and reformer. From the outset, Douglass saw the end of slavery in this war, and he mounted a one-man crusade to win Lincoln to that idea. In his newspaper and on the platform, Douglass thundered at the man in the White House, playing on his personal feelings about slavery, rehearsing the same arguments that Sumner and his colleagues were giving Lincoln in person. You fight the rebels with only one hand, Douglass said. The mission of this war is the destruction of bondage as well as the salvation of the Union. "The very stomach of this rebellion is the negro in the condition of a slave. Arrest that hoe in the hands in the negro, and you smite rebellion in the very seat of its life," he said. "The Negro is the key of the situation — the pivot upon which the whole rebellion turns," he said. "Teach the rebels and traitors that the price they are to pay for the attempt to abolish this Government must be the abolition of slavery," he said. "Hence forth let the war cry be down with treason, and down with slavery, the cause of treason."

The pressure on Lincoln to strike at slavery was unrelenting. In between abolitionist delegations came Sumner and his stern colleagues again, with Vice-President Hannibal Hamlin and Congressman Owen Lovejoy often with them. As the war progressed, they raised still another argument for emancipation, an argument Douglass and members of Lincoln's own Cabinet were also making. In 1862, his armies suffered from manpower shortages on every front. Thanks to repeated Union military failures and to a growing war weariness across the North, volunteering had fallen off sharply; and Union generals bombarded Washington with shrill complaints, insisting that they faced an overwhelming southern foe and must have reinforcements before they could win battles or even fight. While Union commanders often exaggerated rebel strength, Union forces did need reinforcements to carry out a successful offensive war. As Sumner reminded Lincoln, the slaves were an untapped reservoir of strength. "You need more men," Sumner said, "not only at the North, but at the South. You need the slaves." If Lincoln freed them, he could recruit black men into his armed forces, thus helping to solve his manpower woes.

On that score, the slaves themselves were contributing to the pressures on Lincoln to emancipate them. Far from being passive recipients of freedom, as Vincent Harding has rightly reminded us, the slaves *were* engaged in self-liberation, abandoning rebel farms and plantations and escaping to Union lines by the thousands. This in turn created a tangled legal problem that bedeviled the Lincoln administration. What was the status of such "contraband of war," as Union General Benjamin F. Butler designated them? Were they still slaves? Were they free? Were they somewhere in between? The administration tended to follow a look-the-other-way policy, allowing field commanders to solve the contraband problem any way they wished. Some officers sent the fugitives back to the Confederacy, others turned them over to refugee camps, where benevolent organizations attempted to care for them. But with more and more slaves streaming into Union lines, Sumner, several of Lincoln's Cabinet members, Douglass, and many others urged him to grant them freedom and enlist the able-bodied men in the army. "Let the slaves and free colored people be called into service and formed into a liberating army," Douglass exhorted the President, "to march into the South and raise the banner of Emancipation among the slaves."

Lincoln, however, stubbornly rejected a presidential move against slavery. It was "too big a lick," he asserted. "I think Sumner and the rest of you would upset our applecart altogether if you had your way," he told some aggressive Republicans one day. "We didn't go into the war to put down slavery, but to put the flag back; and to act differently at this moment would, I have no doubt, not only weaken our cause, but smack of bad faith.... This thunderbolt will keep."

Nevertheless, Lincoln was sympathetic to the entire range of arguments Sumner and his associates rehearsed for him. Personally, Lincoln hated slavery as much as they did, and many of their points had already occurred to him. In fact, as early as November and December 1861, Lincoln began wavering in his hands-off policy about slavery, began searching about for some compromise — something short of a sweeping emancipation decree. Again he seemed caught in an impossible dilemma: how to remove the cause of the war, keep Britain out of the conflict, cripple the Confederacy and suppress the rebellion, and yet retain the allegiance of Northern Democrats and the critical border?

In March 1862, he proposed a plan to Congress he thought might work: a gradual, compensated emancipation program to commence in the loyal border states. According to Lincoln's plan, the border states would gradually abolish slavery themselves over the next thirty years, and the federal government would compensate slaveowners for their loss. The whole program was to be voluntary; the states would adopt their own emancipation laws without federal coercion.

At the same time, the federal government would sponsor a colonization program, which was also to be entirely voluntary. Without a promise of colonization, Lincoln understood only too well, most Northern whites would never accept emancipation, even if it were carried out by the states. From now on, every time he contemplated some new antislavery move, he made a great fuss about colonization: he embarked on a colonization project in central America and another in Haiti, and he held an interview about colonization with Washington's black leaders, an interview he published in the press. In part, the ritual of colonization was designed to calm white racial fears.

If his gradual, state-guided plan were adopted, Lincoln contended that a presidential decree — federally enforced emancipation — would never be necessary. Abolition would begin on the local level in the loyal border and then be extended into the rebel states as they were conquered. Thus by a slow and salubrious process would the cause of the rebellion be removed and the future of the Union guaranteed.

The plan failed. It failed because the border states refused to act. Lincoln couldn't even persuade Delaware, with its small and relatively harmless slave population, to adopt his program. In desperation, Lincoln on three different occasions — in the spring and summer of 1862 — pleaded with border-state congressmen to endorse his program. In their third meeting, held in the White House on July 12, Lin-

coln warned the border representatives that it was impossible now to restore the Union with slavery preserved. Slavery was doomed. They could not be blind to the signs, blind to the fact that his plan was the only alternative to a more drastic move against slavery, one that would cause tremendous destruction in the South. Please, he said, commend my gradual plan to your people.

But most of the border men turned him down. They thought his plan would cost too much, would only whip the flames of rebellion, would cause dangerous discontent in their own states. Their intransigence was a sober lesson to Lincoln. It was proof indeed that slaveowners — even loyal slaveowners — were too tied up in the slave system ever to free their own Negroes and voluntarily transform their way of life. If abolition must come, it must begin in the rebel South and then be extended into the loyal border later on. Which meant that the president must eradicate slavery himself. He could no longer avoid the responsibility. By mid-July 1862, the pressures of the war had forced him to abandon his hands-off policy and lay a "strong hand on the colored element."

On July 13, the day after his last talk with the border men, Lincoln took a carriage ride with a couple of his cabinet secretaries. His conversation, when recounted in full, reveals a tougher Lincoln than the lenient and compromising president of the legend-building biographies. Lincoln said he was convinced that the war could no longer be won through forbearance toward Southern rebels, that it was "a duty on our part to liberate the slaves." The time had come to take a bold new path and hurl Union armies at "the heart of the rebellion," using the military to destroy the very institution that caused and now sustained the insurrection. Southerners could not throw off the Constitution and at the same time invoke it to protect slavery. They had started the war and must now face its consequences.

He had given this a lot of grave and painful thought, he said, and had concluded that a presidential declaration of emancipation was the last alternative, that it was "a military necessity absolutely essential to the preservation of the Union." Because the slaves were a tremendous source of strength for the rebellion, Lincoln must invite them to desert and "come to us and uniting with us they must be made free from rebel authority and rebel masters." His interview with the border men yesterday, he said, "had forced him slowly but he believed correctly to this conclusion."

On July 22, 1862, Lincoln summoned his cabinet members and read them a draft of a preliminary Emancipation Proclamation. Come January 1, 1863, in his capacity as commander-in-chief of the armed forces in time of war, Lincoln would free all the slaves everywhere in the rebel states. He would thus make it a Union objective to annihilate slavery as an institution in the Confederate South.

Contrary to what many historians have said, Lincoln's projected Proclamation went further than anything Congress had done. True, Congress had just enacted (and Lincoln had just signed) the second confiscation act, which provided for the seizure and liberation of all slaves of people who supported or participated in the rebellion. Still, most slaves would be freed only after protracted case-by-case litigation in the federal courts. Another section of the act did liberate certain categories of slaves without court action, but the bill exempted loyal slaveowners in the rebel South, allowing them to keep their slaves and other property. Lincoln's Proclamation, on the other hand, was a sweeping blow against bondage as an institution in the rebel states, a blow that would free *all* the slaves there — those of secessionists and loyalists alike. Thus Lincoln would handle emancipation himself, avoid judicial red tape, and use the military to vanquish the cornerstone of the Confederacy. Again, he justified this as a military necessity to save the Union.

But Seward and other cabinet secretaries dissuaded Lincoln from issuing his Proclamation in July. Seward argued that the Union had won no clear military victories, particularly in the showcase Eastern theater. As a consequence, Europe would misconstrue the Proclamation as "our last shriek on the retreat," as a wild and reckless attempt to compensate for Union military ineptitude by provoking a slave insurrection behind rebel lines. If Lincoln must give an emancipation order, Seward warned, he must wait until the Union won a military victory.

Lincoln finally agreed to wait, but he was not happy about it: the way George B. McClellan and his other generals had been fighting in the Eastern theater, Lincoln had no idea when he would ever have a victory.

One of the great ironies of the war was that McClellan presented Lincoln with the triumph he needed. A Democrat who sympathized with Southern slavery and opposed wartime emancipation with a passion, McClellan outfought Robert E. Lee at Antietam Creek in September 1862, and forced the rebel army to withdraw. Thereupon Lincoln issued his preliminary Proclamation, with its warning that if the rebellion did not cease by January 1, 1863, the executive branch, including the army and the navy, would destroy slavery in the rebel states.

As it turned out, the preliminary Proclamation ignited racial discontent in much of the lower North, especially the Midwest, and led to significant Democratic gains in the off-year elections of 1862. Many Northern Democrats were already upset with Lincoln's harsh war measures, especially his use of martial law and military arrests. But Negro emancipation was more than they could stand, and they stumped the Northern states that fall, beating the drums of Negrophobia, warning of massive influxes of Southern blacks into the North once emancipation came. When the 1862 ballots were counted, the Democrats had picked up thirty-four congressional seats, won two governorships, and gained control of three state legislatures. While the Republicans retained control of Congress, the future looked bleak indeed if the war ground on into 1864.

Republican analysts — and Lincoln himself — conceded that the preliminary Proclamation was a major factor in the Republican losses. But Lincoln told a delegation from Kentucky that he would rather die than retract a single word in his Proclamation.

As the New Year approached, conservative Republicans begged Lincoln to abandon his "reckless" emancipation scheme lest he shatter their demoralized party and wreck what remained of their country. But Lincoln stood firm. On New Year's day, 1863, he officially signed the final Emancipation Proclamation in the White House. His hand trembled badly, not because he was nervous, but because he had shaken hands all morning in a White House reception. He assured everyone present that he was never more certain of what he was doing. "If my name ever goes into history," he said, "it will be for this act." Then slowly and deliberately he wrote out his full name.

In the final Proclamation, Lincoln temporarily exempted occupied Tennessee and certain occupied places in Louisiana and Virginia. (Later, in reconstructing those states, he withdrew the exemptions and made emancipation a mandatory part of his reconstruction program.) He also excluded the loyal slave states because they were not in rebellion and he lacked the legal authority to uproot slavery there. He would, however, keep goading them to obliterate slavery themselves — and would later push a constitutional amendment that liberated their slaves as well. With the exception of the loyal border and certain occupied areas, the final Proclamation declared that as of this day, all slaves in the rebellious states were *"forever free."* The document also asserted that black men — Southern and Northern alike — would now be enlisted in Union military forces.

Out the Proclamation went to an anxious and dissident nation. Later in the day an interracial crowd gathered on the White House lawn, and Lincoln greeted the people from an open window. The blacks cheered and sang, "Glory, Jubilee has come," and told Lincoln that if he would "come out of that palace, they would hug him to death." A black preacher named Henry M. Turner exclaimed that "it is indeed a time of times," that "nothing like it will ever be seen again in this life."

☆

6

Lincoln's Proclamation was the most revolutionary measure ever to come from an American president up to that time. As Union armies punched into rebel territory, they would rip out slavery as an institution, automatically freeing all slaves in the areas and states they conquered. In this respect (as Lincoln said), the war brought on changes more vast, more fundamental and profound, than either side had expected when the struggle began. Now slavery would perish as the Confederacy perished, would die by degrees with every Union advance, every Union victory.

Moreover, word of the Proclamation hummed across the slave grapevine in the Confederacy; and as Union armies drew near, more slaves than ever abandoned rebel farms and plantations and (as one said) "demonstrated with their feet" their desire for freedom.

The Proclamation also opened the army to black volunteers, and Northern free Negroes and Southern ex-slaves now enlisted as Union soldiers. As Lincoln said, "the colored population is the great *available* and yet unavailed of, force for restoring the Union." And he now availed himself of that force. In all, some 180,000 Negro fighting men — most of them emancipated slaves — served in Union forces on every major battlefront, helping to liberate their brothers and sisters in bondage and to save the Union. As Lincoln observed, the blacks added enormous and indispensable strength to the Union war machine.

Unhappily, the blacks fought in segregated units under white officers, and until late in the war received less pay than whites did. In 1864 Lincoln told Negro leader Frederick Douglass that he disliked the

Men of the Fifty-Fourth Massachusetts (Colored) Infantry Regiment. Organized after the Emancipation Proclamation, the Fifty-Fourth became the most famous black fighting unit in the Union Army. All the men in the regiment were volunteers, and nearly all were free blacks from the North. They enlisted for various reasons: to help free their brothers and sisters from bondage, to prove that black men were not inferior, and to help save the Union. The subject of the brilliant motion picture Glory *(1989), the Fifty-Fourth led the federal assault on Fort Wagner in Charleston Harbor, losing its white officer and almost half its men. Although the attack was repulsed, the men of the Fifty-Fourth proved that black soldiers could fight as well as white soldiers. All told, some 186,000 blacks served in the Union Army: they fought in 450 engagements and won twenty-one Congressional Medals of Honor. (Luis F. Emilio,* A Brave Black Regiment*)*

practice of unequal pay, but that the government had to make some concessions to white prejudices, noting that a great many Northern whites opposed the use of black soldiers altogether. But he promised that they would eventually get equal pay — and they did. Moreover, Lincoln was proud of the performance of his black soldiers: he publicly praised them for fighting "with clenched teeth, and steady eye, and well poised bayonet" to save the Union, while certain whites strove "with malignant heart" to hinder it.

After the Proclamation, Lincoln had to confront the problem of race adjustment, of what to do with all the blacks liberated in the South. By the spring of 1863, he had pretty well written off colonization as unworkable. His colonization schemes all floundered, in part because the white promoters were dishonest or incompetent. But the main reason colonization failed was because most blacks adamantly refused to participate in Lincoln's voluntary program. Across the North, free Negroes denounced Lincoln's colonization efforts — this was their country too! they cried — and they petitioned him to deport slaveholders instead.

As a consequence, Lincoln had just about concluded that whites and liberated blacks must somehow learn how to live together in this country. Still, he needed some device for now, some program that would pacify white Northerners and convince them that Southern freedmen would not flock into their communities, but would remain in the South instead. What Lincoln worked out was a refugee system, installed by his adjutant general in the occupied Mississippi Valley, which mobilized Southern blacks in the South, utilizing them in military and civilian pursuits there. According to the system, the adjutant general enrolled all able-bodied freedmen in the army, employed other ex-slaves as military laborers, and hired still others to work on farms and plantations for wages set by the government. While there were many faults with the system, it was predicated on sound Republican dogma; it kept Southern Negroes out of the North, and it got them jobs as wage earners, thus helping them to help themselves and preparing them for life in a free society.

Even so, emancipation remained the most explosive and unpopular act of Lincoln's presidency. By mid–1863, thousands of Democrats were in open revolt against his administration, denouncing Lincoln as an abolitionist dictator who had surrendered to radicalism. In the Midwest, dissident Democrats launched a peace movement to throw "the shrieking abolitionist faction" out of office and negotiate a peace with the Confederacy that would somehow restore the Union with slavery unharmed. There were large antiwar rallies against Lincoln's war for slave liberation. Race and draft riots flared in several Northern cities.

With all the public unrest behind the lines, conservative Republicans beseeched Lincoln to abandon emancipation and rescue his country "from the brink of ruin." But Lincoln seemed intractable. He had made up his mind to smash the slave society of the rebel South and eliminate "the cruel wrong" of Negro bondage, and no amount of public discontent, he indicated, was going to change his mind. "To use a coarse, but an expressive figure," he wrote one aggravated Democrat, "broken eggs cannot be mended. I have issued the Proclamation, and I cannot retract it." Congressman Owen Lovejoy applauded Lincoln's stand. "His mind acts slowly," Lovejoy said, "but when he moves, it is *forward*."

He wavered once — in August 1864, a time of unrelenting gloom for Lincoln when his popularity had sunk to an all-time low and it seemed he could not be reelected. He confessed that maybe the country would no longer sustain a war for slave emancipation, that maybe he shouldn't pull the nation down a road it did not want to travel. On August 24 he decided to offer Confederate President Jefferson Davis peace terms that excluded emancipation as a condition, vaguely suggesting that slavery would be adjusted later "by peaceful means." But the next day Lincoln changed his mind. With awakened resolu-

tion, he vowed to fight the war through to unconditional surrender and to stick by emancipation come what may. He had made his promise of freedom to the slaves, and he meant to keep it so long as he was in office.

When he won the election of 1864, Lincoln interpreted it as a popular mandate for him and his emancipation policy. But in reality the election provided no clear referendum on slavery, since Republican campaigners had played down emancipation and concentrated on the peace plank in the Democratic platform. Nevertheless, Lincoln used his reelection to promote a constitutional amendment that would guarantee the freedom of all slaves, those in the loyal border as well as those in the rebel South. Since issuing his Proclamation, Lincoln had worried that it might be nullified in the courts or thrown out by a later Congress or a subsequent administration. Consequently he wanted a constitutional amendment that would safeguard his Proclamation and prevent emancipation from ever being overturned.

As it happened, the Senate in May of 1864 had already passed an emancipation amendment — the present Thirteenth Amendment — but the House had failed to approve it. After that Lincoln had insisted that the Republican platform endorse the measure. And now, over the winter of 1864 and 1865, he put tremendous pressure on the House to endorse the amendment, using all his powers of persuasion and patronage to get it through. He buttonholed conservative Republicans and opposition Democrats and exhorted them to support the amendment. He singled out "sinners" among the Democrats who were "on praying ground," and informed them that they had a lot better chance for the federal jobs they desired if they voted for the measure. Soon two Democrats swung over in favor of it. With the outcome still in doubt, Lincoln participated in secret negotiations never made public — negotiations that allegedly involved the patronage, a New Jersey railroad monopoly, and the release of rebels related to Congressional Democrats — to bring wavering opponents into line. "The greatest measure of the nineteenth century," congressman Thaddeus Stevens claimed, "was passed by corruption aided and abetted by the purest man in America." On January 31, 1865, the House adopted the present Thirteenth Amendment by just three votes more than the required two-thirds majority. At once a storm of cheers broke over House Republicans, who danced around, embraced one another, and waved their hats and canes overhead. "It seemed to me I had been born with a new life," one Republican recalled, "and that the world was overflowing with beauty and joy."

Lincoln, too, pronounced the amendment "a great moral victory" and "a King's cure" for the evils of slavery. When ratified by the states, the amendment would end human bondage everywhere in America. Lincoln pointed across the Potomac. "If the people over the river had behaved themselves, I could not have done what I have."

☆

7

Lincoln conceded, though, that he had not controlled the events of the war, but that events had controlled him instead, that God had controlled him. He thought about this a great deal, especially at night when he couldn't sleep, trying to understand the meaning of the war, to understand why it had begun and grown into such a massive revolutionary struggle, consuming hundreds of thousands of lives (the final casualties would come to 620,000 on both sides). By his second inaugural, he had reached an apocalyptic conclusion about the nature of the war — had come to see it as a divine punishment for the "great offense" of slavery, as a terrible retribution God had visited on a guilty people, in North as well as South. Lincoln's vision was close to that of old

John Brown, who had prophesied on the day he was hanged, on that balmy December day back in 1859, that the crime of slavery could not be purged away from this guilty land except by blood. Now, in his second Inaugural Address, Lincoln too contended that God perhaps had willed this "mighty scourge of War" on the United States, "until all the wealth piled by the bondman's two hundred and fifty years of unrequited toil shall be sunk, and until every drop of blood drawn with the lash, shall be paid by another drawn with the sword."

In the last paragraph of his address, Lincoln said he would bind the nation's wounds "with malice toward none" and "charity for all." Yet that did not mean he would be so gentle and forgiving in reconstruction as most biographers have contended. He would be magnanimous in the sense that he wouldn't resort to mass executions or even mass imprisonment of Southern "traitors," as he repeatedly called them. He would not even have the leaders tried and jailed, though he said he would like to "frighten them out of the country." Nevertheless, still preoccupied with the war as a grim purgation which would cleanse and regenerate his country, Lincoln endorsed a fairly tough policy toward the conquered South. After Lee surrendered in April 1865, Lincoln publicly endorsed limited suffrage for Southern blacks, announcing that the intelligent ex-slaves and especially those who had served in Union military forces should have the vote. This put him in advance of most Northern whites. And it put him ahead of most Republicans as well — including many of the so-called radicals — who in April 1865 shrank from Negro suffrage out of fear of their own white constituents. True, Sumner, Salmon Chase, and a few of their colleagues now demanded that all Southern black men be enfranchised in order to protect their freedom. But Lincoln was not far from their position. In a line in his last political speech, April 11, 1865, he granted that the Southern black man deserved the vote, though Lincoln was not quite ready to make that

The strain of war: At left, Abraham Lincoln in Springfield, Illinois, on June 3, 1860. At right, after four years of war, Lincoln posed for photographer Alexander Gardner in Washington, April *10, 1865. (Photo on left: Chicago Historical Society, photo on right: Brown University, McClennan Lincoln Collection)*

mandatory. But it seems clear in what direction he was heading.

Moreover, in a cabinet meeting on Good Friday, 1865, Lincoln and all his Secretaries endorsed the military approach to reconstruction and conceded that an army of occupation might be necessary to control the rebellious white majority in the conquered South. During the war, Lincoln had always thought the military indispensable in restoring civilian rule in the South. Without the army, he feared that the rebellious Southern majority would overwhelm the small Unionist minority there — and maybe even reenslave the blacks. And he was not about to let the latter happen. The army had liber-

ated the blacks in the war, and the army might well have to safeguard their freedom in reconstruction.

☆

8

He had come a long distance from the young Lincoln who entered politics, quiet on slavery lest he be branded an abolitionist, opposed to Negro political rights lest his political career be jeopardized, convinced that only the future could remove slavery in America. He had come a long way indeed. Frederick Douglass, who interviewed Lincoln in the White

House in 1863, said he was "the first great man that I talked with in the United States freely who in no single instance reminded me of the difference between himself and myself, of the difference of color." Douglass, reflecting back on Lincoln's presidency, recalled how in the first year and a half of the war, Lincoln "was ready and willing" to sacrifice black people for the benefit and welfare of whites. But since the preliminary Emancipation Proclamation, Douglass said, American blacks had taken Lincoln's measure and had come to admire and some to love this enigmatic man. Though Lincoln had taxed Negroes to the limit, they had decided, in the roll and tumble of events, that "the how and the man of our redemption had somehow met in the person of Abraham Lincoln."

But perhaps it was Lincoln himself who best summed up his journey to emancipation — his own as well as that of the slaves. In December 1862, after the calamitous by-elections of that year, in the midst of rising racial protest against his emancipation policy, Lincoln asked Congress — and Northern whites beyond — for their support. "The dogmas of the quiet past," he reminded them, "are inadequate to the stormy present. The occasion is piled high with difficulty, and we must rise with the occasion. As our case is new, so we must think anew, and act anew. We must disenthrall our selves, and then we shall save our country.

"Fellow-citizens, *we* cannot escape history. . . . The fiery trial through which we pass, will light us down, in honor or dishonor, to the latest generation. . . . In *giving* freedom to the slave, we *assure* freedom to the *free* — honorable alike in what we give, and what we preserve. We shall nobly save, or meanly lose, the last best, hope of earth."

QUESTIONS TO CONSIDER

1   Most of us are familiar with the story of "Honest Abe" Lincoln, the unambitious rail-splitting man of the people. How does Oates's biographical portrait of Lincoln reveal the complex human being behind this mythical image?

2   How was Lincoln able to reconcile his reverence for the founders and the Constitution with the moral paradox of slavery in a free society? How did Lincoln hope to solve the problems of slavery and racial adjustment in America?

3   What was the so-called slave power conspiracy that Lincoln and many other Republicans feared by the late 1850s? How had the events of that crucial decade seemed to confirm their fears?

4   Oates says that the pressures and problems of fighting a civil war finally caused Lincoln to hurl an executive fist at slavery. What were the forces that led Lincoln to issue his Emancipation Proclamation?

5   Many of Lincoln's contemporaries as well as later scholars accused Lincoln of having made an empty gesture with the Emancipation Proclamation. How does Oates answer these accusations?

XIV

THE WAR THAT MADE
A NATION

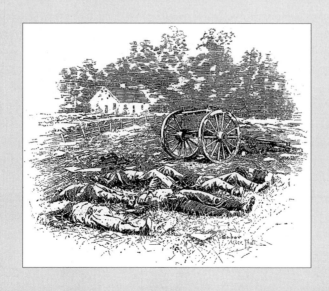

27

Why the Union Won

JAMES M. MCPHERSON

James M. McPherson, one of America's foremost authorities on the Civil War, argues that the rebellious southern states left the Union and formed the Confederacy because they perceived the Black Republican party as a revolutionary threat to their slave-based way of life. For McPherson, secession was therefore "a pre-emptive counterrevolution to prevent the Black Republican revolution from engulfing the South." That the new Confederacy was dedicated to saving slavery, both as a multibillion-dollar labor system and a means of race control, cannot be doubted. The Confederates wrote a constitution that closely resembled the United States Constitution save for one crucial difference: the Confederate document specifically guaranteed slavery and affirmed states' rights. In Savannah, Georgia, rebel vice president Alexander H. Stephens made it unmistakably clear what the Confederacy stood for. "Our new government is founded upon exactly the opposite idea [from that of equality in the Declaration of Independence]; its foundations are laid, its cornerstone rests, upon the great truth that the negro is not equal to the white man; that slavery — subordination to the superior race — is his natural and normal condition. This, our new government, is the first in the history of the world based upon this great physical, philosophical, and moral truth."

From the outset, this new government was beset with internal problems: it lacked sound money, guns, factories, food, railroads, and harmonious political leadership. Still, with its excellent generals and soldiers, the possibility of foreign intervention, and other advantages, the Confederacy faced better odds in its war for independence than had the American colonies. Why, then, did the Confederacy go down to defeat? In the next selection, McPherson examines earlier explanations — that the North had "the strongest battalions," that the South died of internal dissent and loss of will — and finds them lacking. He puts forth a cogent and convincing argument for rebel defeat that reflects an important body of modern thinking about the war. That thinking stresses the overriding importance of military operations, contending that ultimately the war was won or lost on the battlefield. As Lincoln himself said, it was upon "the progress of our arms" that everything else depended — public and soldier morale and political, economic, and social stability. To explain why the Confederacy lost (the "South" didn't lose, because four southern states and one hundred thousand southern men fought for the Union), McPherson offers the theory of contingency — the idea that at certain crucial points in military operations, either side could have won. He discusses four such "moments of contingency," or turning points. The first occurred in the summer of 1862 when it seemed that the South would triumph on the field of arms. The second came in the fall of 1862 when military fortunes swung back in favor of the North. The third took place in July 1863 when the Union won simultaneous victories at Gettysburg and Vicksburg. And the fourth came in the summer of 1864 when the Union war machine bogged down, and northern morale plummeted as a consequence; for a time, it appeared that Lincoln would not be reelected and that a Democrat would become president and negotiate peace with the Confederacy. But Union military victories in Georgia and Virginia hardened northern will to fight on, which "clinched matters for the North."

McPherson goes on to describe the war's most important consequences — the death of slavery and secession, the transformation of the country from a loose confederation of states and regions into an indivisible nation, and the triumph of the northern vision of America and the corresponding loss of the southern vision. This is state-of-the-art analysis, excerpted from McPherson's Pulitzer Prize–winning Battle Cry of Freedom: The Civil War Era *(1988).*

GLOSSARY

ANTIETAM (MARYLAND)   Robert E. Lee and George B. McClellan fought to a draw here, in the bloodiest single day in American military history; the battle ended Lee's first invasion of the North.

ARMY OF THE POTOMAC   The Union's principal fighting force in the eastern theater and its greatest army of the war.

GETTYSBURG (PENNSYLVANIA)   Lee's greatest reversal, in July 1863, ended his second invasion of the North; best known for Pickett's calamitous charge on the third day; Lee suffered such losses that he could never again mount the offensive.

GÖTTERDÄMMERUNG   In German mythology, the destruction of all gods and all things in a final battle with the forces of evil.

PERRYVILLE (KENTUCKY)   A Confederate invasion force under Braxton Bragg lost this battle in October 1862; Bragg's columns and a second rebel invasion force under Kirby Smith fell back into Tennessee.

VICKSBURG (MISSISSIPPI)   Rebel garrison on the Mississippi River; surrendered to Ulysses S. Grant on July 4, 1863, the same day that Lee retreated from Gettysburg.

CONFEDERATE GENERALS:

BEAUREGARD, PIERRE GUSTAVE TOUTANT   Led Confederate forces to victory at First Bull Run (or First Manassas), July 1861.

BRAGG, BRAXTON   Quarrelsome commander of the Army of Tennessee, the Confederacy's main army in the western theater; lost the Battle of Perryville and the battles around Chattanooga, October–November 1863.

HOOD, JOHN BELL   Led the Army of Tennessee to annihilation in the Battle of Nashville, December 1864.

JACKSON, THOMAS J. "STONEWALL"   Defeated three separate Union forces in the Shenandoah Valley, spring 1862; became Lee's most brilliant divisional and corps commander; famous for his flanking march and attack at Chancellorsville, where he was mortally wounded by his own pickets.

JOHNSTON, ALBERT SIDNEY   Many Confederates considered him the best general in the rebel army; commanded the western forces early in the war and was killed in the Battle of Shiloh, Tennessee, April 1862.

JOHNSTON, JOSEPH EGGLESTON   Preferred to fight on the defensive; commanded the main Confederate Army in Virginia in the first half of 1862; fought against McClellan in the Peninsula campaign; was later sent West to coordinate rebel efforts to defend Vicksburg against Grant; contested Sherman's advance against Atlanta in 1864 and in the Carolinas in 1865.

LEE, ROBERT E.   The best rebel commander; preferred to fight on the offensive; led the Army of Northern Virginia, the Confederacy's showcase army, from June 1862 to April 1865, when he surrendered to Grant; won the Seven Days Battles before Richmond, the Second Battle of Bull Run, Fredericksburg, and Chancellorsville against inferior Union generals; promoted to general in chief of all rebel military forces near the end of the war.

PEMBERTON, JOHN   Rebel commander who surrendered Vicksburg, July 1865.

UNION GENERALS:

BURNSIDE, AMBROSE E.   Inept commander of the Army of the Potomac, 1862–1863, who lost to Lee in the Battle of Fredericksburg, December 1862.

GRANT, ULYSSES S.   The North's best general; captured Forts Henry and Donnelson in Tennessee in 1862 and the great river garrison of Vicksburg in 1863; won the battles around Chattanooga in December of that year; became general in chief of all Union forces in 1864, and led the Army of the Potomac against Lee in a series of ferocious engagements around Richmond, finally pinning Lee down in the siege of Petersburg.

HOOKER, JOSEPH   Inept commander of the Army of the Potomac who lost to Lee at Chancellorsville, Virginia, May 1863.

MCCLELLAN, GEORGE B.   Commander of the Army of the Potomac, 1861–1862; orchestrated the glacial-paced Peninsula campaign against Richmond; was driven back by Lee in the Seven Days and recalled to Washington; led the Potomac Army against Lee at Antietam and might have won the battle had he not been overly cautious; finally sacked by Lincoln on the ground that the general had "the slows."

MEADE, GEORGE GORDON   Led the Army of the Potomac in the Battle of Gettysburg, July 1863, and remained titular head of that army during Grant's great offensive against Lee, 1864–1865.

POPE, JOHN   Blusterous, incompetent commander of the Union's Army of Virginia; decisively beaten by Lee and Jackson at Second Bull Run (Second Manassas), August 1863.

SHERMAN, WILLIAM TECUMSEH   Grant's subordinate commander in the West, 1862–1863; became the Union's top general there when Grant was promoted to supreme command; led the Army of Georgia on its famous march through Georgia and the Carolinas, 1864–1865.

The weeks after [Lincoln was assassinated in April 1865] passed in a dizzying sequence of events. Jarring images dissolved and re-formed in kaleidoscopic patterns that left the senses traumatized or elated: Lincoln lying in state at the White House on April 19 as General Grant wept un-abashedly at his catafalque; Confederate armies sur-rendering one after another as [Confederate Presi-dent] Jefferson Davis fled southward hoping to re-establish his government in Texas and carry on the war to victory; Booth killed in a burning barn in Virginia; seven million somber men, women, and children lining the tracks to view Lincoln's funeral train on its way back home to Springfield; the steamboat *Sultana* returning northward on the Mis-sissippi with liberated Union prisoners of war blow-ing up on April 27 with a loss of life equal to that of the *Titanic* a half-century later; Jefferson Davis cap-tured in Georgia on May 10, accused (falsely) of complicity in Lincoln's assassination, imprisoned and temporarily shackled at Fortress Monroe, Vir-ginia, where he remained for two years until re-leased without trial to live on until his eighty-first year and become part of the ex-Confederate literary corps who wrote weighty tomes to justify their Cause; the Army of the Potomac and Sherman's Army of Georgia marching 200,000 strong in a Grand Review down Pennsylvania Avenue on May 23–24 in a pageantry of power and catharsis before being demobilized from more than one million sol-diers to fewer than 80,000 a year later and an even-tual peacetime total of 27,000; weary, ragged Con-federate soldiers straggling homeward begging or stealing food from dispirited civilians who often did not know where their own next meal was coming from; joyous black people celebrating the jubilee of a freedom whose boundaries they did not yet dis-cern; gangs of southern deserters, guerrillas, and outlaws ravaging a region that would not know real peace for many years to come.

The terms of that peace and the dimensions of black freedom would preoccupy the country for a decade or more. Meanwhile the process of chroni-cling the war and reckoning its consequences began immediately and has never ceased. More than 620,000 soldiers lost their lives in four years of con-flict — 360,000 Yankees and at least 260,000 rebels. The number of southern civilians who died as a di-rect or indirect result of the war cannot be known; what *can* be said is that the Civil War's cost in Amer-ican lives was as great as in all of the nation's other wars combined through Vietnam. Was the liberation of four million slaves and the preservation of the Union worth the cost? That question too will proba-bly never cease to be debated — but in 1865 few black people and not many northerners doubted the answer.

In time even a good many southerners came to agree with the sentiments of Woodrow Wilson (a native of Virginia who lived four years of his child-hood in wartime Georgia) expressed in 1880 when he was a law student at the University of Virginia: "*Because* I love the South, I rejoice in the failure of the Confederacy.... Conceive of this Union di-vided into two separate and independent sover-eignties! ... Slavery was enervating our Southern society.... [Nevertheless] I recognize and pay lov-ing tribute to the virtues of the leaders of secession ... the righteousness of the cause which they thought they were promoting — and to the im-mortal courage of the soldiers of the Confederacy." Wilson's words embodied themes that would help reconcile generations of southerners to defeat: their glorious forebears had fought courageously for what they believed was right; perhaps they de-served to win; but in the long run it was a good thing they lost. This Lost Cause mentality took on the proportions of a heroic legend, a southern

Götterdämmerung with Robert E. Lee as a latter-day Siegfried.★

But a persistent question has nagged historians and mythologists alike: if Marse Robert was such a genius and his legions so invincible, why did they lose? The answers, though almost as legion as Lee's soldiers, tend to group themselves into a few main categories. One popular answer has been phrased, from the northern perspective, by quoting Napoleon's aphorism that God was on the side of the heaviest battalions. For southerners this explanation usually took some such form as these words of a Virginian: "They never whipped us, Sir, unless they were four to one. If we had had anything like a fair chance, or less disparity of numbers, we should have won our cause and established our independence." The North had a potential manpower superiority of more than three to one (counting only white men) and Union armed forces had an actual superiority of two to one during most of the war. In economic resources and logistical capacity the northern advantage was even greater. Thus, in this explanation, the Confederacy fought against overwhelming odds; its defeat was inevitable.

But this explanation has not satisfied a good many analysts. History is replete with examples of peoples who have won or defended their independence against greater odds: the Netherlands against the Spain of Philip II; Switzerland against the Hapsburg Empire; the American rebels of 1776 against mighty Britain; North Vietnam against the United States of 1970. Given the advantages of fighting on the defensive in its own territory with interior lines in which stalemate would be victory against a foe who must invade, conquer, occupy, and destroy the capacity to resist, the odds faced by the South were not formida-

ble. Rather, as another category of interpretations has it, internal divisions fatally weakened the Confederacy: the state-rights conflict between certain governors and the Richmond government; the disaffection of non-slaveholders from a rich man's war and poor man's fight; libertarian opposition to necessary measures such as conscription and the suspension of habeas corpus; the lukewarm commitment to the Confederacy by quondam Whigs and unionists; the disloyalty of slaves who defected to the enemy whenever they had a chance; growing doubts among slaveowners themselves about the justice of their peculiar institution and their cause. "So the Confederacy succumbed to internal rather than external causes," according to numerous historians. The South suffered from a "weakness in morale," a "loss of the will to fight." The Confederacy did not lack "the means to continue the struggle," but "the will to do so."

To illustrate their argument that the South could have kept fighting for years longer if it had tried harder, four historians have cited the instructive example of Paraguay. That tiny country carried on a war for six years (1865–71) against an alliance of Brazil, Argentina, and Uruguay whose combined population outnumbered Paraguay's by nearly thirty to one. Almost every male from twelve to sixty fought in the Paraguayan army; the country lost 56 percent of its total population and 80 percent of its men of military age in the war. Indeed, "the Confederate war effort seems feeble by comparison," for a mere 5 percent of the South's white people and 25 percent of the white males of military age were killed. To be sure, Paraguay lost the war, but its "tenacity ... does exhibit how a people can fight when possessed of total conviction."

It is not quite clear whether these ... historians think the South should have emulated Paraguay's example. In any case the "internal division" and "lack of will" explanations for Confederate defeat, while not implausible, are not very convincing either. The problem is that the North experienced

---

★In medieval German mythology, Siegfried slays the dragon Fafnir and wins the hand of Kriemhild, only to be killed at the behest of Queen Brünnhilde, whom he had once promised to wed. — Ed.

similar internal divisions, and if the war had come out differently the Yankees' lack of unity and will to win could be cited with equal plausibility to explain that outcome. The North had its large minority alienated by the rich man's war/poor man's fight theme; its outspoken opposition to conscription, taxation, suspension of habeas corpus, and other war measures; its state governors and legislatures and congressmen who tried to thwart administration policies. If important elements of the southern population, white as well as black, grew disaffected with a war to preserve slavery, equally significant groups in the North dissented from a war to abolish slavery. One critical distinction between Union and Confederacy was the institutionalization of obstruction in the Democratic party in the North, compelling the Republicans to close ranks in support of war policies to overcome and ultimately to discredit the opposition, while the South had no such institutionalized political structure to mobilize support and vanquish resistance.

Nevertheless, the existence of internal divisions on both sides seemed to neutralize this factor as an explanation for Union victory, so a number of historians have looked instead at the quality of leadership both military and civilian. There are several variants of an interpretation that emphasizes a gradual development of superior northern leadership. In [P.G.T.] Beauregard, Lee, the two Johnstons [Albert Sidney and Joseph Eggleston], and [Stonewall] Jackson the South enjoyed abler military commanders during the first year or two of the war, while Jefferson Davis was better qualified by training and experience than Lincoln to lead a nation at war. But Lee's strategic vision was limited to the Virginia theater, and the Confederate government neglected the West, where Union armies developed a strategic design and the generals to carry it out, while southern forces floundered under incompetent commanders who lost the war in the West. By 1863, Lincoln's remarkable abilities gave him a wide edge over Davis as a war leader, while in [Ulysses S.] Grant and [William

Tecumseh] Sherman the North acquired commanders with a concept of total war and the necessary determination to make it succeed. At the same time, in [Secretary of War] Edwin M. Stanton and [Quartermaster General] Montgomery Meigs, aided by the entrepreneurial talent of northern businessmen, the Union developed superior managerial talent to mobilize and organize the North's greater resources for victory in the modern industrialized conflict that the Civil War became.

This interpretation comes closer than others to credibility. Yet it also commits the fallacy of reversibility — that is, if the outcome had been reversed some of the same factors could be cited to explain Confederate victory. If the South had its bumblers like [Braxton] Bragg and [John C.] Pemberton and [John Bell] Hood who lost the West, and Joseph Johnston who fought too little and too late, the North had its [George B.] McClellan and [George Gordon] Meade who threw away chances in the East and its [John] Pope and [Ambrose E.] Burnside and [Joseph] Hooker who nearly lost the war in that theater where the genius of Lee and his lieutenants nearly won it, despite all the South's disadvantages. If the Union had its Stanton and Meigs, the Confederacy had its [Ordnance Chief] Josiah Gorgas and other unsung heroes who performed miracles of organization and improvisation. If Lincoln had been defeated for re-election in 1864, as he anticipated in August, history might record Davis as the great war leader and Lincoln as an also-ran.

Most attempts to explain southern defeat or northern victory lack the dimension of *contingency* — the recognition that at numerous critical points during the war things might have gone altogether differently. Four major turning points defined the eventual outcome. The first came in the summer of 1862, when the counter-offensives of Jackson and Lee in Virginia and Bragg and Kirby Smith in the West arrested the momentum of a seemingly imminent Union victory. This assured a prolongation and intensification of the conflict and created the potential

The outcome of the Civil War, argues James McPherson, was determined on the battlefield. This photograph shows Confederate dead after the 1862 Battle of Antietam, which repelled a rebel in- *vasion of the North and forestalled European recognition of the Confederacy. (Chicago Historical Society)*

for Confederate success, which appeared imminent before each of the next three turning points.

The first of these occurred in the fall of 1862, when battles at Antietam [Maryland] and Perryville [Kentucky] threw back Confederate invasions, forestalled European mediation and recognition of the Confederacy, perhaps prevented a Democratic victory in the northern elections of 1862 that might have inhibited the government's ability to carry on the war, and set the stage for the Emancipation Proclamation which enlarged the scope and purpose of the conflict. The third critical point came in the

summer and fall of 1863 when [Union victories at] Gettysburg, Vicksburg, and Chattanooga turned the tide toward ultimate northern victory.

One more reversal of that tide seemed possible in the summer of 1864 when appalling Union casualties and apparent lack of progress especially in Virginia brought the North to the brink of peace negotiations and the election of a Democratic president. But [Sherman's] capture of Atlanta and [Philip] Sheridan's destruction of [Jubal] Early's [rebel] army in the Shenandoah Valley clinched matters for the North. Only then did it become possible to speak of the in-

A scene during the Battle of Gettysburg, July 1–3, 1863. The summer and fall of that year marked the war's third critical point, when Union victories at Gettysburg, Vicksburg, and Chattanooga "turned the tide toward ultimate northern victory." (Courtesy of the Ann S. K. Brown Military Collection, Brown University Library)

evitability of Union victory. Only then did the South experience an irretrievable "loss of the will to fight."

Of all the explanations for Confederate defeat, the loss of will thesis suffers most from its own particular fallacy of reversibility — that of putting the cart before the horse. Defeat causes demoralization and loss of will; victory pumps up morale and the will to win. Nothing illustrates this better than the radical transformation of *northern* will from defeatism in August 1864 to a "depth of determination . . . to fight to the last" that "astonished" a British journalist a month later. The southern loss of will was a mirror image of this northern determination. These changes of mood were caused mainly by events on the battlefield. Northern victory and southern defeat in the war cannot be understood apart from the contingency that hung over every campaign, every battle, every election, every decision during the war. . . .

Arguments about the causes and consequences of the Civil War, as well as the reasons for northern victory, will continue as long as there are historians to wield the pen — which is, perhaps even for this bloody conflict, mightier than the sword. But certain large consequences of the war seem clear. Secession and slavery were killed, never to be revived during the century and a quarter since Appomattox. These results signified a broader transformation of American society and polity punctuated if not alone achieved by the war. Before 1861 the two words "United States" were generally rendered as a plural noun: "the United States *are* a republic." The war marked a transition of the United States to a singular noun. The "Union" also became the nation, and Americans now rarely speak of their Union except in an historical sense. Lincoln's wartime speeches betokened this transition. In his first inaugural address he used the word "Union" twenty times and the word "nation" not once. In his first message to Congress, on July 4, 1861, he used "Union" thirty-two times and "nation" three times. In his letter to [*New York Tribune* editor] Horace Greeley of August 22, 1862, on the relationship of slavery to the war, Lincoln spoke of the Union eight times and of the nation not at all. Little more than a year later, in his address at Gettysburg, the president did not refer to the "Union" at all but used the word "nation" five times to invoke a new birth of freedom and nationalism for the United States. And in his second inaugural address, looking back over the events of the past four years, Lincoln spoke of one side seeking to dissolve the *Union* in 1861 and the other accepting the challenge of war to preserve the *nation.*

The old federal republic in which the national government had rarely touched the average citizen except through the post-office gave way to a more centralized polity that taxed the people directly and created an internal revenue bureau to collect these taxes, drafted men into the army, expanded the jurisdiction of federal courts, created a national currency and a national banking system, and established the first national agency for social welfare — the Freed-

men's Bureau. [That bureau provided food and schools for the former slaves, helped them find jobs, and made certain they received fair wages.] Eleven of the first twelve amendments to the Constitution had limited the powers of the national government; six of the next seven, beginning with the Thirteenth Amendment in 1865, vastly expanded those powers at the expense of the states.

This change in the federal balance paralleled a radical shift of political power from South to North. During the first seventy-two years of the republic down to 1861 a slaveholding resident of one of the states that joined the Confederacy had been President of the United States for forty-nine of those years — more than two-thirds of the time. In Congress, twenty-three of the thirty-six speakers of the House and twenty-four of the presidents pro tem of the Senate had been southerners. The Supreme Court always had a southern majority; twenty of the thirty-five justices to 1861 had been appointed from slave states. After the war a century passed before a resident of an ex-Confederate state was elected president. For half a century *none* of the speakers of the House or presidents pro tem of the Senate came from the South, and only five of the twenty-six Supreme Court justices appointed during that half-century were southerners.

These figures symbolize a sharp and permanent change in the direction of American development. Through most of American history the South has seemed different from the rest of the United States, with "a separate and unique identity . . . which appeared to be out of the mainstream of American experience." But when did the northern stream become the mainstream? From a broader perspective it may have been the *North* that was exceptional and unique before the Civil War. The South more closely resembled a majority of the societies in the world than did the rapidly changing North during the antebellum generation. Despite the abolition of legal slavery or serfdom throughout much of the western hemisphere and western Europe, most of the world — like the South — had an unfree or quasi-free labor force. Most societies in the world remained predominantly rural, agricultural, and labor-intensive; most, including even several European countries, had illiteracy rates as high or higher than the South's 45 percent; most like the South remained bound by traditional values and networks of family, kinship, hierarchy, and patriarchy. The North — along with a few countries of northwestern Europe — hurtled forward eagerly toward a future of industrial capitalism that many southerners found distasteful if not frightening; the South remained proudly and even defiantly rooted in the past before 1861.

Thus when secessionists protested that they were acting to preserve traditional rights and values, they were correct. They fought to protect their constitutional liberties against the perceived northern threat to overthrow them. The South's concept of republicanism had not changed in three-quarters of a century; the North's had. With complete sincerity the South fought to preserve its version of the republic of the founding fathers — a government of limited powers that protected the rights of property and whose constituency comprised an independent gentry and yeomanry of the white race undisturbed by large cities, heartless factories, restless free workers, and class conflict. The accession to power of the Republican party, with its ideology of competitive, egalitarian, free-labor capitalism, was a signal to the South that the northern majority had turned irrevocably toward this frightening, revolutionary future. Indeed, the Black Republican party appeared to the eyes of many southerners as "essentially a revolutionary party" composed of "a motley throng of Sans culottes ... Infidels and freelovers, interspersed by Bloomer women, fugitive slaves, and amalgamationists." Therefore secession was a pre-emptive counterrevolution to prevent the Black Republican revolution from engulfing the South. "*We* are not revolutionists," insisted James B. D. DeBow and Jefferson Davis during the Civil War, "We are resisting revolution.... We are conservative."

Union victory in the war destroyed the southern vision of America and ensured that the northern vision would become the American vision. Until 1861, however, it was the North that was out of the mainstream, not the South. Of course the northern states, along with Britain and a few countries in northwestern Europe, were cutting a new channel in world history that would doubtless have become the mainstream even if the American Civil War had not happened. Russia had abolished serfdom in 1861 to complete the dissolution of this ancient institution of bound labor in Europe. But for Americans the Civil War marked the turning point. A Louisiana planter who returned home sadly after the war wrote in 1865: "Society has been completely changed by the war. The [French] revolution of '89 did not produce a greater change in the 'Ancien Régime' than this has in our social life." And four years later George Ticknor, a retired Harvard professor, concluded that the Civil War had created a "great gulf between what happened before in our century and what has happened since, or what is likely to happen hereafter. It does not seem to me as if I were living in the country in which I was born." From the war sprang the great flood that caused the stream of American history to surge into a new channel and transferred the burden of exceptionalism from North to South.

QUESTIONS TO CONSIDER

1 McPherson discusses several traditional interpretations of why the Confederacy lost the Civil War. What were they, and which does he consider to be the strongest and the weakest? How does he refute them all?

2 McPherson bases his own explanation of the Confederacy's defeat on the idea of contingency.

What does he mean by this, and what does he consider the critical turning points of the war? When does he think northern victory became inevitable?

3   How does McPherson defend his conviction that the most crucial element in all the developments and consequences of the Civil War, including the political and the social, was what happened on the battlefield? Do you agree? why?

4   Discuss McPherson's argument that the Civil War changed the United States from a union into a nation. What did this change entail and signify?

5   Explain McPherson's idea that, contrary to our usual notion, before the Civil War it was the North and not the South that was exceptional. Do you think this fits in with Douglas Wilson's discussion of presentism in selection 8?

Hayfoot, Strawfoot! The Civil War Soldier Marched to His Own Individual Cadence

BRUCE CATTON

If the Civil War was won or lost on the battlefield, then it is important to acquaint our-selves with the soldiers who did the fighting. First of all, most of the 3 million soldiers in both armies were volunteers who lacked the training and the spit and polish of the profes-sional soldiers of Europe. Second, they were young: a typical Civil War soldier, as James I. Robertson points out in Soldiers Blue and Gray *(1988), was between eighteen and twenty-nine years old; but some were as young as fourteen and others as old as seventy.*

Civil War soldiers endured harsh conditions in camp. Union men subsisted on hard-tack, a kind of cracker that was often infested with weevils and so hard as to be inedible, and salt pork that was frequently tainted, and they washed it all down each day with three or four quarts of strong coffee apiece. That much caffeine must have fried their ner-vous systems. They drank their share of whiskey, too, which they called "bug juice," "rot gut," "bust skull," and consumed homemade concoctions called, "Oh, be joyful" and "knockum stiff." Imbibing too much of such stuff would make you "fire and fall back" (vomit) and leave you "squashmolished" (plagued with a hangover). When sol-diers of both armies secured cherished passes to leave camp and visit the nearest town or city, they often sought out the brothels, where they enjoyed "horizontal refreshments." Enterprising madams often offered lower prices to an entire company or regiment on a sort of group plan.

The sick and wounded of both armies suffered terribly in the dreaded field hospitals. Here a second war was going on that claimed more lives than the shooting war itself. Two-thirds of the Union deaths occurred in the hospitals, where surgeons and nurses, re-lying on primitive medical practices and dubious medicines, fought a losing battle to save wounded or diseased soldiers. Since nobody knew what caused infection, surgeons of both armies worked with unsanitary scalpels and saws in unsanitary conditions. Recalled one surgeon: "We operated in old blood-stained and often pus-stained coats, with undisinfected hands. We used undisinfected instruments and sponges which had been used in prior pus cases and only washed in tap water." The luckless soldier with a bone-breaking woumd in the leg or arm faced certain amputation — it was the only way the surgeons knew to save his life. If he was in a well-stocked hospital, the surgeon would put him mercifully to sleep with chloroform or ether. If both were lacking (and they often were at battlefield hospitals), the poor victim might get a shot of whiskey, or simply a slab of leather placed between his teeth, before the surgeon applied the saw. Because of the horrible conditions in the hospitals and the lack of proper medical treatment, the mortality rate was appalling. Nearly every soldier with an abdominal wound died; some 60 percent of those with other wounds also died.

The real Civil War killer, however, was infectious disease. Dysentery and diarrhea were the worst, sending more men to the grave than bullets and shells on the battlefield. Doctors tried to combat diarrhrea/dysentery with laxatives, opium, castor oil, or Epsom salts, all of which, save the opium, exacerbated the condition horribly. Other killer diseases were malaria and typhoid, which the crude medicines of the day could do little to stop. Doing the best they could with the limited medical knowledge of the day, physicians treated abdominal pains with blisters and "hot fomentation" and intestinal ulcers with oral doses of turpentine, and they sometimes treated headaches with applications of leaches. As other historians have pointed out, a soldier's safety was more imperiled if he had to undergo treatment in an army hospital than if he had fought all three days at Gettysburg.

In his portrait of the Civil War fighting man, the late Bruce Catton, one of the most prolific and preeminent Civil War historians of all time, will introduce you to the daily life, routine, training, combat, and suffering of the soldiers of "the late unpleasantness," as they often called the war. He points out that outmoded battle tactics, combined with murderous new weaponry, turned Civil War battles into bloodbaths. Why did soldiers of the two sides volunteer to fight in such a brutal conflict? Catton touches on this, but two recent books by James M. McPherson, What They Fought For (1994) and For Cause and Comrades (1997), answer that question in depth. Suffice it to say, the Union soldiers fought to preserve the Union and its experiment in popular government; and when Lincoln issued the Emancipation Proclamation, they fought to free the slaves as a means of saving the Union and its free government. As one Union private said, "We have lived, prospered and been protected under a free government, and we wish to preserve the same for the welfare and happiness of our posterity. The welfare of millions yet unborn is dependent upon us, and it behooves us to do all in our power to sustain our government."

Confederates, on the other hand, fought to prevent the hated Yankee invaders from subjugating their region; they fought to protect their homes and families and to create an *independent, slave-based nation, which, they believed, would ensure their liberty as white men. As McPherson points out, the majority of rebel soldiers believed they were fighting "for liberty and slavery, one and inseparable." It did not matter that most Confederate soldiers were non-slaveholders; they were white and were as furiously opposed to the emancipation of black people, whom they hated and feared, as the planters were. As a captain of the Twenty-Eighth Mississippi wrote his wife: "I own no slaves and can freely express my notions without being taxed with any motive of self interest. I know that this country without Negro slave labor would be wholly worthless, a barren waste and desolate plain — we can only live and exist by this species of labor; and hence I am willing to fight to the last."*

Some 260,000 of his southern brothers did fight to the last in a doomed cause, while 360,000 Yankees died to make the United States a nation at last.

GLOSSARY

DRILL SERGEANT   Officer who had to teach the untaught and inexperienced volunteers how to march.

JOHNNY REB   Nickname for a Confederate soldier.

MILITARY TACTICS   Usually defined as "the art or science of disposing specific military or naval forces for battle and maneuvering them in battle."

REGIMENT   Basic army unit, which on paper consisted of about a thousand men divided into ten companies and commanded by a colonel. Four regiments, in turn, constituted a brigade; three or four brigades formed a division; three or more divisions made up a corps; and two or more corps constituted an army.

SPRINGFIELD RIFLE   Standard weapon for Civil War infantry, a .58-caliber muzzle-loading rifled musket that was far more accurate than the outmoded smoothbores.

SUTLER   Civilian merchant licensed by the army to sell additional rations to Union troops.

The volunteer soldier in the American Civil War used a clumsy muzzle-loading rifle, lived chiefly on salt pork and hardtack, and retained to the very end a loose-jointed, informal attitude toward the army with which he had cast his lot. But despite all of the surface differences, he was at bottom blood brother to the G.I. Joe of modern days.

Which is to say that he was basically, and incurably, a civilian in arms. A volunteer, he was still a soldier because he had to be one, and he lived for the day when he could leave the army forever. His attitude toward discipline, toward his officers, and toward the whole spit-and-polish concept of military existence was essentially one of careless tolerance. He refused to hate his enemies — indeed, he often got along with them much better than with some of

From Bruce Catton, "Hayfoot, Strawfoot!" *American Heritage*, vol. 8, no. 3 (April 1957), pp. 30–37. Reprinted by permission of *American Heritage* magazine, a division of Forbes, Inc. Copyright © Forbes, Inc., 1957.

his own comrades — and his indoctrination was often so imperfect that what was sometimes despairingly said of the American soldier in World War II would apply equally to him: he seemed to be fighting chiefly so that he could some day get back to Mom's cooking.

What really set the Civil War soldier apart was the fact that he came from a less sophisticated society. He was no starry-eyed innocent, to be sure — or, if he was, the army quickly took care of that — but the America of the 1860's was less highly developed than modern America. It lacked the ineffable advantages of radio, television, and moving pictures. It was still essentially a rural nation; it had growing cities, but they were smaller and somehow less urban than today's cities; a much greater percentage of the population lived on farms or in country towns and villages than is the case now, and there was more of a backwoods, hay-seed-in-the-hair flavor to the people who came from them.

For example: every war finds some ardent youngsters who want to enlist despite the fact that they are under the military age limit of eighteen. Such a lad today simply goes to the recruiting station, swears that he is eighteen, and signs up. The lad of the 1860's saw it a little differently. He could not swear that he was eighteen when he was only sixteen; in his innocent way, he felt that to lie to his own government was just plain wrong. But he worked out a little dodge that got him into the army anyway. He would take a bit of paper, scribble the number *18* on it, and put it in the sole of his shoe. Then, when the recruiting officer asked him how old he was, he could truthfully say: "I am *over* eighteen." That was a common happening, early in the Civil War; one cannot possibly imagine it being tried today.

Similarly, the drill sergeants repeatedly found that among the raw recruits there were men so abysmally untaught that they did not know left from right, and hence could not step off on the left foot as all soldiers should. To teach these lads how to march, the sergeants would tie a wisp of hay to the left foot and

a wisp of straw to the right; then, setting the men to march, they would chant, "Hay-foot, straw-foot, hay-foot, straw-foot" — and so on, until everybody had caught on. A common name for a green recruit in those days was "strawfoot."

On the drill field, when a squad was getting basic training, the men were as likely as not to intone a little rhythmic chant as they tramped across the sod — thus:

> March! March! March old soldier march!
> Hayfoot, strawfoot,
> Belly-full of bean soup —
> March old soldier march!

Because of his unsophistication, the ordinary soldier in the Civil War, North and South alike, usually joined up with very romantic ideas about soldiering. Army life rubbed the romance off just as rapidly then as it does now, but at the start every volunteer went into the army thinking that he was heading off to high adventure. Under everything else, he enlisted because he thought army life was going to be fun, and usually it took quite a few weeks in camp to disabuse him of this strange notion. Right at the start, soldiering had an almost idyllic quality; if this quality faded rapidly, the memory of it remained through all the rest of life.

Early days in camp simply cemented the idea. An Illinois recruit, writing home from training camp, confessed: "It is fun to lie around, face unwashed, hair uncombed, shirt unbuttoned and everything un-everythinged. It sure beats clerking." Another Illinois boy confessed: "I don't see why people will stay at home when they can get to soldiering. A year of it is worth getting shot for to any man." And a Massachusetts boy, recalling the early days of army life, wrote that "Our drill, as I remember it, consisted largely of running around the Old Westbury town hall, yelling like Devils and firing at an imaginary foe." One of the commonest discoveries that comes from a reading of Civil War diaries is that the chief worry, in training camp, was a fear that the war would be over before the ardent young recruits could get into it. It is only fair to say that most of the diarists looked back on this innocent worry, a year or so afterward, with rueful amusement.

There was a regiment recruited in northern Pennsylvania in 1861 — 13th Pennsylvania Reserves officially, known to the rest of the Union Army as the Bucktails because the rookies decorated their caps with strips of fur from the carcass of a deer that was hanging in front of a butcher shop near their camp — and in mid-spring these youthful soldiers were ordered to rendezvous at Harrisburg. So they marched cross-country (along a road known today as the Bucktail Trail) to the north branch of the Susquehanna, where they built rafts. One raft, for the colonel, was made oversized with a stable; the colonel's horse had to ride, too. Then the Bucktails floated down the river, singing and firing their muskets and having a gay old time, camping out along the bank at night, and finally they got to Harrisburg; and they served through the worst of the war, getting badly shot up and losing most of their men to Confederate bullets, but they never forgot the picnic air of those first days of army life, when they drifted down a river through the forests, with a song in the air and the bright light of adventure shining just ahead. Men do no go to war that way nowadays.

Discipline in those early regiments was pretty sketchy. The big catch was that most regiments were recruited locally — in one town, or one county, or in one part of a city — and everybody more or less knew everybody else. Particularly, the privates knew their officers — most of whom were elected to their jobs by the enlisted men — and they never saw any sense in being formal with them. Within reasonable limits, the Civil War private was willing to do what his company commander told him to do, but he saw little point in carrying it to extremes.

So an Indiana soldier wrote: "We had enlisted to put down the Rebellion, and had to patience with the red-tape tomfoolery of the regular service. The boys recognized no superiors, except in the line of legitimate duty. Shoulder straps waived, a private was ready at the drop of a hat to thrash his commander — a thing that occurred more than once." A New York regiment, drilling on a hot parade ground, heard a private address his company commander thus: "Say, Tom, let's quit this darn foolin' around and go over to the sutler's and get a drink." There was very little of the "Captain, sir" business in those armies. If a company or regimental officer got anything especial in the way of obedience, he got it because the enlisted men recognized him as a natural leader and superior and not just because he had a commission signed by Abraham Lincoln.

Odd rivalries developed between regiments. (It should be noted that the Civil War soldier's first loyalty went usually to his regiment, just as navy man's loyalty goes to his ship; he liked to believe that his regiment was better than all others, and he would fight for it, any time and anywhere.) The army legends of those days tell of a Manhattan regiment, camped near Washington, whose nearest neighbor was a regiment from Brooklyn, with which the Manhattanites nursed a deep rivalry. Neither regiment had a chaplain; and there came to the Manhattan colonel one day a minister, who volunteered to hold religious services for the men in the ranks.

The colonel doubted that this would be a good idea. His men, he said, were rather irreligious, not to say godless, and he feared they would not give the reverend gentleman a respectful hearing. But the minister said he would take his chances; after all, he had just held services with the Brooklyn regiment, and the men there had been very quiet and devout. That was enough for the colonel. What the Brooklyn regiment could do, his regiment could do. He ordered the men paraded for divine worship, announcing that any man who talked, laughed, or even coughed would be summarily court-martialed.

So the clergyman held services, and everyone was attentive. At the end of the sermon, the minister asked if any of his hearers would care to step forward and make public profession of faith; in the Brooklyn regiment, he said, fourteen men had done this. Instantly the New York colonel was on his feet.

"Adjutant!" he bellowed. "We're not going to let that damn Brooklyn regiment beat us at anything. Detail twenty men and have them baptized at once!"

Each regiment seemed to have its own mythology, tales which may have been false but which, by their mere existence, reflected faithfully certain aspects of army life. The 48th New York, for instance, was said to have an unusually large number of ministers in its ranks, serving not as chaplains but as combat soldiers. The 48th, fairly early in the war, found itself posted in a swamp along the South Carolina coast, toiling mightily in semitropical heat, amid clouds of mosquitoes, to build fortifications, and it was noted that all hands became excessively profane, including the one-time clergymen. A visiting general, watching the regiment at work one day, recalled the legend and asked the regiment's lieutenant colonel if he himself was a minister in private life.

"Well, no, General," said the officer apologetically. "I can't say that I was a regularly ordained minister. I was just one of these —— —— local preachers."

Another story was hung on this same 48th New York. A Confederate ironclad gunboat was supposed to be ready to steam through channels in the swamp and attack the 48th's outposts, and elaborate plans were made to trap it with obstructions in the channel, a tangle of ropes to snarl the propellers, and so on. But it occurred to the colonel that even if the gunboat was trapped the soldiers could not get into it; it was sheathed in iron, all its ports would be closed, and men with axes could never chop their way into it. Then the colonel had an inspiration. Remembering that many of his men had been recruited from the less savory districts of New York City, he paraded the regiment and (according to legend) announced:

"Now men, you've been in this cursed swamp for two weeks — up to your ears in mud, no fun, no glory and blessed poor pay. Here's a chance. Let every man who has had experience as a cracksman or a safeblower step to the front." To the last man, the regiment marched forward four paces and came expectantly to attention.

Not unlike this was the reputation of the 6th New York, which contained so many Bowery toughs that the rest of the army said a man had to be able to show that he had done time in prison in order to get into the regiment. It was about to leave for the South, and the colonel gave his men an inspirational talk. They were going, he said, to a land of wealthy plantation owners, where each Southerner had riches of which he could be despoiled; and he took out his own gold watch and held it up for all to see, remarking that any deserving soldier could easily get one like it, once they got down to plantation-land. Half an hour later, wishing to see what time it was, he felt for his watch . . . and it was gone.

If the Civil War army spun queer tales about itself, it had to face a reality which, in all of its aspects, was singularly unpleasant. One of the worst aspects had to do with food.

From first to last, the Civil War armies enlisted no men as cooks, and there were no cooks' and bakers' schools to help matters. Often enough, when in camp, a company would simply be issued a quantity of provisions — flour, pork, beans, potatoes, and so on — and invited to prepare the stuff as best it could. Half a dozen men would form a mess, members would take turns with the cooking, and everybody had to eat what these amateurs prepared or go hungry. Later in the war, each company commander would usually detail two men to act as cooks for the company, and if either of the two happened to know anything about cooking the company was in luck. One army legend held that company officers usually detailed the least valuable soldiers to this job, on the theory that they would do less harm in the cook shack than anywhere else. One soldier, writing after the war, asserted flatly: "A company cook is a most peculiar being; he generally knows less about cooking than any other man in the company. Not being able to learn the drill, and too dirty to appear on inspection, he is sent to the cook house to get him out of the ranks."

When an army was on the march, the ration issue usually consisted of salt pork, hardtack, and coffee. (In the Confederate Army the coffee was often missing, and the hardtack was frequently replaced by corn bread; often enough the meal was not sifted, and stray bits of cob would appear in it.) The hardtack was good enough, if fresh, which was not always the case; with age it usually got infested with weevils, and veterans remarked that it was better to eat it in the dark.

In the Union Army, most of the time, the soldier could supplement his rations (if he had money) by buying extras from the sutler—the latter being a civilian merchant licensed to accompany the army, functioning somewhat as the regular post exchange functions nowadays. The sutler charged high prices and specialized in indigestibles like pies, canned lobster salad, and so on; and it was noted that men who patronized him regularly came down with stomach upsets. The Confederate Army had few sutlers, which helps to explain why the hungry Confederates were so delighted when they could capture a Yankee camp: to seize the sutler's tent meant high living for the captors, and the men in Lee's army were furious when, in the 1864 campaign, they learned that General Grant had ordered the Union Army to move without sutlers. Johnny Reb felt that Grant was really taking an unfair advantage by cutting off this possible source of supply.

If Civil War cooking arrangements were impromptu and imperfect, the same applied to its hospital system. The surgeons, usually, were good men by the standards of that day—which were low since no one on earth knew anything about germs or about how wounds became infected, and antisepsis in the operating room was a concept that had not yet come into existence; it is common to read of a surgeon whetting his scalpel on the sole of his shoe just before operating. But the hospital attendants, stretcher-bearers, and the like were chosen just as the company cooks were chosen; that is, they were detailed from the ranks, and the average officer selected the most worthless men he had simply because he wanted to get rid of men who could not be counted on in combat. As a result, sick or wounded men often got atrocious care.

A result of all of this—coupled with the fact that many men enlisted without being given any medical examinations—was that every Civil War regiment was suffered a constant wastage from sickness. On paper, a regiment was supposed to have a strength ranging between 960 and 1,040 men; actually, no regiment ever got to the battlefield with anything like that strength, and since there was no established system for sending in replacements a veteran regiment that could must 350 enlisted men present for duty was considered pretty solid. From first to last, approximately twice as many Civil War soldiers died of disease—typhoid, dysentery, and pneumonia were the great killers—as died in action; and in addition to those who died a great many more got medical discharges.

In its wisdom, the Northern government set up a number of base hospitals in Northern states, far from the battle fronts, on the theory that a man recovering from wounds or sickness would recuperate better back home. Unfortunately, the hospitals thus established were under local control, and the men in them were no longer under the orders of their own regiments or armies. As a result, thousands of men who were sent north for convalescence never returned to the army. Many were detailed for light work at the hospitals, and in these details they stayed because nobody had the authority to extract them and send them back to duty. Others, recovering their health, simply went home and stayed there. They were answerable to the hospital authorities, not to the army command, and the hospital authorities rarely cared very much whether they returned to duty or not. The whole system was ideally designed to make desertion easy.

On top of all of this, many men had very little understanding of the requirements of military

During the Civil War, there were often long intervals between battles when the soldiers of both sides drilled and relaxed in camp.

This photograph shows Union officers playing dominoes at Camp Winfield Scott, Yorktown, Virginia. (Corbis-Bettmann)

discipline. A homesick boy often saw nothing wrong in leaving the army and going home to see the folks for a time. A man from a farm might slip off to go home and put in a crop. In neither case would the man look on himself as a deserter; he meant to return, he figured he would get back in time for any fighting that would take place, and in his own mind he was innocent of any wrongdoing. But in many cases the date of return would be postponed from week to week; the man might end as a deserter, even though he had not intended to be one when he left.

This merely reflected the loose discipline that prevailed in Civil War armies, which in turn reflected the underlying civilian-mindedness that pervaded the rank and file. The behavior of Northern armies on the march in Southern territory reflected the same thing — and, in the end, had a profound effect on the institution of chattel slavery.

Armies of occupation always tend to bear down hard on civilian property in enemy territory. Union armies in the Civil War, being imperfectly disciplined to begin with — and suffering, furthermore, from a highly defective rationing system — bore down with especial fervor. Chickens, hams, cornfields, anything edible that might be found on a Southern plantation, looked like fair game, and the loose fringe of stragglers that always trailed around the edges of a moving Union army looted with a fine disregard for civilian property rights.

This was made all the more pointed by the fact that the average Northern soldier, poorly indoctrinated though he was, had strong feelings about the evils of secession. To his mind, the Southerners who sought to set up a nation of their own were in rebellion against the best government mankind had ever known. Being rebels, they had forfeited their rights; if evil things happened to them that (as the average Northern soldier saw it) was no more than just retribution. This meant that even when the army command tried earnestly to prevent looting and individual foraging the officers at company and regimental levels seldom tried very hard to carry out the high command's orders.

William Tecumseh Sherman has come down in history as the very archetype of the Northern soldier who believed in pillage and looting; yet during the first years of the war Sherman resorted to all manner of ferocious punishments to keep his men from despoiling Southern porperty. He had looters tied up by the thumbs, ordered courts-martial, issued any number of stern orders — and all to very little effect. Long before he adopted the practice of commandeering or destroying Southern property as a war measure, his soldiers were practicing it against his will, partly because discipline was poor and partly because they saw nothing wrong with it.

It was common for a Union colonel, as his regiment made camp in a Southern state, to address his men, pointing to a nearby farm, and say: "Now, boys, that barn is full of nice fat pigs and chickens. I don't want to see any of you take any of them" — whereupon he would fold his arms and look sternly in the opposite direction. It was also common for a regimental commander to read, on parade, some ukase from higher authority forbidding foraging, and then to wink solemnly — a clear hint that he did not expect anyone to take the order seriously. One colonel, punishing some men who had robbed a chicken house, said angrily: "Boys, I want you to understand that I am not punishing you for stealing but for getting caught at it."

It is more than a century since that war was fought, and things look a little different now than they looked at the time. At this distance, it may be possible to look indulgently on the wholesale foraging in which Union armies indulged; to the Southern farmers who bore the brunt of it, the business looked very ugly indeed. Many a Southern family saw the foodstuffs needed for the winter swept away in an hour by grinning hoodlums who did not need and could not use a quarter of what they took. Among the foragers there were many lawless characters who took watches, jewels, and any other valuable they could find; it is recorded that a squad would now and then carry a piano out to the lawn, take it apart, and use the wires to hang pots and pans over the campfire. . . . The Civil War was really romantic only at a considerable distance.

Underneath his feeling that it was good to add chickens and hams to the army ration, and his belief that civilians in a state of secession could expect no better fate, the Union soldier also came to believe that to destroy Southern property was to help win the war. Under orders, he tore up railroads and burned warehouses; it was not long before he realized that anything that damaged the Confederate economy weakened the Confederate war effort, so he rationalized his looting and foraging by arguing that it was a step in breaking the Southern will to resist. It is at this point that the institution of human slavery enters the picture.

Most Northern soldiers had very little feeling against slavery as such, and very little sympathy for the Negro himself. They thought they were fighting to save the Union, not to end slavery, and except for New England troops most Union regiments contained very little abolition sentiment. Nevertheless, the soldiers moved energetically and effectively to destroy slavery, not because they especially intended to but simply because they were out to do all the damage they could do. They were operating against Southern property — and the most obvious, important, and easily removable property of all was the

As Bruce Catton points out, Civil War armies had no cooks. When in camp, the soldiers received provisions like flour, beans, *or pork, and "prepared the stuff" however they could. These soldiers are cooking a meal over a makeshift fire. (Corbis-Bettmann)*

slave. To help the slaves get away from the plantation was, clearly, to weaken Southern productive capacity, which in turn weakened Confederate armies. Hence the Union soldier, wherever he went, took the peculiar insitution apart, chattel by chattel.

As a result, slavery had been fatally weakened long before the war itself came to an end. The mere act of fighting the war killed it. Of all institutions on earth, the institution of human slavery was the one least adapted to survive a war. It could not survive the presence of loose-jointed, heavy-handed armies of occupation. It may hardly be too much to say that the mere act of taking up arms in slavery's defense doomed slavery.

Above and beyond everything else, of course, the business of the Civil War soldier was to fight. He fought with weapons that look very crude to modern eyes, and he moved by an outmoded system of tactics, but the price he paid when he got into action was just as high as the price modern soldiers pay despite the almost infinite development of firepower since the 1860's.

Standard infantry weapon in the Civil War was the rifled Springfield — a muzzle-loader firing a conical lead bullet, usually of .58 caliber.

To load was rather laborious, and it took a good man to get off more than two shots a minute. The weapon had a range of nearly a mile, and its "effective

Because of deadly weaponry and outmoded infantry tactics, Civil War battles became gruesome bloodbaths. The wounded gathered around makeshift field hospitals, some sullen, others in shock.

These soldiers, two of them fresh off the amputating table, were casualties of the Virginia campaign of 1864. (Archive Photos)

range" — that is, the range at which it would hit often enough to make infantry fire truly effective — was figured at about 250 yards. Compared with a modern Garand, the old muzzle-loader is no better than a museum piece; but compared with all previous weapons — the weapons on which infantry tactics in the 1860's were still based — it was a fearfully destructive and efficient piece.

For the infantry of that day still moved and fought in formations dictated in the old days of smoothbore muskets, whose effective range was no more than 100 yards and which were wildly inaccurate at any distance. Armies using those weapons attacked in solid mass formations, the men standing, literally, elbow to elbow. They could get from effective range to hand-to-hand fighting in a very short time, and if they had a proper numerical advantage over the defensive line they could come to grips without losing too many men along the way.

But in the Civil War the conditions had changed radically; men would be hit while the rival lines were still half a mile apart, and to advance in mass was simply to invite wholesale destruction. Tactics had not yet been adjusted to the new rifles; as a result, Civil War attacks could be fearfully costly, and when the defenders dug entrenchments and got some protection — as the men learned to do, very quickly — a direct frontal assault could be little better than a form of mass suicide.

It took the high command a long time to revise tactics to meet this changed situation, and Civil War battles ran up dreadful casualty lists. For an army to lose 25 per cent of its numbers in a major battle was by no means uncommon, and in some fights — the Confederate army at Gettysburg is an outstanding example — the percentage of loss ran close to one third of the total number engaged. Individual units were sometimes nearly wiped out. Some of the

Union and Confederate regiments that fought at Gettysburg lost up to 80 per cent of their numbers; a regiment with such losses was usually wrecked, as an effective fighting force, for the rest of the war.

The point of all of which is that the discipline which took the Civil War soldier into action, while it may have been very sketchy by modern standards, was nevertheless highly effective on the field of battle. Any armies that could go through such battles as Antietam, Stone's River, Franklin or Chickamauga and come back for more had very little to learn about the business of fighting.

Perhaps the Confederate General D. H. Hill said it, once and for all. The battle of Malvern Hill, fought on the Virginia peninsula early in the summer of 1862, finished the famous Seven Days campaign, in which George B. McClellan's Army of the Potomac was driven back from in front of Richmond by Robert E. Lee's Army of Northern Virginia. At Malvern Hill, McClellan's men fought a rear-guard action — a bitter, confused fight which came at the end of a solid week of wearing, costly battles and forced marches. Federal artillery wrecked the Confederate assault columns, and at the end of the day Hill looked out over the battlefield, strewn with dead and wounded boys. Shaking his head, and reflecting on the valor in attack and in defense which the two armies had displayed, Hill never forgot about this. Looking back on it, long after the war was over, he declared, in substance:

"Give me Confederate infantry and Yankee artillery and I'll whip the world!"

QUESTIONS TO CONSIDER

1   Soldiers of both sides looted and pillaged, but in the Union army the practice evolved into economic warfare against civilians. Was this form of warfare effective? Was it justifiable? How did this form of warfare affect slavery?

2   Why did Confederate soldiers fight? Why did Union soldiers fight? What was the typical Union soldier's attitude toward emancipation? Think about modern military television commercials, urging young Americans to enlist in America's armed forces. Has the basic appeal of enlisting today changed from that of the Civil War period?

3   What was the biggest killer of the Civil War soldier? Why was this the case? Was the medical establishment equipped to handle disease and wounds? What single medical advance would have saved countless soldiers' lives?

4   During the Civil War, what was the difference between battlefield tactics and the advancement in modern weaponry? How did the discrepancy between tactics and weaponry affect Civil War battles? In your opinion, what advances were vital in bringing about a successful military strategy?

RECONSTRUCTION:
"A SPLENDID FAILURE"

29

The New View of Reconstruction

ERIC FONER

"Whatever you were taught or thought you knew about the post–Civil War era is probably wrong in the light of recent study." So went the editorial comment in the issue of American Heritage *in which "The New View of Reconstruction" originally appeared. If you think that Reconstruction was a tragic time when fanatical Radicals like Old Thad Stevens and Charles Sumner took control of Reconstruction away from a moderate Andrew Johnson, sought to "put the colored people on top" in the conquered South, and turned it over to hordes of roguish carpetbaggers, traitorous scalawags, and ignorant and uppity Negroes who "stole the south blind," you will be in for a surprise. The new interpretation of Reconstruction, which broke full force in the 1960s, cast President Andrew Johnson and unrepentant southern whites as the real villains of the drama. It argues that Reconstruction, instead of being a misguided experiment in extremism, was in fact not nearly radical enough. The new view of the postwar years, and the story of how it replaced the traditional interpretation, is the subject of this selection by Eric Foner, today's foremost historian of the Reconstruction era.*

To place his essay in historical context, it would be well to review the attitudes of southern blacks and whites as the war drew to a close, and to describe Johnson's reconstruction policy. For the deeply religious slaves, the Civil War had had profound religious meaning. Hundreds of thousands of them, writes historian Vincent Harding, "believed unswervingly that their God moved in history to deliver his people, and they had been looking eagerly, praying hourly, waiting desperately for the glory of the coming of the Lord. For them, all the raucous, roaring guns of Charleston Harbor and Bull Run, and Antietam and Fort Pillow, of Shiloh and Murfreesboro and Richmond were the certain voice of God, announcing his judgment across the bloody stretches of the South."

During the course of the war, African Americans believed, God did deliver them. With the Confederacy's collapse, as one song went, "slavery chain done broke at last."

> *Slavery chain done broke at last!*
> *Broke at last! Broke at last!*
> *Slavery chain done broke at last!*
> *Gonna praise God till I die!*

Some reacted to their liberation with cautious elation. When a young Virginia woman heard her former masters weeping over the capture of Jefferson Davis, she went down to a spring alone and cried out. "Glory, glory, hallelujah to Jesus! I's free! I's free!" Suddenly afraid, she looked about. What if the white folks had heard her? But seeing no one, she fell to the ground and kissed it, thanking "Master Jesus" over and over. For her, freedom meant hope — hope that she could find her husband and four children who had been sold to a slave trader.

Others celebrated their liberation in public. In Athens, Georgia, they danced around a liberty pole; in Charleston, they paraded through the streets. Many African Americans, however, were wary and uncertain. "You're joking me," one man said when the master told him he was free. He asked some neighbors if they were free also. "I couldn't believe we was all free alike," he said. Some African Americans, out of feelings of obligation or compassion, remained on the home place to help their former masters. But others were hostile. When a woman named Cady heard that the war was over, she decided to protest the cruel treatment she had suffered as a slave. She threw down her hoe, marched up to the big house, found the mistress, and flipped her dress up. She told the white woman, "Kiss my ass!"

For Cady, for the young black woman of Virginia, for hosts of other African Americans, freedom meant an end to the manifold evils of slavery; it meant the right to say what they felt and go where they wanted. But what else did freedom mean to them? As black leaders of Charleston said, it meant that blacks should enjoy full citizenship, have the right to vote and run for political office. It meant federal protection from their former masters lest they attempt to revive slavery. And it meant economic security in the form of land, so that the blacks could exercise self-help and be economically independent of their former masters.

If the end of the war was a time of profound hope for black Americans, it was a monumental calamity for most southern whites. By turns, they were angry, helpless, vindictive, resigned, and heartsick. Their cherished South was not just defeated; it was annihilated. The South's major cities were in ruins, railroads and industry desolated, commerce paralyzed, and two-thirds of the assessed wealth, including billions of dollars in slaves, destroyed. As one historian says, "Many [white southerners] were already grieving over sons, plantations, and fortunes taken by war; losing their blacks was the final blow." Some masters shot or hanged African Americans who proclaimed their freedom. That was a harbinger of the years of Reconstruction, for most white southerners were certain that their cause had been just and were entirely unrepentant about fighting against the Union. A popular ballad captured the mood in postwar Dixie:

> Oh, I'm a good ole Rebel, now that's just what I am
> For this fair land of freedom I do not care a damn.
> I'm glad I fit against it, I only wish't we'd won
> And I don't want no pardon for nothin' what I done. . . .
>
> I hates the Yankee nation and everything they do
> I hates the Declaration of Independence too
> I hates the glorious Union, 'tis dripping with our blood
> And I hate the striped banner, I fit it all I could. . . .
>
> I can't take up my musket and fight 'em now no mo'
> But I ain't gonna love 'em and that is certain sho'
> And I don't want no pardon for what I was and am
> And I won't be reconstructed and I don't care a damn.

In Washington, Republican leaders were jubilant in victory and determined to deal firmly with southern whites in order to preserve the fruits of the war. But what about the new president, Andrew Johnson? A profane, hard-drinking Tennessee Democrat who bragged about his plebeian origins, Johnson had been the only southern senator to oppose secession openly. He had sided with the Union, served as war governor of Tennessee, and became Lincoln's running mate in 1864, on a Union ticket comprising both Republicans and War Democrats. As a result of the assassination of Lincoln, Johnson was now president, and he faced one of the most difficult tasks ever to confront an American chief executive: how to bind the nation's wounds, preserve African American freedom, and restore the southern states to their proper places in the Union.

Lincoln had contemplated an army of occupation for the South, thinking that military force might be necessary to protect the former slaves and prevent the old southern leadership from returning to power. Now there was such an army in the South: some 200,000 Union troops had moved in to restore order there and to perform whatever reconstruction duties Johnson might ask of them.

Initially, Republican leaders were hopeful about Johnson, for in talking about his native region he seemed tough, even uncompromising. But as he set about restoring defeated Dixie, Johnson alarmed and then enraged congressional Republicans by adopting a soft, conciliatory reconstruction policy. The president not only opposed granting blacks the right to vote but allowed former Confederates to return to power in the southern states. He stood by as they adopted black codes that reduced blacks to a virtual condition of peonage, and he hotly opposed congressional interference in the reconstruction process. He even urged southern states to reject the Fourteenth Amendment, pushed through Congress by the Republicans, which would protect southern blacks. The amendment would prevent the states from enacting laws that abridged "the privileges or immunities of citizens of the United States." It would also bar the states from depriving "any person of life, liberty, or property, without due process of law," or from denying any person the "equal protection of the law." Johnson did more than just oppose the amendment; he damned Republican leaders like Charles Sumner of Massachusetts and Thaddeus Stevens of Pennsylvania, calling them tyrants and traitors. He even campaigned against the Republican party in the 1866 off-year elections. As a consequence, he alienated moderate as well as radical Republicans, who soon united against him. When the 1866 elections gave the Republicans huge majorities in both houses of Congress, they took control of Reconstruction and set about reforming the South themselves, enfranchising the freedmen and giving them the right to vote and hold office.

This gives you the proper historical background for Foner's lucid and judicious essay on the new view of Reconstruction and its leading participants. Foner concludes that Reconstruction was "a splendid failure," in that it did not resolve "the debate over the meaning of freedom in American life" and did not provide African Americans with the economic security they needed to be truly free in a capitalist country. Alas, that failure was to plague black Americans for generations to come. But for Foner, the "animating vision" of Reconstruction — an America in which all would enjoy "the right to rise," to go as far as their talent and toil would take them unimpeded by "inherited caste distinctions" — is profoundly relevant to a country "still grappling with the unresolved legacy of emancipation."

GLOSSARY

CARPETBAGGERS   Northerners, most of them former soldiers, who migrated to the South in search of economic opportunities.

DU BOIS, W. E. B.   Great black scholar and author of a seminal work, *Black Reconstruction in America* (1935), which offered "a monumental" reassessment of Reconstruction and damned the historical profession for adhering to the traditional racist interpretation of the era.

FREEDMEN'S BUREAU   Established by congressional statute in March 1865, the Bureau of Freedmen, Refugees, and Abandoned Lands was supposed to provide food and schools for the former slaves, help them secure jobs, and make certain they received fair wages.

FIFTEENTH AMENDMENT Adopted in 1870, it asserted that "the right of citizens of the United States to vote shall not be denied or abridged by the United States or by any State on account of race, color, or previous condition of servitude."

JOHNSON, ANDREW United States president, 1865–1869. Because he defied and obstructed congressional reconstruction measures, the Republican-controlled House of Representatives voted to impeach him, but the Senate failed to convict him by just one vote; it was the first and last attempt to impeach an American president for political reasons.

KU KLUX KLAN Southern white supremacist group organized in response to the Fifteenth Amendment; dressed in white sheets and hoods, Klansmen tried to prevent African Americans from voting by mob violence and other means of intimidation.

LAND DISTRIBUTION Proposal championed by a few Radical Republicans to confiscate the estates of ex-Confederates and distribute the land among the former slaves. Had that been done, Foner writes elsewhere, it "would have had profound consequences for Southern society, weakening the land-based economic and political power of the old ruling class, offering blacks a measure of choice as to whether, when, and under what circumstances to enter the labor market, and affecting the former slaves' conception of themselves." Land confiscation never happened because most Republicans thought it too bold a step and shrank from violating southern whites' property rights.

REDEEMERS Southern whites who overthrew Republican rule in the southern states, thus "redeeming" them.

SCALAWAGS Southern whites who became Republicans; they were "old line Whig Unionists who had opposed secession in the first place" or poor whites who had long resented the planters' rule.

STEVENS, THADDEUS Leading Radical Republican in the national House of Representatives, he was an idealistic reformer who demanded that blacks enjoy full rights as citizens and that former rebel lands be confiscated and distributed among the former slaves; he promoted the Fourteenth Amendment and was the major instigator of the 1867 Reconstruction Acts, which subjected the former Confederate states to military rule and granted universal male suffrage, which gave the freedmen the right to vote. He was also a major force in the impeachment trial of Andrew Johnson.

SUMNER, CHARLES One of the leading Radical Republicans in the U.S. Senate, he too was a committed idealist who advocated complete civil and political equality for African Americans. "More than any of his political contemporaries," writes his biographer, David Herbert Donald, "Sumner realized that the future of American democracy depended upon the ability of the white and black races to live together in peace and equity."

In the past twenty years, no period of American history has been the subject of a more thoroughgoing reevaluation than Reconstruction — the violent, dramatic, and still controversial era following the Civil War. Race relations, politics, social life, and economic change during Reconstruction have all been reinterpreted in the light of changed attitudes toward the place of blacks within American society. If historians have not yet forged a fully satisfying portrait of Reconstruction as a whole, the traditional interpretation that dominated historical writing for much of this century has irrevocably been laid to rest.

Anyone who attended high school before 1960 learned that Reconstruction was an era of unrelieved sordidness in American political and social life. The martyred Lincoln, according to this view, had planned a quick and painless readmission of the Southern states as equal members of the national family. President Andrew Johnson, his successor, attempted to carry out Lincoln's policies but was foiled by the Radical Republicans (also known as Vindictives or Jacobins). Motivated by an irrational hatred of Rebels or by ties with Northern capitalists out to plunder the South, the Radicals swept aside Johnson's lenient program and fastened black supremacy upon the defeated Confederacy. An orgy of corruption followed, presided over by unscrupulous Carpetbaggers (Northerners who ventured south to reap the spoils of office), traitorous scalawags (Southern whites who cooperated with the new governments for personal gain), and the ignorant and childlike freedmen, who were incapable of properly exercising the political power that had been thrust upon them. After much needless suffering, the white community of the South banded together to overthrow these "black" governments and restore home rule

From Eric Foner, "The New View of Reconstruction," American Heritage, vol. 34, no. 6 (October/November, 1983), pp. 1–15. Reprinted by permission of *American Heritage* magazine, a division of Forbes, Inc. Copyright © Forbes, Inc., 1983.

(their euphemism for white supremacy). All told, Reconstruction was just about the darkest page in the American saga.

Originating in anti-Reconstruction propaganda of Southern Democrats during the 1870s, this traditional interpretation achieved scholarly legitimacy around the turn of the century through the work of William Dunning and his students at Columbia University. It reached the larger public through films like *Birth of a Nation* and *Gone With the Wind* and that best-selling work of myth-making masquerading as history, *The Tragic Era* by Claude G. Bowers. In language as exaggerated as it was colorful, Bowers told how Andrew Johnson "fought the bravest battle for constitutional liberty and for the preservation of our institutions ever waged by an Executive" but was overwhelmed by the "poisonous propaganda" of the Radicals. Southern whites, as a result, "literally were put to the torture" by "emissaries of hate" who manipulated the "simple-minded" freedmen, inflaming the negroes' "egotism" and even inspiring "lustful assaults" by blacks upon white womanhood.

In a discipline that sometimes seems to pride itself on the rapid rise and fall of historical interpretations, this traditional portrait of Reconstruction enjoyed remarkable staying power. The long reign of the old interpretation is not difficult to explain. It presented a set of easily identifiable heroes and villains. It enjoyed the imprimatur of the nation's leading scholars. And it accorded with the political and social realities of the first half of this century. This image of Reconstruction helped freeze the mind of the white South in unalterable opposition to any movement for breaching the ascendancy of the Democratic party, eliminating segregation, or readmitting disfranchised blacks to the vote.

Nevertheless, the demise of the traditional interpretation was inevitable, for it ignored the testimony of the central participant in the drama of Reconstruction — the black freedman. Furthermore, it was grounded in the conviction that blacks were unfit to share in political power. As Dunning's Columbia colleague John W. Burgess put it, "A black skin means membership in a race of men which has never of itself succeeded in subjecting passion to reason, has never, therefore, created any civilization of any kind." Once objective scholarship and modern experience rendered that assumption untenable, the entire edifice was bound to fall.

The work of "revising" the history of Reconstruction began with the writings of a handful of survivors of the era, such as John R. Lynch, who had served as a black congressman from Mississippi after the Civil War. In the 1930s white scholars like Francis Simkins and Robert Woody carried the task forward. Then, in 1935, the black historian and activist W.E.B. Du Bois produced *Black Reconstruction in America,* a monumental reevaluation that closed with an irrefutable indictment of a historical profession that had sacrificed scholarly objectivity on the altar of racial bias. "One fact and one alone," he wrote, "explains the attitude of most recent writers toward Reconstruction; they cannot conceive of Negroes as men." Du Bois's work, however, was ignored by most historians.

It was not until the 1960s that the full force of the revisionist wave broke over the field. Then, in rapid succession, virtually every assumption of the traditional viewpoint was systematically dismantled. A drastically different portrait emerged to take its place. President Lincoln did not have a coherent "plan" for Reconstruction, but at the time of his assassination he had been cautiously contemplating black suffrage. Andrew Johnson was a stubborn, racist politician who lacked the ability to compromise. By isolating himself from the broad currents of public opinion that had nourished Lincoln's career, Johnson created an impasse with Congress that Lincoln would certainly have avoided, thus throwing away his political power and destroying his own plans for reconstructing the South.

The Radicals in Congress were acquitted of both vindictive motives and the charge of serving as the stalking-horses of Northern capitalism. They emerged instead as idealists in the best nineteenth-century reform tradition. Radical leaders like Charles Sumner and Thaddeus Stevens had worked for the rights of blacks long before any conceivable political advantage flowed from such a commitment. Stevens refused to sign the Pennsylvania Constitution of 1838 because it disfranchised the state's black citizens; Sumner led a fight in the 1850s to integrate Boston's public schools. Their Reconstruction policies were based on principle, not petty political advantage, for the central issue dividing Johnson and these Radical Republicans was the civil rights of freedmen. Studies of congressional policy-making, such as Eric L. McKitrick's *Andrew Johnson and Reconstruction,* also revealed that Reconstruction legislation, ranging from the Civil Rights Act of 1866 to the Fourteenth and Fifteenth Amendments, enjoyed broad support from moderate and conservative Republicans. It was not simply the work of a narrow radical faction.

Even more startling was the revised portrait of Reconstruction in the South itself. Imbued with the spirit of the civil rights movement and rejecting entirely the racial assumptions that had underpinned the traditional interpretation, these historians evaluated Reconstruction from the black point of view. Works like Joel Williamson's *After Slavery* portrayed the period as a time of extraordinary political, social, and economic progress for blacks. The establishment of public school systems, the granting of equal citizenship to blacks, the effort to restore the devastated Southern economy, the attempt to construct an interracial political democracy from the ashes of slavery, all these were commendable achievements, not the elements of Bowers's "tragic era."

Unlike earlier writers, the revisionists stressed the active role of the freedmen in shaping Reconstruction. Black initiative established as many schools as did Northern religious societies and the Freedmen's Bureau. The right to vote was not simply thrust upon them by meddling outsiders, since blacks began agitating for the suffrage as soon as they were freed. In 1865 black conventions throughout the South issued eloquent, though unheeded, appeals for equal civil and political rights.

With the advent of Radical Reconstruction in 1867, the freedmen did enjoy a real measure of political power. But black supremacy never existed. In most states blacks held only a small fraction of political offices, and even in South Carolina, where they comprised a majority of the state legislature's lower house, effective power remained in white hands. As for corruption, moral standards in both government and private enterprise were at low ebb throughout the nation in postwar years — the era of Boss Tweed, the Credit Mobilier scandal, and the Whiskey Ring. Southern corruption could hardly be blamed on former slaves.

Other actors in the Reconstruction drama also came in for reevaluation. Most carpetbaggers were former Union soldiers seeking economic opportunity in the postwar South, not unscrupulous adventurers. Their motives, a typically American amalgam of humanitarianism and the pursuit of profit, were no more insidious than those of Western pioneers. Scalawags, previously seen as traitors to the white race, now emerged as "Old Line" Whig Unionists who had opposed secession in the first place or as poor whites who had long resented planters' domi-

Black legislators in the South Carolina House of Representatives are voting on an appropriation bill in 1873. African Americans had a majority in the lower house, yet "effective power," as Eric Foner writes, remained in white hands." (North Wind Picture Archives)

411

nation of Southern life and who saw in Reconstruction a chance to recast Southern society along more democratic lines. Strongholds of Southern white Republicanism like east Tennessee and western North Carolina had been the scene of resistance to Confederate rule throughout the Civil War; now, as one scalawag newspaper put it, the choice was "between salvation at the hand of the Negro or destruction at the hand of the rebels."

At the same time, the Ku Klux Klan and kindred groups, whose campaign of violence against black and white Republicans had been minimized or excused in older writings, were portrayed as they really were. Earlier scholars had conveyed the impression that the Klan intimidated blacks mainly by dressing as ghosts and playing on the freedmen's superstitions. In fact, black fears were all too real: the Klan was a terrorist organization that beat and killed its political opponents to deprive blacks of their newly won rights. The complicity of the Democratic party and the silence of prominent whites in the face of such outrages stood as an indictment of the moral code the South had inherited from the days of slavery.

By the end of the 1960s, then, the old interpretation had been completely reversed. Southern freedmen were the heroes, the "Redeemers" who overthrew Reconstruction were the villains, and if the era was "tragic," it was because change did not go far enough. Reconstruction had been a time of real progress and its failure a lost opportunity for the South and the nation. But the legacy of Reconstruction — the Fourteenth and Fifteenth Amendments — endured to inspire future efforts for civil rights. As Kenneth Stampp wrote in *The Era of Reconstruction,* a superb summary of revisionist findings published in 1965, "If it was worth four years of civil war to save the Union, it was worth a few years of radical reconstruction to give the American Negro the ultimate promise of equal civil and political rights."

As Stampp's statement suggests, the reevaluation of the first Reconstruction was inspired in large

In 1871, members of the North Carolina Ku Klux Klan discuss the murder of another victim. As Foner points out, the Klan was a terrorist organization that beat and killed its political opponents to deprive blacks of their newly won rights." (North Wind Picture Archives)

measure by the impact of the second — the modern civil rights movement. And with the waning of that movement in recent years, writing on Reconstruction has undergone still another transformation. Instead of seeing the Civil War and its aftermath as a second American Revolution (as Charles Beard had), a regression into barbarism (as Bowers argued), or a golden opportunity squandered (as the revisionists saw it), recent writers argue that Radical Reconstruction was not really very radical. Since land was not distributed to the former slaves, they remained economically dependent upon their former owners. The planter class survived both the war and Reconstruction with its property (apart from slaves) and prestige more or less intact.

Not only changing times but also the changing concerns of historians have contributed to this latest reassessment of Reconstruction. The hallmark of the past decade's historical writing has been an emphasis upon "social history" — the evocation of the past lives of ordinary Americans — and the downplaying of strictly political events. When applied to Reconstruction, this concern with the "social" suggested that black suffrage and officeholding, once seen as the most radical departures of the Reconstruction era, were relatively insignificant.

Recent historians have focused their investigations not upon the politics of Reconstruction but upon the social and economic aspects of the transition from slavery to freedom. Herbert Gutman's influential study of the black family during and after slavery found little change in family structure or relations between men and women resulting from emancipation. Under slavery most blacks had lived in nuclear family units, although they faced the constant threat of separation from loved ones by sale. Reconstruction provided the opportunity for blacks to solidify their preexisting family ties. Conflicts over whether black women should work in the cotton fields (planters said yes, many black families said no) and over white attempts to "apprentice" black children revealed that the autonomy of family life was a major preoccupation of the freedmen. Indeed, whether manifested in their withdrawal from churches controlled by whites, in the blossoming black fraternal, benevolent, and self-improvement organizations, or in the demise of the slave quarters and their replacement by small tenant farms occupied by individual families, the quest for independence from white authority and control over their own day-to-day lives shaped the black response to emancipation.

In the post–Civil War South the surest guarantee of economic autonomy, blacks believed, was land. To the freedmen the justice of a claim to land based on their years of unrequited labor appeared self-evident. As an Alabama black convention put it, "The property which they [the planters] hold was nearly all earned by the sweat of *our* brows." As Leon Litwack showed in *Been in the Storm So Long,* a Pulitzer Prize–winning account of the black response to emancipation, many freedmen in 1865 and 1866 refused to sign labor contracts, expecting the federal government to give them land. In some localities, as one Alabama overseer reported, they "set up claims to the plantation and all on it."

In the end, of course, the vast majority of Southern blacks remained propertyless and poor. But exactly why the South, and especially its black population, suffered from dire poverty and economic retardation in the decades following the Civil War is a matter of much dispute. In *One Kind of Freedom,* economists Roger Ransom and Richard Sutch indicted country merchants for monopolizing credit and charging usurious interest rates, forcing black tenants into debt and locking the South into a dependence on cotton production that impoverished the entire region. But Jonathan Wiener, in his study of postwar Alabama, argued that planters used their political power to compel blacks to remain on the plantations. Planters succeeded in stabilizing the plantation system, but only by blocking the growth of alternative enterprises, like factories, that might draw off black laborers, thus locking the region into a pattern of economic backwardness.

If the thrust of recent writing has emphasized the social and economic aspects of Reconstruction, politics has not been entirely neglected. But political studies have also reflected the postrevisionist mood summarized by C. Vann Woodward when he observed "how essentially nonrevolutionary and conservative Reconstruction really was." Recent writers, unlike their revisionist predecessors, have found little to praise in federal policy toward the emancipated blacks.

A new sensitivity to the strength of prejudice and laissez-faire ideas in the nineteenth-century North has led many historians to doubt whether the Republican party ever made a genuine commitment to racial justice in the South. The granting of black suffrage was an alternative to a long-term federal responsibility for protecting the rights of the former slaves. Once enfranchised, blacks could be left to fend for themselves. With the exception of a few Radicals like Thaddeus Stevens, nearly all Northern policy-makers and educators are criticized today for assuming that, so long as the unfettered operations of the marketplace afforded blacks the opportunity to advance through diligent labor, federal efforts to assist them in acquiring land were unnecessary.

Probably the most innovative recent writing on Reconstruction politics has centered on a broad reassessment of black Republicanism, largely undertaken by a new generation of black historians. Scholars like Thomas Holt and Nell Painter insist that Reconstruction was not simply a matter of black and white. Conflicts within the black community, no less than divisions among whites, shaped Reconstruction politics. Where revisionist scholars, both black and white, had celebrated the accomplishments of black political leaders, Holt, Painter, and others charge that they failed to address the economic plight of the black masses. Painter criticized "representative colored men," as national black leaders were called, for failing to provide ordinary freemen with effective political leadership. Holt found that black officeholders in South Carolina mostly emerged from the old free mulatto class of Charleston, which shared many assumptions with prominent whites. "Basically bourgeois in their origins and orientation," he wrote, they "failed to act in the interest of black peasants."

In emphasizing the persistence from slavery of divisions between free blacks and slaves, these writers reflect the increasing concern with continuity and conservatism in Reconstruction. Their work reflects a startling extension of revisionist premises. If, as has been argued for the past twenty years, blacks were active agents rather than mere victims of manipulation, then they could not be absolved of blame for the ultimate failure of Reconstruction.

Despite the excellence of recent writing and the continual expansion of our knowledge of the period, historians of Reconstruction today face a unique dilemma. An old interpretation has been overthrown, but a coherent new synthesis has yet to take its place. The revisionists of the 1960s effectively established a series of negative points: the Reconstruction governments were not as bad as had been portrayed, black supremacy was a myth, the Radicals were not cynical manipulators of the freedmen. Yet no convincing overall portrait of the quality of political and social life emerged from their writings. More recent historians have rightly pointed to elements of continuity that spanned the nineteenth-century Southern experience, especially the survival, in modified form, of the plantation system. Nevertheless, by denying the real changes that did occur, they have failed to provide a convincing portrait of an era characterized above all by drama, turmoil, and social change.

Building upon the findings of the past twenty years of scholarship, a new portrait of Reconstruction ought to begin by viewing it not as a specific time period, bounded by the years 1865 and 1877, but as an episode in a prolonged historical process — American society's adjustment to the consequences of the Civil War and emancipation. The Civil War, of course, raised the decisive questions of America's national existence: the relations between local and national authority, the definition of citizenship, the balance between force and consent in generating obedience to authority. The war and Reconstruction, as Allan Nevins observed over fifty years ago, marked the "emergence of modern America." This was the era of the completion of the national railroad network, the creation of the modern steel industry, the conquest of the West and final subduing of the Indians, and the expansion of the mining frontier. Lincoln's America — the world of the small farm and artisan shop — gave way to a rapidly industrialized economy. The issues that galvanized postwar Northern politics — from the question of the greenback currency to the mode of paying holders of the national debt — arose from the economic changes unleashed by the Civil War.

Above all, the war irrevocably abolished slavery. Since 1619, when "twenty negars" disembarked from a Dutch ship in Virginia, racial injustice had haunted American life, mocking its professed ideals even as tobacco and cotton, the products of slave labor, helped finance the nation's economic development. Now the implications of the black presence could no longer be ignored. The Civil War resolved the problem of slavery but, as the Philadelphia diarist Sydney George Fisher observed in June 1865, it opened an even more intractable problem: "What shall we do with the Negro?" Indeed, he went on, this was a problem "*incapable* of any solution that will satisfy both North and South."

As Fisher realized, the focal point of Reconstruction was the social revolution known as emancipation. Plantation slavery was simultaneously a system of labor, a form of racial domination, and the foundation upon which arose a distinctive ruling class within the South. Its demise threw open the most fundamental questions of economy, society, and politics. A new system of labor, social, racial, and political relations had to be created to replace slavery.

The United States was not the only nation to experience emancipation in the nineteenth century. Neither plantation slavery nor abolition were unique to the United States. But Reconstruction was. In a comparative perspective Radical Reconstruction stands as a remarkable experiment, the only effort of a society experiencing abolition to bring the former slaves within the umbrella of equal citizenship. Because the Radicals did not achieve everything they wanted, historians have lately tended to play down the stunning departure represented by black suffrage and officeholding. Former slaves, most fewer than two years removed from bondage, debated the fundamental questions of the polity: What is a republi-

can form of government? Should the state provide equal education for all? How could political equality be reconciled with a society in which property was so unequally distributed? There was something inspiring in the way such men met the challenge of Reconstruction. "I knew nothing more than to obey my master," James K. Greene, an Alabama black politician later recalled. "But the tocsin of freedom sounded and knocked at the door and we walked out like free men and we met the exigencies as they grew up, and shouldered the responsibilities."

"You never saw a people more excited on the subject of politics than are the negroes of the south," one planter observed in 1867. And there were more than a few Southern whites as well who in these years shook off the prejudices of the past to embrace the vision of a new South dedicated to the principles of equal citizenship and social justice. One ordinary South Carolinian expressed the new sense of possibility in 1868 to the Republican governor of the state: "I am sorry that I cannot write an elegant stiled letter to your excellency. But I rejoice to think that God almighty has given to the poor of S. C. a Gov. to hear to feel to protect the humble poor without distinction to race or color. . . . I am a native borned S. C. a poor man never owned a Negro in my life nor my father before me. . . . Remember the true and loyal are the poor of the whites and blacks, outside of these you can find none loyal."

Few modern scholars believe the Reconstruction governments established in the South in 1867 and 1868 fulfilled the aspirations of their humble constituents. While their achievements in such realms as education, civil rights, and the economic rebuilding of the South are now widely appreciated, historians today believe they failed to affect either the economic plight of the emancipated slave or the ongoing transformation of independent white farmers into cotton tenants. Yet their opponents did perceive the Reconstruction governments in precisely this way — as representatives of a revolution that had put the bottom rail, both racial and economic, on top. This perception helps explain the ferocity of the attacks leveled against them and the pervasiveness of violence in the postemancipation South.

The spectacle of black men voting and holding office was anathema to large numbers of Southern whites. Even more disturbing, at least in the view of those who still controlled the plantation regions of the South, was the emergence of local officials, black and white, who sympathized with the plight of the black laborer. Alabama's vagrancy law was a "dead letter" in 1870, "because those who are charged with its enforcement are indebted to the vagrant vote for their offices and emoluments." Political debates over the level and incidence of taxation, the control of crops, and the resolution of contract disputes revealed that a primary issue on Reconstruction was the role of government in a plantation society. During presidential Reconstruction, and after "Redemption," with planters and their allies in control of politics, the law emerged as a means of stabilizing and promoting the plantation system. If Radical Reconstruction failed to redistribute the land of the South, the ouster of the planter class from control of politics at least ensured that the sanctions of the criminal law would not be employed to discipline the black labor force.

An understanding of this fundamental conflict over the relation between government and society helps explain the pervasive complaints concerning corruption and "extravagance" during Radical Reconstruction. Corruption there was aplenty; tax rates did rise sharply. More significant than the rate of taxation, however, was the change in its incidence. For the first time, planters and white farmers had to pay a significant portion of their income to the government, while propertyless blacks often escaped scot-free. Several states, moreover, enacted heavy taxes on uncultivated land to discourage land speculation and force land onto the market, benefiting, it was hoped, the freedmen.

As time passed, complaints about the "extravagance" and corruption of Southern governments found a sympathetic audience among influential Northerners. The Democratic charge that universal suffrage in the South was responsible for high taxes and governmental extravagance coincided with a rising conviction among the urban middle classes of the North that city government had to be taken out of the hands of the immigrant poor and returned to the "best men" — the educated, professional, financially independent citizens unable to exert much political influence at a time of mass parties and machine politics. Increasingly the "respectable" middle classes began to retreat from the very notion of universal suffrage. The poor were no longer perceived as honest producers, the backbone of the social order; now they became the "dangerous classes," the "mob." As the historian Francis Parkman put it, too much power rested with "masses of imported ignorance and hereditary ineptitude." To Parkman the Irish of the Northern cities and the blacks of the South were equally incapable of utilizing the ballot: "Witness the municipal corruptions of New York, and the monstrosities of negro rule in South Carolina." Such attitudes helped to justify Northern inaction as, one by one, the Reconstruction regimes of the South were overthrown by political violence.

In the end, then, neither the abolition of slavery nor Reconstruction succeeded in resolving the debate over the meaning of freedom in American life. Twenty years before the American Civil War, writing about the prospect of abolition in France's colonies, Alexis de Tocqueville had written, "If the Negroes have the right to become free, the [planters] have the incontestable right not to be ruined by the Negroes' freedom." And in the United States, as in nearly every plantation society that experienced the end of slavery, a rigid social and political dichotomy between former master and former slave, an ideology of racism, and a dependent labor force with limited economic opportunities all survived abolition.

Unless one means by freedom the simple fact of not being a slave, emancipation thrust blacks into a kind of no-man's land, a partial freedom that made a mockery of the American ideal of equal citizenship.

Yet by the same token the ultimate outcome underscores the uniqueness of Reconstruction itself. Alone among the societies that abolished slavery in the nineteenth century, the United States, for a moment, offered the freedmen a measure of political control over their own destinies. However brief its sway, Reconstruction allowed scope for a remarkable political and social mobilization of the black community. It opened doors of opportunity that could never be completely closed. Reconstruction transformed the lives of Southern blacks in ways unmeasurable by statistics and unreachable by law. It raised their expectations and aspirations, redefined their status in relation to the larger society, and allowed space for the creation of institutions that enabled them to survive the repression that followed. And it established constitutional principles of civil and political equality that, while flagrantly violated after Redemption, planted the seeds of future struggle.

Certainly, in terms of the sense of possibility with which it opened, Reconstruction failed. But as Du Bois observed, it was a "splendid failure." For its animating vision — a society in which social advancement would be open to all on the basis of individual merit, not inherited caste distinctions — is as old as America itself and remains relevant to a nation still grappling with the unresolved legacy of emancipation.

QUESTIONS TO CONSIDER

1 What was the traditional view of Reconstruction? On what racial and political assumptions was it based? When and why did this view end?

2 What is the new view of Reconstruction? Who are the heroes and the villains in the new scenario? What activities, in the new view, shaped the black response to emancipation? Explain why more recent writers have faulted federal policy toward the liberated blacks. How was their criticism of federal policy different from the criticism of that policy by the traditional Reconstruction historians? Why do some recent writers argue that Radical Reconstruction was not nearly radical enough?

3 What social forces spawned white terrorist groups like the Ku Klux Klan during Reconstruction? What was the purpose of such groups? Why would a white person want to join them?

4 What did historian Alan Nevins mean when he declared that the Civil War and Reconstruction marked "the emergence of modern America"?

5 How does Foner define the plantation-slavery system? Did emancipation and the war destroy all facets of the system?

6 At the end of his essay, Foner quotes W. E. B. Du Bois that Reconstruction was "a splendid failure." How was it splendid? How was it a failure?

30

A New Look at the Carpetbaggers

RICHARD N. CURRENT

The carpetbagger, a northerner who moved to the South after the Civil War, is one of the most maligned and misunderstood players in the drama of Reconstruction. The traditional view portrays the carpetbagger as corrupt and dishonest Yankee who went south after Congress's Reconstruction Acts of 1867 divided the region into military districts and granted political rights to the freedmen. The carpetbaggers, in the old view, entered southern politics, formed coalitions with Negroes and scalawags ("traitorous" southerners who became Republicans), and proceeded to "steal the South blind."

While admitting that there were scoundrels and political tramps among the carpetbaggers, Richard N. Current, an eminent and prolific historian of the Civil War and Reconstruction era, challenges the old view that the whole class of carpetbaggers was evil and predatory. A revisionist like Eric Foner, the author of the preceding selection, Current finds that most carpetbaggers were "men of substance" — civilians and former Union soldiers who went south before 1867, intending to settle in the region, not steal it blind. For them, the South was a new frontier, like the West, where dreams of a prosperous and pleasant new life could be realized. The carpetbaggers became southern businessmen and planters as well as politicians. While some of the last named were guilty of misgovernment and corruption, many others were honest and capable. Because they "disturbed the relations between the races" by favoring Negro political rights, the carpetbaggers earned the undying hatred of native southern whites. Current concludes that the most numerous and most significant carpetbaggers were ambitious, energetic men who "brought their savings or their borrowings to invest, who eventually got into politics for idealistic as well as selfish reasons, and who in office behaved no better and no worse than most of their contemporaries."

GLOSSARY

CLAYTON, POWELL   Carpetbag governor of Arkansas who had owned a plantation there since the end of the Civil War.

FREEDMEN   Former slaves who, instead of being passive recipients of freedom, agitated from the start of Reconstruction for full citizenship and the right to vote.

MORGAN, ALBERT T. AND CHARLES Brothers who moved from Wisconsin to Mississippi, where they invested about $50,000 in lumbering and planting enterprises.

RED SHIRTS   Military clubs of southern white Democrats who, armed with rifles and revolvers, sought to intimidate African Americans and break up Republican meetings.

TOURGÉE, ALBION W.   Ohio man who moved to North Carolina and invested $5,000 in a nursery business.

UNION LEAGUES   Organized by agents of the Freedmen's Bureau and by Federal soldiers, these organizations sought to win the allegiance of the freedmen to the Republican party.

WARNER, WILLARD   Ohio legislator who moved to Alabama in 1868, was elected to the national senate from that state, and bought land with the idea of making an economic career in the South, which he eventually did.

WHITE LEAGUES   Organized in 1874 in Louisiana, they were "Ku Klux without the disguise and secrecy," as one historian described them. They claimed to have formed to preserve the white race and to protect themselves against the "Republican alliances" in the state. In New Orleans, they were "organized, drilled and militant bodies."

The story of the postbellum South is often told as if it were a morality play or a television melodrama. The characters personify Good or Evil, and they are so clearly identified that there is no mistaking the "good guys" and the "bad guys." One of the villains, who deserves the boos and hisses he is sure to get, is the carpetbagger. As usually portrayed, this contemptible Yankee possess as little honor or intelligence as he does property, and he possesses so little property that he can, quite literally, carry all of it with him in a carpetbag. He is attracted southward by the chance for power and plunder that he sees when the vote is given to southern Negroes and taken from some of the southern whites by the Reconstruction Acts of 1867. Going south in 1867 or after, he meddles in the politics of places where, as a mere roving adventurer, he has no true interest. For a time he and his kind run the southern states. At last, when the drama ends, Good has triumphed over Evil, and the carpetbagger has got his comeuppance. But he leaves behind him a trail of corruption, misgovernment, and lastingly disturbed race relations.

That picture may seem an exaggeration, a caricature. If so, it nevertheless has passed for a long time as a true, historical likeness, and it continues to pass as such. A standard dictionary defines *carpetbaggers* as a term of contempt for northern men who went south "to seek private gain under the often corrupt reconstruction governments." Another dictionary, based on "historical principles," contains this definition: "One of the poor northern adventurers who, carrying all their belongings in carpetbags, went south to profit from the social and political upheaval after the Civil War." A recent textbook refers to "the Radical carpetbaggers who had poured into the

---

Reprinted by permission of Louisiana State University Press from Richard N. Current, "Carpetbaggers Reconsidered," in Kenneth M. Stampp and Leon F. Litwack (eds.), *Reconstruction: An Anthology of Revisionist Writings*. Copyright © 1969 by Louisiana State University Press.

The old view of Reconstruction, as Richard N. Current says, portrayed the carpetbagger as "a contemptible Yankee" who "possesses as little honor or intelligence as he does property, and he possesses so little property that he can, quite literally, carry all of it with him in a carpetbag. He is attracted southward by the chance for power and plunder." Current's essay disputes this traditional view. (Corbis-Bettmann)

defeated section after the passage of the First Reconstruction Act of March, 1867." The prevailing conception, than, is that these men were late arrivals who waited till the Negro was given the suffrage and who then went off with their carpetbags, cynically, to take advantage of the colored vote.

Even those who hold that view concede that "a few were men of substance, bent on settling in the South," and that some of them took up residence there before the passage of the Reconstruction Acts. With respect to men of this kind, however, the question has been raised whether they should be considered carpetbaggers at all. Many of the northerners active in Mississippi politics after 1867, the historian of Reconstruction in that state observes, had arrived as would-be planters before 1867. "It is

incorrect, therefore to call them 'carpet baggers,'" this historian remarks. "They did not go South to get offices, for there were no offices for them to fill. The causes which led them to settle there were purely economic, and not political." Thus the brothers Albert T. and Charles Morgan, when they moved from Wisconsin to Mississippi, "came not as carpetbaggers," for they brought with them some $50,000, which they invested in planting and lumbering enterprises (and lost). And the much better-known figure Albion W. Tourgée, who moved from Ohio to North Carolina, was perhaps no carpetbagger, either, for he took with him $5,000 which he put into a nursery business (and also lost).

Now, suppose it could be demonstrated that, among the northern politicians in the South during Reconstruction, men essentially like the Morgans and Tourgée were not the few but the many, not exceptional but fairly typical. Suppose that the majority moved to the South before 1867, before the establishment of the "corrupt reconstruction governments," and hence for reasons other than to seek private gain or political power under such governments. One of two conclusions must follow. Either we must say that true carpetbaggers were much fewer and less significant than has been commonly supposed, or we must seek a new definition of the word.

In redefining it, we should consider the actual usage on the part of southerners during the Reconstruction period. We may learn something of its denotation as well as its connotation if we look at the way they applied it to a specific person: the one-time Union army officer Willard Warner, of Ohio and Alabama.

Warner might seem, at first glance, to exemplify the latecomer rising immediately in southern politics, for he completed his term in the Ohio legislature and was elected to the United States Senate from Alabama in the same year, 1868. But he was not really a new arrival. He had visited Alabama and, with a partner, had leased a plantation there in the fall of 1865. He bought land in the state the next year, and he spent most of the spring and summer of

1866 and most of the autumn and winter of 1867–68 on his Alabama land. He intended to make an economic career in the South (and indeed he was eventually to do so).

At first, Warner had no trouble with his Alabama neighbors. "A Northern man, who is not a fool, or foolish fanatic," he wrote from his plantation in the spring of 1866, "may live pleasantly in Alabama, without abating one jot of his self-respect, or independence." At one time or another, as he was to testify later, the leading Democrats of the state, among them ex-Confederate General James H. Clanton, came to him and said: "General, when we talk about carpetbaggers we want you to understand that we don't mean you; you have come here and invested what means you had in property here, and you have the same interest there that we have."

The Alabamans changed their attitude toward Warner when he was elected to office with Negro support. Afterwards (1871) General Clanton himself explained:

If a man should come here and invest $100,000, and in the next year seek the highest offices, by appealing to the basest prejudices of an ignorant race, we would call him a political carpet-bagger. But if he followed his legitimate business, took his chances with the rest, behaved himself, and did not stir up strife, we would call him a gentleman. General Warner bought land; I fixed some titles for him, and I assured him that when men came there to take their chances with us for life, we would take them by the hand. But we found out his designs. Before his seat in Ohio got cold, he was running the negro machine among us to put himself in office.

Another Alabama Democrat, from Huntsville, in the area where Warner had bought land, elaborated further upon the same theme in testifying before a congressional committee, as follows:

Question: You have used the epithets "carpet-bagger" and "scalawag" repeatedly . . . give us an accurate definition.

Answer: Well, sir, the term carpet-bagger is not applied to northern men who came here to settle in the South, but a carpet-bagger is generally understood to be a man who comes here for office sake, of an ignorant or bad character, and who seeks to array the negroes against the whites; who is a kind of political dry-nurse for the negro population, in order to get office through them.

Question: Then it does not necessarily suppose that he should be a northern man?

Answer: Yes, sir; it does suppose that he is to be a northern man, but it does not apply to all northern men that come here.

Question: If he is an intelligent, educated man, and comes here for office, then he is not a carpet-bagger, I understand?

Answer: No, sir; we do not generally call them carpet-baggers.

Question: If he is a northern man possessed of good character and seeks office he is not a carpet-bagger?

Answer: Mr. Chairman, there are so few northern men who come here of intelligence and character, that join the republican party and look for office alone to the negroes, that we have never made a class for them. . . . They stand *sui generis*. . . . But the term "carpet-bagger" was applied to the office-seeker from the North who comes here seeking office by the negroes, by arraying their political passions and prejudices against the white people of the community.

Question: The man in addition to that, under your definition, must be an ignorant man and of bad character?

Answer: Yes, sir; he is generally of that description. We regard any man as a man of bad character who seeks to create hostility between the races. . . .

Question: Having given the definition of the carpet-bagger, you may now define scalawag.

Answer: A scalawag is his subservient tool and accomplice, who is a native of the country.

So far as these two Alabamans were concerned, it obviously made no difference whether a northerner came before 1867 or after, whether he brought with him and invested thousands of dollars or was penniless, whether he was well educated or illiterate, or whether he was of good or bad character in the ordinary sense. He was, by definition, a carpetbagger and a man of ignorant and bad character if he, at any time, encouraged political activity on the part of the Negroes and thus arrayed the blacks against the whites, that is, the Republicans against the Democrats. He was not a carpetbagger if he steered entirely clear of politics or if he consistently talked and voted as a Democrat or Conservative.

This usage was not confined to Alabama; it prevailed throughout the South. To speak of "economic carpetbaggers," as historians sometimes do, is therefore rather hard to justify on a historical basis. Politics — Republican politics — was the distinguishing mark of the man whom the Democrats and Conservatives after 1867 dubbed a carpetbagger, and they called him by that name whether or not he had gone South originally for economic rather than political reasons. To speak of "Negro carpetbaggers" is also something of an anachronism. Colored men from the North did go south and enter politics, of course, but in the Reconstruction lexicon (with its distinction among carpetbaggers, scalawags, and Negroes) they were put in a category of their own. Northern-born or southern-born, the Negro was a Negro to the southern Conservatives, and they did not ordinarily refer to him as a carpetbagger. From contemporary usage, then, we derive the following as a non-valuational definition: the men called carpetbaggers were *white northerners who went south after the beginning of the Civil War and, sooner or later, became active in politics as Republicans.*

With this definition at hand, we can proceed to make at least a rudimentary survey of the so-called carpetbaggers as a group, in order to find out how well they fit the traditional concept with respect to their background. Lest us consider first the state and local officeholders. There were hundreds of these people, and many of them left too few traces for us now to track them down. Studies have touched upon the subject in some of the states, and though fragmentary, these studies at least suggest that most of the men

under consideration do not conform to the stereotype.

In Arkansas the carpetbag governor (1968–72) Powell Clayton had owned and lived on a plantation since 1865. Many years later he was to gather data showing that the overwhelming majority of the so-called carpetbaggers, who were in office when he was, had arrived in Arkansas before 1867, and that the small minority who came as late as 1867 "did so when the Democrats were in full power, and before the officers to be elected or appointed, together with their salaries and emoluments, had been fixed by the [reconstructed] State Constitution." Clayton adds:

With a very few exceptions, the Northern men who settled in Arkansas came there with the Federal Army, and . . . were so much impressed with its genial climate and great natural resources as to cause them . . . to make it their future home. A number, like myself and my brother William, had contracted matrimonial ties. Many of them had been away from home so long as practically to have lost their identity in the States [from which they had come]. . . . These were the reasons that influenced their settlement in Arkansas rather than the existence of any political expectations.

That, of course, is *ex parte* testimony, from one of the carpetbaggers himself. Still, he supports his conclusion with ample and specific evidence.

And, with respect to some of the other states, southern historians have tended toward similar conclusions. In Alabama, says one of these historians, "many of the carpet-bag politicians were northern men who had failed at cotton planting." In Florida, says another, about a third of the forty-six delegates elected in 1867 to the state constitutional convention were white Republicans from the North. "Most of the Northerners had been in the state for a year or more and were *bona fide* citizens of the commonwealth." "As a class," they were "intellectually the best men among the delegates." In Mississippi, says a third, "the genuine 'carpet baggers' who came after the adoption of the reconstruction policy were comparatively few in number." The vast majority of the so-called carpet-baggers in Mississippi were men who had arrived earlier as planters.

Information is not available regarding all the carpet-bag officeholders in all the reconstructed states. What is needed, then, is information about a representative sample of such officeholders. A sample could be made of the carpetbag governors, of whom the total was nine. Eight of the nine arrived in the South before 1867. Two were officers of the Freedmen's Bureau, two were civilian officials of the federal government, and four were private enterprisers—two of them planters, one lawyer, and the other a minister of the gospel. The single late-comer, Adelbert Ames of Massachusetts and Mississippi, first appeared in Mississippi as a regular army officer and as a military governor, not as an adventurer in search of a political job.

A larger sample consists of the entire body of white northerns who during the Reconstruction period were elected as Republicans to represent southern constituencies in either branch of Congress. Altogether, there were about sixty-two of these men, seventeen in the Senate and forty-five in the House of Representatives. It is impossible to be absolutely precise in listing these congressional carpetbaggers. There were a few borderline cases where, for example, a man was born in the South but raised or educated in the North, and it is hard to know whether he should be classified as a northerner or not.

Of the sixty-two senators and congressmen, practically all were veterans of the Union army. That is not surprising, and it does not alter the accepted stereotype. More surprising, in view of the carpetbagger's reputation for "ignorant or bad character," is the fact that a large proportion were well educated. About two-thirds of the group (forty-three of the sixty-two) had studied law, medicine, or engineering enough to practice the profession, or had attended one or more years of college, or had been school teachers. Of the senators alone, approximately half were college graduates. Seemingly the academic and intellectual attainments of the carpetbaggers in Congress were, on the whole, at least as high as those of the other members of Congress, whether from the North or from the South.

Still more significant is the fact that nearly five-sixths of the entire carpetbag group — fifty of the sixty-two — had arrived in the South before 1867, before the passage of the Reconstruction Acts, before the granting of political rights to the Negro. Of the fifty early arrivals, only fifteen appeared on the southern scene as Treasury Department employees, Freedmen's Bureau officials, or members of the postwar occupation forces (and at least a few of these fifteen soon left the government service and went into private enterprise). Thirty-five of the fifty were engaged in farming or business or the professions from the time of their arrival or soon after.

As for those other twelve of the sixty-two — the twelve who did not begin to live in the South until 1867 or later — more than half (at least seven) took up some private occupation before getting public office. Their comparatively late arrival does not, in itself, signify that they moved south merely for "office sake."

If, then, the sixty-two carpetbag congressmen and senators make up a representative sample, we must conclude that a majority of the carpetbaggers, taken as a whole, do not conform to the traditional view, at least so far as their backgrounds are concerned. With comparatively few exceptions, the so-called carpetbaggers had moved South for reasons other than a lust for offices newly made available by the passage of the Reconstruction Acts. These men were, in fact, a part of the multitude of Union officers and soldiers who, during or soon after the war, chose to remain in or return to the land they had helped to conquer.

To thousands of the young men in blue, at and after the war's end, the South beckoned as a land of wondrous charm, a place of almost magical opportunity. "Northern men are going to do well in every part of the South. The Southern men are too indolent to work and the Yankees are bound to win."

So, for example, a cavalry sergeant wrote from Texas to his sister back home in Ohio in 1866. "I have some idea that I will not remain in Ohio long, and maybe I will locate in the sunny South," he continued. "What think you of roses blooming in open air in November, and the gardens glorious with flowers."

Here, in the South, was a new frontier, another and a better West. Some men compared the two frontiers before choosing the southern one, as did the Morgan brothers, who first looked over Kansas and then decided upon Mississippi. Albert T. Morgan afterwards wrote that the former cry, "Go West, young man,: had been changed to "Go South, young man," and in 1865 the change was "already quite apparent, in the purpose of those of the North who were seeking new homes." Many years later Albion W. Tourgée recalled the hopes and dreams with which, in the fall of 1865, he had settled as a badly wounded veteran in Greensboro, North Carolina:

He expected the future to be as bright and busy within the conquered territory as it had been along the ever-advancing frontier of the West. . . . He expected the whole region to be transformed by the power of commerce, manufactures, and the incursion of Northern life, thought, capital, industry, and enterprise. . . . Because he thought he bore a shattered life he sought a milder clime. He took his young wife with him, and they built their first home-nest almost before the smoke of battle disappeared. . . . His first object was restored health; his next desire, to share the general prosperity.

Once they had been released from the army, thousands of other Union soldiers and officers returned to the South with similar dreams of prosperity and a pleasant life. For the moment, land was cheap and cotton dear. Labor was abundant, and the Negroes were expected to work more willingly for their liberators than for their late masters. So the veterans turned South. At the end of 1865 a newsman from the North learned that, in Alabama alone, there were already five thousand of them "engaged in planting and trading." Even more than the uplands of Alabama, Tennessee, and Georgia, the Mississippi Valley was proving an "attraction to adventurous capital," this traveling reporter found. "Men from the Middle States and the great West were everywhere, buying and leasing plantations, hiring freedmen, and setting thousands of ploughs in motion." No impecunious wanderers were these, but bringers of "adventurous capital." They paid cash for lands or leases, for wages, for supplies. At a time when the South was languishing for money, these newcomers provided it, put it into circulation, and thus gave the economy a lift.

Most of those who thus adventured with their capital were to lose it. They failed for several reasons. At cotton planting the Yankees were novices, unused to local conditions and deluded in their expectations of the Negro as a free worker, or so the southerners said. Actually the southerners as well as the Yankees ran into economic difficulties during the first few years after the war. "Various causes have arisen to prostrate the people, leaving them nearly ruined," a contemporary observed early in 1867, "among which I may more especially mention the following, which could not have been foreseen or provided against: The too great drouth at one season, which destroyed and blasted their corn; too much rain at another season, which injured their cotton; and then the army worm, which came out of the ground in vast numbers, destroyed what was left." There was, besides, the federal cotton tax, which both northern and southern planters denounced as ruinous.

Often, whether as planters or as businessmen, the northerners faced a special disadvantage — the hostility of the people around them. "The rebels will not buy from a Galvanized Yankee, or Loyal Unionist, nor from a Yankee either," a Unionist Virginian complained late in 1865, "the result being that loyal or Northern merchants are failing all over the South." In many places the Yankees were boycotted if they sympathized with or voted for Republicans. "Only one hundred and one men were found base enough to vote for the Radical ticket," a Memphis newspaper reported in April, 1866. "We have held up the names of a portion of these men and written small pox over their doors in order that our people might shun them."

Discouraged and disillusioned after a year or two in their new homes, large numbers of the Yankees abandoned them and returned to the North. Others, of whom some were successful and some were not, remained in the South. Of those who remained, many turned to state and local politics as Republicans in 1867 or after. These comprised the majority of that class of men who eventually came to be known as carpetbaggers.

Before 1867 the northerners in the South possessed only limited opportunities in politics. As Republicans, they could not hope to be elected to office. As newcomers, they often found it difficult even to vote, because of the residence requirements. The Georgia constitution, as remade after the war, extended the residence requirement in that state from six months to two years. "Now it is generally admitted," a northern settler in Georgia protested, "that this change . . . has been effected to prevent loyal men who were obliged to leave here during the war and those who have come here since the war from having any voice in choosing the officers of the State and representatives to Congress." Of course, the newcomers could seek federal jobs, and many of them did so, but again they faced something of a handicap, for they understood that President Johnson preferred "Southern citizens" when "suitable persons" among them could be found.

To the northern settlers remaining in the South the congressional acts of 1867 suddenly brought political opportunity and also, as some of them saw it, political responsibility. Tourgée, for one, sought election to the new constitutional convention in North Carolina because, having failed in business and lost the savings he had brought, he needed the

money he would be paid as a delegate. But he sought election also because he was concerned about Negro rights and wished to do what he could to protect them. A more prosperous settler, a planter of Carroll Parish, Louisiana, who once had been an Ohio school superintendent, took an active interest in southern politics for reasons that he explained, in April, 1867, to Senator John Sherman:

On the closing of my services as a Soldier, I became a member of the firm of Lynch, Ruggles & Co., which was organized in Circleville, Ohio, for the purpose of buying lands in the South and planting. We have located at this point, which is 40 miles above Vicksburg, have purchased lands, have organized most efficient labor forces, & our investment now is on a scale which makes us on *that* account deeply interested in every effort made to bring peace to the South. . . .

I . . . respectfully ask your advice as to the proper course to be pursued by Northern men in the South who sympathize with Congress in the present crisis. . . . I have never held a civil office and never intended to, if I can avoid it; but we have a large force at work, have their confidence, and now as they are voters, they look to our advice, and I want to give it as wisely as possible. Other Northern men are similarly situated. . . .

The position of some of these other northern men was later recalled by C. M. Hamilton, a Pennsylvanian who had gone to Florida in 1864, as a Freedmen's Bureau agent, and had become after 1867 one of the most prominent carpetbaggers of that state. In 1871 he told a congressional committee investigating the Ku Klux Klan:

. . . when the reconstruction acts first passed Congress, the Yankees, as we are called, most of us soldiers who were in the South, rather stood back, did not really feel at that time that they [we] had any particular right to interfere in politics, or to take part in them. But the reconstruction laws were passed; reconstruction was necessary; . . . the democratic party of the South adopted the policy of masterly inactivity . . . ; there was a new element here that had been enfranchised who were without leaders. The northern men in the South, and there were but a handful of them in this State, who had been in the Army, took hold of this matter of reconstruction, and they have perfected it so far as it has been accomplished.

These northerners, already in the South in 1867, felt they had a right and a duty to be where they were and to do what they did. They were Americans. They had fought a war to keep the nation one. South as well as North, it was *their* country. They had chosen to live in the southern part of it. This was now their home, and they had a stake in its future as well as the future of the country as a whole. Their attitude should be quite understandable — as understandable as the feeling of the majority of southern whites.

Naturally, the native Conservatives and Democrats resented the northern Republicans and reviled them with such epithets as "aliens," "birds of passage," and "carpetbaggers." As applied to most of the men, however, these were not objective and descriptive terms. The Union veterans who settled in the South were impelled by a variety and a mixture of motives: restlessness, patriotic idealism, the desire to get ahead, and what not. But so were the pioneers at other times and places in the United States. So were the southerners themselves who moved westward or northward during the Reconstruction period. At that time the newer states of the Southwest (such as Alabama, Mississippi, and especially Arkansas) were filled with fairly recent arrivals from the older states of the Southeast. And at that time there were more southerners residing in the North than northerners in the South. The latter were no more "birds of passage" than the former. Perhaps the frontiersman has been too much idealized for his propensity to rove. Certainly the carpetbagger has been too much condemned for the mere act of moving from one part of the country to another.

Even if all this be conceded, there remain of course the other elements of the carpetbagger stereotype — the charges of misgovernment, corruption, and racial disturbance.

With regard to the charge of misgovernment and corruption, it is hard to generalize about the carpetbaggers as a class. Nevertheless, a few tentative observations may be made. First, the extent and duration of "carpetbag rule" has been exaggerated. In six of the eleven ex-Confederate states (Texas, Tennessee, Alabama, Georgia, Virginia, North Carolina) there was never a carpetbag governor; there was never a majority of carpetbaggers among the Republicans in or out of office; certainly there was never anything approaching carpetbagger domination of state politics. In all those states the Republicans held power only briefly if at all, and they held it, to the extent that they did so, by means of their strength among Negroes and scalawags. In the other five states (Arkansas, Mississippi, Louisiana, Florida, South Carolina) there were carpetbag governors part of the time, but even in these states the carpetbaggers could maintain themselves only with Negro and native white support. Second, the extent of illegal and illegitimate spending by the carpetbag governments has been exaggerated — if spending for schools, transportation, and other social and economic services be considered legitimate. Third, the improper spending, the private use of public funds, was by no means the work of carpetbaggers alone, nor were they the only beneficiaries: heavily involved also were native whites, including Conservatives and Democrats as well as scalawags. Fourth, probably the great majority of the carpetbaggers were no more corrupt than the great majority of contemporary officeholders throughout the United States.

Consider the carpetbag governors, who are generally mentioned as the most conspicuous examples of dishonesty. One of them, Joseph Brooks of Arkansas, did not succeed in exercising uncontested power, for either good or evil, and was soon ousted. Two of the governors, R. K. Scott of South Carolina and W. P. Kellogg of Louisiana, are rather difficult to defend. Four others — Powell Clayton of Arkansas, Harrison

Reed and M. L. Stearns of Florida, and H. C. Warmoth of Louisiana — were loudly accused but never really proved guilty of misusing their offices for private profit. Only one of the four, Warmoth, seems actually to have made much money while in Reconstruction politics, and he made a fortune. While governor, he admitted that there was "a frightful amount of corruption" in Louisiana. He explained, however, that the temptation came from the business interests who offered bribes, and he insisted that the Republicans, black as well as white, had resisted bribery as well as had the Democrats. It might be more true to say that Louisiana corrupted Warmoth (if indeed he was corrupted) than to say that Warmoth corrupted Louisiana. The other two carpetbag governors, Adelbert Ames of Mississippi and D. H. Chamberlain of South Carolina, were economy-minded and strictly honest.

There remains the charge that the carpetbaggers disturbed the relations between the races in the South. Of course, the carpetbaggers did so. Their doing so was the basic cause of the animus against them. This is the reason why the honest ones among them, the men likes Ames and Chamberlain and Warner, were as thoroughly hated and as strongly opposed as were any of the Yankee scoundrels. Most of the southern whites opposed the granting of political rights to the former slaves. The carpetbaggers encouraged the Negroes to exercise such rights. Thus the carpetbaggers upset the pattern of race relationships, the pattern of Negro passivity, which most white southerners considered ideal.

The party struggle in the postwar South amounted to something more than ordinary politics. In some of its aspects it was equivalent to a continuation, or a renewal, of the Civil War.

On the one hand, southern Conservatives thought of themselves as still fighting for home rule and white supremacy — in essence much the same war aims as the Confederacy had pursued. Carpetbaggers, on the other hand, saw their own basic objective as the reunification of the country, which had been in-completely won at Appomattox, and as the emancipation of the Negroes, who had been partially freed by the adoption of the Thirteenth Amendment.

On both sides the methods frequently were those of actual, though irregular, warfare. The Ku Klux Klan, the White league, the Red Shirts, and the various kinds of rifle companies were military or semi-military organizations. So, too, were the state militias, the Union Leagues and Loyal Leagues, and the other partisan institutions of the carpetbaggers and their Negro allies. The carpetbaggers served, so to speak, as officers of frontline troops, deep in enemy territory, "on the picket line of freedom in the South." The embattled Republicans undoubtedly suffered much heavier casualties than did their foes.

True, the Republicans had the advantage of support by the regular United States Army, but often that support was more a potentiality than a fact, and at critical moments it failed to materialize. As for the warriors of white supremacy, they had the backing of northern sympathizers in strength and numbers that would have gladdened the heart of Jefferson Davis in that earlier war time when he was angling for the aid of the Knights of the Golden Circle. The carpetbaggers were divided and weakened by the Republican party schism of 1872, by personal rivalries among themselves, and by jealousies between them and their Negro and scalawag associates. Finally, as some of the carpetbaggers saw it, they were stabbed in the back — abandoned by the government and the people in the North.

The history of this losing campaign has been written almost exclusively from the southern, or Democratic, or disillusioned Republican point of view: the story of the carpetbaggers has been told mainly by their enemies. Historical scholarship has given its sanction to the propaganda of the victorious side in the Reconstruction War. That propaganda, like most, has its elements of truth, and like most, its elements of distortion and downright falsehood. Not that the carpetbaggers were invariably the apostles of righteousness and truth. We would make little progress toward historical understanding if we merely took the same old morality play and switched the labels of Evil and Good. But surely the time has long since passed when we can, uncritically, accept the "carpetbagger" stereotype.

No doubt men can be found who fit it. No doubt there were political tramps who went South to make cynical use of the Negro vote and who contrived to win both office and illicit gain. But such men were few and comparatively unimportant. Far more numerous and more significant were those energetic and ambitious men who, with or without carpetbags, brought their savings or their borrowings to invest, who eventually got into politics for idealistic as well as selfish reasons, and who in office behaved no better and no worse then most of their contemporaries. Some of these men, like some others of their time, proved corrupt. It would be interesting to know whether, as peculators, the carpetbaggers took out more than a small fraction of the money that, as speculators, they had brought in.

Questions to Consider

1 What was the main cause of southern white animosity toward the carpetbaggers? Does this animosity explain why the carpetbaggers were so maligned in early histories of Reconstruction?

2 Does Current make a persuasive case in his reconsideration of the carpetbaggers? What evidence does he use to demonstrate that they were not, as a whole, the Yankee rogues that southern whites made them out to be?

3 Current observes that "the party struggle in the postwar South amounted to something more than ordinary politics. In some of its aspects it was equivalent to a continuation, or a renewal, of the Civil War." Do you agree with this statement? What was the outcome of this postwar struggle? How did these events affect U. S. history? Is this struggle over?

4 How do you think the term "carpetbagger" ought to be defined? Is a "carpetbagger" necessarily bad?

5 From what you have read in Foner's and Current's essays, do you think that Reconstruction was at all successful? In what ways did it succeed? In what ways did it fail? What is the legacy of Reconstruction for modern America?